RATHER MISGUIDED

A Response To Tījānī Samāwī's *Then I Was Guided*

Adapted from *Bal Ḍalalta* by:

Shaykh Khālid al-ʿAsqalānī

WWW.MAHAJJAH.COM

Contents

Foreword 1

Introduction 5

Preface 7

Chapter One - Sunnī-Shīʿī divergence on classifying the Ṣaḥābah 9
- Definition of Ṣaḥābah 11
- Definition of munāfiq 11
- The True Shīʿī Classification of Ṣaḥābah 11
- Refutation of the Shīʿī Categorisation of the Ṣaḥābah 14

Chapter Two - Treaty of Ḥudaybiyyah 31
- Tījānī's position on the Ṣaḥābah at Ḥudaybiyyah 32
- The Ṣaḥābah at Ḥudaybiyyah 34
- Refuting Tījānī on the Ṣaḥābah at Ḥudaybiyyah 43
- Tījānī on ʿUmar at Ḥudaybiyyah 48
- Refuting Tījānī on ʿUmar at Ḥudaybiyyah 48
- The reluctance of the Ṣaḥābah to release themselves from Iḥrām 52
- Reasons for the delay in executing the command of the Prophet ﷺ 53
- Tījānī on ʿUmar's role at Ḥudaybiyyah 54

The Prophet's ﷺ Final Days 57

Tījānī on the Thursday calamity 69
- Refuting Tījānī on the Thursday calamity 70
- Tījānī on the accusation of senseless speech 77
- Refuting Tījānī on the accusation of senseless speech 77
- An alternative perspective 77
- Tījānī on the knowledge of ʿUmar 78
- Tījānī on the Prophets ﷺ treatment of ʿUmar 79
- Refuting Tījānī on the Prophets ﷺ treatment of ʿUmar 79

Tījānī on the Battalion of Usāmah 91
- Tījānī's objectivity 100

Chapter Three - Tījānī's Claim that the Qur'ān Dispraises the Ṣaḥābah 109
1. Tījānī's first proof for Qur'ānic Disparagement of Ṣaḥābah 111
2. Tījānī's second proof for Qur'ānic Disparagement of Ṣaḥābah 121
Context In Which Verses Were Revealed 122
Qur'ān Teaches And Admonishes Ṣaḥābah 123
Ṣaḥābah's Contribution To Tabūk Campaign 125
Divine Pardon 127
Shīʿī Scholars On This Verse 128
Repercussions Of Wanton Tafsīr 130
Allah's Replacing Of Those Who Disobey 132
Allah Loves Them And They Love Him 135
The Prophet's Companions And The Mahdī's Companions 137
Tījānī On The Division Of Ṣaḥābah 143
Were The Ṣaḥābah Disunited? 148
3. Tījānī's third proof for Qur'ānic Disparagement of Ṣaḥābah 150
Tījānī's Distortions 151
Qur'ān Encourages Ṣaḥābah 152
Chapter Four - Tījānī's claim that the Prophet ﷺ Dispraised the Ṣaḥābah 155
1. Tījānī's claim that the Prophet ﷺ Dispraised the Ṣaḥābah 155
Refuting Tījānī's claim that the Prophet ﷺ Dispraised the Ṣaḥābah 155
Tījānī's distortion of text 156
Sunnī interpretation of these Aḥādīth 157
Shīʿī scholars do not apply it to Ṣaḥābah 158
Shīʿī imāms exonerate Ṣaḥābah 160
Further responses to Tījānī's reasoning 163
Variant wordings in the Aḥādīth 164
Tījānī's claim that "most of the Ṣaḥābah substituted and changed" 171
Refuting Tījānī's claim that "most of the Ṣaḥābah substituted and changed 171
2. Tījānī on the Companions competing for worldly motives 172
Refuting Tījānī on the Companions competing for worldly motives 173
Incoherence in Tījānī's reasoning 173
Ṣaḥābah's spending 174
Tījānī's sources 179

Chapter Five - Tījānī's claims that the Ṣaḥābah Vilified One Another **183**
1. The Ḥadīth of Abū Saʿīd al-Khudrī on ʿĪd prayers **183**
Refuting Tījānī's claim from the Ḥadīth of Abū Saʿīd al-Khudrī on ʿĪd prayers 183
2. Tījānī's claim that the Ṣaḥābah Altered the laws of Ṣalāh **187**
Refuting Tījānī's claim that the Ṣaḥābah Altered the laws of Ṣalāh 188
Tījānī's referencing 188
Background to the Ḥadīth of Anas 188
Response to Tījānī's accusation on ʿUthmān and ʿĀ'ishah 191
3. Tījānī's claim that the Ṣaḥābah رضي الله عنهم Testified Against Themselves **195**
Refuting Tījānī's claim that the Ṣaḥābah رضي الله عنهم Testified Against Themselves 196
Chapter Six - Tījānī's Criticisms against Abū Bakr **201**
1. Tījānī's Claims that Abū Bakr Condemned Himself **202**
Refuting Tījānī's Claims that Abū Bakr Condemned Himself 203
Tījānī's referencing 203
The meaning of Abū Bakr's statements 205
2. Tījānī's condemnation of Abū Bakr on the issue of Fadak **212**
Refuting Tījānī's condemnation of Abū Bakr on the issue of Fadak 213
Ibn Qutaybah 214
Al-Imāmah wa al-Siyāsah *215*
Sunnī's denouncing their scholars 217
Shīʿah propaganda tactics 218
Meaning of Shīʿah 219
Were al-Ṭabarī and al-Nasā'ī Shīʿah? 221
Ḥadīth of causing harm to Fāṭimah رضي الله عنها 224
Ḥadīth of ʿĀ'ishah 225
Did Abū Bakr intend to harm Fāṭimah? 230
Relationship between Abū Bakr and Fāṭimah 232
Tījānī's reasoning for the infallibility of Fāṭimah 238
Refuting Tījānī's reasoning for the infallibility of Fāṭimah 238
Ḥadīth of hurting Fāṭimah and infallibility 240
Tījānī and the verse of purification 241
Tījānī's emotional outburst 248

The burial of Fāṭimah 250
Tījānī's predisposed hatred for the Ṣaḥābah 252

3. Tījānī's debates on Abū Bakr 256
Ḥadīth of *Muwaṭṭa'* 256
Libertine translation 257
Reason for Abū Bakr's crying 258
Reliable Aḥādīth on Abū Bakr 258
Consequences of Tījānī's interpretation 261
Commentators of *Muwaṭṭa'* 262
Tījānīs Ḥadīth criticism 268

4. Tījānī's enlightenment and his attitude towards Abū Bakr 276
Responding to Tījānī's enlightenment and his attitude towards Abū Bakr 277
Nomination of Khalīfah 278
The Ḥadīth of Ghadīr 280
Response to the Ḥadīth of Ghadīr 281
Context of the Ḥadīth 281
Why did the Prophet ﷺ say this? 282
The Meaning of Mawlā 282
How was it understood? 286
The alleged congratulatory procession 288
Integrity of Tījānī's Quotes 291
Requirements for Valid Bayʿah 298
Shīʿī Scholars Refute Tījānī's Allegation 300
Tījānī's claim that ʿUmar Objected to Abū Bakr's Appointment 301
Responding to Tījānī's claim that ʿUmar Objected to Abū Bakr's Appointment 302
Tījānī's Claim That ʿAlī objected to Abū Bakr's Appointment 303
Responding to Tījānī's Claim That ʿAlī objected to Abū Bakr's Appointment 303

5. Tījānī's proofs for the superiority of ʿAlī over Abū Bakr 306
Responding to Tījānī's proofs for the superiority of ʿAlī over Abū Bakr 307

6. Tījānī criticises Abū Bakr for applying the Law of Allah 335
Context of the ḥadīth cited by Tījānī 336

Fighting those who refuse to give zakāh 336
Sunnī Explanation 337
Shīʿī Explanation 339
Tījānī's Conundrum 340
ʿUmar's Questioning 341

7. Tījānī's condemnation of Abū Bakr for how he dealt with Khālid ibn al-Walīd 350

Refuting Tījānī's condemnation of Abū Bakr for how he dealt with Khālid ibn al-Walīd 351

Chapter Seven - Tījānī's Criticisms of the Second Khalīfah, ʿUmar ibn al-Khaṭṭāb 369

1. Tījānī's claim that ʿUmar Contradicted the Sunnah 371

Refuting Tījānī's claim that ʿUmar Contradicted the Sunnah 371
Shīʿī scholars accept these narrations 377
Tījānī forges aḥādīth 378

2. Tījānī's claim that ʿUmar was Unjust 381

Refuting Tījānī's claim that ʿUmar was Unjust 382

3. Tījānī accuses ʿUmar of ignorance 384

Refuting Tījānī's accusation of ignorance 384

4. Tījānī accuses ʿUmar of contravening revealed text 387

Refuting Tījānī's accusation of ʿUmar contravening revealed text 387
Mutʿah of Ḥajj 387
Mutʿah of women 389
Tījānī's accusation regarding the knowledge of ʿUmar 395
Refuting Tījānī's accusation regarding the knowledge of ʿUmar 395
Tījānī's accusation on ʿUmar concerning the meaning of Kalālah 397
Refuting Tījānī's accusation on ʿUmar concerning the meaning of Kalālah 398
Tījānī's accusation on ʿUmar concerning the distribution of zakāh 400
Refuting Tījānī's accusation on ʿUmar concerning the distribution of zakāh 400
Tījānī's accusation on ʿUmar preventing Abū Hurayrah from transmitting the ḥadīth of glad tidings 401

Refuting Tījānī's accusation on ʿUmar preventing Abū Hurayrah from transmitting the ḥadīth of glad tidings 402
Tījānī's allegations against the Ahl al-Sunnah concerning the infallibility of the Prophet ﷺ 405
Refuting Tījānī's allegations against the Ahl al-Sunnah concerning the infallibility of the Prophet ﷺ 406
Tījānī's accusation on ʿUmar concerning the Devil fleeing from him 407
Refuting Tījānī's accusation on ʿUmar concerning the Devil fleeing from him 407
Tījānī's accusation that ʿUmar altered the rulings of the Prophet ﷺ 410
Refuting Tījānī's accusation that ʿUmar altered the rulings of the Prophet ﷺ 410

5. Tījānī's Claim That ʿUmar Testified Against Himself 413
Refuting Tījānī's claim that ʿUmar testified against himself 414

6. Tījānī's position on ʿUmar in the discussion, "A conversation with a scholar" 417
Refuting Tījānī's position on ʿUmar in the discussion, "A conversation with a scholar" 418

7. Tījānī's objections to ʿUmar's khilāfah 419
Refuting Tījānī's objections to ʿUmar's khilāfah 419

Chapter Eight - Tījānī's Criticisms of the Third Khalīfah, ʿUthmān ibn ʿAffān 423
Tījānī claims that the Ṣaḥābah unanimously conspired to kill ʿUthmān 428
Refuting Tījānī's claims that the Ṣaḥābah unanimously conspired to kill ʿUthmān 429
Narrations negating the involvement of the Ṣaḥābah 430
Shīʿī scholars deny the Ṣaḥābah's involvement 435
Who killed ʿUthmān? 437
ʿĀ'ishah's role 438
Roles of Ṭalḥah, Zubayr and Muḥammad ibn Abī Bakr 440
ʿUthmān's burial 443
Prophetic inheritance 444
Tījānī criticises ʿUthmān's Ijtihād 445

Chapter Nine - Tījānī's criticism of Sayyidah ʿĀ'ishah, the Prophet's ﷺ wife **451**

1. Tījānī accuses ʿĀ'ishah of sedition and provoking rebellion **456**

Summary of Tījānī's argument 457

Underlying principles 458

The purpose of ʿĀ'ishah's departure was for reconciliation and not battle 459

Tījānī accuses ʿĀ'ishah of adopting the ways of Jāhiliyyah 460

Tījānī asserts that ʿĀ'ishah held a grudge against ʿAlī 461

Was ʿĀ'ishah responsible for bloodshed? 463

Tījānī lies about ʿĀ'ishah hating ʿAlī 466

Tījānī asks why ʿĀ'ishah ignored ʿAlī's merits 468

Who was wrong? 471

Tījānī's slanderous comments 474

Why respect ʿĀ'ishah? 478

Tījānī's insolence 484

Tījānī accuses ʿĀ'ishah of lying 489

Chapter Ten - Tījānī's Criticisms of Ṭalḥah and Zubayr **491**

Tījānī claims that Ṭalḥah and Zubayr gave false testimony 495

Refuting Tījānī's claims that Ṭalḥah and Zubayr gave false testimony 495

Chapter Eleven - Tījānī's criticisms of Muʿāwiyah ibn Abī Sufyān **501**

1. Tījānī accuses Muʿāwiyah of initiating the cursing of ʿAlī. **508**

Refuting Tījānī's accusation that Muʿāwiyah initiated the cursing of ʿAlī. 509

2. Tījānī's claim that Muʿāwiyah was not one of the Prophet's ﷺ scribes **512**

Refuting Tījānī's claim that Muʿāwiyah was not one of the Prophet's ﷺ scribes 512

3. Tījānī's claim that Muʿāwiyah had Ḥujr ibn ʿAdī executed because he refused to curse ʿAlī **513**

Refuting Tījānī's claim that Muʿāwiyah had Ḥujr ibn ʿAdī executed because he refused to curse ʿAlī 514

4. Tījānī's claim that Ḥasan al-Baṣrī disparaged Muʿāwiyah **515**

Refuting Tījānī's claim that Ḥasan al-Baṣrī disparaged Muʿāwiyah 515

5. Tījānī's perspective of Muʿāwiyah during the Fitnah **516**
Refuting Tījānī's perspective of Muʿāwiyah during the Fitnah 518
6. Tījānī's claim that Muʿāwiyah poisoned Ḥasan **526**
Refuting Tījānī's claim that Muʿāwiyah poisoned Ḥasan 526
7. Tījānī's claim that Muʿāwiyah altered the Khilāfah from shūrā to monarchy **527**
Refuting Tījānī's claim that Muʿāwiyah altered the Khilāfah from shūrā to monarchy 528
Chapter Twelve - Tījānī's Criticisms of Abū Hurayrah **533**
1. Tījānī's claims that Abū Hurayrah fabricated aḥādīth from the Prophet ﷺ **533**
Refuting Tījānī's claims that Abū Hurayrah fabricated aḥādīth from the Prophet ﷺ 534
Chapter Thirteen - The Final Study: Miscellaneous Issues **545**
1. Tījānī's Proofs for ʿAlī's immediate succession **545**
The ḥadīth, "I am the city of knowledge and ʿAlī is the door." 545
Analysis of the ḥadīth, "I am the city of knowledge and ʿAlī is the door." 545
The ḥadīth, "O ʿAlī! You hold in relation to me the same position as Haroon held in relation to Moses." 547
Analysis of the ḥadīth, "O ʿAlī! You hold in relation to me the same position as Haroon held in relation to Moses." 548
The ḥadīth, "Whomsoever I am his Mawlā, then this is ʿAlī, he too is his Mawlā." 552
Analysis of the ḥadīth, "Whomsoever I am his Mawlā, then this is ʿAlī, he too is his Mawlā." 553
The ḥadīth, "ʿAlī is from me and I am from ʿAlī" 556
Analysis of the ḥadīth, "ʿAlī is from me and I am from ʿAlī" 557
The ḥadīth, "This is my brother, my trustee and my deputy [caliph] after me." 559
Analysis of the ḥadīth, "This is my brother, my trustee and my deputy [caliph] after me." 559
2. Tījānī's proofs for the obligation of following the Ahl al-Bayt **565**
a. Ḥadīth al-Thaqalayn 565
Analysis of Ḥadīth al-Thaqalayn 567

b. The Ḥadīth, "My Ahl al-Bayt are like the Ark of Noah." 576
Analysing the Ḥadīth, "My Ahl al-Bayt are like the Ark of Noah." 576
c. The Ḥadīth, "Whoever wishes to live and die like me..." 577
Analysing the Ḥadīth, "Whoever wishes to live and die like me..." 578
3. Tījānī's Confusion about the salutation appearing after ʿAlī's name in *Ṣaḥīḥ al-Bukhārī* 580
4. Tījānī's claim that the four Schools of Fiqh are traced back to Jaʿfar al-Ṣādiq 584
Refuting Tījānī's claim that the four Schools of Fiqh are traced back to Jaʿfar al-Ṣādiq 585
5. The Rāfiḍah Deny the Existence of Shīʿī sects which consider ʿAlī Divine 588
6. Tījānī presents al-Khūʾī's defence of the Shīʿah on the issue of distortion 594
7. Tījānī on the significance of the addition in the Adhān, "ʿAlī Walī Allāh" 603
8. The proof for self-flagellation during the commemoration of Ḥusayn's murder 607
9. Explanation of the ḥadīth of division in the Ummah. 609
10. Tījānī distorts the ḥadīth of the Bedouin urinating in the Masjid 611
11. Tījānī's criticism of ʿAbd Allāh ibn ʿUmar 613
12. Tījānī ridicules some of the Ṣaḥābah calling them *al-Munqalibīn* **(those who turned back on their heels) 616**
13. Tījānī associates the term Ahl al-Sunnah wa l-Jamāʿah with Muʿāwiyah 617
14. Tījānī claims that the Prophet صَلَّى ٱللَّٰهُ عَلَيْهِ وَسَلَّمَ **mentioned the Twelve Imāms by name 619**
15. Tījānī claims that the Ṣaḥābah killed ʿAlī 622
16. Another distortion of ḥadīth by Tījānī 623
17. Tījānī claims that the differences between the four Imāms is symptomatic of contradiction between Qurʾān and Ḥadīth 624

Transliteration key

أ إ - ’
آ - ā
ب - b
ت - t
ث - th
ج - j
ح - ḥ
خ - kh
د - d
ذ - dh
ر - r
ز - z
س - s
ش - sh
ص - ṣ
ض - ḍ
ط - ṭ
ظ - ẓ
ع - ‘
غ - gh
ف - f
ق - q
ك - k
ل - l
م - m
ن - n
و - w, ū
ه - h
ي - y, ī

Foreword

For well in excess of a thousand years the Muslim world has been split into a roughly 90% mainstream of Ahl al-Sunnah, and a 10% minority of Shīʿah belonging to a range of persuasions. This character of this sectarian divide has never remained static and uniform. It has seen, and continues to witness, periods of both war and precarious peace, of cooperation and of treason, and of oppression as well as of justice. It has also seen a great deal of polemical literature.

The present work responds to a particular type of polemic: the conversion story of an ex-Sunnī, in this case, the Tunisian Muḥammad Tījānī Samāwī. A visit to ʿIrāq in the late 70s led not only to his conversion to Shīʿism, but also to authorship of a slew of polemical books which were feted and celebrated in the Shīʿī world, printed in large quantities in various international languages for circulation among Sunnīs.

The power of the conversion story is self-evident. Shīʿī polemicists from Ibn Ṭāwūs in the 6th/12th century, to ʿAbd al-Ḥusayn Sharaf al-Dīn in the 14th/20th have remained unable to resist the temptation of the strawman conversion story. While the strawman element is not directly present in Tījānī Samāwī's work, the wholesale reliance he places on ʿAbd al-Ḥusayn Sharaf al-Dīn's works, especially *al-Murājaʿat* in which he magisterially fabricates a discourse between himself and Shaykh Salīm al-Bishrī—the Shaykh of al-Azhar who died two decades before he dared to publish his work—makes his own works as vulnerable to the strawman charge as any other. Other than the contemporary convert angle, his works offer preciously little that is original.

That the success of Irān's 1979 Revolution introduced a new era of Sunnī-Shīʿī interaction and coexistence is beyond question. The great emphasis that Irān's leadership placed on Sunnī-Shīʿī unity appears, ironically, not to have dimmed the enthusiasm for proselytisation in Sunnī communities, despite the obvious consequences of such a policy. Similarly, the deep sense of hurt and outrage that was shared by Sunnī and Shīʿī alike in the wake of the publication of Rushdie's *Satanic Verses* and the Danish cartoons does not appear to have given Shīʿī proselytisers any appreciation of the hurt experienced by the Ahl al-Sunnah when Shīʿism embarks—as it inevitably must—upon the character assassination of the

Ṣaḥābah in the name of historical objectivity. And while the Shīʿī leadership have from time to time made the requisite perfunctory statements, those statements are immediately contradicted, if not utterly belied, by the active encouragement that the circulation of books such as Tījānī Samāwī's receive from the very same quarters.

The irony of building unity on the one hand, and destroying it on the other, cannot be more pronounced. It reminds of the verse of the Qur'ān in which Allah says, "And do not be like she who untwisted her spun thread after it was strong [by] taking your oaths as [means of] deceit between you because one community is more plentiful [in number or wealth] than another community. Allah only tries you thereby. And He will surely make clear to you on the Day of Resurrection that over which you used to differ."[1]

It is for this very reason that the cycle of polemic followed by counter-polemic has no option but to continue, as vicious as it might be perceived in some quarters. Among the various responses to Tījānī, Khālid al-ʿAsqalānī's *Bal Ḍalalta* stands out as a comprehensive study that critically assesses each of Tījānī's arguments. The present work is an adapted translation of al-ʿAsqalānī's work.

As I pen the final words to this introduction, I would ask that a moment be spared to think of the silent and silenced sector that, but for circumstances, would have formed an important participant in the field of conversion-based Sunnī-Shīʿī polemics. These are the hundreds upon hundreds of victims of the Iranian regime's relentless suppression of Shīʿī conversion to Sunnism in Irān. Many of them "disappeared" during Irān's dark years that ran from 1981 to 1985[2]. Many more continue to languish in Iranian jails under the charge of "Wahhabism." The double standards of calling for unity whilst perpetuating proselytisation not only continues, but has sunk to an unprecedented level of depravity in the human catastrophe being perpetrated against the Sunnī population of Syria by Shīʿism's triple entente of Irān, Hezbollah, and their supporting brigades of Iraqi, Afghan, and Pakistani volunteers.

---

1 Sūrah al-Naḥl: 92.

2 More than 7900 Iranian political prisoners were executed between 1981 and 1985—at least seventy-nine times the number killed between 1971 and 1979. Laura Secor: *Children of Paradise*, p. 91.

The indications and implications of such heedless and relentless pursuit of a geographically contiguous Shīʿī crescent cannot be ignored. If anything, it underlines the need for polemics to continue.

MT Karaan

Introduction

All praises are due to Allah, Sustainer of the entire universe. Peace and salutations upon his trustworthy Messenger, Muḥammad, son of ʿAbd Allāh, and upon his family and all his Companions.

A Jew by the name ʿAbd Allāh ibn Sabaʾ instituted the belief that the Imāmah of ʿAlī رضي الله عنه was compulsory and publicly vilified Abū Bakr, ʿUmar, and ʿUthmān رضي الله عنهم. His Zoroastrian disciples continued his legacy, causing mischief, division, and separation in the Ummah with claims such as the pre-emptive right of ʿAlī رضي الله عنه to khilāfah, his superiority over all the Companions and the annual commemoration of the horrific killing of Ḥusayn ibn ʿAlī رضي الله عنهما at Karbalāʾ.

Although these issues should have ended there, the Rawāfiḍ[1] continued their attempts to reignite and resuscitate them. When these arguments did not deceive the intelligent, they began exposing their true nature by claims that all but three or seven of the Companions abandoned Islam; that the Twelve Imāms are infallible; that revelation descends upon them; that angels even greater than Jibrīl and Mīkāʾīl come to them; that they are superior to the Prophets; that they have knowledge of the past, present, and future; and that whoever does not believe in their Imāmah is a disbeliever.

The greatest calamity is that a large numbers of Muslims continue to be goaded by them. They spread amongst them their venom and instil within them hatred and rancour for the Ummah, to the extent that individuals thus deceived believe themselves to be upon truth, when in reality they have drifted closer to falsehood.

---

1 Rafiḍī (plural: Rawāfiḍ) and Rāfiḍah is a name which pejoratively refers to the Shīʿah.
Al-Kulaynī has reported in *Al-Rawḍah min al-Kāfī* a lengthy narration from Muḥammad ibn Salmān, who reported from his father. A portion of it makes mention:

> Abū Baṣīr said to Imām Jaʿfar, "May I be sacrificed for you! There are words that are constantly thrown at us breaking our backs, killing our hearts and used as justification by the rulers to kill us. It is a narration reported by their jurists."
>
> Imām Jaʿfar asked, "Do you refer to the narration pertaining to The Rāfiḍah?"
> Abū Baṣīr replied in the affirmative.
>
> Imām Jaʿfar then said, "They are not the ones who have given you all this name, instead it is Allah who has named you such." (vol. 8 p. 28).

One wishes that the issue would end here. However, the rancour and hatred which they implant is not against the Jew and the Christian. Instead it is against the greatest personalities of the Ummah: the Companions of Muḥammad صَلَّى ٱللَّٰهُ عَلَيْهِ وَسَلَّمَ. When they claim that the Book revealed by Allah is interpolated, do you imagine that it is to the Injīl or Tawrāh that they refer? By no means! It is to the Protected Book of Allah that they refer—that book which no falsehood can approach and regarding which Allah has said, "*Verily, We have revealed the Remembrance; and verily, We are its protectors.*"[1]

In this context there appeared a book, *Thumma Ihtadayt* (*Then I was guided*) by Muḥammad Tījānī Samāwī. This book, while zealously confirming the error and deviation of Shīʿism, served as a violent wake up call to all those who continue to believe that the Shīʿah are advocates of Sunnī-Shīʿī rapprochement. The passage of time proved that what they promote is not unity, but destruction. How else, when every book they release is laced with deception and embroidered with falsehood? *Then I was guided* is a clear example of this. The two principles on which the author relies and upon which his conclusions rest are fabrications and contradictions.

Tījānī clearly does not know much about the sect to which he has been "guided", nor does he appear to have acquainted himself with any of their reliable books. The truth is certainly within reach, but only to an objective investigator who purges himself of bias and prejudice.

The present study will facilitate the way for seekers of truth. It incorporates evidence from the books of the Ahl al-Sunnah as well as the books of the Shīʿah.

In conclusion, I wish to express appreciation to all those whose concern led to this study being undertaken and completed, as well as those who sincerely contributed effort and time. May Allah سُبْحَانَهُ وَتَعَالَىٰ make it a means of reward for them in this world and a cause for entry into Jannah in the hereafter.

I beseech Allah to make this work sincerely for his pleasure, to resurrect us with the Companions of His Messenger Muḥammad صَلَّى ٱللَّٰهُ عَلَيْهِ وَسَلَّمَ, and make our final abode the Everlasting Paradise. *Āmīn*.

1 Sūrah al-Ḥijr: 9.

Preface

Tījānī divides his book into two parts. The first part mentions his travels through certain Muslim countries and his interaction with some of the Shīʿah who he claims had a positive effect in guiding him from darkness to light, and in differentiating between truth and falsehood.

In the second part of his book, he mentions his research and his subsequent arrival at what he believes to be true about the Companions رَضِيَ ٱللَّهُ عَنْهُمْ. He also describes how he realized that the Ahl al-Sunnah deviated from the truth, and discovered that the straight path was the way of the Twelver Shīʿah.

The second part, which represents the majority of the book, deals with the Companions رَضِيَ ٱللَّهُ عَنْهُمْ. Since this issue lies at the very heart of this controversy, it is from here that I must proceed. Thereafter, I turn to the remaining misconceptions in Tījānī's book.

Chapter One

Sunnī-Shīʿī divergence on classifying the Ṣaḥābah

Tījānī begins his investigation with what he considers to encapsulate the difference between the Ahl al-Sunnah and the Shīʿah: the lives of the Companions رَضِيَ اللَّهُ عَنْهُمْ. He begins his examination by comparing the manner in which the Companions are classified by the Ahl al-Sunnah and the Shīʿah respectively. He mentions that the Shīʿah divide the Companions into three categories:

> **Through my discussions with the scholars of the Shīʿah, I have concluded that the Companions, according to the Shīʿah, can be divided into three categories:**
>
> - **The select Companions, who truly knew Allah and his Messenger صَلَّى اللَّهُ عَلَيْهِ وَسَلَّمَ, who pledged their allegiance to him up to death, who accompanied him with truth and sincerity, and did not change after him but rather remained firm on their covenant. Allah praises them abundantly in the noble Qur'ān. The Messenger of Allah صَلَّى اللَّهُ عَلَيْهِ وَسَلَّمَ also commends them in many places. The Shīʿah, like the Ahl al-Sunnah mention them with respect and reverence and invoke Allah's pleasure on them.**
>
> - **The Companions who embraced Islam and followed the Messenger of Allah صَلَّى اللَّهُ عَلَيْهِ وَسَلَّمَ out of either greed or fear. They considered their Islam as a favour upon the Messenger of Allah صَلَّى اللَّهُ عَلَيْهِ وَسَلَّمَ. They would occasionally cause harm to him and would not submit to his commands and prohibitions. Instead, they would give preference to their own opinions, directly contradicting explicit text, to the extent that verses would occasionally be revealed to rebuke or warn them. Allah disgraced them in many verses and the Messenger of Allah صَلَّى اللَّهُ عَلَيْهِ وَسَلَّمَ warned against them in many aḥādīth. The Shīʿah mention them by their actions, with no respect or reverence.**
>
> - **The hypocrites who accompanied the Messenger of Allah صَلَّى اللَّهُ عَلَيْهِ وَسَلَّمَ to conspire against him. They curried favour in order to conspire against Islam and Muslims. Allah revealed an entire sūrah concerning them, mentioned them in many places, and threatened them with the lowest level of Jahannam. The Messenger of Allah mentioned them, warned against them, and taught some of his Companions رَضِيَ اللَّهُ عَنْهُمْ their names**

> **and their signs. The Shī'ah and the Ahl al-Sunnah agree on them being cursed and disowned.**[1]

This is the Shīʿī classification of the Companions رضي الله عنهم, as mentioned by Tījānī in his book. In addition, there is a special category of Companions who have distinction on account of their close relationship and innate merit and disposition. They are the Ahl al-Bayt, the household of the Messenger صلى الله عليه وسلم, may Allah be pleased with them all.

Thereafter, Tījānī discusses the beliefs of the Ahl al-Sunnah concerning the Companions رضي الله عنهم, and says:

> **As for the Ahl al-Sunnah, although they respect, honour and favour the Ahl al-Bayt, they do not recognise this typology, nor do they consider the hypocrites amongst the Companions. Rather, in their opinion, they consider the Companions as the best creation of Allah after the Messenger of Allah صلى الله عليه وسلم. If there is to be any categorisation, it should be from the perspective of virtue, embracing Islam earlier, and enduring tribulation. They therefore give preference to the Rightly Guided Khulafā' at the highest level, then the six remaining people who were given glad tidings of Jannah, according to what they narrate.**[2]

This is how Tījānī represents the Sunnī view of the Ṣaḥābah.

Before I begin my refutation of the Twelver Shīʿī classification of the Companions, it is necessary to first define who is a Ṣaḥābī and who is a hypocrite, from a lexical and technical perspective. Thereafter it will be necessary to understand who the targets of this Shīʿī classification are, in light of their most relied upon sources. This will make it easy for the reader, be he Sunnī or Shīʿī to distinguish between truth and falsehood.

I now commence the refutation and exposé of the Shīʿī classification of the Companions رضي الله عنهم. And to Allah is my recourse.

---

1 *Then I was guided*, p. 78 - 79.

2 Ibid.

Definition of Ṣaḥābah

Lexically: The word Ṣaḥābah derives from the Arabic root *ṣ-ḥ-b*. This root denotes accompaniment or companionship. Thus the word Ṣāḥib means companion, the plural of which is Ṣaḥābah.

Technically: A Ṣaḥābī is someone who met the Messenger صَلَّى ٱللَّٰهُ عَلَيْهِ وَسَلَّمَ, whilst believing in him, and eventually passed away a believer. This definition implies that one who saw the Messenger صَلَّى ٱللَّٰهُ عَلَيْهِ وَسَلَّمَ without believing in him and died upon disbelief does not fall in the category of those termed as Ṣaḥābah.

Definition of munāfiq

Lexically: The root *n-f-q* produces the word *nāfiqā'* which denotes the holes in which a Jerboa hides, escaping from one to the other. It also produces the word *nafaq*, a tunnel. What these words have in common is a sense of concealment. The word *nifāq* (hypocrisy) arises from this same lexical meaning.

Technically: A munāfiq is one who outwardly portrays to have embraced Islam and to follow the Messenger صَلَّى ٱللَّٰهُ عَلَيْهِ وَسَلَّمَ while concealing his disbelief and enmity towards Allah and His Messenger صَلَّى ٱللَّٰهُ عَلَيْهِ وَسَلَّمَ.

Having understood this explanation of the two terms, *ṣaḥābī* and *munāfiq*, it becomes clear that they are mutually exclusive, both lexically and technically. Thus, a Ṣaḥābī is one who believed in the Messenger صَلَّى ٱللَّٰهُ عَلَيْهِ وَسَلَّمَ and passed away with Īmān, whereas a munāfiq is one who outwardly pretends to believe while concealing disbelief in his heart. It is therefore as impossible for a Ṣaḥābī to be a munāfiq as it is for a munāfiq to be a Ṣaḥābī.

The question might be asked: "How do we differentiate between a Ṣaḥābī and a munāfiq?" To this I respond that a munāfiq possesses characteristics and attributes clearly mentioned in the Qur'ān and Sunnah that allow for differentiation between him and the Ṣaḥābah. These characteristics will be mentioned in our critical assessment of the Shīʿī classification of Ṣaḥābah.

The True Shīʿī Classification of Ṣaḥābah

Tījānī mentions that the Shīʿah divide the Ṣaḥābah into three categories. The fact of the matter is that they divide them into two categories, with no third. This stands confirmed in the statements of their scholars and the testimony of their own books.

Tījānī's first category with whom the Shīʿah are well pleased in fact number no less than three and no more than seven. Their main authority on ḥadīth narrators, al-Kashshī, reports with a chain of narration deemed reliable by Shīʿī standards that Imām Muḥammad al-Bāqir said:

> "All the people became *murtadd* (apostate) except for three: Salmān, Abū Dharr and al-Miqdād."
>
> The narrator says, "So I asked about ʿAmmār and he said, 'He fell into a predicament initially, but later returned.'"[1]

Another narration states:

> ... after sometime the people returned (to Islam). The first to return was Abū Sāsān al-Anṣārī, ʿAmmār, Abū ʿUmayrah and Shatīrah. So they were seven, and even Amīr al-Mu'minīn did not know anyone besides these seven.[2]

Al-Kulaynī, the most senior ḥadīth scholar of the Twelver Shīʿah and author of *al-Kāfī*[3] one of their four major ḥadīth collections narrates from Ḥumrān ibn Aʿyan:

> I said to Abū Jaʿfar (al-Bāqir), "May I be sacrificed for you! How few are we in number! Were we to gather for one sheep we would not be able to finish it."
>
> He said, "Should I not tell you of something stranger than that? The Muhājirīn and the Anṣār left Islam, except (gesturing with his hand) three."[4]

It is narrated in *al-Rawḍah* from ʿAbd al-Raḥīm al-Qaṣīr, who said:

---

1 *Ḥaqq al-Yaqīn fī Maʿrifat Uṣūl al-Dīn*, vol. 1 p. 370 – 371; *Rijāl al-Kashshī*, p. 17; *Tafsīr al-ʿAyyāshī*, vol. 1 p. 223.

2 Ibid.

3 ʿAbd al-Ḥusayn al-Mūsawī says in his book *Al-Murājaʿāt* (p. 334), "The best of these compilations are the Four Books, which are the main sources for the Shīʿah in the primary and secondary aspects of their faith, from the earliest generation until present. They are *al-Kāfī*, *al-Tahdhīb*, *al-Istibṣār*, and *Man lā Yaḥḍurhu al-Faqīh*. They are all *mutawātir* (mass transmitted) and their contents categorically established to be authentic. *Al-Kāfī* precedes the others and is the most superior, most distinguished and excellent."

4 *Al-Uṣūl min al-Kāfī*, vol. 2 p. 191; *Rijāl al-Kashshī*, p. 13; *Tafsīr al-Ṣāfī*, vol. 1 p. 359.

> I said to Abū Jaʿfar, "Indeed the people become agitated when we say, 'The people became apostate'."
>
> He said, "O ʿAbd al-Raḥīm! All the people returned to Jāhiliyyah after the demise of the Messenger of Allah ﷺ. The Anṣār withdrew but they did not withdraw in goodness. They pledged their allegiance to Saʿd, while singing the poetry of the period of Jāhiliyyah, 'O Saʿd! You are the man of our hopes, your mane is well-groomed and your steed runs hard.'"[1]

To the Shīʿah, this is then the first category of the Companions upon whom they look with approval.

As for the second category, to the Shīʿah they are the rest of the Ṣaḥābah رضي الله عنهم who were not mentioned in the first category. The Shīʿah regard them as people of hypocrisy, apostasy and betrayal. At the head of them are the Three Khulafā', then the remaining Six who were given glad-tidings of Paradise, and thereafter the remaining Ṣaḥābah. This is what the Shīʿah believe concerning the Ṣaḥābah as taken from their original sources.

Why would Tījānī divide the Ṣaḥābah into three categories? The reason: To mislead, especially the Sunnī reader, by creating the false impression that these Ṣaḥābah were not apostates, but only men who desired worldly gain or feared the Messenger ﷺ (which is inevitably hypocrisy). This insertion of an intermediate category in his chapter on the Companions is a shrewd tactic on Tījānī's part; he thus enables the reader to place any of the Companions into the category of the apostates. Later in his book, Tījānī combines the categories of hypocrites and apostates into one. Thereby, the Companions become divided into two groups: a group with whom Allah is pleased and a group who apostatized. This makes it easy to persuade the reader to accept the Shīʿī classification of the Companions. Any misgivings that by the term "hypocrite" Tījānī is referring to ʿAbd Allāh ibn Ubayy ibn Salūl and his companions will soon be put to rest when Tījānī comes to the defence of Ibn Ubayy in connection with the Messenger ﷺ performing the funeral prayer over him.[2]

1 *Al-Rawḍah min al-Kāfī*, p. 246.

2 *Then I was guided*, p. 90.

Refutation of the Shīʿī Categorisation of the Ṣaḥābah

1. Since the Shīʿah do not consider īmān to be a condition for being Ṣaḥābī they include the Munāfiqīn amongst the Ṣaḥābah. If this were true, the Jews and Christians and idolaters who saw the Prophet صلى الله عليه وسلم should also be termed Ṣaḥābah. Such a statement can only be made by a witless fool. If the Shīʿah admit that a Ṣaḥābī is one who saw the Prophet صلى الله عليه وسلم while believing in him and who died upon that belief, then their claim that a munāfiq is a Ṣaḥābī becomes void.

2. Without specifying who is a Munāfiq and who is a Ṣaḥābī, this definition has flung the door wide open and any Ṣaḥābī, including those who he approves of like ʿAlī رضي الله عنه, can be included in the category of the Munāfiqīn. This would give any individual the right to believe that any Companion of the Prophet صلى الله عليه وسلم is a munāfiq, by resting upon the notion that the Munāfiqīn can be considered as Companions. Such a concept would enable the atheists, the godless, and the Orientalists to vilify Islam and its adherents.

3. Tījānī leads his readers to conclude that the true Ṣaḥābah were few, far outnumbered by the Munāfiqīn who seized central leadership. Tījānī himself says in the third category of Ṣaḥābah that the Munāfiqīn outwardly displayed Islam and concealed their kufr, constantly drawing closer in order to plot against Islam and the Muslims. If this was their objective, and they were the majority, why did they not besiege the Messenger صلى الله عليه وسلم and his Ṣaḥābah, annihilate them, and destroy the fledgling Islamic state? Reality, however, testifies that Islam was victorious, spread to every region of the world, and raised its standard, while every flag of kufr collapsed before it. Consider therefore, dear reader, how the perceptions of the Shīʿah clash with both reason and historical fact.

4. The hypocrites were not unknown entities within the society of Madīnah; instead, they were a small yet notorious group. Some of them were known by name and others by the qualities they possessed which are mentioned in the Qurʾān. This reality is explained in the ḥadīth of Kaʿb ibn Mālik رضي الله عنه who was one of the three who stayed behind during the Battle of Tabūk. He said:

   > Whenever I went out amongst the people after the Messenger of Allah left, I would roam around amongst them and it would sadden me that the only

people I would see is either a man known as an open hypocrite or a man whom Allah excused due to weakness.[1]

The Qur'ān has identified the symptoms of Nifāq and exposed the salient features of the hypocrites in numerous places:

- They mock the faith and the faithful.[2]
- They transgress and choose deviation at the expense of guidance.[3, 4]
- They are distracted and lazy during *'ibādah* (worship).[5]
- They are neither with the believers nor the disbelievers.[6]
- They take false and vain oaths in the name of Allah.[7]
- They lack understanding of Islam.[8]

1 *Ṣaḥīḥ al-Bukhārī*, Ḥadīth no. 4156.

2 Sūrah al-Nisā: 140; Sūrah al-Tawbah: 65, 79.

3 Ibn 'Abd al-Barr reports that 'Alī رضي الله عنه was asked about those who fought against him in Nahrawān (i.e. the Khawārij):

"Are they kuffār?"
'Alī رضي الله عنه replied, "It is from kufr that they have fled!"
He was asked, "Are they then munafiqīn?"
'Alī رضي الله عنه replied: "Verily the munafiqīn do not remember Allah except a little."
He was then asked, "So what are they?"
'Alī رضي الله عنه answered, "They are people who have been afflicted by a trial, and have thus become blind and deaf. They rebelled against us and fought us, so we fought them" (Ibn Qudāmah: *Al-Mughnī*, vol. 12 p. 241 – 241).

Subḥān Allāh! So when 'Alī رضي الله عنه negates the quality of nifāq from the Khawārij, regarding whom the Messenger صلى الله عليه وسلم said, "The Khawārij are the dogs of Hell," simply because they would remember Allah and Allah stated in the Qur'ān that the munafiqīn do not remember Allah except a little, what then can be said about the Ṣaḥābah of the Messenger صلى الله عليه وسلم, whom Allah described as *Muḥammad* صلى الله عليه وسلم *is Allah's Messenger and those with him are severe against the kuffār and compassionate among themselves. You will see them sometimes bowing, sometimes prostrating, seeking Allah's bounty and His pleasure. Their hallmark is on their faces because of the effect of prostration.* (Sūrah al-Fatḥ: 29) Astonishing indeed is the deviation of the Shī'ah!

4 Sūrah al-Baqarah: 16.

5 Sūrah al-Nisā: 142.

6 Sūrah al-Nisā: 143.

7 Sūrah al-Tawbah: 56; Sūrah al-Munāfiqīn: 2.

8 Sūrah al-Baqarah: 13.

- They are miserly.[1]
- They lack faith in Allah and the Last Day.[2]
- They are saddened when the believers receive good or assistance, and they celebrate when the believers go through any difficulty or trials.[3]
- They patiently await the changing tide against the believers.[4]
- They refrain from spending in the path of Allah.[5]
- They are pleased when they are left behind from jihād.[6]
- They take oaths in the name of Allah in order to protect themselves against the rejection of Muslims.[7]
- They cause division amongst believers and are treacherous in times of dispute.[8]
- They delay ṣalāh to its latest possible time, abstain from congregational ṣalāh and find Fajr and ʿIshā the most difficult of the prayers.[9]

These are some of the qualities of the hypocrites, as described by Allah. So, by Allah, is this the description given to those who accompanied the Prophet ﷺ? Are these descriptions befitting of those who are categorised as Ṣaḥābah? There is no doubt that the Ṣaḥābah of the Messenger ﷺ are the furthest of people from these qualities. They are deserving of the pleasure of Allah and His approval, so much so that Allah says about them:

كُنْتُمْ خَيْرَ أُمَّةٍ أُخْرِجَتْ لِلنَّاسِ تَأْمُرُوْنَ بِالْمَعْرُوْفِ وَتَنْهَوْنَ عَنِ الْمُنْكَرِ وَتُؤْمِنُوْنَ بِاللّٰهِ

1 Sūrah al-Tawbah: 76-78.
2 Sūrah al-Tawbah: 45.
3 Sūrah Āl ʿImrān: 120; Sūrah al-Tawbah: 50.
4 Sūrah al-Tawbah: 98.
5 Sūrah al-Tawbah: 67; Sūrah al-Munāfiqīn: 7.
6 Sūrah al-Tawbah: 81.
7 Sūrah al-Munāfiqīn: 2.
8 Sūrah al-Tawbah: 47-48.
9 *Ṭarīq al-Hijratayn wa Bāb al-Saʿādatayn*, p. 666 - 667.

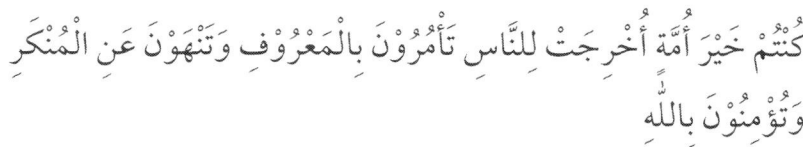

You are the best of nations who have been raised for mankind. You command the good, prohibit the evil and believe in Allah.[1]

Allah also says:

يٰٓأَيُّهَا النَّبِىُّ حَسْبُكَ اللّٰهُ وَمَنِ اتَّبَعَكَ مِنَ الْمُؤْمِنِيْنَ

Sufficient for you is Allah, and those believers who follow you.[2]

مُحَمَّدٌ رَّسُوْلُ اللّٰهِ ۚ وَ الَّذِيْنَ مَعَهٗٓ أَشِدَّآءُ عَلَى الْكُفَّارِ رُحَمَآءُ بَيْنَهُمْ تَرٰيهُمْ رُكَّعًا سُجَّدًا يَّبْتَغُوْنَ فَضْلًا مِّنَ اللّٰهِ وَ رِضْوَانًا ۚ

Muḥammad ﷺ is Allah's Messenger and those with him are severe against the kuffār and compassionate among themselves. You will see them sometimes bowing, sometimes prostrating, seeking Allah's bounty and His pleasure. Their hallmark is on their faces because of the effect of prostration.[3]

وَالَّذِيْنَ اٰمَنُوْا وَهَاجَرُوْا وَجٰهَدُوْا فِىْ سَبِيْلِ اللّٰهِ وَالَّذِيْنَ اٰوَوْا وَّنَصَرُوْٓا أُولٰٓئِكَ هُمُ الْمُؤْمِنُوْنَ حَقًّا ۚ لَهُمْ مَّغْفِرَةٌ وَّرِزْقٌ كَرِيْمٌ

As for those who believe, migrate and strive in the path of Allah, and those who help and assist, they are the true believers. For them is forgiveness and a noble sustenance.[4]

Those who believed, migrated and strove, they are the Muhājirīn. And those who assisted and helped, they are the Anṣār. All of whom are Ṣaḥābah. Allah describes them collectively as true believers.

Who then, with a vestige of intellect and sanity, would place the Ṣaḥābah and the Munāfiqīn in the same trench?

5. It is an agreed fact, acknowledged also by Tījānī, that the Prophet ﷺ taught a few Ṣaḥābah the names of the Munāfiqīn. It has also been established that the Prophet ﷺ was pleased with his Ṣaḥābah and made loving them, praising them, and defending their honour compulsory. He said:

---

1 Sūrah Āl ʿImrān: 110.

2 Sūrah al-Anfāl: 64.

3 Sūrah Fatḥ: 29.

4 Sūrah al-Anfāl: 74.

لا تسبوا أصحابي فو الذي نفسي بيده لو أن أحدكم أنفق مثل أحد ذهبا ما بلغ مد أحدهم ولا نصيفه

Do not revile my Ṣaḥābah, for I swear by the One Who controls my life, if any of you have to spend gold equal to Mount Uḥud, it will never equal one *mudd*[1] spent by the Ṣaḥābah, and not even half.[2]

The Messenger ﷺ also said:

من سب اصحابي فعليه لعنة الله والملائكة والناس اجمعين

Whoever curses my Ṣaḥābah, may the curse of Allah, the angels and the entire humanity, be upon him.[3]

إحفظوني في أصحابي ثم الذين يلونهم ثم الذين يلونهم

Protect me by protecting my Ṣaḥābah, then those after them, then those after them.[4]

This proves with certainty the ʿ*adālah* (religious integrity) of all the Ṣaḥābah. It is absolutely impossible to insert the munāfiqīn into the meaning of these aḥādīth. Verily Allah has revealed concerning the Munāfiqīn:

إِنَّ الْمُنٰفِقِيْنَ فِى الدَّرْكِ الْأَسْفَلِ مِنَ النَّارِ ۚ

Indeed, the munāfiqīn will be in the lowest depths of the Fire.[5]

The ال in the word Munāfiqīn is to indicate *istighrāq* (inclusiveness), i.e. to include every single one of the munāfiqīn. The only exception would be if, Allah forbid, the Prophet ﷺ contradicted himself in his statements, and that could never be.

1 A measurement of volume equivalent to approximately 750 ml.

2 *Ṣaḥīḥ al-Bukhārī*, Ḥadīth no. 3470.

3 Ṭabarānī: *al-Muʿjam al-Kabīr*, vol. 12, Ḥadīth no. 12709; Abū Nuʿaym: *Ḥilyah*, vol. 7 p. 103; Ibn Abī ʿĀsim: *Al-Sunnah*, Ḥadīth no. 1000.

4 *Musnad Aḥmad*, Ḥadīth no. 177, with an authentic chain of narration. *Ibn Mājah*, Ḥadīth no. 2363; *Ḥākim*, vol. 1 p. 114, corroborated by al-Dhahabī as authentic by the standards of al-Bukhārī and Muslim.

5 Surah al-Nisāʾ: 145.

6. We ask the "guided" Tījānī what he means by categorising the Ṣaḥābah into two groups: Category One who followed the Messenger صَلَّى اللَّهُ عَلَيْهِ وَسَلَّمَ, which he claims were the minority of the Ṣaḥābah; and Categories Two and Three, the vilified, who followed the Messenger صَلَّى اللَّهُ عَلَيْهِ وَسَلَّمَ for worldly gain, out of fear, or out of hypocrisy, as well as those who later turned on their heels.

   If the majority of the Ṣaḥābah were deserters or hypocrites, it would mean that the Prophet صَلَّى اللَّهُ عَلَيْهِ وَسَلَّمَ was not capable of instilling truth and integrity in his Ṣaḥābah. Allah forbid! Did he only manage to train three or seven Ṣaḥābah in all the time of his Prophethood? Such allegations against him are far-fetched indeed! May our parents be sacrificed for him, peace and salutations be upon him.

   To a real seeker of truth I say: Is this not a direct insult against the Prophet صَلَّى اللَّهُ عَلَيْهِ وَسَلَّمَ? By Allah, what did he accomplish over the length of this period with his Ṣaḥābah? And did they only learn evil from him? Subḥān Allāh! Is this the great Prophet who prepared a single nation of mankind, through whom Allah conquered the world, and through them saved mankind from the worship of creation and brought them to the worship of the Creator, from the tyranny of other religions to the justice of Islam, and from the darkness of ignorance to the light of freedom? Through them people entered the religion of Allah from every deep corner in droves and groups, and even Jews and Christians acknowledge the greatness of this generation.

   Yet, fifteen centuries later, we still hear the claims of Ibn Saba's followers telling us that this same generation of Ṣaḥābah were hypocrites who turned on their heels and are destined for the Fire.

7. Whoever studies the biography of our Prophet صَلَّى اللَّهُ عَلَيْهِ وَسَلَّمَ will know that Islam was not plagued by hypocrisy during the Makkan period on account of the persecution which the Muslims faced during that time. Instead, it emerged in Madīnah after Allah had firmly established His Prophet صَلَّى اللَّهُ عَلَيْهِ وَسَلَّمَ there and Islam had become an accepted reality. There is consensus that Abū Bakr, ʿUmar, ʿUthmān, and others رَضِيَ اللَّهُ عَنْهُمْ embraced Islam at the very dawn of its emergence in Makkah. This alone should make it clear that they were the furthest people from hypocrisy.

8. Verily Allah unmasked the munāfiqīn in two sūrahs—Surah al-Munāfiqūn and Surah al-Tawbah—exposing their condition, their conspiracies, and that which their hearts concealed with regards to the believers. This is why Sūrah al-Tawbah is called *al-Fāḍiḥah* (The Exposer) and *al-Mudamdamah* (The Annihilator). It then reveals the condition of the people of Īmān, the noble Ṣaḥābah, through the testimony of Allah.

   Sūrah al-Munāfiqūn was revealed concerning the leader of the hypocrites, ʿAbd Allāh ibn Ubayy ibn Salūl, and his companions. It is reported by al-Bukhārī in his *Ṣaḥīḥ*, under the commentary of Sūrah al-Munāfiqūn, from Zayd ibn Arqam رضي الله عنه:

   > I was in an expedition when I heard ʿAbd Allāh ibn Ubayy saying, "Do not spend on those who are with the Messenger of Allah, until they disperse from him. And if we return from him, the honoured will definitely expel the weak." So I mentioned that to my paternal uncle — or to ʿUmar — so he mentioned it to the Prophet صلى الله عليه وسلم. He then summoned me and I told him what I had heard. The Messenger of Allah صلى الله عليه وسلم sent a message to ʿAbd Allāh ibn Ubayy and his companions, but they took an oath that they had not said such a thing. The Messenger of Allah refuted what I had said and believed him. This caused me such grief that I had never experienced before. So I remained at home, and my uncle said to me, "What did you expect, except that the Messenger of Allah would belie you and detest you." Allah then revealed, "*When the munāfiqīn come to you...*" (Sūrah al-Munāfiqūn). The Prophet صلى الله عليه وسلم summoned me and read the verses, after which he said, "Verily Allah has attested to the truth of what you said, O Zayd."

   Perhaps Tījānī will contest this, so let me elaborate:

   I recommend that he study the book *Majmaʿ al-Bayān fī Tafsīr al-Qurʾān* by al-Ṭabarsī, one of their leading scholars, who confirms that Sūrah al-Munāfiqūn was revealed regarding Ibn Ubay: "The verses were revealed concerning ʿAbd Allāh ibn Ubay, the hypocrite, and his companions."

   He then mentions the narrations of al-Bukhārī which supports this. It is also established that each of the companions of Ibn Ubayy were known to the Ṣaḥābah. This is very clear from the context of the ḥadīth.

With regards to Sūrah al-Tawbah, it mentions the Munāfiqīn explicitly on many occasions and brings to the fore many of their qualities, such as in the statement of Allah :

إِنَّمَا يَسْتَأْذِنُكَ الَّذِيْنَ لَا يُؤْمِنُوْنَ بِاللّٰهِ وَالْيَوْمِ الْأٰخِرِ وَ ارْتَابَتْ قُلُوْبُهُمْ فَهُمْ فِيْ رَيْبِهِمْ يَتَرَدَّدُوْنَ

Only those would ask permission of you who do not believe in Allah and the Last Day and whose hearts have doubted, and they, in their doubt, are hesitating.

وَلَوْ أَرَادُوا الْخُرُوْجَ لَأَعَدُّوْا لَهٗ عُدَّةً وَّلٰكِنْ كَرِهَ اللّٰهُ انْبِعَاثَهُمْ فَثَبَّطَهُمْ وَقِيْلَ اقْعُدُوْا مَعَ الْقٰعِدِيْنَ

And if they had intended to go forth, they would have prepared for it [some] preparation. But Allah disliked their being sent, so He kept them back, and they were told, "Remain [behind] with those who remain."

لَوْ خَرَجُوْا فِيْكُمْ مَّا زَادُوْكُمْ إِلَّا خَبَالًا وَّلَأَوْضَعُوْا خِلٰلَكُمْ يَبْغُوْنَكُمُ الْفِتْنَةَ وَفِيْكُمْ سَمّٰعُوْنَ لَهُمْ ۗ وَاللّٰهُ عَلِيْمٌۢ بِالظّٰلِمِيْنَ

Had they gone forth with you, they would not have increased you except in confusion, and they would have been active among you, seeking [to cause] you fitnah. And among you are avid listeners to them. And Allah is Knowing of the wrongdoers.

لَقَدِ ابْتَغَوُا الْفِتْنَةَ مِنْ قَبْلُ وَقَلَّبُوْا لَكَ الْأُمُوْرَ حَتّٰى جَآءَ الْحَقُّ وَظَهَرَ أَمْرُ اللّٰهِ وَهُمْ كٰرِهُوْنَ

They had already desired dissension before and had upset matters for you until the truth came and the ordinance of Allah appeared, while they were averse.

وَمِنْهُمْ مَّنْ يَّقُوْلُ ائْذَنْ لِّيْ وَلَا تَفْتِنِّيْ ۗ أَلَا فِي الْفِتْنَةِ سَقَطُوْا ۗ وَ إِنَّ جَهَنَّمَ لَمُحِيْطَةٌۢ بِالْكٰفِرِيْنَ

And among them is he who says, "Permit me [to remain at home] and do not put me to trial." Unquestionably, into trial they have fallen. And indeed, Hell will encompass the disbelievers. [1]

It is common knowledge that all of the Ṣaḥābah went out with the Messenger ﷺ to fight, with the exception of a few. Initially, Abū Dharr and Abū Khaythamah رضي الله عنهما remained behind, but they too left soon thereafter and joined the Prophet ﷺ. Amongst the Ṣaḥābah who remained behind were three and they were Kaʿb ibn Mālik, Hilāl ibn Umayyah, and Murārah ibn al-Rabīʿ رضي الله عنهم; who were from the Anṣār.

The manner in which Allah forgave them and accepted their repentance will be discussed shortly. The Munāfiqīn and those who were exempted from jihād remained in Madīnah. I have previously mentioned the statement of Kaʿb ibn Mālik رضي الله عنه, one of the three who remained behind, that no one stayed behind except the person whom Allah had excused or the person who was known for open hypocrisy. This indicates that the Munāfiqīn had signs by which the Ṣaḥābah knew them, and they were not unfamiliar with them:

يَحْذَرُ الْمُنٰفِقُوْنَ أَنْ تُنَزَّلَ عَلَيْهِمْ سُوْرَةٌ تُنَبِّئُهُمْ بِمَا فِيْ قُلُوْبِهِمْ ۚ قُلِ اسْتَهْزِءُوْا ۚ إِنَّ اللّٰهَ مُخْرِجٌ مَّا تَحْذَرُوْنَ

The munāfiqīn fear that a sūrah may be revealed about them, informing them of what is in their hearts. Say: "(Go ahead and) Mock! Certainly Allah will expose that which you fear". [2]

Ibn Kathīr mentions under the commentary of this verse:

Mujāhid said, "They say something amongst themselves then they say, 'We hope that Allah will not expose this secret of ours.'" This verse is similar to Allah's statement, *When they come to you, they greet you in a manner in which Allah does not greet you, and they say within themselves, 'why does Allah not punish us for what we say?' Jahannam will be sufficient for them, they will burn in it and what an evil destination.* This means that Allah will reveal to His Messenger ﷺ that which will expose you and clarify to you your affair. Similarly, the statement

1 Sūrah al-Tawbah: 45 – 49.

2 Sūrah al-Tawbah: 64.

of the Most High, Do those in whose hearts there is disease think that Allah will not expose their grudges?... until and surely you will know them by the tone of their speech.[1] It is for this reason that Qatādah said, "This sūrah used to be known as The Exposer, i.e. the exposer of the Munāfiqīn."[2]

In other words, Allah has exposed them to the entire creation and has made their true nature clear to humanity, whereas previously their plans were made stealthily and in secret. After having understood this, only those who are enveloped by compound ignorance will say that the Munāfiqīn and the Ṣaḥābah are in one category.

As for the verses:

سَيَحْلِفُونَ بِاللَّهِ لَكُمْ إِذَا انقَلَبْتُمْ إِلَيْهِمْ لِتُعْرِضُوا عَنْهُمْ ۖ فَأَعْرِضُوا عَنْهُمْ ۖ إِنَّهُمْ رِجْسٌ ۖ وَمَأْوَاهُمْ جَهَنَّمُ جَزَاءً بِمَا كَانُوا يَكْسِبُونَ

They will swear by Allah to you when you return to them that you would leave them alone. So leave them alone; indeed they are evil; and their refuge is Hell as recompense for what they had been earning.

يَحْلِفُونَ لَكُمْ لِتَرْضَوْا عَنْهُمْ ۖ فَإِن تَرْضَوْا عَنْهُمْ فَإِنَّ اللَّهَ لَا يَرْضَىٰ عَنِ الْقَوْمِ الْفَاسِقِينَ

They swear to you so that you might be satisfied with them. But if you should be satisfied with them - indeed, Allah is not satisfied with a defiantly disobedient people.[3]

These verses were revealed concerning those Munāfiqīn who remained behind during the Battle of Tabūk. They were approximately eighty people, who came to present their excuses before the Prophet ﷺ when he returned, and none of them were amongst the elite Ṣaḥābah رضي الله عنهم.

In *Ṣaḥīḥ al-Bukhārī*, the narration of ʿAbd Allāh ibn Kaʿb discusses the reason of the revelation of verses 107-108 of Sūrah al-Tawbah:

---

1 Sūrah Muḥammad: 29.

2 *Tafsīr Ibn Kathīr*, vol. 2 p. 381.

3 Sūrah al-Tawbah: 95 - 96.

وَالَّذِينَ اتَّخَذُوا مَسْجِدًا ضِرَارًا وَكُفْرًا وَتَفْرِيقًا بَيْنَ الْمُؤْمِنِينَ وَإِرْصَادًا لِّمَنْ حَارَبَ اللَّهَ وَرَسُولَهُ مِن قَبْلُ ۚ وَلَيَحْلِفُنَّ إِنْ أَرَدْنَا إِلَّا الْحُسْنَىٰ ۖ وَاللَّهُ يَشْهَدُ إِنَّهُمْ لَكَاذِبُونَ

And [there are] those [hypocrites] who took for themselves a mosque for causing harm and disbelief and division among the believers and as a station for whoever had warred against Allah and His Messenger before. And they will surely swear, "We intended only the best." And Allah testifies that indeed they are liars.

لَا تَقُمْ فِيهِ أَبَدًا ۚ لَّمَسْجِدٌ أُسِّسَ عَلَى التَّقْوَىٰ مِنْ أَوَّلِ يَوْمٍ أَحَقُّ أَن تَقُومَ فِيهِ ۚ فِيهِ رِجَالٌ يُحِبُّونَ أَن يَتَطَهَّرُوا ۚ وَاللَّهُ يُحِبُّ الْمُطَّهِّرِينَ

Do not stand [for prayer] within it - ever. A masjid founded on righteousness from the first day is more worthy for you to stand in. Within it are men who love to purify themselves; and Allah loves those who purify themselves.[1]

This verse also exposes the Munāfiqīn. It refers to the incident when they built Masjid Ḍirār for Abū ʿĀmir, the sinful monk, in order to fight the believers. They requested the Prophet ﷺ to perform ṣalāh in it, but Jibrīl عليه السلام informed him of their reality. Allah instructed His Prophet ﷺ to destroy it and he in turn ordered a few of his Ṣaḥābah to carry out the task. On the contrary, they were instructed to perform ṣalāh in the masjid whose foundations was laid on *taqwā* (piety).

There is no doubt that those who built Masjid Ḍirār were known to the Ṣaḥābah, but in Tījānī's prejudiced view the majority of the Ṣaḥābah were Munāfiqīn. Reason dictates that the masjid in which the Messenger ﷺ performed ṣalāh was the masjid of the Ṣaḥābah, whereas the masjid which was ordered to be destroyed was the masjid of the Munāfiqīn. It begs the question: If the majority of the Ṣaḥābah were Munāfiqīn and the Messenger ﷺ then performed ṣalāh in the masjid of the hypocrites, then did the Messenger ﷺ destroy the masjid of the believers? Was this only so that

1 Sūrah al-Tawbah: 107 - 108.

ṣalāh could be performed in the masjid of the Munāfiqīn? Understand, O people of intellect!

And in this very same Sūrah, Allah expresses His pleasure with the Ṣaḥābah, the first forerunners of the Muhājirīn and the Anṣār, by saying:

وَالسّٰبِقُوْنَ الْاَوَّلُوْنَ مِنَ الْمُهٰجِرِيْنَ وَالْاَنْصَارِ وَالَّذِيْنَ اتَّبَعُوْهُمْ بِاِحْسَانٍ ۙ رَّضِيَ اللّٰهُ عَنْهُمْ وَرَضُوْا عَنْهُ وَاَعَدَّ لَهُمْ جَنّٰتٍ تَجْرِيْ تَحْتَهَا الْاَنْهٰرُ خٰلِدِيْنَ فِيْهَآ اَبَدًا ؕ ذٰلِكَ الْفَوْزُ الْعَظِيْمُ

And the forerunners of the Muhājirīn and the Anṣār and also those who followed them in goodness. Allah is pleased with them and they are pleased with Him. He has prepared for them gardens under which rivers flow, to dwell therein forever. That is the ultimate success.[1]

Thus did Allah express His pleasure with the Ṣaḥābah, the Muhājirīn and the Anṣār.

So woe to those who hate them or abuse them, or hate or abuse some of them, especially the leader of the Ṣaḥābah after the Messenger ﷺ, and the best of them and most virtuous, the greatest friend and the best successor: Abū Bakr ibn Abī Quḥāfah رضي الله عنه. Undoubtedly the disgraced cult of the Rāfiḍah oppose the noblest of Ṣaḥābah, hate them and abuse them—may Allah protect us from that. What is the state of their faith in relation to the Qur'ān if they curse those whom Allah is pleased with? As for the Ahl al-Sunnah, they express their pleasure with those with whom Allah is pleased, curse those whom Allah and His Messenger ﷺ curse, befriend those whom Allah befriends, and oppose those whom Allah opposes.

They are adherents and not innovators; they follow and do not formulate their own ideas. This is why they are the successful *Ḥizb Allāh* (army of Allah) and His believing servants.

Allah سبحانه وتعالى says:

1 Sūrah al-Tawbah: 100.

لَقَدْ تَّابَ اللّٰهُ عَلَى النَّبِيِّ وَ الْمُهٰجِرِيْنَ وَ الْأَنْصَارِ الَّذِيْنَ اتَّبَعُوْهُ فِيْ سَاعَةِ الْعُسْرَةِ مِنْۢ بَعْدِ مَا كَادَ يَزِيْغُ قُلُوْبُ فَرِيْقٍ مِّنْهُمْ ثُمَّ تَابَ عَلَيْهِمْ ؕ إِنَّهُ بِهِمْ رَءُوْفٌ رَّحِيْمٌ

Verily, Allah has pardoned the Prophet, the Muhājirīn and the Anṣār, who followed him in the hour of difficulty, after the hearts of a group of them nearly deviated. He then pardoned them. Verily, He is Most Kind, Most Merciful unto them.[1]

This verse is also very clear in its praise for the Muhājirīn and Anṣār, and testifies to their purity of heart. The testimony of Allah in these two verses explicitly proves the integrity of these chosen Ṣaḥābah. Furthermore, Allah was pleased with the three who stayed behind and included them amongst the larger group of the Ṣaḥābah, as opposed to the Munāfiqīn who stayed behind and made excuses that the Messenger ﷺ accepted on account of their outward appearance.

This is the greatest proof of the vast difference between the Ṣaḥābah, who were declared people of integrity by Allah despite their mistakes, and the Munāfiqīn whom Allah exposed in His Noble Book. And all praise belongs to Allah, Lord of the entire universe.

9. It is imperative that I now quote the opinion of a very senior Twelver Shīʿī scholar, who Allah caused to speak the truth. In his *Tafsīr* Abū Naṣr Muḥammad ibn Masʿūd al-ʿAyyāshī reports a narration from Imām Muḥammad al-Bāqir (who is regarded as the fifth Imām by the Shīʿah) under the commentary of the verse:

إِنَّ اللّٰهَ يُحِبُّ التَّوَّابِيْنَ وَ يُحِبُّ الْمُتَطَهِّرِيْنَ

Verily Allah loves those who repent and He loves those who are pure.[2]

This narration explicitly negates any form of hypocrisy from the Ṣaḥābah of the Prophet ﷺ. He reports that Imām Muḥammad al-Bāqir said:

1 Sūrah al-Tawbah: 117.

2 Sūrah al-Baqarah: 222.

كنت عند ابي جعفر عليه السلام فدخل عليه حمران بن اعين فساله عن اشياء فلما هم حمران بالقيام قال لابي جعفر عليه السلام اخبرنا اطال الله بقاك و امتعنا بك انا ناتيك فما نخرج من عندك حتى ترق قلوبنا و تسلوا انفسنا عن الدنيا و تهون علينا ما في ايدي الناس من هذه الاموال ثم نخرج من عندك فاذا صرنا مع الناس و التجار احببنا الدنيا ؟ قال فقال ابو جعفر عليه السلام انما هي القلوب مرة يصعب عليها الامر و مرة يسهل ثم قال ابو جعفر اما ان اصحاب رسول الله صلى الله عليه و سلم قالوا يا رسول الله نخاف علينا النفاق قال فقال لهم و لم تخافون ذلك ؟ قالوا انا اذا كنا عندك فذكرتنا روعنا و وجلنا نسينا الدنيا و زهدنا فيها حتى كانا نعاين الاخرة و الجنة و النار و نحن عندك فاذا خرجنا من عندك و دخلنا هذه البيوت وشممنا الاولاد و راينا العيال و الاهل و الاولاد و المال يكاد ان نحول عن الحال التي كنا عليها عندك و حتى كأنا لم نكن على شيء افتخاف علينا ان يكون هذا النفاق؟ فقال لهم رسول الله صلى الله عليه و سلم كلا! هذا من خطوات الشيطان ليرغبنكم في الدنيا والله لو انكم تدومون على الحال التي تكونون عليها و انتم عندي في الحال التي و صفتم انفسكم بها لصافحتكم الملائكة و مشيتم على الماء و لو لا انكم تذنبون فتستغفرون الله لخلق خلقا لكي يذنبوا ثم يستغفروا فيغفر لهم ان المؤمن مفتن تواب اما تسمع لقوله ﴿ إِنَّ اللّٰهَ يُحِبُّ التَّوَّابِيْنَ ﴾ وقال ﴿اِسْتَغْفِرُوْا رَبَّكُمْ ثُمَّ تُوْبُوْا اِلَيْهِ﴾

I was with Abū Jaʿfar (Imām al-Bāqir) when Ḥumrān ibn Aʿyan entered and asked him about some matters. When Ḥumrān stood to leave, he said to Abū Jaʿfar, "Inform us, may Allah keep you amongst us for a long time and allow us to benefit from you: we come to you and do not leave without our hearts being softened and our souls forgetting about the world, and we consider insignificant the wealth which people possess. Then (why is it) when we leave you, and mingle with people and businessmen, that we love the world?"

Abū Jaʿfar said, "It is only but the heart. Occasionally things are difficult and sometimes things are easy."

Then Abū Jaʿfar said, "Did not the Ṣaḥābah of the Messenger of Allah say, 'O Messenger of Allah, do you fear hypocrisy for us?' He enquired, 'And why do you fear that?' They said, 'When we are with you, and you remind us of our fears and apprehensions, we forget the world and withdraw from it; as if we see the hereafter and Jannah and Jahannam, while we are with you. But when we leave from you, and enter these houses, see our children, look at our dependants, our wives, our children and our wealth, we almost entirely deviate from the condition we were in when we were with you. Do you fear for us that this might be hypocrisy?' So the Messenger of Allah said to them, 'Never! This is of the footsteps of Shayṭān, to make you desirous of the world. By Allah, if you were to stay in the condition that you were in while you were with me, as you described to me, then the angels would have been shaking hands with you and you would walk on water. Were it not for you committing sin and seeking forgiveness from Allah, He would have created a creation who would sin, and then seek forgiveness, so He could forgive them. Indeed, the believer is one who errs and seeks forgiveness. Have you not heard His statement, *Verily, Allah loves those who repent.* He also said, *seek forgiveness from your Lord then repent unto Him*.'"[1]

Imām al-Ḥasan al-ʿAskarī is regarded as the eleventh Imām by the Shīʿah. In his *Tafsīr* he provides clear proof for the lofty status of the Ṣaḥābah. He reports that when Prophet Mūsā عليه السلام asked Allah a number of questions, one of them was:

هل في صحابة الانبياء اكرم عندك من صحابتي قال الله عز و جل: يا موسى اما علمت ان فضل صحابة محمد على صحابة المرسلين كفضل ال محمد على جميع ال النبين و كفضل محمد على جميع المرسلين

"Are there amongst the Ṣaḥābah of the Messengers people who are more honourable than my Ṣaḥābah?"

Allah replied, "O Mūsā! Do you not know that the superiority of the Ṣaḥābah of Muḥammad over all the companions of the Messengers is like the superiority of the family of Muḥammad over all the families of the Prophets, and like the superiority of Muḥammad over all the Messengers."[2]

I conclude with the memorable words of ʿAlī ibn Abī Ṭālib رضي الله عنه about the Ṣaḥābah:

---

1 *Tafsīr al-ʿAyyāshī*, vol. 1 p. 128.

2 *Tafsīr al- Ḥasan al-ʿAskarī*, commentary on Sūrah al-Baqarah p. 11.

لقد رايت اصحاب محمد صلى الله عليه و سلم فما ارى احدا يشبههم منكم
لقد كانوا يصبحون شعثا غبرا و قد باتوا سجدا و قياما يراوحون بين جباههم
و خدودهم و يقفون على مثل الجمر من ذكر معادهم كأن بين اعينهم ركب
المعزي من طول سجودهم اذا ذكر الله هملت اعينهم حتى تبل جيوبهم و
مادوا كما يميد الشجريوم الريح العاصف خوفا من العقاب و رجاء للثواب

> Indeed, I have seen the Ṣaḥābah of Muḥammad صلى الله عليه وسلم and I do not see anyone amongst you who resembles them. They would rise in the morning, unkempt and covered with dust, because they had spent the night in prostration and standing. They would alternate between their foreheads and their cheeks, while it felt as if they were standing on coals, when thinking of their return to the hereafter. It is as if between their eyes there were marks like knees of goats due to the length of their prostration. When they would remember Allah, their eyes would drip until their bosoms would become wet. They would shake as a tree shakes on a terribly windy day, fearing punishment and hoping for reward.[1]

The Shīʿī scholar, Ibrāhīm al-Thaqafī, mentioned in his book *al-Ghārāt*—which is amongst the classical works of the Shīʿah—the following exchange between ʿAlī رضي الله عنه and his companions:

> "O Amīr al-Mu'minīn! Inform us about your comrades."
>
> He asked, "About which comrades of mine?"
>
> They said, "About the Ṣaḥābah of Muḥammad."
>
> He said, "All of the Ṣaḥābah of Muḥammad are my comrades."[2]

This is the statement concerning the Ṣaḥābah of the Prophet صلى الله عليه وسلم by their greatest Imām. Yet, the "guided" Tījānī and other Shīʿah claim that the majority of these Ṣaḥābah were Munāfiqīn. Will they rescind this vile statement of theirs and control their tongues concerning the noble Ṣaḥābah رضي الله عنهم, or else refrain from claiming to have īmān?

---

1 *Nahj al-Balāghah* with commentary of Muḥammad ʿAbduh, p. 225.

2 Al-Thaqafī: *Al-Ghārāt*, vol. 1 p. 177.

I thus encourage you, dear reader, to refer to the proofs mentioned here in order to determine how accurately we have represented the Shīʿī position on the majority of the Ṣaḥābah, especially their claim that the Three Khulafāʾ were amongst the Munāfiqīn who turned apostate.

Chapter Two

Treaty of Ḥudaybiyyah

After dividing the Ṣaḥābah into three categories, Tījānī claims that he will base his research on impartiality and objectivity, drawing on sound logic and reason:

> **This is what I know from the Sunnī scholars, and that is what I heard from the Shī'ī scholars regarding the classification of the Companions; and that is what made me start my detailed study with the issue of the Companions. I promised my God — if He led me on the right path — to rid myself from emotional bias and to be neutral and objective and to listen to what the two sides said, then to follow what was best, basing my conclusions on two premises:**
>
> 1. **A sound and a logical premise: that is to say that I would only depend upon what everybody is in agreement with, regarding the commentary on the Book of Allah, and the correct parts of the honourable Sunnah of the Prophet.**
> 2. **The mind: for it is the greatest gift that Allah has given to human beings, and through it He honoured them and distinguished them from the rest of creation.**[1]

He thus claims to rely on the Noble Qur'ān, the authentic Sunnah, and reason.

It is a fact accepted by novices, let alone advanced students, that the understanding of the Qur'ān must be taken from its original sources and from the statements of qualified scholars, and must be based on knowledge of its principles. To understand the Sunnah it is necessary to refer to the scholars of ḥadīth and the science of *al-Jarḥ wa al-Ta'dīl* (narrator discreditation and accreditation) who verify aḥādīth based on the chain of transmission and the text.

It is also necessary for the individual to exercise his reason in order to know correct from incorrect, provided that he does not overstep into irrationality.

So, how truthful is Tījānī in his claims of impartiality and relying on reason and logic? We shall see.

---

1 *Then I was guided*, pg. 64.

Tījānī's position on the Ṣaḥābah at Ḥudaybiyyah

The first matter which Tījānī brings up in context of indictments against the Ṣaḥābah is the Truce of Ḥudaybiyyah. He says:

> **Briefly the story is as follows:**
>
> **In the sixth year after the Hijrah (emigration of the Prophet from Mecca to Madinah), the Messenger of Allah with one thousand and four hundred of his Companions marched towards Mecca to do the Umrah. They camped in "Dhū al-Hulayfah" where the Prophet صَلَّى ٱللَّٰهُ عَلَيْهِ وَسَلَّمَ ordered his Companions to put down their arms and wear the Ihram (white gowns worn especially for the purpose of the pilgrimage and the Umrah), then they dispatched al-Hady (an offering for sacrifice) to inform Quraysh that he was coming as a visitor to do the Umrah and not as a fighter. But Quraysh, with all its arrogance, feared that its reputation would be dented if the other Arabs heard that Muhammad had entered Mecca by force. Therefore, they sent a delegation led by Suhayl ibn Amr ibn Abd Wadd al-Amiri to see the Prophet and ask him to turn back that year, but said that they would allow him to visit Mecca for three days the year after. In addition to that, they put down some harsh conditions, which were accepted by the Messenger of Allah as the circumstances warranted such acceptance, and as revealed to him by his God, Glory and Might be to Him.**
>
> **A few of the Companions did not like the Prophet's action and opposed him very strongly, and Umar ibn al-Khattab came and said to him, "Are you not truly the Prophet of Allah?"**
>
> **He answered, "Yes, I am."**
>
> **Umar asked, "Are we not right and our enemy wrong?"**
>
> **The Prophet answered, "Yes."**
>
> **Umar asked, "Why do we then disgrace our religion?"**
>
> **The Messenger of Allah صَلَّى ٱللَّٰهُ عَلَيْهِ وَسَلَّمَ said, "I am the Messenger of Allah and I will never disobey Him and He is my support."**
>
> **Umar asked, "Did you not tell us that we would come to the House of Allah and go around it?"**
>
> **The Prophet answered, "Yes, and did I tell you that we were coming this year?"**

Umar answered, "No."

The Prophet said, "Then you are coming to it and going around it."

Umar later went to Abu Bakr and asked him, "O Abu Bakr, is he not truly the Prophet of Allah?"

He answered, "Yes."

Umar then asked him the same questions he had asked the Messenger of Allah, and Abu Bakr answered him with the same answers and added, "O Umar he is the Messenger of Allah, and he will not disobey his God, Who is his support, so hold on to him."

When the Prophet had finished signing the treaty, he said to his Companions, "Go and slaughter (sacrifices) and shave your heads." And by Allah [not] one of them stood up until he had said it three times. When nobody obeyed his orders, he went to his quarters, then came out and spoke to no one, and slaughtered a young camel with his own hands, and then asked his barber to shave his head. When the Companions saw all that, they went and slaughtered (sacrifices), and shaved one another, until they nearly killed one another

This is the summary of the story of the peace treaty of al-Hudaibiyah, which is one of the events whose details both the Shia and Sunnah agree upon, and it is cited by many historians and biographers of the Prophet such as al-Tabari, Ibn al-Athir, Ibn Saad, al-Bukhari and Muslim.

I stopped here, for I could not read this kind of material without feeling rather surprised about the behaviour of those Companions towards their Prophet. Could any sensible man accept some people's claims that the Companions may Allah bless them, always obeyed and implemented the orders of the Messenger of Allah ﷺ, for these incidents expose their lies, and fall short of what they want! Could any sensible man imagine that such behaviour towards the Prophet is an easy or acceptable matter or even an excusable one! Allah, the Almighty, said:

فَلَا وَرَبِّكَ لَا يُؤْمِنُوْنَ حَتّٰى يُحَكِّمُوْكَ فِيْمَا شَجَرَ بَيْنَهُمْ ثُمَّ لَا يَجِدُوْا
فِيْٓ أَنْفُسِهِمْ حَرَجًا مِمَّا قَضَيْتَ وَيُسَلِّمُوْا تَسْلِيمًا

But no, by your Lord, they will not (truly) believe until they make you, (O Muḥammad), judge concerning that over which they dispute among

themselves and then find within themselves no discomfort from what you have judged and submit in (full, willing) submission.[1]

The Ṣaḥābah at Ḥudaybiyyah

Before proceeding with the refutation of Tījānī's assessment of the Ṣaḥābah's conduct at Ḥudaybiyyah it will only be fair to the reader that the incident of Ḥudaybiyyah be recounted in as much detail as to establish some context. The truncated version reproduced by Tījānī conveniently overlooks major elements of the entire incident and zooms-in, in high definition, on the alleged elements of misconduct.

The Messenger of Allah ﷺ had a vision that he had entered Makkah and circumambulated the Kaʿbah. The Companions of the Prophet ﷺ were overjoyed when the Prophet ﷺ told them about the vision since they esteemed and revered Makkah. The opportunity of paying a visit had been denied to them for a long time but nobody had cause to think of the Holy City. They had been yearning to make the journey to Makkah all those years and were looking forward to the day when their hearts' desire would be fulfilled and they could pay homage to the first House erected for the worship of Allah. The Muhājirīn were especially consumed by longing since Makkah was their birthplace. They had grown up in that city but had been forced to abandon it. As soon as the Prophet ﷺ informed the Companions of the vision, almost all of them promptly agreed to accompany him and started making preparations for the journey.

It was the month of Dhū al-Qaʿdah, in the sixth year of hijrah, when the Messenger of Allah ﷺ set out for Makkah with the intention of performing ʿUmrah along with 1400 of his noble Companions رضي الله عنهم; clad in the garb of pilgrims [Iḥrām] along with the sacrificial animals, so that everybody would know that he was going not for war but to pay a visit to the Kaʿbah.

When he drew nearer he sent a scout from the tribe of Khuzāʿah to assess the attitude of Quraysh. He was informed that Khālid ibn al-Walīd was camped at Kurāʿ al-Ghamīm with his cavalry acting as Quraysh's vanguard. He was further informed that the Quraysh had conscripted mercenaries from other tribes to engage with the Muslims were they to approach; all of this to dissuade them from proceeding towards Makkah.

1 Sūrah al-Nisā': 65.

To avoid confrontation with Quraysh, the Prophet صَلَّى ٱللَّهُ عَلَيْهِ وَسَلَّمَ took detours and tread alternate routes until he was very close to Makkah. Suddenly the Prophet's صَلَّى ٱللَّهُ عَلَيْهِ وَسَلَّمَ mount, called al-Qaswā', knelt down and would not get up. The men around the Messenger صَلَّى ٱللَّهُ عَلَيْهِ وَسَلَّمَ started talking rapidly, "Al-Qaswā' has become stubborn!" But the Messenger صَلَّى ٱللَّهُ عَلَيْهِ وَسَلَّمَ said, "Al-Qaswā' has not refused for such is not her nature. The one who restrained the elephants is keeping her back. I swear by Him Who holds my life that if they propose anything to me by which the sanctuaries of Allah are dignified, I will certainly accede to their request." The Messenger صَلَّى ٱللَّهُ عَلَيْهِ وَسَلَّمَ then prodded the camel which at once sprang up on her legs, but changed her direction and started off towards Ḥudaybiyyah. She came to a halt near a water-hole that contained but little water. Certain persons complained to the Messenger صَلَّى ٱللَّهُ عَلَيْهِ وَسَلَّمَ that they were thirsty. He took out an arrow from his quiver and asked them to throw it in the ditch. Thereupon water gushed forth and everyone drank to their satisfaction.

The Prophet صَلَّى ٱللَّهُ عَلَيْهِ وَسَلَّمَ called upon 'Umar ibn al-Khaṭṭāb رَضِيَ ٱللَّهُ عَنْهُ to send him to Makkah as an emissary to Quraysh and to negotiate the terms of their entry. 'Umar feared that he would not succeed in convincing Quraysh, and that the enmity he displayed towards them and the harsh manner in which he treated them would compromise the negotiation. In turn he responded, "I will suggest to you a man they respect more than myself, 'Uthmān ibn 'Affān."

The Messenger صَلَّى ٱللَّهُ عَلَيْهِ وَسَلَّمَ then summoned 'Uthmān ibn 'Affān رَضِيَ ٱللَّهُ عَنْهُ and sent him to Abū Sufyān and the rest of Quraysh to tell them that he had not come to war but merely to perform the 'Umrah. The Prophet صَلَّى ٱللَّهُ عَلَيْهِ وَسَلَّمَ also asked 'Uthmān رَضِيَ ٱللَّهُ عَنْهُ to invite the Quraysh to Islam and to bring joy to the believing men and women still in Makkah with the glad tidings that Islam's dominance was imminent and a time would soon come when they no longer would need to conceal their faith.

'Uthmān رَضِيَ ٱللَّهُ عَنْهُ went to Makkah and delivered the Prophet's صَلَّى ٱللَّهُ عَلَيْهِ وَسَلَّمَ message to Abū Sufyān and other leaders of the Quraysh. After the Makkans had heard the message that 'Uthmān رَضِيَ ٱللَّهُ عَنْهُ had brought them his love for the Prophet صَلَّى ٱللَّهُ عَلَيْهِ وَسَلَّمَ was put to test when the they said to him, "If what you want is to do *Ṭawāf* [circumambulation of the Ka'bah], then you are free to do so now". He declined their offer saying, "I will not do so until the Messenger صَلَّى ٱللَّهُ عَلَيْهِ وَسَلَّمَ has gone round the Ka'bah."

The Quraysh then kept ʿUthmān رَضِيَ ٱللَّهُ عَنْهُ as their prisoner after he declined their offer of Ṭawāf. When the Messenger صَلَّى ٱللَّهُ عَلَيْهِ وَسَلَّمَ was misinformed that ʿUthmān رَضِيَ ٱللَّهُ عَنْهُ had been killed, he summoned the people to take an oath to avenge ʿUthmān's death. "We will not leave before engaging them in battle!" he said. Everybody gathered around the Messenger صَلَّى ٱللَّهُ عَلَيْهِ وَسَلَّمَ who was standing under the shade of a tree. The Messenger صَلَّى ٱللَّهُ عَلَيْهِ وَسَلَّمَ took the oath one by one from the fourteen hundred standing around him. After they had all taken the oath, the Messenger صَلَّى ٱللَّهُ عَلَيْهِ وَسَلَّمَ struck one of his hands on the other, saying, "This is the pledge on behalf of ʿUthmān." Thus was the pledge of Riḍwān, taken under a tree, which finds eternal mention in the Qur'ān:

لَقَدْ رَضِيَ اللَّهُ عَنِ الْمُؤْمِنِينَ إِذْ يُبَايِعُونَكَ تَحْتَ الشَّجَرَةِ فَعَلِمَ مَا فِي
قُلُوبِهِمْ فَأَنْزَلَ السَّكِينَةَ عَلَيْهِمْ وَأَثَابَهُمْ فَتْحًا قَرِيبًا

Allah was well pleased with the believers when they swore allegiance unto you beneath the tree, and He knew what was in their hearts, and He sent down the peace of reassurance on them, and has rewarded them with a near victory.[1]

After his return from Makkah certain Muslims said to ʿUthmān, "O Abū ʿAbd Allāh, you have been fortunate enough to fulfil your heart's desire by circumambulating the Kaʿbah."

"Do not be unfair to me," replied ʿUthmān, "I declare by Him who holds my life that if I were detained there for a whole year and the Prophet صَلَّى ٱللَّهُ عَلَيْهِ وَسَلَّمَ were to remain in Ḥudaybiyyah, I would not have circumambulated the Kaʿbah until the Prophet صَلَّى ٱللَّهُ عَلَيْهِ وَسَلَّمَ had done so. Truly, the Quraysh did invite me to circumambulate the House of Allah, but I declined."

While this was going on, Budayl ibn Warqa' al-Khuzāʿī arrived, accompanied by others of the Khuzāʿah tribe. They were the trusted confidants of the Messenger of Allah صَلَّى ٱللَّهُ عَلَيْهِ وَسَلَّمَ. Budayl said, "I have just left Kaʿb ibn Lu'ay and ʿĀmir ibn Lu'ay who have encamped at the Ḥudaybiyyah wells; they have with them their camels with their young. They are going to prevent you from reaching the Kaʿbah."

The Prophet صَلَّى ٱللَّهُ عَلَيْهِ وَسَلَّمَ responded, "We have not come to fight anyone. We have come to make a pilgrimage. Quraysh have been consumed by the warfare! It has

---

1 Sūrah al-Fatḥ: 18.

ruined them. If they want, I will give them respite for a period. They should then give me access to the people. If it (Islam) prevails, and they wish to join into what the people have entered, they could do so. Otherwise, they will have gained in numbers. If they refuse this, then I swear by Him who holds my soul in His hand, I will battle them in this cause of mine until I perish! Allah's command will be fulfilled!"

Budayl tried, unsuccessfully, to persuade the Quraysh. ʿUrwah ibn Masʿūd al-Thaqafī, who was present when the Quraysh dismissed Budayl's proposal arose and said, "O People, am I not as your father?"

"Yes, you are," they told him.

Then he asked, "...and are you not as my children?"

"Yes, indeed," they replied.

"Do you mistrust me?"

"No," they answered.

"Do you not know that I called to the people of ʿUkaẓ to come forth to war alongside me and that when they put me off I came to you with my family and my son, and all who obeyed me?"

"Yes indeed," they replied.

This man (the Messenger ﷺ) has offered you a reasonable proposal accept it and allow me to go to him."

They said, "Go to him."

So, he went to the Messenger ﷺ and started talking to him. The Messenger ﷺ told him the same as he told Budayl.

ʿUrwah then said, "O Muḥammad! What do you think would happen if you vanquished your own people (Quraysh)? By Allah, I do not see dignified people. What I do see is people from various tribes who would flee and forsake you."

Abū Bakr sternly rebuked him, "Go suck Lāt's clitoris! Do you think we would flee and forsake him?"

ʿUrwah said, "Who is this man?"

They replied, "He is Abū Bakr."

ʿUrwah said to Abū Bakr, "By Him Who has control of my life, had it not been for a favour which you did for me, which I did not compensate, I would reply to you."

ʿUrwah then continued speaking to the Messenger ﷺ clutching his beard whenever he said something. Meanwhile Mughīrah ibn Shuʿbah was standing near the Messenger ﷺ, holding a sword and wearing a helmet. Whenever ʿUrwah stretched his hand out to the beard of the Messenger ﷺ, Mughīrah would hit his hand away with the handle of his sword and say (to ʿUrwah), "Remove your hand from the beard of the Messenger."

ʿUrwah raised his head and asked, "Who is this?"

The people said, "He is Mughīrah ibn Shuʿbah."

ʿUrwah said, "O treacherous one! Am I not doing my best to prevent the evil consequences of your treachery?"

Before embracing Islam Mughīrah accompanied some people and killed them. He then took their property, came (to Madīnah), and embraced Islam. The Messenger ﷺ said (to him), "As for your Islam, I accept it, but as for the property I have nothing to do with it."

ʿUrwah, after observing the Ṣaḥābah, returned to his people and said, "O people! By Allah, I have been to the kings and to Caesar, Chosroe and the Negus, yet I have never seen any of them respected by his courtiers as much as Muḥammad is respected by his Ṣaḥābah. By Allah, Muḥammad did not spit except that it fell in the hands of one of them (the Ṣaḥābah) who would rub it on his face and skin; when he ordered them to do something they hastened to carry out his command; when he performed ablution, they would struggle to take the remaining water; and when they spoke to him, they would lower their voices and would not stare at him out of respect."

A man of Banū Kinānah then asked to be allowed to go to see him and Quraysh agreed. As he was approaching, the Messenger of Allah ﷺ commented, "This is so-and-so; he is from a tribe who much venerate sacrificial camels. Send them out to him." They were put out for him and people greeted him chanting *Labbayk* 'at Your service, O Lord'. When he saw this, he said, "Subḥān Allah! It is not right for these people to be kept from the Kaʿbah!" He returned to his companions after that and told them, "I have seen the sacrificial camels necklaced and decorated, and I do not think they should be kept from the Kaʿbah?"

Thereafter, one of their men named Mikraz ibn Ḥafṣ said, "Let me go to him," to which they agreed. When he approached, the Messenger صَلَّىٱللَّهُعَلَيْهِوَسَلَّمَ said, "This is Mikraz; he is an immoral man." As Mikraz began to speak Suhayl ibn ʿAmr arrived and the Prophet صَلَّىٱللَّهُعَلَيْهِوَسَلَّمَ commented, "Your affair has been eased! [*Suhila*]."[1]

Suhayl then came and said, "Come on now, let us write an agreement between us."

The Prophet صَلَّىٱللَّهُعَلَيْهِوَسَلَّمَ asked for a document to be brought and said, "Write down, *BismiLlāhi al-Raḥmān al-Raḥīm* (in the name of Allah, the Most Merciful and Most Beneficent)."

But Suhayl objected, "As for that term *al-Raḥmān*, I swear I don't know what that is. Instead, put down *Bismik Allāhumma* (In your name, O Allah), like you used to write."

The Muslims insisted, "By Allah, we will write it only BismiLlāhi al-Raḥmān al-Raḥīm!"

But the Prophet صَلَّىٱللَّهُعَلَيْهِوَسَلَّمَ said, "Write down Bismik Allāhumma."

He then said, "This is what Muḥammad, the Messenger of Allah, has agreed..."

Suhayl objected, "By Allah, if we knew you to be the Messenger of God, we would not have blocked your access to the Kaʿbah, nor would we have fought you. Rather, write down, 'Muḥammad, son of ʿAbd Allāh'."

The Messenger صَلَّىٱللَّهُعَلَيْهِوَسَلَّمَ then said, "I certainly am the Messenger of Allah, even though you call me a liar! Write down, 'Muḥammad, son of ʿAbd Allāh'."

He صَلَّىٱللَّهُعَلَيْهِوَسَلَّمَ began negotiations by expressing his wish that the Quraysh not hinder the passage of the Muslims to the House of Allah; and that they should thus be allowed to do Ṭawāf of the Kaʿbah.

1 The Prophet صَلَّىٱللَّهُعَلَيْهِوَسَلَّمَ took a good omen from his name Suhayl, which means ease.

Suhayl said, "You shall return this year and not enter Makkah lest the Arabs say that Quraysh were pliant to you in making this agreement. Next year we will make way for you; and your people may enter and stay for three nights, each rider bearing his own weapons—swords in sheaths, that is—and bringing in no other weapons."

The agreement went on thus: 'This is the peace agreement made by Muḥammad, son of ʿAbd Allāh, with Suhayl ibn ʿAmr. They have made peace by agreeing to put aside warfare from each other for ten years. During this period, people will be safe and leave one another alone. Provided that if anyone from Quraysh comes to Muḥammad without permission of his guardian, then he must send him back to them. If, however, anyone goes to Quraysh from Muḥammad, they are not to send him back to him. There are to be no secret agreements, bad faith or antagonism between us. Anyone wishing to enter into a pact or agreement with Muḥammad may do so. Anyone wishing to enter into an agreement or pact with Quraysh may do so.'

The Muslims objected, "How could someone be returned to the polytheists if he came as a Muslim!"

While this discussion was in progress Abū Jandal, son of Suhayl, came running dragging his chains, having escaped from Makkah. He threw himself at the feet of the Muslims seeking sanctuary.

Suhayl said, "This fellow, O Muḥammad, is the first whom I charge you to return to me."

The Prophet ﷺ said, "But we have not completed the agreement yet?"

"In that case," Suhayl insisted, "I will never make a pact with you over anything."

The Prophet ﷺ said, "Release him to my custody."

"I will not release him to you," Suhayl replied.

"I insist that you release him!" the Prophet pleaded.

"That I will not do," Suhayl retorted.

Abū Jandal then exclaimed, "O Muslims, shall I be returned to the polytheists? I have come to you as a Muslim. Can you not see how I have been treated?" He had been brutally tortured on account of his faith.

The Messenger صَلَّى ٱللَّهُ عَلَيْهِ وَسَلَّمَ said, "Be patient, O Abū Jandal! Allah will provide a solution and relief for you and the others with you who are powerless. We have made a peace pact with the enemy and we and they have sworn to this in Allah's name; we cannot act falsely with them."

ʿUmar رَضِيَ ٱللَّهُ عَنْهُ jumped up and walked along beside Abū Jandal, saying, "Be patient! They are only polytheists, their blood is worth no more than that of dogs!" He kept the hilt of his sword close to Abū Jandal. ʿUmar used to say, "I was hoping he would take the sword and strike his father with it! But the man spared his father, and the matter was settled."

ʿUmar رَضِيَ ٱللَّهُ عَنْهُ said, 'So I went to the Messenger of Allah صَلَّى ٱللَّهُ عَلَيْهِ وَسَلَّمَ, and asked, "Are you not truly the Messenger of Allah?"

"Yes, indeed," he replied.

"Are we not in the right? And our enemy in error?"

"Certainly," was the response.

"Why, then, are we accepting lowliness in our religion?"

He صَلَّى ٱللَّهُ عَلَيْهِ وَسَلَّمَ replied, "I am the Messenger of Allah, and I will not disobey him; He is my helper."

"Did you not tell us we would make Ṭawāf of the Kaʿbah?"

"Indeed I did, but did I tell you we would do so this year?"

ʿUmar رَضِيَ ٱللَّهُ عَنْهُ replied "No."

"Well," said the Prophet صَلَّى ٱللَّهُ عَلَيْهِ وَسَلَّمَ, "you will definitely make Ṭawāf."

ʿUmar went on, "I then went down to Abū Bakr and asked, 'O Abū Bakr, is he not Allah's Prophet?'

"Yes, indeed," replied Abū Bakr.

"Are we not in the right and our enemy in error?..."

A similar discussion ensued until Abū Bakr said, "Look, he is indeed the Messenger of Allah and he will not disobey Him; He is his helper. Trust him; he is right."

Umar said, "I have gone on fasting, giving alms, praying and freeing slaves because of what I did that day and out of fear for what I said that day, until I felt that I had made up."

Once the Messenger ﷺ concluded the agreement he told his Companions, "Sacrifice your animals and shave."

The Companions were in a state of gloom and sadness that when the instruction was given they did not act immediately. The Prophet ﷺ went to Umm Salamah رضي الله عنها and told her of the morale of the Ṣaḥābah and their delay in sacrificing their animals and shaving their heads. Umm Salamah said, "O Prophet of Allah, go on out without speaking a word to anyone and sacrifice your camel. Then call for your barber and have him shave your head. They will follow you."

He went out and spoke to no one until he had done this. When they saw this, they stood up, sacrificed their animals. Then some so hurriedly shaved the heads of others that it appeared that they were fighting one another to get it done.

Thereafter some believing women went to see the Prophet ﷺ and Allah revealed, "*O you who believe! If believing women should come to you as emigrants, then test them ...*" Until the words, "*... nor shall you hold on to bonds of marriage with disbelieving women.*"[1]

That day ʿUmar divorced two women who had been his wives while he was a polytheist. Muʿāwiyah ibn Abī Sufyān married one of these, while Ṣafwān ibn Umayyah married the other.

Al-Bukhārī relates with his chain to Zayd ibn Aslam, from his father, that the Messenger of Allah ﷺ was travelling one night in the company of ʿUmar ibn al-Khaṭṭāb رضي الله عنه when ʿUmar asked him a question on some matter, but the Messenger ﷺ gave him no reply. ʿUmar asked him again and yet again, received no reply from him. ʿUmar then thought to himself "O ʿUmar, your mother is as good as bereaved of you! You persisted three times in asking the Messenger of Allah ﷺ, and despite that he would not respond to you."

ʿUmar continued, "So I moved my mount away and advanced to the front of the Muslims, fearing that there was going to be a revelation about me. But immediately

1 Sūrah al-Mumtaḥinah: 10.

I heard someone shouting at me. I said to myself eerily, 'I fear this revelation is certainly about me.' Then I went to the Prophet ﷺ and greeted him. He said, 'Tonight a Sūrah has been revealed to me that is more pleasing to me than anything over which the sun rises.' He then recited, '*We have granted you a clear victory!*'"[1] (The opening verses of Sūrah al-Fatḥ)

Having concluded the incident at Ḥudaybiyyah with sufficient detail I believe that you, esteemed reader, have preliminary understood the role of the Ṣaḥābah in context. It is time to proceed with the critical analysis of Tījānī's assessment of the entire episode.

Refuting Tījānī on the Ṣaḥābah at Ḥudaybiyyah

1. It is apparent that Tījānī has summarised this narration a great deal to the extent that he cautiously concealed the important portion of it, which indicates his ill intent and bias against the Ṣaḥābah. Notwithstanding claims of impartiality he deliberately omitted these words of ʿUrwah ibn Masʿūd which form part of this narration:

    This man (the Messenger ﷺ) has offered you a reasonable proposal accept it and allow me to go to him."

    They said, "Go to him."

    So, he went to the Messenger ﷺ and started talking to him. The Messenger ﷺ told him the same as he told Budayl.

    ʿUrwah then said, "O Muḥammad! What do think would happen if you vanquished your own people (Quraysh)? By Allah, I do not see dignified people. What I do see is people from various tribes who would flee and forsake you."

    Abū Bakr rebuked him sternly, "Go suck Lāt's clitoris![2] Do you think we would flee and forsake him?"

    ʿUrwah said, "Who is this man?"

    They replied, "He is Abū Bakr."

1 Sūrah al-Fatḥ: 1.

2 Later the author will forward a footnote with regards to the view of Ibn Ḥajar which states the legality of using vulgar language in order to deter the one deserving of it.

> 'Urwah said to Abū Bakr, "By Him Who has control of my life, had it not been for a favour which you did for me, which I did not compensate, I would reply to you."
>
> 'Urwah then continued speaking to the Messenger صلى الله عليه وسلم clutching his beard whenever he said something. Meanwhile Mughīrah ibn Shu'bah was standing near the Messenger صلى الله عليه وسلم, holding a sword and wearing a helmet. Whenever 'Urwah stretched his hand out to the beard of the Messenger صلى الله عليه وسلم, Mughīrah would hit his hand away with the handle of his sword and say (to 'Urwah), "Remove your hand from the beard of the Messenger."
>
> 'Urwah raised his head and asked, "Who is this?"
>
> The people said, "He is Mughīrah ibn Shu'bah."
>
> 'Urwah said, "O treacherous one! Am I not doing my best to prevent the evil consequences of your treachery?"
>
> Before embracing Islam Mughīrah accompanied some people and killed them. He then took their property, came (to Madīnah), and embraced Islam. The Messenger صلى الله عليه وسلم said (to him), "As for your Islam, I accept it, but as for the property I have nothing to do with it."
>
> 'Urwah then started looking at the Ṣaḥābah and said, "By Allah, the Messenger of Allah did not spit except that it fell in the hands of one of them (the Ṣaḥābah) who would rub it on his face and skin; when he ordered them to do something they hastened to carry out his command; when he performed ablution, they would struggle to take the remaining water; and when they spoke to him, they would lower their voices and would not stare at him out of respect. By Allah, I have been to the kings and to Caesar, Chosroe and the Negus, yet I have never seen any of them respected by his courtiers as much as Muḥammad is respected by his Ṣaḥābah!"

These were the Ṣaḥābah رضي الله عنهم. They honoured their Prophet صلى الله عليه وسلم. An idolater testifies to this. Subḥān Allāh! Do you not see, beloved reader, how this "fair and objective" Tījānī conceals this important part of the ḥadīth? However, he might be excused for this concealment since it would undo his arguments from beginning to end. How could it be congruent with his exaggerations?

2. The Ṣaḥābah did not "strongly" oppose the Messenger ﷺ as Tījānī claims and there is nothing apparent in the ḥadīth to indicate that they intended to oppose their Messenger ﷺ. Rather, they acted as they did out of love for their faith and anger at the disbelievers. They thought—as any human being would—that the resolutions of the treaty were prejudiced of the Muslims. This was clear and apparent from this treaty. The Ṣaḥābah were not infallible and did not receive revelation from Allah as the Messenger ﷺ did. Also, how is it possible that the Ṣaḥābah disobeyed their Messenger ﷺ and failed to execute his command, yet Allah says about them:

لَقَدْ رَضِيَ اللَّهُ عَنِ الْمُؤْمِنِينَ إِذْ يُبَايِعُونَكَ تَحْتَ الشَّجَرَةِ فَعَلِمَ مَا فِي قُلُوبِهِمْ فَأَنْزَلَ السَّكِينَةَ عَلَيْهِمْ وَأَثَابَهُمْ فَتْحًا قَرِيبًا

Allah was indeed Allah pleased with the believers when they pledged allegiance to you, [O Muḥammad], under the tree, and He knew what was in their hearts, so He sent down tranquillity upon them and rewarded them with an imminent conquest.[1]

This verse was revealed in relation to the very Treaty of Ḥudaybiyyah. How do we reconcile these two things: Allah who knows the seen and the unseen informs us of His pleasure with the Ṣaḥābah because of His knowledge of the state of their hearts, and also gives them glad tidings of imminent victory—yet Tījānī seeks to cast doubt on their intentions and devotion to the Prophet ﷺ.

3. The line of reasoning presented in *Then I was guided* portrays the behaviour of the Prophet ﷺ in a very erratic, unpredictable manner. How do we reconcile the 'fact' that they deliberately disobeyed the Prophet ﷺ and caused him distress when the Prophet ﷺ himself says of those present at Ḥudaybiyyah, "You are the best people on earth!"[2] One might concede that this was said in a moment of euphoria after granting the pledge of Riḍwān, but the behaviour of the Companions رضي الله عنهم subsequent to that angered the Prophet ﷺ. However, this interpretation of events becomes increasingly

1 Sūrah al-Fatḥ: 18.

2 *Ṣaḥīḥ al-Bukhārī*, Ḥadīth no. 4154, Narrated by Jābir: "The Messenger of Allah ﷺ said to us at al-Ḥudaybiyyah, 'You are the best people on earth!' We were 1,400; and were I able today to see, I would show you the place where the tree stood."

problematic when we consider what the Prophet صَلَّى ٱللَّهُ عَلَيْهِ وَسَلَّمَ said at a time long after Ḥudaybiyyah.

Jābir رَضِيَ ٱللَّهُ عَنْهُ narrates, "A slave belonging to Ḥāṭib came to the Messenger of Allah صَلَّى ٱللَّهُ عَلَيْهِ وَسَلَّمَ complaining about him. He said, 'O Messenger of Allah, Ḥāṭib will surely enter hell-fire!'

The Messenger صَلَّى ٱللَّهُ عَلَيْهِ وَسَلَّمَ replied, 'You have erred; he will not enter hell; he was present at Badr and Ḥudaybiyyah.'"[1]

Umm Mubashshir رَضِيَ ٱللَّهُ عَنْهَا relates that she heard the Messenger of Allah صَلَّى ٱللَّهُ عَلَيْهِ وَسَلَّمَ say, when he was with Ḥafṣah رَضِيَ ٱللَّهُ عَنْهَا, "None, if God wills it, will enter the Fire from those who made the pledge beneath the tree."[2]

These aḥādīth are unquestionable in terms of a Prophetic reference for the good conduct of the Ṣaḥābah رَضِيَ ٱللَّهُ عَنْهُمْ at Ḥudaybiyyah. The question begs though: Is there anyone who can better elaborate about the Prophet's صَلَّى ٱللَّهُ عَلَيْهِ وَسَلَّمَ assessment of Ḥudaybiyyah than the Prophet صَلَّى ٱللَّهُ عَلَيْهِ وَسَلَّمَ himself?

4. To make it even clearer for the reader, I present the narration of *Ṣaḥīḥ Muslim* concerning the Treaty of Ḥudaybiyyah, which Tījānī himself makes reference to in the footnotes of his book. It is a different narration to the one in *Ṣaḥīḥ al-Bukhārī* which makes specific mention of those Ṣaḥābah who "strongly opposed" the command of the Messenger صَلَّى ٱللَّهُ عَلَيْهِ وَسَلَّمَ and "refused" to submit to his instruction. *Ṣaḥīḥ Muslim* records the words of Barā' ibn ʿĀzib رَضِيَ ٱللَّهُ عَنْهُ:

> When the Messenger صَلَّى ٱللَّهُ عَلَيْهِ وَسَلَّمَ was prevented from the Kaʿbah, the people of Makkah made a treaty with him that he could enter Makkah and stay for three days, he would not enter except with swords in their sheaths and arms encased in their covers, that none of its inhabitants left with him and that he did not prevent anyone who came with him from remaining.
>
> He said to ʿAlī ibn Abī Ṭālib, "Write down the conditions between us! 'In the Name of Allah, the Most Gracious, the Most Merciful. This is the covenant concluded by Muḥammad, the Messenger of Allah صَلَّى ٱللَّهُ عَلَيْهِ وَسَلَّمَ."

1 *Ṣaḥīḥ Muslim*, The Book of the Merits of the Companions, The chapter on the virtues of Ḥāṭib ibn Abī Baltaʿah and the people of Badr.

2 *Ṣaḥīḥ Muslim*, The Book of the Merits of the Companions, Chapter: The Virtues Of The Companions Of The Tree.

> Then the polytheists said, "If we knew you to be the Messenger of Allah we would have followed you. Instead write Muḥammad, the son of ʿAbd Allāh."
>
> The Messenger ﷺ then commanded ʿAlī to erase it (i.e. the words "the Messenger of Allah") but ʿAlī refused and said, "Never, By Allah! I will not erase it."
>
> The Messenger of Allah ﷺ then said, "Show me its place." He showed him. The Messenger ﷺ erased it and wrote, "The son of ʿAbd Allāh." He then remained in Ḥudaybiyyah for three days.[1]

Now if I wished to employ Tījānī's approach, his line of thinking, and claimed objectivity, then I could say, "I stopped here, for I could not read this kind of material without feeling rather surprised about the behaviour of this Companion towards his Prophet ﷺ. Could any sensible person accept the claim of some people that this Companion obeyed and implemented the orders of the Messenger of Allah ﷺ, for these incidents expose their lies, and fall short of what they want! Could any sensible man imagine that such behaviour towards the Prophet is an easy or acceptable matter or even an excusable one? Does he think himself greater than the Prophet ﷺ in his desire to please Allah to the extent that he left him—may my parents be sacrificed for him—to erase it and rewrite it with his own noble hands? I don't think any intelligent person would say that this act of opposition to the Messenger ﷺ is insignificant, acceptable or excusable."

Tījānī's approach opens the door for every ignorant person to interpret the actions of any Ṣaḥābī with the Messenger ﷺ as a misdemeanour against him, a failure to execute his command, and bad behaviour with him. Let us not for the moment burden ourselves with citing the explanations of these incidents given by the ḥadīth commentators. I simply say to Tījānī: would you accept this explanation in relation to ʿAlī ibn Abī Ṭālib رضي الله عنه with regards to his "opposition" to the Messenger ﷺ? If you accept that, then it is necessary to judge ʿAlī رضي الله عنه in the same manner that you judged the rest of the Ṣaḥābah. However, if this reasoning does not appear to you then you have revealed your bias against the Ṣaḥābah رضي الله عنهم. Your reasoning is self-incriminating, and all praise is to Allah.

---

1 *Ṣaḥīḥ Muslim*, The Book of Jihād and Siyar, The chapter of the Treaty of Ḥudaybiyyah.

Tījānī on ʿUmar at Ḥudaybiyyah

Tījānī goes on to say:

> **Did Umar ibn al-Khattab succumb to them and find no difficulty in accepting the order of the Messenger ﷺ? Or was he reluctant to accept the order of the Prophet? Especially when he said, "Are you not truly the Prophet of Allah? Did you not tell us? ..." etc., and did he succumb after the Messenger of Allah gave him all these convincing answers? No he was not convinced by his answers, and he went and asked Abu Bakr the same questions. But did he succumb after Abu Bakr answered him and advised him to hold on to the Prophet? I do not know if he actually succumbed to all that and was convinced by the answers of the Prophet ﷺ and Abu Bakr! For why did he say about himself, "For that I did so many things..." Allah and His Messenger know the things which were done by Umar.**
>
> **Furthermore, I do not know the reasons behind the reluctance of the rest of the Companions after that, when the Messenger of Allah said to him, "Go and slaughter [sacrifices] and shave your heads." Nobody listened to his orders even when he repeated them three times, and then in vain.**
>
> **Allah, be praised! I could not believe what I had read. Could the Companions go to that extent in their treatment of the Messenger. If the story had been told by the Shia alone, I would have considered it a lie directed towards the honourable Companions. But the story has become so well known that all the Sunni historians refer to it. As I had committed myself to accept what had been agreed on by all parties, I found myself resigned and perplexed. What could I say? What excuse could I find for those Companions who had spent nearly twenty years with the Messenger of Allah, from the start of the Mission to the day of al-Hudaibiyah, and had seen all the miracles and enlightenment of the Prophethood? Furthermore the Qur'an was teaching them day and night how they should behave in the presence of the Messenger, and how they should talk to him, to the extent that Allah had threatened to ruin their deeds if they raised their voices above his voice.**

Refuting Tījānī on ʿUmar at Ḥudaybiyyah

1. There is no doubt that ʿUmar رضي الله عنه accepted what the Messenger ﷺ told him. He did, however, display some disinclination towards the conditions agreed upon because the wisdom did not reveal itself clearly to him. This is especially plausible if we consider that he directed his questions to the

Messenger ﷺ and subsequently to Abū Bakr رضي الله عنه, after the Mushrikīn had placed these strenuous conditions upon the Messenger ﷺ, amongst which was that if a person came as a Muslim (to Madīnah) he was to be returned (to Makkah). It is reported in a ḥadīth:

> Suhayl said, "And on condition that no man from amongst us comes to you, even if he is upon your religion, except that you return him to us."
>
> The Muslims exclaimed, "Subḥān Allāh! How can he be returned if he comes to us as a Muslim?"
>
> While they were discussing this, Abū Jandal ibn Suhayl ibn ʿAmr appeared bound in shackles coming from the lower parts of Makkah in order to present himself to the Muslims. Suhayl then said, "This is the first person I demand from you to return to me."
>
> The Messenger ﷺ then said, "We have not yet completed the agreement."
>
> He said, "Then I will never enter into any treaty with you."
>
> The Messenger ﷺ said, "Then permit him (to stay with us) for my sake."
>
> He replied, "I do not permit him for you."
>
> The Messenger ﷺ said, "Permit him!"
>
> Suhayl said, "I will not!"
>
> Mikraz said, "Rather, we permit him for you."[1]
>
> Abū Jandal then exclaimed, "O Muslims! Am I to be returned to the Mushrikīn and I have come as a Muslim? Do you not see what I have endured?"
>
> He had suffered severe punishment.
>
> ʿUmar said, "Then I went to the Messenger ..."

It was at that point that ʿUmar رضي الله عنه asked those questions. It was because of this that the command was difficult for ʿUmar رضي الله عنه to accept; in fact, it was difficult upon most of the Ṣaḥābah.

1 Abū Jandal was not allowed to remain with the Muslims, rather he was returned as agreed.

Added to that, let us consider ʿUmar's question to the Messenger ﷺ, "Did you not inform us that we would come to the Kaʿbah and circumambulate it?" This was because the Messenger ﷺ had informed the Ṣaḥābah that he saw in his dream that he and his Ṣaḥābah entered the Kaʿbah. This is what made it difficult for them to bear when the delay became evident.[1] It was because of these reasons that ʿUmar رضي الله عنه questioned the conditions agreed upon by the Messenger ﷺ. It was out of desire to humble the Mushrikīn and to grant victory to the Muslims. His questions are clear in this regard. It was not a matter of doubt, as in one narration it is reported that Abū Bakr رضي الله عنه said to him, "Hold fast onto his stirrup as he is the Messenger of Allah," and ʿUmar رضي الله عنه said, "And I bear witness that he is the Messenger of Allah."[2]

Ibn Ḥajar therefore says:

> What is apparent is that ʿUmar's questioning the treaty was an interlude from him in order to discover the wisdom of the incident and remove uncertainty. Similar to this is the incident in which he questioned the Messenger ﷺ performing funeral prayer over the known hypocrite ʿAbd Allāh ibn Ubay. In the first case (i.e. Ḥudaybiyyah), however, his discernment did not coincide with divine decree whereas in the second (funeral prayer on Ibn Ubay) it did. He only did the mentioned actions for this reason. Therefore, everything which came from him was excusable, in fact rewardable, as he acted in conformity with his best discretion.[3]

A ḥadīth in *Ṣaḥīḥ Muslim* clarifies that ʿUmar رضي الله عنه paused in order to discover the wisdom behind the treaty and to clarify the ambiguity:

> Revelation then descended upon the Messenger ﷺ giving him glad tidings of the victory. The Messenger ﷺ then sent for ʿUmar and read it to him. ʿUmar said, "Is this a victory?" The Messenger ﷺ replied, "Indeed it is," and ʿUmar was content and returned.[4]

In Sūrah al-Fatḥ, Allah revealed:

---

1 *Fatḥ al-Bārī*, vol. 5 p. 408.

2 Ibid. vol. 5 p. 409.

3 Ibid.

4 *Ṣaḥīḥ al-Muslim*.

لَقَدْ رَضِيَ اللَّهُ عَنِ الْمُؤْمِنِينَ إِذْ يُبَايِعُونَكَ تَحْتَ الشَّجَرَةِ فَعَلِمَ مَا فِي قُلُوبِهِمْ فَأَنْزَلَ السَّكِينَةَ عَلَيْهِمْ وَأَثَابَهُمْ فَتْحًا قَرِيبًا

Certainly Allah was pleased with the believers when they pledged allegiance to you, [O Muḥammad], under the tree, and He knew what was in their hearts, so He sent down tranquillity upon them and rewarded them with an imminent conquest.[1]

Imām Aḥmad narrates a ḥadīth in his *Musnad* from Jābir رضي الله عنه that the Messenger صلى الله عليه وسلم said: "A man who witnessed Badr and Ḥudaybiyyah will never enter the Fire."[2]

Indeed, Allah informs us about His pleasure with the believers who gave the pledge to the Messenger صلى الله عليه وسلم under the tree, and He confirms their entry into Paradise. Why? It is because He knew the purity of their hearts and actions, and no doubt ʿUmar رضي الله عنه was from amongst the foremost of them. If the "guided" Tījānī criticises the Ṣaḥābah while Allah, the Knower of the Unseen, tells us that their hearts were pure then is he not questioning Allah Himself?

2. Tījānī states that ʿUmar رضي الله عنه said, "For that reason I did some actions," and thereafter comments, "Allah and His Messenger alone know the actions which ʿUmar undertook," if anything these words indicate the scope of his ignorance. What ʿUmar رضي الله عنه intended has been mentioned explicitly.

> Ibn Isḥāq's narration states that ʿUmar used to say, "I continued giving charity, fasting, praying, and emancipating slaves because of what I did; out of fear for the words which I spoke." And al-Wāqidī has reported a ḥadīth of Ibn ʿAbbās رضي الله عنه who narrated that ʿUmar رضي الله عنه said, "I set free on account of it many slaves and kept fast for many days."[3]

The context of the ḥadīth shows that ʿUmar رضي الله عنه acted out of honest discernment. These deeds of expiation were also the product of his discretion. They present clear evidence of his conscientiousness, piety, and willingness

1 Sūrah al-Fatḥ: 18.

2 *Musnad Aḥmad*, Ḥadīth no. 15262.

3 *Fatḥ al-Bārī* vol. 5 p. 408, authenticated by Albānī and Arna'ūṭ.

to submit to truth. The context of the ḥadīth indicates that his actions at Ḥudaybiyyah were intended to demonstrate the might of the Muslims and to humiliate the disbelievers.

3. Tījānī failed to notice the element of ʿUmar's رضي الله عنه compliance with the command of Allah when he divorced two of his wives after the verses prohibiting marriage to women who remained in Shirk. The verses of Sūrah al-Mumtaḥinah were revealed within the context of the episode at Ḥudaybiyyah. This further demonstrates the reason for ʿUmar's interlude being one of seeking further clarity rather than delaying to fulfil the divine instruction.

The reluctance of the Ṣaḥābah to release themselves from Iḥrām

> **Furthermore, I do not know the reasons behind the reluctance of the rest of the Companions after that, when the Messenger of Allah said to him, "Go and slaughter [sacrifices] and shave your heads."**

To this say I say: I have explained in light of the ḥadīth in *Ṣaḥīḥ Muslim* that ʿAlī رضي الله عنه was from amongst the Ṣaḥābah present at Ḥudaybiyyah, that he was amongst those who opposed the conditions imposed upon the Muslims, and that he held the same view as ʿUmar ibn al-Khaṭṭāb رضي الله عنه. The ḥadīth states that when the Messenger صلى الله عليه وسلم said, "Go slaughter and shave your heads," none stood up. There is no doubt that ʿAlī رضي الله عنه was amongst them and that he did not execute the command of the Messenger صلى الله عليه وسلم. Despite that Tījānī says:

> **What could I say? What excuse could I find for those Companions who had spent nearly twenty years with the Messenger of Allah, from the start of the Mission to the day of al-Hudaibiyah, and had seen all the miracles and enlightenment of the Prophethood?**

It seems as if it has escaped you that ʿAlī رضي الله عنه was one of these Ṣaḥābah. Therefore, if you are able to make an excuse for ʿAlī رضي الله عنه for this incident then I believe that it will be considered an excuse for the rest of the Ṣaḥābah رضي الله عنهم as well. If, however, you are unable to find an excuse for ʿAlī رضي الله عنه then the criticism you have levelled against the Ṣaḥābah is definitely directed to ʿAlī رضي الله عنه as well.

Reasons for the delay in executing the command of the Prophet صَلَّى ٱللَّٰهُ عَلَيْهِ وَسَلَّمَ

As for the failure of the Ṣaḥābah to immediately execute the commands of the Messenger صَلَّى ٱللَّٰهُ عَلَيْهِ وَسَلَّمَ, this could have been for a number of reasons, which Ibn Ḥajar has explained:

a. They thought that the command may have been a recommendation rather than an obligation.

b. They hoped that revelation would descend and cancel the afore-mentioned treaty.

c. That special permission would descend for them to enter Makkah that year in order to complete their rituals of ʿUmrah.

d. That this pause may have occurred during a period of abrogation and was thus permissible for them.

e. They were distracted and engrossed in thought of their humiliation despite having the ability to meet their goal and fulfil their rituals by force or conquest.

f. They delayed in submitting, believing that the unqualified command did not necessitate immediate compliance.

All of these are plausible reasons for all of them. There is no proof in this incident that the command necessitated immediate compliance or not. Similarly, there is no proof that the command was for obligation and not a recommendation, because of the possibility which this incident allows for.

Similar to this is what happened during the Conquest when the Messenger صَلَّى ٱللَّٰهُ عَلَيْهِ وَسَلَّمَ instructed his Ṣaḥābah to break their fast in Ramaḍān. When they hesitated, he took a drinking bowl and drank. When they saw him do this, they did the same.[1]

These are the explanations which the scholars have made for the noble Ṣaḥābah. As for the ignorant, the resentment and dislike that they have for the Ṣaḥābah induced them to see the actions of the Ṣaḥābah in the most sinister and unfavourable light. Against such glaring prejudice we seek Allah's protection.

1 Ibid. vol. 5 p. 409.

Tījānī on ʿUmar's role at Ḥudaybiyyah

He now goes on to say:

> **And what leads me to believe that ʿUmar was the one who led the Ṣaḥābah present in hesitating to execute the command of the Messenger صَلَّى ٱللَّٰهُ عَلَيْهِ وَسَلَّمَ, in addition to his own confession, is that he performed "actions" which he did not wish to mention, and which he himself mentions in other places, "I continued to fast, give charity and emancipate slaves out of the fear for the words that I uttered", and other such statements regarding this matter.**
>
> **All of which gives us the impression that ʿUmar himself realised the folly of the position which he took on that day. Indeed it is an amazing and strange story, but true.** [1]

1. This is a cheap ploy against the noble Companion ʿUmar ibn al-Khaṭṭāb رَضِيَ ٱللَّٰهُ عَنْهُ. How could he know that ʿUmar رَضِيَ ٱللَّٰهُ عَنْهُ prompted the rest of the Ṣaḥābah to delay in executing the instruction of the Messenger صَلَّى ٱللَّٰهُ عَلَيْهِ وَسَلَّمَ? Does he know what is in the heart of ʿUmar رَضِيَ ٱللَّٰهُ عَنْهُ or did he receive revelation? This is nothing but bias against ʿUmar رَضِيَ ٱللَّٰهُ عَنْهُ. Upon what evidence is his accusation based against ʿUmar رَضِيَ ٱللَّٰهُ عَنْهُ? Is there anything in the ḥadīth which indicates to that? If so, then let him show us instead of speaking recklessly about the best of people.

2. Does this statement not also demonstrate his indictment of the rest of the Ṣaḥābah who he claims abandoned the instruction of the Messenger صَلَّى ٱللَّٰهُ عَلَيْهِ وَسَلَّمَ in favour of the position of ʿUmar رَضِيَ ٱللَّٰهُ عَنْهُ? Bear in mind that this would include ʿAlī رَضِيَ ٱللَّٰهُ عَنْهُ as well. This is the slippery slope that this "guided one" has created: first laying the foundation of indicting all the great Ṣaḥābah, and thereby leading people to accept the Shīʿī theory of mass apostasy by the Ṣaḥābah with none but three or seven exceptions. Does he not realise that he is criticising his first Imām, ʿAlī ibn Abī Ṭālib رَضِيَ ٱللَّٰهُ عَنْهُ, who was one of the Ṣaḥābah who hesitated in executing the instruction of the Messenger صَلَّى ٱللَّٰهُ عَلَيْهِ وَسَلَّمَ.

   As for his statement:

   > **In addition to his own confession, is that he performed "actions" which he did not wish to mention.**

---

1 This passage was omitted in the English translation; it appears in the original on page 98 (*Mu'assasat al-Fajr* London).

And

> **… which he himself mentions in other places, "I continued to fast, give charity …"**

One wonders if this man knows what he is writing. How could ʿUmar رضي الله عنه do actions which he did not wish to mention and then mentions in other places what he did? Here he intends to give the reader the impression that there were other actions which were concealed by ʿUmar رضي الله عنه. It appears that Tījānī has a sixth sense through which he can uncover what the commentators of ḥadīth were unable to. What does he mean with his statement, "other occasions"? Are these not "other" narrations for this ḥadīth? What makes you hold onto the narration of al-Bukhārī, which states that ʿUmar رضي الله عنه said, "Therefore, I did actions," but you doubt the narrations which clarify what these "actions" are, especially when the speaker in all these narrations is ʿUmar رضي الله عنه himself? Why would he confess to do actions which he did not want to mention?

Tījānī's words, "***…and other such narrations from him on this matter,***" beg the question what else has been narrated on this matter? When you encounter the clear and explicit statement of ʿUmar رضي الله عنه, you regard them as ambiguous. If you could find clear and explicit evidence to convict ʿUmar you would have filled your book with it, but you couldn't so you try to give the impression that you did.

The Prophet's ﷺ Final Days

It is amazing how malleable an incident taken out of context can be. The fabric of reality almost shifts and a culprit can be portrayed a victim; a hero projected as a villain. After realizing the serious consequences of Tījānī's truncated version of what happened at Ḥudaybiyyah and his imaginative reinterpretation of events, I am confident that you, beloved reader, will appreciate some details of the final moments in the life of the Prophet ﷺ. This will serve as a background against which you will align the events that transpired. I have no doubt that your informed decision will be guided by context and discernment.

After the Conquest of Makkah, Islam spread throughout the Arabian Peninsula. Deputations of Arab tribes followed one after another in rapid succession to announce their entry into the fold of Islam and to pledge their allegiance to the Prophet ﷺ. This surge in the growth of Islam alludes to the inevitable dominance of Islam.

إِذَا جَآءَ نَصْرُ اللّٰهِ وَ الْفَتْحُ ﴿١﴾ وَ رَأَيْتَ النَّاسَ يَدْخُلُوْنَ فِيْ دِيْنِ اللّٰهِ
أَفْوَاجًا ﴿٢﴾ فَسَبِّحْ بِحَمْدِ رَبِّكَ وَ اسْتَغْفِرْهُ ۚ إِنَّهُ كَانَ تَوَّابًا ﴿٣﴾

When the victory of Allah has come and the conquest. And you see the people entering into the religion of Allah in multitudes. Then exalt [Him] with praise of your Lord and ask forgiveness of Him. Indeed, He is ever Accepting of repentance.[1]

The tenth year after the Hijrah witnessed a series of unique events signalling the Prophet's ﷺ mission in this world had been fulfilled and that his end was near. These were subtle signs which were picked up on by the Prophet ﷺ and some of his close Companions. ʿIrbāḍ ibn Sāriyah رَضِيَ اللَّهُ عَنْهُ relates:

> One day, the Messenger of Allah ﷺ stood up among us and delivered a deeply moving speech that melted our hearts and caused our eyes to flow. It was said to him, "O Messenger of Allah, it is as though you have delivered a speech of farewell, so enjoin something upon us." He said, "I urge you to fear Allah, and to listen and obey, even if (your leader) is an Abyssinian slave. After I am gone, you will see great conflict. I urge you to adhere to my Sunnah and

---

1 Sūrah al-Naṣr.

> the path of the Rightly-Guided Khulafā', and cling to it with your molars. And beware of newly-invented matters, for every innovation is a deviation."[1]

The Prophet's صلى الله عليه وسلم usual practise during the final days of Ramaḍān was that he would seclude himself for devotions in I'tikāf for ten days. However, he withdrew into seclusion for a period of twenty days that year.

In addition to this he would complete the recitation of the Qur'ān once every Ramaḍān when he was visited by Jibrīl عليه السلام. That year he completed the recitation twice.[2]

'Umar ibn al-Khaṭṭāb رضي الله عنه as well as Ibn 'Abbās رضي الله عنه understood the above verses to suggest the imminence of the Prophet's صلى الله عليه وسلم demise. Ibn 'Abbās رضي الله عنه said:

> 'Umar used to ask me questions in front of the Companions of the Prophet صلى الله عليه وسلم. So 'Abd al-Raḥmān ibn 'Awf said to him, "Why do you ask him, while we have children his age?'"
>
> 'Umar said to him, "It is because of what you know (about him)."
>
> So he asked me about this verse, '*When the victory of Allah has come and the Conquest*.' I said, "It is only regarding the (end of the) life span of the Messenger of Allah صلى الله عليه وسلم, which Allah informed him of."
>
> I then recited the Sūrah until its end. So 'Umar said, "By Allah! I do not understand it except the way you have."[3]

The Messenger of Allah صلى الله عليه وسلم frequently recited these words just before he passed away, "*Subḥānaka Rabbanā wa biḥamdika Astaghfiruka wa atūbu ilaika* [Glory be to You, Our Lord and praise be to You; I seek Your forgiveness and turn to You in repentance]"

'Ā'ishah رضي الله عنها asked him, "O Messenger of Allah! What are these new words which I hear from you repeatedly?"

He replied, "A sign has been appointed for me relating to my people that I should repeat these words at the appearance of that sign." Then he recited Sūrah al-Naṣr.[4]

---

1 *Abū Dāwūd*, Ḥadīth no. 3607; *al-Tirmidhī*, Ḥadīth no. 2676.

2 *Ṣaḥīḥ al-Bukhārī*, Ḥadīth no. 3624.

3 *Ṣaḥīḥ al-Bukhārī*, Ḥadīth no. 4430.

4 *Ṣaḥīḥ Muslim*, Ḥadīth no. 484.

He undertook the journey for Ḥajj that year as well. During his Ḥajj he encouraged his people to take the rites of Ḥajj from him as he was not aware if he would perform Ḥajj in the future.

The verse in Sūrah al-Mā'idah, "*This day I have perfected for you your religion and completed My favour upon you and have approved for you Islam as your religion...*"[1] was revealed during the Ḥajj.

Upon his return to Madīnah, the Messenger ﷺ visited the graves of those slain at Uḥud and prayed for them. He also visited the graves of his Companions in al-Baqīʿ [the cemetery in Madīnah]; almost as if he were bidding them farewell from this realm. ʿUqbah ibn ʿĀmir رضي الله عنه said:

> One day the Messenger of Allah ﷺ went out and sought Allah's forgiveness for the martyrs of the battle of Uḥud after eight years. It seemed that by so doing, he bid farewell to the living and the dead. He then came back, ascended the pulpit and said, "I shall be one who goes ahead; I am a witness for you (before Allah), and I will be present before you at the Pond (*Ḥawḍ al-Kawthar*). By Allah I can see with my own eyes the Ḥawḍ from this place. I am not afraid that you will associate anything with Allah in worship after (my demise), but I fear that you will vie with one another for the life of the world." It was the last time that I saw the Messenger of Allah ﷺ.[2]

Two days prior to his illness the Prophet ﷺ prepared an army under the leadership of Usāmah ibn Zayd رضي الله عنه. The army was to proceed to Greater Syria. Senior companions from the Muhājirīn and Anṣār were enlisted in this detachment. Among those enlisted was ʿUmar ibn al-Khaṭṭāb رضي الله عنه. Concerns were expressed regarding the ability of Usāmah to lead a 3000 strong detachment considering his age. The Messenger ﷺ addressed them:

> If you criticize his appointment it is as if you criticize the appointment of his father before him. He is indeed worthy of office as was his father. He (Zayd) was among the most beloved to me and this (Usāmah) is the most beloved after him.[3]

---

1 Sūrah al-Mā'idah: 3.

2 *Ṣaḥīḥ al-Bukhārī*, Ḥadīth no. 4042.

3 *Ṣaḥīḥ al-Bukhārī*, Ḥadīth no. 4467.

The army was camped at al-Jurf, 5 kilometers outside Madīnah. When the news of the Prophet's صَلَّى ٱللَّهُ عَلَيْهِ وَسَلَّمَ illness reached Usāmah, he delayed his departure. The army was later dispatched during the Khilāfah of Abū Bakr رَضِيَ ٱللَّهُ عَنْهُ; and it was one of the first duties he fulfilled after assuming leadership.

Abū Muwayhibah, the freed-slave of the Messenger of Allah صَلَّى ٱللَّهُ عَلَيْهِ وَسَلَّمَ said:

> The Messenger of Allah صَلَّى ٱللَّهُ عَلَيْهِ وَسَلَّمَ sent for me during the middle of the night, saying, "Abū Muwayhibah, I have been ordered to ask for forgiveness for those in Baqī'; so come with me."
>
> I left with him and when he stood among them, he said, "Peace be upon you, O people in the graves! You can be content that you do not experience the same as people here. Tests encroach like dark portions of the night, following one another in succession, the last being worse than the first."
>
> He then came over to me and said, "Abū Muwayhibah, I have been given the keys to the treasures of the world, remaining here a long time, and the (going to) paradise. I have been given the choice between this and meeting my Lord and (going to) paradise (soon)."
>
> I said, "May my parents be ransomed for you, choose the keys of the treasures of this world, a long life here, and then Paradise."
>
> He replied, "No, Abū Muwayhibah. Rather I chose to meet my Lord and Paradise."
>
> He then proceeded to pray for forgiveness for those buried in al-Baqī', and then left. And soon thereafter began the illness in which Allah took him."[1]

The next day he began complaining of a headache. He was at the house of Maymūnah رَضِيَ ٱللَّهُ عَنْهَا while visiting his wives in turn, when his pain persisted and became severe. His family assembled, and it was suggested that he be given medicine through the corner of his mouth. He gestured with his hand, meaning to say, "Do not pour medicine in my mouth."

It was assumed that he did so in the same way as a patient dislikes medicines. When he improved and felt a little better, he said, "Did I not forbid you to pour medicine in my mouth?"

1 al-Bayhaqī: *Dalā'il al-Nubuwwah*, vol. 7 p. 162.

His family responded, "(We thought it was because of) the dislike, patients have for medicines."

He said, "Let everyone present in the house be given medicine by pouring it in his mouth while I am looking at him, except ʿAbbās as he was not present."[1]

Thereafter he began asking, "Where shall I stay tomorrow?", "Where am I tomorrow?" They understood that he was seeking permission of his wives to be nursed in the home of ʿĀ'ishah رضي الله عنها. So they all agreed for him to be nursed there. He moved to ʿĀ'ishah's house supported on either side by al-Faḍl ibn ʿAbbās and Alī ibn Abī Ṭālib رضي الله عنهم. One can imagine the sadness experienced by his family as they saw his head wrapped in a bandage and his feet dragging on the ground as he was being supported; as he was too weak to walk. It was there that he spent the last week of his life.

When he arrived at the home of ʿĀ'ishah رضي الله عنها he requested the water of seven water-skins—the mouths of which have not been untied—be poured on him as a remedy, so that he would gain strength to advise his Companions. He sat in a big basin belonging to his wife Ḥafṣah رضي الله عنها, and his wives then started to pour water on him from these water skins until he experienced relief. Then he went out to the people and led them in prayer and addressed them. He ascended the pulpit, praised Allah as He deserves to be praised and delivered his final sermon which included the following statements:

> "May Allah's curse be on the Jews and Christians for they took the graves of their Prophets as places of worship."
>
> "Do not make my grave an idol that is worshipped."
>
> "I advise you to treat the Anṣār well. They are my family and with them I found shelter. They have acquitted themselves credibly of the responsibility that fell upon them and now there remains what is for them. The believers will increase, but the Anṣār will diminish to the extent that they would be among men as salt is in food. Whoever among you occupies a position of responsibility and is powerful enough to do harm or good to people should fully acknowledge and appreciate the favour that these benefactors have shown, and overlook their faults."[2]

---

1 *Dalā'il al-Nubuwwah*, vol. 7 p. 168-9; *Ṣaḥīḥ al-Bukhārī*, Ḥadīth no. 4458; *Musnad Ahmad*, vol. 6 p. 438.

2 *Ṣaḥīḥ al-Bukhārī*, Ḥadīth no. 3799-3801 *Ṣaḥīḥ Muslim*, Ḥadīth no. 2510.

Abū Saʿīd Al-Khudrī relates:

> The Prophet ﷺ delivered a sermon and said, "Allah gave a choice to one of (His) slaves either to choose this world or what is with Him in the Hereafter. He chose the latter."
>
> Abū Bakr began to weep. I said to myself, "What is this old man weeping for, if Allah gave a choice to one (of His) slaves either to choose this world or what is with Him in the Hereafter and he chose the latter?" (However) that slave was Allah's Messenger ﷺ; he was referring himself. Abū Bakr was more knowledgeable than us.
>
> The Prophet ﷺ said, "O Abū Bakr! Do not cry."
>
> The Prophet ﷺ then added, "Abū Bakr has favoured me much with his property and company. If I were to take a Khalīl (close friend) other than Allah, I would certainly have taken Abū Bakr. It is enough that we share the Islamic bond of brotherhood and friendship. No door leading into the Masjid is to be left open besides the door of Abū Bakr."[1]

Saʿīd ibn Jubayr narrates

> I heard Ibn ʿAbbās رضي الله عنهما saying, "Thursday! And you know not what Thursday is?" and then he wept till the stones on the ground were moist with his tears.
>
> On that I asked, "What is (about) Thursday?"
>
> He said, "When the health of the Messenger ﷺ deteriorated, he said, 'Bring me a bone, so that I may write something for you after which you will never go astray.'
>
> The people argued their opinions although it was inappropriate to dispute in front of a prophet, they said, "What is his condition? Is he speaking senselessly? Ask him for clarity."
>
> The Prophet ﷺ replied, "Leave me as I am in a better state than what you are asking me to do." Then the Prophet ﷺ advised them with three things saying, "Expel the Mushrikīn from the Arabian Peninsula, be hospitable to all foreign delegates as I used to do." The narrator added, "The third order

1 *Ṣaḥīḥ al-Bukhārī*, Ḥadīth no. 3654.

> was something beneficial which either Ibn ʿAbbās did not mention, or he mentioned but I forgot."[1]

The narration above—which has been narrated with variant wording—is one of the issues which will be discussed at length in the refutation below. The focal point of the debate is the document that was proposed to be written.

If the esteemed reader would indulge me and pause for a moment. Let us not speculate the contents of the document since it was never written. The famous Muḥaddith and historian, ʿImād al-Dīn ibn Kathīr has presented a very objective approach to understanding this element of the ḥadīth. He says:

> Orthodox scholars accept what is fully established and reject what might be viewed as allegorical. This is the methodology of those firmly rooted in knowledge. This area is one of those where the feet of many of the noisome slip. Orthodox scholars do not manipulate events to suit the narrative of their prescribed leaning, rather they pursue the truth alone, moving with it along whatever path it leads.
>
> We do not suggest that we know what was intended; but if we were to apply discernment at what the Prophet ﷺ potentially might have intended we can apply those aḥādīth that lend themselves to a clear, unambiguous interpretation.
>
> Imām Aḥmad narrates with his chain from ʿĀ'ishah رضي الله عنها, "When the Messenger of Allah ﷺ was suffering from that illness from which he succumbed to, he said, 'Summon Abū Bakr and his son, so that no one will desire afterwards or aspire to Abū Bakr's role.' He went on, 'Allah would not allow it to be otherwise, and the believers.' He said this twice."
>
> Imām Aḥmad also narrates—with another chain— from ʿĀ'ishah رضي الله عنها, "When the illness of the Messenger of Allah ﷺ worsened, he told ʿAbd al-Raḥmān, Abū Bakr's son, 'Bring me a shoulder bone or a tablet so that I can write a document for Abū Bakr about which no one can dispute.' When ʿAbd al-Raḥmān went to do this, he said, 'Allah and the believers reject there being any disagreement over you, O Abū Bakr!'"
>
> Al-Bukhārī narrates with an alternate chain from ʿĀ'ishah رضي الله عنها who said, "The Prophet ﷺ said, 'I felt like sending for Abū Bakr and his son, and appoint

1 *Ṣaḥīḥ al-Bukhārī*, Ḥadīth no. 4431; *Ṣaḥīḥ Muslim*, Ḥadīth no. 1637.

> him lest some people claim something or some others desire something, but then I said (to myself), 'Allah would not allow it to be otherwise, and the Muslims would prevent it from being otherwise.'"
>
> There is a ḥadīth which appears both in al-Bukhārī and Muslim from Muḥammad ibn Jubayr ibn Muṭʿim رضي الله عنه, who quoted his father as saying, "A woman came to the Messenger of Allah صلى الله عليه وسلم, and he told her to return to him again. She asked, 'Suppose I come and no longer find you?' She seemed to be implying his death. He replied, 'If you do not find me, then go to Abū Bakr.'"
>
> It seems obvious— though Allah knows best—that she said that to the Messenger of Allah صلى الله عليه وسلم, during his final illness.
>
> On the Thursday, five days before he passed away, the Messenger of Allah صلى الله عليه وسلم had delivered an address in which he had asserted the excellence of Abū Bakr over the other Companions, in addition to his explicit instructions that Abū Bakr lead them in prayer. It may perhaps be that this address should be viewed as a substitution for what he intended to write in the document.
>
> He had washed himself prior to making that noble address. They had sprinkled over him water from seven water-skins, the openings of which had not been untied as mentioned in the *Ṣaḥīḥ* collections.

Jundub ibn ʿAbd Allāh al-Bajalī رضي الله عنه related:

> I heard from the Messenger of Allah صلى الله عليه وسلم five days before his death that he said, "I stand acquitted before Allah of taking any one of you as a friend; for Allah has taken me as His friend, as he took Ibrāhīm as His friend. Had I taken any one of my Ummah as a friend, I would have taken Abū Bakr as a friend. Beware of those who preceded you and used to take the graves of their prophets and righteous men as places of worship, but you must not take graves as masjids; I forbid you to do that."[1]

The Prophet صلى الله عليه وسلم departed from this world on a Monday morning. Five days prior to that would be the Thursday.

The Ahl al-Sunnah consider the decision of leadership the responsibility of the Muslim community. The mention of Abū Bakr in the previous narrations, in

1 *Ṣaḥīḥ Muslim*, Ḥadīth no. 532.

addition to his appointment to lead the Ṣalāh, are strong suggestions from the Prophet ﷺ for his preferred candidate.

The Prophet ﷺ did not appoint a successor as can be learnt from the narration involving ʿAlī ibn Abī Ṭālib رضي الله عنه and ʿAbbās ibn al-Muṭṭalib رضي الله عنه

Al-Bukhārī narrated with his complete chain to ʿAbd Allāh ibn ʿAbbās رضي الله عنه who said:

> ʿAlī ibn Abī Ṭālib came out of the Messenger's ﷺ home during his fatal illness. The people asked, "O Abū al-Ḥasan, how is the health of Allah's Messenger ﷺ this morning?"
>
> ʿAlī replied, "He has recovered with the Grace of Allah."
>
> ʿAbbās grabbed him by the hand and said to him, "In three days you will be ruled (by somebody else), and by Allah, I feel that Allah's Messenger will not survive this ailment. I know the look of death on the faces of the offspring of ʿAbd al-Muṭṭalib. Let us go to the Messenger ﷺ and ask him who will take over the Khilāfah. If it is given to us we will know, and if it is given to somebody else, we will inform him so that he may tell the new ruler to take care of us."
>
> ʿAlī said, "By Allah, if we asked the Messenger ﷺ for it (the Khilāfah) and he denied us it now, the people will never give it to us after that. By Allah, I will not ask Allah's Messenger ﷺ for it." [1]

The mother of Ibn ʿAbbās رضي الله عنهما, Umm al-Faḍl رضي الله عنها said:

> The Messenger of Allah ﷺ came out to us with his head bandaged from his illness. He prayed Maghrib, reciting (Sūrah) al-Mursalāt." [She said:] "He did not pray it again until he met Allah." [2]

The Messenger ﷺ sent Abū Bakr رضي الله عنه forward to lead the people in ṣalāh until he passed away. After the Maghrib prayer the Prophet ﷺ experienced difficulty and repeatedly lost consciousness. When he instructed that Abū Bakr رضي الله عنه lead the prayer ʿĀ'ishah رضي الله عنها suggested that ʿUmar be appointed instead. The Prophet ﷺ insisted that only Abū Bakr رضي الله عنه lead the prayer. Perhaps the

---

1 *Ṣaḥīḥ al-Bukhārī*, Ḥadīth no. 4447.

2 *Al-Tirmidhī*, Ḥadīth no. 308; *Ṣaḥīḥ al-Bukhārī*, Ḥadīth no. 4429.

Prophet ﷺ wanted to leave no room for misunderstanding in his suggested candidate.

Imām al-Bukhārī narrates from Abū Mūsā رضي الله عنه:

> The Messenger ﷺ was ill and when his illness intensified, He said, "Order Abū Bakr to lead the people in ṣalāh!"
>
> ʿĀ'ishah then said, "Indeed, he is a soft-hearted man. When he stands in your place he will be unable to lead the people in ṣalāh."
>
> She then repeated herself and he said, "Order Abū Bakr to lead the ṣalāh! Indeed you are of the women of Yūsuf!"
>
> He then came to the Messenger and he led the people in ṣalāh during the life of the Messenger ﷺ.[1]

ʿUbayd Allāh ibn ʿAbd Allāh reported that he visited ʿĀ'ishah رضي الله عنها and asked her to tell him about the illness of the Messenger of Allah ﷺ. She agreed and said:

> The Prophet ﷺ was seriously ill and he asked whether the people had prayed. We said, "No, they are waiting for you, Messenger of Allah."
>
> The Prophet ﷺ said, "Put some water in the tub for me."
>
> We did accordingly and the Prophet ﷺ took a bath. When he was about to move with difficulty, he fainted. After regaining consciousness, he again asked, "Have the people prayed?"
>
> We said, "No, they are waiting for you, Messenger of Allah."
>
> He again said, "Put some water for me in the tub."
>
> We did accordingly and he took a bath, but when he was about to move with difficulty he fainted After regaining consciousness, he asked whether the people had prayed and again we said, "No, they are waiting for you, Messenger of Allah."
>
> He said, "Put some water for me in the tub."
>
> We did accordingly and he took a bath and he was about to move with difficulty when he fainted. When he regained consciousness, he asked, "Have the people prayed?"

1 *Ṣaḥīḥ al-Bukhārī*, The Book of Congregation, Ḥadīth no. 646.

We said, "No, they are waiting for you, Messenger of Allah."

The people were staying in the masjid and waiting for the Messenger of Allah صَلَّى ٱللَّهُ عَلَيْهِ وَسَلَّمَ to lead the 'Ishā prayer. The Messenger of Allah صَلَّى ٱللَّهُ عَلَيْهِ وَسَلَّمَ sent (instructions) to Abū Bakr to lead the people in prayer. When the messenger came, he told him (Abū Bakr), "The Messenger of Allah صَلَّى ٱللَّهُ عَلَيْهِ وَسَلَّمَ has ordered you to lead the people in prayer."

Abū Bakr who was a man of very tenderly feelings asked 'Umar to lead the prayer. 'Umar said, "You are more entitled to that." Abū Bakr led the prayers during those days. Afterwards the Messenger of Allah صَلَّى ٱللَّهُ عَلَيْهِ وَسَلَّمَ felt some relief and he went out supported by two men, one of them was 'Abbās, to the noon prayer. Abū Bakr was leading the people in prayer. When Abū Bakr saw him, he began to withdraw, but the Messenger of Allah صَلَّى ٱللَّهُ عَلَيْهِ وَسَلَّمَ told him not to withdraw. He told his two companions to seat him beside him (Abū Bakr). They seated him by the side of Abū Bakr. Abū Bakr said the prayer standing while following the prayer of the Prophet صَلَّى ٱللَّهُ عَلَيْهِ وَسَلَّمَ and the people prayed (standing) while following the prayer of Abū Bakr. The Prophet صَلَّى ٱللَّهُ عَلَيْهِ وَسَلَّمَ was seated.

'Ubayd Allāh said:

I visited 'Abd Allāh ibn 'Abbās, and said, "Should I repeat to you what 'Ā'ishah had told me about the illness of the Prophet صَلَّى ٱللَّهُ عَلَيْهِ وَسَلَّمَ?"

He said, "Go ahead."

I repeated to him what had been transmitted by her. He objected to none of it, only asking whether she had named the man who accompanied 'Abbās. I said, "No." He replied, "It was 'Alī."[1]

On Sunday, a day before his departure from this world, the Prophet صَلَّى ٱللَّهُ عَلَيْهِ وَسَلَّمَ set his slaves free, paid as a charity the seven Dīnārs he owned, and gave his weapons as an endowment to be used by the Muslims. Even his armour was mortgaged as a security with a Jew for thirty ṣā' of barley.

Anas ibn Mālik رَضِيَ ٱللَّهُ عَنْهُ said:

Abū Bakr used to lead the people in prayer during the fatal illness of the Prophet صَلَّى ٱللَّهُ عَلَيْهِ وَسَلَّمَ until it was Monday. When the people aligned (in rows) for

---

1 *Ṣaḥīḥ al-Bukhārī*, Ḥadīth no. 687.

> the prayer, the Prophet صَلَّى ٱللَّهُ عَلَيْهِ وَسَلَّمَ lifted the curtain of his house and started looking at us and was standing at that time. His face was (glittering) like a page of the Muṣḥaf, and he smiled cheerfully. We were about to be put to trial for the pleasure of seeing the Prophet. Abū Bakr retreated to join the row as he thought that the Prophet صَلَّى ٱللَّهُ عَلَيْهِ وَسَلَّمَ would lead the prayer. The Prophet صَلَّى ٱللَّهُ عَلَيْهِ وَسَلَّمَ beckoned us to complete the prayer and he let the curtain fall. He passed away on that very day.[1]

ʿĀ'ishah رَضِيَ ٱللَّهُ عَنْهَا narrates:

> Once Fāṭimah came walking and her gait resembled the gait of the Prophet صَلَّى ٱللَّهُ عَلَيْهِ وَسَلَّمَ. The Prophet صَلَّى ٱللَّهُ عَلَيْهِ وَسَلَّمَ said, "Welcome, O my daughter!" Then he made her sit on his right or on his left side, after which he told her a secret and she started weeping.
>
> I asked her, "Why are you weeping?" He again told her a secret and she started laughing. I said, "I never saw happiness so near to sadness as I saw today."
>
> I asked her what the Prophet صَلَّى ٱللَّهُ عَلَيْهِ وَسَلَّمَ had told her and she replied, "I would never disclose the secret of Allah's Messenger صَلَّى ٱللَّهُ عَلَيْهِ وَسَلَّمَ."
>
> When the Prophet صَلَّى ٱللَّهُ عَلَيْهِ وَسَلَّمَ passed away, I asked her about it. She replied, "The Prophet صَلَّى ٱللَّهُ عَلَيْهِ وَسَلَّمَ said, 'Every year Jibrīl used to revise the Qur'ān with me once only, but this year he has done so twice. I think this indicates my death, and you will be the first of my family to follow me.' So I started weeping. Then he said, 'Do you not like to be the leader of all the women of Paradise or the leader of the believing women?' So I laughed for that."[2]

When the pangs of death started, ʿĀ'ishah رَضِيَ ٱللَّهُ عَنْهَا supported him against her. She used to say, "One of Allah's bounties upon me is that the Messenger of Allah صَلَّى ٱللَّهُ عَلَيْهِ وَسَلَّمَ passed away in my house, on my day. His soul departed with his head between my chest and neck while he was leaning against me. Allah mixed his saliva with mine at his death.[3]

1 *Ṣaḥīḥ al-Bukhārī*, Ḥadīth no. 680.

2 Note that this merit of Fāṭimah رَضِيَ ٱللَّهُ عَنْهَا has been narrated by ʿĀ'ishah رَضِيَ ٱللَّهُ عَنْهَا.

3 *Ṣaḥīḥ al-Bukhārī*, Ḥadīth no. 4096.

Tījānī on the Thursday calamity

Tījānī says:

Briefly the story is as follows:

The Companions were meeting in the Messenger's house, three days before he died. He ordered them to bring him a bone and an ink pot so that he could write a statement for them which would prevent them from straying from the right path, but the Companions differed among themselves and some of them disobeyed the Prophet and accused him of talking nonsense. The Messenger of Allah became very angry and ordered them out of his house without issuing any statement.

This is the story in some details:

Ibn Abbas said: Thursday, and what a Thursday that was! The Messenger's pain became very severe, and he said, "Come here, I will write you a document which will prevent you from straying from the right path." But Umar said that the Prophet was under the spell of the pain, and that they had the Qur'ān which was sufficient being the Book of Allah. Ahl al-Bayt then differed and quarrelled amongst themselves, some of them agreeing with what the Prophet said, while others supported Umar's view. When the debate became heated and the noise became louder, the Messenger of Allah said to them, "Leave me alone."

Ibn Abbas said: The disaster was that the disagreement among the Companions prevented the Messenger from writing that document for them.

The incident is correct and there is no doubt about its authenticity, for it was cited by the Shii scholars and their historians in their books, as well as by the Sunni scholars and historians in their books. As I was committed to consider the incident, I found myself bewildered by Umar's behaviour regarding the order of the Messenger of Allah. And what an order it was! "To prevent the nation from going astray", for undoubtedly that statement would have had something new in it for the Muslims and would have left them without a shadow of doubt.[1]

He continues and says:

This type of reasoning would not be accepted by simple-minded people, let alone by the scholars. I repeatedly tried to find an excuse for Umar but

1 *Then I was guided*, p. 67.

> **the circumstances surrounding the incident prevented me from finding an excuse. Even if I changed the words "He is talking nonsense" - God forbid - to "the pain has overcome him", I could not find any justification for Umar when he said, "You have the Qur'ān, and it is sufficient being the Book of Allah." Did he know the Qur'ān better than the Messenger of Allah, for whom it was revealed? Or was the Messenger of Allah - God forbid - unaware of what he was? Or did he seek, through his order, to create division and disagreement among the Companions - God forbid.[1]**

Refuting Tījānī on the Thursday calamity

1. Tījānī combined in this ḥadīth more than one narration. He mentioned that the Ṣaḥābah accused the Messenger ﷺ of senseless speech, but that word does not exist in the ḥadīth which he mentions. In the ḥadīth he also relates the words of Ibn ʿAbbās, "Thursday, and what was Thursday? The pain intensified upon the Messenger ﷺ..." This sentence is not in the ḥadīth which he references to *Ṣaḥīḥ al-Bukhārī* in the margins of his book.

   However, this sentence together with the word "*yahjur*" appears in a different ḥadīth which Tījānī pretends to be unaware of as it clarifies some pertinent points about this incident. It is the narration of Saʿīd ibn Jubayr who said:

   > Ibn ʿAbbās said, "Thursday, and what was Thursday? The pain intensified upon the Messenger ﷺ who then said, 'Come, let me write for you a letter after which you will never stray.'
   >
   > They then disputed and a dispute is not appropriate in the presence of the Messenger ﷺ. They said, 'What is his condition? Is he speaking senselessly? Ask him for clarity.'
   >
   > So they went to him and he said, 'Leave me, for indeed, what I am in is better for me than what you call me towards.'
   >
   > He then exhorted them with three things. He said, 'Expel the Mushrikīn from the Arabian Peninsula, and give gifts to the delegations as I used to,' he either did not mention the third or the narrator said, 'I forgot it.'"[2]

2. It is necessary for a Muslim to believe that the Messenger ﷺ was infallible in terms of lying and from changing any Islamic law in good health

1 *Then I was guided*, p. 68.

2 *Ṣaḥīḥ al-Bukhārī*, The Book of Expeditions, Ḥadīth no. 4178.

or illness. His infallibility extends to the duty of explaining what he was commanded to explain and conveying that which Allah commanded him to convey.[1]

When we recognise this, it becomes clear to us that if he was commanded to convey something during health or illness he would convey it without doubt. If he intended to write something indispensable, it is inconceivable that he would have neglected it whether on account of their disagreement or anything else, just as he never previously failed to convey his message despite the opposition he faced. He was always guided by the command of Allah:

بَلِّغْ مَآ أُنْزِلَ إِلَيْكَ

Announce that which has been revealed to you.[2]

This indicates that what the Messenger صَلَّى ٱللَّٰهُ عَلَيْهِ وَسَلَّمَ intended to write was something optional and not compulsory. Indeed, the Messenger صَلَّى ٱللَّٰهُ عَلَيْهِ وَسَلَّمَ lived another four days after that and did not re-issue the instruction for them to write. His statement in the narration which Tījānī concealed, "and he exhorted them with three things," indicates the fact that what the Messenger صَلَّى ٱللَّٰهُ عَلَيْهِ وَسَلَّمَ intended to write was not a mandatory matter. If it was something which he was commanded to convey he would not have neglected it on account of possible disagreement. Allah would have punished the one who prevented him from fulfilling his duty. Had there been an imperative command the Prophet صَلَّى ٱللَّٰهُ عَلَيْهِ وَسَلَّمَ would have conveyed it verbatim as he did in the case of expelling the Mushrikīn.[3]

3. Tījānī says:

But can we find a sensible explanation to this hurtful incident which angered the Messenger so much that he ordered them to leave?[4]

I say:

---

1 *Ṣaḥīḥ Muslim* with commentary, Kitāb al-Wasiyyah vol. 11 p. 131.

2 Sūrah al-Mā'idah: 67.

3 *Fatḥ al-Bārī*, vol. 7 p. 741.

4 *Then I was guided*, p. 68.

There is no indication of the Messenger displaying any anger towards the Ṣaḥābah رضي الله عنهم or his instruction to expel them. None of the seven versions of this Ḥadīth in *Ṣaḥīḥ al-Bukhārī* seem to convey this notion. Instead, the severity of the pain experienced by the Messenger ﷺ resulted in his request for them to stop arguing amongst themselves. This is evident since the narration continues wherein the Messenger ﷺ advised them with three matters and this transpired after their argument. There is, therefore, absolutely no evidence to suggest that the Messenger ﷺ was angry with them, or that he dismissed them.

Let us assume for the sake of argument that he was angry with them. This is not impossible as they were not infallible and could well do something to incur anger. However, the Messenger ﷺ would sometimes become angry and then later become pleased. Indeed, his anger towards his Ṣaḥābah was a source of goodness for them. Imām al-Bukhārī narrates a ḥadīth in his *Ṣaḥīḥ* from Abū Hurayrah رضي الله عنه that he heard the Messenger ﷺ saying:

اللّٰهم فأيّما مؤمن سببته فاجعل ذلك له قربة إليك يوم القيامة

O Allah! If I should ever abuse a believer, please let that be a means of bringing him closer to You on the Day of Judgment.[1]

There is also a ḥadīth in *Musnad Aḥmad* and al-Ṭabarānī's *al-Muʿjam al-Kabīr* in which the Prophet ﷺ states:

أيّما رجل من أمتي سببته سبّة في غضبى أو لعنته لعنة فإنّما أنا من ولد آدم أغضب كما يغضبون وإنّما بعثني رحمة للعالمين فاجعلها صلاة عليه يوم القيامة

If there is any man from my Ummah whom I cursed in anger, then indeed I am but a son of Ādam. I become angry like they become angry. Allah sent me as a mercy unto the worlds, therefore let it be a mercy for them on the Day of Judgement.[2]

---

1 *Ṣaḥīḥ al-Bukhārī*, The Book of Supplications vol. 5, Ḥadīth no. 6000.

2 *Musnad Aḥmad*, vol. 9, Ḥadīth no. 23767; Ṭabarānī: *al-Muʿjam al-Kabīr* vol. 6, Ḥadīth no. 6156-6157; *Abū Dāwūd* vol. 5, Ḥadīth no. 4659 with an authentic chain.

Tījānī's inability to find a reasonable explanation for the Prophet's ﷺ anger at the Companions is of no consequence. Imām al-Bukhārī reports the following ḥadīth:

> One night the Messenger ﷺ knocked on the door of ʿAlī ibn Abī Ṭālib رضي الله عنه and asked, "Are you not praying?"
>
> ʿAlī replied, "O Messenger of Allah! Our souls are in the hands of Allah. If He wills, he wakes us up."
>
> Thereupon the Messenger ﷺ left and did not say anything in return.
>
> ʿAlī says, "As he turned around I heard him hit his hand against his thigh saying:
>
> وَكَانَ الْإِنْسَانُ أَكْثَرَ شَيْءٍ جَدَلًا
>
> *But man has ever been, more than anything, [prone to] dispute.*[1]

Has Tījānī found a reasonable explanation for ʿAlī's رضي الله عنه remonstration with the Messenger ﷺ and invoking predestination as an argument causing the Messenger ﷺ to hit his thigh in exasperation saying in opposition, "*But man has ever been prone to dispute.*"

If he has found a reasonable explanation for ʿAlī's رضي الله عنه remonstration, then the Messenger's ﷺ action with regards to the argumentation of the Ṣaḥābah is understandable.

4. Ibn ʿAbbās's رضي الله عنهما crying and his naming it "a great calamity" do not constitute an argument against the Ahl al-Sunnah. Ibn ʿAbbās رضي الله عنهما used to cry retrospectively when narrating the incident and not at the time when it occurred. All the narrations concur upon that. It is possible that he remembered the passing of the Messenger ﷺ which increased his grief. In addition the failure to write the letter would certainly be a great loss for one who doubted the succession of Abū Bakr رضي الله عنه. If the Messenger ﷺ had written the letter then all doubts would have been removed. Also, Ibn ʿAbbās رضي الله عنهما called that incident the "great calamity" because, although, he himself was amongst those who concurred with the nomination of Abū

1 *Ṣaḥīḥ al-Bukhārī*, The Book of Supplications vol. 1, Ḥadīth no. 1075.

Bakr رضي الله عنه there appeared in his time people whose rejection of Abū Bakr's رضي الله عنه Khilāfah led them to embroil the Ummah in great strife and bloodshed. Considering that this letter could possibly have averted all this bloodshed, its non-writing could certainly be considered a loss.

5. Tījānī says:

The Sunnis say that Umar recognized that the Prophet's illness was advancing, so he wanted to comfort him and relieve him from any pressure. This type of reasoning would not be accepted by simple-minded people, let alone by the scholars.

I say:

There is no doubt, according to us, that this explanation of the scholars is logically acceptable, especially when we realise that the ḥadīth states that the Messenger's صلى الله عليه وسلم pain intensified. However, this was not the only reason which caused ʿUmar رضي الله عنه to say what he said. Rather, a sign became apparent to him which indicated that the instruction of the Messenger صلى الله عليه وسلم was not peremptory. Therefore, he applied his discretion. This is the same as ʿAlī رضي الله عنه did when the Messenger صلى الله عليه وسلم called him to prayer and he cited predestination as an argument; the Messenger صلى الله عليه وسلم did not say it in a peremptory manner.

Tījānī claims that the Ahl al-Sunnah make the excuse that ʿUmar رضي الله عنه intended to grant the Messenger صلى الله عليه وسلم respite out of compassion for him. The picture he presents of the view of the Ahl al-Sunnah is hopelessly incomplete. I will therefore cite the views of the scholars explaining the position of ʿUmar رضي الله عنه, to illustrate to the reader the strength of the Ahl al-Sunnah's position. It will also demonstrate the difference between the explanation of the coarsely ignorant and the scholar firmly rooted in his knowledge.

Al-Māzarī says about this incident:

> It was permissible for the Ṣaḥābah to disagree about this letter, despite his clear instruction to them concerning it, because instructions are sometimes accompanied with that which indicates non-compulsion. It was as if an indication became apparent that the instruction was not mandatory in nature but rather optional and therefore their opinions differed. ʿUmar decided to

abstain because it became apparent to him that the instruction was not issued with firm intent. The Messenger's ﷺ instruction could be rooted either in revelation or discretion. If it was on account of revelation, then he left it because of revelation and if it was on account of discretion then he left it because of discretion.[1]

Imām al-Bayhaqī says towards the end of his book, *Dalā'il al-Nubuwwah*:

'Umar merely intended to create ease for the Messenger ﷺ when he saw him overcome by pain. If the Messenger ﷺ intended to write something indispensable for them he would not have neglected it on account of their disagreement or anything else because Allah says, "Convey what was revealed to you." The Messenger ﷺ never allowed the opposition of enemies to prevent conveyance of instructions as in the case of the instruction to expel the Jews from the Arabian Peninsula, and other matters mentioned in the ḥadīth.[2]

Imām al-Qurṭubī says:

I'tūnī (bring me) is an instruction and it is the duty of the instructed to hasten to the execution of the instruction. However, it was apparent to 'Umar, as well as to a group of the Ṣaḥābah, that the instruction was not mandatory in nature and that it fell under the realm of guidance to that which was most beneficial. Therefore, they disliked burdening him with that which would cause him difficulty, keeping in mind Allah's words:

مَا فَرَّطْنَا فِي الْكِتَابِ مِنْ شَيْءٍ

Nothing have we omitted from the Book.[3]

تِبْيَانًا لِكُلِّ شَيْءٍ

We have sent down to you the Book explaining all things.[4]

It was for this reason that 'Umar رضي الله عنه said, "The book of Allah suffices us."

1 *Fatḥ al-Bārī*, The Book of Expeditions.

2 *Ṣaḥīḥ Muslim* with its explanation, The Book of Bequests.

3 *Sūrah al-An'ām*: 38.

4 Sūrah al-Naḥl: 89.

It was, however, apparent to another group of Ṣaḥābah that the best course of action was for him to write the letter as it would serve as additional clarification. His commanding them to stand and leave indicates that his initial instruction was optional. That is why the Messenger صلى الله عليه وسلم did not repeat the instruction even though he lived for a few days thereafter. If it was mandatory he would not have neglected it on account of their disagreement because he did not neglect conveying on account of any opposition. At times when he was not assertive in his instruction the Ṣaḥābah would confer with him. But when he was assertive they would execute without hesitation.[1]

Evidence of the understanding and knowledge of ʿUmar رضي الله عنه is found in these aḥādīth:

ʿĀ'ishah رضي الله عنها narrates that the Messenger صلى الله عليه وسلم said, "Amongst the people before you there were those who were *muḥaddathūn* (divinely inspired). If there is anyone from my Ummah, it is ʿUmar."[2]

Abū Saʿīd al-Khudrī رضي الله عنه narrates that the Messenger صلى الله عليه وسلم said, "While I was sleeping, people were presented to me wearing shirts. Some had shirts reaching their chests, and others less than that. Then ʿUmar passed by wearing a shirt which he dragged behind him." They enquired, "How do you interpret that O Messenger of Allah?" He said, "The Religion."[3]

Ibn ʿUmar رضي الله عنهما narrates that the Messenger صلى الله عليه وسلم said, "While I was sleeping a bowl of milk was brought to me. I drank from it until I quenched my thirst to the point where I saw it exiting my nails. Then I gave my surplus to ʿUmar." They asked, "How do you interpret it, O Messenger of Allah?" He said, "Knowledge."[4]

ʿAlī ibn Abī Ṭālib رضي الله عنه praised ʿUmar رضي الله عنه and testified to his integrity and steadfastness. This is mentioned in the authoritative Shīʿī book, *Nahj al-Balāghah*, compiled by their scholar, Sharīf al-Raḍī. In a portion of his sermon, ʿAlī رضي الله عنه said:

1 *Fatḥ al-Bārī*, The Book of Knowledge.

2 *Ṣaḥīḥ al-Bukhārī*, The Book Concerning the Virtues of the Ṣaḥābah, vol. 3, Ḥadīth no. 3486. *Ṣaḥīḥ Muslim* with its commentary, vol. 15, Ḥadīth no. 2398, The Book of the Virtues of the Ṣaḥābah.

3 *Ṣaḥīḥ Muslim* with its commentary, vol. 15, Ḥadīth no. 2390, The Book Concerning the Virtues of the Ṣaḥābah.

4 *Ṣaḥīḥ al-Bukhārī*, The Book concerning the Virtues of the Ṣaḥābah, Ḥadīth no. 3478.

> A ruler governed them who was just and steadfast, until religion reached the point of ultimate satiation.[1]

Ibn Abī al-Ḥadīd, the Shīʿī commentator on *Nahj al-Balāghah* says, "This governor is ʿUmar ibn al-Khaṭṭāb."[2]

Tījānī on the accusation of senseless speech

> **Even if I changed the words "He is talking nonsense" - God forbid - to "the pain has overcome him", I could not find any justification for Umar when he said, "You have the Qur'ān, and it is sufficient being the Book of Allah."**

Refuting Tījānī on the accusation of senseless speech

Nothing in any of the versions of the ḥadīth indicates that the person who made this statement was ʿUmar رضي الله عنه. What ʿUmar رضي الله عنه said was *ghalabahū al-wajaʿ* (the pain overcame him), to insinuate that he actually said "*yahjur*" (speaking senselessly) by suggesting replacing one term for the other is nothing less than Tījānī's own prejudicial delusion.

The actual word in the ḥadīth is *a hajara*? (Is he speaking senselessly?). The ḥadīth clearly mentions that this question was asked by several persons. The purpose of the question was to refute those who said, "do not write!" They were in essence saying, "How can we delay? Do you think he is like anyone else that speaks incoherently when he is sick?" In further refutation of this notion, they said, "Ask him for clarity."

If we should assume these words came from one of the Ṣaḥābah then perhaps the matter was unclear to this particular person. The person who made this statement might also have been a recent Muslim or someone so stricken with emotion at seeing the Messenger صلى الله عليه وسلم in this condition that he harshly rebuked those who thought it best not to write.

An alternative perspective

Hajr literally means to speak in a jumbled and incoherent manner. There are two types of it. One is where speech is unclear, the voice is hoarse, and the tongue is dry

1 *Nahj al-Balāghah*, p. 794.

2 Ibn al-Ḥadīd: *Sharḥ Nahj al-Balāghah*, vol. 4 p. 519.

on account of heat during a high fever. This is something that even the Prophets are susceptible to. There is consensus among the historians that the Messenger ﷺ was afflicted with hoarseness of voice during the illness which led to his demise.

The second type is when speech is incoherent due to fainting spells caused by the fever. Scholars differ about whether this could affect the Prophets. Some of them accept that it could occur to them comparing it to sleep while others deny it.

Perhaps the person who made this statement intended the first category. In other words, he found the Prophet's ﷺ manner of speech different to his normal way of talking. Therefore, it is possible that he could not understand his words on account of weakness in his voice. Viewed from this perspective there is nothing objectionable.

Tījānī on the knowledge of ʿUmar

Tījānī says:

> **Did he know the Qur'ān better than the Messenger of Allah ﷺ, for whom it was revealed?**

Tījānī's statement only confirms his ignorance. The statement of ʿUmar رضي الله عنه, "The book of Allah is sufficient for us," was in refutation of those who argued with him and not a rebuttal of the Messenger ﷺ. Added to that is the fact that it became clear to him that the Messenger ﷺ was not peremptory. He therefore made his statement relying on the words of Allah:

ٱلْيَوْمَ أَكْمَلْتُ لَكُمْ دِينَكُمْ

This day have I perfected your religion for you.[1]

مَا فَرَّطْنَا فِي الْكِتَابِ مِنْ شَيْءٍ

We did not omit anything in the book.[2]

This, as we explained before, was confirmation of ʿUmar's رضي الله عنه deep understanding and knowledge. The Messenger ﷺ was fully aware of what he himself said

1 Sūrah al-Mā'idah: 3.

2 Sūrah al-Anʿām: 38.

and what ʿUmar رضي الله عنه said. The fact that he did not refute ʿUmar رضي الله عنه indicates that he regarded ʿUmar's رضي الله عنه statement as correct, also realising that this matter would not cause division amongst the Ṣaḥābah. This is exactly what happened as the Muslims nominated Abū Bakr رضي الله عنه and thereby thwarted any form of disagreement.

Tījānī on the Prophets صلى الله عليه وسلم treatment of ʿUmar

> **Even if the Sunni reasoning was right, then the Messenger of Allah صلى الله عليه وسلم would have realized the good will of Umar and thanked him for that and perhaps asked him to stay, instead of feeling angry at him and telling them to leave his house.**

Refuting Tījānī on the Prophets صلى الله عليه وسلم treatment of ʿUmar

Had he applied his mind logically he would have concluded that the Messenger's صلى الله عليه وسلم silence on ʿUmar's رضي الله عنه statement and subsequent abandonment of writing indicate that he agreed with ʿUmar رضي الله عنه. Here Tījānī commits another sleight of hand. By slyly insinuating that the command *Ukhrujū ʿannī* (leave me) was addressed at ʿUmar رضي الله عنه, he violates the rules of Arabic grammar. The form of the word *Ukhrujū* (leave) indicates that it was addressed at a group of people and not one particular individual. All those present were commanded to leave.[1]

Tījānī's words in fact prove that the Messenger صلى الله عليه وسلم was silent on ʿUmar's رضي الله عنه statement and did not object to it. It was only when the noise and disagreement became unbearable that he said, "Leave me!" However, nothing here indicates specific dismissal of ʿUmar's رضي الله عنه words, especially if we consider that the ḥadīth goes on to state that he imparted three instructions thereafter.

Then Tījānī says:

> **May I ask why did they abide by his order when he asked them to leave the room and did not say then that he was "talking nonsense"? Was it because they had succeeded in their plot to prevent the Prophet from writing the**

---

1 One of the persons present in the room was ʿAlī ibn Abī Ṭālib رضي الله عنه. He states in a ḥadīth documented in *Musnad Aḥmad* (vol. 1 p. 90) and *al-Sunan al-Kubrā* (vol. 5 p. 17) of al-Bayhaqī.

> We were with the Prophet صلى الله عليه وسلم when he commanded me to bring him paper on which to write something after by which his Ummah will not go astray after him. I feared that he would die before I could bring the paper.

> **document, so that there was no need for them to stay any longer? Thus, we find them creating noise and difference in the presence of the Messenger, and divided into two parties: one agreeing with the Messenger of Allah about writing that document, while the other agreed with Umar "that he was talking nonsense".[1]**

Allāhu Akbar! Did the Ṣaḥābah scheme against the Messenger ﷺ in order to prevent him from writing? By Allah, this is the belief of one who has no love and respect for the Ṣaḥābah of the Messenger ﷺ in his heart. These are the same Ṣaḥābah who befriended him and assisted him and followed the light which descended upon him and ransomed their souls and their families and everything they owned, and because of it, Allah opened for them the world and debased for them the Persians and the Romans, all because of their assisting the Messenger ﷺ.

Then Tījānī comes along and claims that they schemed against the Messenger of Allah ﷺ? Is this the pure and intelligent logic which led him to contradict reason and revelation? Subḥān Allāh! All this interpolation only to make the text serve the outrageous goal of belittling the Ṣaḥābah. He then repeats his entirely defeated argument that ʿUmar رضي الله عنه said that the Messenger ﷺ spoke senselessly. The truth is manifestly clear.

Tījānī continues:

> **The matter is not just concerned with Umar alone, for if it was so, the Messenger of Allah would have persuaded him that he could not be talking nonsense and that the pain could not overcome him in matters of the nation's guidance and of preventing it from going astray. But the situation became much more serious, and Umar found some supporters who seemingly had a prior agreement on their stand, and so they created the noise and the disagreement among themselves and forgot, or perhaps pretended to forget, the words of Allah - the Most High:**
>
> يَٰٓأَيُّهَا ٱلَّذِينَ ءَامَنُوا۟ لَا تَرْفَعُوٓا۟ أَصْوَٰتَكُمْ فَوْقَ صَوْتِ ٱلنَّبِيِّ وَلَا تَجْهَرُوا۟ لَهُۥ بِٱلْقَوْلِ كَجَهْرِ بَعْضِكُمْ لِبَعْضٍ أَن تَحْبَطَ أَعْمَٰلُكُمْ وَأَنتُمْ لَا تَشْعُرُونَ

1 *Then I was guided*, p. 68.

> ***O you who believe! Raise not your voices above the voice of the Prophet, nor speak aloud to him in talk, as you may speak aloud to one another, lest your deeds become vain and you perceive not.*** [1]

What an astonishing claim! If indeed the Messenger صَلَّى ٱللَّهُ عَلَيْهِ وَسَلَّمَ was angry with ʿUmar رَضِيَ ٱللَّهُ عَنْهُ and commanded him and others to leave him was he then not able to silence ʿUmar? And the ḥadīth itself states that the Messenger صَلَّى ٱللَّهُ عَلَيْهِ وَسَلَّمَ thereafter still imparted three instructions to them. In light of this, his not silencing ʿUmar رَضِيَ ٱللَّهُ عَنْهُ is proof that he agreed with him and approved of what he said.

To Tījānī's insinuation that in their excessive clamour they pretended to forget the words of Allah, I respond: The Ṣaḥābah did not raise their voice above the voice of the Messenger صَلَّى ٱللَّهُ عَلَيْهِ وَسَلَّمَ; rather some raised their voices above the voices of others which does not violate the verse. The argument is therefore self-defeating.

Now Tījānī reveals his malice as follows:

> **In this incident they went beyond raising their voices and talking loud to accusing the Messenger of Allah of talking nonsense - God forbid - then they increased their noise and differences until it became a battle of words in his presence.**
>
> **I think the majority of the Companions were with Umar, and that is why the Messenger of Allah found it useless to write the document, because he knew that they would not respect him and would not abide by the command of Allah by not raising their voices in his presence, and if they were rebellious against the command of Allah, then they would never obey the order of His Messenger.**
>
> **Thus, the wisdom of the Messenger ruled that he was not to write the document because it had been attacked during his lifetime, let alone after his death.**
>
> **The critics would say that he was talking nonsense, and perhaps they would doubt some of the orders he passed whilst on his death-bed, for they were convinced that he was talking nonsense.**
>
> **I ask Allah for forgiveness, and renounce what has been said in the presence of the holy Messenger, for how could I convince myself and my free conscience that Umar ibn al- Khattab was acting spontaneously, whereas his friends**

---

1 Sūrah al-Ḥujurāt: 2.

> **and others who were present at the incident cried until their tears wet the stones, and named the incident "the misfortune of the Muslims". I therefore decided to reject all the justifications given to explain the incident, and even tried to deny it so that I could relax and forget about the tragedy, but all the books referred to it and accepted its authenticity but could not provide sound justification for it.[1]**

Here Tījānī gives clear evidence of his lack of objectivity. He claims that the Messenger ﷺ thought it best not to argue about the writing of the letter, and considered it wiser not to pursue it because the Ṣaḥābah would neither submit nor execute his instruction, but would criticise him for it? Let us imagine for a moment that this was true: Is it at all conceivable that the Messenger ﷺ—whose fundamental responsibility is to convey the divine message—would have any hesitation about writing that which he was commanded to covey? What choice did he have in the matter when Allah commands:

يَاأَيُّهَا الرَّسُولُ بَلِّغْ مَا أُنْزِلَ إِلَيْكَ مِنْ رَبِّكَ وَإِنْ لَمْ تَفْعَلْ فَمَا بَلَّغْتَ رِسَالَتَهُ وَاللَّهُ يَعْصِمُكَ مِنَ النَّاسِ

O Messenger, announce that which has been revealed to you from your Lord, and if you do not, then you have not conveyed His message. And Allah will protect you from the people.[2]

وَمَا يَنْطِقُ عَنِ الْهَوَىٰ إِنْ هُوَ إِلَّا وَحْيٌ يُوحَىٰ

Nor does he speak from [his own] inclination. It is not but a revelation revealed.[3]

It was necessary for the Messenger ﷺ to convey, whether by writing or speech. As such he issued commands like the one to expel the Mushrikīn from the Arabian Peninsula. Tījānī's claim is an indictment on the Messenger ﷺ. How could he hesitate about conveying because of mere criticism?

Any person who reads the Qur'ān knows the extent of Tījānī's ignorance of the reality of Prophethood. All the Prophets were confronted with various forms of

---

1 *Then I was guided*, p. 69.

2 Sūrah al-Mā'idah: 67.

3 Sūrah al-Najm: 3,4.

physical and psychological abuse, but these abuses did not dissuade them from conveying the message of Allah. Our Prophet ﷺ—the Seal of the Prophets—was also confronted with a variety of temptations, threats and torments in order to dissuade him from conveying his message. The Mushrikīn abused and tormented him and his Ṣaḥābah, forced them to take refuge in the mountain passes of Makkah, hurled derision and ridicule at him with insults such as "magician" and "insane"—but none of these pressures stood in the way of conveying the religion of Allah completely without any deficiencies. He and his Companions strove in the path of Allah until Allah gave him dominion on earth and raised his religion above all other religions.

Then this Rāfiḍī comes along and claims that the most resolute of all the Prophets ﷺ refused to convey the order of Allah which would protect the Ummah from misguidance. Why? Because of nothing other than disrespect, disobedience to his instruction, and criticism of it. Nothing can be further from the character of our beloved Prophet ﷺ! It was his duty to convey the message and disclose the truth even if the entire earth waged war against him so that truth may prevail over falsehood. It is for this reason that Allah sent Prophets as givers of glad tidings and warnings to the people. This informs us that what the Messenger ﷺ intended to write was not revelation.

Tījānī accuses the Ṣaḥābah of not respecting the Messenger ﷺ, of not fulfilling his command, and of criticising him. Sometimes he writes that Ibn ʿAbbās cried to such an extent that his tears moistened the ground, and sometimes he writes that the Ṣaḥābah cried until their tears moistened the ground; but at the same time they schemed to prevent the Messenger ﷺ from writing, most of them siding with the view of ʿUmar.

He then rallies to the defence of his partisans and says:

> **I tend to agree with the Shii point of view in explaining the incident because I find it logical and very coherent.**
>
> **I still remember the answer which al-Sayyid Muhammad Baqir al-Sadr gave me when I asked him, "How did our master Umar understand, among all the Companions what the Messenger wanted to write, namely the appointment of Ali as his successor- as you claim - which shows that he was a clever man?"**

> **Al-Sayyid al-Sadr said: Umar was not the only one who anticipated what the Messenger was going to write. In fact most of the people who were present there understood the situation the same way as Umar did, because the Messenger of Allah had previously indicated the issue when he said, "I shall leave you with two weighty things: the Book of Allah and the members of my Family (Ahl al-Bayt) and their descendants, if you follow them, you will never go astray after me." And during his illness he said to them, "Let me write you a document, if you follow its contents, you will never go astray." Those who were present, including Umar, understood that the Messenger of Allah wanted to reiterate, in writing, what he had already said in Ghadir Khum, and that was to follow the Book of Allah and Ahl al-Bayt and that Ali was the head of it. It was as if the holy Prophet صَلَّى ٱللَّٰهُ عَلَيْهِ وَسَلَّمَ was saying, "Follow the Qur'ān and Ali." He said similar things on many occasions, as has been stated by many historians.**
>
> **The majority of Quraysh did not like Ali because he was young and because he smashed their arrogance and had killed their heroes; but they did not dare oppose the Messenger of Allah, as they had done at the "Treaty of al-Hudaibiyah", and when the Messenger prayed for Abdullah ibn Abi al-Munafiq, and on many other incidents recorded by history. This incident was one of them, and you see that the opposition against writing that document during the Prophets illness encouraged some of those who were present to be insolent and make so much noise in his presence.**[1]

Tījānī claims that the explanation of the Shīʿah is logical and has many supporting proofs. May I ask what these proofs are? Is it Bāqir al-Ṣadr's analysis of the position of the Ṣaḥābah? Does Bāqir al-Ṣadr know the unseen or receive revelation? I am amazed, and continue to be amazed, by his statement:

> **Umar was not the only one who anticipated what the Messenger was going to write. In fact most of the people who were present then understood the situation the same way as Umar did.**

Bāqir al-Ṣadr must have opened up the chests of the Ṣaḥābah to know what they contained.

Then Tījānī says:

> **Because the Messenger of Allah had previously indicated the issue when he said, "I shall leave you with two weighty things."**

1 *Then I was guided*, p. 69-70.

He alludes to the ḥadīth of Ghadīr Khumm which (allegedly) bears the statement of the Messenger صَلَّى ٱللَّهُ عَلَيْهِ وَسَلَّمَ, "Whomsoever, I am his Mawlā, then ʿAlī رَضِيَ ٱللَّهُ عَنْهُ is his Mawlā."

I say to Tījānī and his guide: Seeing that the Messenger صَلَّى ٱللَّهُ عَلَيْهِ وَسَلَّمَ previously said "the like of it"— as you claim —why did he repeat it? According to your interpretation these aḥādīth and the ones transmitted by the Ahl al-Sunnah in their authentic compilations already explicitly state that. Do you not find it odd that he needs to repeat it? Do these aḥādīth not suffice as a proof against the Ahl al-Sunnah?

What is truly strange is that the Shīʿah have constantly been boxing our ears to point out that the Messenger صَلَّى ٱللَّهُ عَلَيْهِ وَسَلَّمَ stated that ʿAlī رَضِيَ ٱللَّهُ عَنْهُ will be his successor in categorically unambiguous texts. Yet they continue citing aḥādīth such as, "This is my brother, my advisor, and my successor amongst you, therefore listen to him and obey him," which can be interpreted in a variety of different manners.

Al-Mūsawī in his book *al-Murājaʿāt*[1] claims that there are forty clear aḥādīth concerning the successorship of ʿAlī, while in the book *Ḥaqq al-Yaqīn*[2] their great scholar, ʿAbd Allāh Shubbar, produces thirteen explicit aḥādīth establishing the successorship of ʿAlī رَضِيَ ٱللَّهُ عَنْهُ. Why then, after all this, does he cling to straws, reiterating that the Messenger صَلَّى ٱللَّهُ عَلَيْهِ وَسَلَّمَ intended to write a letter stating in it the successorship of ʿAlī ibn Abī Ṭālib رَضِيَ ٱللَّهُ عَنْهُ? If you say it is because the Ahl al-Sunnah deny it or explain it away, then I say: If the Ahl al-Sunnah deny these "unambiguous" texts, along with the events of Ghadīr Khumm that occurred in the presence of a mass of people, then it is more likely that they would deny a dubious letter where only a small group of people were present.

Tījānī goes on to say:

> **The majority of Quraysh did not like Ali because he was young and because he smashed their arrogance and had killed their heroes.**

Who does he intend with the word "Quraysh" here? Is it the Mushrikīn of Makkah or the Ṣaḥābah of the Messenger صَلَّى ٱللَّهُ عَلَيْهِ وَسَلَّمَ? If it is the Mushrikīn of Makkah, then was ʿAlī رَضِيَ ٱللَّهُ عَنْهُ the only one who shattered, crushed and killed their heroes? Was he the only one who fought at Badr, Uḥud and other expeditions? Did not all the

1 *Murājaʿāt* 48, p. 169-181.

2 ʿAbd Allāh Shubbar: *Ḥaqq al-Yaqīn fī Maʿrifat Uṣūl al-Dīn*, vol. 1 p. 174-282.

Ṣaḥābah share in that, at the forefront Abū Bakr, ʿUmar, ʿUthmān, Ṭalḥah, Zubayr, and others? If that is the case—and indeed it is—then there is no distinction for ʿAlī رَضِيَ ٱللَّهُ عَنْهُ above the rest of the Ṣaḥābah.

If by "Quraysh" he means the Ṣaḥābah—which is most likely intended considering the context, since Abū Bakr, ʿUmar, ʿUthmān, and most of the Muhājirīn were from the Quraysh—then here I ask: Did ʿAlī shatter the grandeur of these Ṣaḥābah and kill their heroes, or did these Ṣaḥābah enter into Islam out of desire or fear? What sense does this make when the Messenger صَلَّى ٱللَّهُ عَلَيْهِ وَسَلَّمَ said:

> This matter of leadership will be amongst the Quraysh—no person will oppose them except that Allah will drag him on his face into the Fire—as long as they maintain the religion.[1]

Ibn ʿUmar رَضِيَ ٱللَّهُ عَنْهُمَا narrates another ḥadīth in which the Messenger صَلَّى ٱللَّهُ عَلَيْهِ وَسَلَّمَ said:

> This matter will remain amongst the Quraysh as long as two of them remain.[2]

ʿAlī رَضِيَ ٱللَّهُ عَنْهُ himself said in a sermon in *Nahj al-Balāghah* which is from amongst the most highly revered works of the Shīʿah:

> Indeed, the leaders are from the Quraysh.[3]

It was for that reason the four khulafāʾ were from the Quraysh, amongst them ʿAlī ibn Abī Ṭālib رَضِيَ ٱللَّهُ عَنْهُ. So what do these Shīʿah ramble about? It should rather be said from the outset that reason and historical fact prove that the remainder of the Persians—whose grandeur ʿAlī رَضِيَ ٱللَّهُ عَنْهُ and the Ṣaḥābah ruined and whose heroes they killed—embraced Islam and it is they who then conspired against the Ṣaḥābah, using the Ahl al-Bayt as a pretext.

They pretended to cry for the Ahl al-Bayt and assist them, and shed false tears for them. Thereafter, they started destroying the foundations of this religion by criticising those who conveyed and preserved the Qur'ān and Sunnah, namely the trustworthy Ṣaḥābah, may Allah be pleased with all of them.

---

1 *Ṣaḥīḥ al-Bukhārī*, The Book of Laws, Ḥadīth no. 6720, *Ṣaḥīḥ Muslim* with commentary, vol. 12, Ḥadīth no. 1821.

2 Ibid.

3 *Nahj al-Balāghah*, p. 305.

If by writing the letter the Messenger ﷺ intended to instate or appoint someone as his successor he would have given it to Abū Bakr رضي الله عنه as that is what the evidence suggests. Qāsim ibn Muḥammad, the grandfather of Imām al-Bāqir, is reports from ʿĀ'ishah رضي الله عنها:

> The Messenger ﷺ said, "Indeed, I was on the verge of calling Abū Bakr and his son, and entrust leadership to him for fear that people might speak or aspire to things. But Allah and the Believers refuse to have anyone but Abū Bakr.[1]

In *Ṣaḥīḥ Muslim*, ʿUrwah narrates that ʿĀ'ishah رضي الله عنها said:

> The Messenger ﷺ said to me, "Call Abū Bakr and your brother for me so that I may write a letter. Indeed I fear that some aspiring person might say I am more deserving, but Allah and the Believers refuse to have anyone but Abū Bakr."[2]

Al-Bukhārī and Muslim narrate that Jubayr ibn Muṭʿim said:

> A woman came to the Messenger ﷺ and he instructed her to return to him later. She said, "What should I do if I return and I do not find you?" It was as if she was implying death.
>
> He replied, "If you do not find me then go to Abū Bakr."[3]

Al-Bukhārī and Muslim narrate also from Abū Hurayrah رضي الله عنه that he heard the Messenger ﷺ say:

> While I was sleeping I saw myself standing over a well with a bucket on it. I drew from it as much as Allah decreed. Then the son of Abū Quḥāfah (Abū Bakr) took it and drew a bucket or two. His drawing was somewhat weak but Allah overlooked it. Then it turned into a big bucket and (ʿUmar) Ibn al-Khaṭṭāb took it. I never saw a giant, draw water like he did, until people were fully satiated.[4]

---

1 *Ṣaḥīḥ al-Bukhārī*, The Book of Laws, vol. 6, Ḥadīth no. 6791.

2 *Ṣaḥīḥ Muslim* with the commentary, vol. 15, Ḥadīth no. 2387.

3 *Ṣaḥīḥ al-Bukhārī*, The Chapter on the Merits of the Ṣaḥābah, Ḥadīth no. 3459; *Ṣaḥīḥ Muslim* with its commentary, The Chapter on the Merits of the Ṣaḥābah, vol. 15, Ḥadīth no. 2386.

4 Op. Cit. Ḥadīth no. 4364.

It is reported from Abū Bakrah رضي الله عنه:

> The Messenger صلى الله عليه وسلم said one day, "Who amongst you had a dream?"
>
> A man replied, "I saw as if a scale descended from the heavens. Then you (the Messenger صلى الله عليه وسلم) and Abū Bakr were weighed, and you outweighed Abū Bakr. Then Abū Bakr and 'Umar were weighed, and Abū Bakr outweighed 'Umar. Then 'Umar and 'Uthmān were weighed, and 'Umar outweighed 'Uthmān. Then the scale was lifted."
>
> Abū Bakrah said, "This upset the Messenger صلى الله عليه وسلم and he then said, 'A khilāfah of Nubuwwah, then Allah will give the kingdom to whomever he wills thereafter.'"[1]

The Messenger صلى الله عليه وسلم sent Abū Bakr رضي الله عنه forward to lead the people in ṣalāh until he passed away. Imām al-Bukhārī narrates from Abū Mūsā رضي الله عنه:

> The Messenger صلى الله عليه وسلم was ill and when his illness intensified, He said, "Order Abū Bakr to lead the people in ṣalāh!"
>
> 'Ā'ishah then said, "Indeed, he is a soft-hearted man. When he stands in your place he will be unable to lead the people in ṣalāh."
>
> She then repeated herself and he said, "Order Abū Bakr to lead the ṣalāh! Indeed you are of the women of Yūsuf."
>
> He then came to the Messenger and he led the people in ṣalāh during the life of the Messenger صلى الله عليه وسلم.[2]

It has been narrated from Zuhrī, who reported from Anas ibn Mālik رضي الله عنه:

> Abū Bakr used to lead them in ṣalāh during the illness of the Messenger صلى الله عليه وسلم in which he passed away. On Monday while they were standing in their rows, the Messenger صلى الله عليه وسلم opened the curtain of the room and stood there gazing at us. As if his face was a page of the Qur'ān. He smiled and we were tempted to break our prayer out of happiness at the sight of the Messenger صلى الله عليه وسلم. Abū Bakr stepped backwards to reach the row behind him thinking that the Messenger صلى الله عليه وسلم had come out to the prayer. The Messenger صلى الله عليه وسلم,

---

1 *Sunan Abū Dāwūd*, The Chapter on the Sunnah, Ḥadīth no. 4635; *Sunan al-Tirmidhī*, The Chapters of Dreams, Ḥadīth no. 2403.

2 *Ṣaḥīḥ al-Bukhārī*, The Book of Congregation, Ḥadīth no. 646.

> however, motioned to him to complete the prayer. He then lowered the screen and passed away later that day.[1]

The Messenger ﷺ sending Abū Bakr رضي الله عنه forward is an indication towards his rightful leadership over the Muslims and this is exactly what happened. The view of Ahl al-Sunnah is that if the Messenger ﷺ indeed intended to entrust anyone with leadership by writing a letter that person would have been Abū Bakr رضي الله عنه. They based this contention on evidence that is more powerful and persuasive, possesses greater clarity, and in no way contradicts logic.

This stands in stark contrast with the empty claims of the Shīʿah that are too fragile and weak for any sane mind to accept. I have overlooked the rest of Tījānī's discussion on this matter, as it is a tedious repetition of what was already mentioned. Further, I have refuted all the questions that have been brought up surrounding this ḥadīth. And all praise is due to Allah in the beginning and at the end.

1 *Ṣaḥīḥ al-Bukhārī*, Ḥadīth no. 648.

Tījānī on the Battalion of Usāmah

Tījānī says:

> **The story in brief is as follows:**
>
> **The Prophet ﷺ organized an army to be sent to Asia Minor two days before his death. He appointed Usamah ibn Zayd ibn Haritha, (who was eighteen years old), as its commander in chief, then the holy Prophet attached some important men, both Muhajireen and Ansar, to this expedition, such as Abu Bakr, Umar, Abu Obaydah and other well-known Companions. Some people among them[1] criticized the Prophet for appointing Usamah as the commander in chief of that army, and asked how could he have appointed so young a man as their commander. In fact the same people had previously criticized the Prophet for appointing Usamah's father as an army commander before him. They went on criticizing until the Prophet became so angry that he left his bed, feverish and with his head bandaged, with two men supporting him and his feet barely touching the ground (may my parents be sacrificed for him) because of the severe exhaustion he was experiencing[2].He ascended the pulpit, praised Allah highly then said,**
>
>> **O People ! I have been informed that some of you object to my appointing Usamah as commander of the detachment. You now object to my appointing Usamah as commander in chief as you objected to me appointing his father commander in chief before him. By Allah, his father was certainly competent for his appointment as commander in chief and his son is also competent for the appointment.**
>
> **Then he exhorted them to start without further delay and kept saying,**
>
>> **"Send the detachment of Usamah; deploy the detachment of Usamah, send forward the detachment of Usamah." He kept repeating the exhortations but the Companions were still sluggish, and camped by al-Jurf and nearly did not do it.[3]**

Tījānī references this summary of the incident to four sources: *Ṭabaqāt ibn Saʿd*, *Tārīkh ibn al-Athīr*, *al-Sīrah al-Ḥalabiyyah* and *Tārīkh al-Ṭabarī*. Here I find myself compelled

1 This passage was omitted in the English translation.

2 This passage was omitted in the English translation.

3 *Then I was guided*, p. 71-72.

to reproduce the narration concerning the army of Usāmah ibn Zayd رضي الله عنه from the very books cited as reference in order to see whether Tījānī summarised and transmitted correctly or if he blatantly lied.

Ibn Saʿd, in his book *al-Ṭabaqāt al-Kubrā*, says:

> Then with regards to the battalion of Usāmah ibn Zayd ibn Ḥārithah to the people of Ubnā, the land of al-Sarāt in the direction of Balqā, They said: On Monday, four nights before the end of Ṣafar during eleventh year after Hijrah, the Messenger صلى الله عليه وسلم commanded the people to prepare for an assault on the Romans. The next day he called Usāmah ibn Zayd and said, "Travel to the land where your father was killed and attack them with your infantry. I have placed you in charge of this army. Attack the people of Ubnā in the morning and set a fire upon them and hasten the journey so that you precede the reports. If Allah grants you victory, then remain a short while amongst them. Take guides with you and send spies and your vanguard ahead of you."
>
> On Wednesday, the (final) illness of the Messenger صلى الله عليه وسلم began and he became feverish and suffered from headaches. When he woke the Thursday morning he tied the flag for Usāmah with his own hand and said, "Sally forth in the name of Allah and in his path. Fight those who disbelieve in Allah." Usāmah then left with his flag tied and handed it to Buraydah ibn Ḥuṣayb al-Aslamī and camped at Jurf. There were none amongst the prominent first Muhājirīn and Anṣār except that he was deputed for that battle. Amongst them were Abū Bakr, ʿUmar ibn al-Khaṭṭāb, Abū ʿUbaydah ibn al-Jarrāḥ, Saʿd ibn Abī Waqqāṣ, Saʿīd ibn Zayd, Qatādah ibn Nuʿmān, and Salamah ibn Aslam ibn Ḥuraysh.
>
> Then a group said, "This youngster is being placed above the first Muhājirīn?" The Messenger صلى الله عليه وسلم became intensely angry and came out having placed a bandage on his head and a cloth over him. He then ascended the pulpit, praised, and glorified Allah, then said, "O people what is this that has reached me from some of you concerning my appointment of Usāmah? Indeed, if you criticised my appointment of Usāmah then you criticised my appointment of his father before him. By Allah, indeed he was suitable for leadership and indeed his son too is suitable for leadership. Verily, he was of the most beloved of people to me and indeed they (father and son) are inspired towards all good. I exhort you to be good towards him (Usāmah) for indeed he is from the best amongst you." He then descended and entered his home.

> That was the Saturday, ten days having passed of Rabīʿ al-Awwal. Those Muslims who were to leave with Usāmah رَضِيَ ٱللَّهُ عَنْهُ came out, bid their farewells to the Messenger صَلَّى ٱللَّهُ عَلَيْهِ وَسَلَّمَ, and proceeded to camp at al-Jurf. The illness of the Messenger صَلَّى ٱللَّهُ عَلَيْهِ وَسَلَّمَ intensified and he started saying, "Dispatch the army of Usāmah!" On the Sunday the pain of the Messenger صَلَّى ٱللَّهُ عَلَيْهِ وَسَلَّمَ intensified. Usāmah therefore came from his camp and entered upon the Messenger صَلَّى ٱللَّهُ عَلَيْهِ وَسَلَّمَ who was overcome with pain. That was the day they inserted medicine into his mouth. Usāmah lowered his head and kissed him but the Messenger صَلَّى ٱللَّهُ عَلَيْهِ وَسَلَّمَ could not speak. He raised his hands towards the heaven and placed them on Usāmah. Usāmah said, "I realised that he was supplicating for me."
>
> Usāmah returned to his camp. He then returned the Tuesday. The Messenger صَلَّى ٱللَّهُ عَلَيْهِ وَسَلَّمَ awoke in a stable condition and said to him, "March forward upon the blessing of Allah." Usāmah then bid him farewell, went out to his camp and instructed his army to get ready to leave. While he was about to mount his conveyance the messenger of his mother, Umm Ayman, arrived and said, "Indeed the Messenger صَلَّى ٱللَّهُ عَلَيْهِ وَسَلَّمَ is dying." Usāmah, ʿUmar, and Abū ʿUbaydah proceeded towards Madīnah and went to the Messenger صَلَّى ٱللَّهُ عَلَيْهِ وَسَلَّمَ who was in his final moments. The Messenger صَلَّى ٱللَّهُ عَلَيْهِ وَسَلَّمَ passed away as the sun fell, twelve nights of the month of Rabīʿ al-Awwal having passed. The Muslims who were camping at al-Jurf entered Madīnah with Buraydah ibn Ḥuṣayb holding the flag of Usāmah until he reached the door of the Messenger صَلَّى ٱللَّهُ عَلَيْهِ وَسَلَّمَ where he entrenched it.[1]

Ibn al-Athīr says in his book *al-Kāmil fī al-Tārīkh* under the discussion relating to the events of the eleventh year:

> In the month of Muḥarram of this year the Messenger صَلَّى ٱللَّهُ عَلَيْهِ وَسَلَّمَ sent a group to Shām (the Levant) under the leadership of Usāmah ibn Zayd, the freed slave of the Messenger صَلَّى ٱللَّهُ عَلَيْهِ وَسَلَّمَ. He commanded Usāmah to camp in the vicinity of al-Balqā' and Dārūm in the land of Palestine. The hypocrites spoke (disparagingly) about his leadership and said, "He appointed a youngster to be the commander of the senior Muhājirīn and Anṣār?"
>
> The Messenger صَلَّى ٱللَّهُ عَلَيْهِ وَسَلَّمَ then said, "If you are criticising his appointment (as the leader) then indeed you criticised the appointment of his father before. Indeed he is as suitable for command as was his father before him." He included (in the army) with Usāmah some of the first amongst the Muhājirīn

1 Ibn Saʿd: *al-Ṭabaqāt al-Kubrā*, p. 189-191.

including Abū Bakr and ʿUmar. As people were busy with that the illness of the Messenger صلى الله عليه وسلم began.[1]

ʿAlī al-Ḥalabī in his *al-Sīrah al-Ḥalabiyyah* says with regards to the detachment of Usāmah:

> On Monday, four days remaining of the month of Ṣafar, the eleventh year after Hijrah, the Messenger صلى الله عليه وسلم commanded the Ṣaḥābah to prepare for an assault on the Romans. The next day he called Usāmah and said to him, "Travel to the place of your father (the place where his father, Zayd ibn Ḥārithah, had been martyred) and attack them with your infantry. Indeed I have placed you in charge of this army. Attack the people of Ubnā in the morning and set fire upon them. Make haste in your journey so that you reach before the reports. If Allah grants you victory over them then minimise your stay amongst them. Take with you guides and send your spies and scouts forth before you." That Wednesday the pain of the Messenger صلى الله عليه وسلم began. He became feverish and suffered from headaches. When he awoke on Thursday, the Messenger صلى الله عليه وسلم tied the flag for Usāmah with his hand and said, "March forward in the name of Allah, in the path of Allah, and fight the one who disbelieves in Allah!" Usāmah then set out with his flag tied and handed it over to Buraydah and camped at al-Jurf. There were none amongst the prominent Muhājirīn and Anṣār except that he hastened towards it, amongst them Abū Bakr, ʿUmar, Abū ʿUbaydah, and Saʿd ibn Abī Waqqāṣ. Some people said, "This youngster is being placed in charge of the first Muhājirīn and Anṣār." This is because Usāmah was eighteen, nineteen, or sixteen years old at the time.
>
> ...When their statement and criticism concerning his age reached the Messenger صلى الله عليه وسلم, he became extremely angry. He came out of his room with a bandage on his head and a cloth over him. He ascended the pulpit, praised Allah and said, "What is this statement which has reached me from some of you concerning my appointment of Usāmah as the leader? Indeed, if you criticise my appointment of Usāmah, then you criticise my appointment of his father. By Allah, he was eligible for command and after him his son is eligible for command. He is of the most beloved of people to me and all good could be expected of them. Therefore, show goodwill towards him as he is amongst the best of you." It was stated before that Usāmah رضي الله عنه was called *al-Ḥibb ibn al-Ḥibb* (the beloved, son of the beloved) and that when he was young the Messenger صلى الله عليه وسلم used to wipe his nose with his own clothes.

1 Ibn al-Athīr: *al-Kāmil fī al-Tārīkh*, p. 182.

He then descended and entered his home. That was the Saturday, ten days having passed of the month of Rabīʿ al-Awwal, the eleventh year after the migration. The Muslims who were leaving with Usāmah came, bid farewell to the Messenger ﷺ and went to the camp at al-Jurf. The Messenger's ﷺ illness intensified and he started saying, "Send out the army of Usāmah!"

At this point the Messenger ﷺ exempted Abū Bakr and instructed him to lead the people in ṣalāh. Therefore, there is no contradiction between the view that Abū Bakr was part of the army and that he stayed behind, as he was initially part of the army and then stayed behind when the Messenger ﷺ instructed him to lead the people in ṣalāh. With this understanding of events the accusation of the Shīʿah against Abū Bakr for lagging behind the army of Usāmah is debunked, for you now know that his staying behind was on account of the instruction of the Messenger ﷺ for him to lead the people in ṣalāh. The view of this Rāfiḍī as well as his claim that the Messenger ﷺ cursed the one who lagged behind the army of Usāmah is rejected as there is no basis for the curse in the ḥadīth whatsoever.

The Sunday, the pain intensified upon the Messenger ﷺ. Usāmah came from his camp and entered the room of the Messenger ﷺ while the Messenger ﷺ was overcome with pain. He lowered his head and kissed him but the Messenger ﷺ could not speak. He then started raising his hands toward the heaven and then placed it on Usāmah. Usāmah said, "I realised that he was supplicating for me." He returned to the camp and then visited the Messenger ﷺ again on Monday. He said to Usāmah, "March forward with the blessings of Allah." Usāmah then bid him farewell, went out to his camp, and commanded the people to prepare for departure. Just as he intended to mount his horse, the messenger of his mother, Umm Ayman, came to him and said, "Indeed the Prophet is dying."

Another narration states, "Then Usāmah moved until he reached al-Jurf where his wife, Fāṭimah bint Qays, sent word to him saying, "Do not hasten, for indeed the Messenger of Allah has grown seriously ill." He approached Madīnah along with ʿUmar and Abū ʿUbaydah. They reached the Messenger ﷺ as he was dying. The Messenger ﷺ then passed on as the sun dropped.[1]

---

1 *ʿAlī ibn Burhān al-Dīn al-Ḥalabī*, vol. 3 p. 207.

Al-Ṭabarī mentions in his book *Tārīkh al-Umam wa l-Mulūk* two narrations concerning the Battalion of Usāmah ibn Zayd in the chapter concerning the events which occurred during the eleventh year after Hijrah.

The first narration reads:

> From ʿUbayd ibn Ḥunayn — the freed slave of the Messenger صلى الله عليه وسلم — from Abū Muwayhibah — also the freed slave of the Messenger صلى الله عليه وسلم — who says, "The Messenger returned to Madīnah after he performed the complete Ḥajj and the journey came to an end. He then chose a group from amongst the people and placed in charge of them Usāmah ibn Zayd. He commanded him to attack Ābil al-Zayt on the highlands of Syria, the land in Jordan. The hypocrites then spoke about Usāmah's appointment but the Messenger صلى الله عليه وسلم rebuffed them, saying, "He is eligible for command and if you say (something unkind) about him then indeed you said (something unkind) about his father before, and he was suitable for it as well.'"

In the second narration, ʿIkrimah narrates from Ibn ʿAbbās رضي الله عنه, who said:

> The Messenger صلى الله عليه وسلم arranged the military detachment of Usāmah. The hypocrites criticised the appointment of Usāmah as the leader. When the Messenger صلى الله عليه وسلم learnt of this, he came out to the people; his head bandaged on account of a headache, and said, "Indeed, I saw in a dream last night two gold bracelets on my forearm. I disliked it and so I removed it. It then flew away. I interpret it to refer to these two liars, the one from Yamāmah and the one from Yemen. I have heard that some people are criticising the command of Usāmah. By my life, if they criticised his command, indeed they criticised his father's command before him. Indeed his father was eligible for command and indeed he too is suitable for it. Dispatch the military battalion of Usāmah!" He also said, "May Allah curse those who take the graves of their Prophets as places of worship." Usāmah then went out and set up camp at al-Jurf and gathered the people in the camp. Ṭulayḥah (another false prophet) appeared and the people lingered. The Messenger صلى الله عليه وسلم became seriously ill and the army of Usāmah was not dispatched. People waited for one another until Allah took his Messenger.[1]

---

1 *Tārīkh al-Ṭabarī*, p. 224-225. Also refer to *al-Iḥtijāj* of al-Ṭabarsī vol. 1 p. 71; *al-Sīrat al-Nabawiyyah* of Ibn Hishām vol. 4 p. 299; *Nūr al-Yaqīn* of Muḥammad al-Khidr p. 16, *al-Bidāyah wa al-Nihāyah* vol. 5 p. 195, *al-Muntaẓam* of Ibn al-Jawzī vol. 4 p. 16, *al-Mawāhib* vol. 1 p. 647, *Subul al-Hudā wa al-Rashād* vol. 6 p. 248.

This is all that these four historians have mentioned in their books about the Battalion of Usāmah ibn Zayd رضي الله عنه; they have not mentioned anything else.

When comparing it with what Tījānī mentions in his book, which he claims to have quoted and summarised from these four sources, we come to the following conclusions:

1. Tījānī claims that the senior Ṣaḥābah, amongst them Abū Bakr and ʿUmar رضي الله عنهما, criticised the appointment of Usāmah رضي الله عنه as the leader. He says:

> **The holy Prophet attached some important men, both Muhajireen and Ansar, to this expedition, such as Abu Bakr, Umar, Abu Obaydah and other well-known Companions. Some people among them[1] criticized the Prophet for appointing Usamah as the commander in chief of that army, and asked how could he have appointed so young a man as their commander. In fact the same people had previously criticized the Prophet for appointing Usamah's father as an army commander before him. They went on criticizing until...**

It is implied that Abū Bakr, ʿUmar, Abū ʿUbaydah, and the senior well-known Ṣaḥābah رضي الله عنهم were the ones who criticised the appointment of Usāmah رضي الله عنه and of his father before him, and that they were excessive in their criticism. However, when we consult the four sources cited by Tījānī we do not find a trace of proof for this fabrication. Ibn Saʿd in his *Ṭabaqāt* and al-Ḥalabī in his *Sīrah* say:

> There was none amongst the prominent first Muhājirīn and Anṣār except that he was deputed for that battle. Amongst them were Abū Bakr, ʿUmar ibn al-Khaṭṭāb, Abū ʿUbaydah ibn al-Jarrāḥ, Saʿd ibn Abī Waqqāṣ, Saʿīd ibn Zayd, Qatādah ibn Nuʿmān, and Salamah ibn Aslam ibn Ḥuraysh. Then a group spoke...

The members of this "group" are unnamed and unidentified. Therefore, if the author of the cited source intended these Ṣaḥābah he would have identified them as such.

The remaining sources also contain no identification of this sort. From this we come to know that these noble and senior Ṣaḥābah, Abū Bakr, ʿUmar, Abū ʿUbaydah, and others رضي الله عنهم, were in no way involved in criticising Usāmah رضي الله عنه and his father.

---

1 This passage was omitted in the English translation.

2. Abū Bakr رَضِيَ اللَّهُ عَنْهُ was not part of the army of Usāmah رَضِيَ اللَّهُ عَنْهُ because it has been authentically narrated that the Messenger صَلَّى اللَّهُ عَلَيْهِ وَسَلَّمَ appointed him to lead the ṣalāh. We have previously mentioned the aḥādīth pertaining to that. One of those is the ḥadīth which clarifies that Abū Bakr رَضِيَ اللَّهُ عَنْهُ led the Muslims in ṣalāh the day of the Messenger's صَلَّى اللَّهُ عَلَيْهِ وَسَلَّمَ passing when he removed the curtain of the room and saw the Ṣaḥābah in rows behind Abū Bakr رَضِيَ اللَّهُ عَنْهُ. How could he then have been in the army of Usāmah رَضِيَ اللَّهُ عَنْهُ?

3. To stir up the emotions of the reader, Tījānī opts for exaggeration to the extent that he clashes headlong with the documented record of history. He says:

   He left his bed, feverish and with his head bandaged, with two men supporting him and his feet barely touching the ground (may my parents be sacrificed for him) because of the severe exhaustion he was experiencing.

   Subḥān Allāh! What sort of honesty and integrity is it that allows for words to be ripped from their proper context? What the historians narrate is that the Messenger صَلَّى اللَّهُ عَلَيْهِ وَسَلَّمَ "came out after he had just wrapped his head with a bandage and then ascended the pulpit." As for him being "carried out between two men with his feet sketching a line in the ground," this was not narrated by a single one of them. The reader will soon see in my rebuttals that Tījānī based his book upon flagrant falsifications and astonishing contradictions.

4. Tījānī now blames the Ṣaḥābah with this statement:

   Then he exhorted them to start without further delay and kept saying,

   "Send the detachment of Usamah; deploy the detachment of Usamah, send forward the detachment of Usamah."

   He kept repeating the exhortations but the Companions were still sluggish, and camped by al-Jurf and nearly did not do it.[1]

   What do the authors of the cited sources actually mention on this matter? They mention that the Messenger صَلَّى اللَّهُ عَلَيْهِ وَسَلَّمَ said, "Dispatch the army of Usāmah!" That was the Saturday. Then Usāmah came to visit the Messenger صَلَّى اللَّهُ عَلَيْهِ وَسَلَّمَ on Sunday to bid farewell, and the Messenger صَلَّى اللَّهُ عَلَيْهِ وَسَلَّمَ said, "March

1 *Then I was guided*, p. 71.

forward with the blessings of Allah!" When Usāmah رضي الله عنه intended to leave and instructed the army to prepare for departure the news came to him that the Messenger صلى الله عليه وسلم was dying. This is as much as they mention; nothing more. Tījānī, however, found it easy and convenient to fabricate against the Ṣaḥābah and then falsely claim that they tarried and were sluggish in executing the instruction of the Messenger صلى الله عليه وسلم.

5. Who were the critics of Usāmah's رضي الله عنه appointment? The evidence presented above makes it abundantly clear that the prominent Muhājirīn and Anṣār did not criticise the appointment of Usāmah رضي الله عنه, and that those who spoke disparagingly about it were unidentified persons. Al-Ṭabarī and Ibn al-Athīr, both cited by Tījānī, mentioned that the critics Usāmah's رضي الله عنه appointment were the hypocrites. Had they been from the Ṣaḥābah, at least one historian would have mentioned it. At the beginning of this book, I have established that the hypocrites were never counted amongst the Ṣaḥābah. From this we know that the Ṣaḥābah were completely innocent of criticising the appointment of Usāmah رضي الله عنه, and with that all the webs spun by Tījānī around this matter are conclusively blown away.

6. The tragedy is not that Tījānī cites sources which contradict him rather the real tragedy is in the clear double standards and mental acrobatics he gets into when searching for the weaknesses of the Ṣaḥābah. Tījānī's claim that the Ṣaḥābah—at the head of them Abū Bakr رضي الله عنه by implication—criticised the appointment of Usāmah رضي الله عنه is completely without precedent. This is because his entire motivation in this matter is to search for any incident which he can use to criticise the Ṣaḥābah. After his failure to find any point of criticism of the Ṣaḥābah despite studying it from various angles he resorts to blatant forgery and distortion. This is exactly what Tījānī did in relation to this incident. But what did his Shīʿī predecessors do? They too studied the various angles of this incident hoping to find something with which to criticise the Ṣaḥābah. But they were more productive than Tījānī. The author of *al-Sīrah al-Ḥalabiyyah* says:

> With this understanding of events the accusation of the Shīʿah against Abū Bakr for lagging behind the army of Usāmah is debunked, for you now know that his staying behind was on account of the instruction of the Messenger

> صَلَّىٰ ٱللَّٰهُ عَلَيْهِ وَسَلَّمَ for him to lead the people in ṣalāh. The view of this Rāfiḍī as well as his claim that the Messenger صَلَّىٰ ٱللَّٰهُ عَلَيْهِ وَسَلَّمَ cursed the one who lagged behind the army of Usāmah is rejected as there is no basis for the curse in the ḥadīth whatsoever.

Do you see the contradiction? Sometimes the claim is that Abū Bakr رَضِيَ ٱللَّٰهُ عَنْهُ was one of those who criticised Usāmah's appointment, implying that he was part of the army; and sometimes they claim that he lagged behind. What is the crime of this innocent Ṣaḥābī when it is these people who fabricate and distort history in order to criticise him. In doing so they fail to realise that they contradict themselves. Their blatant fabrications turn into a proof against them rather than for them. Is this the sound reasoning Tījānī promised us in the beginning?

Tījānī's objectivity

Tījānī says:

> **As usual, when I read about those events which touch on the integrity of the Companions, I try to deny or ignore them, but it is impossible to do so when all the historians and scholars, Shia and Sunnis, agree on their authenticity.**
>
> **I have promised my God to be fair, and I shall never be biased in favour of my creed, and will never use anything but the truth as my criterion. But the truth here is so bitter, and the holy Prophet صَلَّىٰ ٱللَّٰهُ عَلَيْهِ وَسَلَّمَ said, "Say the truth even if it is about yourself, and say the truth even if it is bitter..." The truth in this case is that the Companions who criticized the appointment of Usamah disobeyed all the clear texts that could not be doubted or misinterpreted, and there is no excuse for that, although some people make flimsy excuses in order to preserve the integrity of the Companions and "the virtuous ancestors". But the free and sensible person would not accept such feeble excuses, unless he is one of those who cannot comprehend any saying, or is perhaps one of those who are blinded by their own prejudice to the extent that they cannot differentiate between the obligatory task that must be obeyed and the prohibition that must be avoided. I thought deeply to find an acceptable excuse for those people, but without success.[1]**

I leave it to the vigilant leader to judge the truth of his pledge to be fair, not to be biased towards his school of thought, and to set store by nothing but the truth. I

1 *Then I was guided*, p. 72.

leave the vigilant reader to judge the falseness and deceit of his statements for themselves.

His claim that the Ṣaḥābah opposed the command of the Creator, the explicit texts which do not accept doubt and interpretation, without any justification indicates only ignorance and lack of aptitude. When and how did the Ṣaḥābah oppose the command of their Creator? And where are those "explicit texts" which "do not accept doubt and do not accept interpretation"? The truth of the matter is that the Messenger صلى الله عليه وسلم appointed Usāmah رضي الله عنه as commander of the army and some people criticised his appointment. Therefore the Messenger صلى الله عليه وسلم spoke about it and those who criticised retracted their criticism and obeyed his command. It should be remembered that the people during this time used to consult the Messenger صلى الله عليه وسلم in many matters but once he asserted his decision they would follow. In this particular matter all of the people followed the instruction of their Messenger صلى الله عليه وسلم, included amongst them those who criticised the appointment of Usāmah رضي الله عنه.

He states, "*Some people make flimsy excuses in order to preserve the integrity of the Companions and "the virtuous ancestors"*. But the free and sensible person would not accept such feeble excuses ..." this, by Allah, is one of his most amazing comments. The one who reads it would think that the Ṣaḥābah were highway robbers, hooligans, or fools. What need do these noble Ṣaḥābah have for anyone to defend their honour after Allah defended them, expressed his pleasure at them, testified to their excellence and strength of Īmān, and chose them for the companionship of His Messenger صلى الله عليه وسلم. The lands which they treaded on and the countries which they conquered testify to their exaltedness. Then along comes this buffoon with this casuistry which not even a fool would accept.

Then Tījānī says:

> **I read the points of view of the Sunnis which provide us with an excuse based on the fact that these people were the elders of Quraysh, and were among the early followers of Islam, whereas Usamah was a young man who had not fought in the decisive battles that gave Islam its glory, such as Badr, Uhud and Hunayn; and that he was a young man with no experience of life when the Messenger of Allah appointed him military commander. Furthermore, they thought that human nature, by its inclination, makes it difficult for elderly people to be led by young men, therefore they [i.e. the Companions]**

criticized the appointment and wanted the Messenger of Allah to appoint a prominent and respectable Companion.

It is an excuse which is not based on any rational or logical premise, and any Muslim who reads the Qur'an and understands its rules must reject such an excuse, because Allah- the Almighty - says:

وَمَآ آتَاكُمُ الرَّسُوْلُ فَخُذُوْهُ وَمَا نَهَاكُمْ عَنْهُ فَانْتَهُوْا

***So take what the Messenger assigns to you, and deny yourselves that which he withholds from you.*[1]**

وَمَا كَانَ لِمُؤْمِنٍ وَلَا مُؤْمِنَةٍ إِذَا قَضَى اللّٰهُ وَرَسُوْلُهُ أَمْرًا أَنْ يَكُوْنَ لَهُمُ الْخِيَرَةُ مِنْ أَمْرِهِمْ وَمَنْ يَعْصِ اللّٰهَ وَرَسُوْلَهُ فَقَدْ ضَلَّ ضَلَالًا مُبِيْنًا

***It is not fitting for a believer, man or woman, when a matter has been decided by Allah and His Messenger to have any option about their decision: if any one disobeys Allah and His Messenger, he is indeed on a clearly wrong Path.*[2, 3]**

I challenge Tījānī to produce one Sunnī source that exonerates the Ṣaḥābah with excuses of the kind he mentioned. As explained earlier, not a single historian ever said that the critics of Usāmah's appointment were those Ṣaḥābah who were the elders of the Quraysh. Tījānī claims to have read the excuses made by the Ahl al-Sunnah. Since the reader has the advantage over the one who has not read, the onus rests on him to identify the source in which he read those excuses.

Tījānī then says:

If we are to carefully analyse this incident we find the second Khalīfah (ʿUmar) among the most distinguished role-players and most famous advocates [for the dismissal of Usāmah] since it was he, after the death of Messenger, who went to Abū Bakr and requested him to dismiss Usāmah from his position of leadership and replace him with someone else. However, Abū Bakr said to him, "May your mother mourn you ʿUmar! Are you instructing me to remove him when the Messenger instated him?" How does the 'inspired' ʿUmar fare

1 Sūrah al-Ḥashr: 7.

2 Sūrah al-Aḥzāb: 36.

3 *Then I was guided*, p. 72-73.

in this matter, whose reality Abū Bakr perceived? Or is there some secret in the matter, concealed from the historians; or is it they who conceal it to preserve ʿUmar's honour — as is their habit — just as they substituted the expression "yahjur" with the expression "ghalabahū al-wajaʿ".[1]

The narration which Tījānī cites is a weak narration. In its chain of transmitters is Sayf ibn ʿUmar al-Ḍabbī whom ʿUqaylī lists as an unreliable transmitter.[2] Al-Dhahabī says in *Mīzān al-Iʿtidāl*:

> He composed works on the Conquests and Apostasy, etc. Like al-Wāqidī, he narrated from Hishām ibn ʿUrwah, ʿUbayd Allāh ibn ʿUmar, Jābir al-Juʿfī, and many other unknown narrators. He was an informed historian. Jubārah ibn al-Mughallis, Abū Maʿmar al-Qaṭīʿī, and al-Naḍr ibn Ḥammād al-ʿAtakī, and others narrated from him.
>
> ʿAbbās reports from Yaḥyā that he is unreliable.
>
> Muṭayyan narrated from Yaḥyā (that he said), "A copper coin is better than him."
>
> Abū Dāwūd said, "Worthless as a transmitter."
>
> Abū Ḥātim said, "*Matrūk* (suspected of ḥadīth forgery)."
>
> Ibn Ḥibbān said, "He was accused of *zandaqah* (heresy)
>
> Ibn ʿAdī said, "Most of his aḥādīth lack corroboration."[3]

The ḥadīth is weak at best and inadmissible as proof, firstly, because of Sayf ibn ʿUmar and secondly because Tījānī omitted an important part of the ḥadīth: The part stating that ʿUmar رضي الله عنه made this request from Abū Bakr رضي الله عنه at the instruction of Usāmah رضي الله عنه. The ḥadīth states:

> Usāmah stood amongst the people and then said to ʿUmar, "Return to the khalīfah of the Messenger of Allah and ask him to permit me to return with the people for indeed with us are some of the most prominent people and I do not feel safe for the khalīfah of the Messenger of Allah...[4]

1 *Then I was guided*, p. 90.

2 Al-ʿUqaylī: *al-Ḍuʿafāʾ al-Kabīr* vol. 2 p. 175, biography no. 694.

3 Al-Dhahabī: *Mīzān al-Iʿtidāl*, vol. 2 p. 255, biography no. 3637.

4 *Al-Ṭabarī* vol. 2 p. 246.

Tījānī, however, concealed all of this in order to prove his "fairness". And for further confirmation of his "fairness" and his "not attacking" the Ṣaḥābah—with ʿUmar at the forefront—is that he only cites such narrations which he in his ignorance believes to serve his goals, and overlooks others. Indeed, in al-Ṭabarī there is another narration which precedes this narration about ʿUmar رَضِيَ ٱللَّهُ عَنْهُ, stating that it was not ʿUmar who requested that, but rather, the general public because of widespread apostasy in the Arabian Peninsula. Tījānī, however, conveniently avoids mentioning it as there is no demerit against Abū Bakr and ʿUmar رَضِيَ ٱللَّهُ عَنْهُمَا in it.

How could ʿUmar رَضِيَ ٱللَّهُ عَنْهُ have been one of the most chief critics of Usāmah's رَضِيَ ٱللَّهُ عَنْهُ appointment when it was he who informed the Messenger صَلَّى ٱللَّهُ عَلَيْهِ وَسَلَّمَ about them?[1] May I remind the reader that Tījānī did not praise the position taken by Abū Bakr in the matter of dispatching the army of Usāmah but rather completely ignored it. However, when he comes across an incident which he thinks contains something which disparages this noble Ṣaḥābī, then he blows it up and builds castles in the air.

The tongue-in-cheek manner in which Tījānī here tries to cast aspersions on ʿUmar رَضِيَ ٱللَّهُ عَنْهُ actually provides an excellent opportunity to assess the objectivity that he is constantly at pains to convince the readers of. The full report, as it appears in al-Ṭabarī's *Tārīkh*, runs like this:

> Al-Ṭabarī narrates—with his chain of transmission—from al-Ḥasan al-Baṣrī, who said that the Prophet صَلَّى ٱللَّهُ عَلَيْهِ وَسَلَّمَ mobilized an army comprising fighters from Madīnah and the neighbouring tribes and appointed Usāmah ibn Zayd as their leader. ʿUmar ibn al-Khaṭṭāb was also enlisted. The Prophet صَلَّى ٱللَّهُ عَلَيْهِ وَسَلَّمَ passed away before the army had departed.
>
> (Considering the imminent danger to Madīnah) Usāmah kept the army back and sent ʿUmar back saying, "Return to the Khalīfah and seek his permission for me to return with the army since most of the people of counsel are with me. I fear the safety of the Khalīfah and the Muslims (not wanting to put them at risk by departing with the bulk of the fighting force)."
>
> (On his way) Some of the Anṣār tasked him with an additional request saying, "If he insists that the army deploys, tell him that we request he replaces Usāmah with someone senior."

1 *Fatḥ al-Bārī* vol. 7 p. 759.

ʿUmar complied with Usāmah's orders and duly conveyed his concerns to Abū Bakr. Abū Bakr responded emphatically, "I will not withhold the execution of orders given by the Messenger of Allah ﷺ, even if it results in me being gnawed at by dogs and wolves!" ʿUmar then conveyed the request of the Anṣār; that Abū Bakr replace him with someone senior. Upon hearing this Abū Bakr lunged up from his seat and grabbed ʿUmar's beard reprimanding him, "May your mother be barren of you, O son of Khaṭṭāb! He was appointed by the Prophet ﷺ and you want me to replace him!"

ʿUmar returned to the camp and they asked him what transpired. He said, "Proceed, may your mothers be barren of all of you! I had to face the wrath of the Khalīfah on your account!"

Abū Bakr then approached their camp, summoned the army and began escorting them on their departure. He escorted them on foot, whilst Usāmah was mounted and ʿAbd al-Raḥmān ibn ʿAwf held the reigns of Abū Bakr's mount. Usāmah addressed Abū Bakr saying, "O Khalīfah, I insist that you mount the animal or I will descend from mine." Abū Bakr responded, "By Allah, neither will you dismount nor will I mount. Why should I not get my feet dusty in the path of Allah even if it be for a short while? The fighter will receive seven hundred rewards for every step he takes; and seven hundred sins will be wiped away and he will be elevated by seven hundred stages."

After saying this Abū Bakr turned to Usāmah once again saying, "If you permit, allow ʿUmar to remain behind and assist me." Usāmah consented to this request. Then Abū Bakr addressed the entire army, "O people; Halt! I advise you with ten things and remember them well:

Do not commit treachery; or act unfaithfully.

Do not deceive.

Do not mutilate [the corpses of your enemy];

Do not kill a young child, nor an old man, nor a woman;

You shall not fell palm trees or burn them,

You shall not cut down [any] fruit-bearing tree;

You shall not slaughter a sheep or a cow or a camel except for food.

> You will pass people who occupy themselves in monasteries; leave them alone, and leave them with what they busy themselves with.
>
> You will come to a people who will bring you vessels in which are varieties of food; if you eat anything from [those dishes], mention the name of God over them.
>
> You will meet a people who have shaven the middle of their head and have left around it [a ring of hair] like turbans; tap them lightly with the sword.
>
> Go ahead, in Allah's name; may Allah make you perish through wounds and plague!"[1]

It has already been placed on record that this report suffers a serious lack of authenticity due to the presence of Sayf ibn ʿUmar in its chain. This weakness is further exacerbated by the interruption between Ḥasan al-Baṣrī and the putative witnesses to the event—an interruption of which the ḥadīth experts have long rejected as being wholly unsubstantial due to Ḥasan's complete lack of discretion in who he received ḥadīth from.

But as much as Tījānī's claim of complete objectivity is damaged by passing of decidedly unauthentic reports as authentic history, the manner in which he carefully hides from the readers' sight elements in the text of the report that would damage his purpose leaves his claims of objectivity utterly ruined.

Consider that by severely truncating a (20) line report into a mere (3) lines, he has actually done the following:

- Concealed from his reader the fact that ʿUmar's رضي الله عنه return to Madīnah was at the behest of his commander, Usāmah رضي الله عنه;
- Hid from them that the request to appoint someone else in Usāmah's stead came from some of the Anṣār who feared that matters had changed substantially when the demise of the Prophet صلى الله عليه وسلم was followed by widespread apostasy in the Arabian Peninsula;
- Studiously shielded his reader from learning about the resolute response of Abū Bakr رضي الله عنه to both requests.

1 *Tārīkh al-Ṭabarī*, vol. 3 p. 225-227.

Then he says:

> **I am surprised that those Companions angered the Prophet on that Thursday and accused him of talking "nonsense", and said, "It is sufficient for us that we have the Book of Allah", while the Book of Allah says to them in its clear verses:**
>
> قُلْ إِنْ كُنْتُمْ تُحِبُّونَ اللَّهَ فَاتَّبِعُونِي يُحْبِبْكُمُ اللَّهُ
>
> ***Say, [O Muhammad], "If you should love Allah , then follow me.[1]***
>
> **As if they were more knowledgeable about the Book of Allah and its rules than he to whom it had been revealed. There they were, two days after that great misfortune, and two days before he [the holy Prophet] went up to meet his High Companion, angering him even more by criticizing him for appointing Usamah, and not obeying his orders. Whereas he was ill and bed-ridden in the first misfortune, in the second one he had to come out, with his head bandaged and covered by a blanket and supported by two men with his feet barely on the ground, and address them from the top of the pulpit. He started his speech with the profession of the unity of Allah and praised Him in order to make them feel that he was not talking nonsense, then he informed them about what he knew regarding their criticism of his orders.**
>
> **Furthermore, he reminded them of an incident which had occurred four years previously, in which he was criticized by them. After all that, did they really think that he was talking nonsense or that his illness had overcome him so that he was unaware of what he was saying?[2]**

I am amazed once again that Tījānī comes up with an argument that serves as a proof against him rather than for him. Seeing that the Messenger صَلَّى ٱللَّٰهُ عَلَيْهِ وَسَلَّمَ came out to refute those who criticised the appointment of Usāmah رَضِيَ ٱللَّٰهُ عَنْهُ and also reminded them of the criticism of Zayd ibn Ḥārithah رَضِيَ ٱللَّٰهُ عَنْهُ four years earlier, why did he not remind them also about that other important matter: the alleged appointment of ʿAlī ibn Abī Ṭālib رَضِيَ ٱللَّٰهُ عَنْهُ?

If the Messenger صَلَّى ٱللَّٰهُ عَلَيْهِ وَسَلَّمَ was allegedly pressurised by the Ṣaḥābah in the incident of the Thursday Calamity, then here, in front of all the people, why did he not

1 Sūrah Āl ʿImrān: 31.

2 *Then I was guided*, p. 73-74.

command the letter to be written or announce the succession of ʿAlī رضي الله عنه? Here, he could guarantee that no one could prevent him.

If Tījānī asserts that the Messenger صلى الله عليه وسلم did not mention it because he knew that they would reject his statement, then what was the point of the Messenger صلى الله عليه وسلم coming out, delivering a complete sermon, refuting their criticism of Usāmah رضي الله عنه and his father if he knew that his instruction would not be obeyed.

If this matter was of such great importance, then the Messenger صلى الله عليه وسلم would have mentioned it to the people with great emphasis. This is the greatest proof that the matter was not one which he was commanded to convey. Rather, he was clearly given a choice in it.

Chapter Three

Tījānī's Claim that the Qur'ān Dispraises the Ṣaḥābah

Tījānī commences this discussion as follows:

> **First of all, I must say that Allah - praise be to Him the Most High - commended, in many places in His Holy Book, the Companions of the Messenger of Allah who loved, obeyed and followed the Messenger without personal greed and without opposition or arrogance, and only wanted the acceptance of Allah and His Messenger; those Companions have pleased Allah and He pleased them, and that is the way for those who fear Allah.**
>
> **This group of the Companions are appreciated by the Muslims because of their attitudes towards the Prophet صَلَّى ٱللَّٰهُ عَلَيْهِ وَسَلَّمَ and their works with him, therefore they are liked and respected by all Muslims, and they are appreciated whenever people mention their names.**
>
> **My study does not concern itself with this group of Companions who are respected by both the Sunnis and the Shia, nor is it concerned, with those who were well known for their hypocrisy, and who are cursed by all Muslims, Shia and Sunnis, whenever their names are mentioned.**
>
> **However, my study is concerned with the group of Companions about whom the Muslims have expressed different views. There are verses in the Holy Qur'an where they are rebuked and threatened because of their attitudes in certain positions, and the Messenger of Allah صَلَّى ٱللَّٰهُ عَلَيْهِ وَسَلَّمَ warned them on many occasions, and warned other people about them.**
>
> **The outstanding differences between the Shia and the Sunnis, is concerned with this group of Companions ...**[1]

This entire passage attempts to portray a common categorization of Ṣaḥābah among both Ahl al-Sunnah and Shīʿah; the difference only being with a single category among them. Conveniently Tījānī forgets, perhaps genuinely, that he previously stated that the Ahl al-Sunnah do not, from the outset, divide the Ṣaḥābah into groups.[2] Instead they consider all the Ṣaḥābah of the Messenger صَلَّى ٱللَّٰهُ عَلَيْهِ وَسَلَّمَ as trustworthy; and affirm their moral integrity as an undeniable fundamental of

1 *Then I was guided*, p. 98.

2 Refer to p. 9 of this book.

the religion. Therefore, Tījānī's claim that the Ahl al-Sunnah merely differ with the Shīʿah in the categorization of the Ṣaḥābah is a bitter mistruth. Under no circumstances are the Munāfiqīn considered from the Ṣaḥābah. Despite all claims of fair treatment, impartiality and comprehensive considerations, Tījānī insists on using only the Shīʿī tripartite division of the Ṣaḥābah. This strategy completely ignores the view of the Ahl al-Sunnah concerning the Ṣaḥābah; and facilitates the opportunity to manipulate the interpretation of Qur'ānic text to submit itself to preconceived ideas about the Companions of the Messenger ﷺ. Sūrah al-Tawbah is one of the later Sūrahs in terms of sequence of revelation. It was revealed in relation to the expedition of Tabūk. One of the distinct themes that runs throughout this Sūrah is the contrast between the Munāfiqīn and the Ṣaḥābah. Let us look at the Qur'ānic division of the people around the Messenger ﷺ.

The hypocrites are identified with specific moral indicators; and are grouped with the disbelievers in the next life.

أَلْمُنٰفِقُوْنَ وَالْمُنٰفِقٰتُ بَعْضُهُم مِّنْۢ بَعْضٍ ۘ يَأْمُرُوْنَ بِالْمُنكَرِ وَيَنْهَوْنَ عَنِ الْمَعْرُوْفِ وَيَقْبِضُوْنَ أَيْدِيَهُمْ ۚ نَسُوا اللّٰهَ فَنَسِيَهُمْ ۗ إِنَّ الْمُنٰفِقِيْنَ هُمُ الْفٰسِقُوْنَ وَعَدَ اللّٰهُ الْمُنٰفِقِيْنَ وَالْمُنٰفِقٰتِ وَالْكُفَّارَ نَارَ جَهَنَّمَ خٰلِدِيْنَ فِيهَا ۚ هِىَ حَسْبُهُمْ ۚ وَلَعَنَهُمُ اللّٰهُ ۖ وَلَهُمْ عَذَابٌ مُّقِيْمٌ

The hypocrite men and hypocrite women are of one another. They enjoin what is wrong and forbid what is right and close their hands. They have forgotten Allah, so He has forgotten them [accordingly]. Indeed, the hypocrites - it is they who are the defiantly disobedient. Allah has promised the hypocrite men and hypocrite women and the disbelievers the fire of Hell, wherein they will abide eternally. It is sufficient for them. And Allah has cursed them, and for them is an enduring punishment.[1]

Thereafter the outstanding characteristics of the Ṣaḥābah are listed. Notice that the Qur'ānic description does not divide the Ṣaḥābah into two groups.

وَالْمُؤْمِنُوْنَ وَالْمُؤْمِنٰتُ بَعْضُهُمْ أَوْلِيَآءُ بَعْضٍ ۚ يَأْمُرُوْنَ بِالْمَعْرُوْفِ وَيَنْهَوْنَ

1 Sūrah al-Tawbah: 67-68.

عَنِ الْمُنكَرِ وَيُقِيمُونَ الصَّلَوٰةَ وَيُؤْتُونَ الزَّكَوٰةَ وَيُطِيعُونَ اللَّهَ وَرَسُولَهُ ۚ أُولَٰئِكَ سَيَرْحَمُهُمُ اللَّهُ ۗ إِنَّ اللَّهَ عَزِيزٌ حَكِيمٌ وَعَدَ اللَّهُ الْمُؤْمِنِينَ وَالْمُؤْمِنَاتِ جَنَّاتٍ تَجْرِي مِن تَحْتِهَا الْأَنْهَارُ خَالِدِينَ فِيهَا وَمَسَاكِنَ طَيِّبَةً فِي جَنَّاتِ عَدْنٍ ۚ وَرِضْوَانٌ مِّنَ اللَّهِ أَكْبَرُ ۚ ذَٰلِكَ هُوَ الْفَوْزُ الْعَظِيمُ

The believing men and believing women are allies of one another. They enjoin what is right and forbid what is wrong and establish prayer and give zakāh and obey Allah and His Messenger. Those - Allah will have mercy upon them. Indeed, Allah is Exalted in Might and Wise. Allah has promised the believing men and believing women gardens beneath which rivers flow, wherein they abide eternally, and pleasant dwellings in gardens of perpetual residence; but approval from Allah is greater. It is that which is the great attainment.[1]

The following verse eliminates any attempt of grouping the Ṣaḥābah with the Munāfiqīn.

يَا أَيُّهَا النَّبِيُّ جَاهِدِ الْكُفَّارَ وَالْمُنَافِقِينَ وَاغْلُظْ عَلَيْهِمْ ۚ وَمَأْوَاهُمْ جَهَنَّمُ ۖ وَبِئْسَ الْمَصِيرُ

O Prophet, fight against the disbelievers and the hypocrites and be harsh upon them. And their refuge is Hell, and wretched is the destination.[2]

1. Tījānī's first proof for Qur'ānic Disparagement of Ṣaḥābah

He begins by citing what he calls *āyat al-inqilāb* (the verse of turning on the heels), and quotes the verse:

وَمَا مُحَمَّدٌ إِلَّا رَسُولٌ قَدْ خَلَتْ مِنْ قَبْلِهِ الرُّسُلُ أَفَإِنْ مَاتَ أَوْ قُتِلَ انْقَلَبْتُمْ عَلَىٰ أَعْقَابِكُمْ وَمَنْ يَنْقَلِبْ عَلَىٰ عَقِبَيْهِ فَلَنْ يَضُرَّ اللَّهَ شَيْئًا وَسَيَجْزِي اللَّهُ الشَّاكِرِينَ

1 Sūrah al-Tawbah: 71-72.

2 Sūrah al-Tawbah: 73.

> *Muḥammad is no more than a Messenger: many were the Messengers that passed away before him. If he died or were slain, will you then turn back on your heels? If any did turn back on his heels, not the least harm will he do to Allah; but Allah [on the other hand] will swiftly reward those who [serve Him] with gratitude.*[1]

In commenting on this verse he says:

> **This Qur'anic verse is clear about how the Companions will turn back upon their heels, and only a few will stand their ground, as the above Qur'anic verse indicated in the expression of Allah about them. Those who stand their ground and do not turn back are the grateful, for the grateful are only a small minority, as in the words of Allah- the Most High:**
>
> وَقَلِيلٌ مِنْ عِبَادِيَ الشَّكُورُ
>
> ***But few of my servants are grateful.***[2]
>
> **Also there are many sayings of the Holy Prophet ﷺ which explain the "turning back", and we will refer to some of them soon...**[3]

Our response:

Interpretation of Qur'ān is either undertaken independently by an expert in the field, or is transmitted from one. The science of *Tafsīr* (Exegesis) is governed by hermeneutic standards and interpretative guidelines. The instruments used within this framework include, contextual devices like *Asbāb al-Nuzūl* (circumstances surrounding revelation) and *Naskh* (abrogation) as well as semantic devices which include concepts of *ʿĀm* (general) and *Khāṣ* (specific). This framework is the standard against which all Tafsīr is evaluated. Al-Zarkashī says in his *al-Burhān*:

> Tafsīr refers, technically, to the knowledge of the revelation of the verse, chapter, narrations and subtle indications, then (knowledge of) the sequence of Makkī and Madanī verses, the elements of the verses whether categorical or allegorical, general or specific, qualified or unqualified, concise or detailed. Some have added to the definition, "the knowledge of its ḥalāl and ḥarām, promises and warnings, commands and prohibitions, lessons and parables."[4]

---

1 Sūrah Āl ʿImrān: 144.

2 Sūrah Saba': 13.

3 *Then I was guided*, p. 99.

4 Al-Zarkashī: *al-Burhān fī ʿUlūm al-Qur'ān*, vol. 2 p. 148; Also refer to *Bayn al-Shīʿah wa al-Sunnah* by ʿAlī al-Sālūs p. 11.

We have already established that the novice may not undertake the task of interpretation independently. He ought to refer to the experts lest he falls into conjecture. The tragedy is that despite displaying no expertise in the subject, Tījānī fails to adhere to either approach in his interpretation of the verses. The hermeneutic framework is ignored since there is absolute disregard of context; and the given interpretation suffers the lack of precedent.

The scholars of Tafsīr have agreed that the circumstances surrounding the revelation of this verse was the defeat of the Muslims at Uḥud when Shayṭān exclaimed, "Indeed, Muḥammad has been killed!" and some of the hypocrites said, "Indeed, Muḥammad has been killed! So give them your hands for they are only your brothers!" Some of the Ṣaḥābah said, "If Muḥammad has been killed will you not continue on the path your Prophet tread so that you may meet up with him?" Allah سُبْحَانَهُ وَتَعَالَى then revealed the verse:

وَمَا مُحَمَّدٌ إِلَّا رَسُوْلٌ قَدْ خَلَتْ مِنْ قَبْلِهِ الرُّسُلُ

Muḥammad is no more than a Messenger: many were the Messengers that passed away before him.[1]

Senior scholars of the Twelver Shīʿah acknowledge this as the context in which this verse was revealed.[2] The verse, therefore, is to be understood as Allah's reprimanding of the Ṣaḥābah for their anxiety and apprehension on the Day of Uḥud, when news spread that "Muḥammad has been killed". [3]

Another scholar expresses it in the following manner:

> If Muḥammad صَلَّى ٱللَّٰهُ عَلَيْهِ وَسَلَّمَ died or was killed, then his death is no reason to abandon his religion and teachings since every soul shall taste death. Neither was Muḥammad صَلَّى ٱللَّٰهُ عَلَيْهِ وَسَلَّمَ, nor they, sent to remain in this world forever. Rather, they are expected to live and eventually die on Islam and *tawḥīd* (monotheism); whether the Prophet صَلَّى ٱللَّٰهُ عَلَيْهِ وَسَلَّمَ died or remained with them since death is inevitable.[4]

1 Sūrah Āl ʿImrān: 144.

2 Refer to *Majmaʿ al-Bayān* of al-Ṭabarsī, vol. 2 p. 215.

3 *Tafsīr al-Ṭabarī*, vol. 3 p. 455.

4 Ibn Qayyim: *Badāiʿ al-Tafsīr*, vol. 1 p. 515.

A later scholar elaborates on the meaning of this verse as follows:

أَفَإِنْ مَاتَ أَوْ قُتِلَ انْقَلَبْتُمْ عَلَىٰ أَعْقَابِكُمْ

If he died or were slain, will you then turn back on your heels?

How can you renegade and leave his religion when he dies or is killed despite knowing that there were Messengers before him whose followers held firm to their religion even when they (the Messengers) went missing on account of death or murder.[1]

He goes on to say:

وَمَنْ يَنْقَلِبْ عَلَىٰ عَقِبَيْهِ

If any did turn back on his heels.

Meaning: By turning his back from fighting or turning apostate from Islam.

فَلَنْ يَضُرَّ اللَّهَ شَيْئًا

Not the least harm will he do to Allah.

Meaning: No harm will come to Allah; instead such a person only harms himself.

وَسَيَجْزِي اللَّهُ الشَّاكِرِينَ

But Allah [on the other hand] will swiftly reward those who [serve Him] with gratitude.

Meaning: Those who displayed patience, fought, and were martyred; that is how they expressed gratitude to Allah for the favour of Islam upon them.[2]

This verse is clear proof of Abū Bakr's رَضِيَ اللَّهُ عَنْهُ lofty status, bravery and firmness on truth. It was this verse which he recited the day the Messenger صَلَّى اللَّهُ عَلَيْهِ وَسَلَّمَ passed away.

1 al-Shawkānī: *Fatḥ al-Qadīr,* vol. 1 p. 571.

2 Ibid.

Ibn ʿAṭiyyah has alluded to this:

> His steadiness in that situation, and afterwards in the way he dealt with the widespread apostasy, is among his many accolades. This is especially significant since the Munāfiqīn became bold after the news of the Prophet's demise spread. Their antagonistic behaviour nearly resulted in a confrontation (with the Muslims). The sad news was so difficult on ʿUmar that he insisted the Prophet ﷺ had not been taken. He stood up in the Masjid and began delivering his famous, heart-rending address about the Prophet's ﷺ (imminent) return. The ambitions of the hypocrites were put to rest with this fervent sermon. Thereafter Abū Bakr رضي الله عنه arrived; observing ʿUmar delivering his fiery speech. After seeing the Prophet ﷺ, Abū Bakr رضي الله عنه returned to the Masjid and interrupted ʿUmar رضي الله عنه saying, "Be silent!" But ʿUmar continued with his speech. Then (while ʿUmar was speaking) Abū Bakr recited the *tashahhud* (declaration of faith) and the people listened to him and turned their attention away from ʿUmar. He said, "Whoever used to worship Allah, indeed Allah is alive and will not die. And whoever worshipped Muḥammad, indeed Muḥammad has passed away. Muḥammad is but a Messenger. Messengers have passed before him..." completing the verse. The Ṣaḥābah began to weep. Everyone started reciting that very verse. It was as though they had never heard it before that day. ʿĀ'ishah says in (a ḥadīth related by) al-Bukhārī, "Allah benefited the people with the khuṭbah of ʿUmar. Then He benefited them afterwards with the khuṭbah of Abū Bakr. This was one of those situations where Abū Bakr's gratitude[1] was evidently clear; and on his account the gratitude of the people."[2]

Compare this to Tījānī's anomalous interpretation:

> **The important thing is that the "turning back" verse refers to the Companions who lived with the Messenger of Allah in al-Medinah al- Munawwarah, and indicates the immediate "turning back" after the Prophet's death.**

Tījānī's understanding of this verse stands in contrast to fourteen centuries of Qur'ānic exegesis. Furthermore, his approach breaches the protocols of interpretation. Given that he veils the meaning of the verse as Allah's unmistakeable 'glad tidings' to the Companions رضي الله عنهم, that they were going to 'turn on their heels'

---

1 This is in reference to the word used in the verse quoted by al-Tījānī (al-Shākirīn).

2 *Al-Muḥarrar al-Wajīz*, vol. 3 p. 248-249.

in the near future; Tījānī thus asserts that the Qur'ān predicted the imminent transformation of the bulk of Ṣaḥābah even though the Prophet ﷺ was still alive. He goes on to advocate with full certainty that they renegaded immediately after the Prophet's ﷺ passing.

Proceeding from his assertion that they 'turned on their heels' immediately after the Prophet's demise, it is imperative for him to clarify who those Ṣaḥābah are, i.e. identify the deserters from the resolute. Failure to provide clarification will leave the entire Ummah in disarray. The need for clarification is further compounded if one considers the Shī'ah tripartite categorization. Who are those 'upon whom the Shī'ah and Ahl al-Sunnah differ'?

It ought to be noted at this point that the Qur'ānic description of Ṣaḥābah and Munāfiqīn does not leave room for speculation. I do not suppose that Tījānī is able to say with confidence that the 'resolute' Ṣaḥābah—whose resoluteness the Rāfiḍah acknowledge and with whom they are pleased—were only three to seven[1] in number. Any such claim clearly contradicts the established narrations, quoted earlier, which prove that Abū Bakr and 'Umar did not turn on their heels.

What about the other Ṣaḥābah? What can be said of the likes of Sa'd ibn Abī Waqqāṣ — whose bow was broken (due to his repeated firing) — and Ṭalḥah ibn 'Ubayd Allāh, regarding whom the Prophet ﷺ said in the battle of Uḥud, "Ṭalḥah has made Jannah compulsory for himself," and Qatādah ibn Nu'mān — whose eye was struck and returned to its socket with the blessed hand of the Prophet ﷺ which resulted in it being better than before? All of this during the Battle of Uḥud in which they (allegedly) "turned on their heels"; is it possible that such individuals would renegade immediately after the Prophet's ﷺ demise? This has also been acknowledged by al-Ṭabarsī in *Majma' al-Bayān fī Tafsīr al-Qur'ān*.

All of these Companions are not from the resolute Ṣaḥābah according to Rāfiḍī categorization. So how does one account for their exemplary behaviour within the Shī'ī paradigm?

If considered from another perspective, failure to identify the 'resolute' Ṣaḥābah from the 'deserters' is an indirect charge of incoherence against the Noble Qur'ān. It praises the Ṣaḥābah, bears testimony to their Īmān and confirms their inner and

1 Refer to p. 12 onwards of this book.

outer piety at many places; yet at others is disapproves of them and gives 'glad tidings' of their apostasy.

Every Muslim must know that the Ṣaḥābah were human beings who may have at times erred, but at the same time were people of religious integrity and honesty. The Qur'ān testifies to that at many places:

وَالسَّابِقُوْنَ الْأَوَّلُوْنَ مِنَ الْمُهَاجِرِيْنَ وَالْأَنْصَارِ وَالَّذِيْنَ اتَّبَعُوْهُمْ بِإِحْسَانٍ رَضِيَ اللّٰهُ عَنْهُمْ وَرَضُوْا عَنْهُ وَأَعَدَّ لَهُمْ جَنَّاتٍ تَجْرِيْ تَحْتَهَا الْأَنْهَارُ خَالِدِيْنَ فِيْهَا أَبَدًا ذٰلِكَ الْفَوْزُ الْعَظِيْمُ

The forerunners from the Muhājirīn and Anṣār and those who follow them in [all] good deeds, well-pleased is Allah with them, as are they with Him. He has prepared for them gardens under which rivers flow, to dwell therein forever, that is the supreme felicity.[1]

This is glad tidings from Allah سبحانه وتعالى for the Ṣaḥābah. In essence Allah is informing us of three groups of people. The first two groups He is pleased with. As for the third group, they only deserve His divine pleasure if they follow the first two groups in excellence. Allah is not forewarning their apostasy and 'turning their backs on the religion'. Is it conceivable that Allah would be pleased with people who would later 'turn their backs on the religion'; further still encourage others to be their followers?

Another proof of the moral integrity of the Ṣaḥābah is the Prophet's صلى الله عليه وسلم statement:

لا تسبّوا أصحابي فلو أنّ أحدكم أنفق مثل أحد ذهبا ما بلغ مدّ أحدهم ولا نصيفه

Do not revile my Ṣaḥābah! I swear by Him in whose control lies my life, if any of you have to spend gold equal to Mount Uḥud, it would not equate even one mudd spent by the Ṣaḥābah, and not even half a mudd.[2]

1 Sūrah al-Tawbah: 100.

2 *Ṣaḥīḥ al-Bukhārī*, Ḥadīth no. 3470.

All the Ṣaḥābah, therefore; were trustworthy and of moral integrity according to the transmitted text and sound logic.

It is imperative than consideration be given to sequence, structure and coherence between verses of the Qur'ān when one attempts to interpret it. Verses of the Qur'ān are interconnected and are to be understood in harmony with the verses before and after. The verse which Tījānī cites as proof relates to the Battle of Uḥud and the mistakes which occurred in it. The chapter (or parts of it) concerns itself with Allah's سُبْحَانَهُ وَتَعَالَىٰ admonishing the believers for their mistakes during this battle. Allah سُبْحَانَهُ وَتَعَالَىٰ refutes the notion that one will be entered into Jannah merely on Īmān, without having to undergo jihād, trials, and tests. Allah سُبْحَانَهُ وَتَعَالَىٰ says:

أَمْ حَسِبْتُمْ أَنْ تَدْخُلُوا الْجَنَّةَ وَلَمَّا يَعْلَمِ اللَّهُ الَّذِيْنَ جَاهَدُوْا مِنْكُمْ وَيَعْلَمَ الصَّابِرِيْنَ وَلَقَدْ كُنْتُمْ تَمَنَّوْنَ الْمَوْتَ مِنْ قَبْلِ أَنْ تَلْقَوْهُ فَقَدْ رَأَيْتُمُوْهُ وَأَنْتُمْ تَنْظُرُوْنَ

Or do you think that you will enter Jannah while Allah has not yet made evident those of you who fight in His cause and made evident those who are steadfast? And you had certainly wished for martyrdom before you encountered it, and you have [now] seen it [before you] while you were looking on.[1]

Immediately after that Allah mentions:

وَمَا مُحَمَّدٌ إِلَّا رَسُوْلٌ

Muḥammad is no more than a Messenger.[2]

This verse is a continuation of their admonishment because of their mistakes during that battle. Allah سُبْحَانَهُ وَتَعَالَىٰ then reminds them in the verses following it, that in previous nations there were *ṣāliḥūn* (righteous believers) who fought alongside their Prophets and did not lose heart, weaken in their resolve, or become despondent as some of you had (i.e. the Ṣaḥābah).

Allah سُبْحَانَهُ وَتَعَالَىٰ confirms the Īmān of the Ṣaḥābah in the next verse, and warns them from obeying the unbelievers:

1 Sūrah Āl ʿImrān: 142-143.

2 Sūrah Āl ʿImrān: 144.

يٰأَيُّهَا الَّذِيْنَ اٰمَنُوْا إِنْ تُطِيْعُوا الَّذِيْنَ كَفَرُوْا يَرُدُّوْكُمْ عَلٰى أَعْقَابِكُمْ فَتَنْقَلِبُوْا خَاسِرِيْنَ

O you who have believed, if you obey those who disbelieve, they will turn you back on your heels, and you will [then] become losers.[1]

And after admonishing them — a few verses later — Allah سُبْحَانَهُ وَتَعَالَىٰ mentions that He pardoned those who turned away the day of fighting:

إِنَّ الَّذِيْنَ تَوَلَّوْا مِنْكُمْ يَوْمَ الْتَقَى الْجَمْعَانِ إِنَّمَا اسْتَزَلَّهُمُ الشَّيْطَانُ بِبَعْضِ مَا كَسَبُوْا وَلَقَدْ عَفَا اللّٰهُ عَنْهُمْ إِنَّ اللّٰهَ غَفُوْرٌ حَلِيْمٌ

Indeed, those of you who turned back on the day the two armies met, it was Shayṭān who caused them to slip because of some [blame] they had earned. But Allah has already forgiven them. Indeed, Allah is All Forgiving and All Forbearing.[2]

Thereafter Allah mentions that the believers responded to the Messenger's صَلَّى ٱللَّهُ عَلَيْهِ وَسَلَّمَ call, after being afflicted with wounds in the Battle of Uḥud, to pursue Abū Sufyān at Ḥamrā al-Asad. Allah says:

الَّذِيْنَ اسْتَجَابُوْا لِلّٰهِ وَالرَّسُوْلِ مِنْۢ بَعْدِ مَا أَصَابَهُمُ الْقَرْحُ ۚ لِلَّذِيْنَ أَحْسَنُوْا مِنْهُمْ وَاتَّقَوْا أَجْرٌ عَظِيْمٌ الَّذِيْنَ قَالَ لَهُمُ النَّاسُ إِنَّ النَّاسَ قَدْ جَمَعُوْا لَكُمْ فَاخْشَوْهُمْ فَزَادَهُمْ إِيْمَانًا وَقَالُوْا حَسْبُنَا اللّٰهُ وَنِعْمَ الْوَكِيلُ فَانْقَلَبُوْا بِنِعْمَةٍ مِنَ اللّٰهِ وَفَضْلٍ لَمْ يَمْسَسْهُمْ سُوْءٌ وَاتَّبَعُوْا رِضْوَانَ اللّٰهِ وَاللّٰهُ ذُوْ فَضْلٍ عَظِيْمٍ

Those [believers] who responded to Allah and the Messenger after injury had struck them. For those who did good among them and feared Allah is a great reward. Those to whom hypocrites said, "Indeed, the people have gathered against you, so fear them." But it [merely] increased them in faith, and they said, "sufficient for us is Allah, and [He

1 Sūrah Āl ʿImrān: 149.

2 Sūrah Āl ʿImrān: 155.

> *is] the best Disposer of affairs." So they returned with favour from Allah and bounty, no harm having touched them. And they pursued the pleasure of Allah, and Allah is the possessor of great bounty.*[1]

There is no doubt that the Ṣaḥābah are the ones described with these qualities and praise; and it is they who returned with the favour and bounty of Allah سُبْحَانَهُ وَتَعَالَىٰ. Is it not then ludicrous to assert that the verse quoted by Tījānī is a Qur'ānic prediction of the apostasy of the Ṣaḥābah after the Prophet's صَلَّى ٱللَّٰهُ عَلَيْهِ وَسَلَّمَ demise?

Then Tījānī says:

> **We could not explain the Qur'anic verse with reference to Tulayha, Sujah and al-Aswad al-Ansi, out of respect for the Companions, because the above-mentioned Companions have turned back and abandoned Islam, and even claimed the prophecy during the lifetime of the Messenger of Allah who fought them and finally defeated them.**[2]

Subḥān Allah! What imaginative speculation! Did the Messenger صَلَّى ٱللَّٰهُ عَلَيْهِ وَسَلَّمَ fight the apostates and gain victory over them? How and when? Musaylamah and al-Aswad al-ʿAnsī emerged just before the passing of the Messenger صَلَّى ٱللَّٰهُ عَلَيْهِ وَسَلَّمَ and it was only al-ʿAnsī who passed away before the Prophet صَلَّى ٱللَّٰهُ عَلَيْهِ وَسَلَّمَ. As for Ṭulayḥah and Sajāḥ; it is a matter of consensus among historians that their apostasy manifested only after the Prophet's صَلَّى ٱللَّٰهُ عَلَيْهِ وَسَلَّمَ demise. It was Khālid ibn Walīd رَضِيَ ٱللَّٰهُ عَنْهُ who fought Ṭulayḥah in the Battle of al-Baẓẓakhah and defeated him. Ṭulayḥah subsequently fled to al-Shām but shortly returned to the fold of Islam. Then the soothsayer, Sajāḥ bint Ḥārith, appeared and one of her ardent followers was Mālik ibn Nuwayrah. A group from Banū Tamīm opposed her which resulted in fighting between them. Then, Sajāḥ travelled with her army to Yamāmah after defeating Aws ibn Khuzaymah and met Musaylamah. Musaylamah married her and she returned to her homeland, ʿIrāq. As for Musaylamah al-Kadhdhāb (the liar); Khālid ibn Walīd and his companions, ʿIkrimah ibn Abī Jahl, and Shuraḥbīl ibn Ḥasanah رَضِيَ ٱللَّٰهُ عَنْهُمْ defeated him in the famous Battle of Yamāmah.

The question remains; where is the historic evidence of the Prophet fighting the apostates? Respected reader, fourteen centuries of transmitted history have been disregarded simply to accuse the Prophet's صَلَّى ٱللَّٰهُ عَلَيْهِ وَسَلَّمَ Companions of apostasy!

1 Sūrah Āl ʿImrān: 172-174.

2 *Then I was guided*, p. 99.

It comes as no surprize that Tījānī would defend Mālik ibn Nuwayrah and his followers who desisted from giving the zakāh. He justifies this by insinuating that the Prophet صلى الله عليه وسلم nominated ʿAlī ibn Abī Ṭālib رضي الله عنه as his successor at Ghadīr Khum.[1] Mālik ibn Nuwayrah was thus surprised to learn that Abū Bakr رضي الله عنه was the one to whom allegiance was given; therefore, he desisted from handing over the zakāh.

I seek protection in Allah from 'objectivity' that leads to defence of apostates and accusations of apostasy against the Companions of the Messenger صلى الله عليه وسلم!

The detailed discussion on Mālik ibn Nuwayrah will be covered under the allegations against Khālid ibn Walīd رضي الله عنه.

2. Tījānī's second proof for Qur'ānic Disparagement of Ṣaḥābah

Tījānī puts forward a second verse from the Qur'ān which he alleges condemns the Ṣaḥābah رضي الله عنهم. He refers to this verse from Sūrah al-Tawbah as 'the verse of Jihād'.

يَٰأَيُّهَا الَّذِيْنَ أٰمَنُوْا مَا لَكُمْ إِذَا قِيْلَ لَكُمُ انْفِرُوْا فِيْ سَبِيلِ اللّٰهِ اثَّاقَلْتُمْ إِلَى
الْأَرْضِ أَرَضِيْتُمْ بِالْحَيٰوةِ الدُّنْيَا مِنَ الْأٰخِرَةِ فَمَا مَتَاعُ الْحَيٰوةِ الدُّنْيَا فِي
الْأٰخِرَةِ إِلَّا قَلِيْلٌ . إِلَّا تَنْفِرُوْا يُعَذِّبْكُمْ عَذَابًا أَلِيمًا وَيَسْتَبْدِلْ قَوْمًا غَيْرَكُمْ
وَلَا تَضُرُّوْهُ شَيْئًا وَاللّٰهُ عَلٰى كُلِّ شَيْءٍ قَدِيرٌ

O you who have believed, what is [the matter] with you that, when you are told to go forth in the cause of Allah, you adhere heavily to the earth? Are you satisfied with the life of this world rather than the hereafter? But what is the enjoyment of worldly life compared to the hereafter except a [very] little. If you do not go forth, He will punish you with a painful punishment and will replace you with another people, and you will not harm Him at all. And Allah is over all things competent.[2]

This Qur'anic verse is clear about the reluctance of the Companions to go and fight in the Holy War [Jihad], and how they chose to be content with the

1 The commentary on the proof-worthiness of the ḥadīth of Ghadīr Khumm will be discussed later (p. 280 onwards of this book).

2 Sūrah al-Tawbah: 38-39.

life on earth, in spite of their knowledge of its short duration. Their action warranted a rebuke and a threat from Allah – the Almighty - that a terrible torture was awaiting them, and that He would change them for others who were true believers.

Our comment:

Context In Which Verses Were Revealed

The scholars agree that this verse was revealed as motivation for the Ṣaḥābah to participate in the Expedition of Tabūk. This was subsequent to the Conquest of Makkah and the Battles at Ṭā'if and Ḥunayn. Their instruction to deploy came in the heart of summer; when the date orchids were laden with fruit which were about to ripen. The military strategy usually adopted by the Prophet ﷺ was to only reveal the destination after the army departed. Due to the difficulty ahead, unforgiving heat, arduous journey, large enemy and many other formidable obstacles, the Messenger ﷺ disclosed the destination on this occasion prior to departure. When considering all these factors, some of the Ṣaḥābah رضي الله عنهم were initially overwhelmed by the onerous task. Allah سبحانه وتعالى revealed these verses inciting them towards jihād, and warning them about being sluggish.

In *Majma' al-Bayān al-Ṭabarsī* concurs with the above as being the context within which the verses were revealed.[1]

The verse is therefore understood as Allah's exhorting the believers towards military engagement with the Romans; the Expedition of Tabūk.[2]

No doubt the languid demeanour was not the disposition of all the Ṣaḥābah. It is improbable that all of them were sluggish and unenergetic. This form of expression is common and well-known in the Qur'ān; addressing all while referring to some.[3]

It is important to note that the demur of some of the companions was not the result of aversion for jihād. Consider that recently they had participated in a series of battles, and after a difficult year their crops were finally beginning to ripen. These

1 Refer to *Majma'*, vol. 3 p. 62.

2 *Tafsīr al-Ṭabarī*, vol. 6 p. 372.

3 *Fatḥ al-Qadīr*, vol. 2 p. 526. Ṭabarsī related in his tafsīr, *Majma' al-Bayān*: "Jabbā'ī says, "this slow-footedness was specific to a group of the believers and not all of them were sluggish in relation to (departing for) jihād.""

verses descended rebuking them in one sense, yet encouraging them towards jihād in another.

Qur'ān Teaches And Admonishes Ṣaḥābah

Let us also not forget that the Ṣaḥābah were human beings, subject to all elements of human nature including procrastination. Therefore; many verses of the Qur'ān were revealed to teach the Ṣaḥābah, to give them direction, to further motivate them, and nurture them so that they would be exemplars for those after them. Anyone who reflects on the Qur'ān would recognize this divine nurturing; especially through the mode of address:

يٰأَيُّهَا الَّذِيْنَ أٰمَنُوْا

O you who believe!

This manner of addressing the Ṣaḥābah appears 89 times throughout the Qur'ān. Each time they are being guided, taught, and nurtured. The following verses demonstrate this:

يٰأَيُّهَا الَّذِيْنَ أٰمَنُوْا كُتِبَ عَلَيْكُمُ الْقِصَاصُ

O you who believe! The law of equality is prescribed to you in cases of murder.[1]

يٰأَيُّهَا الَّذِيْنَ أٰمَنُوْا ادْخُلُوْا فِيْ السِّلْمِ كَافَّةً

O you who believe! Enter into Islam whole-heartedly.[2]

يٰأَيُّهَا الَّذِيْنَ أٰمَنُوْا أَنْفِقُوْا مِمَّا رَزَقْنَاكُمْ

O you who believe! Spend out of [the bounties] we have provided for you.[3]

يٰأَيُّهَا الَّذِيْنَ أٰمَنُوْا اتَّقُوْا اللّٰهَ وَذَرُوْا مَا بَقِيَ مِنَ الرِّبَا

O you who believe! Fear Allah, and give up what remains of your demand for usury.[4]

1 Sūrah al-Baqarah: 178.
2 Sūrah al-Baqarah: 208.
3 Sūrah al-Baqarah: 254.
4 Sūrah al-Baqarah: 278.

يَأَيُّهَا الَّذِيْنَ اٰمَنُوْا اتَّقُوا اللّٰهَ حَقَّ تُقَاتِه

O you who believe! Fear Allah as He should be feared.[1]

يٰاَيُّهَا الَّذِيْنَ اٰمَنُوْا لَا تَتَّخِذُوْا بِطَانَةً

O you who believe! Take not into your intimacy.[2]

يٰاَيُّهَا الَّذِيْنَ اٰمَنُوْا إِنْ تُطِيْعُوْا الَّذِيْنَ كَفَرُوْا

O you who believe! If you obey the unbelievers.[3]

يٰاَيُّهَا الَّذِيْنَ اٰمَنُوْا أَوْفُوْا بِالْعُقُوْدِ

O you who believe! Fulfil (all) obligations.[4]

يٰاَيُّهَا الَّذِيْنَ اٰمَنُوْا لَا تَقْرَبُوْا الصَّلٰوةَ وَأَنْتُمْ سُكَارٰى

O you who believe! Approach not prayers when you are intoxicated.[5]

يٰاَيُّهَا الَّذِيْنَ اٰمَنُوْا لَا تَتَّبِعُوْا خُطُوَاتِ الشَّيْطَانِ

O you who believe! Follow not Satan's footsteps.[6]

يٰاَيُّهَا الَّذِيْنَ اٰمَنُوْا اسْتَجِيْبُوْا لِلّٰهِ وَلِلرَّسُوْلِ

O you who believe! Give your response to Allah and His Messenger.[7]

يٰاَيُّهَا الَّذِيْنَ اٰمَنُوْا لَا تَدْخُلُوْا بُيُوتًا غَيْرَ بُيُوْتِكُمْ

O you who believe! Enter not houses other than your own.[8]

---

1 Sūrah Āl ʿImrān: 102.

2 Sūrah Āl ʿImrān: 118.

3 Sūrah Āl ʿImrān: 149.

4 Sūrah al-Māʾidah: 1.

5 Sūrah al-Nisāʾ: 43.

6 Sūrah al-Nūr: 21.

7 Sūrah al-Anfāl: 24.

8 Sūrah al-Nūr: 27.

It is for this reason that Ibn Mas'ūd رضي الله عنه says:

> Whenever you hear Allah saying, "O you who believe," then harken to it as it is either good being commanded, or evil prohibited.[1]

The Qur'ānic context therefore dictates that these types of verses appeared for the purpose of teaching the Ṣaḥābah good conduct and prohibiting them from evil. Unfortunately, the Rāfiḍah have conjured an aura of infallibility with which they have anointed their Imāms. Thereafter they use the same self-conjured infallibility as the yardstick against which the Companions ought to be measured. Any mistake or shortcoming on the part of the Ṣaḥābah is then misinterpreted as a cardinal offense.

The following part of the verse is a warning for neglecting Jihād:

إِلَّا تَنْفِرُوْا يُعَذِّبْكُمْ عَذَابًا أَلِيْمًا

Unless you go forth, He will punish you with a grievous penalty.

Ibn 'Abbās رضي الله عنهما says:

> The Messenger of Allah صلى الله عليه وسلم called on a community of Arabs for battle but they were sluggish; so Allah withheld rain from them. That was their punishment.[2]

It is well-known that the Ṣaḥābah رضي الله عنهم set out with the Messenger صلى الله عليه وسلم for Tabūk and were never afflicted by any form of punishment.

Ṣaḥābah's Contribution To Tabūk Campaign

Before proceeding any further it is necessary to point out that no allegation of procrastination or lethargy can be cast against Abū Bakr, 'Umar, and 'Uthmān رضي الله عنهم. We will soon read of their eager contribution and wilful participation.

Abū Bakr رضي الله عنه contributed all his wealth to this expedition; leaving nothing for his family. When he brought his wealth, the Messenger صلى الله عليه وسلم asked him what he kept behind for his family, "Allah and His Messenger," was his reply.[3]

---

1 al-Suyūṭī: *Al-Itqān fī 'Ulūm al-Qur'ān*, vol. 2 p. 92-93.

2 *Al-Ṭabarī*, vol. 6 p. 373; *al-Baghawī*, vol. 4 p. 48; and *al-Muḥarrar al-Wajīz*, vol. 8 p. 183.

3 *Sunan al-Tirmidhī*, The Chapter of the Virtues, Ḥadīth no. 3675; Refer also to *Ṣaḥīḥ al-Tirmidhī*, Ḥadīth no. 2902.

Add to this Allah's affirmation of Abū Bakr's Companionship with the Messenger صَلَّى ٱللَّٰهُ عَلَيْهِ وَسَلَّمَ. In the verse that immediately follows the one we are discussing Allah says:

إِلَّا تَنْصُرُوْهُ فَقَدْ نَصَرَهُ اللّٰهُ إِذْ أَخْرَجَهُ الَّذِيْنَ كَفَرُوْا ثَانِيَ اثْنَيْنِ إِذْ هُمَا فِي
الْغَارِ إِذْ يَقُوْلُ لِصَاحِبِهِ لَا تَحْزَنْ إِنَّ اللّٰهَ مَعَنَا

If you do not aid him [the Messenger صَلَّى ٱللَّٰهُ عَلَيْهِ وَسَلَّمَ] — Allah has already aided him when those who disbelieved had driven him out [of Makkah] as one of two, when they were in the cave and he said to his companion, "Do not grieve; indeed, Allah is with us."[1]

It is for that reason that Ḥusayn ibn al-Faḍl said, "Anyone who denies that Abū Bakr was the Prophet's صَلَّى ٱللَّٰهُ عَلَيْهِ وَسَلَّمَ Companion is a disbeliever because of his denying the clear text of the Qur'ān." Sha'bī said, "In this verse Allah سُبْحَانَهُ وَتَعَالَىٰ rebukes all people on earth besides Abū Bakr."[2]

'Umar رَضِيَ ٱللَّٰهُ عَنْهُ brought half of his wealth to the Prophet صَلَّى ٱللَّٰهُ عَلَيْهِ وَسَلَّمَ; while 'Uthmān رَضِيَ ٱللَّٰهُ عَنْهُ brought one thousand *dīnārs* (gold coins) and scattered it in the lap of the Prophet صَلَّى ٱللَّٰهُ عَلَيْهِ وَسَلَّمَ. Later 'Uthmān رَضِيَ ٱللَّٰهُ عَنْهُ pledged three hundred camels fully laden with provisions. This was used to prepare the *jaysh al-'usrah* (the army of scarcity). The Prophet صَلَّى ٱللَّٰهُ عَلَيْهِ وَسَلَّمَ repaid 'Uthmān's altruism with a guarantee of paradise. Twice he said to 'Uthmān رَضِيَ ٱللَّٰهُ عَنْهُ, "No harm can come to 'Uthmān whatever he does after this day."[3]

As for 'Abd al-Raḥmān ibn 'Awf, the Prophet صَلَّى ٱللَّٰهُ عَلَيْهِ وَسَلَّمَ prayed behind him during the expedition of Tabūk.

What about those who cried because they were unable to participate due to lack of conveyance? They were called the *bakkā'ūn* (those who cried). They were seven in number; and it is they whom Allah referred to in the verse:

وَلَا عَلَى الَّذِيْنَ إِذَا مَا أَتَوْكَ لِتَحْمِلَهُمْ قُلْتَ لَا أَجِدُ مَا أَحْمِلُكُمْ عَلَيْهِ تَوَلَّوْا
وَأَعْيُنُهُمْ تَفِيْضُ مِنَ الدَّمْعِ حَزَنًا أَلَّا يَجِدُوْا مَا يُنْفِقُوْنَ

---

1 Sūrah al-Tawbah: 40.

2 *Tafsīr al-Baghawī*, vol. 4 p. 49.

3 *Sunan al-Tirmidhī*, vol. 5: Chapter on the Virtues of the Ṣaḥābah, Ḥadīth no. 3701; Refer also to *Ṣaḥīḥ al-Tirmidhī*, Ḥadīth no. 2920.

Nor [is there blame] upon those who, when they came to you that you might give them mounts, you said, "I can find nothing for you to ride upon." They turned back while their eyes overflowed with tears out of grief that they could not find something to spend [for the cause of Allah].[1]

Are these examples of people who were sluggish and uneager to strive for the cause of Islam?

Divine Pardon

Without doubt, a small group of Muslims lagged behind this expedition which include Kaʿb ibn Mālik, Hilāl ibn Umayyah, and Murārah ibn Rabīʿ رَضِيَ اللَّهُ عَنْهُمْ. They were "The Three"[2] who lagged behind the expedition. Abū Khaythamah and Abū Dharr also lagged behind but then caught up with the army which numbered thirty thousand. Allah سُبْحَانَهُ وَتَعَالَى later forgave "The Three".

Allah سُبْحَانَهُ وَتَعَالَى says:

لَقَدْ تَابَ اللّٰهُ عَلَى النَّبِيِّ وَالْمُهَاجِرِيْنَ وَالْأَنْصَارِ الَّذِيْنَ اتَّبَعُوْهُ فِيْ سَاعَةِ الْعُسْرَةِ مِنْۢ بَعْدِ مَا كَادَ يَزِيْغُ قُلُوْبُ فَرِيْقٍ مِّنْهُمْ ثُمَّ تَابَ عَلَيْهِمْ إِنَّهُ بِهِمْ رَءُوْفٌ رَحِيْمٌ

Allah has already forgiven the Prophet and the Muhājirīn and the Anṣār who followed him in the hour of difficulty after the hearts of a party of them had almost inclined [to doubt], and then He forgave them. Indeed, He was to them Most Kind and Most Merciful.[3]

This is divine praise for the Messenger of Allah صَلَّى اللَّهُ عَلَيْهِ وَسَلَّمَ, the Muhājirīn, the Anṣār, and the rest of the Ṣaḥābah. The verse bears glad tidings of His forgiveness after they left to Tabūk in a state of anxiety, initially inclining towards comfort and rest. However, Allah سُبْحَانَهُ وَتَعَالَى made their feet firm, strengthened their resolve and forgave them.

---

1 Sūrah al-Tawbah: 92.

2 Referred to in the verse of Sūrah al-Tawbah, "*And [He also forgave] the three who were left behind [and regretted their error] to the point that the earth closed in on them in spite of its vastness and their souls confined them and they were certain that there is no refuge from Allah except in Him. Then He turned to them so they could repent. Indeed, Allah is the Accepting of repentance, the Merciful.*" 118.

3 Sūrah al-Tawbah: 117.

Bear in mind the statement of Ibn ʿAbbās ﵄, "Whoever Allah forgives will never be punished."[1]

Al-Jaṣṣāṣ comments on this verse in his book *Aḥkām al-Qur'ān*:

> In this verse is praise for the Ṣaḥābah of the Prophet ﷺ who strove with him. It also informs us of their inner spiritual perfection and purity. Allah does not announce His forgiveness, except those with whom He is pleased and whose actions please Him. It is an unequivocal refutation of their critics and of those who describe them in a manner other than with the inner purity and virtue He ascribes to them. May Allah, be pleased with them.[2]

Let us not forget that the expedition of Tabūk was the last military campaign undertaken by the Prophet ﷺ with his Companions ﵃. Have the Ṣaḥābah not proven their bravery during all the other expeditions with the Prophet ﷺ; at Badr, Uḥud, and al-Khandaq, then the Conquest of Makkah, and the campaigns of Ḥunayn and Mu'tah? Then, after the demise of the Prophet ﷺ did they not continue with jihād; and through their jihād the religion was fortified from the plague of apostasy? Did Allah not grant victory at their hands in the conquests of territories in Irān, ʿIrāq, the Levant, and Egypt? Would it then be fair to cast unqualified allegations at the Ṣaḥābah; that they were sluggish about jihād and chose reliance upon this worldly life? Is this a conclusion based on impartiality and fair-mindedness?

Shīʿī Scholars On This Verse

The position of the Twelver Shīʿah on the Ṣaḥābah is no mystery. One would expect that if these verses had the potential to condemn the Ṣaḥābah, such condemnation would surface in Shīʿī books of Tafsīr. After consulting many Shīʿī Tafsīr books, on the commentary of this verse in particular, we failed to find a single scholar of theirs who understood it as dispraise for the Ṣaḥābah.

Al-Ṭabarsī, a scholar of significant repute among the Shīʿah, commented on the verse in the following manner:

> Then Allah admonished the Ṣaḥābah with regards to sluggishness about jihād.

1 *Tafsīr al-Baghawī*, vol. 4 p. 105.

2 *Aḥkām al-Qur'ān* by al-Jaṣṣāṣ, vol. 3 p. 160.

He said:

يَاأَيُّهَا الَّذِيْنَ أٰمَنُوْا مَا لَكُمْ إِذَا قِيْلَ

O you who believe! What is the matter with you, that, when you are asked.[1]

In other words, the Messenger ﷺ of Allah called you and said, "Go forth in the cause of Allah," that is go out and struggle against the Mushrikīn. Here it is reference to the expedition of Tabūk... It is reported from al-Ḥasan and Mujāhid about the phrase "you cling heavily to the earth," it means, you are sluggish and inclined towards the world you are upon.

Al-Jubbā'ī says, "This slow-footedness was peculiar to a group of the believers since all of them were not dither about jihād. It is an example of a general statement intended for a specific group of believers. This is evident from the words, 'do you prefer the life of this world to the hereafter?' This is interrogative expression implies reprimand; meaning, "do you prefer this temporal worldly life over the everlasting hereafter and eternal bliss?"[2]

Al-Ṭabarsī did not find anything in the verse to indicate criticism against the Ṣaḥābah. Instead his interpretation resembles that of the Ahl al-Sunnah. Simply put, it served as both a rebuke for their initial hesitancy, and a motivation for their participation in the expedition of Tabūk. Their hebetude was a result of the unenviable circumstance they found themselves in.

Al-Kāshānī says in his tafsīr, *al-Ṣāfī*:

يَاأَيُّهَا الَّذِيْنَ أٰمَنُوْا مَا لَكُمْ إِذَا قِيْلَ لَكُمُ انْفِرُوْا فِيْ سَبِيْلِ اللّٰهِ اثَّاقَلْتُمْ إِلَى الْأَرْضِ

O you who believe! What is the matter with you, that, when you are asked to go forth in the cause of Allah, you cling heavily to the earth.[3]

You delay, tending to your land and residing in your homes. It states in al-Jawāmiʿ that it refers to the expedition of Tabūk, in the tenth year, after their

1 Sūrah al-Tawbah: 38-39.

2 *Majmaʿ al-Bayān*, vol. 3 p. 62.

3 Sūrah al-Tawbah: 38-39.

> return from Ṭā'if. They were summoned for this expedition during a time of drought and unforgiving heat. In addition to this the unpropitious distance and sizeable enemy were factors that contributed to their hesitancy. Then al-Qummī transmits a narration concerning the background to this battle and says, "Then the Messenger ﷺ instructed his Companions to prepare for Tabūk, which is near al-Bulqā. He sent for the tribes around him, those in Makkah and those who entered Islam from the tribes of Khuzāʿah, Muzaynah, and Juhaynah; exhorting them towards jihād. The Messenger ﷺ also called for his camp-site to be set up, which was done at Thaniyyat al-Wadāʿ. He also instructed the people of Juddah to assist those who needed support; and encouraged those who had provisions to share with those who did not; thus strengthening the army. Then he delivered a sermon in which he encouraged them towards jihād. He (al-Qummī) says: "The Arab tribes who were summoned arrived; whereas a group among the Munāfiqīn and others besides them decided not to come..."[1]

Can the readers perceive any form of dispraise of the Ṣaḥābah in al-Kāshānī's account? Is there anything to indicate that they forsook jihād for worldly gain? Instead, the opposite is true. Al-Kāshānī's commentary of this verse does not differ with that of the Ahl al-Sunnah. The attentive reader would also have noticed that al-Kāshānī, a Twelver Shīʿī scholar, inadvertently acknowledges that the Ṣaḥābah were a single group; distinct from the Munāfiqīn. He mentioned that the Prophet ﷺ instructed his Companions to prepare for jihād using the word "Aṣḥāb" in a general manner. In other words, it refers to all of the Ṣaḥābah. He also mentioned that a group from the hypocrites decided not to come. Now, if the hypocrites were from the body of Ṣaḥābah, as some claim, then al-Kāshānī would have said, "a group from the hypocrite Ṣaḥābah, decided not to come for the jihād." Subḥān Allah! This clearly demonstrates that the tripartite categorization is flawed.

Repercussions Of Wanton Tafsīr

The reader might find the objection to Tījānī's wanton approach to Tafsīr a tad harsh. We wish to demonstrate the ramifications of interpreting the Word of Allah with complete disregard for the hermeneutic standards and indifference to the protocols of Tafsīr.

---

1 Fayḍ al-Kāshānī: *Tafsīr al-Ṣāfī*, vol. 2 p. 342-343.

Allah سُبْحَانَهُ وَتَعَالَىٰ says:

يَاأَيُّهَا النَّبِيُّ اتَّقِ اللَّهَ وَلَا تُطِعِ الْكَافِرِينَ وَالْمُنَافِقِينَ إِنَّ اللَّهَ كَانَ عَلِيمًا حَكِيمًا

O Prophet صَلَّى ٱللَّٰهُ عَلَيْهِ وَسَلَّمَ, fear Allah and do not obey the disbelievers and the hypocrites. Indeed, Allah is ever Knowing and Wise.[1]

This could be said to mean that Allah سُبْحَانَهُ وَتَعَالَىٰ threatened his Prophet صَلَّى ٱللَّٰهُ عَلَيْهِ وَسَلَّمَ and instructed him to fear Him and not to obey the unbelievers and hypocrites. A libertine approach to interpreting the Divine Word allows one to understand this as proof that the Prophet صَلَّى ٱللَّٰهُ عَلَيْهِ وَسَلَّمَ was not conscious of Allah سُبْحَانَهُ وَتَعَالَىٰ in his daʿwah; and that he was amenable to the hypocrites and unbelievers. Disregard for the principles of Tafsīr has parlous repercussions.

Another example from Sūrah al-Mā'idah:

يَاأَيُّهَا الرَّسُولُ بَلِّغْ مَا أُنْزِلَ إِلَيْكَ مِنْ رَبِّكَ وَإِنْ لَمْ تَفْعَلْ فَمَا بَلَّغْتَ رِسَالَتَهُ وَاللَّهُ يَعْصِمُكَ مِنَ النَّاسِ إِنَّ اللَّهَ لَا يَهْدِي الْقَوْمَ الْكَافِرِينَ

O Messenger صَلَّى ٱللَّٰهُ عَلَيْهِ وَسَلَّمَ, announce that which has been revealed to you from your Lord, and if you do not, then you have not conveyed His message. And Allah will protect you from the people. Indeed, Allah does not guide the disbelieving people.[2]

An unbridled interpretation allows for the outrageous idea that Allah سُبْحَانَهُ وَتَعَالَىٰ was rebuking the Prophet صَلَّى ٱللَّٰهُ عَلَيْهِ وَسَلَّمَ for his complacency in conveying what was revealed to him. The objections to this type of ludicrous interpretations are identical to Tījānī's preposterous allegations against the Companions on the basis of unprincipled interpretation. Furthermore, it is degrading to the Qur'ān, the source of light and guidance, that it be subject to wanton interpretation. Disregard for the hermeneutical standards, and failure to restrict oneself to one's limitations, inevitably produces absurd interpretations of the Book of Allah. It is for this very reason that the scholars have restricted the novice; and cautioned him from departure from the transmitted opinions.

1 Sūrah al-Aḥzāb: 1.

2 Sūrah al-Mā'idah: 67.

It is ironic that Tījānī has the following to say:

> **The Book of Allah is silent and could be interpreted in various ways, and it contains what is vague and what is similar, and to understand it we have to refer to those who are well endowed with knowledge as regards the Qur'an, and to Ahl al-Bayt, as regards to the Prophet's traditions.**[1]

Has Tījānī referred to those deeply rooted in knowledge, and the Ahl al-Bayt? Has he been faithful to the principles he quoted, or has he followed his fancies in his attack on the men of the best generation (the Ṣaḥābah رضي الله عنهم), blinding him and resulting in his preposterous allegations

Allah's Replacing Of Those Who Disobey

Then Tījānī says:

> **The threat to change them came in many Qur'anic verses which indicate clearly that they showed their reluctance to fight in al-Jihad- Holy War - more than once, and Allah- the Most High - says:**

وَإِنْ تَتَوَلَّوْا يَسْتَبْدِلْ قَوْمًا غَيْرَكُمْ ثُمَّ لَا يَكُونُوا أَمْثَالَكُمْ

And if you turn away, He will replace you with another people; then they will not be the likes of you.[2]

I say: This is merely a part of the verse which was revealed encouraging them to spend in Allah's path. The complete verse goes like this:

هَاأَنْتُمْ هَٰؤُلَاءِ تُدْعَوْنَ لِتُنْفِقُوا فِي سَبِيلِ اللَّهِ فَمِنْكُمْ مَنْ يَبْخَلُ وَمَنْ يَبْخَلْ
فَإِنَّمَا يَبْخَلُ عَنْ نَفْسِهِ وَاللَّهُ الْغَنِيُّ وَأَنْتُمُ الْفُقَرَاءُ وَإِنْ تَتَوَلَّوْا يَسْتَبْدِلْ قَوْمًا
غَيْرَكُمْ ثُمَّ لَا يَكُونُوا أَمْثَالَكُمْ

Here you are — those invited to spend in the cause of Allah — but among you are those who withhold [out of greed]. And whoever withholds only withholds [benefit] from himself; and Allah is Free of need, while you are the needy. And if you turn away, He will replace you with another people; then they will not be the likes of you.

---

1 *Then I was guided* p. 152.

2 Sūrah Muḥammad: 38.

The scholars of Qur'ānic exegesis have explained this verse thus, "You are being called to spend in the way of Allah that which has been prescribed for you; yet among you there are those who are miserly. Whoever is miserly is essentially miserly with his own self and deprives himself of Allah's reward. Allah is Independent, completely without need of what you spend; while you are entirely in need of Him. If you turn away from His obedience, He will replace you with another people. That is to say He will bring them in your place and they will not be like you; in turning away from His obedience. Rather, they will be obedient to Him."

Let us focus on these words:

وَإِنْ تَتَوَلَّوْا يَسْتَبْدِلْ قَوْمًا غَيْرَكُمْ ثُمَّ لَا يَكُونُوا أَمْثَالَكُمْ

And if you turn away, He will replace you with another people; then they will not be the likes of you.

It means: If you turn away from the obedience of Allah سُبْحَانَهُ وَتَعَالَى and following his path then soon he will replace you with a people other than you. They will listen, be more obedient than you, and will not be niggardly about spending in the path of Allah. This is the tafsīr of all the Ahl al-Sunnah. Is there any clue in this verse that leads to Tījānī's bizarre conclusion of the Ṣaḥābah being sluggish about jihād on many occasions? The verse has no mention of jihād at all! Has anyone before Tījānī come with this interpretation? Is this even the tafsīr of the Rāfiḍah?

Abū ʿAlī al-Ṭabarsī says concerning the meaning of this verse:

> "*Here you are — those invited to spend in the cause of Allah,*" (al-Ṭabarsī says) It refers to that which was obligatory from their wealth. In other words, "you have only been instructed to take out that which was mandatory and spend it in the obedience of Allah. "*But among you are those who withhold,*" what was mandatory; zakāh, "*and whoever withholds only withholds [benefit] from himself,*" because they deprive themselves of a great reward; and huge punishment is binding on them. Then Allah says, "*Allah is Free of need,*" of whatever wealth you possess, "*while you are the needy,*" of Allah's goodness, bounties and mercy. In other words, He does not command you to spend out of His need, rather, so that you may benefit in the hereafter. "*And if you turn away,*" in other words, you resist from His obedience and the instruction of his Messenger then, "*he will replace you with another people,*" more submissive and obedient than you,

> "*then they will not be the likes of you,*" rather they will be better than you and more obedient to Allah...[1]

Muḥammad Mughniyyah states in his *Tafsīr:*

> "*Here you are — those invited*" is a reference to the wealthy. "*Invited to spend in the cause of Allah*", Allah سُبْحَانَهُ وَتَعَالَى says "*invited*", he did not say we command you. It is as if Allah سُبْحَانَهُ وَتَعَالَى is coaching the wealthy and encouraging them to spend from the goodness of their hearts. Even clearer than this verse concerning encouraging the believers to spend in the path of Allah is the verse of *istiqrāḍ ḥasan* (this is in reference to the verses where Allah سُبْحَانَهُ وَتَعَالَى seeks a 'loan' from the believers with the promise of a great reward for them in the hereafter). "*And whoever withholds only withholds [benefit] from himself,*" because spending is a protection from the fire and the anger of Allah سُبْحَانَهُ وَتَعَالَى. It comes in the ḥadīth, "*Fortify your wealth with zakāh.*" "*Allah is Free of need, while you are the needy,*" even if you own the universe with its earth and its heaven you are still in need of Allah سُبْحَانَهُ وَتَعَالَى for its maintenance and its arrangement. "*He will replace you with another people,*" who will glorify him with his praises and comply with his command.[2]

Again we see that Tījānī's interpretation lacks any precedent. The Shīʿī scholars could not find fault with the Ṣaḥābah in these verses; yet the one seeking the path of guidance sees in it what none before him has seen.

Tījānī insists that his interpretation has some substance:

> **It is like the words of Allah:**
>
> يَٰٓأَيُّهَا الَّذِينَ آمَنُوا مَنْ يَرْتَدَّ مِنْكُمْ عَنْ دِينِهِ فَسَوْفَ يَأْتِي اللَّهُ بِقَوْمٍ
> يُحِبُّهُمْ وَيُحِبُّونَهُ أَذِلَّةٍ عَلَى الْمُؤْمِنِينَ أَعِزَّةٍ عَلَى الْكَافِرِينَ يُجَاهِدُونَ
> فِي سَبِيلِ اللَّهِ وَلَا يَخَافُونَ لَوْمَةَ لَائِمٍ ذَٰلِكَ فَضْلُ اللَّهِ يُؤْتِيهِ مَنْ يَشَاءُ
> وَاللَّهُ وَاسِعٌ عَلِيمٌ
>
> ***O you who have believed, whoever of you should revert from his religion - Allah will bring forth [in place of them] a people He will love and who***

---

1 *Majmaʿ al-Bayān*, vol. 6 p. 48.

2 Muḥammad Mughniyyah: *Tafsīr al-Mubīn*, p. 677-678.

> ***will love Him [who are] humble toward the believers, powerful against the disbelievers; they strive in the cause of Allah and do not fear the blame of a critic. That is the favour of Allah; He bestows it upon whom He wills. And Allah is All Encompassing and All Knowing.***[1,2]

Our comment:

This verse is among the greatest proofs for the magnificence of the Ṣaḥābah; and it is they who are intended by the group "*whom Allah loves and they love Him*". A number of early experts including Ḥasan, al-Ḍaḥḥāk and Ibn Jurayj say that it was revealed in connection with Abū Bakr رضي الله عنه and his companions. Al-Ṭabarī mentions in his Tafsīr that ʿAlī ibn Abī Ṭālib رضي الله عنه said, "This verse was revealed concerning Abū Bakr and his companions." Some have opined that it refers to the Anṣār; while others say it refers to the people of Yemen, the people of Abū Mūsā al-Ashʿarī. Whatever the case may be, the verse is general concerning all the Ṣaḥābah. There is no doubt that the first of them is Abū Bakr, ʿUmar, ʿUthmān, ʿAlī, and the remaining Ṣaḥābah رضي الله عنهم.

Al-Ṭabarsī concurs in his commentary of the above verse:

> There is a difference of opinion concerning who was described with these qualities among them. It has been said that it refers to Abū Bakr and his companions who fought the apostates; this has been narrated from Ḥasan, Qatādah, and al-Ḍaḥḥāk. It has been said that they are the Anṣār; this has been narrated from al-Suddī. It has been said that it refers to the people of Yemen; this has been narrated from Mujāhid. It has been said that it refers to the Persians and it has been said that they are ʿAlī and his companions.[3]

Allah Loves Them And They Love Him

The proof that the Ṣaḥābah were primarily intended in this verse is this expression:

فَسَوْفَ يَأْتِي اللّٰهُ بِقَوْمٍ يُحِبُّهُمْ وَيُحِبُّونَهُ

Allah will bring forth [in place of them] a people He will love and who will love Him.

1 Sūrah al-Mā'idah: 54.

2 *Then I was guided*, p. 101-102.

3 *Majmaʿ al-Bayān*, vol. 2 p. 122-123.

There is no doubt that Allah loves the Ṣaḥābah of his Prophet صَلَّى ٱللَّٰهُ عَلَيْهِ وَسَلَّمَ. It is they who sheltered him, assisted him, struggled with him, stood by his side in adversity and ease, and therefore deserved the pleasure of Allah.

Allah says:

وَالسَّابِقُوْنَ الْأَوَّلُوْنَ مِنَ الْمُهَاجِرِيْنَ وَالْأَنْصَارِ وَالَّذِيْنَ اتَّبَعُوْهُمْ بِإِحْسَانٍ رَضِيَ اللّٰهُ عَنْهُمْ وَرَضُوْا عَنْهُ وَأَعَدَّ لَهُمْ جَنَّاتٍ تَجْرِيْ تَحْتَهَا الْأَنْهَارُ خَالِدِيْنَ فِيْهَا أَبَدًا ذٰلِكَ الْفَوْزُ الْعَظِيْمُ

The forerunners from the Muhājirīn and Anṣār and those who follow them in [all] good deeds, well-pleased is Allah with them, as are they with Him. He has prepared for them gardens under which rivers flow, to dwell therein forever, that is the supreme felicity.[1]

لَقَدْ رَضِيَ اللّٰهُ عَنِ الْمُؤْمِنِيْنَ إِذْ يُبَايِعُوْنَكَ تَحْتَ الشَّجَرَةِ فَعَلِمَ مَا فِيْ قُلُوْبِهِمْ فَأَنْزَلَ السَّكِيْنَةَ عَلَيْهِمْ وَأَثَابَهُمْ فَتْحًا قَرِيْبًا

Certainly was Allah pleased with the believers when they pledged allegiance to you, [O Muḥammad], under the tree, and He knew what was in their hearts, so He sent down tranquillity upon them and rewarded them with an imminent conquest.[2]

There is no doubt that the Muhājirīn and the Anṣār, and those who took the pledge with him صَلَّى ٱللَّٰهُ عَلَيْهِ وَسَلَّمَ under the tree, the noble Ṣaḥābah, are being referred to in the verse. At their helm stand the four khulafā' رَضِيَ ٱللَّٰهُ عَنْهُمْ. Necessity demands that their actions and disposition were motivated by love.

As for the words of Allah, "*humble toward the believers, powerful against the disbelievers,*" it is a clear sign and unmistakeable trait of the Ṣaḥābah.

Consider how they are described by Allah سُبْحَانَهُ وَتَعَالَىٰ:

مُحَمَّدٌ رَّسُوْلُ اللّٰهِ وَالَّذِيْنَ مَعَهٗ أَشِدَّآءُ عَلَى الْكُفَّارِ رُحَمَآءُ بَيْنَهُمْ

1 Sūrah al-Tawbah: 100.

2 Sūrah al-Fatḥ: 18.

Muḥammad is the Messenger of Allah; and those with him are forceful against the disbelievers, merciful among themselves.[1]

It is an undeniable fact that 'those with him' were the Ṣaḥābah and at the forefront was Abū Bakr, then ʿUmar, then ʿUthmān, then ʿAlī, then the rest of them according to their status and virtue. It comes in the ḥadīth that the Prophet صَلَّى ٱللَّٰهُ عَلَيْهِ وَسَلَّمَ said:

The most compassionate of my Ummah upon my Ummah is Abū Bakr...[2]

As for his words, "*they strive in the cause of Allah and do not fear the blame of a critic,*" it is well-known that the Ṣaḥābah were the first of those who struggled in the path of Allah سُبْحَانَهُ وَتَعَالَىٰ. The verses of the Qur'ān which support this are abundant. This description appearing in the aḥādīth are more famous than require mention. This is a lasting quality of theirs.

It is deplorable to accuse the Ṣaḥābah of apostasy on the premise of the verse under discussion. During Abū Bakr's رَضِيَ ٱللَّٰهُ عَنْهُ khilāfah it was the Ṣaḥābah who fought the apostates and were victorious over them. It is therefore inconceivable that the apostates were triumphant over the believers. There is also no doubt that this jihād is also a proof for the validity of the khilāfah of Abū Bakr, ʿUmar, and ʿAlī رَضِيَ ٱللَّٰهُ عَنْهُمْ as they fought in the path of Allah during the life of the Prophet صَلَّى ٱللَّٰهُ عَلَيْهِ وَسَلَّمَ and fought the apostates after him. Whoever displays these qualities is indeed a friend of Allah سُبْحَانَهُ وَتَعَالَىٰ.[3]

The Prophet's Companions And The Mahdī's Companions

When Tījānī mentioned this verse as proof for the apostasy of the Ṣaḥābah رَضِيَ ٱللَّٰهُ عَنْهُمْ; he also intended to clarify that the praiseworthy qualities mentioned in it applied to ʿAlī رَضِيَ ٱللَّٰهُ عَنْهُ and his partisans. Therefore, we find ʿAlī al-Qummī commenting on this verse:

As for Allah's words, "*O you who have believed, whoever of you should revert from his religion - Allah will bring forth [in place of them] a people He will love and who will love Him [who are] humble toward the believers, powerful against the disbelievers; they strive in the cause of Allah and do not fear the blame of a critic,*" it is an address

1 Sūrah al-Fatḥ: 29.

2 *Sunan al-Tirmidhī*, vol. 5 Kitāb al-Manāqib: Ḥadīth no. 3790; Refer (also) to *Ṣaḥīḥ al-Tirmidhī*, Ḥadīth no. 2981.

3 al-Qurṭubī: *Al-Jāmiʿ li Aḥkām al-Qur'ān*, vol. 6 p. 142.

> towards the Ṣaḥābah of the Messenger ﷺ who appropriated from the family of Muḥammad ﷺ their right and turned apostate from the religion of Allah سُبْحَانَهُ وَتَعَالَى. "*Allah will bring forth [in place of them] a people He will love and who will love Him*," descended in relation to the Qā'im and his Ṣaḥābah, "*they strive in the cause of Allah and do not fear the blame of a critic*."[1]

If this verse was revealed in relation to the 'imaginary' Qā'im and his companions, then let us investigate the jihād of the *Imām al-Waṣī* ('Alī ibn Abī Ṭālib) and his twelve successors as they were the predecessors. Thus we shall get a glimpse of what can be expected from the companions of the 'Qā'im' since they are the successors — so that the reader and seeker of the truth may decide whether this verse applies to them or not. It is from the books of the Shī'ah that we reproduce the words of the Imāms, lest we be accused of prejudice or bias!

'Alī ibn Abī Ṭālib رَضِيَ اللَّهُ عَنْهُ is quoted in *Nahj al-Balāghah*, one of the most reliable books to them, describing the jihād of his partisans:

> As for what follows: Indeed, jihād is a door from the doors of Jannah which Allah opened for His select friends. It is the garment of taqwā, and Allah's fortified coat of armour, and His firm shield. Whoever leaves it loathing it, Allah will clothe him with the garment of disgrace and wrap him in trial. He will be kicked with scorn, his heart will be veiled, and the truth will be removed from him on account of neglecting jihād. Debasement will be ordained and justice will be denied.
>
> Behold! Indeed, I called you to fight these people day and night, secretly and openly, and I said to you, "Attack them before they attack you." By Allah a nation is never attacked in their homeland except that they are disgraced.
>
> Then you pretended to trust (Allah) and deceived one another until the enemy incursions raided you and took possession of the land...[2]
>
> Amazing! Amazing! Allah stifles the heart and brings anxiety on account of the gathering (unity) of these people upon their falsehood while you dispute about truth. How grievous it is for you that you have become the target shot at, you are attacked and do not attack, incursions are made against you and you make no incursions, Allah is disobeyed and you are contented with that.

1 *Tafsīr al-Qummī*, vol. 1 p. 177-178.

2 Where is the honour?

> When I instruct you to move towards them during the hot days you say, "This is extreme heat, give us respite until the heat withdraws," and when I instruct you to move towards them in the winter you say, "This is extreme cold, give us respite until the cold withdraws." All of this to flee from the heat and the cold. By Allah, it is rather from the sword that you flee.
>
> O those who resemble men but are not really men! Your intelligence is that of children and your wit is that of the occupants of the curtained canopies (women kept in seclusion from the outside world). I hoped I had not seen you and I had not known you. Your acquaintance has brought regret and followed it up with grief. Indeed, you have filled my heart with pus, and filled my chest with anger, and made me swallow gulps of grief, and you have spoiled my opinion through your disobedience and disgrace.[1]

At another place he says:

> O people, your bodies are together but your desires are divergent. Your talk softens the hard stones and your action attracts your enemy towards you. You claim in your sittings that you would do this and that, but when fighting approaches, you say to war, "turn thou away..."
>
> By Allah! Deceived is the one whom you have deceived while, by Allah, he who is successful with you receives only useless arrows! You are like broken arrows thrown over the enemy. By Allah! I am now in the position that I neither confirm your views nor hope for your support, nor challenge the enemy through you.[2]

On another occasion he said:

> Woe to you. I am tired of rebuking you. Do you accept this worldly life in place of the next life? Or disgrace in place of dignity? When I invite you to fight your enemy your eyes revolve as though you are in the clutches of death, and in the senselessness of your last moments. My pleadings are not understood by you and you remain stunned. It is as though your hearts are affected with madness hence you do not understand. Your example is that of the camels whose protector has disappeared, so that if they are collected from one side they disperse away from the other side.

1 *Nahj al-Balāghah*, p. 88-91.

2 Ibid. p. 94-96.

> By Allah, how bad are you for igniting flames of war. You are intruded against but do not intrude (against the enemy). Your boundaries are decreasing but you do not get enraged over it. Those against you do not sleep but you are unmindful.[1]

Then he said on another occasion:

> By Allah, whoever is supported by people like you must suffer disgrace; and whoever fires arrows with your support is as if he throws arrows that are broken both at head and tail. By Allah, within the courtyard you are quite numerous but under the banner you are only a few.
>
> May Allah disgrace your faces and destroy you. You do not understand the right as you understand the wrong and do not crush the wrong as you crush the right.[2]

In another place he says:

> I called you towards jihād but you did not turn towards it, I made you hear but you did not listen, I called you in private and public but you did not respond, and I advised you but you did not accept... I wish, by Allah, Muʿāwiyah could trade with me like the trading of *dīnārs* (gold coins) with *dirhams* (silver coins) then he could take ten amongst you and I could take one man from amongst them.[3]

Ḥasan ibn ʿAlī رضي الله عنه once said describing his 'extraordinary' disciples after they criticised him:

> By Allah, I believe that Muʿāwiyah is better for me than these who claim to be my followers. They desire my death, seize my strength, and take my wealth. By Allah, for me to take a covenant with Muʿāwiyah through which I save my blood and remain safe amongst my family is better for me than for these people to allow my murder, and (as a result) my household and my family are ruined.[4]

And here is Ḥusayn رضي الله عنه directing his speech to the 'heroes' of the Shīʿah:

---

1 Ibid. p. 104 and 105.

2 Ibid. p. 143 and 144.

3 Ibid. p. 224.

4 al-Ṭabarsī: *Al-Iḥtijāj*, vol. 2 p. 300.

> Woe unto you, O congregation. May you be filled with grief and deprivation! When you called us for assistance while you were perplexed and we called you for assistance agitating (you for it). You sharpened a sword against us which was in our hands, and fuelled a fire against us (which we) kindled for your, and our enemy. Then you became a people united in their enmity towards your friends and a hand against your enemies without an exchange. There is no hope for you with them and there was no wrongdoing from us to you. Why then shall there not be for you distress seeing that you disliked us when the sword was vigilant and the heart was at peace...[1]

And here is Muḥammad al-Bāqir, the fifth Imām of the Twelver Shīʿah, describing his disciples:

> Had all people been our followers three quarters of them would doubt us and the other quarter would be fools.[2]

As for Imām Mūsā ibn Jaʿfar, the seventh Imām of the Twelver Shīʿah, revealing to us the true apostates he said:

> If my disciples were mixed (with others) I would not find them save having deplorable qualities, and if I were to test them I would not find them save apostate, and if I had to sift them none would remain save what belonged to me. Indeed, whenever they recline on sofas they say, "We are the disciples of ʿAlī." Verily the disciples of ʿAlī are those whose words are validated by their actions.[3]

If these are the followers of ʿAlī and his sons, then I tremor at the thought of the Qā'im and his followers!

After ʿAlī رَضِيَ اللَّهُ عَنْهُ rebuked his companions with the aforementioned speech, he did not forget to produce for them an example to be followed, and emulated, and to take lesson from. For this he did not find but the Ṣaḥābah. He said:

> Indeed, I have seen the Ṣaḥābah of Muḥammad صَلَّى اللَّهُ عَلَيْهِ وَسَلَّمَ and I do not see anyone amongst you who resembles them. They would rise in the morning, unkempt

1 Ibid. p. 224.

2 *Rijāl al-Kashshī*, p. 179.

3 *Al-Rawḍah min al-Kāfī*, vol. 8 p. 191 under the chapter: the Shīʿah of ʿAlī are those whose words honour their actions.

> and covered with dust, because they had spent the night in prostration and standing. They would alternate between their foreheads and their cheeks, while it felt as if they were standing on coals, when thinking of their return to the Hereafter. It is as if between their eyes there were marks like knees of goats due to the length of their prostration. When they would remember Allah, their eyes would drip until their bosoms would become wet. They would shake as a tree shakes on a terribly windy day, fearing punishment and hoping for reward.[1]

Then he described his fighting with the Ṣaḥābah during the Prophet's صلى الله عليه وسلم era:

> We (the Ṣaḥābah) were with the Prophet صلى الله عليه وسلم fighting our fathers, sons, brothers, and uncles; that did not increase us save in faith and submission. We passed (many days during this time) upon morsels, and in patience upon the anguish of pain, and in determination in fighting the enemy. A man amongst us and one from our enemy would compete with one another the way two studs competed glancing at one another stealthily which one would quench the other with the cup of death. At times it went our way and other times it went the way of our enemy. Then, when Allah saw our truthfulness he sent upon our enemy subjugation and upon us victory to the extent that Islam was settled, firmly established, and its lands settled. By my life, if we had done what you did[2] there would be no pillars for the religion and there be no revival of faith. By my life, if we had also behaved like you, no pillar of (our) religion could have been raised, nor could the tree of faith have borne leaves. By Allah, certainly you will now milk our blood (instead of milk) and eventually you will face shame.[3]

Those were the companions of ʿAlī and his children رضي الله عنهم. Compare them to the Ṣaḥābah of Muḥammad صلى الله عليه وسلم. We have seen them both through the eyes of ʿAlī رضي الله عنه, as preserved in the books of the Shīʿah. Sadly, Tījānī and al-Qummī have shown us that they are blind to reason, and deaf to the words of the Imāms.

1 These are the persons whom al-Qummī and al-Tījānī say are apostate!

2 Here he is referring to his disciples.

3 *Nahj al-Balāghah*, p. 129-130.

Tījānī On The Division Of Ṣaḥābah

Then Tījānī continues and says:

> **If we want to investigate the Qur'anic verses which emphasize this issue and talk about the classification of the Companions, which the Shia advocate, then we would need a special book for it. The Holy Qur'an expressed all that in the most direct and eloquent way when Allah says:**
>
> وَلْتَكُنْ مِّنْكُمْ أُمَّةٌ يَّدْعُوْنَ إِلَى الْخَيْرِ وَيَأْمُرُوْنَ بِالْمَعْرُوْفِ وَيَنْهَوْنَ عَنِ الْمُنْكَرِ وَأُولٰئِكَ هُمُ الْمُفْلِحُوْنَ وَلَا تَكُوْنُوا كَالَّذِيْنَ تَفَرَّقُوْا وَاخْتَلَفُوْا مِنْ بَعْدِ مَا جَآءَهُمُ الْبَيِّنَاتُ وَأُولٰئِكَ لَهُمْ عَذَابٌ عَظِيْمٌ . يَوْمَ تَبْيَضُّ وُجُوْهٌ وَتَسْوَدُّ وُجُوْهٌ فَأَمَّا الَّذِيْنَ اسْوَدَّتْ وُجُوْهُهُمْ أَكَفَرْتُمْ بَعْدَ إِيْمَانِكُمْ فَذُوْقُوا الْعَذَابَ بِمَا كُنْتُمْ تَكْفُرُوْنَ . وَأَمَّا الَّذِيْنَ ابْيَضَّتْ وُجُوْهُهُمْ فَفِيْ رَحْمَةِ اللّٰهِ هُمْ فِيْهَا خَالِدُوْنَ
>
> ***And let there be [arising] from you a nation inviting to [all that is] good, enjoining what is right and forbidding what is wrong, and those will be the successful. And do not be like the ones who became divided and differed after the clear proofs had come to them. And those will have a great punishment. On the Day [some] faces will turn white and [some] faces will turn black. As for those whose faces turn black, [to them it will be said]: "Did you disbelieve after your belief? Then taste the punishment for what you used to reject." But as for those whose faces will turn white, [they will be] within the mercy of Allah. They will abide therein eternally.***[1]

These Qur'anic verses, as every intelligent scholar knows, are addressing the Companions, and warning them of the division and disagreement among themselves after they have already been shown the Right Path. They also tell them that a great torture is awaiting them, and divide them in two groups: The first group: when they will be resurrected on the Day of Judgement, every one of them would have a white face, and those are the grateful who deserve the mercy of Allah. The second group: when they will be resurrected

1 Sūrah Āl 'Imrān: 104-107.

on the Day of Judgement, everyone of them would have a black face, and those are the apostates, whom Allah - the Almighty - promised the great torture.[1]

Our comment:

The scholars say concerning this verse:

"*And let there be [arising] from you,*" O believers, a group calling the people towards good, Islam, and the sharīʿah. The word "من" from the word "منكم" (from you) in the verse gives the meaning of 'some' i.e. 'let there be some of you...' because commanding towards the good and forbidding evil is from the *furūḍ kifāyāt* (communal obligations).

Regarding the part, "*And do not be like the ones who became divided and differed after the clear proofs had come to them,*" majority say it refers to the Jews and the Christians. Others say they are the *mubtadiʿah* (innovators) of this Ummah. Abū Umāmah says that they are the *Ḥarūriyyah* (the Khawārij).[2]

As for Allah's statement, "*On the Day [some] faces will turn white and [some] faces will turn black. As for those whose faces turn black,*" the scholars of tafsīr have differed in identifying them. Ibn ʿAbbās رضي الله عنهما says, "The faces of the Ahl al-Sunnah will be lit and the faces of the people of *bidʿah* (innovation) will be in gloom."

Al-Ḥasan al-Baṣrī says, "They are the hypocrites. They pronounce their faith with their tongues but rejected it with their hearts and actions."

Abū Umāmah رضي الله عنه says, "They are the Khawārij."

Abū Ghālib says, "Abū Umāmah saw mutilated heads positioned at the entrance of Damascus and said, "Dogs of the fire, the worst of the fallen (killed in battle) under the sky, the best of the fallen are those who they killed," and then he recited the verse, "*On the Day [some] faces will turn white and [some] faces will turn black. As for those whose faces turn black.*" I said to Abū Umāmah, "Did you hear that from the Messenger of Allah صلى الله عليه وسلم?" He said, "I heard it not once, but twice, but thrice, but four times (until he came to seven). If I did not hear it I would not have narrated it to you."[3]

---

1 *Then I was guided* pg. 101.

2 *Jāmiʿ al-Qurṭubī*, vol. 4 p. 107; Also see *al-Baghawī*, vol. 2 p. 86.

3 *Jāmiʿ al-Qurṭubī*, vol. 4 p. 107 and 108; *al-Ṭabarī*, vol. 3 p. 386-387; *al-Muḥarrar al-Wajīz*, vol. 3 p. 190-191; *al-Baghawī*, vol. 2 p. 87; *Fatḥ al-Qadīr*, vol. 1 p. 88.

Qatādah says it refers to the apostates and he held another opinion that it applied to the people of bidʿah.

Asmā' bint Abī Bakr رضي الله عنهما said that the Messenger of Allah صلى الله عليه وسلم said:

إني فرطكم على الحوض حتى أنظر من يرد علي منكم و سيؤخذ الناس دوني فأقول يا رب مني و من أمتي.فيقال لي هل شعرت ما عملوا بعدك؟ و الله ما برحوا يرجعون على أعقابهم

Indeed, I will precede you to the ḥawḍ (special fountain of the Prophet صلى الله عليه وسلم from which the believers will drink) so that I can see who comes to me from amongst you. People will be taken before they reach me and I will say, "O my Lord, they are from me and from my nation," and then it will be said to me, "Do you know what they did after you?" By Allah, they will continue being returned upon their heels.[1]

Ubayy ibn Kaʿb رضي الله عنه said, "It is that īmān from the time of Ādam, before people disputed in religion. When Allah took a covenant of servitude from them. They were created with the inclination for Islam. A time when they were all one nation, submitters."

Ibn Jarīr al-Ṭabarī says, "The most accurate view in this matter is the one we have quoted from Ubayy ibn Kaʿb; that all of the unbelievers are referred to by it. That the īmān which they abandoned, and for which they were rebuked, is the īmān which they admitted to the day it was said to them:

أَلَسْتُ بِرَبِّكُمْ قَالُوْا بَلٰى شَهِدْنَا

Am I not your Lord [who cherishes and sustains you]?"- They said: "Certainly! We do testify! [2,3]

In brief, this is what the scholars have said about this verse. Not a single scholar understood it to apply to the Companions of the Prophet صلى الله عليه وسلم. The mystery is how could anyone arrive at the conclusion that it is Qur'ānic disparagement of Ṣaḥābah رضي الله عنهم.

1 *Tafsīr al-Baghawī*, vol. 2 p. 88.

2 Sūrah al-Aʿrāf: 172.

3 *Al-Ṭabarī*, vol. 3 p. 387.

Let us see what the Shīʿī scholars have said about this verse.

Al-Faḍl al-Ṭabarsī says in *Majmaʿ al-Bayān* under the commentary of this verse:

> "*And do not be like the ones who became divided...*" about the religion. They are the Jews and the Christians. "*And differed after the clear proofs had come to them,*" it has been said that its meaning is *tafarraqū* (to be divided) also. "*On the Day [some] faces will turn white and [some] faces will turn black. As for those whose faces turn black,*" only the faces of the believers will be luminous that day as a reward for their belief and obedience; and the faces of the unbelievers will be blackened in gloom as a punishment for their disbelief and sins. The reason for this appears in the words that follow, "*did you disbelieve after your belief? Then taste the punishment for what you used to reject.*" In other words, it will be said to them, '*did you disbelieve after believing*?' There is a difference of opinion concerning who is intended by it:
>
> 1. They are those who disbelieved after displaying belief with hypocrisy ... as reported from Ḥasan.
> 2. They are all unbelievers; because of rejecting of Tawḥīd when Allah made them witness over themselves when He said "*Am I not your Lord [who cherishes and sustains you]?" They said: "Certainly! We do testify!*" He will then say to them, "*did you disbelieve after your belief on the day of the covenant?*" as reported from Ubay.
> 3. That they are the Ahl al-Kitāb. They belied the Prophet ﷺ after their belief in him... as stated by ʿIkrimah and preferred by al-Zajāj and al-Jubbā'ī
> 4. That they are the people of innovation and dissension from this Ummah, as reported from ʿAlī. A Similar view is ascribed to Qatādah with the addition of those who apostatised. It has been related from the Prophet ﷺ that he said, "... will come to me at the Ḥawḍ..." Al-Thaʿlabī mentions in his tafsīr that Abū Umāmah al-Bāhilī said, "They are the Khawārij and it has been transmitted from the Prophet ﷺ that they will pierce through Islam like an arrow pierces through prey."[1]

1 *Majmaʿ al-Bayān*, vol. 2 p. 160-162.

Despite mentioning multiple views on the interpretation for this verse, al-Ṭabarsī did not mention a single view implicating the Ṣaḥābah. The discussion on the ḥadīth of the Ḥawḍ will follow later. The group which will be kept from the Ḥawḍ are the apostates, the people of dissension such as the Khawārij and their likes.

Let us take a look at *al-Tafsīr al-Ṣāfī* by Fayḍ al-Kāshānī. He mentions under the commentary of this verse:

> "*And do not be like the ones who became divided...*" like the Jews and the Christians. They differed amongst themselves on monotheism, *tanzīh* (declaring Allah to be unlike his creation), and the realities of the hereafter.
>
> "*After the clear proofs had come to them,*" it refers to the verses and the clear proofs for accepting him as the Messenger of Allah.
>
> "*On the Day [some] faces will turn white and [some] faces will turn black. As for those whose faces turn black,*" allusions to the apparent delight of joy and the distress of fear in it.
>
> "*As for those whose faces turn black, [to them it will be said] 'did you disbelieve after your belief?*" it will be asked of them in condemnation and amazement, "did you disbelieve?" In *al-Majma'* it is reported from Amīr al-Mu'minīn ('Alī) that they are the people of innovation, dissension and false views from this Ummah. It is reported from the Prophet ﷺ that he said, "They will come to me at the Ḥawḍ..."[1]

This commentary is like the one before it. There is no explicit declaration that those intended in the verse are the Ṣaḥābah.

Tījānī is not done ranting:

> **These Qur'anic verses, as every intelligent scholar knows, are addressing the Companions, warning them of the division...**

Perhaps the reader is beginning to notice the departure from principle at so many places that repeating the mantra might prove monotonous. A Qur'ānic reference about the Jews and Christians is being stripped of context; cloaked in the garb of wild conjecture and presented as revealed truth about the Ṣaḥābah رضي الله عنهم.

1 *Tafsīr al-Ṣāfī*, vol. 1 p. 341.

Were The Ṣaḥābah Disunited?

Tījānī goes on to say:

> **It is well-known that the Companions were divided after the death of the Messenger of Allah. They disagreed among themselves to such an extent that they fought each other bloody wars which led to the regression and the backwardness of the Muslims and made them easy target for their enemies. The above Qur'anic verse could not be interpreted in any other way except that which is readily accepted by people.**[1]

There is no disunity to speak of among the Ṣaḥābah during the era of Abū Bakr رضي الله عنه nor in the era of ʿUmar رضي الله عنه. It is an accepted historical fact that the Ṣaḥābah رضي الله عنهم were responsible for keeping the tide of apostasy at bay through the *Riddah* wars. Were it not for their efforts then who knows what future Islam would have taken. Whose efforts expanded the Islamic territories? At whose hands did Allah grant victory in the East and West? Who was it that brought crushing defeat to the Roman and Persian empires? The fear for the Ṣaḥābah in the hearts of their enemies, and the humiliation they experienced, is an inescapable reality. This is a fact attested to by even the enemies of this Ummah.

For the sake of being fair I will present statements from the one considered the Waṣī of the Messenger صلى الله عليه وسلم by the Shīʿah. Let us witness his description of the state of the Ummah during the eras of the first two khulafā', Abū Bakr and ʿUmar رضي الله عنهما. I will restrict myself to some of the most important and reliable books of the Shīʿah, *Nahj al-Balāghah*, of Sharīf al-Raḍī and *al-Ghārāt* of al-Thaqafī.

ʿAlī ibn Abī Ṭālib رضي الله عنه recalls the occasion when he gave his pledge of allegiance to Abū Bakr رضي الله عنه:

> At that point I walked to Abū Bakr and gave him the *bayʿah* and dealt with those matters so that falsehood dissipates and vanishes. The word of Allah was elevated even if the disbelievers disliked it. Abū Bakr then took charge of the affairs. He combined forbearance with firmness, ease with moderation, and I accompanied him as an advisor and obeyed him as long as he obeyed Allah, striving hard.[2]

1 *Then I was guided*, p. 101.

2 al-Thaqafī: *Al-Ghārāt*, vol. 2 p. 305 and 307.

ʿAlī رضي الله عنه had the following to say about the second khalīfah, ʿUmar ibn al-Khaṭṭāb رضي الله عنه:

> For Allah is the effort of *fulān* (referring to ʿUmar). He straightened the curve, remedied the sickness, subdued mischief and established the Sunnah. He left with a clean slate and few faults. He attained the good of this world and escaped its evil. He fulfilled his obedience to Allah and feared Him as He deserved. He departed from this world leaving the people in varying paths, wherein the deviant is unable to attain guidance and the guided uncertain of his fate.[1]

What does Tījānī have to say about this? This is the Imām and Waṣī telling us what he thinks of Abū Bakr and ʿUmar, and the state of the Ummah during their reign. These are his words found in the books of the Shīʿah. Tījānī claims his transition came about after reaching inner conviction by reading a number of Shīʿī books including *Aṣl al-Shīʿah wa Uṣūlihā*. Let us read what Muḥammad ibn Ḥusayn Āl Kāshif al-Ghiṭā mentioned in his book when describing the reason for ʿAlī's رضي الله عنه bayʿah to the two khulafā':

> When he saw that the two khulafā', here I mean the first and the second, exerting all their energy in spreading tawḥīd, preparing armies, expanding the conquered territories; without claiming monopoly or being autocratic he gave his bayʿah and submitted.[2]

It was at the end of ʿUthmān's khilāfah when the fitnah[3] emerged because of the handiwork of a Jewish conspirator. ʿAbd Allāh ibn Saba', a Jew, instituted the belief that the Imāmah of ʿAlī رضي الله عنه was compulsory.[4]He is the source of extremist patronage for the Ahl al-Bayt.

After that, the civil wars followed one after the other. The protagonists being the Rāfiḍah at times and the Khawārij at others. As for the Ṣaḥābah, they had no hand in igniting the flame of *fitnah*. In this regard we find a notable Shīʿī scholar, al-Ṣadūq ibn Bābuwayh, narrating in his book *al-Khiṣāl* — from Hishām ibn Sālim — from Abū ʿAbd Allāh (al-Ṣādiq):

---

1 *Nahj al-Balāghah*, p. 509.

2 *Aṣl al-Shīʿah wa Uṣūlihā*, p. 132-133; Beirut: Dār al-Aḍwā.

3 This is reference to the civil strife which occurred during the fourth decade of Islam.

4 Ahead of those who came before him, Abū Bakr, ʿUmar and ʿUthmān رضي الله عنهم.

> The Companions of the Messenger ﷺ were twelve thousand, eight thousand from Madīnah, two thousand from Makkah and two thousand from the *Ṭulaqā'* (those who accepted Islam after the Conquest of Makkah). Not a single Qadarī, Murji'ī, *Ḥarūrī* (Khārijī), or Mu'tazilī, or person of vain desire, was seen amongst them. They cried during the night and day; and would say, "Take our souls before we eat the leavened bread."[1]

This is testimony from the books of the Shī'ah!

3. Tījānī's third proof for Qur'ānic Disparagement of Ṣaḥābah

Tījānī cites as a proof what he calls the verse of *khushū'* (lit. Humility):

أَلَمْ يَأْنِ لِلَّذِينَ آمَنُوا أَنْ تَخْشَعَ قُلُوبُهُمْ لِذِكْرِ اللَّهِ وَمَا نَزَلَ مِنَ الْحَقِّ وَلَا يَكُونُوا كَالَّذِينَ أُوتُوا الْكِتَابَ مِنْ قَبْلُ فَطَالَ عَلَيْهِمُ الْأَمَدُ فَقَسَتْ قُلُوبُهُمْ وَكَثِيرٌ مِنْهُمْ فَاسِقُونَ

Has not the time arrived for the Believers that their hearts in all humility should engage in the remembrance of Allah and of the Truth which has been revealed (to them), and that they should not become like those to whom was given Revelation before, but long ages passed over them and their hearts grew hard? For many among them are rebellious transgressors.[2]

In *al-Durr al-Manthur* by Jalal al-Din al-Suyuti, the author says: when the Companions of the Messenger of Allah ﷺ came to al-Medinah and started to enjoy a higher standard of living after having lived through many hardships, they seemed to slow down, so they were punished for that, and hence the verse "Has not the time yet come for those who believe" was revealed. Another version of the story, which came from the Prophet ﷺ, was that Allah- the Most High- found some reluctance in the Muhajereen seventeen years after the first revelation of the Holy Qur'an, and therefore Allah revealed the verse "Has not the time yet come for those who believe". If those Companions - who are the best people according to the Sunnis - did not feel humble before the name of Allah or His right revelation of seventeen

1 al-Qummī: *Al-Khiṣāl*.

2 Sūrah al-Ḥadīd: 16.

> **years, so that Allah found them slowing down, and rebuked and warned them for their hardened hearts which were leading them to corruption, we cannot blame the people of Quraysh who only entered Islam in the seventh Hijri year after the conquest of Makkah.[1]**

The first narration mentioned by Tījānī from *al-Durr al-Manthūr* of al-Suyūṭī, is a narration from A'mash and not attributed to the Prophet ﷺ at all. Al-Suyūṭī said:

> Ibn Mubārak, 'Abd al-Razzāq, and Ibn al-Mundhir quote A'mash as saying, "When the Ṣaḥābah of the Messenger ﷺ arrived in Madīnah they found prosperity after enduring gruelling hardships in the past. It was as if they had become too comfortable and were hence rebuked. Then the verse, "*has not the time arrived for the Believers...*"[2]

The narration is suspended on A'mash, who in addition to be known for *tadlīs* (concealing his source), is uncorroborated in this narration. The entire narration is therefore not the Prophet's ﷺ words as claimed by Tījānī. Let us also not forget Tījānī's distortion of the words in this narration since it is found in *al-Durr al-Manthūr* with the word 'rebuked'; but Tījānī distorted it by substituting it with the word 'punished' so that it aligns with his 'unbiased', 'sincere' search for guidance.

Tījānī's Distortions

This is what al-Suyūṭī had to say about the other narration quoted by Tījānī:

> Ibn Mardawayh narrated this narration from Anas. I am only aware of the Marfū' version of it where the Prophet ﷺ said, "Allah considered (the progress of) the hearts of the Muhājirīn slow after seventeen years since the revelation of the Qur'ān and therefore revealed the verse, "has not the time arrived for the Believers that their hearts in all humility should engage in the remembrance of Allah..."[3]

This narration quoted by Ibn Mardawayh from Anas رضي الله عنه is not found in any of the reliable books of Tafsīr. In addition to this it contradicts the sound narration recorded by Muslim in his *Ṣaḥīḥ* from 'Abd Allāh ibn Mas'ūd رضي الله عنه wherein he said:

1 *Then I was guided*, p. 101-102.

2 *Al-Durr al-Manthūr fī Tafsīr al-Ma'thūr*, vol. 6 p. 254.

3 *Al-Durr al-Manthūr fī Tafsīr al-Ma'thūr*, vol. 6 p. 253.

مَا كَانَ بَيْنَ إِسْلَامِنَا وَبَيْنَ أَنْ عَاتَبَنَا اللّٰهُ بِهَذِهِ الْآيَةِ (أَلَمْ يَأْنِ لِلَّذِيْنَ آمَنُوْا أَنْ تَخْشَعَ قُلُوْبُهُمْ لِذِكْرِ اللّٰهِ) إِلَّا أَرْبَعُ سِنِيْنَ

There were only four years between our Islam and Allah reprimanding us with this verse, "has not the time arrived for the Believers that their hearts in all humility should engage in the remembrance of Allah..."[1]

Ibn Mas'ūd رضي الله عنه was from the earliest in Islam and was more acquainted with the revelation of Qur'ān.

The narration of Ibn Mardawayh is therefore weak and anomalous. It has *Shudhūdh* (anomaly) since it contradicts the stronger narration of Ibn Mas'ūd; and has *Nakārah* (incongruity) because of Ibn Mardawayh being the only source to transmit it without any shāhid or mutābi'.[2]

I would like to bring to the attention of the respected reader that al-Suyūṭī recorded twenty narrations in total under this verse, including the narration of 'Abd Allāh ibn Mas'ūd رضي الله عنه. Regrettably Tījānī only noticed two; and resorted to distortion in one of them in order to give credence to his wanton commentary.

Citing al-Suyūṭī as reference was merely theatrics and window-dressing for his unsuspecting audience. It is known by the 'ulamā' that al-Suyūṭī applied no criteria of reliability in what he included in *al-Durr al-Manthūr* as he quotes weak and even fabricated narrations. The mere reference to this work does not indicate reliability.

Assuming that the two narrations cited by Tījānī were indeed authentic; Allah's words would simply be understood as an admonishment for the Ṣaḥābah, and an encouragement to increase in humility and to remain in constant fear of Allah سبحانه وتعالى The Ṣaḥābah رضي الله عنهم were certainly not infallible; and were subject to the elements of human nature like forgetfulness and temporal oversight.

Qur'ān Encourages Ṣaḥābah

You might remember that earlier I mentioned that the Qur'ān was revealed to train

1 *Ṣaḥīḥ Muslim ma'a Sharḥ*, vol. 18, The Chapter of Tafsīr, Ḥadīth no. 3027.

2 A term used by ḥadīth scholars for particular types of corroborating reports.

the Ṣaḥābah for the task of taking leadership, and to encourage them towards good, and forbid them from vice. Ibn Masʿūd رضي الله عنه says:

> Whenever you hear Allah saying, "O you who believe," then harken to it as it is either good being commanded, or evil prohibited.[1]

The verse we are currently discussing was revealed to rekindle the Ṣaḥābah's spirit; and to encourage them towards humility. Further, it informs them of the Jews and the Christians who were afflicted with hardness of the hearts with the passing of lengthy passages of time. Hardheartedness overcame them due to insufficient remembrance of Allah and resulted in them becoming sinful. This verse came to warn the Ṣaḥābah of the laxness of this path so as they might avoid it.

This, without doubt, is considered part of their training. If rebuking them was not permitted they would be considered angels and not human beings.

The Prophet صلى الله عليه وسلم was even rebuked, as seen in the story of Ibn Umm Maktūm رضي الله عنه. The verse, "He [the Prophet] frowned and turned away,"[2] was subsequently revealed. If Allah's rebuking the Ṣaḥābah is considered a disparagement, then what will Tījānī say about Allah's سبحانه وتعالى rebuke of the Prophet صلى الله عليه وسلم?

The Qur'ān was revealed to teach the Prophet صلى الله عليه وسلم and guide him.

Allah سبحانه وتعالى says:

يَاأَيُّهَا النَّبِيُّ اتَّقِ اللّٰهَ وَلَا تُطِعِ الْكَافِرِيْنَ وَالْمُنَافِقِيْنَ

O Messenger, fear Allah and do not obey the disbelievers and the hypocrites. Indeed, Allah is ever Knowing and Wise.[3]

فَإِنْ كُنْتَ فِي شَكٍّ مِمَّا أَنْزَلْنَا إِلَيْكَ فَاسْأَلِ الَّذِيْنَ يَقْرَءُوْنَ الْكِتَابَ مِنْ قَبْلِكَ

So if you are in doubt, [O Muḥammad], about that which We have revealed to you, then ask those who have been reading the Scripture before you.[4]

1 al-Suyūṭī: *Al-Itqān*, vol. 2 p. 92-93.
2 Sūrah ʿAbasa: 1.
3 Sūrah al-Aḥzāb: 1.
4 Sūrah Yūnus: 95.

What will Tījānī say about the Prophet ﷺ? We have already demonstrated the repercussions of disregarding the principles of Qur'ānic interpretation.[1]

In conclusion I reiterate what I previously stated, that ʿAlī رضي الله عنه praised the Ṣaḥābah when teaching and rebuking his disciples. He encouraged them to take the Ṣaḥābah as an example when he said:

> Indeed, I have seen the Ṣaḥābah of Muḥammad ﷺ and I do not see anyone amongst you who resembles them. They would rise in the morning, unkempt and covered with dust, because they had spent the night in prostration and standing. They would alternate between their foreheads and their cheeks.

In addition to the statement of Jaʿfar al-Ṣādiq when he described the Ṣaḥābah of the Messenger ﷺ with his words:

> They would wake up dishevelled and pass the night in prostration and standing alternating between their foreheads and their cheeks.[2]

If this is how the Imāms described the Ṣaḥābah; what objectivity has Tījānī displayed in his critical analysis of them?

In closing I leave you with the words of Ḥasan al-ʿAskarī, the eleventh infallible Imām of the Shīʿah. He said about those who hate the Ṣaḥābah:

> ان رجلا ممن يبغض آل محمد و اصحابه الخيرين و واحدا منهم لعذبه الله عذابا لو قسم على مثل عدد خلق الله تعالى لأهلكهم اجمعين
>
> Surely a man who hates the family of Muḥammad ﷺ and his Ṣaḥābah, the best two and even one of them, Allah will inflict upon them such a punishment that if it were to be dispersed amongst the entire creation it would destroy them all.[3]

---

1 Refer to p. 130 of this book.

2 Ibid.

3 *Tafsīr al-Ḥasan al-ʿAskarī*, p. 157, under the words of Allah, "And they said, 'Our hearts are wrapped.'" (Sūrah al-Baqarah: 88)

Chapter Four

1. Tījānī's claim that the Prophet صَلَّى ٱللَّٰهُ عَلَيْهِ وَسَلَّمَ Dispraised the Ṣaḥābah

Tījānī commences this chapter with a discussion around a Ḥadīth which the Shīʿah commonly refer to as the Ḥadīth of the *Ḥawḍ* (Pond):

> **The Messenger of Allah صَلَّى ٱللَّٰهُ عَلَيْهِ وَسَلَّمَ said: As I was standing, there came a group of people whom I recognized, and a man stood between the group and myself, then said: "Let us go." I said, "Where to?" He said, "To Hell, by Allah!" I asked, "What have they done?" He answered, "They turned back after you had departed, and I expect only a few will reach salvation."**
>
> **The Messenger of Allah صَلَّى ٱللَّٰهُ عَلَيْهِ وَسَلَّمَ also said:**
>
>> **I shall arrive at the pool before you, and he who passes by me will drink, and whoever drinks from it will never feel thirsty. There will come to me people that I know and they know me, but we shall be separated, then I shall say, "My companions". An answer shall come, "You do not know what they did after you left." Then I shall say, "Away with those who changed after me."**
>
> **When we look deeply at the various sayings that have been referred to by the Sunnis in their books, we will have no doubt that most of the Companions changed or even became apostates after the departure of the Messenger of Allah, except a few who were considered to be the minority. The above sayings could not be applied to the third type [of Companions], for they were the hypocrites, and the text states: I shall say, "My companions."[1]**

Refuting Tījānī's claim that the Prophet صَلَّى ٱللَّٰهُ عَلَيْهِ وَسَلَّمَ Dispraised the Ṣaḥābah

There are a number of fundamental elements which cannot be compromised in any objective research project. One of these key features is the reliability and accuracy of the collected data. Another element is faithful representation of that data. I leave it to the reader to assess Tījānī's adherence to these principles in his citing of these narrations, as well as his interpretations thereof.

---

1 *Then I was guided*, p. 103.

Tījānī's distortion of text

Neither of the two versions of the Ḥadīth which Tījānī referenced to the *Ṣaḥīḥ* collections of al-Bukhārī or Muslim are worded as such in those collections. As a matter of fact, the first ḥadīth cited by Tījānī appears to have been distorted and truncated. We have come to notice a recurring pattern of misdirection and manipulation of data in Tījānī's assessment of text in the past chapters; and he has not failed in maintaining that consistency here as well.

The complete narration in *Ṣaḥīḥ al-Bukhārī* as reported by Abū Hurayrah رضي الله عنه from the Prophet صلى الله عليه وسلم is reproduced below:

> بينا أنا نائم إذا زمرة حتى إذا عرفتهم خرج رجل من بيني وبينهم فقال هلم فقلت أين ؟ قال إلى النار والله قلت وما شأنهم ؟ قال إنهم ارتدوا بعدك على أدبارهم القهقرى . ثم إذا زمرة حتى إذا عرفتهم خرج رجل من بيني وينهم فقال هلم قلت أين ؟ قال إلى النار والله قلت ما شأنهم ؟ قال إنهم ارتدوا بعدك على أدبارهم القهقرى فلا أراه يخلص منهم إلا مثل همل النعم
>
> While I was sleeping, a group were brought close to me, and when I recognised them, a man (an angel) emerged between me and them, and said to them, "Come along." I asked, "Where?" He said, "To the Hell-Fire, by Allah." I asked, "What is wrong with them?" He said, "They turned back after you left." Then behold! Another group were brought close to me, and when I recognised them, a man (an angel) emerged between me and them. He said (to them), "Come along." I asked, "Where?" He said, "To the Hell-Fire, by Allah." I asked, "What is wrong with them?" He said, "They turned back after you left." So I did not see anyone of them escaping except a few who were like camels without a shepherd.[1]

Notice the word *Nā'im* (sleeping) which appears in al-Bukhārī has been substituted for the word *Qā'im* (standing) in Tījānī's citation of the Ḥadīth.

The misdirection does not end here. Tījānī referenced the Ḥadīth to both al-Bukhārī and Muslim. The Ḥadīth under discussion is found only in al-Bukhārī; Muslim does not narrate it!

Yes, such aḥādīth are recorded in the reliable Ḥadīth books of the Ahl al-Sunnah. Tījānī, however; conveniently ignores the explanation offered by the Ahl al-Sunnah

1 *Ṣaḥīḥ al-Bukhārī*, vol. 5, Kitāb al-Raqā'iq, Ḥadīth no. 6215.

throughout the centuries. Instead he applies his oblique approach to understanding texts; completely disregarding the prescribed framework of interpretation. For the sake of fairness it is my duty to present the explanations given by the Ahl al-Sunnah on this ḥadīth.

Sunnī interpretation of these Aḥādīth

The scholars have offered a number of explanations on the meaning of the word Riddah as well as the intended party mentioned in the ḥadīth. Some scholars have said that they are the people of innovation and heretical tendencies.

Qabīṣah says, "They are those who turned apostate during the era of Abū Bakr and remained upon disbelief until they were killed or died upon it."

Al-Khaṭṭābī says, "Not a single Ṣaḥābī turned apostate. The only ones to turn apostate were from the Bedouin Arabs who did not assist the religion at all; and that does not imply criticism against the well-known Ṣaḥābah."

Ibn Ṭīn says, "It is possible that they are the munāfiqīn or those who committed major sins."[1]

Ibn Ḥajar says, "It has been said that they are a group from the Bedouin Arabs who had not wholeheartedly entered into Islam."[2]

Further he says, "It has been said that they are the perpetrators of major sins and bidʿah but died upon Islam."

Imām al-Nawawī says, "This is from those matters about which the scholars differ. It has been said that they are the munāfiqīn apostates, it has also been said that they are those were in the era of the Prophet صَلَّى ٱللَّٰهُ عَلَيْهِ وَسَلَّمَ then turned apostate after him."[3]

At another place he says, "It has also been said that those intended are the perpetrators of major sins and crimes who died upon tawḥīd; and also the people of bidʿah but remained within the fold of Islam."[4]

1 *Fatḥ al-Bārī*, vol. 11 p. 393.

2 Ibid.

3 *Ṣaḥīḥ Muslim maʿa al-Sharḥ*, vol. 3 p. 173.

4 *Ṣaḥīḥ Muslim maʿa al-Sharḥ*, vol. 3 p. 173.

Imām Ibn ʿAbd al-Barr says, "Each person who innovated in the religion will be of those repelled from the Ḥawḍ; such as the Khawārij, the Rawāfiḍ, and all other people of heretical tendencies."[1]

Abū Isḥāq al-Shāṭibī says, The most plausible interpretation is that it refers to individuals of this Ummah. This is because of the identifying features of *ghurrah* and *taḥjīl* (a radiance that will appear on the limbs washed during wuḍū') which will not be seen on the disbelievers. It is inconsequential whether their disbelief was from the outset or subsequent apostasy.

Furthermore, the words, "they changed after you", were used in the ḥadīth. Had reference been made to disbelief, the words "they disbelieved after you", would have been used. The most accurate manner of understanding it is that they substituted the Sunnah. This applies aptly to the people of innovation. If one applied the meaning to the hypocrites it would also be plausible since the hypocrites adopted the religion to conceal their beliefs; not for the sake of worship. In so doing they have substituted true religion for alternative matters; this is the essence of innovation.

This clearly establishes that those intended by the words 'turning back' were the hypocrites and innovators. Therefore, it is evident that the Ṣaḥābah were not intended in the ḥadīth.

In order to further demonstrate Tījānī's bigotry I will present the writings of the Shīʿah, since even they have inadvertently demonstrated some objectivity in this matter.

Shīʿī scholars do not apply it to Ṣaḥābah

Under his commentary of the verse:

فَأَمَّا الَّذِينَ اسْوَدَّتْ وُجُوهُهُمْ أَكَفَرْتُم بَعْدَ إِيمَانِكُمْ

As for those whose faces turn black, [to them it will be said]: "Did you disbelieve [i.e., reject faith] after your belief?"

Faḍl al-Ṭabarsī writes in *Majmaʿ al-Bayān*, "They differ concerning who is intended..." He then mentions four views, the last of them being:

1 Ibid.

> They are the people of bid'ah and heretical tendencies from this Ummah...

As proof for the fourth view he cites the Ḥadīth of the Ḥawḍ:

> The fourth view is that they are the people of innovations and dissension from this Ummah, as reported from 'Alī رضي الله عنه. A similar view is ascribed to Qatādah with the addition of those who apostatised. It has been related from the Prophet صلى الله عليه وسلم that he said, "By He in whose control lays my soul, people from those who accompanied me will come to me at the Ḥawḍ. When I see them they will be prevented from approaching and I will say, 'My companions!' It will then be said, 'You do not know what they innovated after you. They turned on their heels.' Al-Tha'labī mentions in his Tafsīr that Abū Umāmah al-Bāhilī said, "They are the Khawārij and it has been transmitted from the Prophet صلى الله عليه وسلم that they will pierce through Islam like an arrow pierces through prey."[1]

This is al-Ṭabarsī's commentary of this ḥadīth—that they were the people of bid'ah like the Khawārij—which conforms entirely to the interpretation of the Ahl al-Sunnah. Note that he did not imply in any way that it referred to the Ṣaḥābah of the Prophet صلى الله عليه وسلم.

Al-Kāshānī comments on this verse, citing this ḥadīth as a proof that the people of bid'ah and heretical tendencies are referred to in it. He says:

> In *al-Majma'* it is reported from Amīr al-Mu'minīn ('Alī) that they are the people of innovation, dissension and false views from this Ummah. It is reported from the Prophet صلى الله عليه وسلم that he said, "By He in whose control lays my soul, people from those who accompanied me will come to me at the Ḥawḍ. When I see them they will be prevented from approaching and I will say, 'My companions!' It will then be said, 'you do not know what they innovated after you. They turned on their heels.'". Al-Tha'labī mentions it in his *Tafsīr*.[2]

The Shī'ah have unjustly criticised the Ṣaḥābah at many places in their Qur'ānic exergies, yet despite their animosity and condemnable allegations they have not understood this ḥadīth to apply to the Ṣaḥābah. Tījānī does not cite the interpretation given by the Shī'ah since they did not give the slightest indication of it applying to the Ṣaḥābah.

---

1 *Majma' al-Bayān*, vol. 2 p. 160-162.

2 *Tafsīr al-Ṣāfī*, vol. 2 p. 162.

Thus we safely establish that the ḥadīth does not refer to them. The Ṣaḥābah were not apostates, nor innovators who followed heretical beliefs. Once again we refer the honourable reader to the discussion on the division of the Ṣaḥābah.

Shīʿī imāms exonerate Ṣaḥābah

If any further doubt remains regarding the Ṣaḥābah being free from any form of innovation and *irtidād* (apostasy); I will now present statements from the likes of ʿAlī ibn Abī Ṭālib رضي الله عنه and other 'Infallible' Imāms as recorded in Shīʿī sources which exonerate the Ṣaḥābah رضي الله عنهم from these outlandish allegations.[1]

We find the likes of Zayn al-ʿĀbidīn[2] praising the Companions of the Messenger صلى الله عليه وسلم, seeking mercy and forgiveness for them in his supplications. This positive attitude towards them is acknowledgement of their support for the Prophet صلى الله عليه وسلم and their contribution to the spread of Islam.[3]

---

1 Refer to Chapter 1 p. 28-29 and Chapter 3 p. 148 onwards of this book.

2 The reader will notice that the narrations quoted from the Twelver Shīʿah are often self-contradictory. It is barely possible to find a narration from an Imām except that you will find another which contradicts it. This inconsistency and self-contradiction merely affirms the claim of fabrication within the Shīʿī tradition. Surprising still is their own confession of these contradictions.

Muḥammad al-Ṭūsī said in the introduction to his book *Tahdhīb al-Aḥkām* (p. 45), one of the four relied-upon books of the Twelver Shīʿī school:

> All praise is for Allah, the owner of praise and the one deserving of it. Salutations upon the choicest of his creation, Muḥammad صلى الله عليه وسلم. A friend of mine, may Allah strengthen him, reminded me about the phenomenon of contradictory aḥādīth to the point where there is hardly a report except that there is another which contradicts it or is in conflict with it.
>
> This has allowed our opponents to level some of the greatest criticisms against our school to the point where they falsify our beliefs.

3 They say that our scholars, past and present, continue to criticise their opponents on the premise of the differences amongst them in matters of worship, and they (Shīʿī scholars) attack them on account of their differences also in the furūʿ (subsidiary matters)...

Here they mean that the Ahl al-Sunnah disagree in the subsidiary (legal) matters with which there is latitude. Shīʿī scholars say it is not permissible to worship Allah in light of the aforementioned differences. That being said, we find them in a position worse than that of their opponents since these difference are meant to be preserved by infallibles. Furthermore, these differences are in the essential beliefs rather than in the subsidiary matters. The differences among the narrations within the Sunnī legacy can be resolved through various modes of reconciliation; whereas the contradictions within the Shīʿī tradition are irreconcilable as acknowledged by Shīʿī scholars themselves. All of this is an undeniable proof that the source of their narrations is not one. *continued ...*

This is part of a supplication rendered by ʿAlī ibn Ḥusayn Zayn al-ʿĀbidīn in ṣalāh:

> ... And include them in Your forgiveness and pleasure. O Allah, especially the Ṣaḥābah of Muḥammad ﷺ who were excellent companions, who endured great hardships in supporting him, who stood by his side and welcomed him eagerly. They hastened to his call, and surrendered to him when he conveyed the proof of his message. They endured the pain of separation from their wives and children in promoting his message, and fought their fathers and sons to affirm his Prophethood and through him were victorious. Their love for him was pure and intense and they anticipated great reward on account of it. They are the ones whose families ostracised them when they held firm onto his rope and whose relationships were annulled when they remained in the shadow of his relationship. Do not forget, O Allah, what they sacrificed for Your sake. Grant them Your divine pleasure because they were with Your Messenger. They were callers towards You. Compensate them for abandoning the homes of their people for Your sake, and for forsaking prosperity for narrowness of life. Grant them this because of the many who were oppressed for the establishment of your religion.
>
> O Allah, grant the greatest of Your rewards to those who followed in their way; those who say O Allah, forgive us and our brothers who preceded us in faith;

---

continued from page 160

A leading Shīʿī scholar, Dildār al-Lakhnawī, says in his book *Asās al-Uṣūl* on page 51:

> The aḥādīth transmitted from the Imāms vary considerably. It is hard to find a ḥadīth except that there is another contradicting it to the extent that it caused some to turn away from the true belief.

This is the school of the Twelver Shīʿah Indeed, Allah speaks the truth when he says:

إِنَّكُمْ لَفِيْ قَوْلٍ مُّخْتَلِفٍ يُؤْفَكُ عَنْهُ مَنْ أُفِكَ قُتِلَ الْخَرَّاصُوْنَ

> Indeed, you are in differing speech. Deluded away from it [i.e. the Qur'ān] is he who is deluded. Destroyed are the falsifiers. (Sūrah al-Dhāriyāt: 7-10)

They say at one place that the Ṣaḥābah are disbelievers while at another they say they are the best of people. Likewise, they say at one place that fasting on the day of ʿĀshūrā is a major sin and at another that it is of the best of deeds (refer to *Wasā'il al-Shīʿah* by al-Ḥurr al-ʿĀmilī, vol. 5; The Chapter of Fast; p. 337-339). Similarly, they say that the Qur'ān is distorted at one place, then deny any distortion occurred at another place, then they claim to have uncovered a new Qur'ān. Likewise, sometimes they say that mutʿah (temporary marriage) is a good deed and at other times they say that only the worst of people practice it (refer to *Wasā'il al-Shīʿah*, vol. 14; The Chapter of Marriage; p. 456).

> those who pursued their example and strove to tread their path, following in their footsteps; not doubting, being steered by the light of their guidance, accepting their teachings as religion, and being led by their guidance. Send your rewards to those who do not dispute about them and do not accuse them falsely. O Allah, send salutations upon those who follow them (the Ṣaḥābah) from this day to the Day of Judgement, and upon their wives and families, and upon those who obey You. Send such a salutation which will safeguard them from Your disobedience and extend for them (their abodes) in Your gardens of Paradise and save them from the scheme of Shayṭān...[1]

The most senior Shīʿī scholar of ḥadīth, al-Kulaynī produces the following narration in his book, *Uṣūl al-Kāfī*: [2]

> Manṣūr Ibn Ḥāzim narrates, "I asked Imām Jaʿfar al-Ṣādiq, 'Why is it that when I ask you concerning a matter you respond to me with an answer then someone else comes to you (with the same question) and you respond to him with another answer?'
>
> He said, 'We respond to the people with additions and omissions.'
>
> I then said, 'Tell me about the Companions of the Messenger صَلَّى ٱللَّٰهُ عَلَيْهِ وَسَلَّمَ; were they honest concerning Muḥammad صَلَّى ٱللَّٰهُ عَلَيْهِ وَسَلَّمَ or did they lie concerning him?'
>
> He said, 'Rather, they were honest.'
>
> I said, 'Why do they differ concerning them?'
>
> He replied, 'Do you not know that a man would come to the Prophet صَلَّى ٱللَّٰهُ عَلَيْهِ وَسَلَّمَ and he would respond to him with an answer then he would give him an answer which abrogated that answer. In that way the ḥadīth, some abrogated others.'[3]

Imām Ḥasan al-ʿAskarī, the eleventh Imām, in the *Tafsīr* attributed to him, elaborates on a communication between Mūsā عَلَيْهِ ٱلسَّلَامُ and his Lord during which some questions were asked. This is one of the questions asked by Mūsā عَلَيْهِ ٱلسَّلَامُ:

---

1 Imām Zayn al-ʿĀbidīn: *Al-Ṣaḥīfah al-Kāmilah al-Sajādiyyah*, p. 26-27; Published in Irān, Mu'assasah Anṣāriyān.

2 Refer to *al-Murājaʿāt* of ʿAbd al-Ḥusayn al-Mūsawī, p. 334.

3 *Uṣūl al-Kāfī*, vol. 1 p. 52; The Chapter on the Virtues of Knowledge. *Uṣūl al-Kāfī* is one of the four books considered to be the chief resources for the fundamental and subsidiary matters of the Twelver school.

"Is there anyone nobler than my companions in previous nations?"

Allah said, "O Mūsā, do you not know that the superiority of the Companions of Muḥammad ﷺ over the companions of other Messengers is like the superiority of the family of Muḥammad over all the families of other prophets; and like the superiority of Muḥammad ﷺ over all other prophets."[1]

He also said:

Indeed a (single) man from the prominent Companions of the best Prophet ﷺ would outweigh all the companions of other prophets عليهم السلام if weighed against them.[2]

After all of these explanations it becomes clear to the reader that the noble Ṣaḥābah رضي الله عنهم were innocent of apostasy or turning on their heels according to both Sunnī scholars, and the Imāms of the Shīʿah. All that remains is the charge of bidʿah and heretical beliefs.

Al-Qummī writes in *al-Khiṣāl*—from Hishām ibn Sālim—from Imām Jaʿfar who said:

The Companions of the Messenger ﷺ were twelve thousand, eight thousand from Madīnah, two thousand from Makkah and two thousand from the *Ṭulaqā'* (those who accepted Islam after the Conquest of Makkah). Not a single Qadarī, Murjiʿī, *Ḥarūrī* (Khārijī), or Muʿtazilī, or person of vain desire, was seen amongst them. They cried during the night and day; and would say, "Take our souls before we eat the leavened bread."[3]

From this we learn that the Ṣaḥābah رضي الله عنهم are exonerated from the charge of bidʿah by the Imāms of the Ahl al-Bayt in the narrations found in the books of leading Shīʿī scholars. It appears that Tījānī could not conceal his bias no matter how often he assured us that his point of departure was from a position of neutrality and impartiality.

Further responses to Tījānī's reasoning

There are a few more elements in Tījānī's argument that require attention. Let us begin with his insinuation from the word *aṣḥābī* (my companions) in the ḥadīth.

---

1 *Tafsīr al-Ḥasan al-ʿAskarī*, p. 11; Sūrah al-Fātiḥah.

2 Ibid. al-Baqarah: 88; p. 157.

3 al-Qummī: *Kitāb al-Khiṣāl*, p. 239-240; Chapter 12.

He asserts that this is proof that those prevented from the Ḥawḍ are none other than the Ṣaḥābah of the Messenger صلى الله عليه وسلم. This interpretation is farfetched since it ignores the need to harmonise between the various narrations of this ḥadīth. An intelligent person would be consistent in his speech and the only way to understand him objectively is to reconcile all the various wordings used so that the intended party becomes clear. We are left with no choice but to analyse the various expressions found in the ḥadīth in order to accurately determine who is intended by the word aṣḥābī in this context.

The word Ṣaḥābah is general and unrestricted in its application in language. Through convention it later became associated with the Companions of the Prophet صلى الله عليه وسلم. However, the Prophet صلى الله عليه وسلم did not qualify the meaning of this word nor did he define its application. Since the conventional understanding of this word cannot be applied to the ḥadīth retrospectively, the only plausible meaning is that it refers to anyone whom the Prophet صلى الله عليه وسلم had seen or met.[1]

There is no debate about the fact that the Prophet صلى الله عليه وسلم had seen the munāfiqīn, and was aware of them during his lifetime. Similarly those Bedouin Arabs who later turned apostate were seen by him too. This undeniable fact clarifies the position of those who understood the ḥadīth to apply to the subsequent apostates and hypocrites.

Variant wordings in the Aḥādīth

Imām Aḥmad and al-Ṭabarānī transmit a ḥadīth which is narrated with an acceptable chain from Abū Bakrah رضي الله عنه that the Prophet صلى الله عليه وسلم said:

> Men from those who accompanied me and saw me will come to me at the Ḥawḍ.[2]

Al-Bukhārī and Muslim transmit narrations in which the Messenger of Allah صلى الله عليه وسلم mentioned those prevented from the Ḥawḍ using the diminutive form of the noun.

Anas رضي الله عنه relates that the Prophet صلى الله عليه وسلم said:

1 *Minhāj al-Sunnah al-Nabawiyyah*, vol. 8 p. 387.

2 Refer to *Fatḥ al-Bārī*, vol. 11 p. 393.

ليردن على الحوض رجال ممن صاحبنى حتى إذا رأيتهم ورفعوا إلى اختلجوا دونى فلأقولن أى رب أصيحابى أصيحابى.فليقالن لى إنك لا تدرى ما أحدثوا بعدك

Men from amongst those who accompanied me will come to me at the Ḥawḍ. When I see them and they approach me they will be obstructed and I will say, "O Lord, Uṣayḥābī! Uṣayḥābī! (In each instance the diminutive form of the noun is used)." It will be said to me, "Indeed, you do not know what they innovated after you."[1]

This further clarifies what is meant in the additions found in other narrations which read, "They are from my Ummah," and in another, "Men from amongst you," and in yet another, "A group (from amongst you)".

It is therefore incorrect to interpret the meaning of the ḥadīth in light of the wording of one narration alone, which in itself does not give credence to the meaning promoted by Tījānī. Citing one ḥadīth and ignoring all other variant wordings displays a lack of objectivity and academic discretion.

As for the Messenger's ﷺ statement in the ḥadīth that "he recognised them", it does not mean, necessarily, that he knew them personally. Rather, it means that he recognised them through some distinguishing features possessed by them as clarified by the ḥadīth of Abū Hurayrah in *Ṣaḥīḥ Muslim* wherein the Messenger of Allah ﷺ said:

ترد على أمتى الْحوض وأنا أذود الناس عنه كما يذود الرجل إبل الرجل عن إبله قالوا يا نبى الله أتعرفنا قال نعم لكم سيما ليست لأحد غيركم تردون على غرا محجلين من آثار الوضوء وليصدن عنى طائفة منكم فلا يصلون فأقول يا رب هؤلاء من أصحابى فيجيبنى ملك فيقول وهل تدرى ما أحدثوا بعدك

"My Ummah will come to me at the Ḥawḍ and I will ward off people from it like a man wards off the camels of another man from his camels."

They (the companions) said, "O Messenger of Allah, will you recognise us?"

1 *Ṣaḥīḥ Muslim maʿa Sharḥ*, Ḥadīth no. 2304, vol. 15; *Ṣaḥīḥ al-Bukhārī*, The Chapter of Riqāq, Ḥadīth no. 2611.

> He said, "Yes, you will have distinguishing features that others besides you will not have. You will come to me *c*[1] from the effects of wuḍū'. A group from amongst you will be obstructed and will not reach me and I will say, 'O Lord, my Companions!' An angel will respond to me and say, 'Do you know what they did after you?'"[2]

This ḥadīth implies that even the people of innovation and hypocrisy will be raised with the distinguishing marks of radiance from the limbs washed during Wuḍū'.

The word *minkum* (from amongst you) in the ḥadīth implies that all of them will be resurrected with the same distinguishing marks of the believers as it comes in the ḥadīth of the *Ṣirāṭ* (the Bridge) in which he said, "and this Ummah will remain, amongst them the munāfiqīn..."[3]

The abovementioned ḥadīth points to the fact that the munāfiqīn will be resurrected with the believers.

After this detailed explanation we can confidently assert that it is irrational to conclude that the Ṣaḥābah will be the ones prevented from the Ḥawḍ based on the ḥadīth for the following reasons:

The Prophet ﷺ was pleased with them and defended them. He ﷺ said:

> خير الناس قرني ثم الذين يلونهم ثم الذين يلونهم ثم يجيء أقوام تسبق شهادة أحدهم يمينه ويمينه شهادته
>
> The best people are those living in my generation, and then those who will follow them, and then those who will follow the latter. Then there will come some people who will bear witness before taking oaths, and take oaths before bearing witness.[4]

In this ḥadīth the Prophet ﷺ affirms the superiority of the Ṣaḥābah over all the subsequent generations.

1 These words refer to the light which emanate from the limbs of wuḍū' on the Day of Judgement.

2 *Ṣaḥīḥ Muslim ma'a Sharḥ*, vol. 3, Ḥadīth no. 247, The Chapter of Ṭahārah.

3 *Al-Fatḥ*, vol. 11, p. 393.

4 *Ṣaḥīḥ al-Bukhārī*, vol. 3, The Chapter concerning the virtues of the Ṣaḥābah, Ḥadīth no. 3451, from ʿAbd Allāh ibn Masʿūd.

Muslim relates a ḥadīth from Abū Burdah, from his father, that the Prophet ﷺ raised his head to the heavens and said:

النجوم أمنة للسماء فإذا ذهبت النجوم أتى السماء ما توعد وأنا أمنة لأصحابي فإذا ذهبت أتى أصحابي ما يوعدون وأصحابي أمنة لأمتي فإذا ذهب أصحابي أتى أمتي ما يوعدون

> The stars are a source of security for the sky and when the stars disappear there comes to the sky, (i.e. it meets the same fate) as it has been promised (it would plunge into darkness). And I am a source of safety and security to my Ṣaḥābah and when I would go away there would fall to the lot (of my Ṣaḥābah) what they have been promised and my Ṣaḥābah are a source of security for the Ummah and as they would go there would fall to the lot of my Ummah what (its people) have been promised.[1]

Al-Nawawī says in his *Sharḥ Muslim*:

> "My Ṣaḥābah are a source of security for the Ummah and as they would go there would fall to the lot of my Ummah what (its people) have been promised," it refers to the appearance of bidʿah and innovations in the religion and sedition in it, the emergence of the horns of Shayṭān, the victory of the Romans and others over the Muslims, and the violation (of the sanctity) of Makkah and Madīnah and other places. This is from his miracles (his prophecies which came to pass).[2]

In addition to the narrations above the Prophet ﷺ gave glad tidings of Jannah to some Ṣaḥābah during their lifetimes.

ʿAbd al-Raḥmān ibn ʿAwf رضي الله عنه said that the Messenger ﷺ said:

أبو بكر في الجنة وعمر في الجنة وعثمان في الجنة وعلي في الجنة وطلحة في الجنة والزبير في الجنة وعبد الرحمن بن عوف في الجنة وسعد في الجنة وسعيد في الجنة وأبو عبيدة بن الجراح في الجنة

> Abū Bakr is in Jannah, ʿUmar is in Jannah, ʿUthmān is in Jannah, ʿAlī is in Jannah, Ṭalḥah is in Jannah, Zubayr is in Jannah, ʿAbd al-Raḥmān ibn ʿAwf is

---

1 *Ṣaḥīḥ Muslim maʿa Sharḥ*, vol. 16, The chapter concerning the virtues of the Ṣaḥābah, Ḥadīth no. 2531.

2 op. cit, p. 125.

> in Jannah, Sa'd (ibn Abī Waqqāṣ) is in Jannah, Sa'īd (ibn Zayd) is in Jannah, and Abū 'Ubaydah ibn al-Jarrāḥ is in Jannah.[1]

Imām Aḥmad narrates from Jābir ibn 'Abd Allāh رَضِيَ ٱللَّهُ عَنْهُ that the Prophet صَلَّى ٱللَّهُ عَلَيْهِ وَسَلَّمَ said:

> The man who witnessed Badr and Ḥudaybiyyah will never enter the Fire.[2]

Also, the Prophet صَلَّى ٱللَّهُ عَلَيْهِ وَسَلَّمَ passed away while being pleased with the Ṣaḥābah رَضِيَ ٱللَّهُ عَنْهُمْ.

It has also never been proven that any of the Muhājirīn or the Anṣār became apostate.

Imām 'Abd al-Qādir al-Baghdādī says in his book *al-Farq bayn al-Firaq*:

> The Ahl al-Sunnah are unanimous in that those who turned apostate after the Prophet's صَلَّى ٱللَّهُ عَلَيْهِ وَسَلَّمَ death were from Kindah, Ḥanīfah, Fazārah, Banū Asad, and Banū Bakr ibn Wā'il. None of them were from the Muhājirīn or the Anṣār; who accepted Islam before the Conquest of Makkah.
>
> They also agree that the title of Muhājirīn is only for those who migrated before the Conquest of Makkah and that they, through the grace of Allah, remained upon the straight path.[3]

An intelligent person is always understood to be coherent and consistent in what he says or does. Tījānī's assertions imply, by necessity, that the Prophet صَلَّى ٱللَّهُ عَلَيْهِ وَسَلَّمَ contradicted himself. Anyone who buys into Tījānī's ridiculous idea is actually accepting that the Prophet صَلَّى ٱللَّهُ عَلَيْهِ وَسَلَّمَ was incoherent, inconsistent, and self-contradictory in his speech. How else would the Prophet صَلَّى ٱللَّهُ عَلَيْهِ وَسَلَّمَ give glad tidings of Paradise to the Companions yet predict that they would be chased from his Ḥawḍ in the Hereafter?

Al-Ṭabarānī transmits a ḥadīth with an acceptable chain of narrators from Abū al-Dardā' رَضِيَ ٱللَّهُ عَنْهُ that he asked the Prophet صَلَّى ٱللَّهُ عَلَيْهِ وَسَلَّمَ afterwards:

---

1 *Sunan al-Tirmidhī*, The book of Manāqib, The chapter about 'Abd al-Raḥmān ibn 'Awf; Refer also to *Ṣaḥīḥ al-Tirmidhī*, Ḥadīth no. 2947.

2 *Musnad Aḥmad*, vol. 5, Ḥadīth no. 15262, p. 213; Refer also to *al-Silsilah al-Ṣaḥīḥah*, vol. 5, Ḥadīth no. 2160.

3 *Al-Farq bayn al-Firaq*, p. 318-319.

I said, "O Messenger of Allah ﷺ, pray to Allah that I am not amongst them!"

He said, "You are not amongst them."[1]

Did the Prophet ﷺ not know the condition of Abū al-Dardā'? Did he pray for him only that he turns out to be an apostate?

If the Prophet ﷺ was not aware of the conditions of the Ṣaḥābah in the Hereafter he would not have said about Abū Bakr رضي الله عنه, his closest, most honoured, and beloved Companion:

أنت عتيق الله من النار

You are Allah's *'Atīq* (one who is emancipated) from the Fire.[2]

And about 'Umar رضي الله عنه he said:

دخلت الجنة فإذا أنا بقصر من ذهب فقلت لمن هذا القصر قالوا لشاب من قريش فظننت أني أنا هو فقلت ومن هو فقالوا عمر بن الخطاب

I entered Jannah and I was before a palace of gold. So I said, "Whose palace is this?"

They said, "A youth from the Quraysh."

So I thought that I was him. I asked, "And who is he?"

They said, "'Umar ibn al-Khaṭṭāb."[3]

And about 'Uthmān رضي الله عنه he said:

You are in Jannah.[4]

Over 80 of the Ṣaḥābah رضي الله عنهم including Abū Hurayrah رضي الله عنه narrate the Ḥadīth of the Ḥawḍ. If they were renegades and apostates why would they bother to narrate

1 Refer to *Fatḥ al-Bārī*, vol. 11, p. 393.

2 *Sunan al-Tirmidhī*, The book of virtues, Ḥadīth no. 3679; Refer also to *Ṣaḥīḥ al-Tirmidhī*, Ḥadīth no. 2905, from 'Ā'ishah رضي الله عنها.

3 *Sunan al-Tirmidhī*, The book of virtues, Ḥadīth no. 3688, from Anas; Also refer to *Ṣaḥīḥ al-Tirmidhī*, Ḥadīth no. 2911; And refer to *Bukhārī* for a similar narration, Ḥadīth no. 3476.

4 See p. 167 of this book.

this ḥadīth of the Messenger ﷺ after his demise since it would implicate them in the first degree?

Let us for a moment assume the plausibility of Tījānī's interpretation. The ḥadīth that he has cited is general which means all the Companions ought to be included. If all are subject to inclusion it stands to reason that even those Companions with whom the Prophet ﷺ was pleased according to Tījānī's definition like ʿAlī ibn Abī Ṭālib, Ḥasan, Ḥusayn, ʿAmmār ibn Yāsir, Abū Dharr al-Ghifārī, Salmān al-Fārisī, Miqdād ibn Aswad, Khuzaymah ibn Thābit, and Ubayy ibn Kaʿb all deserve to be included. The onus is upon Tījānī to provide proof for the exclusion of the aforesaid Companions. If he says that the Prophet ﷺ has mentioned virtues of these Companions which preclude them; our response is simply that the other Companions also have virtues which preclude them.

As for the statement, "You do not know what they innovated after you," it is an accepted fact that the Ṣaḥābah did not substitute or innovate after the death of the Prophet ﷺ. Sayyid Muḥammad Ṣiddīq Ḥasan al-Qanūjī says in his book *al-Dīn al-Khāliṣ*:

> A Rāfiḍī asked a Sunnī, "What do you say concerning the Ṣaḥābah?"
>
> He replied, "I say about them what Allah says about them in his book when he says:
>
> رَضِيَ اللّٰهُ عَنْهُمْ وَرَضُوْا عَنْهُ
>
> Allah being pleased with them; and they with Him.
>
> The Rāfiḍī then said, "Indeed, they innovated after the Prophet ﷺ."
>
> The Sunnī then said, "Allah says:
>
> وَمَا بَدَّلُوْا تَبْدِيْلًا
>
> And they did not alter [the terms of their commitment] by any alteration.
>
> And we do not believe in a Lord who informs about something not knowing that things would change thereafter."

Tījānī's claim that "most of the Ṣaḥābah substituted and changed"

Tījānī said, "Most of the Ṣaḥābah substituted and changed (things within the religion), rather, most of them turned apostate after him except for a few who he referred to as *Haml al-Naʿam*."

Refuting Tījānī's claim that "most of the Ṣaḥābah substituted and changed

Tījānī is finding it increasingly difficult to hide bigotry. His failure to comprehend the Prophet's ﷺ words reveal to us his myopia when processing information. The words "*Haml al-Naʿam*" refer to those who came close to the Ḥawḍ in that vision and nearly reached it but were obstructed from it. It does not refer to everyone who came to the Ḥawḍ.

In another narration the word *rahṭ* [group] is used. Abū Hurayrah رضي الله عنه narrates that the Prophet ﷺ said:

يرد على يوم القيامة رهط من أصحابي فيحلئون عن الحوض فأقول يا رب أصحابي فيقول إنك لا علم لك بما أحدثوا بعدك إنهم ارتدوا على أدبارهم القهقرى

> A *rahṭ* [group] from my companions will come to me on the Day of Judgement but they will be prevented from the Ḥawḍ and I will say, "O my Lord, my companions!" He will say, "Indeed you have no knowledge about what they innovated after you. Indeed they turned on their heels after you."[1]

The word Rahṭ, as everyone is aware, refers to a group of men who do not exceed ten in number.[2]

Lastly, I say: Tījānī wants us to arrive at a particular conclusion. That conclusion is that majority of the Ṣaḥābah رضي الله عنهم turned apostate. But what are the implications of arriving at such a conclusion? It implies that this dīn, which we have been practicing for the last fourteen centuries, this Qur'ān with us today, the Sunnah which we attempt to emulate, the ṣalāh, the pillars of the dīn which we have established in our lives and any other act of worship in general; all of the aforementioned is incorrect as it was transmitted to us via apostates.

1 *Ṣaḥīḥ al-Bukhārī* with *Fatḥ al-Bārī*, vol. 11 p. 473, Ḥadīth no. 6585.

2 *Mukhtār al-Ṣiḥāḥ*, p. 109.

This also means that the '*murtaddīn*' [apostates] who conquered the lands of the East and subjugated the lands of the West did so not to humble people to the worship of Allah but to enter them into the door of apostasy.

This also means that Musaylamah al-Kadhdhāb, Sajāḥ, and others were the people of the truth as they did not turn murtadd from Islam but rather turned away from the people of apostasy.

2. Tījānī on the Companions competing for worldly motives

Tījānī says:

> **The Messenger of Allah ﷺ said:**
>
> > **I lead you and am your witness, and by Allah I now look at my pool and have been given the keys to the treasures of the earth [for the earth's keys], and by Allah I am not worried that you become polytheist after me, but I am worried that you will compete for it.**
>
> **The Messenger of Allah ﷺ was right. They competed for this world to the extent that they fought against each other, and each party accused the other of blasphemy. Some of the famous Companions were eager to collect gold and silver, and historians such as al-Masudi in Muruj al-Dhahab and al-Tabari and others stated that the wealth of al-Zubayr on its own came to fifty thousand Dinars and a thousand horses with one thousand slaves and many holdings in Basra, al-Kufa, Egypt and many other places.**
>
> **The agricultural products from Iraq alone brought Talhah one thousand Dinars every day, and perhaps more than that.**
>
> **Abdul Rahman ibn Awf had one hundred horses, one thousand camels and ten thousand sheep. After his death, quarter of his wealth which was divided among his wives came to eighty four thousand Dinars.**
>
> **Uthman ibn Affan left on the day of his death one hundred and fifty thousand Dinars apart from an enormous wealth of land, cattle and villages.**
>
> **Zayd ibn Thabit left an amount of gold and silver that had to be broken by hammers! Apart from money and agricultural holdings which came to one hundred thousand Dinars..**
>
> **These were just a few historical examples. Since we do not want to go into detailed analysis of their importance at the moment, we only mention them**

> **as a proof and support of the sayings, that they [these companions] were more interested in the present life.[1]**

Refuting Tījānī on the Companions competing for worldly motives

I am still trying to find any indication in this ḥadīth that portrays a number of Ṣaḥābah رضي الله عنهم with ownership of abundance of wealth or worldly possessions. The ḥadīth informs us that in the future this Ummah would own the treasures of this world and that people will compete with one another in it. This is from the miracles of the Messenger صلى الله عليه وسلم and sign of Prophethood that he prophesized future events that came to be.

That being said, the ḥadīth does not apply to the Ṣaḥābah رضي الله عنهم as they never owned the treasures of the world.

In addition to the above, the fighting which took place among them did not occur on account of competing for the petty wealth of this world, but on account of the fitnah which occurred as a result of the murder of ʿUthmān, even though they did not intend to fight one another.

In general, each of the two groups will be rewarded for its *Ijtihād* (scholarly discretion) on the matter. More clarity will be given concerning this topic later in this book.

Incoherence in Tījānī's reasoning

Without realizing it Tījānī proves that the Ṣaḥābah رضي الله عنهم were not apostates. Whatever arguments he presented in the previous section, are responded to by evidence that he has furnished. In the previous discussion he claimed that the majority of the Ṣaḥābah turned apostate; yet here he cites a ḥadīth which clearly states that the Messenger صلى الله عليه وسلم did not fear apostasy for his Ṣaḥābah رضي الله عنهم. Rather, he feared that they would compete with one another in worldly things.

Again, without realizing he implies criticism against ʿAlī ibn Ṭālib رضي الله عنه and his companions as the (verb used in the) ḥadīth is in its plural form, *tanāfasū ʿalā al-dunyā* (they competed with one another in worldly things), which includes both sides. In fact, Tījānī admits to that when he says:

---

1 *Then I was guided*, p. 105.

The Messenger of Allah ﷺ was right. They competed for this world to the extent that they fought against each other, and each party accused the other of blasphemy.

It is an accepted fact that the fighting which took place was between Ṭalḥah and Zubayr's رضي الله عنهما army against ʿAlī's رضي الله عنه army. By accepting the apparent meaning of the ḥadīth he has to concede that both sides were at fault (as the verb in the ḥadīth is in the plural form as mentioned before).

The corollary of this line of argument is that ʿAlī ibn Abī Ṭālib competed for wealth, leadership and power by fighting his adversaries. Allah forbid.

He goes on to say:

Some of the famous Companions were eager to collect gold and silver.

There is no doubt that wealth which the Ṣaḥābah رضي الله عنهم owned does not warrant dispraise or reprimand. The accomplishments of these noble Companions—who are accused of hoarding their wealth—clearly establish that they were from the choicest of the Ṣaḥābah رضي الله عنهم.

Ṣaḥābah's spending

To demonstrate ties let us take the example of the third Khalīfah', ʿUthmān ibn ʿAffān رضي الله عنه, who was among the closest people to the Messenger ﷺ, and extremely generous. ʿAbd al-Raḥmān ibn Samurah رضي الله عنه said about him:

عن عبد الرحمن بن سمرة قال جاء عثمان إلى النبي صلى الله عليه وسلم بألْف دينار قال الحسن بن واقع وكان في موضع آخر من كتابي في كمه حين جهز جيش العسرة فنثرها في حجره قال عبد الرحمن فرأيت النبي صلى الله عليه وسلم يقلبها في حجره ويقول ما ضر عثمان ما عمل بعد اليوم مرتين

ʿUthmān went to the Messenger ﷺ with one thousand dīnārs. Ḥasan ibn Wāqiʿ (one of the narrators) said, "And in another place in my book, 'went to the Messenger ﷺ with one thousand dīnārs in his garment,'" when the 'army of difficulty' (during the expedition of Tabūk) was being prepared. So he poured them into the Messenger's ﷺ lap." ʿAbd al-Raḥmān said, "So

I saw the Messenger ﷺ turning them over in his lap, saying, 'Whatever 'Uthmān does after today will not harm him,' he said it twice."[1]

The Messenger ﷺ once said:

من يحفر بئر رومة فله الجنة فحفرها عثمان

Whoever digs the well of Rūmah will be rewarded with Jannah. (The narrator of the ḥadīth says,) "'Uthmān then dug it."[2]

We can clearly see that ʿUthmān رضي الله عنه used his wealth in the obedience of Allah سبحانه وتعالى and His Messenger ﷺ.

Similarly, Ṭalḥah ibn ʿUbayd Allāh رضي الله عنه was given the glad tidings of Jannah by the Prophet ﷺ.[3] He was also from those who strove in the path of Allah, defending the Messenger ﷺ during the Battle of Uḥud which resulted in his hand becoming paralysed.

Zubayr رضي الله عنه said:

عن الزبير قال كان على رسول الله صلى الله عليه وسلم يوم أحد درعان فنهض إلى صخرة فلم يستطع فأقعد تحته طلحة فصعد النبي صلى الله عليه وسلم حتى استوى على الصخرة فقال سمعت النبي صلى الله عليه وسلم يقول أوجب طلحة

On the Day of Uḥud, the Messenger of Allah ﷺ wore two coats of mail. He tried to get up on a boulder, but was not able to, so Ṭalḥah squatted under him, lifting the Messenger ﷺ upon it, such that he could sit on the boulder. So he said: "It (Paradise) is obligatory for Ṭalḥah."[4]

Ṭalḥah رضي الله عنه used to fear sleeping the night after he had gathered a bit of wealth. Ṭalḥah ibn Yaḥyā رضي الله عنه reports that Saʿdā bint ʿAwf al-Mariyyah, the wife of Ṭalḥah رضي الله عنه, said:

---

1 *Sunan al-Tirmidhī*, Kitāb Al-Faḍā'il, bāb Faḍā'il ʿUthmān ibn ʿAffān, Ḥadīth no. 3701; Also refer to *Ṣaḥīḥ al-Tirmidhī*, Ḥadīth no. 2920.

2 *Ṣaḥīḥ al-Bukhārī*, Kitāb al-Waṣāyā, bāb idhā waqafa arḍ wa bi'r, Ḥadīth no. 2626.

3 Refer to p. 167 of this book.

4 *Sunan al-Tirmidhī*, Kitāb al-Manāqib, bāb Ṭalḥah ibn ʿUbayd Allāh, Ḥadīth no. 3738; Refer also to *Ṣaḥīḥ al-Tirmīdhī*, Ḥadīth no. 2939.

> I went to Ṭalḥah one day while he was dreary. I said, "What is the matter? Is there something about your family that is unsettling you?"
>
> He said, "No, you are a good wife. I have some wealth that is bothering me."
>
> I said, "What about it bothers you? Divide it amongst your people."
>
> He said (to his servant), "Call my people!" He then divided it amongst them.
>
> I asked the treasurer, "How much did he give?" and he said, "Four hundred thousand."[1]

Ḥasan al-Baṣrī said that Ṭalḥah ibn ʿUbayd Allāh رضي الله عنه sold a piece of land which he owned for seven hundred thousand. That night he could not sleep. The next morning he woke up and dispersed the wealth.

As for Zubayr ibn al-ʿAwwām رضي الله عنه, the Messenger صلى الله عليه وسلم gave him the glad tidings of Jannah.[2] He was also the *ḥawārī*[3] of the Messenger صلى الله عليه وسلم.

ʿAlī ibn Abī Ṭālib رضي الله عنه narrates that the Messenger of Allah صلى الله عليه وسلم said:

> عن علي بن أبي طالب رضى الله عنه قال قال رسول الله إن لكل نبي حواريا وإن حواري الزبير بن العوام
>
> Indeed, every Messenger has a Ḥawārī, and my Ḥawārī is Zubayr ibn al-ʿAwwām.[4]

Is it possible for one who has excessive love for wealth, and desires to horde gold and silver, that he would impart the following advice on his death bed? He urged his son, ʿAbd Allāh ibn Zubayr رضي الله عنه to cover his debts just before his death. Al-Bukhārī transmits a ḥadīth from ʿAbd Allāh ibn Zubayr رضي الله عنه, who said:

> عبد الله بن الزبير، رضي الله عنهما، قال: لما وقف الزبير يوم الجمل دعاني فقمت إلى جنبه، فقال: يا بني إنه لا يقتل اليوم إلا ظالم أو مظلوم ،وإني لا أرانى إلا سأقتل اليوم مظلوما، وإن من أكبر همي لديني، أفترى ديننا يبقي

---

1 *Siyar Aʿlām al-Nubalāʾ*, Imām al-Dhahabī, vol. 1 p. 32; The muḥaqqīq of the book said: "Its narrators are reliable."

2 This ḥadīth has been cited before on p. 167 of this book.

3 Ḥawārī: it has been said that its meaning is the one suitable for leadership, or it means minister, or helper, or the sincere one. Refer to *al-Fatḥ*, vol. 7 p. 100.

4 *Ṣaḥīḥ al-Bukhārī*, vol. 3 p. 32, Ḥadīth no. 3514; See also *Tirmidhī*, vol. 5, Ḥadīth no. 3744.

من مالنا شيئًا؟ ثم قال: يا بني بع مالنا واقض ديني، وأوصى بالثلث وثلثه لبنيه، يعني لبني عبد الله بن الزبير ثلث الثلث. قال فإن فضل من مالنا بعد قضاء الدين شيء فثلثه لبنيك ، قال هشام : وكان بعض ولد عبد الله قد وازى بعض بني الزبير خبيب وعباد، وله يومئذ تسعة بنين وتسع بنات. قال عبد الله : فجعل يوصيني بدينه ويقول: يا بنى إن عجزت عن شيء منه فاستعن عليه بمولاي. قال فوالله ما دريت ما أراد حتى قلت: يا أبت من مولاك؟ قال: الله. قال: فوالله ما وقعت في كربةٍ من دينه إلا قلت: يا مولى الزبير اقض عنه دينه، فيقضيه

When Zubayr, got ready to fight in the Battle of al- Jamal, he called me and said, "My son, whoever is killed today will be either a wrongdoer or a wronged one. I expect that I shall be the wronged one today. I am much worried about my debts. Do you think that anything will be left over from our property after the payment of my debt?"

He then said, "My son, sell our property and pay off my debts."

Zubayr then willed one-third of that portion to his sons; namely ʿAbd Allāh's sons. He said, "One-third of the one-third. If any property is left after the payment of debts, one-third (of the one-third that is left) is to be given to your sons."

(Hishām, a sub-narrator added, "Some of the sons of ʿAbd Allāh were equal in age to the sons of Zubayr, e.g. Khubayb and ʿAbbād. ʿAbd Allāh had nine sons and nine daughters at that time.")

He kept on instructing me about his debts and then said, "My son, should you find yourself unable to pay any portion of my debt then beseech my Master for His help."

By Allah, I did not understand what he meant and asked, "Father, who is your Master?"

He said, "Allah."

By Allah! Whenever I faced a difficulty in discharging any portion of his debt; I would pray, "O Master of Zubayr, discharge his debt," and He discharged it.[1]

1 Ibid. vol. 3, Kitāb Farḍ al-Khumus, Ḥadīth no. 2961.

ʿAbd al-Raḥmān ibn ʿAwf رضي الله عنه was a noble Ṣaḥābī to whom the Messenger صلى الله عليه وسلم gave the glad tidings of Jannah. He had the honour of the Messenger صلى الله عليه وسلم praying behind him.[1] In addition he took the responsibility of overseeing the spending on the wives of the Messenger صلى الله عليه وسلم after his demise. ʿĀ'ishah رضي الله عنها said that the Messenger صلى الله عليه وسلم used to say:

> عن عائشة أن رسول الله صلى الله عليه وسلم كان يقول إن أمركن مما يهمني بعدي ولن يصبر عليكن إلا الصابرون قال ثم تقول عائشة فسقى الله أباك من سلسبيل الجنة تريد عبد الرحمن بن عوف وقد كان وصل أزواج النبي صلى الله عليه وسلم بمال بيعت بأربعين ألفا
>
> Indeed your affair [referring to his wives] is from that which concerns me after I am gone. None shall bear this responsibility except the patient ones.
>
> Then ʿĀ'ishah said to Abū Salamah, "May Allah give your father drink from the Salsabil (a fountain) of Paradise."
>
> Referring to ʿAbd al-Raḥmān ibn ʿAwf (Abū Salamah is the son of ʿAbd al-Raḥmān ibn ʿAwf). And he had seen to the finances of the Prophet's صلى الله عليه وسلم wives with property that had been sold for four hundred thousand.[2]

Abū Salamah says:

> عن أبي سلمة أن عبد الرحمن بن عوف أوصى بحديقة لأمهات المؤمنين بيعت بأربعمائة ألف
>
> ʿAbd al-Raḥmān ibn ʿAwf left a garden for the Ummahāt al-Mu'minīn that was sold for four hundred thousand.[3]

This is ʿAbd al-Raḥmān ibn ʿAwf رضي الله عنه who, Tījānī claims, was greedy for gold and silver.

As for the Ṣaḥābī Zayd ibn Thābit رضي الله عنه, he was one of the four who collected the (entire) Qur'ān during the Prophet's صلى الله عليه وسلم life.

---

1 This ḥadīth has been cited before on p. 167-168.

2 *Sunan al-Tirmidhī*, Kitāb Al-Faḍā'il, Ḥadīth no. 3749; See also *Ṣaḥīḥ al-Tirmidhī*, Ḥadīth no. 2983.

3 Op. cit, Ḥadīth no. 3750; See also *Ṣaḥīḥ al-Tirmidhī*, Ḥadīth no. 2949.

Anas رضي الله عنه said:

جمع القرْآن على عهد رسول الله صلى الله عليه وسلم أربعة كلهم من الأنصار معاذ بن جبل وأبى بن كعب وزيد بن ثابت وأبو زيد

> Four persons collected the Qur'ān during the lifetime of Allah's Messenger ﷺ and all of them were of the Anṣār: Muʿādh ibn Jabal, Ubayy ibn Kaʿb, Zayd ibn Thābit, and Abū Zayd.[1]

Al-Bukhārī narrates with his chain to al-Barā' ibn ʿĀzib رضي الله عنه who said that the Messenger ﷺ said:

ادع لي زيدا وليجئ باللوح والدواة والكتف أو الكتف والدواة ثم قال اكتب لا يستوي القاعدون

> Call Zayd for me and let him bring the board, the inkpot and the scapula bone (or the scapula bone and the ink pot).
>
> Then he said: "Write: 'Not equal are those believers who sit...'"[2]

He was also one of those whom Abū Bakr رضي الله عنه recommended for the job of compiling the Qur'ān during his Khilāfah, and about whom the Messenger ﷺ said:

> The most learned in the field of inheritance is Zayd ibn Thābit.[3]

These are the Ṣaḥābah رضي الله عنهم; loved by the Prophet ﷺ but reviled by Tījānī. They are the ones whose honesty, integrity, and moral conduct was attested to by the Messenger ﷺ. All of their actions were in their acquisition of the pleasure of Allah and Jannah.

Tījānī's sources

Tījānī could only find material from a historian who is not from the Ahl al-Sunnah.

Al-Masʿūdī is *majrūḥ* (discredited) according to the Ahl al-Sunnah. Ibn Ḥajar writes in the biography of al-Masʿūdī in his book *Lisān al-Mīzān*:

---

1 *Sunan al-Tirmidhī*, Kitāb Al-Faḍā'il, Ḥadīth no. 3794; See also: *Ṣaḥīḥ al-Tirmidhī*, Ḥadīth no. 2983.

2 *Ṣaḥīḥ al-Bukhārī*, Kitāb Al-Faḍā'il al-Qur'ān, bāb Jamʿ al-Qur'ān, Ḥadīth no. 4701.

3 *Siyar Aʿlām al-Nubalā'*, vol. 2 p. 431, The muḥaqqiq states in the margin, "Its chain is sound."

> His books are replete with proofs that he was a Shīʿī Muʿtazilī.[1]

Ibn Taymiyyah said about his book, *Murūj al-Dhahab*:

> In the *Tārīkh* of al-Masʿūdī are so many lies that none besides Allah can encompass them.

Therefore, Tījānī's citing of al-Masʿūdī as his source is another disappointment since it is compromised by prejudice and bias. Al-Qummī, one of the senior scholars of the Shīʿah, mentions al-Masʿūdī in his book *al-Kunā wa l-Alqāb*, confirming that he was a Shīʿī and not of the Ahl al-Sunnah:

> He was the shaykh of the historians and their pillar of reliance. He is Abū al-Ḥasan ʿAlī ibn al-Ḥusayn ibn ʿAlī al-Masʿūdī, al-Hudhalī... Ibn Muṭahhar al-Ḥillī, mentions him in the first section of al-Khulāṣah and said, "He authored a book in the discipline of Imāmah among other works, which include a book affirming the Waṣiyyah to ʿAlī ibn Abī Ṭālib. He is the author of *Murūj al-Dhahab*..." ʿAllāmah al-Majlisī says in the introduction of *al-Biḥār*, "Masʿūdī: Al-Najāshī counts him, in his *al-Fihrist*, amongst the Shīʿī transmitters."[2]

Even though Tījānī quotes from Murūj what he believes to be disparagement of ʿUthmān, he conveniently omitted what al-Masʿūdī was unable to conceal:

> ʿUthmān was a man of the highest levels of generosity, kindness, forbearance, and spending on the near and distant relatives. His governors and many people of his era followed his example and emulated him in his actions.[3]

It is the preconceived resentment and prejudice which leads Tījānī to deception and concealment of the truth. Tījānī cited al-Masʿūdī as reference for his claim that an eighth of ʿAbd al-Raḥmān ibn ʿAwf's wealth, which was distributed among his wives, amounted to 84 000. This detail could not be found in *al-Murūj* despite prolonged efforts and continuous searching.

In conclusion, Tījānī says:

---

1 Refer to *Minhāj al-Sunnah*, vol. 4, p. 85.

2 al-ʿAbbās al-Qummī: *Al-Kunā wa l-Alqāb*, vol. 3 p. 175, publisher: Maktabah al-Ṣadr: Irān, and in the publication of Intishārāt p. 153.

3 al-Masʿūdī: *Murūj al-Dhahab*, vol. 2 p. 332, publisher: Dār al-Andalus: Beirut.

> **These were just a few historical examples. Since we do not want to go into detailed analysis of their importance at the moment, we only mentions them as a proof and support of the sayings ...**

All I can say about this 'reassuring' claim is that I hope in future Tījānī finds more 'corroborating proofs' so that we, and the readers, are not conveniently fed selected bits of information!

Chapter Five

Tījānī's claims that the Ṣaḥābah Vilified One Another

1. The Ḥadīth of Abū Saʿīd al-Khudrī on ʿĪd prayers

Tījānī says:

> **Abu Saeed al-Khudari said: On the first days of 'Id al-Fitr [breaking the fast of Ramadan] and 'Id al-Adha [celebrating the end of the Pilgrimage], the first thing the Messenger of Allah صلى الله عليه وسلم used to do was to say his prayers in the mosque, then he went to see the people, who sat in rows in front of him, and then he started to deliver advice or orders or even finalize outstanding issues, and after all that he would leave. Abu Saeed added: The situation continued to be like that, until one day, either Fitr or Adha, I went with Marwan, who was the governor of al-Medinah. When we arrived at the mosque, which had a new pulpit built by Kathir ibn al-Salt, Marwan headed for the pulpit (before praying), so I pulled him by his clothes, but he pushed me and went up on to the pulpit. He addressed the people before he prayed, so I said to him, "By Allah you have changed it." He replied, "O Abu Saeed, what you know has gone." I said, "By Allah, what I know is better than what I do not know." Marwan then said, "People did not sit for us after the prayers, so I put [it] before the prayers."**
>
> **I looked for the reasons which led those Companions to change the Sunnah [the tradition] of the Messenger of Allah صلى الله عليه وسلم...[1]**

Refuting Tījānī's claim from the Ḥadīth of Abū Saʿīd al-Khudrī on ʿĪd prayers

Tījānī attempts to give credence to his sweeping claim by citing the Ḥadīth of Abū Saʿīd al-Khudrī رضي الله عنه. This narration is meant to prove that it was common for the Ṣaḥābah رضي الله عنهم to vilify one another.

The reader will notice that the person whose actions are criticized in this narration is Marwān. Before proceeding any further it is important to establish whether Marwān was a Companion in the technical sense to begin with. It is illogical to make a sweeping statement of the Ṣaḥābah vilifying one another if one of the parties in a particular incident is not a Ṣaḥābī.

---

1 *Then I was guided*, p. 105.

The scholars have debated the status of Marwān; whether he is a Ṣaḥābī or not. Shams al-Dīn al-Dhahabī—who is considered one of the greatest historians and ḥadīth experts—considers Marwān from the Tābiʿīn and not from amongst the Ṣaḥābah رضي الله عنهم.[1] At the time of the Messenger's صلى الله عليه وسلم demise he had not yet reached puberty, he was barely 10 years old.

It is highly unethical and greatly misleading to throw allegations at the entire spectrum of the Ṣaḥābah if an isolated incident involves a Ṣaḥābī and Tābiʿī. What a misleading heading, "*Their testifying against themselves that they altered the Sunnah*."

Look at the extent of the prejudice and bias in Tījānī's accusation. Can any fair-minded, objective, intelligent person still accept that this 'journey of guidance' began from a position of impartiality and neutrality?

If one refers to the original Arabic of Tījānī's book the plural form is used to emphasize the dispute, thus insinuating that all the Companions were at each other's throats condemning, criticizing and vilifying each other. What a dishonest representation of reality!

Tījānī's unqualified expression in the original Arabic gives rise to another perplexing situation as the allegation does not exempt any of the Ṣaḥābah from blame. The allegation thus includes those whom they accept as righteous Ṣaḥābah; such as ʿAlī ibn Abī Ṭālib, Abū Dhar, and ʿAmmār ibn Yāsir رضي الله عنهم. On what basis can they be excluded from the rest of the Companions?

If the issue of ʿĪd prayer was something contested so greatly that 'they testified against themselves that they altered the Sunnah', how do we account for the ḥadīth which appears immediately after the one cited by Tījānī? Is there any indication of the Sunnah being altered in this narration?

Ibn ʿAbbās رضي الله عنه says:

شهدت العيد مع رسول الله صلى الله عليه وسلم وأبي بكر وعمر وعثمان ـ رضى الله عنهم ـ فكلهم كانوا يصلون قبل الخطبة

> I offered the ʿĪd prayer with the Messenger of Allah صلى الله عليه وسلم, Abū Bakr, ʿUmar, and ʿUthmān; all of them offered the prayer before delivering the Khuṭbah.[2]

---

1 *Siyar Aʿlām al-Nubalā'*, vol. 3 p. 476.

2 *Ṣaḥīḥ al-Bukhārī*, vol. 1, Kitāb al-ʿĪdayn, Ḥadīth no. 920.

Let us assume for a moment some actions of the Ṣaḥābah did not conform exactly with what Tījānī considers to be Sunnah, this does not warrant any blame as they were not infallible. It is not impossible that their Ijtihād on a particular matter leads them to a conclusion that does not represent the Sunnah entirely. This would not be considered disregard for the Sunnah since we know from their practise they would retract their opinion if it became clear to them that it was in conflict with the Sunnah.

For the sake of brevity let us limit the examples which demonstrate the haste in which the Ṣaḥābah رضي الله عنهم and Tābiʿīn retracted their rulings based on Ijtihād in favour of opinions aligned with the Sunnah when they were made aware of it.

Al-Shāfiʿī says:

> Someone who I trust related to me—from Ibn Abī Dhi'b—from Makhlad ibn Khafāf—who said, "I bought a slave and earned revenue through him. Later, a defect of his came to my attention and I took the matter to ʿUmar ibn ʿAbd al-ʿAzīz who decreed that I may return it (to the original owner) but that I return the revenue received. I then went to ʿUrwah (ibn Zubayr) and informed him (about ʿUmar's decree). He then said, "I am going to him this afternoon. I will inform him that ʿĀ'ishah رضي الله عنها related to me from the Messenger صلى الله عليه وسلم that he ruled in a matter similar to this (and said):
>
> الخراج بالضمان
>
> Profit belongs to the one who bears responsibility.
>
> I then hastened to ʿUmar and informed him about what ʿUrwah had related to me from ʿĀ'ishah رضي الله عنها, from the Messenger صلى الله عليه وسلم. ʿUmar then said, "This is easier for me than a decree which I gave. O Allah! Surely you know that I did not intend thereby (my decree) except the truth. Then a Sunnah from the Messenger صلى الله عليه وسلم reached me so I overruled the decree of ʿUmar and executed the Sunnah of the Messenger صلى الله عليه وسلم."ʿUrwah then went to him and he decreed that I take revenue from the one who he decreed I should give it to.[1]

The details of this incident are not the major concern here. What is majorly significant is the readiness on the part of ʿUmar ibn ʿAbd al-ʿAzīz to retract his verdict in favour of a Sunnah which reached him from the Messenger صلى الله عليه وسلم.

1 *Iʿlām al-Mūqiʿīn ʿan Rabb al-ʿĀlamīn*, Ibn Qayyim al-Jawzī, vol. 2 p. 200.

Zayd ibn Thābit رضي الله عنه considered it prohibited for a menstruating woman to return home before performing *Ṭawāf al-Wadāʿ* (Final Ṭawāf of Ḥajj). He and ʿAbd Allāh ibn ʿAbbās رضي الله عنهما debated this matter. Eventually, ʿAbd Allāh ibn 'Abbās رضي الله عنه said to him, "If you do not accept my opinion on the matter then ask so-and-so woman from the Anṣār if the Messenger صلى الله عليه وسلم instructed her with that." Zayd رضي الله عنه then returned laughing and said, "You have spoken the truth." A similar narration appears in *Ṣaḥīḥ al-Bukhārī*.[1]

We have previously established that Ahl al-Sunnah do not regard the Ṣaḥābah رضي الله عنهم infallible. The reactions of the Ṣaḥābah رضي الله عنهم in situations such as these indicate their enthusiasm and unrelenting zeal for the Sunnah. It is absurd to assert otherwise.

Marwān's decisions appear to be motivated by Ijtihād. However they were not in conformity with the Sunnah, which resulted in Abū Saʿīd's رضي الله عنه stern objection. If anything, it shows the extent to which the Companions were attentive towards the observance of the Sunnah.

There are a few cases where even ʿAlī ibn Abī Ṭālib رضي الله عنه issued certain *fatāwā* (legal opinions) which were not considered in harmony with the Sunnah.

We present, as an example, his fatwā that the ʿiddah of a pregnant woman will continue until the later of childbirth or prescribed waiting period.

A woman who has been divorced, or whose husband passed away, must undergo a waiting period called ʿiddah. The waiting period differs between divorce and death of husband. A divorced woman must wait for the duration of three menstrual cycles or three periods of cleanliness between her cycles; whereas a woman whose husband has passed away will wait for four months and ten days. If a woman is pregnant before her ʿiddah, the ʿiddah will terminate upon childbirth. The established Sunnah of the Prophet صلى الله عليه وسلم is that the ʿiddah terminates on childbirth.

Similarly, ʿAlī رضي الله عنه issued a fatwā that the dowry [*mahr*] of a woman assigned the power of divorce [*mufawwaḍah*] is void upon death; whereas Ibn Masʿūd رضي الله عنه and others held that she is entitled to the equivalent mahr of her peers. Their ruling is on account of a ḥadīth from the Messenger صلى الله عليه وسلم when he ruled on the matter of Burūʿ bint Wāshiq.

1 Op. cit. vol. 2 p. 203.

The Ahl al-Sunnah love and revere ʿAlī ibn Abī Ṭālib رضي الله عنه. The reason for presenting these cases is not to detract from his lofty status. Rather it is to demonstrate that ʿAlī ibn Ṭālib رضي الله عنه exercised his Ijtihād, but appears to have not coincided with the Sunnah. He will never be accused of changing the Prophet's Sunnah. The Ahl al-Sunnah would look for plausible reasons for his Ijtihād not aligning with the Sunnah; perhaps the ḥadīth on this issue did not reach him.

The approach used by the Ahl al-Sunnah is comprehensive, fair, and consistent. Matters are accounted for in a plausible manner that accurately reflects reality.

Compare that with the wanton approach of a college teacher, untrained in the Islamic sciences who objects to the action of a single Tābiʿī in an error of Ijtihād; seizing that opportunity to criticise the entire fraternity of Ṣaḥābah. In the process, an isolated incident of rectification is inflated into a distorted portrait of reality. Is this anything but the result of an anarchist attitude towards established history?

2. Tījānī's claim that the Ṣaḥābah Altered the laws of Ṣalāh

Tījānī says:

> **Anas ibn Malik said: I knew nothing during the lifetime of the Prophet صلى الله عليه وسلم better than the prayer. He said: Have you not lost what you have lost in it?**
>
> **Al-Zuhri said: I went to see Anas ibn Malik in Damascus, and found him crying, I asked him, "What is making you cry?" He answered, "I have known nothing but these prayers and they have been lost."**
>
> **I would like to make it clear that it was not the followers who implemented the changes after all the intrigues and civil wars; rather it was the caliph Uthman who first made changes in the Prophet's tradition regarding the prayers. Also Umm al-Mumineen Aishah was involved in these changes. Al-Bukhari and Muslim both stated in their books that the Messenger of Allah صلى الله عليه وسلم performed two prayers at Mina, and Abu Bakr after him, then Umar; and Uthman who later performed four prayers.**
>
> **Muslim also stated in his book that al-Zuhri asked 'Urwah, "Why did Aishah complete her prayers during the journey?" He answered, "She improvised in the same way as Uthman did."[1]**

---

1 *Then I was guided*, p. 109.

Refuting Tījānī's claim that the Ṣaḥābah Altered the laws of Ṣalāh

Tījānī's referencing

Tījānī combines two aḥādīth into one. The first ḥadīth is narrated by Mahdī—from Ghaylān—from Anas ibn Mālik رضي الله عنه who said:

ما أعرف شيئا مما كان على عهد النبي صلى الله عليه وسلم.قيل الصلاة. قال أليس ضيعتم ما ضيعتم فيها

"I do not recognize anything as they were at the time of the Prophet ﷺ."

Somebody asked, "The prayer?"

Anas said, "Have you not wasted it as is done now?"[1]

The second ḥadīth is from 'Uthmān ibn Abī Rawwād, the brother of 'Abd al-'Azīz who said:

سمعت الزهري، يقول دخلت على أنس بن مالك بدمشق وهو يبكي فقلت ما يبكيك فقال لا أعرف شيئا مما أدركت إلا هذه الصلاة، وهذه الصلاة قد ضيعت

I heard Al-Zuhrī saying, "I visited Anas ibn Mālik in Damascus and found him weeping. I asked him why he was weeping and he (Anas) replied, 'I do not recognize anything which I witnessed (during the lifetime of the Messenger of Allah) except this prayer which is being lost (not offered as it should be)."[2]

Background to the Ḥadīth of Anas

What is intended by the statement of Anas ibn Mālik رضي الله عنه in the first ḥadīth, "*have you not wasted it as is done now?*" is the delay of ṣalāh beyond its prescribed time. This occurred during the era of Ḥajjāj not during the era of the Ṣaḥābah as Tījānī claims.

To further understand the context of the ḥadīth let us consider the details given by the narrators. The person communicating with Anas رضي الله عنه in this ḥadīth is Abū

1 *Ṣaḥīḥ al-Bukhārī*, vol. 1, Kitāb Mawāqīt al-Ṣalāh, Bāb Taḍyī' al-Ṣalāh 'an Waqtihā, Ḥadīth no. 506.
2 Op. cit. vol. 1 p. 507.

Rāfiʿ. Imām Aḥmad narrates a similar ḥadīth by way of detail from ʿUthmān ibn Saʿd:

فقال أبو رافع يا أبا حمزة ولا الصّلوة فقال أوليس قد علمت ما صنع الحجّاج في الصّلاة

Abū Rāfiʿ then said, "O Abū Ḥamzah, not even the ṣalāh?"

He said, "You know what Ḥajjāj has done regarding prayer."[1]

Under the biography of Anas رضي الله عنه in *al-Ṭabaqāt*, Ibn Saʿd gives the reason for the statement of Anas رضي الله عنه in a narration from ʿAbd al-Raḥmān ibn al-ʿUryān, he said, I heard Thābit al-Bunānī saying:

كنا مع أنس بن مالك فأخر الحجاج الصلاة فقام أنس يريد أن يكلمه فنهاه إخوانه شفقة عليه منه فخرج فركب دابته فقال في مسيره ذلك والله ما أعرف شيئا مما كنا عليه على عهد النبي صلى الله عليه و سلم إلا شهادة أن لا إله إلا الله فقال رجل فالصلاة يا أبا حمزة قال قد جعلتم الظهر عند المغرب أفتلك كانت صلاة رسول الله صلى الله عليه و سلم وأخرجه ابن أبي عمر في مسنده من طريق حماد عن ثابت مختصرا

We were with Anas ibn Mālik when Ḥajjāj delayed the ṣalāh. Anas رضي الله عنه stood up wanting to say something to him but his brothers prevented him out of compassion for him. He then left and mounted his conveyance. He said during that journey, "By Allah! I do not recognise any of our traditions during the era of the Messenger صلى الله عليه وسلم besides the *shahādah* (testimony of acceptance of Islam)."

A man said, "(What about) the ṣalāh, O Abū Ḥamzah?"

He said, "You made Ẓuhr at the time of Maghrib! Was that the ṣalāh of the Messenger of Allah صلى الله عليه وسلم?"

Ibn Ḥajar says that Ibn Abī ʿUmar narrates this ḥadīth in his *Musnad* from Ḥammād, from Thābit, abridged.[2]

1 *Fatḥ al-Bāri*, vol. 2 p. 507.

2 Ibid.

The second ḥadīth of Anas رضي الله عنه is narrated by Zuhrī. This was also during the period when Ḥajjāj was the governor in ʿIrāq. Anas رضي الله عنه had just arrived in Damascus to complain about Ḥajjāj to the Khalīfah, Walīd ibn ʿAbd al-Malik. Again, his statement, "*I do not recognise anything which I witnessed (during the Prophetic era) except this prayer which has been spoiled (not offered as it should be),*" refers to the delay in prayer beyond its prescribed time. It is well-known that Ḥajjāj, Walīd, and others from the Banū Umayyah used to delay the ṣalāh beyond its prescribed times.

ʿAbd al-Razzāq narrates from Ibn Jurayj, from ʿAṭāʾ, who said:

أخر الوليد الجمعة حتى أمسى فجئت فصليت الظهر قبل أن أجلس ثم صليت العصر وأنا جالس إيماء وهو يخطب

> Walīd delayed the Jumuʿah until it became dark. I came and performed Ẓuhr before I sat down then (later) I performed ʿAṣr through gestures (Īmāʾ) while sitting during the sermon.[1]

This is further corroborated by a narration recorded by Abū Nuʿaym in *Kitāb al-Ṣalāh*, from Abū Bakr ibn ʿUtbah, who said:

صليت إلى جنب أبي جحيفة فمسى الحجاج بالصلاة فقام أبو جحيفة فصلى ومن طريق ابن عمر أنه كان يصلي مع الحجاج فلما أخر الصلاة ترك أن يشهدها معه

> I performed ṣalāh next to Abū Juḥayfah when Ḥajjāj delayed the ṣalāh. Abū Juḥayfah stood up and performed ṣalāh. The narration of Ibn ʿUmar relates that he used to perform ṣalāh with Ḥajjāj but when Ḥajjāj postponed the ṣalāh Ibn ʿUmar stopped (performing) it with him.[2]

The ḥadīth of Anas is not to be understood in a general sense that the delaying of prayer was in vogue throughout the Muslim territories. Rather, it should be interpreted in light of what Anas observed in al-Shām and Baṣrah specifically. Upon arriving in Madīnah, Anas رضي الله عنه once remarked:

ما أنكرت شيئا إلا أنكم لا تقيمون الصفوف

1 Ibid. vol. 2 p. 18.

2 Ibid.

والسبب فيه أنه قدم المدينة وعمر بن عبد العزيز أميرها حينئذ

I do not find anything strange except that you do not straighten the rows.

Ibn Ḥajar, author of *Fatḥ al-Bārī* says: "The reason for it is that 'Umar ibn 'Abd al-'Azīz was the *Amīr* (leader) at that time."[1]

Response to Tījānī's accusation on 'Uthmān and 'Ā'ishah

Tījānī accuses both 'Uthmān and 'Ā'ishah رضي الله عنهما of changing the prayer. This callous allegation is general and without any merit as we shall see.

The issue is whether the traveller shortens the prayer or prays it in full? Anyone remotely familiar with the subject of fiqh would be well-aware of the difference of opinion on this issue.

It has reached us that the Ṣaḥābah رضي الله عنهم differed on this matter. It has been narrated about 'Uthmān رضي الله عنه, and Sa'd ibn Abī Waqqāṣ رضي الله عنه, Ibn Mas'ūd رضي الله عنه, Ibn 'Umar رضي الله عنه, and 'Ā'ishah رضي الله عنها, that they all preferred performing the ṣalāh in full while on travel. In fact, this is the view of the majority of the Ṣaḥābah رضي الله عنهم and Tābi'īn.

It has been narrated from 'Ā'ishah رضي الله عنها that the Messenger صلى الله عليه وسلم would sometimes perform his ṣalāh in full and sometimes shorten it when on travel.

A man once asked 'Abd Allāh ibn 'Abbās رضي الله عنه about shortening prayers on journey and he said:

كنت أتم الصلاة في السفر فلم يأمر بالإعادة

I used to perform my ṣalāh in full and he did not instruct (me) to repeat it.[2]

It has come in the Sunnah that shortening the ṣalāh when on travel is a *rukhṣah* (concession). Allah سبحانه وتعالى says:

فَلَيْسَ عَلَيْكُمْ جُنَاحٌ أَنْ تَقْصُرُوْا مِنَ الصَّلَاةِ إِنْ خِفْتُمْ أَنْ يَفْتِنَكُمُ الَّذِيْنَ كَفَرُوْا

1 Ibid.

2 Ibn Qudāmah: *Al-Mughnī*, vol. 3 p. 124, with the research of 'Abd Allāh al-Turkī and 'Abd al-Fattāḥ al-Ḥalw.

And when you travel throughout the land, there is no blame upon you for shortening the prayer [especially] if you fear that those who disbelieve may disrupt [or attack] you.[1]

Muslim narrates from Yaʿlā ibn Umayyah, who said:

قلت لعمر بن الخطاب { لَيْسَ عَلَيْكُمْ جُنَاحٌ أَنْ تَقْصُرُوْا، مِنَ الصَّلاَةِ إِنْ خِفْتُمْ أَنْ يَفْتِنَكُمُ الَّذِيْنَ كَفَرُوْا} فقد أمن الناس فقال عجبت مما عجبت منه فسألت رسول الله صلى الله عليه وسلم عن ذلك فقال صدقة تصدق الله بها عليكم فاقبلوا صدقته

I said to ʿUmar ibn al-Khaṭṭāb ﷺ that Allah says, "*You may shorten the prayer if you fear that those who are unbelievers may afflict you*," the people are now safe?

He replied, "I wondered about it in the same way as you wonder about it, so I asked the Messenger of Allah ﷺ about it and he said, 'It is a charity which Allah given you, so accept His charity.'"[2]

If Tījānī bases his argument on the statement of ʿAbd Allāh ibn Masʿūd رضي الله عنه recorded in both al-Bukhārī and Muslim:

صلى بنا عثمان بمنى أربع ركعات فقيل ذلك لعبد الله بن مسعود فاسترجع ثم قال صليت مع رسول الله صلى الله عليه وسلم بمنى ركعتين وصليت مع أبي بكر الصديق بمنى ركعتين وصليت مع عمر بن الخطاب بمنى ركعتين فليت حظي من أربع ركعات ركعتان متقبلتان[3]

ʿUthmān led us in four rakaʿāt of ṣalāh at Minā. It was related to ʿAbd Allāh ibn Masʿūd and he said, "To Allah do we belong and to Him surely shall we return."

He then said, "I prayed with the Messenger of Allah ﷺ at Minā two rakaʿāt of prayer. I prayed with Abū Bakr al-Ṣiddīq two rakaʿāt of prayer at Minā. I prayed with ʿUmar ibn al-Khaṭṭāb two rakaʿāt of prayer at Minā. I wish I had my share of the two rakaʿāt acceptable (to Allah) of the four rakaʿāt."

---

1 Sūrah al-Nisā': 101.

2 *Ṣaḥīḥ Muslim* with Nawāwi's commentary, vol. 5, Kitāb Ṣalāh al-Musāfirīn, Ḥadīth no. 686.

3 *Ṣaḥīḥ al-Bukhārī*, vol. 1, Kitāb Taqṣīr al-Ṣalāh, Ḥadīth no. 1034.

As for Ibn Masʿūd's رضي الله عنه statement: "I wish I had my share of the two rakaʿāt acceptable (to Allah) of the four rakaʿāt," the word 'من' (translated as 'of' in the translation above) denotes substitution, similar to the verse:

أَرَضِيتُم بِالْحَيَوٰةِ الدُّنْيَا مِنَ الْأٓخِرَةِ

Are you satisfied with the life of this world rather than the hereafter?

This proves that ʿAbd Allāh ibn Masʿūd رضي الله عنه considered the full prayer valid. Otherwise, if he considered it invalid he would not have asked for acceptance of two rakaʿāt from four.

The reason for Ibn Masʿūd's response with "To Allah do we belong and to Him surely shall we return." was on account of the ideal manner of prayer not being maintained. This is further supported by a narration found in *Abū Dāwūd*:

أن عبد الله صلى أربعا قال فقيل له عبت على عثمان ثم صليت أربعا قال الخلاف شر

> ʿAbd Allāh ibn Masʿūd once prayed four rakaʿāt (of ṣalāh while on a journey). Someone commented, "You criticised ʿUthmān but you pray four?"
>
> He replied, "Dissension is evil."[1]

Ibn Ḥajar says in *Fatḥ al-Bārī*:

> A narration in al-Bayhaqī relates, "I dislike dissension." Aḥmad also has a ḥadīth from Abū Dharr رضي الله عنه similar to the first.

Ibn Qudāmah says:

> The famous position transmitted to us about Aḥmad's position (on the matter) is that the individual had the choice (between the two) even though he believed shortening to be the better. This is the view of the majority of the Ṣaḥābah and Tābiʿīn.[2]

Let us consider the interpretations of ʿUthmān رضي الله عنه and ʿĀʾishah رضي الله عنها.

---

1 Refer to *Abū Dāwūd*, Kitāb al-Manāsik, Bāb al-Ṣalāh bi Minā, Ḥadīth no. 1960; Refer also to *Ṣaḥīḥ Abū Dāwūd* of al-Albānī, Ḥadīth no. 1726.

2 *Fatḥ al-Bārī*, vol. 2 p. 657-658.

Some of the scholars have said:

> They were of the opinion that the Messenger صلى الله عليه وسلم only shortened the ṣalāh out of compassion for the Ummah as it was the easier of the two options. The two of them, however, decided to take the tougher of the two options by themselves.

Zuhrī said:

> ʿUthmān ibn ʿAffān رضي الله عنه performed the full prayer because of the Bedouins. They were substantial in number that year (during the ḥajj) so he decided to perform the ṣalāh in full in order that they know that the ṣalāh has four rakaʿāt.

Ibn Ḥajar says in *al-Fatḥ*:

> The reason ʿUthmān رضي الله عنه prayed the ṣalāh in full is because he believed that shortening was only for the weak traveller. As for the one who settled in Makkah for the duration of his journey, the ruling of the resident applied to him and therefore, he must pray his ṣalāh in full.[1]

Ibn Ḥajar then says:

> There is nothing preventing, in my opinion, this being the root cause for (ʿUthmān's) praying the ṣalāh in full. This does not contradict the view which I have adopted. Rather, it strengthens it from the angle that taking up residency during a journey is closer to general residency than what it is to travelling. This is what the Ijtihād of ʿUthmān led to.[2]

As for ʿĀ'ishah رضي الله عنها her reason has been mentioned explicitly. Al-Bayhaqī narrated from Hishām ibn ʿUrwah, from his father that she used to pray full while travelling. Once it was said to her, "Why do you not shorten the prayer?"

She replied, "O my nephew, it is not difficult for me."

The chain of transmission for this report is authentic. This proves that she understood shortening to be a concession and that praying the full prayer better for the one who finds no difficulty in it.[3]

---

1 Ibid. vol. 2 p. 665.

2 Ibid. vol. 2 p. 665.

3 Ibid.

To summarize:

Tījānī disguises his distortion when he alleges that the Ṣaḥābah interfered with the manner in which Ṣalāh was performed "in order to dispel the belief that the Tābi'īn were the ones who altered," He converges the issues of one Ḥadīth in the next; attempting to link the objection of Anas رضي الله عنه to the actions of 'Uthmān and 'Ā'ishah رضي الله عنها.

We have proven from the narrations of Anas رضي الله عنه that he was objecting to the delay of prayer during the era of Ḥajjāj. As for the actions of 'Uthmān رضي الله عنه and 'Ā'ishah رضي الله عنها, we have demonstrated that it is a matter of Fiqh which is subject to interpretation and none of the Ṣaḥābah accused them of changing the prayer.

3. Tījānī's claim that the Ṣaḥābah رضي الله عنهم Testified Against Themselves

Tījānī says:

> **Anas ibn Malik said that the Messenger of Allah صلى الله عليه وسلم said to al-Ansar: You will notice after me some great selfishness, but be patient until you meet Allah and His Messenger by the pool. Anas said: We were not patient.**
>
> **Al-Ala ibn al-Musayyab heard his father saying: I met, al-Bara ibn Azib - May Allah honour them both - and said to him, "Bless you, you accompanied the Prophet صلى الله عليه وسلم and you voted for him under the tree." He said, "My son, you do not know what we have done after him"**
>
> **This early Companion, who was one of those who voted for the Prophet under the tree, and who received the blessing of Allah, for Allah knew what was in their hearts, testifies against himself and his companions that they did not keep the tradition. This testimony is confirmation of what the Prophet صلى الله عليه وسلم talked about and predicted in that his Companions would break with his tradition and fall back on their heels.**
>
> **How could any sensible person, after all this evidence, believe in the righteousness of all the Companions, as the Sunnis do?**
>
> **He, who believes that, is definitely reversing the order of logic and scholarship, and there will be no intellectual criteria for the researcher to use in his quest for the truth.[1]**

1 *Then I was guided*, p. 110-111.

Refuting Tījānī's claim that the Ṣaḥābah رضي الله عنهم Testified Against Themselves

The narration cited by Tījānī could not be found with that wording. Instead we find the narration from Zuhrī, who said:

أنّ أناسا من الأنصار قالوا، يوم حنين، حين أفاء الله على رسوله من أموال هوازن ما أفاء. فطفق رسول الله صلّى الله عليه وسلّم يعطي رجالا من قريش. المائة من الإبل. قالوا: يغفر الله لرسول الله. يعطي قريشا ويتركنا وسيوفنا تقطر من دمائهم!. قال أنس بن مالك فحدّث ذلك رسول الله صلّى الله عليه وسلّم، من قولهم. فأرسل إلى الأنصار فجمعهم في قبّة من أدم. فلمّا اجتمعوا جاءهم رسول الله صلّى الله عليه وسلّم. فقال ما حديث بلغني عنكم؟ فقال له فقهاء الأنصار أمّا ذوو رأينا يا رسول الله فلم يقولوا شيئا. وأمّا أناس منّا حديثة أسنانهم قالوا يغفر الله لرسوله. يعطي قريشا ويتركنا، وسيوفنا تقطر من دمائهم!، فقال رسول الله صلّى الله عليه وسلّم فإنّي أعطي رجالا حديثي عهد بكفر أتألّفهم. أفلا ترضون أن يذهب النّاس بالأموال وترجعون إلى رحالكم برسول الله صلّى الله عليه وسلّم؟ فو الله! لما تنقلبون به خير ممّا ينقلبون به فقالوا بلى يا رسول الله! قد رضينا قال فإنّكم ستجدون أثرة شديدة فاصبروا حتّى تلقوا الله ورسوله. فإنّي على الحوض قالوا سنصبر [1]
قال أنس فلم نصبر

Anas ibn Mālik reported to me that on the Day of Ḥunayn Allah conferred upon His Messenger of صلى الله عليه وسلم the riches of Ḥawāzin. The Messenger of Allah صلى الله عليه وسلم set about distributing to some persons of Quraysh one hundred camels and upon this they said, "May Allah grant pardon to the Messenger of Allah صلى الله عليه وسلم that he gave (these camels) to the people of the Quraysh, and he ignored us, whereas our swords are still dripping blood."

Their statement was conveyed to the Messenger of Allah صلى الله عليه وسلم and he sent someone to the Anṣār and gathered them under a tent (made) of leather. When they had assembled, the Messenger of Allah صلى الله عليه وسلم came to them and said, "What is this news that has reached me from you?"

The wise people of the Anṣār said, "O Messenger of Allah, so far as the knowledgeable amongst us are concerned they have said nothing, but we

1 *Ṣaḥīḥ al-Bukhārī*, Kitāb Farḍ al-Khumus, vol. 3, Ḥadīth no. 2978.

have amongst us persons of immature age; they said, 'May Allah grant pardon to the Messenger of Allah ﷺ that he gave to the Quraysh and ignored us (despite the fact) that our swords are besmeared with their blood."

Upon this the Messenger of Allah ﷺ said, "I give (at times material gifts) to persons who were quite recently in the state of unbelief, so that I may incline them towards the truth. Do you not feel delighted that people should go with riches, and you should go back to your places with the Messenger of Allah ﷺ? By Allah, that with which you return with is better than that with which they return with."

They said, "Yes, O Messenger of Allah, we are pleased."

The Messenger said, "You will encounter marked preference in future, so you should show patience till you meet Allah سُبْحَانَهُ وَتَعَالَىٰ and His Messenger ﷺ. I will be at the Ḥawḍ."

They said, "We will be patient."

Anas related, "We were not patient."

This ḥadīth proves the high status and merit of the Anṣār. How can this not be true when the Messenger ﷺ said:

الأنصار لا يحبهم إلا مؤمن، ولا يبغضهم إلا منافق، فمن أحبهم أحبه الله، ومن أبغضهم أبغضه الله

None loves the Anṣār but a believer, and none hates them but a hypocrite. Allah loves the one who loves them, and He detests the one who hates them.[1]

آية الإيمان حب الأنصار، وآية النفاق بغض الأنصار

Love for the Anṣār is a sign of Īmān and hatred for the Anṣār is a sign of nifāq.[2]

In the ḥadīth the Messenger ﷺ also said, "Do you not feel delighted that people should go with riches, and you should go back to your places with the Messenger of Allah ﷺ?"

Would he have said that to anyone but the best of people?

1 *Ṣaḥīḥ al-Bukhārī*, Kitāb Faḍā'il al-Ṣaḥābah, Ḥadīth no. 3572, from Barā' ibn 'Āzib.

2 Ibid. Ḥadīth no. 3573, from Anas Ibn Mālik.

The statement of Anas رضي الله عنه, "We were not patient," is nothing more than his opinion. It is careless to use it to construct an argument against the Ṣaḥābah that they testified against themselves. A humble person never considers his accomplishments or acknowledges his status.

It is not permissible, on the basis of a vague statement from a Ṣaḥābī, to reject the many clear verses in the Qur'ān which praise the Ṣaḥābah in general and the Anṣār specifically. This is in addition to the fact that the ḥadīth is intended to praise the Anṣār.

Perhaps Anas رضي الله عنه intended by this statement the role in the Anṣār played initially when there was disagreement regarding leadership of the Ummah after the Prophet's صلى الله عليه وسلم demise; and their arguing with the Muhājirīn at the Saqīfah.

This is supported by a ḥadīth narrated by Anas رضي الله عنه from Usayd ibn Ḥuḍayr رضي الله عنه that a man from the Anṣār came to the Messenger of Allah صلى الله عليه وسلم and said, "Will you not use me (as a governor) as you have used such and such a person?" The Messenger صلى الله عليه وسلم then said:

إنكم ستلقون بعدي أثرة، فاصبروا حتى تلقوني على الحوض

> You will encounter much favouritism after me. Be patient until you meet me at the Ḥawḍ.[1]

This is especially true if we recognise that the preference mentioned in this ḥadīth refers to worldly matters.[2]

Tījānī also quoted the words of al-Barā' ibn ʿĀzib رضي الله عنه, "You do not know what we did after him."

Clearly these words have been taken out of context and given a dose of steroids. Al-Barā' ibn ʿĀzib was referring to the battles which were fought between the Muslims. He feared the evil outcome in the Hereafter that might result from that. This is indicative of his virtue and piety.[3]

---

1 *Ṣaḥīḥ Muslim* with its commentary, Kitāb al-Imārah, Bāb al-Amr bi al-Ṣabr 'ind Ẓulm al-Wulāt wa Isti'thārihim, Ḥadīth no. 1845.

2 *Sharḥ Muslim*, vol. 12 p. 331.

3 *Al-Fatḥ*, vol. 7 p. 516.

Also, it is well-known that ʿAlī ibn Abī Ṭālib رَضِيَ ٱللَّهُ عَنْهُ was among those who participated in those battles and therefore, the address, according to Tījānī's interpretation, includes him. The corollary of Tījānī's reasoning implicates ʿAlī ibn Abī Ṭālib as well. Whatever argument is made to exclude ʿAlī رَضِيَ ٱللَّهُ عَنْهُ applies to the rest of the Ṣaḥābah as well.

In reality it is impossible for these two aḥādīth to refute the collection of proofs from the Qur'ān and Sunnah which praise the Ṣaḥābah رَضِيَ ٱللَّهُ عَنْهُمْ and express Allah's سُبْحَانَهُ وَتَعَالَىٰ and His Messenger's صَلَّى ٱللَّهُ عَلَيْهِ وَسَلَّمَ pleasure with them. The Ṣaḥābah falling into error does not negate their virtue or their inner and outer purity.

Chapter Six

Tījānī's Criticisms against Abū Bakr

Tījānī has singled out Abū Bakr رَضِيَ اللَّهُ عَنْهُ for the bulk of his criticisms. He has isolated a number of incidents as evidence upon which he pronounces judgement against Abū Bakr رَضِيَ اللَّهُ عَنْهُ. I will attempt— with Allah's help— to analyse all the points of criticism and reconnect them to their context. This will be the most feasible strategy in defending this noble Ṣaḥābī رَضِيَ اللَّهُ عَنْهُ about whom the Prophet صَلَّى اللَّهُ عَلَيْهِ وَسَلَّمَ said:

أبرأ إلى كل خليل من خله ولو كنت متخذا خليلا لاتخذت ابن أبي قحافة خليلا وإن صاحبكم خليل الله

I distance myself from taking anyone as a *khalīl* (close friend). Were I to take a khalīl I would have taken Abū Bakr. Indeed, your companion is the Khalīl of Allah.[1]

Consider the great status of Abū Bakr رَضِيَ اللَّهُ عَنْهُ when the Qur'ān bears testimony to his Īmān:

إِلَّا تَنْصُرُوْهُ فَقَدْ نَصَرَهُ اللّٰهُ إِذْ أَخْرَجَهُ الَّذِيْنَ كَفَرُوْا ثَانِيَ اثْنَيْنِ إِذْ هُمَا فِي الْغَارِ إِذْ يَقُوْلُ لِصَاحِبِه لَا تَحْزَنْ إِنَّ اللّٰهَ مَعَنَا فَأَنْزَلَ اللّٰهُ سَكِيْنَتَهٗ عَلَيْهِ وَأَيَّدَهٗ بِجُنُودٍ لَّمْ تَرَوْهَا وَجَعَلَ كَلِمَةَ الَّذِيْنَ كَفَرُوا السُّفْلٰى وَكَلِمَةُ اللّٰهِ هِيَ الْعُلْيَا وَاللّٰهُ عَزِيْزٌ حَكِيْمٌ

If you do not aid him [i.e. the Prophet صَلَّى اللَّهُ عَلَيْهِ وَسَلَّمَ] — Allah has already aided him when those who disbelieved had driven him out [of Makkah] as one of two, when they were in the cave and he [i.e. Muḥammad صَلَّى اللَّهُ عَلَيْهِ وَسَلَّمَ] said to his Companion, "Do not grieve; indeed Allah is with us." And Allah sent down His tranquillity upon him and supported him with soldiers [i.e. angels] you did not see and made the word of those who disbelieved the lowest while the word of Allah — that is the highest. And Allah is Exalted in Might and Wise.

1 *Sunan al-Tirmidhī*, Kitāb al-Manāqib, Ḥadīth no. 3655; Refer also to *Ṣaḥīḥ al-Tirmidhī*, Ḥadīth no. 2889; Its origin is in *Bukhārī*, Ḥadīth no. 3456.

The esteemed reader will be well aware that we have already disproved Tījānī's insinuation that Abū Bakr was enlisted in Usāmah's رَضِيَ ٱللَّهُ عَنْهُ army; as well as his allegation that Abū Bakr objected to Usāmah's appointment. Prior to his demise the Prophet صَلَّى ٱللَّهُ عَلَيْهِ وَسَلَّمَ appointed Abū Bakr to lead the Muslims in ṣalāh.

After the Prophet's صَلَّى ٱللَّهُ عَلَيْهِ وَسَلَّمَ passing, Abū Bakr رَضِيَ ٱللَّهُ عَنْهُ was the most determined to dispatch the army of Usāmah رَضِيَ ٱللَّهُ عَنْهُ despite the uncertainty of others who feared an attack from the enemy. When it was suggested to him that the army rather remain in Madīnah for a while he said, "I will not undo the standard which was fastened by the Messenger of Allah!" Abū Bakr's insistence on dispatching the battalion of Usāmah رَضِيَ ٱللَّهُ عَنْهُ immediately after his appointment as Khalīfah is considered one of his greatest accomplishments.[1] This fact has been completely ignored by Tījānī despite it being a matter of consensus among historians.

It is worthy of noting that Tījānī conveniently failed to mention Abū Bakr's steadfastness at Ḥudaybiyyah. This was an occasion which even great companions like ʿUmar and ʿAlī رَضِيَ ٱللَّهُ عَنْهُمَا expressed their discontentment with the terms laid down by the Quraysh. It serves as a solemn reminder that incidents stripped of context are malleable in the hand of 'objective researchers'.

1. Tījānī's Claims that Abū Bakr Condemned Himself

Tījānī says:

> **Like history records about Abū Bakr the following (incident). He looked at a bird on a tree, then said, "Well done bird ... You eat the fruits, you stand on the trees and you are not accountable to anybody nor indeed can anybody punish you. I wish I was a tree by the road and that a camel would come along and eat me. Then relieve me with his bowel evacuation ... I wish that I had been all that, rather than a human being."**
>
> **He also said, I wish that my mother had not given birth to me ... I wish I was a straw in the mud.**
>
> **These are some texts that I used just as examples and not for any specific reason.[2]**

1 See *Minhāj al-Sunnah*, vol. 6 p. 319.

2 *Then I was guided*, p. 111-112.

Refuting Tījānī's Claims that Abū Bakr Condemned Himself

Tījānī's referencing

Tījānī ascribes the first narration to *Tārīkh al-Ṭabarī, al-Riyāḍ al-Naḍirah, Kanz al-ʿUmmāl* and *Minhāj al-Sunnah* of Ibn Taymiyyah. This narration is not found in *Minhāj al-Sunnah, Riyāḍ al-Naḍirah*, or *Tārīkh al-Ṭabarī*. The only source where it is found is *Kanz al-ʿUmmāl.*

For the second narration he referenced it to the same sources mentioned above, but this narration is neither found in *Kanz al-ʿUmmāl, Tārīkh al-Ṭabarī*, or *Riyāḍ al-Naḍirah.* The only book wherein it is mentioned is *Minhāj al-Sunnah.*

Tījānī tries to create an impression that the compilers of the books which he has referenced are in agreement with him. At the very least it is meant to convince the reader that he has spared no effort in collecting material and has proven his claim from Sunnī sources. Let us now raise the curtain on these references and see for ourselves the tricks which Tījānī has kept under his sleeve.

The book *Minhāj al-Sunnah al-Nabawiyyah fī Naqd Kalām al-Shīʿah* was authored by Taqī al-Dīn Aḥmad ibn Taymiyyah in refutation of the book *Minhāj al-Karāmah fī Ithbāt al-Imāmah* by the Rāfiḍī cleric Ibn al-Muṭahhar al-Ḥillī. The narration under discussion was actually recorded by Ibn al-Muṭahhar al-Ḥillī, the Rāfiḍī, in *Minhāj al-Karāmah*; which was subsequently refuted by Ibn Taymiyyah. So Tījānī's reference to *Minhāj al-Sunnah* is nothing but deception.

As for the book *al-Riyāḍ al-Naḍirah* which Tījānī consistently cites, its full title is *al-Riyāḍ al-Naḍirah fī Manāqib al-ʿAsharah* (The ripe gardens concerning the virtues of the ten). The 'ten' refers to the ten Ṣaḥābah who were given the glad tidings of Jannah. They were Abū Bakr, ʿUmar, ʿUthmān, ʿAlī, Ṭalḥah, Zubayr, Saʿd ibn Abī Waqqāṣ, Saʿīd ibn Zayd, ʿAbd al-Raḥmān ibn ʿAwf and Abū ʿUbaydah رضي الله عنهم. The author of the book in his title alludes to the famous ḥadīth of the Prophet صلى الله عليه وسلم in which he gave the glad tidings of paradise to these Ṣaḥābah رضي الله عنهم on Mount Uḥud.[1] The Rāfiḍah reject this ḥadīth. How is it then that they cite it as a proof in their favour?

1 *Sunan al-Tirmidhī*, Kitāb al-Manāqib, Ḥadīth no. 3747; and *al-Mishkāt* of al-Tabrīzī, *Kitāb al-Manāqib*, Bāb Manāqib al-ʿAsharah; See also *Ṣaḥīḥ al-Tirmidhī*, Ḥadīth no. 2946.

Secondly the two statements of Abū Bakr are not mentioned in the book. The author affirms that Abū Bakr رضي الله عنه was the most suitable person for khilāfah after the Prophet[1] صلى الله عليه وسلم. He discusses ʿAlī's pledge to Abū Bakr and debunks the allegations of the Rāfiḍah.[2] More than one quarter of the book is devoted to Abū Bakr رضي الله عنه. Does Tījānī think nothing of his readers!

Tārīkh al-Ṭabarī was provided as reference for the statements of Abū Bakr رضي الله عنه. I refer the reader to *Tārīkh al-Ṭabarī*, to the events of the year eleven to the end of the year thirteen. There is no trace of these two narrations found in this reference.

The book *Kanz al-ʿUmmāl fī Sunan al-Aqwāl wa al-Afʿāl* was compiled by ʿAlā' al-Dīn al-Hindī. All its narrations are not considered authoritative since the compiler did not restrict himself to collecting only authentic narrations. Instead it is an encyclopaedic index for over 90 books. His objective being to collect whatever has been narrated from the Prophet صلى الله عليه وسلم; whether it be reliable or forged.

It is interesting to note that the compiler of *Kanz al-ʿUmmāl* dedicated a special section for aḥādīth which criticise the Rāfiḍah despite knowing that Sunnī Ḥadīth scholars have not authenticated a single ḥadīth of this nature. These are the same ḥadīth scholars who Tījānī accuses of declaring weak the aḥādīth of the merits of the Ahl al-Bayt; and of fabricating aḥādīth about the virtues of the Ṣaḥābah رضي الله عنهم.

If this accusation had any substance we would expect to see the Sunnī scholars of *al-Jarḥ wa al-Taʿdīl* authenticating all the aḥādīth which criticise the Rāfiḍah. That, however, is not the case as the authentication of aḥādīth is subject to specific criteria which the ḥadīth scholars have agreed upon; based on the evaluation of the sanad and text.

In addition to that al-Hindī, the compiler of *Kanz al-ʿUmmāl*, dedicated a special chapter on the Ṣaḥābah and their merits. This chapter has three sub-sections the first of them dedicated to the four khulafā' (Abū Bakr, ʿUmar, ʿUthmān, and ʿAlī رضي الله عنهم) indicating to their superiority and their precedence in Islam and khilāfah.[3]

One wonders how long Tījānī assumed the act would last.

---

1 *Riyāḍ al-Naḍirah*, p. 169.

2 Ibid. p. 242-246.

3 Refer to *Kanz al-ʿUmmāl*, p. 525.

The meaning of Abū Bakr's statements

It is unfortunate that the words of the Ṣaḥābah رضي الله عنهم seem to be deliberately interpreted in the worst possible way. Likewise, their actions seem to be considered in the worst possible light. It appears almost as if Tījānī goes out of his way to strip their statements and actions from their original context. In so doing he finds opportunity to depict their behaviour in the unfavourable manner which is preconceived in his mind.

Let us return to the quotations from Abū Bakr رضي الله عنه. We find that even if we ignore Tījānī's lies in terms of referencing and suppose we assume their authenticity; do they necessarily mean that Abū Bakr رضي الله عنه condemned himself? If one gives careful consideration to the personality of Abū Bakr رضي الله عنه one will find that these statements ascribed to him merely illustrate the strength of his īmān and his fear of Allah.

Let us not forget the story which appears in the *Ṣaḥīḥayn*[1,2] about a man who instructed his family to cremate his body after his death, and to scatter half of his ashes in the sea and the other half in the land. In addition to the ḥarām act of cremating he did no good during his life. He remarked before his death, "If Allah should get hold of me he will punish me like He punished no other before me." Allah سبحانه وتعالى commanded the land and it gathered his ashes and commanded the sea and it gathered his ashes. Allah سبحانه وتعالى asked him, "What caused you to do this?" He replied, "Out of fear of Your punishment, O my Lord." Allah then forgave him.[3]

His belief in Allah's ability to resurrect him was defective; hence he requested his ashes to be dispersed over land and see. Despite his defective belief he was forgiven on account of his genuine fear of Allah. We learn from this incident that the fear of Allah سبحانه وتعالى is one of the greatest sources for Allah's سبحانه وتعالى forgiveness.[4]

Numerous incidents of this nature have been reported from different Companions. Aḥmad ibn Ḥambal narrates from Masrūq, he said:

1 Referring to *Ṣaḥīḥ al-Bukhārī* and *Ṣaḥīḥ Muslim.*

2 *Ṣaḥīḥ al-Bukhārī*, Kitāb al-Tawḥīd, Ḥadīth no. 7067; *Muslim* with it commentary, Kitāb al-Tawbah, Ḥadīth no. 2756.

3 *Minhāj al-Sunnah*, vol. 5 p. 484.

4 Ibid.

A man once remarked in the company of ʿAbd Allāh ibn Masʿūd رضي الله عنه, "I do not wish to be amongst the Aṣḥāb al-Yamīn. I prefer to be amongst the Muqarrabīn."ʿAbd Allāh ibn Masʿūd رضي الله عنه then said, "There is a man here (referring to himself) who wishes not to be resurrected (at all)."[1]

Al-Tirmidhī and Ibn Mājah narrate in their *Sunan*, from Abū Dharr رضي الله عنه that the Messenger of Allah صلى الله عليه وسلم said:

إني أرى ما لا ترون وأسمع ما لا تسمعون أطت السماء وحق لها أن تئط ما فيها موضع أربع أصابع إلا وملك واضع جبهته ساجدا لله لو تعلمون ما أعلم لضحكتم قليلا ولبكيتم كثيرا وما تلذذتم بالنساء على الفرش ولخرجتم إلى الصعدات تجأرون إلى الله لوددت أني كنت شجرة تعضد

Indeed I see what you do not see, and I hear what you do not hear. The Heavens moan and they have the right to moan. There is no spot, the size of four fingers in them, except that there is an angel placing his forehead in it, prostrating to Allah. By Allah! If you knew what I know, then you would laugh little and cry much. And you would not taste the pleasures of your women in the beds, and you would go out to the open fields imploring Allah. I wish that I was but a felled tree.[2]

Al-Tirmidhī concludes the narration as follows:

ويروى من غير هذا الوجه أن أبا ذر قال لوددت أني كنت شجرة تعضد

It has been related in many other narrations that Abū Dharr said, "I wish that I was a felled tree."[3]

What does Tījānī have to say about the Prophet صلى الله عليه وسلم? Will he claim that the Prophet صلى الله عليه وسلم condemned himself when he said:

لوددت أني كنت شجرة تعضد

I wish that I was a felled tree.

---

1 Ibid. vol. 5 p. 483.

2 *Sunan al-Tirmidhī*, Kitāb al-Zuhd, Ḥadīth no. 2312; *Sunan Ibn Mājah*, Kitāb al-Zuhd, Bāb al-Ḥuzn wa al-Bukā, Ḥadīth no. 4190; See also *Ṣaḥīḥ al-Tirmidhī*, Ḥadīth no. 3378.

3 Ibid.

This Ḥadīth shares the same sentiments as the statement of Abū Bakr رضي الله عنه. Why treat them differently. The complaint of unprincipled interpretation is ever-recurring in *Then I was guided*.

Abū Dharr رضي الله عنه is considered from the first group of Ṣaḥābah رضي الله عنهم; those who were true to the cause. Al-Tirmidhī has provided us with evidence that Abū Dharr رضي الله عنه repeated a similar statement. Does this incriminate Abū Dharr رضي الله عنه as well? The explanation given to exonerate Abū Dharr is the same for Abū Bakr.

These sentiments have been echoed by even ʿAlī رضي الله عنه. Certainly they do not warrant criticism. Muḥammad Bāqir al-Majlisī records in his book *Biḥār al-Anwār*[1] that ʿAlī ibn Abī Ṭālib رضي الله عنه said:

> If only the predators ripped my flesh. If only my mother had not given birth to me so I do not hear the mention of the Fire (of Jahannam).[2]

Does this statement of ʿAlī رضي الله عنه not indicate strength of īmān and genuine fear of Allah?

Then Tījānī goes on to say:

> **This is the book of Allah giving glad tidings to his believing slaves saying:**
>
> أَلَا إِنَّ أَوْلِيَآءَ اللّٰهِ لَا خَوْفٌ عَلَيْهِمْ وَلَا هُمْ يَحْزَنُوْنَ الَّذِيْنَ اٰمَنُوْا
> وَكَانُوْا يَتَّقُوْنَ لَهُمُ الْبُشْرٰى فِي الْحَيٰوةِ الدُّنْيَا وَفِي الْاٰخِرَةِ لَا تَبْدِيْلَ
> لِكَلِمَاتِ اللّٰهِ ذٰلِكَ هُوَ الْفَوْزُ الْعَظِيْمُ
>
> ***Unquestionably, [for] the allies of Allah there will be no fear concerning them, nor will they grieve. Those who believed and feared Allah for them are good tidings in the worldly life and in the hereafter. No change is there in the words [i.e., decrees] of Allah. That is the great attainment.***[3]
>
> **He also says:**

---

1 *Biḥār al-Anwār* is one of the most accepted works in Twelver tradition.

2 *Biḥār al-Anwār*, vol. 43 p. 89.

3 Sūrah Yūnus: 62-64.

إِنَّ الَّذِيْنَ قَالُوْا رَبُّنَا اللّٰهُ ثُمَّ اسْتَقَامُوْا تَتَنَزَّلُ عَلَيْهِمُ الْمَلَآئِكَةُ أَلَّا تَخَافُوْا وَلَا تَحْزَنُوْا وَأَبْشِرُوْا بِالْجَنَّةِ الَّتِيْ كُنْتُمْ تُوْعَدُوْنَ (٣٠) نَحْنُ أَوْلِيَآؤُكُمْ فِي الْحَيٰوةِ الدُّنْيَا وَفِي الْأٰخِرَةِ وَلَكُمْ فِيهَا مَا تَشْتَهِي أَنْفُسُكُمْ وَلَكُمْ فِيهَا مَا تَدَّعُوْنَ (٣١) نُزُلًا مِنْ غَفُوْرٍ رَحِيْمٍ (٣٢) وَمَنْ أَحْسَنُ قَوْلًا مِمَّنْ دَعَا إِلَى اللّٰهِ

Indeed, those who have said: "Our Lord is Allah" and then remained on a right course — the angels will descend upon them, [saying], "do not fear and do not grieve but receive good tidings of Jannah, which you were promised. We [angels] were your allies in worldly life and [are so] in the hereafter. And you will have therein whatever your soul's desire and you will have therein whatever you request [or wish]. Accommodation from a [Lord who is] All Forgiving and Most Merciful."[1]

How could the two Shaykhs, Abu Bakr and Umar, wish that they were not from the human race, which Allah honoured and put it above all His creation?[2]

Our response:

In no way do these verses negate the slave's fear of his Creator. We mentioned previously the Prophet's ﷺ fear of Allah as well as those of his Ṣaḥābah رضي الله عنهم.

As for the verse in Sūrah Yūnus:

أَلَا إِنَّ أَوْلِيَآءَ اللّٰهِ لَا خَوْفٌ عَلَيْهِمْ وَلَا هُمْ يَحْزَنُوْنَ

Unquestionably, [for] the allies of Allah there will be no fear concerning them, nor will they grieve...

Ibn Kathīr says in his commentary of this verse:

> Allah سبحانه وتعالى informs (us in this verse) that His allies are those who believe in Him and are conscious (have taqwā) of Him. Therefore, whoever is conscious

1 Sūrah al-Fuṣṣilāt: 30-32.

2 *Then I was guided*, p. 112.

> of Allah is a friend of Allah; and "there will be no fear" (for them) of what is to come in the Hereafter, "nor will they grieve" over what they left behind in the world.[1]

The fear spoken about in this verse refers to fear in the Hereafter. All the Ṣaḥābah رضي الله عنهم feared Allah in the world.

As for this part of the verse "nor will they grieve", it refers to what they left behind in the world. There is no doubt that the fear of Abū Bakr and the Ṣaḥābah رضي الله عنهم does not indicate that they grieved about anything in the world.

As for the verse:

إِنَّ الَّذِينَ قَالُوا رَبُّنَا اللَّهُ ثُمَّ اسْتَقَامُوا تَتَنَزَّلُ عَلَيْهِمُ الْمَلَائِكَةُ

> *Indeed, those who have said, "Our Lord is Allah," and then remained on a right course — the angels will descend upon them...*

Ibn Jarīr al-Ṭabarī says in his commentary of this verse:

> Allah سبحانه وتعالى says, "*Indeed, those who have said, "Our Lord is Allah,*" alone without partner, and dissociate themselves from deities other than Allah سبحانه وتعالى and partners (falsely ascribed to him)...
>
> "*And then remained on a right course,*" (in other words), upon the belief of the oneness of Allah سبحانه وتعالى and stayed clear from associating a partner with Allah سبحانه وتعالى and they resorted to His obedience concerning what He commanded and prohibited.[2]

Imām al-Ṭabarī then forwards a number of aḥādīth from Abū Bakr رضي الله عنه in order to explain the meaning of expression, "*and then remained on a right course* (referring to istiqāmah)." From amongst them, from Saʿīd ibn ʿImrān, he said:

> I read this verse in the presence of Abū Bakr, "*Indeed, those who have said, 'our Lord is Allah, and then remained on a right course,'* and he remarked, 'They are those who did not ascribe any partner unto Allah سبحانه وتعالى.'"[3]

1 Ibn Kathīr: *Tafsīr al-Qur'ān al-ʿAẓīm*, vol. 2 p. 438.

2 *Tafsīr al-Ṭabarī*, vol. 11 p. 106.

3 Ibid.

From the above we learn that Tījānī's interpretation of the verse is incorrect and does not apply to the first khalīfah, Abū Bakr رضي الله عنه. No person with the slightest amount of intelligence will say that Abū Bakr رضي الله عنه—the person who fought the Mushrikīn and the murtaddīn and strove firmly against them and whom Allah رضي الله عنه used to protect the Muslim community—is a mushrik.

Subḥān Allāh!

Tījānī further states:

> **Even the ordinary believer, who keeps on the straight path during his lifetime, receives the angels to tell him about his place in heaven, and that he should not fear the torture of Allah, nor be depressed about his legacy in life, and that he has the good news while he is in this life before reaching the life Hereafter. Then how could the great Companions, who are the best of creation after the Messenger of Allah (so we have been taught), wish they were excrement or a hair or a straw when the angels had given them the good news that they would go to heaven? They could not have wished to have all the gold on earth to ransom themselves from the torture of Allah before meeting Him. Allah says:**
>
> وَلَوْ أَنَّ لِكُلِّ نَفْسٍ ظَلَمَتْ مَا فِي الْأَرْضِ لَافْتَدَتْ بِهِ وَأَسَرُّوا النَّدَامَةَ لَمَّا رَأَوُا الْعَذَابَ وَقُضِيَ بَيْنَهُمْ بِالْقِسْطِ وَهُمْ لَا يُظْلَمُونَ
>
> ***And if each soul that wronged had everything on earth, it would offer it in ransom. And they will confide regret when they see the punishment; and they will be judged in justice, and they will not be wronged.[1]***

(At another place He says:)

> وَلَوْ أَنَّ لِلَّذِينَ ظَلَمُوا مَا فِي الْأَرْضِ جَمِيعًا وَمِثْلَهُ مَعَهُ لَافْتَدَوْا بِهِ مِنْ سُوءِ الْعَذَابِ يَوْمَ الْقِيَامَةِ وَبَدَا لَهُمْ مِنَ اللَّهِ مَا لَمْ يَكُونُوا يَحْتَسِبُونَ وَبَدَا لَهُمْ سَيِّئَاتُ مَا كَسَبُوا وَحَاقَ بِهِمْ مَا كَانُوا بِهِ يَسْتَهْزِئُونَ
>
> ***And if those who did wrong had all that is in the earth entirely and the like of it with it, they would [attempt to] ransom themselves thereby from the worst of the punishment on the Day of Resurrection. And***

1 Sūrah Yūnus: 54.

> ***there will appear to them from Allah that which they had not taken into account. And there will appear to them the evils they had earned, and they will be enveloped by what they used to ridicule.[1]***

Our response:

Tījānī fails to realize the difference between verses that refer to the Hereafter and those that refer to this world. In the two verses which have been quoted, Allah informs us about the punishment of the Hereafter when regret and repentance will be of no avail to anyone. It does not refer to regret in this world. Every intelligent person knows the difference between the slave's fear of Allah in the world and his fear of Him in the Hereafter.

Abū Nuʿaym reports in *Ḥilyah* from Shaddād ibn ʿAws رضي الله عنه; and Ibn Mubārak narrates in *Zuhd* from al-Ḥasan that the Messenger صلى الله عليه وسلم said:

> قال الله عز وجل و عزتي لا أجمع لعبدي أمنين و لا خوفين ، إن هو أمنني في الدنيا أخفته يوم أجمع فيه عبادي ، و إن هو خافني في الدنيا أمنته يوم أجمع فيه عبادي
>
> Allah سبحانه وتعالى says, "By My Might, I will not combine two states of peace and two states of fear for My slave. If he felt safe from Me[2] in the world, I will cause him to fear Me the day I gather in it My slaves. However, if he feared Me in the world then I will cause him to be at peace the day I gather in it My slaves.[3]

The venerated Twelver scholar al-Ṣadūq ibn Bābuwayh al-Qummī narrates something similar in his book, *al-Khiṣāl*, from al-Ḥasan, who narrates that the Messenger صلى الله عليه وسلم said:

> قال الله عز وجل و عزتي و جلالي لا أجمع على عبدي خوفين ، و لا أجمع له أمنين. فإذا أمنني في الدنيا أخفته يوم القيامة ، و إن هو خافني في الدنيا أمنته يوم القيامة
>
> Allah سبحانه وتعالى says, "By My Strength and My Honour, I will not combine two states of fear upon My slave and I will not combine for him two states of peace.

---

1 Sūrah al-Zumar: 47 and 48.

2 i.e. he felt safe from Allah's سبحانه وتعالى punishment.

3 *Al-Ḥilyah* of Abū Nuʿaym, vol. 6 p. 98; *al-Zuhd* of Ibn Mubārak, p. 157; Refer also to *al-Silsilah al-Ṣaḥīḥah*, vol. 2, Ḥadīth no. 742.

> If he was safe from Me in the world I will cause him to be in a state of fear on the Day of Judgement. However, if he feared Me in the world, I will cause him to be in a state of peace on the Day of Judgement.[1]

The above is for the person who has the slightest understanding of this reality. Whoever fears Allah سُبْحَانَهُ وَتَعَالَىٰ in the world, Allah سُبْحَانَهُ وَتَعَالَىٰ, will cause him to be in a state of peace on the Day of Judgement. That is because the slave's fear of Allah سُبْحَانَهُ وَتَعَالَىٰ in the world is rewarded (in the Hereafter).

Whoever equates the believer's fear of his Creator in the world with an unbeliever's fear in the Hereafter is like the one who equates darkness with light, and equates shade with heat, and equates the dead with the living.[2]

2. Tījānī's condemnation of Abū Bakr on the issue of Fadak

Tījānī's rant against Abū Bakr رَضِيَ ٱللَّهُ عَنْهُ is far from over. This time the charge against Abū Bakr is that he caused grief to the daughter of the Prophet صَلَّى ٱللَّهُ عَلَيْهِ وَسَلَّمَ. Tījānī opens his arguments with the following statements:

> **I also recall the chain of events that took place after the death of the Messenger of Allah, and the hurt and lack of recognition that afflicted his daughter al-Zahra. The Messenger of Allah صَلَّى ٱللَّهُ عَلَيْهِ وَسَلَّمَ said, "Fāṭimah is part of me, he who angers her angers me."**
>
> **Fāṭimah said to Abu Bakr and Umar: I ask you in the name of Allah - the Most High - did you not hear the Messenger of Allah صَلَّى ٱللَّهُ عَلَيْهِ وَسَلَّمَ saying, "The satisfaction of Fāṭimah is my satisfaction, and the anger of Fāṭimah is my anger, he who loves my daughter Fāṭimah loves me, and he who satisfies Fāṭimah satisfies me, and he who angers Fāṭimah angers me?" They said, "Yes, we heard it from the Messenger of Allah صَلَّى ٱللَّهُ عَلَيْهِ وَسَلَّمَ." Then she said, "Therefore, I testify before Allah and the angels that you have angered me and did not please me, and if I meet the Prophet I will complain to him about you."**
>
> **Let us leave this tragic story for the time being, but Ibn Qutaybah, who is considered to be one of the great Sunni scholars, and was an expert in many disciplines and wrote many books on Qur'anic commentary. Ḥadīth Linguistics, grammar and history might well have been converted to Shiism, as somebody I know once claimed when I showed him Ibn Qutaybah's book "History of the Caliphs."**

---

1 al-Qummī: *Kitāb al-Khiṣāl*, Bāb al-Ithnayn, vol. 1 p. 79.

2 *Minhāj al-Sunnah al-Nabawiyyah*, vol. 6 p. 16.

> **This is the type of propaganda that some of our scholars use when they lose the argument. Similarly al-Tabari was a Shi'ite, and al-Nisa'i, who wrote a book about the various aspects of Imām Ali, was a Shiite, and Taha Husayn, a contemporary scholar who wrote "Al-Fitnah al-Kubra" and other facts, was also a Shi'ite!**
>
> **The fact is that all of these were not Shiites, and when they talked about the Shia, they said all sorts of dishonourable things about them, and they defended the fairness of the Companions with all their might.[1]**

Refuting Tījānī's condemnation of Abū Bakr on the issue of Fadak

In the preamble to this discussion Tījānī has cautiously cloaked his allegations in a smokescreen of deliberate misdirection and embellished them with a series of straw man arguments. This strategy is aimed at keeping one busy with secondary discussions thereby distracting one from focusing on the fallacy in the primary argument. The esteemed reader would have noticed that in his opening comments on this issue Tījānī has asserted the following:

- Abū Bakr's position on the issue of Fadak was unjustified
- The ḥadīth 'Fāṭimah is a part of me...' is connected to Fadak
- Abū Bakr and ʿUmar acted in their own interests and were well aware of the hurt they caused to Fāṭimah by denying her inheritance
- Ibn Qutaybah is a celebrated authority whose opinions are unquestionably accepted
- Ibn Qutaybah accepts a version of events that is similar to the views promoted by the Shīʿah
- The narration from Ibn Qutaybah is credible and worthy of acceptance
- To avoid dealing with problematic views, Sunni's conveniently resort to the strategy of disowning their own scholars who hold views which align with the Shīʿah
- Many Sunni scholars support the Shīʿī narrative of what transpired regarding the inheritance of Fadak

---

1 *Then I was guided*, p. 113 - 114.

Some of the points Tījānī raised in the preamble will resurface with greater detail later on in his discussion. Our comments on these allegations will not necessarily follow the sequence above. Instead, our responses will address the arguments that Tījānī raises in support of his allegations as they appear in his discussion.

There are a few questions that one ought to keep in mind. When did the Prophet صَلَّى ٱللَّٰهُ عَلَيْهِ وَسَلَّمَ say, "Fāṭimah is a part of me. I am hurt by what hurts her"? To whom was this said? Is this an unrestricted criterion of judgement?

Ibn Qutaybah

The narration which serves as the foundation upon which Tījānī's argument lies is the one which speaks of Fāṭimah رَضِيَ ٱللَّٰهُ عَنْهَا complaining about Abū Bakr and ʿUmar رَضِيَ ٱللَّٰهُ عَنْهُمَا. He transmitted it from the book *al-Imāmah wa al-Siyāsah*. This book is known by an alternate name, *Tārīkh al-Khulafā'*, and is attributed to Ibn Qutaybah. The onus is upon Tījānī to prove the reliability of this narration since there is no isnād for it; nor is it found in any of the reliable books of ḥadīth. As far as we are concerned it has absolutely no academic value, and is by no means reliable since there is no objective way of establishing how it was transmitted.

Before proceeding we need to establish the credentials of Ibn Qutaybah and the status of his book *al-Imāmah wa al-Siyāsiyah*, or *Tārīkh al-Khulafā'*.

ʿAbd Allāh ibn Muslim ibn Qutaybah, Abū Muḥammad al-Dīnawarī (213-276) was born in Kūfah, ʿIrāq, and lived in the East. He served as a judge in Dīnawar. He was considered a polymath who wrote on diverse topics including tafsīr, fiqh, ḥadīth, grammar, history, theology and philosophy. He was well-known for his contributions to Arabic literature as well as his work on reconciling conflicting ḥadīth titled *Ta'wīl Mukhtalif al-Ḥadīth*.

Opinions regarding him varied in the subjects of ḥadīth and theology. Al-Dhahabī said:

> The man is not an authority in ḥadīth even though he is an accomplished scholar who was grounded in diverse disciplines and skilled at important subjects.[1]

1 *Siyar Aʿlām al-Nubalā'*, vol. 13 p. 300.

Ibn Qutaybah has a respected position amongst the scholars. He is, according to them, from the Ahl al-Sunnah and reliable in his knowledge and his dīn.

Al-Silafī says, "Ibn Qutaybah was of the reliable scholars and of the Ahl al-Sunnah."

Ibn Ḥazm says, "He was reliable in his dīn and his knowledge."

Ibn Taymiyyah says, "Ibn Qutaybah was of those who subscribed to Aḥmad, and Isḥāq, and the supporters of the famous schools of the Ahl al-Sunnah."[1]

Al-Imāmah wa al-Siyāsah

There remains the issue of the book *al-Imāmah wa al-Siyāsah,* or *Tārīkh al-Khulafā'*; what is its status and is it correctly ascribed to Ibn Qutaybah?

If the book is proven to be spuriously ascribed to Ibn Qutaybah the entire argument of Tījānī collapses since this narration is at the heart of his argument. If the book is falsely ascribed to ibn Qutaybah it stands to reason that it has been authored by an anonymous author. If we have no idea about who the author of this book is, it is absolutely certain that the material in the book cannot be relied upon. Therefore, every argument that is supported by this narration is to be disregarded.

Ibn Qutaybah was a renowned scholar and many scholars have compiled biographical notes about him, as well as an index of his works. None of Ibn Qutaybah's biographers have mentioned the book *al-Imāmah wa al-Siyāsah* among his works. The only books attributed to him in the subject of history are *Kitāb al-Ma'ārif* and *Tārīkh Ibn Qutaybah.*[2]

Ibn Qutaybah is not known to have travelled; in fact he never left Baghdād except for Dīnawar.[3]There are passages in the book *al-Imāmah wa al-Siyāsah* which are inconsistent with all his other works. These passages infer that he travelled to Damascus and transmitted from its scholars. How is it possible for him to have transmitted from the scholars of Damascus when he had restricted himself to the East? Why is there no indication of these details in all his other works?

1 'Abd Allāh 'Īlān: *Kitāb al-Imāmah wa al-Siyāsah fī Mizān al-Taḥqīq al-'Ilmī*, p. 28.

2 'Abd Allāh 'Īlān: *Kitāb al-Imāmah wa al-Siyāsah fī Mizān al-Taḥqīq al-'Ilmī*, p. 23.

3 Op. cit. p. 23.

The content of *al-Imāmah wa al-Siyāsah* contradicts many accepted facts; even details Ibn Qutaybah himself attests to. We present the following example of a contradiction of fact; he mentions under the section titled, "ʿAlī's refusal to give Abū Bakr his pledge':

> Then ʿAlī was brought to Abū Bakr saying, "I am the slave of Allah and the brother of His Messenger!" When it was said to him, "Give your pledge to Abū Bakr," he replied, "I have more right to this matter (the position of khilāfah). I will not give my pledge. It is more appropriate that you give your pledge to me!"[1]

Besides these, the book *al-Imāmah wa al-Siyāsah* contains an abundance of clear historical mistakes. For example, he speaks of Abū al-ʿAbbās and al-Saffāḥ as if they were two separate individuals; whereas Abū al-ʿAbbās al-Saffāḥ is one person. He also makes Hārūn al-Rashīd the direct successor of al-Mahdī. Also, he asserts that Hārūn al-Rashīd entrusted the khilāfah to his son al-Ma'mūn (first) and after him to his (other) son al-Amīn. When we review Ibn Qutaybah's *Kitāb al-Maʿārif* he provides us with accurate accounts about al-Saffāḥ and Hārūn al-Rashīd, contradicting what the author of *al-Imāmah wa al-Siyāsah* stated.[2] The factual and historical contradictions in *al-Imāmah wa al-Siyāsah* with Ibn Qutaybah's other works are too obvious to ignore.

The methodology and style of the author of *al-Imāmah wa al-Siyāsah* is completely inconsistent with that of Ibn Qutaybah in his other books. Ibn Qutaybah is famous for lengthy introductions wherein he outlines his methodology and the purpose behind the compilation; whereas the introduction to *al-Imāmah wa al-Siyāsah* does not exceed three lines. We have not seen this in any of Ibn Qutaybah's other works.[3]

What is also noticeable from the book *al-Imāmah wa al-Siyāsah* is that the author does not pay much attention to structure and flow of ideas in his writing. He mentions a narration, then another, then returns later to complete the first. This haphazard, jumbled style is inconsistent with Ibn Qutaybah's other works which are distinguished by their excellent structure and flow.

---

1 Ibid. p. 17.

2 Ibid.

3 Ibid. p. 24.

From the book one gets the impression that the author is relating the conquest of Andalus directly from some contemporaries as it was occurring. It is well-known that the conquest of Andalus occurred during the year 92 A.H, close to 120 years before the birth of Ibn Qutaybah.

The narrations in *al-Imāmah wa al-Siyāsah* show Ibn Qutaybah to have directly transmitted from Ibn Abī Laylā. Muḥammad ibn ʿAbd al-Raḥmān ibn Abī Laylā was a famous jurist and judge in Kūfah, who died in the year 148 A.H; whereas Ibn Qutaybah was only born in the year 213 A.H. How is it possible for him to have heard ḥadīth from a teacher who passed away 65 years before he, Ibn Qutaybah, was born?[1]

Ibn Qutaybah's teachers, whom he usually transmits from in all his other works, are completely absent throughout *al-Imāmah wa al-Siyāsah.*[2] Furthermore, the author of *al-Imāmah wa al-Siyāsah* narrates from transmitters whom Ibn Qutaybah has never narrated from in any of his other books, such as Abū Maryam and Ibn ʿUfayr.[3] The author of *al-Imāmah wa al-Siyāsah* narrates from two senior scholars of Egypt. Ibn Qutaybah never visited Egypt and never took knowledge from any of its scholars.

If one considers all these inconsistencies, flaws, and contradictions, it becomes increasingly evident that the book *al-Imāmah wa al-Siyāsah* is indeed a forgery and falsely ascribed to Ibn Qutaybah. Even the Orientalists examined the origins of this book and they all came to the same conclusion; that it is impossible to ascribe it to Ibn Qutaybah.[4]

Sunnī's denouncing their scholars

Tījānī claims to have experienced a tendency with the Ahl al-Sunnah, whenever they are presented with a problematic statement of one of their own scholars, from which they have no escape, they simply claim the scholar was a Shīʿī.

Tījānī indirectly gives the impression that his arguments are so convincing that he is nearly invincible in a debate scenario. He could have saved the Shīʿah scholars a great deal of grief and spared the rise of Sunnī-Shīʿah sectarian violence.

1 Ibid. p. 24.

2 Ibid. p. 25.

3 Ibid. p. 26.

4 Ibid. p. 22-23.

The life of Iḥsān Ilāhī Ẓahīr, who was brutally assassinated by the Shīʿah, could have been spared if Tījānī had intervened. Incapable of responding to his arguments, the Shīʿah resorted to assassination. An explosive device was placed beneath the stage he was speaking from and sadly he was killed in the blast in 1987.

Similarly, when Aḥmad al-Kasrawī, originally a Shīʿī, stood up to refute their false claims with proofs and evidences in defense of the Ahl al-Sunnah wal-Jamāʿah[1] the Shīʿah had him shot. He did, however, recover after undergoing an operation. After his recovery, they raised a complaint to him and he was invited to verify the matter. However, at the last of those meetings in the year 1324 A.H he was shot once more, and attacked with a dagger. He died shortly thereafter with more than twenty nine wounds found on his body.[2]

Let us return to Tījānī's statement:

> **This is the type of propaganda that some of our scholars use when they lose the argument. Similarly al-Tabari was a Shi'ite, and al-Nisa'i, who wrote a book about the various aspects of Imām Ali, was a Shiite ...**

Our comment:

I would like to pause for a moment and reflect on this statement of Tījānī. When he says 'our scholars', is he saying this as a Sunnī or a Shīʿī? If he says it as a Shīʿī I would have to agree with him on two counts.

Shīʿah propaganda tactics

Firstly, in our interactions with the Shīʿah we have noticed their propaganda strategy wherein they give the innocent target the impression that so many Sunnī scholars were actually Shīʿah, or became Shīʿah. These are some of the very names that they use, "Did you know that al-Nasāʾī was a Shīʿī? Did you know that ʿAbd al-Razzāq was a Shīʿī? One of the first scholars to compile a textbook on the sciences of ḥadīth, al-Ḥākim al-Naysābūrī, was a Shīʿī..."

Secondly, when the Sunnī's quote from reliable books of the Shīʿah, the Shīʿah desperately denounce their own scholars when they are at a loss for answers. Due to the length of this section, and it not being the core argument, I will merely present one such example where the Shīʿah denounce their own scholars due to

1 Refer to his book *al-Tashayyuʿ wa al-Shīʿah.*

2 Ibid.

their inability to answer the incriminating evidence found in his book. Take the case of Ibn Abī al-Ḥadīd al-Madā'inī[1], the author of *Sharḥ Nahj al-Balāghah.* When the Shī'ah are presented with quotations from his book the most convenient exit strategy is to say, "He was a Sunnī." How are they going to explain away the glowing praise for him by numerous Shī'ī scholars; the likes of al-Khuwānasārī[2] and al-Majlisī?[3] Not only did they praise him, but they acknowledged him as a committed Shī'ī with excessive attachment to the Noble household.

Meaning of Shī'ah

Getting back to my original comment; when Tījānī says 'our scholars' does he refer to Sunnī scholars? Unfortunately this description lacks credibility. Perhaps it is necessary to clarify something which is oftentimes confusing to many, be they from Ahl al-Sunnah or the Shī'ah.

The term Shī'ah lexically means a group or partisans. Technically it refers to those who aligned themselves with 'Alī ibn Abī Ṭālib رضي الله عنه and considered themselves his partisans. The term Shī'ah, however, is very comprehensive and covers a broad spectrum of applications. On one end of the spectrum it refers to one with an extra attachment to 'Alī رضي الله عنه; whereas the other end includes those who deify him. The term Shī'ah, therefore, is very encompassing and the common feature in all described with *Tashayyu'*[4] is their attachment to 'Alī ibn Abī Ṭālib رضي الله عنه.

---

1 Ibn Abī al-Ḥadīd al-'Irāqi: 'Abd al-Ḥamīd ibn Hibat Allāh ibn Muḥammad ibn Muḥammad ibn al-Ḥusayn, Abū Ḥāmid, Ibn Abī al-Ḥadīd, 'Izz al-Dīn al-Madā'inī; the man of letters, the eloquent poet, the extremist Shī'ī. He is the author of a commentary on *Nahj al-Balāghah* in 20 volumes. He was born at Madā'in in the year 586. Then he went to Baghdad and became one of the poets in the court of the Khalīfah. He enjoyed the favour of the wazīr Ibn al-'Alqamī, on account of the two of them having literature and Shī'ism in common. *al-Bidāyah wal-Nihāyah*, vol. 9 p. 82.

2 *Rawḍāt al-Jannāt*, vol. 5 p. 19-20.

3 *Biḥār al-Anwār*, vol. 108 p. 72-73.

4 In general Tashayyu' is patronage to 'Alī, love for him, and preferring him over all the Ṣaḥābah after Abū Bakr and 'Umar.

Abū al-Qāsim al-Balkhī said:

> A man asked Sharīk ibn 'Abd Allāh ibn Abī Namir, "Who is better, Abū Bakr or 'Alī?"
>
> He replied, "Abū Bakr."
>
> The questioner said to him, "You say this and you are from amongst the Shī'ah?"
>
> He said, "Yes, a Shī'ī is the one who holds this view. By Allah one day 'Alī ascended this mimbar and said, 'Indeed, Abū Bakr is the best of this Ummah after the Prophet صلى الله عليه وسلم, then 'Umar.' Should we reject his statement? Should we belie him? By Allah he was not a liar."*continued...*

On the other hand there is another term used frequently, Rāfiḍah. Lexically, it is the plural of the word Rāfiḍī, which means one who rejects or abandons. Technically it refers to an extreme brand within the spectrum of Shīʿah where the status of ʿAlī رضي الله عنه cannot be accepted without rejecting Abū Bakr and ʿUmar رضي الله عنهما. Therefore every Rāfidī is a Shīʿī, but not every Shīʿī is necessarily a Rāfiḍī.

The Twelver Shīʿah, also called Imāmiyyah or Jaʿfariyyah, are considered Rāfiḍah[1]. However, due to this brand of Shīʿism being the largest in number and the most

---

continued from page 219

See *Minhāj al-Sunnah*, vol. 1 p. 13-14; Refer also to the book *Tathbīt Dalāʾil al-Nubuwwah*, Qāḍī ʿAbd al-Jabbār al-Ḥamdānī, vol. 1 p. 549 with the research of Dr. ʿAbd al-Karīm ʿUthmān, published by Dār al-ʿArabiyyah, Beirut.

1 Ibn Ḥajar says in the introduction of his book, *Fatḥ al-Bārī*:

> Tashayyuʿ is love for ʿAlī and preferring him among the Ṣaḥābah. The one who prefers him over Abū Bakr and ʿUmar is extreme in his Tashayyuʿ and (sometimes) the term Rāfiḍī is applied to him, otherwise the term Shīʿī will apply. If cursing or explicit hatred is added to that then he is extreme in his Rafḍ. If he believes in rajʿah then he is even more extreme (in his Rafḍ).

Ibn Taymiyyah says:

> The word Rāfiḍah only became widespread when they abandoned Zayd ibn ʿAlī ibn Ḥusayn during the khilāfah of Hishām... From the time of Zayd's rebellion the Shīʿah have been split into Rāfiḍah and Zaydiyyah. When he (Zayd) was asked about Abū Bakr and ʿUmar رضي الله عنهما, he prayed for Allah's mercy upon them. Consequently, they abandoned him and he remarked, "Rafaḍtumūnī (you have forsaken me)" and from that point on they were called the Rāfiḍah because of their abandoning him. The person who did not abandon him of the Shīʿah was called a Zaydī because of his (continued) allegiance to him.

Once Muḥammad Taqī Lisān al-Mulk, a Shīʿī scholar, said:

> When Zayd's companions came out with him they asked him about Abū Bakr and ʿUmar. He replied, "I have nothing but good to say about them and I heard nothing but good from my family about them." They then said to him, "You are not our companion (leader)," and abandoned him. Zayd then said, "They abandoned me today," and from that day they were called the Rāfiḍah...
>
> Zayd prevented them from cursing the Ṣaḥābah and when they realised that he was not going to dissociate himself from Shaykhayn, Abū Bakr and ʿUmar, they abandoned him and split from him. After that episode this word was applied to every person who was extreme in the school and permitted the cursing of the Ṣaḥābah.

See *Nāsikh al-Tawārīkh*, vol. 3 p. 590 under the statements of Zayn al-ʿĀbidīn; Also refer to *al-Shīʿah wa Ahl al-Bayt* of Iḥsān Ilāhī Ẓahīr.

politicised since the Safavid invasion in Persia; and due to the proselytizing in the wake of the 1979 Iranian Revolution; the term Shīʿah evolved and is almost exclusively associated with this brand of extreme Shīʿism.

Hence we find people often applying the restricted modern application of this term to the comprehensive usage of it in the classical period of Islamic history. Therefore, a person called a Shīʿah in former times might have been someone who fought alongside ʿAlī رضي الله عنه against Muʿāwiyah رضي الله عنه, or favoured ʿAlī رضي الله عنه over Muʿāwiyah رضي الله عنه during the Fitnah, but this person would condemn the beliefs which later formed into Twelver Shīʿism.

If one is able to distinguish the diverse usage of this term, it will clarify much of the confusion that has resulted out of applying a modern conventional usage of a term to interpret a history where that term has been applied comprehensively.

Ḥasan ibn Mūsā al-Nawbakhtī, a theologian of the Twelver Shīʿah said that cursing Abū Bakr and ʿUmar رضي الله عنهما was not found amongst the early partisans of ʿAlī and that the first person to spread cursing was the Jew, ʿAbd Allāh ibn Saba'. He says:

> He was amongst those who spread cursing of Abū Bakr, ʿUmar, ʿUthmān, and the rest of the Ṣaḥābah and dissociation from them.[1]

Sadly this dishonest strategy of exploiting the public's confusion in this matter has been employed by many Shīʿī scholars and preachers before Tījānī. I would like to remind the reader once again about Tījānī's pledge of objectivity and impartiality.

Were al-Ṭabarī and al-Nasā'ī Shīʿah?

The list of Sunnī scholars who are said to be Shīʿah is very long. Tījānī has alluded to al-Ṭabarī and al-Nasā'ī. There might have been a few isolated statements by these scholars which might have resulted in some scholars claiming that they had a tinge of Tashayyuʿ in them.

Let us take the case of al-Nasā'ī. Al-Nasā'ī said to his student:

> When I entered Damascus I found many people who were against ʿAlī رضي الله عنه, so I wrote *'Khaṣā'iṣ ʿAlī'* (on the Virtues of ʿAlī) hoping that Allah will guide them through this book.

---

1 al-Nawbakhtī: *Firaq al-Shīʿah*, p. 23.

> Then I (al-Nasā'ī) was asked, "Why don't you write on the virtues of Muʿāwiyah رضي الله عنه (specifically, as he already collected aḥādīth with praise of Ṣaḥābah in general which include Muʿāwiyah)?"
>
> He replied, "What should I write for him? Should I write the ḥadīth which states: 'May Allah not fill his belly.'?"[1]

At first glance this might be interpreted as a very slight form of Shīʿism.

What will we say when we see what al-Nasā'ī had to say about Muʿāwiyah? When questioned about specific authentic aḥādīth, al-Nasā'ī had nothing to offer. However, when considering the status of companionship in Muʿāwiyah رضي الله عنه this is what al-Nasā'ī had to say:

> Indeed Islam is like a home with a door. The door of Islam is the Companions. So whoever causes harm to the Companions in essence wishes to cause harm to Islam just as one who knocks at the door intends to enter that home. As for those who seek out Muʿāwiyah, they only want to get to the Companions.[2]

Compare this to the belief of those who condemn Abū Bakr for carrying out the instruction of Allah's Messenger صلى الله عليه وسلم in regards to Fadak!

As for Ṭāhā Ḥusayn, I have no reason to comment since his writings indicate that he held heretical beliefs. By no definition is he considered from the Ahl al-Sunnah. It serves no purpose to bring up a twentieth century literary critic, who was not remotely considered from the fraternity of Sunnī scholarship; unless the motive is to mislead an innocent reader by employing ancient Shīʿah propaganda strategies.

Tījānī goes on to say:

> **Let us return to the incident mentioned by Ibn Qutaybah in which Fāṭimah allegedly was angered by Abu Bakr and Umar. If I doubt the authenticity of that story, then I could not doubt the authenticity of al-Bukhari's book, which we consider to be the most correct book after the Book of Allah. As we have committed ourselves to the fact that it is correct, then the Shiites have the right to use it in their protestation against us and force us to keep**

1 Al-Dhahabī: *Tadhkirat al-Ḥuffāẓ*, vol.2 p. 194.

2 Al-Mizzī: *Tahdhīb al-Kamāl*, vol. 1 p. 45, 'Al-Ḥākim has narrated with his chain to Abū al-Ḥasan ʿAlī ibn Muḥammad al-Qābisī who said, 'I heard Abū al-Ḥasan ibn Hilāl saying: Abū ʿAbd al-Raḥmān al-Nasā'ī was asked about Muʿāwiyah ibn Abī Sufyān, the Companion of the Messenger of Allah صلى الله عليه وسلم...'"

to our commitment, as is only fair for sensible people. In his book, al-Bukhari writes in a chapter entitled "The virtues of the relatives of the Messenger of Allah" the following: The Messenger of Allah ﷺ said, "Fāṭimah is part of me, and whoever angers her angers me." Also in a chapter about "The Khaybar Raid" he wrote: According to Aishah, Fāṭimah- may Allah's peace be upon her - daughter of the Prophet, sent a message to Abu Bakr asking him for her share of the inheritance of the Messenger of Allah, but he refused to pay Fāṭimah anything of it. Fāṭimah became so angry at Abu Bakr that she left him and never spoke to him before her death.

The final result is one, al-Bukhari mentioned it briefly and Ibn Qutaybah talked about it in some detail, and that is: the Messenger of Allah ﷺ is angry when Fāṭimah is angry, and he is satisfied when Fāṭimah is satisfied, and that she died while she was still angry with Abu Bakr and Umar.

If al-Bukhari said: She died while she was still angry at Abu Bakr, and did not speak to him before she died, then the end result is quite clear. If Fāṭimah is "the leading lady among all the ladies" as al-Bukhari declared in the section al-Isti'dhan, and if Fāṭimah is the only lady in this nation whom Allah kept clean and pure, then her anger could not be but just, therefore Allah and His Messenger get angry for her anger. Because of that Abu Bakr said, "May Allah – the Most High - save me from His anger and Fāṭimah's anger." Then he cried very bitterly when she said, "By Allah, I will curse you in every prayer that I do." He came out crying and said, "I do not need your pledge of allegiance and discharge me from my duties."... Furthermore, before she died, she asked to be buried secretly, and at night, so that none of them could be present at her funeral.[1]

Our comment:

Tījānī has linked the narration attributed to Ibn Qutaybah with the narrations found in al-Bukhārī. He argues for the condemnation of Abū Bakr based on the ḥadīth where the Prophet ﷺ says, "I am hurt by what hurts her..." He also insinuates that withholding the distribution of the Prophet's ﷺ wealth after his demise is a crime worthy of rebuke. He stresses on the point of Fāṭimah رضي الله عنها departing from this world whilst she was still angry with Abū Bakr and refused to speak to him until her death.

1 *Then I was guided*, p. 114-116.

Ḥadīth of causing harm to Fāṭimah رَضِيَ اللّٰهُ عَنْهَا

Previously we had suggested that the reader reflect when this ḥadīth was mentioned, in what context and about whom. If we ignore the context then the ḥadīth is subject to wanton interpretation, and misleading application. Let us examine the context in which the Prophet ﷺ said these words.

Al-Bukhārī narrates:

عن المسور بن مخرمة قال سمعت رسول الله صلى الله عليه و سلم يقول وهو على المنبر أن بني هشام بن المغيرة استأذنوا في أن ينكحوا ابنتهم علي بن أبي طالب فلا آذن ثم لا آذن ثم لا آذن إلا أن يريد ابن أبي طالب أن يطلق ابنتي وينكح ابنتهم فأنما هي بضعة مني يريبني ما أرابها ويؤذيني ما أذاها

Miswar ibn Makhramah رَضِيَ اللّٰهُ عَنْهُ said, "I heard the Messenger ﷺ saying while on the mimbar, 'Indeed, Banū Hishām ibn al-Mughīrah sought permission (from me) to marry their daughter to ʿAlī ibn Abī Ṭālib. I do not grant them permission! I do not grant them permission! I do not grant them permission! Except if ʿAlī ibn Abī Ṭālib divorces my daughter and marries their daughter. She is a part of me, what alarms her alarms me and what hurts her hurts me.'"[1]

Muslim also narrates this ḥadīth with the same wording from Miswar ibn Makhramah رَضِيَ اللّٰهُ عَنْهُ in his Ṣaḥīḥ.[2]

It appears that this ḥadīth was said in rebuke of ʿAlī رَضِيَ اللّٰهُ عَنْهُ. The corollary to Tījānī's arguments against Abū Bakr رَضِيَ اللّٰهُ عَنْهُ is that ʿAlī رَضِيَ اللّٰهُ عَنْهُ deserves the same level of criticism since he hurt her by seeking the hand of the daughter of Abū Jahl. If hurting Fāṭimah رَضِيَ اللّٰهُ عَنْهَا is a sin, is ʿAlī رَضِيَ اللّٰهُ عَنْهُ still infallible? Was ʿAlī acting on the instruction of the Prophet ﷺ or was it a personal interest that he pursued? Was ʿAlī رَضِيَ اللّٰهُ عَنْهُ accorded the latitude of repentance? If ʿAlī could repent from a proposal, which was a personal matter which caused harm to Fāṭimah, surely Abū Bakr is in a greater position for repentance since he did not act in his personal interest but in fulfilment of the command of the Prophet ﷺ.

---

1 Refer to Ṣaḥīḥ al-Bukhārī, Kitāb al-Nikāḥ: bāb Dhabb al-Rajul ʿan Ibnatih fī al-Ghayrah wa al-Inṣāf, Ḥadīth no. 4932.

2 Ṣaḥīḥ Muslim, Kitāb Faḍāʾil al-Ṣaḥābah, bāb Faḍāʾil Fāṭimah, Ḥadīth no. 2449.

Objectivity and impartiality demand equal treatment in this matter. Whatever reason is given to exonerate ʿAlī رضي الله عنه applies even greater to Abū Bakr رضي الله عنه since he had nothing to gain from his actions.

Ḥadīth of ʿĀ'ishah

If Tījānī even bothered to refer to *Ṣaḥīḥ al-Bukhārī* and find this ḥadīth then he sacrificed all claims to objectivity when he chose only to present the portion of it which he believed served his purpose. If he did not refer to the original text in *Ṣaḥīḥ al-Bukhārī* but relied on what he read in the books of the Shīʿah, then he has disappointed us by breeching our trust and going against his pledge to us.

Here I am obliged to transmit the ḥadīth of ʿĀ'ishah رضي الله عنها in its entirety so that it may become clear to the objective reader, who seeks the truth.

> عن عائشة أن فاطمة بنت رسول الله صلى الله عليه وسلم أرسلت إلى أبي بكر الصديق تسأله ميراثها من رسول الله صلى الله عليه وسلم مما أفاء الله عليه بالمدينة وفدك وما بقي من خمس خيبر فقال أبو بكر إن رسول الله صلى الله عليه وسلم قال لا نورث ما تركنا صدقة إنما يأكل آل محمد صلى الله عليه وسلم في هذا المال وإني والله لا أغير شيئا من صدقة رسول الله صلى الله عليه وسلم عن حالها التي كانت عليها في عهد رسول الله صلى الله عليه وسلم ولأعملن فيها بما عمل به رسول الله صلى الله عليه وسلم فأبى أبو بكر أن يدفع إلى فاطمة شيئا فوجدت فاطمة على أبي بكر في ذلك قال فهجرته فلم تكلمه حتى توفيت وعاشت بعد رسول الله صلى الله عليه وسلم ستة أشهر فلما توفيت دفنها زوجها علي بن أبي طالب ليلا ولم يؤذن بها أبا بكر وصلى عليها علي وكان لعلي من الناس وجهة حياة فاطمة فلما توفيت استنكر علي وجوه الناس فالتمس مصالحة أبي بكر ومبايعته ولم يكن بايع تلك الأشهر فأرسل إلى أبي بكر أن ائتنا ولا يأتنا معك أحد كراهية محضر عمر بن الخطاب فقال عمر لأبي بكر والله لا تدخل عليهم وحدك فقال أبو بكر وما عساهم أن يفعلوا بي إني والله لآتينهم فدخل عليهم أبو بكر فتشهد علي بن أبي طالب ثم قال إنا قد عرفنا يا أبا بكر فضيلتك وما أعطاك الله ولم ننفس عليك خيرا ساقه الله إليك ولكنك استبددت علينا

بالأمر وكنا نحن نرى لنا حقا لقرابتنا من رسول الله صلى الله عليه وسلم فلم يزل يكلم أبا بكر حتى فاضت عينا أبي بكر فلما تكلم أبو بكر قال والذي نفسي بيده لقرابة رسول الله صلى الله عليه وسلم أحب إلي أن أصل من قرابتي وأما الذي شجر بيني وبينكم من هذه الأموال فإني لم آل فيها عن الحق ولم أترك أمرا رأيت رسول الله صلى الله عليه وسلم يصنعه فيها إلا صنعته فقال علي لأبي بكر موعدك العشية للبيعة فلما صلى أبو بكر صلاة الظهر رقي على المنبر فتشهد وذكر شأن علي وتخلفه عن البيعة وعذره بالذي اعتذر إليه ثم استغفر وتشهد علي بن أبي طالب فعظم حق أبي بكر وأنه لم يحمله على الذي صنع نفاسة على أبي بكر ولا إنكارا للذي فضله الله به ولكنا كنا نرى لنا في الأمر نصيبا فاستبد علينا به فوجدنا في أنفسنا فسر بذلك المسلمون وقالوا أصبت فكان المسلمون إلى علي قريبا حين راجع الأمر المعروف

ʿĀ'ishah narrates that Fāṭimah, the daughter of the Messenger ﷺ, sent someone to Abū Bakr to ask him for her share of the Messenger's ﷺ estate from what Allah سُبْحَانَهُ وَتَعَالَىٰ gave him in Madīnah, and Fadak, and what was left from the fifth of the income (annually received) from Khaybar.

Abū Bakr said, "The Messenger of Allah ﷺ said, 'We, the Prophets, do not have any heirs; what we leave behind is given in charity. The household of the Messenger of Allah ﷺ will eat from this wealth (revenue generated from properties).' By Allah, I will not alter the charity of the Messenger ﷺ from the condition it was in during his time. I will do the same with it as the Messenger of Allah ﷺ used to do."

Abū Bakr, therefore, refused to hand over anything to Fāṭimah, who became upset with him for this reason.

He (the narrator) said, "She avoided him and did not talk to him until the end of her life. She lived for six months after the death of the Messenger of Allah ﷺ. When she died, her husband, ʿAlī ibn Abī Ṭālib, buried her during the night and did not inform Abū Bakr and offered the funeral prayer over her himself.

During the lifetime of Fāṭimah, ʿAlī received (special) regard from the people. After she died, he sensed disaffection in the faces of the people towards him.

He, therefore, sought to make peace with Abū Bakr and offer his allegiance to him. He had not yet (publicly) given his allegiance to him as khalīfah during the previous months. He sent for Abū Bakr to come and see him and to come alone not wanting the presence of ʿUmar (at this meeting). ʿUmar said (to Abū Bakr), 'Do not go alone,' but Abū Bakr replied, 'What do you think they will do to me? I am going to them!'

Abū Bakr went to them and ʿAlī testified to the oneness of Allah and said, 'Indeed, we know your virtue and what Allah has given you and we were not jealous of any good which Allah has steered in your direction. However, you acted independently on the matter (of khilāfah) and surprised us and we thought ourselves worthy of a portion (an opinion) in the matter on account of our relationship with the Messenger of Allah.'

(ʿAlī spoke) until tears flowed from Abū Bakr. When Abū Bakr spoke he said, 'By the One Who has control of my life, to maintain good ties with the relatives of the Messenger ﷺ is more beloved to me than maintaining good ties with my own relatives. As for what has transpired between you and me concerning this wealth, (Fadak and the inheritance of the Messenger), I have not deviated from the right course and I have not given up doing what the Messenger of Allah ﷺ used to do with it.'

ʿAlī then said to Abū Bakr, 'I will meet you this afternoon for the (public) pledge of allegiance.' (Later that afternoon) when Abū Bakr had completed his Ẓuhr Ṣalāh he ascended the mimbar, read the tashahhud, extolled ʿAlī's virtues and mentioned the excuse ʿAlī gave him for delaying his pledge and sought Allah's forgiveness. (Then) ʿAlī read the tashahhud, highlighted the right of Abū Bakr and told (the people) that it was not jealousy of Abū Bakr or denial of what Allah preferred him with that caused him to do what he did (referring to postponement of his pledge). Rather, (he said), "We felt that we had a portion in this matter but it was taken despite us (without our consultation) and for that reason we were upset." The Muslims were pleased with that (his speech and explanation) and said, "You have done the right thing." The Muslims felt closer to ʿAlī after he took that position.[1]

Muslim also narrates this ḥadīth in his *Ṣaḥīḥ* from ʿĀ'ishah رضي الله عنها with the same wording.[2]

1 *Ṣaḥīḥ al-Bukhārī*, Kitāb al-Maghāzī, bāb Ghazwah al-Khaybar, Ḥadīth no. 3997.

2 *Ṣaḥīḥ Muslim*, Kitāb al-Jihād wa al-Siyar, bāb Qawl al-Nabī ﷺ 'lā nūrath', Ḥadīth no. 1759.

Let us consider some of the details covered by this narration.

It is evident from this narration that the monetary rights of the Ahl al-Bayt were fulfilled by Abū Bakr رضي الله عنه from the alms of Madīnah Munawwarah, the income of Fadak, and the booty of Khaybar during his khilāfah. However, these assets were not handed over to them and distributed in the form of inheritance due to the edict of the Messenger صلى الله عليه وسلم.

Furthermore, it is also understood that Abū Bakr رضي الله عنه did not use his own discretion in fulfilling their monetary rights and hence did not expropriate their rights. Rather, he fulfilled them exactly as the Messenger صلى الله عليه وسلم did when he was alive.

This narration also establishes that he gave preference to the Ahl al-Bayt in (maintaining relations with them, being loyal to them and fulfilling their rights) over himself and his family.

Another point to be noted is that there was no objection from ʿAlī رضي الله عنه to Abū Bakr's رضي الله عنه policy regarding the wealth left behind by the Prophet صلى الله عليه وسلم; nor in the manner in which the wealth was been administered.

The Rāfiḍah are known to deny ʿAlī's pledge of allegiance to Abū Bakr. Since Tījānī has 'committed' to accept this narration he has to acknowledge that the pledge of allegiance took place indeed.

As for Abū Bakr not giving Fāṭimah the inheritance, these are the reasons:

The Prophet صلى الله عليه وسلم said:

مَا نُورَثُ مَا تَرَكْنَا صَدَقَةٌ

We are not inherited from. What we leave behind is a charity

Abū Bakr, ʿUmar, ʿUthmān, ʿAlī, Ṭalḥah, Zubayr, Saʿd, ʿAbd al-Raḥmān ibn ʿAwf, ʿAbbās, Abū Hurayrah and the wives of the Prophet صلى الله عليه وسلم all narrate this ḥadīth. The transmission of this ḥadīth is established in the *Ṣiḥāḥ* and the *Masānīd*. There is, therefore, without doubt, an *Ijmāʿ* (consensus) of the Ṣaḥābah upon it (the implication of this ḥadīth). Abū Bakr practising upon the bequest of the Messenger cannot be blameworthy.

There are also other authentic aḥādīth which support this fact. Al-Bukhārī narrates in his Ṣaḥīḥ from Abū Hurayrah رضي الله عنه that the Messenger صلى الله عليه وسلم said:

لا يقتسم ورثتي دينارا ما تركت بعد نفقة نسائي ومؤونة عاملي فهو صدقة

> My heirs will not share a dīnār. What I leave behind, after the expenses of my wives and the salaries of my workers, is a charity.[1]

Abū Dāwūd narrates in his Sunan in a portion of the ḥadīth of Abū Dardā' رضي الله عنه that the Prophet صلى الله عليه وسلم said:

وإن العلماء ورثة الأنبياء وإن الأنبياء لم يورثوا دينارا ولا درهما ورثوا العلم فمن أخذه أخذ بحظ وافر

> And indeed the scholars are the heirs of the ambiyā', and the ambiyā' did not leave behind a dīnār or a dirham, rather they left behind knowledge; so whoever takes it has taken a huge portion.[2]

How can a person be censured for acting on the ḥadīth of the Prophet صلى الله عليه وسلم?

This last ḥadīth is not exclusively found in the books of Ahl al-Sunnah. The celebrated Shīʿī scholar al-Kulaynī quotes it in *al-Uṣūl min al-Kāfī.*

Al-Kulaynī narrates in his *Uṣūl*, in the chapter concerning the reward of the *ʿālim* (the learned scholar) and the *mutaʿallim* (the student) — from ʿAlī ibn Ibrāhīm — from his father — from Ḥammād ibn ʿĪsā — from al-Qaddāḥ — from Abū ʿAbd Allāh (al-Ṣādiq), he said:

> The Messenger said, "Whoever treads a path seeking in it knowledge, Allah takes him on a path to Jannah. Indeed the angels lower their wings for the student of knowledge out of satisfaction with him and the inhabitants of the heaven and earth, even the fish in the ocean, pray for the forgiveness for the student of knowledge. The superiority of the ʿālim over the *ʿābid* (worshipper) is like the superiority of the moon—on the night of the full moon—over all of the stars. **Indeed, the scholars are the heirs of the ambiyā' and the**

1 *Ṣaḥīḥ al-Bukhārī*, Kitāb al-Waṣāyā, Ḥadīth no. 2624; And *Ṣaḥīḥ Muslim*, Kitāb al-Jihād wa al-Siyar, Ḥadīth no. 1760.

2 *Sunan Abī Dāwūd*, Kitāb al-ʿIlm, bāb Faḍl al-ʿIlm, Ḥadīth no. 3641; Refer also to *Ṣaḥīḥ Abī Dāwūd*, Ḥadīth no. 3096.

ambiyā' did not leave behind a dīnār or a dirham but they left behind knowledge. The one who takes therefrom has taken a great portion."[1]

Did Abū Bakr intend to harm Fāṭimah?

Abū Bakr did not claim this wealth for himself or for his family. He was not of the beneficiaries of this charity. The consequence of withholding the distribution of this inheritance included his daughter, ʿĀ'ishah رضي الله عنها. Likewise he did not distribute it among any of the wives of the Messenger صلى الله عليه وسلم. If Abū Bakr denied the right of Fāṭimah رضي الله عنها then he was indiscriminate since he gave nothing to his own daughter.

Al-Bukhārī and Muslim narrate from ʿUrwah—from ʿĀ'ishah رضي الله عنها that after the Prophet's صلى الله عليه وسلم demise his wives considered sending ʿUthmān to Abū Bakr to ask for their inheritance. Then ʿĀ'ishah رضي الله عنها said, did the Prophet صلى الله عليه وسلم not say:

ما نورث ما تركنا صدقة

We are not inherited from. What we leave behind is a charity.[2]

Abū Bakr gave ʿAlī and his family control of the wealth which the Prophet left behind and ʿUmar did the same. If they intended to cause harm, why hand over the administration of the revenue from these properties to the Prophet's صلى الله عليه وسلم family?

Abū Bakr رضي الله عنه ensured Fāṭimah رضي الله عنها of her financial security. Abū Hurayrah رضي الله عنه narrates:

جات فاطمة إلى ابي بكر فقالت من يرثك ؟ قال أهلي وولدي قالت فما لي لا أرث ابي ؟ فقال ابو بكر سمعت رسول الله صلى الله عليه و سلم يقول لا نورث ولكني أعول من كان رسول الله صلى الله عليه و سلم يعوله وأنفق على من كان رسول الله صلى الله عليه و سلم ينفق عليه

Fāṭimah came to Abū Bakr and said, "Who will inherit from you?" He said, "My family and my children." She said, "Why is it then that I do not inherit

---

1 *Al-Uṣūl min al-Kāfī*, al-Kulaynī, vol. 1 p. 26-27, Kitāb Faḍl al-ʿIlm.

2 *Ṣaḥīḥ Muslim*, Kitāb al-Jihād wa al-Siyar, Ḥadīth no. 1758; *Ṣaḥīḥ al-Bukhārī*, Kitāb al-Farā'iḍ, ḥadīth: 6349.

> from my father?" Abū Bakr replied, "I heard the Messenger saying, 'We are not inherited from', but I will support those whom the Messenger of Allah ﷺ used to support, and I will spend upon those whom the Messenger of Allah ﷺ spent upon."[1]

Abū Bakr is among those who spent his wealth during the lifetime of the Prophet, is it conceivable that he would harm the Prophet's ﷺ daughter by withholding her wealth?

Ibn ʿAbbās and Abū Hurayrah رضي الله عنهما narrate that the Prophet ﷺ said, "No one's wealth has benefited as Abū Bakr's wealth has benefited me."[2]

Abū Hurayrah رضي الله عنه reported Allah's Messenger ﷺ as saying:

> If anyone contributes a pair of anything for the sake of Allah, he would be invited to enter Paradise (with these words), "O servant of Allah, it is good (for you)." Those who engage in prayer will be invited to enter by the gate of prayer; those who take part in Jihād will be invited to enter by the gate of Jihād; those who give charity will be invited to enter by the gate of charity; and those who observe fast will be invited to enter by the gate al-Rayyān.
>
> Abū Bakr said, "O Messenger of Allah, is it necessary that a person be invited through only one of these gates? Will anyone be invited to enter by all those gates?"
>
> The Messenger of Allah ﷺ said, "Yes, and I hope you will be one of them."

It must be known that Abū Bakr رضي الله عنه loved the family of the Prophet ﷺ dearly and respected them. It is for this reason that he said:

والله لقرابة رسول الله صلى الله عليه و سلم أحب الي أن أصل من قرابتي

> By Allah! To maintain a good relationship with the family of the Prophet ﷺ is more beloved to me than to maintain a good relationship with my own family.[3]

---

1 *Sunan al-Tirmidhī*, Kitāb al-Siyar, Ḥadīth no. 1608; Refer also to *Ṣaḥīḥ al-Tirmidhī*, Ḥadīth no. 1310.

2 *Ṣaḥīḥ al-Bukhārī*, Kitāb al-Salāt, Ḥadīth no. 467, *Sunan al-Tirmidhī*, Kitāb al-Manāqib, Ḥadīth no. 4022.

3 *Ṣaḥīḥ al-Bukhārī*, Kitāb al-Maghāzī, vol. 4, Ḥadīth no. 3810.

ارقبوا محمدا صلى الله عليه و سلم في أهل بيته

Honour Muḥammad through his family.[1]

Now, after presenting the reasons for Abū Bakr's position, is it acceptable to attack him, accuse him of harming and angering Fāṭimah رضي الله عنها, and oppressing her of her right? I leave it to the fair and objective reader to decide.

Relationship between Abū Bakr and Fāṭimah

It would be prudent to clarify a few points which might linger in the mind of the esteemed reader concerning Fāṭimah's رضي الله عنها anger towards Abū Bakr رضي الله عنه over the inheritance, and her burial at night.

The scholars of the Ahl al-Sunnah confirm that the position which is in line with the dictates of the Prophet صلى الله عليه وسلم is the one taken by Abū Bakr رضي الله عنه. Therefore, they have sought out plausible explanations for her reactions which are in line with the lofty status of Fāṭimah رضي الله عنها.

Bear in mind that Fāṭimah رضي الله عنها in no way resembles the Munāfiqīn about whom Allah سبحانه وتعالى says:

وَمِنْهُم مَّن يَلْمِزُكَ فِي الصَّدَقَاتِ فَإِنْ أُعْطُوا مِنْهَا رَضُوا وَإِن لَّمْ يُعْطَوْا مِنْهَا إِذَا هُمْ يَسْخَطُونَ وَلَوْ أَنَّهُمْ رَضُوا مَا آتَاهُمُ اللَّهُ وَرَسُولُهُ وَقَالُوا حَسْبُنَا اللَّهُ سَيُؤْتِينَا اللَّهُ مِن فَضْلِهِ وَرَسُولُهُ إِنَّا إِلَى اللَّهِ رَاغِبُونَ

And among them are some who criticise you concerning the [distribution of] charities. If they are given from them, they approve; but if they are not given from them, at once they become angry. If only they had been satisfied with what Allah and His Messenger صلى الله عليه وسلم *gave them and said, "Sufficient for us is Allah; Allah will give us of His bounty, and [so will] His Messenger* صلى الله عليه وسلم*; indeed, we are desirous toward Allah," [it would have been better for them].*[2]

1 *Ṣaḥīḥ al-Bukhārī*, Kitāb Faḍā'il al-Ṣaḥābah, bāb Manāqib Qarābah Messenger, Ḥadīth no. 3509.

2 Sūrah al-Tawbah: 58-59.

As a matter of fact, those who insist that she was upset because of not receiving her wealth are inadvertently likening her to the Munāfiqīn who became angry when they were not given wealth even when it was Allah's command.

There are two approaches by which the scholars have clarified this issue. The first approach is based on the methods of the Fuqahā'. This is how they deal with this objection:

> Despite Abū Bakr's argument based on the ḥadīth (as his proof), it was because she understood the ḥadīth differently to Abū Bakr. It is as if she believed that there was an exception to the rule when it came to the Prophet's صَلَّى ٱللَّهُ عَلَيْهِ وَسَلَّمَ statement, "We are not inherited from," and that there was no harm in inheriting from the land and property which Messenger صَلَّى ٱللَّهُ عَلَيْهِ وَسَلَّمَ left behind, whereas Abū Bakr held on to the general meaning of the ḥadīth. They therefore differed in a matter which allows for difference in interpretation. When he Abū Bakr persisted in his position, she avoided him.[1]

Imām al-Nawawī says in *Sharḥ Ṣaḥīḥ Muslim*:

> As for what he mentioned about Fāṭimah's avoidance of Abū Bakr, it refers to her withdrawing from meeting him and it is not the forbidden hijrān which refers to not greeting the person and turning away from him in a gathering.
>
> His words in the ḥadīth, "She did not speak to him," means she did not speak to him concerning this matter, or because of her withdrawal she did not request anything from him and was not compelled to meet him and speak to him. It has not been narrated that they met and she did not greet him and did not speak to him.[2]

The alternate method is in keeping with the method of the Muḥaddithīn. In this particular issue it appears that the method of the Muḥaddithīn seems more likely.

The scholars have listed all the narrations from ʿĀ'ishah رَضِيَ ٱللَّهُ عَنْهَا and compared the various versions of the ḥadīth. They have concluded that the expressions *Ghaḍab* (anger), *Wajd* (disillusionment), *Hijran* (avoidance) and *ʿAdam al-Takallum* (not wanting to talk), are not part of the actual narration. Instead it is the assumption of the narrator who, in his narration had added his understanding of the situation. If

1 *Fatḥ al-Bārī*, vol. 6 p. 233.

2 *Muslim* with the *Sharḥ*, vol. 12 p. 111.

one goes back to the narration, the entire episode of anger and not speaking to Abū Bakr رضي الله عنه appears after the words, 'He said'[1]. Upon investigation it became evident which narrator was most likely responsible for providing his understanding of events while narrating this ḥadīth. It appears to be Imām Muḥammad ibn Muslim ibn Shihāb al-Zuhrī.

It is stated regarding al-Zuhrī, that he had a habit of explaining the ḥadīth wherein he would add explanatory notes or his opinions to the ḥadīth. At times he would add these notes by means of words and phrases that would make them distinct from the actual ḥadīth and at times without doing so.

If we take either the interpretation on the method of the Fuqahā' or the ḥadīth-based explanation, there is evidence to suggest the anger was not permanent, nor was it merely for the sake of wealth. This is further supported by what is related by Imām Aḥmad in his *Musnad* with an interrupted chain:

> Ja'far ibn 'Amr ibn Umayyah said, "Fāṭimah entered upon Abū Bakr and said, 'The Messenger of Allah صلى الله عليه وسلم told me that I will be the first of his household to meet him.'"[2]

Al-Bayhaqī narrates from Sha'bī:

---

1 Maulana Muḥammad Nāfi' writes in his book, *Ruḥamā' Baynahum* pg 90:

Some of the narrations of this incident are emphatic whilst others are not. And by doing a comprehensive study of all of them, I have reached the following conclusions:

1. Out of the total thirty six narrations, eleven are narrated from other Sahabah besides 'A'ishah رضي الله عنها. For example, Abū Hurayrah, Abū al-Ṭufayl, 'Āmir ibn Wāthilah, and Umm Hāni' رضي الله عنهم, etc. Similarly, they are narrated from other narrators besides Ibn Shihab al-Zuhrī, and in none of them is Fāṭimah's displeasure mentioned.
2. The remaining twenty-five narrations are narrated by 'A'ishah رضي الله عنها and through the transmission of Ibn Shihab al-Zuhrī. They are of two types:
    - Nine of the twenty five narrations make no mention whatsoever of her displeasure.
    - The balance of them, which is sixteen narrations, make mention of her displeasure.
3. Furthermore the narrations indicating her displeasure mention it after the words "he said" and not after the words "she said" which means that the additions to come are not from 'A'ishah رضي الله عنها rather they are of a narrator who has narrated this incident from her.

2 *Musnad Aḥmad*, Ḥadīth no. 26420.

> Abū Bakr visited Fāṭimah and ʿAlī said to her, "It is Abū Bakr seeking permission to see you."
>
> She said to him, "Would you like me to grant him permission?"
>
> He replied, "Yes," and she permitted him to enter.
>
> Abū Bakr رضي الله عنه entered and spoke to her until she was pleased.

Even if this ḥadīth is *mursal* (ends with the Tābiʿī) its sanad leading to Shaʿbī is authentic and with it the confusion concerning Fāṭimah's avoidance of Abū Bakr رضي الله عنه is resolved.[1]

Al-Suyūṭī says:

> The *mursalāt* (plural of mursal) of Shaʿbī are authentic according to the leaders in knowledge of ḥadīth criticism. ʿIjlī says, "The mursal of Shaʿbī is authentic. When he narrates a mursal ḥadīth it is almost always authentic."[2]

Tījānī's citation of the narration falsely ascribed to Ibn Qutaybah in the book *Tārīkh al-Khulafā'* is clearly a lie and forgery. This narration, which includes the statement of Abū Bakr, reads, "I seek refuge by Allah from his anger and your anger, O Fāṭimah," then Abū Bakr's رضي الله عنه crying until he nearly died and his statement, "I do not need your pledge. Discharge me from my pledge (office)." By comparing this narration with the other narrations we have further advanced our earlier argument. It is also proof that Tījānī's linking the narration ascribed to Ibn Qutaybah with the narration in al-Bukhārī is flawed since the disparity between the two narrations is too great to be ignored.

Thus we come to see the fallacy in this statement of his:

> **The final result is one, al-Bukhari mentioned it briefly and Ibn Qutaybah talked about it in some detail, and that is: the Messenger of Allah صلى الله عليه وسلم is angry when Fāṭimah is angry, and he is satisfied when Fāṭimah is satisfied, and that she died while she was still angry with Abu Bakr and Umar.**

Then Tījānī says:

> **Many of our historians and scholars admit that Fāṭimah - may Allah's peace be upon her - challenged Abu Bakr in many cases such as the donations, the**

---

1 *Fatḥ al-Bārī*, vol. 6 p. 233.

2 *Musnad Fāṭimah al-Zahrā*, Jalāl al-Dīn al-Suyūṭī.

inheritance and the shares of the relatives, but her challenge was dismissed, and she died angry at him. However, our scholars seem to pass over these incidents without having the will to talk about them in some detail, so that they could as usual, preserve the integrity of Abu Bakr. One of the strange things that I have read regarding this subject, is what one of the writers said after he had mentioned the incident in some detail: God forbid that Fāṭimah should claim something that does not rightly belong to her, and God forbid that Abu Bakr denied her rights.

The writer thought that through this weak reasoning, he would be able to solve the problem and convince the researchers. He appears to be saying something similar to the following: God forbid that the Holy Qur'an should say anything but the truth, and God forbid that the sons of Israel should worship the calf. We have been plagued with scholars who say things that they cannot comprehend, and believe in the object and its antithesis, simultaneously. The point is that Fāṭimah claimed and Abu Bakr dismissed her claim, so she was either a liar - God forbid - or Abu Bakr treated her unjustly. There could be no third solution for the case, as some of our scholars would wish.[1]

Our comment:

Tījānī is being dishonest when he accuses the scholars of the Ahl al-Sunnah of overlooking the issue of Fadak. If anything, our comments in the previous paragraphs indicate the abundance of literature on this topic. Ibn Taymiyyah clarified this matter in his invaluable work, *Minhāj al-Sunnah al-Nabawiyyah*[2]. Likewise, Ibn Ḥajar explained the meaning of the ḥadīth in his commentary of *al-Bukhārī*, *Fatḥ al-Bārī*. Al-Nawawī, also explained this ḥadīth in his commentary on *Ṣaḥīḥ Muslim*, as mentioned previously. Let us not forget the book *Tuḥfah al-Ithnā al-ʿAshariyyah* of Shāh ʿAbd al-ʿAzīz al-Dehlawī and its abridged version by Maḥmūd Shukrī al-Ālūsī. Other scholars who have commented on the subject include Mubārakpūrī and the martyr, Iḥsān Ilāhī Ẓahīr.[3]

For a moment let us forget the scholars of the Ahl al-Sunnah. Let us see what the 'infallible' Imāms had to say. Ibn Abī al-Ḥadīd the Shīʿī commentator of *Nahj al-Balāghah*[4] writes:

1 *Then I was guided*, p. 115.

2 Refer to *Minhāj*, vol. 4 p. 193-264.

3 Here I refer to his book *al-Shīʿah wa Ahl al-Bayt*.

4 Refer to p. 219, footnote 1 of this book.

> Kathīr al-Nawā' states that he asked Imām Muḥammad al-Bāqir, "May my life be sacrificed upon you please tell me, 'Did Abū Bakr and 'Umar usurp your rights?'"
>
> Imām Muḥammad al-Bāqir replied, "I take an oath in that being who has revealed the glorious Qur'ān upon his slave they have not usurped our rights not even to the extent of a mustard seed."
>
> I further inquired, "Should I love them or disassociate myself from them?"
>
> Imām Muḥammad al-Bāqir said, "Love them in this world and in the Hereafter. I am responsible if you happen to incur harm because of loving them."
>
> He then said, "May Allah curse Mughīrah and Bannān for ascribing such lies to us, the Ahl al-Bayt."[1]

1. This statement of Imām Muḥammad al-Bāqir proves that Abū Bakr did not oppress the Ahl al-Bayt.
2. Abū Bakr and 'Umar fulfilled all the rights of the Ahl al-Bayt and had not usurped any of them.
3. Imām Muḥammad al-Bāqir encouraged love and veneration for Abū Bakr and 'Umar.
4. The narrations portraying them to be oppressors and usurpers are fabrications of the likes of Mughīrah ibn Sa'īd and Bannān, confounded liars

Ibn Abī al-Ḥadīd cites the following narration in *Sharḥ Nahj al-Balāghah*:

> Zayd ibn 'Alī ibn al-Ḥusayn said, "By Allah, if I were given the option of administering these funds I would adopt the same method as Abū Bakr."[2]

Ibn Abī al-Ḥadīd stated further in *Sharḥ Nahj al-Balāghah*:

> Abū Bakr would grant them enough to satisfy their needs from the revenue of Fadak and would distribute the rest among the poor. 'Umar had done the same after him, and so had 'Uthmān and 'Alī.[3]

---

1 *Sharḥ Nahj al-Balāghah*, vol. 4 p. 113.

2 Ibid.

3 *Sharḥ Nahj al-Balāghah*, vol. 2 p. 292.

Tījānī's reasoning for the infallibility of Fāṭimah

> **Logical reasoning and traditional proofs prevent the Mistress of Ladies from being accused of lying, due to the confirmation of her father (s) in his saying: "Fāṭimah is a part of me, and whoever hurts her hurts me." Hence, intuitively, whoever lies does not deserve this kind of statement (of honour) by the Messenger of Allah صَلَّى ٱللَّهُ عَلَيْهِ وَسَلَّمَ. Therefore, the saying itself is a clear indication of her infallibility. The purification verse from the Holy Qur'an is another indication of her infallibility, and it was revealed in her honour and the honour of her husband and her two sons, as Aishah herself testified. Hence, there is nothing left for sensible people but to accept the fact that she was unjustly treated, and that she was easy to be branded a liar by somebody who was willing to let her burn unless the remaining people in her house came out to vote for him.**
>
> **Because of all of that, she - may Allah's peace be upon her - refused entry to Abu Bakr and Umar when they asked her permission. Even when Ali allowed them to enter, she turned her face to the wall and refused to look at them.**
>
> **Furthermore, before she died, she asked to be buried secretly, and at night, so that none of them could be present at her funeral, and to this day, the grave of the Prophet's صَلَّى ٱللَّهُ عَلَيْهِ وَسَلَّمَ daughter is unknown.**
>
> **I would like to ask why our scholars remain silent about these facts, and are reluctant to look into them, or even to mention them. They give us the impression that the Companions are like angels, infallible and sinless.[1]**

Refuting Tījānī's reasoning for the infallibility of Fāṭimah

Tījānī's claims are beginning to evolve. His condemnation of Abū Bakr is no longer limited to linking the issue of Fadak with the ḥadīth of hurting Fāṭimah. The abundance of aḥādīth supporting the position of Abū Bakr رَضِيَ ٱللَّهُ عَنْهُ are too many to deny. Fāṭimah رَضِيَ ٱللَّهُ عَنْهَا, therefore, has to be elevated to a status by virtue of which anyone who disagrees with her must be in error. It is absolutely necessary for her to be proven infallible. Otherwise, how is Tījānī going to deal with the *mutawātir* (mass transmitted) aḥādīth on the Prophets not being inherited? What answer has he produced to the fact that all the Khulafā' subsequent to Abū Bakr رَضِيَ ٱللَّهُ عَنْهُ, including ʿAlī رَضِيَ ٱللَّهُ عَنْهُ, made no changes to the manner in which the assets were being administered, and revenue being distributed? How is he going to deal with the

1 *Then I was guided*, p. 115-116.

statements of al-Bāqir and Zayd ibn ʿAlī which endorse the actions of Abū Bakr?

Tījānī's objectivity, which amounts to defending a preconceived idea; despite the overwhelming evidence to the contrary, demands that Fāṭimah ﴿رَضِيَ اللَّهُ عَنْهَا﴾ be infallible. His attempt to prove her infallibility is based on the following sequence:

- It is impossible for her to lie. Here he is insinuating that the position taken by the Ahl al-Sunnah necessitates that she was a liar.
- It was impossible for her to lie because of the ḥadīth stating that hurting Fāṭimah ﴿رَضِيَ اللَّهُ عَنْهَا﴾ causes hurt to the Prophet ﴾صَلَّى اللَّهُ عَلَيْهِ وَسَلَّمَ﴿.
- This ḥadīth, therefore proves, that she is infallible.
- Her infallibility is also proven from 'The verse of Purification'.

True to the fish-and-chips tradition of free salt, pepper, and a napkin; Tījānī has thrown in a few free red herrings from his own side.

- Abū Bakr threatened to burn down the house of Fāṭimah.
- She refused him entry. When he entered she turned her face away from him in protest.
- She requested to be buried at night so that they could not attend her funeral.
- Scholars from the Ahl al-Sunnah refuse to discuss this issue.
- The Companions of the Prophet ﴾صَلَّى اللَّهُ عَلَيْهِ وَسَلَّمَ﴿ are portrayed as angels by the Ahl al-Sunnah, despite their alleged oppression on the 'infallible' daughter of the Prophet ﴾صَلَّى اللَّهُ عَلَيْهِ وَسَلَّمَ﴿.

Our responses will not follow the exact sequence above. However, we aim to pay attention to the core allegations. Some of the objections raised by Tījānī have already been adequately dealt with and his repetition of the same argument does not make it free from fallacy.

The Ahl al-Sunnah have never said that Fāṭimah ﴿رَضِيَ اللَّهُ عَنْهَا﴾ was a liar. If it is a crime to question the position of Fāṭimah ﴿رَضِيَ اللَّهُ عَنْهَا﴾ on any matter of Fiqh, and the accusation is that one accuses her of lying, what will be said about a ḥadīth narrated by Jaʿfar ibn Muḥammad (al-Ṣādiq) who relates from his father Muḥammad ibn ʿAlī (al-Bāqir), who said:

> We came to Jābir and asked him about the Ḥajj of the Prophet ﷺ. He told us that the Messenger of Allah ﷺ said, "Had I known when I set out what I know now, I would not have brought the *Hady* (sacrificial animals) with me and I would have made it 'Umrah. Whoever does not have a Hady with him, let him remove Iḥrām and make it 'Umrah,"
>
> 'Alī رضي الله عنه, came from Yemen with Hady and the Messenger of Allah ﷺ brought Hady from al-Madīnah. Fāṭimah had put on a dyed garment and applied kohl to her eyes, and he ('Alī) said, "I went to the Prophet to complain about that and enquire (whether he permitted her to do so) I said, 'O Messenger of Allah, Fāṭimah had put on a dyed garment and applied kohl to her eyes, and she said, the Messenger of Allah told me to do that.' He said, 'She is telling the truth, she is telling the truth, I told her to do that.'"[1]

If it was impossible for her to lie, why did 'Alī رضي الله عنه have to clarify the matter with the Prophet ﷺ? The Ahl al-Sunnah do not claim that it was impossible for her to lie. No doubt it was possible, but it was her fear of Allah and her scrupulousness that prevented her from ever stating a mistruth.

Ḥadīth of hurting Fāṭimah and infallibility

> **Logical reasoning and traditional proofs prevent the Mistress of Ladies from being accused of lying, due to the confirmation of her father (s) in his saying: "Fāṭimah is a part of me, and whoever hurts her hurts me." Hence, intuitively, whoever lies does not deserve this kind of statement (of honour) by the Messenger of Allah ﷺ. Therefore, the saying itself is a clear indication of her infallibility.**

Let us take a moment to reflect on Tījānī's argument for the infallibility of Fāṭimah رضي الله عنها. It is impossible for Fāṭimah رضي الله عنها to lie because the Prophet ﷺ said, "Fāṭimah is a part of me, I am hurt by what hurts her." Since she does not lie, she must be infallible. Is there any relationship between it being impossible to lie and the Prophet ﷺ saying "Fāṭimah is a part of me..."? How does this lead to infallibility? Honestly, does the esteemed reader see any logical reasoning in this?

If Fāṭimah رضي الله عنها were infallible, why is it that the Prophet ﷺ made her the example for carrying out prescribed punishments? It is an indictment on the

1 *Ṣaḥīḥ Muslim*, Kitāb al-Ḥajj, Ḥadīth of Jābir on Ḥajj, Ḥadīth no. 1218.

Prophet ﷺ that he use an example of an individual who is infallible since he ﷺ would be describing an impossible scenario.

ʿĀ'ishah رضي الله عنها narrates:

> The Quraysh were very concerned about the case of a woman from the Makhzūm tribe who had committed theft. They wondered who should intercede for her with the Messenger of Allah ﷺ. It was suggested that Usāmah ibn Zayd intercede due to the Prophet's ﷺ love for him. Usāmah spoke to him about that matter and the Prophet ﷺ said to him, "Do you intercede when one of the legal punishments ordained by Allah has been violated?" Then he got up and addressed the people saying, "The nations before you were ruined because when a noble person amongst them committed theft, they would leave him, but if a weak person amongst them committed theft, they would execute the legal punishment on him. By Allah, if Fāṭimah, the daughter of Muḥammad, were to commit the theft, I would have cut off her hand!"[1]

We would expect much more convincing evidence to argue the case of infallibility.

If ʿAlī رضي الله عنه is infallible, as Tījānī is going to argue later, how does one reconcile the fact that an 'infallible' caused hurt to another 'infallible' when he proposed for the daughter of Abū Jahl. The pain that the first 'infallible' caused to the second 'infallible' resulted in the undisputed infallible, the Messenger of Allah ﷺ, to be upset. The case for infallibility is definitely not in this ḥadīth.

Tījānī and the verse of purification

Tījānī says:

> **The purification is another proof of her infallibility as it was revealed concerning her and her husband and her two sons, as Aishah herself testifies**

Our response:

The verse of purification that he is referring to appears in Sūrah al-Aḥzāb. In this verse Allah speaks about removing the impurity, and purification of Ahl al-Bayt. The expression Ahl al-Bayt is comprehensive. The context of the verses reveals to

1 *Ṣaḥīḥ al-Bukhārī*, ḥadīth 6788; *Ṣaḥīḥ Muslim*, ḥadīth 1688 a.

us that the Qur'ānic address is towards the wives of the Prophet ﷺ. Tījānī claims that this verse applies exclusively to ʿAlī, Fāṭimah, Ḥasan and Ḥusayn رضي الله عنهم. Let us study the verse in question, along with the verses which precede it and those which follow it. Allah سبحانه وتعالى says:

يَا نِسَاءَ النَّبِيِّ مَنْ يَأْتِ مِنْكُنَّ بِفَاحِشَةٍ مُبَيِّنَةٍ يُضَاعَفْ لَهَا الْعَذَابُ ضِعْفَيْنِ
وَكَانَ ذٰلِكَ عَلَى اللّٰهِ يَسِيرًا وَمَنْ يَقْنُتْ مِنْكُنَّ لِلّٰهِ وَرَسُولِهِ وَتَعْمَلْ صَالِحًا
نُؤْتِهَا أَجْرَهَا مَرَّتَيْنِ وَأَعْتَدْنَا لَهَا رِزْقًا كَرِيمًا يَا نِسَاءَ النَّبِيِّ لَسْتُنَّ كَأَحَدٍ
مِنَ النِّسَاءِ إِنِ اتَّقَيْتُنَّ فَلَا تَخْضَعْنَ بِالْقَوْلِ فَيَطْمَعَ الَّذِي فِي قَلْبِهِ مَرَضٌ
وَقُلْنَ قَوْلًا مَعْرُوفًا . وَقَرْنَ فِي بُيُوتِكُنَّ وَلَا تَبَرَّجْنَ تَبَرُّجَ الْجَاهِلِيَّةِ الْأُولَىٰ
وَأَقِمْنَ الصَّلٰوةَ وَآتِينَ الزَّكٰوةَ وَأَطِعْنَ اللّٰهَ وَرَسُولَهُ إِنَّمَا يُرِيدُ اللّٰهُ لِيُذْهِبَ
عَنْكُمُ الرِّجْسَ أَهْلَ الْبَيْتِ وَيُطَهِّرَكُمْ تَطْهِيرًا وَاذْكُرْنَ مَا يُتْلَىٰ فِي بُيُوتِكُنَّ
مِنْ آيَاتِ اللّٰهِ وَالْحِكْمَةِ إِنَّ اللّٰهَ كَانَ لَطِيفًا خَبِيرًا

O wives of the Prophet, whoever of you should commit a clear immorality—for her the punishment would be doubled two fold, and ever is that, for Allah, easy. And whoever of you devoutly obeys Allah and His Messenger and does righteousness—We will give her reward twice; and We have prepared for her a noble provision. O wives of the Prophet, you are not like anyone among women. If you fear Allah, then do not be soft in speech [to men] lest he in whose heart is disease should covet, but speak with appropriate speech and abide in your houses and do not display yourselves as [was] the display of the former times of ignorance. And establish ṣalāh and give zakāh and obey Allah and His Messenger. Allah intends only to remove from you the impurity [of sin], O people of the [Prophet's] household, and to purify you with [extensive] purification. And remember what is recited in your houses of the verses of Allah and wisdom. Indeed, Allah is ever Subtle and Acquainted [with all things].[1]

The verse is clearly addressing the Prophet's ﷺ wives. The instruction, the prohibition, the promise and the threat is directed at them. That being said, we do not restrict these verses to the Prophet's ﷺ wives. We believe that the

1 Sūrah al-Aḥzāb: 30-34.

entire Ahl al-Bayt is included on account of the general nature of the verse. ʿAlī, Fāṭimah, Ḥasan, and Ḥusayn رضي الله عنهم are included by virtue of the Prophet's صلى الله عليه وسلم supplication for them.

The term Ahl al-Bayt certainly applies to the wife of a person, and there is no indication from the Arabic language, nor from the Prophetic usage of this term that excludes the wives.

Al-Bukhārī narrates in his *Ṣaḥīḥ* from ʿAbd al-Raḥmān ibn Abī Laylā, he said:

سألنا رسول الله صلى الله عليه و سلم فقلنا يا رسول الله كيف الصلاة عليكم أهل البيت فإن الله قد علمنا كيف نسلم عليكم؟ قال (قولوا اللهم صل على محمد وعلى آل محمد كما صليت على إبراهيم وعلى آل إبراهيم إنك حميد مجيد اللهم بارك على محمد وعلى آل محمد كما باركت على إبراهيم وعلى آل إبراهيم إنك حميد مجيد

We asked the Messenger صلى الله عليه وسلم, "Allah has taught us how to say salām upon you, O Messenger of Allah, but how do we say the *ṣalāt* (singular of ṣalawāt) upon you and your household?"

The Messenger صلى الله عليه وسلم said, "Say, 'O Allah send ṣalāt upon Muḥammad and the family of Muḥammad as you sent ṣalāt upon Ibrāhīm and the family of Ibrāhīm, indeed You are Praiseworthy, Honourable. O Allah bless Muḥammad and the family of Muḥammad as you blessed Ibrāhīm and the family of Ibrāhīm, indeed you are Praiseworthy, Honourable.'"[1]

There is no doubt that the 'Ahl al-Bayt' intended (in the above ḥadīth) are his wives and his progeny as is clarified in the ḥadīth narrated in *Ṣaḥīḥ al-Bukhārī* from ʿAmr ibn Salīm al-Zuraqī, who related that the Ṣaḥābah said:

يا رسول الله كيف نصلي عليك؟ فقال رسول الله صلى الله عليه و سلم قولوا اللهم صل على محمد وأزواجه وذريته كما صليت على إبراهيم وبارك على محمد وأزواجه وذريته كما باركت على آل إبراهيم إنك حميد مجيد

"O Messenger of Allah, how do we send ṣalāt upon you?"

1 *Ṣaḥīḥ al-Bukhārī*, Kitāb al-Ambiyā, Ḥadīth no. 3190.

The Messenger ﷺ said, "Say, 'O Allah, send ṣalāt upon Muḥammad and his wives and his progeny as you sent ṣalāt upon Ibrāhīm and bless Muḥammad and his wives and his progeny as you blessed Ibrāhīm, indeed you are Praiseworthy, Honourable.'"[1]

It is narrated in a lengthier ḥadīth related by Anas in *al-Bukhārī*:

فخرج النبي صلى الله عليه و سلم فانطلق إلى حجرة عائشة فقال السلام عليكم أهل البيت ورحمة الله فقالت وعليك السلام ورحمة الله فتقرى حجر نسائه كلهن يقول لهن كما يقول لعائشة

The Prophet ﷺ came out (one day) and went to ʿĀ'ishah's room and said, "Greetings upon you, Ahl al-Bayt, and the mercy of Allah."

She replied, "And upon you greetings and the mercy of Allah..."

He then went to all of his wives and said to them what he said to ʿĀ'ishah.[2]

Who constitute the Ahl al-Bayt? Muslim narrates in his *Ṣaḥīḥ* from Yazīd ibn Ḥayyān that the Prophet ﷺ said:

وأهل بيتى أذكركم الله فى أهل بيتى أذكركم الله فى أهل بيتى أذكركم الله فى أهل بيتى. فقال له حصين ومن أهل بيته يا زيد أليس نساؤه من أهل بيته قال نساؤه من أهل بيته ولكن أهل بيته من حرم الصدقة بعده قال ومن هم قال هم آل على وآل عقيل وآل جعفر وآل عباس قال كل هؤلاء حرم الصدقة قال نعم

(The Prophet ﷺ said,) "And my household, I remind you about my household, I remind about you my household, I remind you about my household."

Ḥuṣayn (the narrator transmitting the ḥadīth from the Ṣaḥābī) enquired, "Who makes up his household, O Zayd (Ibn Arqam, the Ṣaḥābī narrating the ḥadīth)? Are his wives not part of his household?"

Zayd رضي الله عنه said, "His wives are from his household. However, his household are (also) those persons whom the ṣadaqah (charity) is prohibited upon after him."

1 Ibid. 3189.
2 Ibid. 4515.

Ḥuṣayn asked, "Who are they?"

Zayd replied, "The family of ʿAlī, the family of ʿAqīl, the family of Jaʿfar and the family of ʿAbbās."

Ḥuṣayn asked, "Is the charity forbidden for all of them?"

Zayd replied: "Yes."[1]

Lexically, the word 'Ahl' includes wives. Al-Fayrūzābādī says:

Ahl al-Amr (lit. people of the matter) refers to its governors, in relation to the house it refers to its inhabitants, in relation to a madh-hab it refers to those who ascribe to it. For the (ordinary) man his wife is like his family, for the Prophet it is his wives his daughters, his son in law, ʿAlī...[2]

Ibn Manẓūr says:

Ahl al-Bayt refers to the inhabitants of the house, the family of the man, and the closest people to him. The Ahl al-Bayt of the Prophet refers to his wives, his daughters, and his son in law, ʿAlī... it has been said that it refers to the wives of the Prophet...[3]

Similarly, the usage of the word "ahl" in the Qur'ān applies to the wives. Allah سُبْحَانَهُ وَتَعَالَىٰ says:

إِذْ قَالَ مُوسَىٰ لِأَهْلِهِ إِنِّي آنَسْتُ نَارًا سَآتِيكُم مِّنْهَا بِخَبَرٍ

[Mention] when (Prophet) Mūsā said to his family [his wife], "Indeed, I have perceived a fire. I will bring you from there information."[4]

قَالَتْ مَا جَزَاءُ مَنْ أَرَادَ بِأَهْلِكَ سُوءًا إِلَّا أَن يُسْجَنَ...

She said, "What is the recompense of one who intended evil for your Ahl (wife) but that he is imprisoned..."[5]

1 *Ṣaḥīḥ Muslim*, Kitāb Faḍā'il al-Ṣaḥābah, bāb Faḍā'il ʿAlī, Ḥadīth no. 2408.

2 *Al-Qāmūs al-Muḥīṭ*, bāb al-Lām, Faṣl al-Ḥamzah, p. 1245.

3 *Lisān al-ʿArab*, Ibn Manẓūr, Ḥarf al-Lām, p. 290.

4 Sūrah Yūsuf: 25.

5 Sūrah Yūsuf: 25.

The person making the above statement is Zulaykhā, the wife of the ʿAzīz, according to all of the mufassirīn. Also, Allah سُبْحَانَهُ وَتَعَالَىٰ says:

فَأَنْجَيْنَاهُ وَأَهْلَهُ إِلَّا امْرَأَتَهُ

So we saved him and his family, except for his wife.[1]

The word *illā* (except) is a device of exception (*adāt al-istithnā*) which means his wife was part of his family but was excluded for the reason that is known by all.

Even the Shīʿī Qur'ānic commentaries indicate that the word "Ahl" refers to the wives.

ʿAlī al-Qummī says in his commentary of the words (of Allah سُبْحَانَهُ وَتَعَالَىٰ):

فَلَمَّا قَضَىٰ مُوسَى الْأَجَلَ وَسَارَ بِأَهْلِهِ

And when (Prophet) Mūsā had completed the term and was traveling with his family.[2]

> When the year came to an end (Prophet) Mūsā عَلَيْهِ السَّلَام took his wife, and Shuʿayb provided provisions for him, and he took his livestock... Shuʿayb said to him, "Go! Allah has selected you." He then drove his livestock and left (Madyan) heading for Egypt. When he reached a desert strip of land, his family with him, an intense coldness, and darkness and wind came over them and the darkness covered them. Mūsā عَلَيْهِ السَّلَام saw a fire that had become apparent as Allah says, "And when Mūsā had completed the term and was traveling with his family..."[3]

Abū ʿAlī al-Ṭabarsī says in the commentary of Allah's سُبْحَانَهُ وَتَعَالَىٰ words:

إِذْ قَالَ مُوسَىٰ لِأَهْلِهِ

[Mention] when Mūsā said to his family.

> This is concerning Mūsā when he said to his family, his wife, the daughter of Shuʿayb.[4]

1 Sūrah al-Naml: 57.

2 Sūrah al-Qaṣaṣ: 29.

3 *Tafsīr al-Qummī*, vol. 2 p. 116-117, Sūrah al-Naml.

4 *Majmaʿ al-Bayān*, vol. 5 p. 168, Sūrah al-Naml.

He (al-Ṭabarsī) repeats at his commentary of the words:

إِذْ رَأَى نَارًا فَقَالَ لِأَهْلِهِ امْكُثُوا

When he saw a fire and said to his family, "Stay here..."[1]

> His statement, "to his family," she is the daughter of Shuʿayb. He married her in Madyan...[2]

If we take all of this into consideration the term Ahl al-Bayt includes the wives. There is nothing in the verse that proves the infallibility of Fāṭimah رضي الله عنها or anyone else, for the following reasons:

Firstly, the ḥadīth of ʿĀ'ishah رضي الله عنها that Tījānī alluded to, in which she said:

> خرج النبى صلى الله عليه وسلم غداة وعليه مرط مرحل من شعر أسود فجاء الحسن بن على فأدخله ثم جاء الحسين فدخل معه ثم جاءت فاطمة فأدخلها ثم جاء على فأدخله ثم قال إِنَّمَا يُرِيدُ اللَّهُ لِيُذْهِبَ عَنكُمُ الرِّجْسَ أَهْلَ الْبَيْتِ وَيُطَهِّرَكُمْ تَطْهِيرًا
>
> The Prophet صلى الله عليه وسلم came out wearing a blanket made of black hair with patterns on it. Ḥasan came and he entered him under it. Thereafter, Ḥusayn came and he entered him under it. Then Fāṭimah came and he entered her into it and ʿAlī came and he entered him into it as well and said, "Allah intends only to remove from you the impurity [of sin], O people of the [Prophet's] household, and to purify you with [extensive] purification."[3]

The ḥadīth is clearly a supplication from the Messenger for Allah to remove impurity from them and to purify them. If they were infallible, what was the point of the supplication? On the other hand, if they were in need of purification and the removal of impurity what claim do they have to infallibility?

Allah addresses the participants at Badr, reminding them that He removed impurity from them as well.

---

1 Sūrah Ṭāhā: 10.

2 *Majmaʿ al-Bayān*, vol. 4 p. 89, Sūrah Ṭāhā.

3 *Ṣaḥīḥ Muslim*, Kitāb Faḍā'il al-Ṣaḥābah, Ḥadīth no. 2424.

إِذْ يُغَشِّيكُمُ النُّعَاسَ أَمَنَةً مِّنْهُ وَيُنَزِّلُ عَلَيْكُم مِّنَ السَّمَاءِ مَاءً لِّيُطَهِّرَكُم بِهِ
وَيُذْهِبَ عَنكُمْ رِجْزَ الشَّيْطَانِ وَلِيَرْبِطَ عَلَىٰ قُلُوبِكُمْ وَيُثَبِّتَ بِهِ الْأَقْدَامَ

[Remember] when He overwhelmed you with drowsiness [giving] security from Him and sent down upon you from the sky, rain by which to purify you and remove from you the evil [suggestions] of Satan and to make steadfast your hearts and plant firmly thereby your feet.[1]

Allah purified the believers in general when He said:

مَا يُرِيدُ اللَّهُ لِيَجْعَلَ عَلَيْكُم مِّنْ حَرَجٍ وَلَٰكِن يُرِيدُ لِيُطَهِّرَكُمْ وَلِيُتِمَّ نِعْمَتَهُ
عَلَيْكُمْ لَعَلَّكُمْ تَشْكُرُونَ

Allah does not intend to make difficulty for you, but He intends to purify you and complete His favour upon you that you may be grateful.[2]

Allah سُبْحَانَهُ وَتَعَالَىٰ informs us in the above verse that He intends to purify His slaves and complete His favour upon them as a mercy from Him. He does not mention anything about making them infallible. This verse is similar to the previous one with no difference (in meaning).

What is there to indicate that Fāṭimah رَضِيَ اللَّهُ عَنْهَا was infallible? The verse of 'Purification' is general and applies to the wives of the Prophet, and the rest of the Ahl al-Bayt. The ḥadīth indicates that the Prophet صَلَّى اللَّهُ عَلَيْهِ وَسَلَّمَ supplicated for the purification of Ḥasan, Ḥusayn, ʿAlī, and Fāṭimah. If they were primarily intended by the verse what need was there of the Prophet to supplicate for their purification? The concept of purification does not entail infallibility since the participants of Badr were purified, as are the rest of the believers.

Tījānī's emotional outburst

Tījānī's deficit of convincing evidence has compelled him to tread the path of emotion. He believes that fabricated narrations which are loaded with emotion will

1 Sūrah al-Anfāl: 11.

2 Sūrah al-Mā'idah: 6.

win the sympathy of the reader. He has the forged book ascribed to ibn Qutaybah as collateral. He draws attention away from the liabilities in his reasoning and suggests they focus on the brutality of Abū Bakr and ʿUmar رضي الله عنهما. Little does he realize that this fabricated narration portrays ʿAlī رضي الله عنه as a defenseless coward; such is the nature of forgeries!

Tījānī says:

> **Hence, there is nothing left for sensible people but to accept the fact that she was unjustly treated, and that she was easy to be branded a liar by somebody who was willing to let her burn unless the remaining people in her house came out to vote for him.**
>
> **Because of all of that, she - may Allah's peace be upon her - refused entry to Abu Bakr and Umar when they asked her permission. Even when Ali allowed them to enter, she turned her face to the wall and refused to look at them.**

Our comment:

On the contrary, there is nothing left for sensible people but to accept that Abū Bakr رضي الله عنه treated her with kindness. The two narratives paint diametrically opposite portraits of Abū Bakr رضي الله عنه.

This is a narration from *Ṣaḥīḥ al-Bukhārī* which portrays a kind and just Abū Bakr:

والله لقرابة رسول الله صلى الله عليه و سلم أحب الي أن أصل من قرابتي

> By Allah! To maintain a good relationship with the family of the Prophet صلى الله عليه وسلم is more beloved to me than to maintain a good relationship with my own family.[1]

The other is a narration in a book falsely attributed to Ibn Qutaybah and portrays a brutal Abū Bakr رضي الله عنه.

Which of the two is more accurate in its description of Abū Bakr رضي الله عنه; and which is most consistent with this statement of the Prophet صلى الله عليه وسلم, "No one's wealth has benefited as Abū Bakr's wealth has benefited me."?[2]

---

1 *Ṣaḥīḥ al-Bukhārī*, Kitāb al-Maghāzī, vol. 4, Ḥadīth no. 3810.

2 *Ṣaḥīḥ al-Bukhārī*, Kitāb al-Salāt, Ḥadīth no. 467, *Sunan al-Tirmidhī*, Kitāb al-Manāqib, Ḥadīth no. 4022.

As for the allegation of coercion in pledging allegiance, let us read what Abū Naḍrah relates:

> When the people gathered around Abū Bakr رضي الله عنه (to pledge their allegiance to him) he said, "I do not see ʿAlī?" Some men amongst the Anṣār went to call ʿAlī رضي الله عنه and when he arrived Abū Bakr said to him, "O ʿAlī, the cousin of the Messenger and his son in law?"
>
> ʿAlī replied, "There is no objection O khalīfah of the Messenger صلى الله عليه وسلم, extend your hand."
>
> Abū Bakr رضي الله عنه extended his hand and ʿAlī رضي الله عنه pledged his allegiance. Then Abū Bakr رضي الله عنه said, "Why is it that I do not see Zubayr?" Some men amongst the Anṣār went to call him and Abū Bakr رضي الله عنه said to him, "I said (to myself) the cousin of the Messenger صلى الله عليه وسلم and his disciple (*ḥawārī*)?"
>
> Zubayr replied, "There is no objection, O khalīfah of the Messenger صلى الله عليه وسلم, extend your hand," and he pledged his allegiance to Abū Bakr رضي الله عنه.[1]

This is an authentic accepted narration. Compare it to what has been ascribed to Ibn Qutaybah. If they had any objection to his Khilāfah they would have made this public. Zubayr رضي الله عنه was martyred at Jamal, his concerns were no secret. ʿAlī رضي الله عنه was present at Jamal and Ṣiffīn, if he had any objection it would have been made public. This is the brave and courageous ʿAlī رضي الله عنه that the Ahl al-Sunnah know.

The burial of Fāṭimah

The matter of her requesting to be buried secretly during the night so that neither Abū Bakr رضي الله عنه nor ʿUmar رضي الله عنه would attend her Ṣalāt al-Janāzah is indeed strange. Is this mentioned in the narrations; or is it the imagination of 'objective' minds that will spare no trouble in condemning Abū Bakr?

Tījānī references the ḥadīth to *al-Ṣaḥīḥ al-Bukhārī*. The narration, however, reads quite differently:

> فوجدت فاطمة على أبي بكر في ذلك فهجرته فلم تكلمه حتى توفيت وعاشت بعد النبي صلى الله عليه و سلم ستة أشهر فلما توفيت دفنها زوجها علي ليلا ولم يؤذن بها أبا بكر

---

1 *Kitāb al-Sunnah*, ʿAbd Allāh ibn Aḥmad ibn Ḥambal, vol. 2, Ḥadīth no. 1296; the Muḥaqqiq said, "Its sanad is authentic."

> Fāṭimah became angry with Abū Bakr concerning that and avoided him and did not speak to him until she passed away. She lived for six months after the Prophet ﷺ. When she died her husband, ʿAlī, buried her during the night and did not inform Abū Bakr.

Is there any mention in this report that Fāṭimah bequeathed that she be buried at night so that Abū Bakr and ʿUmar رضي الله عنهما not be present at the Ṣalāt al-Janāzah?

Once again, the esteemed reader will be reminded of our discussion on the explanations of al-Zuhrī when narrating ḥadīth. This narration is part of the lengthy narration by ʿĀ'ishah رضي الله عنها which is transmitted by al-Zuhrī. It seems increasingly likely that this is al-Zuhrī's assumption of what occurred.[1]

If the relations were soured between the Abū Bakr رضي الله عنه and the household of ʿAlī رضي الله عنه; how is it that Asmā' bint ʿUmays رضي الله عنها, the wife of Abū Bakr رضي الله عنه, was involved in the nursing of Fāṭimah رضي الله عنها during her final illness? The relationship was not limited to extended periods of nursing, but it included Fāṭimah رضي الله عنها requesting Asmā' to prepare a canopy over her bier so that the shape of her body would not be exposed during burial. Asmā' participated in washing the blessed body of Fāṭimah رضي الله عنها after her passing, as well as shrouding her. Does this speak of any animosity between Abū Bakr رضي الله عنه and the family of ʿAlī رضي الله عنه?

For the sake of fairness I will quote Shīʿī narrations on this issue.

Abū Jaʿfar al-Ṭūsī writes in his *Amālī*:

> ʿAlī used to nurse her and Asmā' bint ʿUmays would constantly help him in seeing to her.[2]

Al-Majlisī writes in *Jilā' al-ʿUyūn*:

> ʿAlī had carried out her bequest, he had himself paid attention to her nursing and Asmā' bint ʿUmays had helped him in seeing to her... Shaykh al-Ṭūsī has narrated with a reliable chain of transmission that the first bier to ever be made in Islam was the bier of Fāṭimah. The reason that prompted this was that when the sickness that claimed her life befell her she said to Asmā' bint ʿUmays, "O Asmā'! I have become very weak and sickly and I am beginning to

1 Refer to p. 234 of this book.

2 *Amālī*, vol. 1 p. 107.

lose a lot of weight, is there anything that you can make for me that will cover my body from it being seen by men (after I pass away)?" She said, "I noticed the people of Abyssinia doing something during my stay there, I can do the very same for you as well if you want." Fāṭimah replied in the positive. She subsequently brought planks of wood and placed them on the floor, then she asked for branches of date palms to be brought and placed them on top of those planks and thereafter covered it (the bier that she made) with material (forming a canopy like covering over the bier). She said to Fāṭimah, "This is what I have seen them doing in Abyssinia." Fāṭimah said, "Can you make something similar to this for me as well and cover my body from the gazes of men falling upon it, Allah may save your body from the fire of Jahannam?"[1]

Tījānī's predisposed hatred for the Ṣaḥābah

Tījānī cannot tolerate favourable mention of the Ṣaḥābah. He is enraged by the Ṣaḥābah رضي الله عنهم.

Why our scholars remain silent about these facts, and are reluctant to look into them, or even to mention them. They give us the impression that the Companions are like angels, infallible and sinless.

Our response:

We do not say anything more than what Allah says about them in the Qur'ān:

كُنْتُمْ خَيْرَ أُمَّةٍ أُخْرِجَتْ لِلنَّاسِ تَأْمُرُوْنَ بِالْمَعْرُوْفِ وَتَنْهَوْنَ عَنِ الْمُنْكَرِ وَتُؤْمِنُوْنَ بِاللّٰهِ

You are the best nation produced [as an example] for mankind. You enjoin what is right and forbid what is wrong and believe in Allah.[2]

مُحَمَّدٌ رَّسُوْلُ اللّٰهِ وَالَّذِيْنَ مَعَهُ أَشِدَّآءُ عَلَى الْكُفَّارِ رُحَمَآءُ بَيْنَهُمْ تَرَاهُمْ رُكَّعًا سُجَّدًا يَّبْتَغُوْنَ فَضْلًا مِّنَ اللّٰهِ وَرِضْوَانًا سِيْمَاهُمْ فِيْ وُجُوْهِهِمْ مِنْ أَثَرِ السُّجُوْدِ ذٰلِكَ مَثَلُهُمْ فِي التَّوْرَاةِ وَمَثَلُهُمْ فِي الْإِنْجِيْلِ كَزَرْعٍ أَخْرَجَ شَطْأَهٗ

1 *Jilā' al-'Uyūn*, p. 172, p. 175.
2 Sūrah Āl 'Imrān: 110.

فَآزَرَهُ فَاسْتَغْلَظَ فَاسْتَوَى عَلَى سُوقِهِ يُعْجِبُ الزُّرَّاعَ لِيَغِيظَ بِهِمُ الْكُفَّارَ وَعَدَ اللَّهُ الَّذِينَ آمَنُوا وَعَمِلُوا الصَّالِحَاتِ مِنْهُم مَّغْفِرَةً وَأَجْرًا عَظِيمًا

Muḥammad is the Messenger of Allah; and those with him are forceful against the disbelievers, merciful among themselves. You see them bowing and prostrating [in prayer], seeking bounty from Allah and [His] pleasure. Their mark [i.e. sign] is on their faces [i.e. foreheads] from the trace of prostration. That is their description in the Torah. And their description in the Injīl is as a plant which produces its offshoots and strengthens them so they grow firm and stand upon their stalks delighting the sowers – so that He [i.e. Allah] may enrage by them the disbelievers. Allah has promised those who believe and do righteous deeds among them forgiveness and a great reward.[1]

وَالَّذِينَ آمَنُوا وَهَاجَرُوا وَجَاهَدُوا فِي سَبِيلِ اللَّهِ وَالَّذِينَ آوَوا وَّنَصَرُوا أُولَـٰئِكَ هُمُ الْمُؤْمِنُونَ حَقًّا لَّهُم مَّغْفِرَةٌ وَرِزْقٌ كَرِيمٌ

But those who have believed and emigrated and fought in the cause of Allah and those who gave shelter and aided—it is they who are the believers, truly. For them is forgiveness and noble provision.[2]

لَـٰكِنِ الرَّسُولُ وَالَّذِينَ آمَنُوا مَعَهُ جَاهَدُوا بِأَمْوَالِهِمْ وَأَنفُسِهِمْ وَأُولَـٰئِكَ لَهُمُ الْخَيْرَاتُ وَأُولَـٰئِكَ هُمُ الْمُفْلِحُونَ

But the Messenger and those who believed with him fought with their wealth and their lives. Those will have [all that is] good and it is those who are the successful. [3]

يَا أَيُّهَا النَّبِيُّ حَسْبُكَ اللَّهُ وَمَنِ اتَّبَعَكَ مِنَ الْمُؤْمِنِينَ

O Prophet ﷺ*, sufficient for you is Allah and for whoever follows you of the believers.*[4]

This is not what we say about the Ṣaḥābah, rather it is what the Prophet ﷺ says:

---

1 Sūrah al-Fatḥ: 29.

2 Sūrah al-Anfāl: 74.

3 Sūrah al-Tawbah: 88.

4 Sūrah al-Anfāl: 64.

يأتي على الناس زمان فيغزو فئام من الناس، فيقولون فيكم من صاحب رسول الله صلى الله عليه وسلم فيقولون نعم فيفتح لهم ثم يأتي على الناس زمان فيغزو فئام من الناس، فيقال هل فيكم من صاحب أصحاب رسول الله صلى الله عليه وسلم فيقولون نعم. فيفتح لهم، ثم يأتي على الناس زمان فيغزو فئام من الناس، فيقال هل فيكم من صاحب من صاحب أصحاب رسول الله صلى الله عليه وسلم فيقولون نعم. فيفتح لهم

A time will come when crowds of people will fight in the path of Allah and they will say, "Are there amongst you those who accompanied the Messenger ﷺ?" They will reply, "Yes," and victory will be granted to them. Then a time will come when crowds of people will fight in the path of Allah and it will be asked, "Are there amongst you those who accompanied those who accompanied the Messenger ﷺ?" They will reply, "Yes," and victory will be granted to them. Then a time will come and it will be asked, "Are there amongst you those who accompanied those who accompanied the Companions of the Messenger ﷺ?" They will reply, "Yes," and they will be granted victory.[1]

لا تسبوا أصحابي فلو أن أحدكم أنفق مثل أحد ذهبا ما بلغ مد أحدهم ولا نصيفه

Do not curse my Ṣaḥābah! Indeed, if you were to spend the equivalent of Uḥud in gold it would not compare to the mudd[2] of one of them, or even half of that.

If we defend the Companions of Muḥammad ﷺ it is because we seek to defend the dignity of Muḥammad ﷺ. How could a smear campaign against the Companions of Muḥammad ﷺ not be an indictment on him? He has alerted us to this reality:

الرجل على دين خليله فلينظر أحدكم من يخالل

A man is upon the religion of his close friend. Therefore, be careful who you befriend.[3]

1 *Ṣaḥīḥ al-Bukhārī*, Faḍā'il al-Ṣaḥābah, Ḥadīth no. 3449.

2 A measurement of volume approximately equal to 750 ml.

3 *Sunan Abī Dāwūd*, Kitāb al-Adab, Ḥadīth no. 4833 vol. 5; Also *Sunan al-Tirmidhī*, Kitāb al-Zuhd, Ḥadīth no. 2378, vol. 4.

ولو كنت متخذا من أمتي خليلا لاتخذت، أبا بكر ولكن أخي وصاحبي

If I were to take a close friend I would take Abū Bakr but (he is) my brother and my Ṣaḥābī.[1]

The Messenger ﷺ remained amongst his Ṣaḥābah for a significant period of time. Did his words contradict his actions? Was his effect on mankind so dismal that the entire generation of his Companions deserted his religion immediately after his passing?

A campaign of disparagement against the Ṣaḥābah is an insult to Allah. How can one take an offensive attitude with the Ṣaḥābah after Allah praised them in the Qur'ān in this manner:

لَقَدْ رَضِيَ اللّٰهُ عَنِ الْمُؤْمِنِيْنَ إِذْ يُبَايِعُوْنَكَ تَحْتَ الشَّجَرَةِ فَعَلِمَ مَا فِيْ قُلُوْبِهِمْ فَأَنْزَلَ السَّكِيْنَةَ عَلَيْهِمْ وَأَثَابَهُمْ فَتْحًا قَرِيْبًا وَمَغَانِمَ كَثِيْرَةً يَأْخُذُوْنَهَا وَكَانَ اللّٰهُ عَزِيْزًا حَكِيْمًا

Certainly was Allah pleased with the believers when they pledged allegiance to you, [O Muḥammad], under the tree, and He knew what was in their hearts, so He sent down tranquillity upon them and rewarded them with an imminent conquest. And much war booty which they will take. And ever is Allah Exalted in Might and Wise.[2]

وَالسَّابِقُوْنَ الْأَوَّلُوْنَ مِنَ الْمُهَاجِرِيْنَ وَالْأَنْصَارِ وَالَّذِيْنَ اتَّبَعُوْهُمْ بِإِحْسَانٍ رَّضِيَ اللّٰهُ عَنْهُمْ وَرَضُوْا عَنْهُ وَأَعَدَّ لَهُمْ جَنَّاتٍ تَجْرِيْ تَحْتَهَا الْأَنْهَارُ خَالِدِيْنَ فِيْهَآ أَبَدًا ذٰلِكَ الْفَوْزُ الْعَظِيْمُ

The forerunners from the Muhājirīn and Anṣār and those who follow them in [all] good deeds, well-pleased is Allah with them, as are they with Him. He has prepared for them, gardens under which rivers flow to dwell therein forever; that is the supreme felicity.[3]

1 *Ṣaḥīḥ al-Bukhārī.*

2 Sūrah al-Fatḥ: 17-18.

3 Sūrah al-Tawbah: 100.

Here is the statement of Muḥsin al-Mulk Muḥammad Mahdī ʿAlī, formerly a Shīʿī Mujtahid, whom Allah had truly guided. His journey to guidance from the Rāfiḍī faith was a result of a deep and critical study of the status of the Ṣaḥābah as portrayed in the Qur'ān versus the Shīʿī Rāfiḍī portrayal of Ṣaḥābah. He said:

> The reality is that what the Shīʿah believe concerning the noble Ṣaḥābah results in directing suspicion towards the Prophet and stirring doubts about Islam in the hearts of those who study its doctrines. That is because the one who believes concerning those who believed in the Prophet ﷺ that they were untruthful in their belief and were unbelievers in their hearts (may Allah protect us), to the extent that they turned apostate directly after the Prophet's ﷺ demise; such a person is unable to believe in the nubuwwah of Muḥammad ﷺ. That is because if the Prophet ﷺ had been truthful in his nubuwwah his teachings would have been effective and he would have found some who believed in him from the depths of their hearts. Also, he would have found amongst the number of people who believed (in him) a few hundreds who remained steadfast upon īmān. If the Ṣaḥābah were deficient in their īmān and Islam, as they (the Rāfiḍah) claim, then who was affected with the guidance of the Prophet ﷺ and what was the number of those who benefitted from his nubuwwah? If the Ṣaḥābah, besides a few, were munāfiqīn murtaddīn (may Allah protect us) then who submitted to Islam and who benefitted from the teachings of the Messenger ﷺ and his nurturing?[1]

3. Tījānī's debates on Abū Bakr

Tījānī reminisces over a debate in which he prevailed against a Sunnī, whom he claims was a scholar. The details of the debate are lengthy; therefore the salient features will be focused on in the course of our discussion.

Ḥadīth of *Muwaṭṭa'*

Tījānī says:

> **I quickly went home and brought back two books, "al-Muwatta of Imam Malik" and "The Sahih of al-Bukhari". Then said, "Sir, what made me doubt Abu Bakr was the Messenger of Allah himself." I opened al-Muwatta and read: He said to the martyrs of Uhud, "Those, I bear witness against." Abu**

1 *Al-Āyāt al-Bayyināt*, vol. 1 p. 6-7; see also Ṣūratān Mutaḍāddatān, Abū al-Ḥasan al-Nadwī, p. 55.

> **Bakr then said, "O Messenger of Allah ﷺ, are we not their brothers? Did we not become Muslims as they did? Did we not fight as they did?"**
>
> **The Messenger ﷺ replied, "Yes, but I do not know what you are going to do after me."**
>
> **On hearing that, Abu Bakr cried bitterly and said, "We are going to alter many things after your departure."**
>
> **After having read the Ḥadīths, the looks on the faces of the scholarly Shaykh and that of the audience changed. They looked at each other and waited for the scholar, who was too shocked at what he had heard, to reply. All he did was to raise his eye brows, as a sign of astonishment and then said:**
>
> وَقُلْ رَبِّ زِدْنِيْ عِلْمًا
>
> ***And say: My Lord, increase me in knowledge.***[1,2]

Our response:

Despite the interrupted chain in this ḥadīth, its meaning has largely been corroborated by other texts[3]. Perhaps it was Tījānī's marred interpretation of it that rendered the Sunnī speechless. It could not have been the adapted translation that appears in *Then I was guided* which has been embellished to accommodate Tījānī's interpretation.

Libertine translation

Compare the translation undertaken by Aishah Bewley with the translation above:

> Abu'n-Nadr, the mawlā of Umar ibn Ubaydullah, that it has reached him that the Messenger of Allah, may Allah bless him and grant him peace, said over the martyrs of Uhud, "I testify for them." Abu Bakr as-Siddiq said, "Messenger of Allah! Are we not their brothers? We entered Islam as they entered Islam and we did jihād as they did jihād." The Messenger of Allah, may Allah bless him and grant him peace, said, "Yes, but I do not know what you will do after me." Abu Bakr wept profusely and said, "Are we really going to out-live you!"

---

1 Sūrah Ṭāhā: 114.

2 *Then I was guided* 128-129.

3 *Al-Tamhīd*, vol. 21 p. 228.

The statement of Abū Bakr, "Are we really going to out-live you!" has conveniently been adapted to "*We are going to alter many things after your departure.*"

Reason for Abū Bakr's crying

Abū Bakr's crying was clearly on account of the thought of living on after the Prophet's ﷺ demise. The Prophet ﷺ clearly acknowledged the Islam and Jihād of the Ṣaḥābah رضي الله عنهم when Abū Bakr رضي الله عنه asked him, "Are we not their brothers? We entered Islam as they entered Islam and we did jihād as they did jihād."

What the Messenger of Allah ﷺ meant by his statement, "but I do not know what you will do after me", is that he would testify for the physical actions of those who were martyred at Uḥud based on his knowledge. Since there would be individuals who lived after the Messenger's ﷺ demise he would not be able to testify for those deeds as he ﷺ does not have knowledge of those righteous actions. It is an accepted fact that the Prophet ﷺ had no knowledge of the unseen except what was revealed to him. Allah says in the Qur'ān:

قُلْ لَآ أَمْلِكُ لِنَفْسِي نَفْعًا وَّلَا ضَرًّا إِلَّا مَا شَآءَ اللّٰهُ ۚ وَلَوْ كُنْتُ أَعْلَمُ الْغَيْبَ لَاسْتَكْثَرْتُ مِنَ الْخَيْرِ وَمَا مَسَّنِيَ السُّوْٓءُ ۚ إِنْ أَنَا إِلَّا نَذِيْرٌ وَّبَشِيْرٌ لِّقَوْمٍ يُّؤْمِنُوْنَ

Say, "I hold not for myself (the power of) benefit or harm, except what Allah has willed. And if I knew the unseen, I could have acquired much wealth, and no harm would have touched me. I am not except a warner and a bringer of good tidings to a people who believe."[1]

Reliable Aḥādīth on Abū Bakr

The converse interpretation is ludicrous as it would imply that the Prophet ﷺ contradicted himself. How is it possible that the Prophet would praise Abū Bakr رضي الله عنه in the glowing manner described by Abū Hurayrah رضي الله عنه who reported Allah's Messenger ﷺ as saying:

---

1 Sūrah al-Aʿrāf: 188.

> If anyone contributes a pair of anything for the sake of Allah, he would be invited to enter Paradise (with these words), "O servant of Allah, it is good (for you)." Those who engage in prayer will he invited to enter by the gate of prayer; those who take part in Jihād will be invited to enter by the gate of Jihād; those who give charity will be invited to enter by the gate of charity; and those who observe fast will be invited to enter by the gate al-Rayyān.
>
> Abū Bakr said, "O Messenger of Allah, is it necessary that a person be invited through (only) one of these gates? Will anyone be invited to enter by all those gates?"
>
> The Messenger of Allah ﷺ said, "Yes, and I hope you will be one of them."[1]

Al-Tirmidhī , as well as al-Ṭabarānī in *al-Muʿjam al-Kabīr*, narrate from ʿĀ'ishah رضي الله عنها that Abū Bakr رضي الله عنه visited the Prophet ﷺ, and the Prophet ﷺ said to him:

أنت عتيق الله من النار

You are Allah's freed slave from the fire.[2]

In a lengthy ḥadīth found in *al-Bukhārī* Abū Mūsā al-Ashʿarī رضي الله عنه narrates:

فجاء أبو بكر فدفع الباب فقلت من هذا فقال أبو بكر فقلت على رسلك قال ثم ذهبت فقلت يا رسول الله هذا أبو بكر يستأذن فقال ائذن له وبشره بالجنة قال فأقبلت حتى قلت لأبي بكر ادخل ورسول الله صلى الله عليه وسلم يبشرك بالجنة

> Then Abū Bakr came and knocked on the door and I said, "Who is it?"
>
> He replied, "Abū Bakr," and I said to him, "One moment."
>
> I went (to the Prophet ﷺ) and said, "O Messenger of Allah, it is Abū Bakr seeking permission to enter."
>
> He said, "Let him in and give him the glad tidings of Jannah."

1 *Ṣaḥīḥ al-Bukhārī*, Kitāb al-Ṣawm, Ḥadīth no. 1897; *Ṣaḥīḥ Muslim*, Kitāb al-Zakāt, Ḥadīth no. 1027.

2 *Sunan al-Tirmidhī*, Kitāb al-Manāqib, Ḥadīth no. 3679; Ṭabarānī in his *al-Kabīr*, vol. 1, Ḥadīth no: 7-10; Refer also to *Ṣaḥīḥ al-Tirmidhī*, Ḥadīth no: 2905.

I approached until I said to Abū Bakr, "Enter and the Prophet ﷺ gives you the glad tidings of Jannah."[1]

Al-Tirmidhī transmits from ʿAbd al-Raḥmān ibn ʿAwf رضي الله عنه, he said that the Messenger of Allah ﷺ said:

أبو بكر في الجنة

Abū Bakr is in Jannah.[2]

Al-Tirmidhī also transmits from ʿAlī ibn Abī Ṭālib رضي الله عنه that he said:

كنت مع رسول الله صلى الله عليه وسلم إذ طلع أبو بكر وعمر فقال رسول الله صلى الله عليه وسلم هذان سيدا كهول أهل الجنة من الأولين والاخرين إلا النبيين والمرسلين يا علي لا تخبرهما

I was with the Messenger of Allah ﷺ when Abū Bakr and ʿUmar appeared. The Messenger of Allah ﷺ then said, "These two are the forerunners of the middle-aged men of Jannah from the first to the last except for the ambiyā' and rusul. O ʿAlī, do not inform them."[3]

Allah has confirmed the Companionship of this noble Ṣaḥābī with his words:

إِلَّا تَنْصُرُوْهُ فَقَدْ نَصَرَهُ اللّٰهُ إِذْ أَخْرَجَهُ الَّذِيْنَ كَفَرُوْا ثَانِيَ اثْنَيْنِ إِذْ هُمَا فِي الْغَارِ إِذْ يَقُوْلُ لِصَاحِبِهٖ لَا تَحْزَنْ إِنَّ اللّٰهَ مَعَنَا

If you do not aid him (i.e. the Prophet)—Allah has already aided him when those who disbelieved had driven him out (of Makkah) as one of two when they were in the cave and he (i.e. the Prophet) said to his companion, "Do not grieve; indeed Allah is with us."[4]

The verse is a timeless virtue for Abū Bakr as he had the exclusive good fortune of accompanying the Messenger of Allah ﷺ on the Hijrah protecting him with his life.[5] It is for that reason that Sufyān ibn ʿUyaynah and others have said:

1 *Ṣaḥīḥ al-Bukhārī*, Kitāb Faḍā'il al-Ṣaḥābah, Ḥadīth no: 3471, vol. 3.

2 *Sunan al-Tirmidhī*, Kitāb al-Manāqib, Bāb Manāqib ʿAbd al-Raḥmān ibn ʿAwf, Ḥadīth no: 3747.

3 Ibid. Ḥadīth no: 3665.

4 Sūrah al-Tawbah: 40.

5 *Fatḥ al-Bārī*, vol. 7 p. 12.

> Indeed, Allah admonishes the entire creation regarding His Prophet except for Abū Bakr. Whoever denies the Companionship of Abū Bakr is a disbeliever as he has belied the Qur'ān.[1]

Consequences of Tījānī's interpretation

Tījānī says with confidence that these are forgeries since they contradict his interpretation of the ḥadīth in *Muwaṭṭa'*.

If we have to concede in favour of Tījānī's explanation then we have no recourse but to say that the consistent application of understanding would apply in the following ḥadīth too. Khārijah ibn Zayd relates that the Prophet صلى الله عليه وسلم said, "By Allah, I do not know what Allah will do with me though I am Allah's Messenger.[2]" If this narration is understood in light of Tījānī's explanation of the ḥadīth in *Muwaṭṭa'* it would imply that the Prophet صلى الله عليه وسلم testified against himself! We seek Allah's protection from such blasphemy!

We are faced with two antithetical possibilities:

1. The ḥadīth in *Muwaṭṭa'* is sound, but is vague and needs to be understood in light of the abundant explicit narrations which speak of the virtues of Abū Bakr رضي الله عنه and the Prophet's صلى الله عليه وسلم assurance of his place in Paradise.
2. The ḥadīth in *Muwaṭṭa'* is sound and the other narrations are forged because they are incoherent with a particular understanding of this ḥadīth.

Since the chain of the ḥadīth in *Muwaṭṭa'* is interrupted and is not independently relied upon, we have to take into consideration the manner in which the scholars have understood the ḥadīth. This is prudent as they have only verified it on the basis of each element of it having corroboration in the Sunnah. There is nothing to corroborate the fact that Abū Bakr رضي الله عنه considered himself one who will alter the Sunnah; instead there is Prophetic advice to seek out Abū Bakr's counsel after the Prophet's صلى الله عليه وسلم passing. If we consider this in addition to the repugnant consequence of judging the ḥadīth of Khārijah consistently with Tījānī's understanding of the ḥadīth in *Muwaṭṭa'*, we have no alternative but to understand the ḥadīth in *Muwaṭṭa'* against the backdrop of all the other aḥādīth which mention Abū Bakr رضي الله عنه favourably and assure his position in Paradise.

---

1 *Minhāj al-Sunnah*, vol. 8 p. 381.

2 *Ṣaḥīḥ al-Bukhārī*, Kitāb al-Janā'iz, Ḥadīth no. 1243.

Commentators of *Muwaṭṭa'*

Inadvertently Tījānī has acknowledged the need to refer to scholars in complicated matters:

> **The Book of Allah is silent and could be interpreted in various ways, and it contains what is vague and what is similar, and to understand it we have to refer to those who are well endowed with knowledge as regards the Qur'an, and to Ahl al-Bayt, as regards to the Prophet's ﷺ traditions.[1]**

Many scholars have penned commentaries on the *Muwaṭṭa'* of Mālik. Note that their explanations are in harmony with what has been mentioned by us earlier. We present what they have written in explanation of this ḥadīth.

Al-Zurqānī says:

> "*These I will testify for*," with regards to sacrificing their bodies and souls, and orphaning their children, for those who had children.
>
> "*Abū Bakr al-Ṣiddīq said, 'Are we not their brothers, O Messenger of Allah? We accepted Islam as they accepted Islam and strove as they strove*'" Why are they singled out for your testimony (in their favour)?
>
> The Prophet said, "*Rather, you are their brothers*,' to the end of his statement. "*I do not know what you will do (tuḥdithūn) after me*," that is the reason why I limited the testimony to them.
>
> "*Abū Bakr cried and cried*," he cried incessantly on account of the great sadness (he felt upon the thought) of being separated from the Prophet. Then he said, "*Will we exist after you?*" (meaning) will we live "*after you?*" This is an expression borne out of sadness and not an actual question as it is inconceivable for such a question to come from Abū Bakr after the Prophet informed him.[2]

Imām al-Bājī says:

> Abū Bakr's statement, "*O Messenger of Allah, are we not their brothers? Did we not accept Islam as they accepted Islam and strive as they strove*," was an attempt to gain favour with the Prophet ﷺ because of what he saw of their (the martyrs of Uḥud) exclusivity in a ruling he wished his portion in it would be

1 There is no doubt in the falseness of this statement but I have cited it to clarify the scope of Tījānī's continuous contradictions.

2 *Sharḥ al-Zurqānī 'alā Muwaṭṭa' al-Imām Mālik*, vol. 3 p. 49-50.

> great and the portion of those Ṣaḥābah who participated in it (the Battle of Uḥud) would be confirmed.
>
> Therefore, he said, "*Our actions were similar to their actions*," (it was) in reference to Īmān which is the root and jihād which was the last of their actions and he asked, "*Will you be a witness for us as you will be a witness for them?*" The Prophet صَلَّى ٱللَّهُ عَلَيْهِ وَسَلَّمَ replied, "*I do not know what you will do after me.*"
>
> Some scholars have said that the statement, even though it was directed to Abū Bakr, refers to others besides him whom the Prophet صَلَّى ٱللَّهُ عَلَيْهِ وَسَلَّمَ was unaware what their end condition and action would be and what they would die upon. As for Abū Bakr رَضِيَ ٱللَّهُ عَنْهُ, he was informed that he was of the people of Jannah. The Prophet صَلَّى ٱللَّهُ عَلَيْهِ وَسَلَّمَ bore testimony to that by virtue of his apparent good actions and because it was revealed to him, and was informed about Allah's pleasure with him. However, when Abū Bakr رَضِيَ ٱللَّهُ عَنْهُ asked the question in a general sense and did not specify himself asking about his own personal condition, the answer too was general. The Prophet's صَلَّى ٱللَّهُ عَلَيْهِ وَسَلَّمَ preferring him and informing him about what Allah سُبْحَانَهُ وَتَعَالَىٰ has preserved for him of good, a great reward, and a generous return; make clear that he was not of those who did actions nullifying what they did after the Prophet صَلَّى ٱللَّهُ عَلَيْهِ وَسَلَّمَ.

He goes on to say:

> There is another possible interpretation, in my opinion. It is that the Prophet صَلَّى ٱللَّهُ عَلَيْهِ وَسَلَّمَ meant, "These persons I will testify to what I witnessed of their actions in jihād which led to their death in the path of Allah." He did not say that he is a witness for the one who witnessed this day and fought (in it) and was saved from death in it such as ʿAlī and Ṭalḥah and Abū Ṭalḥah, who stood the test of that day, and others who were better than most of those who died on that day. However, the Prophet صَلَّى ٱللَّهُ عَلَيْهِ وَسَلَّمَ specified this ruling (his testimony) for the one whom he witnessed his jihād to the point where he was killed as a martyr. This is what the Prophet صَلَّى ٱللَّهُ عَلَيْهِ وَسَلَّمَ meant with his statement to Abū Bakr رَضِيَ ٱللَّهُ عَنْهُ, "*I do not know what you will do after me.*" The Prophet صَلَّى ٱللَّهُ عَلَيْهِ وَسَلَّمَ did not refer to actions which would contravene the sharīʿah. Rather, he intended all actions, those that were in conformity with the sharīʿah and those that opposed it. The meaning of that (statement) is, "I will not witness what you do after me. Therefore, I cannot testify on your behalf in relation to it even though I know that amongst you are those who will die upon what pleases Allah سُبْحَانَهُ وَتَعَالَىٰ of good actions but those actions have not been identified to me. (For example),

it has been said to me that such a person will strive in jihād in such a place, and one of you will kill Zayd, or ʿAmr will kill him. For that reason, I cannot be a witness for you for the same actions and its details in the manner that I will testify to the details of the actions of these and what I witnessed of some of you in terms of general practice upon the revelation and the instruction of Allah سُبْحَانَهُ وَتَعَالَىٰ. Upon this interpretation the meaning of his words are, "I do not know what you will do after me," addressing all the Ṣaḥābah, Abū Bakr رَضِيَ اللَّهُ عَنْهُ and others besides him.

As for his statement, "*then Abū Bakr wept and wept and said, 'are we going to exist after you;*'" it means he wept for an extended time. He clarified the reason for his weeping with his words, "are we going to exist after you?" It was out of sadness at the thought of remaining behind after the Prophet صَلَّى اللَّهُ عَلَيْهِ وَسَلَّمَ, and being alone after him, and being deprived of his blessings and Allah's سُبْحَانَهُ وَتَعَالَىٰ favour on account of him (his presence). All of the aforementioned indicates that Abū Bakr رَضِيَ اللَّهُ عَنْهُ understood from the Prophet's صَلَّى اللَّهُ عَلَيْهِ وَسَلَّمَ statement, "*I do not know what you are going to do after me,*" that the Prophet صَلَّى اللَّهُ عَلَيْهِ وَسَلَّمَ did not fear or (even) imagine that Abū Bakr رَضِيَ اللَّهُ عَنْهُ would do something in contradiction of the sharīʿah and consequently oppose the precedent of the Prophet صَلَّى اللَّهُ عَلَيْهِ وَسَلَّمَ as weeping for that reason would have been more appropriate. If that was indeed the case, he would have said, "*Are we going to innovate such actions which will repel from your path and oppose your precedent?*" Because he did not say that or cry on account of that and he only cried on account of his separation from the Prophet صَلَّى اللَّهُ عَلَيْهِ وَسَلَّمَ we know that he understood (from the Prophet's صَلَّى اللَّهُ عَلَيْهِ وَسَلَّمَ statement) what we explained before. And Allah سُبْحَانَهُ وَتَعَالَىٰ knows best.[1]

As for his statement:

I said, "If the Messenger of Allah صَلَّى اللَّهُ عَلَيْهِ وَسَلَّمَ was the first to doubt Abu Bakr, and did not bear witness against him, because the Messenger did not know what would happen after him ..."

Our comment:

Does this mean that the Prophet صَلَّى اللَّهُ عَلَيْهِ وَسَلَّمَ was the first to doubt himself since Khārijah ibn Zayd relates that he صَلَّى اللَّهُ عَلَيْهِ وَسَلَّمَ said, "*By Allah, I do not know what Allah will do with me though I am Allah's Messenger.*[2]"

---

1 *Al-Muwaṭṭa' Sharḥ al-Bājī*, vol. 3 p. 207-209.

2 *Ṣaḥīḥ al-Bukhārī*, Kitāb al-Janā'iz, Ḥadīth no. 1243.

Did the Prophet ﷺ doubt him when he appointed Abū Bakr رضي الله عنه to lead the prayers during his final illness?

What about when he came out in his fatal illness with a piece of cloth tied round his head and sat on the pulpit. After thanking and praising Allah he ﷺ said, "There is no one who had done more favour to me with his life and property than Abū Bakr. If I were to take a Khalīl other than Allah, I would certainly have taken Abū Bakr but the Islamic brotherhood and friendship are sufficient."

Earlier in the book, 'Umar رضي الله عنه is wrongfully accused of claiming that the Prophet ﷺ was incoherent in his speech. I ask you, esteemed reader, does Tījānī's interpretation not imply that the Prophet ﷺ was incoherent?

Tījānī goes on to say:

> **It is within my right to doubt and not to have a preference for anybody until I know the truth. Evidently, these Ḥadīths contradict and nullify all the known Ḥadīths in favour of Abu Bakr and Umar, because they are more realistic than these which mention their alleged virtues.**
>
> **The audience said, "How could that be?" I said, "The Messenger of Allah ﷺ did not bear witness against Abu Bakr and said: I do not know what they will do after me! This sounds very reasonable. History has proved that, and the Holy Qur'an and history bear witness that they did change after him. Because of that Abu Bakr cried for he changed and angered Fatimah al-Zahra, daughter of the Messenger as we explained before, and he changed until he repented and wished that he was not a human being. As for the Ḥadīth: If the faith of my nation and the faith of Abu Bakr were put on balance, the faith of Abu Bakr would weigh heavier", it is invalid and implausible. It is not possible for the faith of a man, who spent forty years of his life believing in polytheism and worshipping idols, to be greater than the faith of the entire nation of Muhammad, which has many God-fearing and pious people and martyrs and Imams, who spent all their lives fighting for the sake of Allah.**
>
> **How could Abu Bakr fit into this Ḥadīth? If it was true, he would not, in later life have finished that he was not a human being. Further, if his faith was greater than the faith of the entire nation of Muhammad, Fatimah, the daughter of the Messenger of Allah and the leading lady, would not have been angry at him or asked Allah to punish him in each prayer she prayed."[1]**

1 *Then I was guided*, p. 129-130.

Our comment:

We have come to realize the extent of Tījānī's objectivity, even if it implies that the Prophet ﷺ doubts himself. Tījānī has proven to us, repeatedly, that he has already taken a stance on Abū Bakr. With the aid of the vagueness in a few narrations he sets himself up in the perfect position to reject all the authentic explicit narrations.

We have also come to realize that there are no objective academic criteria that he is prepared to subject himself to. It stands to reason that he can doubt whom he wishes, condemn whom he wishes, accept what he wishes, and reject what he wishes.

As for his statement:

> **The Holy Qur'an and history bear witness that they did change after him.**

Do these verses give any hint that the Ṣaḥābah رضي الله عنهم were going to change after the Prophet's ﷺ demise?

> لٰكِنِ الرَّسُوْلُ وَالَّذِيْنَ اٰمَنُوْا مَعَهٗ جَاهَدُوْا بِأَمْوَالِهِمْ وَأَنْفُسِهِمْ وَأُولٰٓئِكَ لَهُمُ الْخَيْرَاتُ وأُولٰٓئِكَ هُمُ الْمُفْلِحُوْنَ أَعَدَّ اللّٰهُ لَهُمْ جَنَّاتٍ تَجْرِيْ مِنْ تَحْتِهَا الْأَنْهَارُ خَالِدِيْنَ فِيْهَا ذٰلِكَ الْفَوْزُ الْعَظِيْمُ
>
> *But the Messenger of Allah and those who believed with him fought with their wealth and their lives. Those will have [all that is] good and it is those who are the successful. Allah has prepared for them gardens beneath which rivers flow, wherein they will abide eternally. That is the great attainment.*[1]

Did the Prophet ﷺ fight the Mushrikīn at Badr, when their numbers reached one thousand fighters, and at Uḥud, when their numbers reached three thousand, and other battles, with a band of true believers whose number did not exceed ten?

Was Allah unaware of the status of the Ṣaḥābah when He made them role models to be followed?

1 Sūrah al-Tawbah: 88-89.

وَالسَّابِقُوْنَ الْأَوَّلُوْنَ مِنَ الْمُهَاجِرِيْنَ وَالْأَنْصَارِ وَالَّذِيْنَ اتَّبَعُوْهُمْ بِإِحْسَانٍ رَّضِيَ اللّٰهُ عَنْهُمْ وَرَضُوْا عَنْهُ وَأَعَدَّ لَهُمْ جَنَّاتٍ تَجْرِيْ تَحْتَهَا الْأَنْهَارُ خَالِدِيْنَ فِيْهَا أَبَدًا ذٰلِكَ الْفَوْزُ الْعَظِيْمُ

And the first forerunners [in the faith] among the Muhājirīn and the Anṣār and those who followed them with good conduct—Allah is pleased with them and they are pleased with Him, and He has prepared for them gardens beneath which rivers flow, wherein they will abide forever. That is the great attainment.[1]

Allah سُبْحَانَهُ وَتَعَالَى says:

لِلْفُقَرَاءِ الْمُهَاجِرِيْنَ الَّذِيْنَ أُخْرِجُوْا مِنْ دِيَارِهِمْ وَأَمْوَالِهِمْ يَبْتَغُوْنَ فَضْلًا مِّنَ اللّٰهِ وَرِضْوَانًا وَيَنْصُرُوْنَ اللّٰهَ وَرَسُوْلَهُ ۚ أُولٰئِكَ هُمُ الصَّادِقُوْنَ ۚ وَالَّذِيْنَ تَبَوَّؤُا الدَّارَ وَالْإِيْمَانَ مِنْ قَبْلِهِمْ يُحِبُّوْنَ مَنْ هَاجَرَ إِلَيْهِمْ وَلَا يَجِدُوْنَ فِيْ صُدُوْرِهِمْ حَاجَةً مِّمَّا أُوْتُوْا وَيُؤْثِرُوْنَ عَلٰى أَنْفُسِهِمْ وَلَوْ كَانَ بِهِمْ خَصَاصَةٌ ۚ وَمَنْ يُّوْقَ شُحَّ نَفْسِهِ فَأُولٰئِكَ هُمُ الْمُفْلِحُوْنَ

For the poor emigrants who were expelled from their homes and their properties, seeking bounty from Allah and [His] approval and supporting Allah and His Messenger, [there is also a share]. Those are the truthful and [also for] those who were settled in the Home [i.e. Madīnah] and [adopted] the faith before them. They love those who emigrated to them and find not any want in their breasts of what they [i.e. the emigrants] were given but give [them] preference over themselves, even though they are in privation. And whoever is protected from the stinginess of his soul—it is those who will be the successful.[2]

We do not expect any commentary from Tījānī. Let the 'infallible' Imām of the Twelver Shīʿah, ʿAlī ibn Ḥusayn, elaborate on these verses. ʿAlī ibn Abī al-Fatḥ al-relates his book *Kashf al-Ghummah fī Maʿrifat al-A'immah* from ʿAlī ibn Ḥusayn:

1 Sūrah al-Tawbah: 100.

2 Sūrah al-Ḥashr: 8-9.

A group of people came to him from ʿIrāq and made some disparaging remarks about Abū Bakr, ʿUmar, and ʿUthmān. When they completed what they had to say, he said to them, "Are you from the group (described by the verse), 'for the first emigrants who were expelled from their homes and their properties, seeking bounty from Allah and [His] approval and supporting Allah and His Messenger of Allah. Those are the truthful'?" They answered, "No."

He asked, "Are you then from the group (described by the verse), 'those who were settled in the Home [i.e. Madīnah] and [adopted] the faith before them. They love those who emigrated to them and find not any want in their breasts of what they [i.e., the emigrants] were given but give [them] preference over themselves, even though they are in privation'?" They answered, "No."

ʿAlī ibn Ḥusayn then said, "As for you, you have distanced yourselves from being either one of these two groups and I testify that you are not amongst those whom Allah says about them:

وَالَّذِيْنَ جَآءُوْا مِنْۢ بَعْدِهِمْ يَقُوْلُوْنَ رَبَّنَا اغْفِرْ لَنَا وَلِإِخْوَانِنَا الَّذِيْنَ سَبَقُوْنَا بِالْإِيْمَانِ وَلَا تَجْعَلْ فِيْ قُلُوْبِنَا غِلًّا لِّلَّذِيْنَ اٰمَنُوْا رَبَّنَا إِنَّكَ رَءُوْفٌ رَّحِيْمٌ

And (there is a share for) those who came after them, saying: "Our Lord, forgive us and our brothers who preceded us in faith and put not in our hearts (any) resentment toward those who have believed. Our Lord, indeed You are Kind and Merciful.[1,2]

Be gone from me, Allah will do with you what He wills.[3]

Tījānīs Ḥadīth criticism

Tījānī writes:

> **As for the Ḥadīth: If the faith of my nation and the faith of Abu Bakr were put on balance, the faith of Abu Bakr would weigh heavier", it is invalid and implausible. It is not possible for the faith of a man, who spent forty years of**

1 Sūrah al-Ḥashr: 10.

2 Ibid.

3 *Kashf al-Ghummah*, vol. 2 p. 291, under the heading Faḍā'il al-Imām Zayn al-ʿĀbidīn.

his life believing in polytheism and worshipping idols, to be greater than the faith of the entire nation of Muhammad ﷺ.

Our comment:

This has been a journey of sorts and we have often found Tījānī venturing off into the wilderness without a compass. This time Tījānī veers off the course of academic ḥadīth criticism and rejects a narration based solely on its content. The alarming indiscretion is not Tījānī's rejection of this narration; it is the reason for rejection.

Tījānī ignored the procedure of studying the chain of transmission in order to establish the reliability of the report or not. This approach of his speaks volumes for the inconsistency in his evaluation of facts. His outright rejection means that he was not even prepared to entertain the content value of such a narration.

The report, "Had the īmān of Abū Bakr been compared with the īmān of the Ummah," is a statement of ʿUmar ibn al-Khaṭṭāb رضي الله عنه which has been narrated by Isḥāq ibn Rāhūyah, and al-Bayhaqī in *al-Shuʿab* with an authentic chain.

Al-Sakhāwī says:

> Hudhayl ibn Shuraḥbīl narrates it from ʿUmar. Likewise, (it has been recorded) by Ibn Mubārak in al-Zuhd, and Muʿādh ibn al-Muthannā in *Ziyādāt Musnad Musaddad*. Ibn ʿAdī also narrates it in the biography of ʿĪsā ibn ʿAbd Allāh in *al-Kāmil*, and in *Musnad al-Firdows* with the ḥadīth of Ibn ʿUmar which leads to the Prophet with the wording, "If the īmān of Abū Bakr is weighed against the īmān of the Ummah, his īmān will outweigh it." Appearing in the chain of this ḥadīth is ʿĪsā ibn ʿAbd Allāh ibn Sulaymān, who is considered a weak transmitter. That being said, he is not the only person to narrate it in this manner. Ibn ʿAdī narrates this ḥadīth (reaching the Prophet ﷺ) from a different transmitter with the wording, "If the īmān of Abū Bakr is weighed against the īmān of the people of the world it would outweigh theirs." There is also a *shāhid* (corroborating narration) in the *Sunan* from Abū Bakrah, from the Prophet ﷺ. It reads, "A man came to the Prophet ﷺ and said, 'O Messenger of Allah, I saw (in dream) it was as if a scale descended from the sky and you weighed against Abū Bakr and you were heavier than him. Then Abū Bakr was weighed against the rest and he outweighed (the rest)...'"[1]

1 *Al-Maqāṣid al-Ḥasanah*.

We thus find that the ḥadīth was a subject of discussions among Sunnī scholars. The statement from ʿUmar رضي الله عنه is further corroborated by the narration appearing in the *Sunan*. Is it plausible that Tījānī deliberately chose to overlook this and reject it because it doesn't agree with his worldview?

Is it implausible that Abū Bakr Īmān could outweigh the rest of the Ummah despite being responsible for the Islam of five of the ten promised Jannah? ʿUthmān ibn ʿAffān, al-Zubayr ibn al-ʿAwwām, ʿAbd al-Raḥmān ibn al-ʿAwf, Saʿd ibn Abī Waqqāṣ, and Ṭalḥah ibn ʿUbayd Allah all entered into Islam through the efforts of Abū Bakr. Is it farfetched that he will share in all their reward? Abū Bakr has the lion's share of setting slaves free in the Makkan period, does this account for nothing?

Abū Bakr رضي الله عنه accepted Islam without hesitation. The Prophet صلى الله عليه وسلم said:

ما عرضت الإسلام على أحد إلا كانت له عنده كبوة أو تردد غير أبي بكر فإنه لم يتلعثم

> I did not present Islam to anyone except that he had a stumble or hesitation except for Abū Bakr, he did not hesitate.[1]

Compare Tījānī's rejection of the ḥadīth with the question Muḥammad ibn ʿAlī ibn Abī Ṭālib (known as ibn al-Ḥanafiyyah) asked his father:

قلت لأبي أى الناس خير بعد رسول الله صلى الله عليه وسلم قال أبو بكر. قلت ثم من قال ثم عمر وخشيت أن يقول عثمان قلت ثم أنت قال ما أنا إلا رجل من المسلمين

> "Who is the best of all people after the Messenger of Allah صلى الله عليه وسلم?"
>
> "Abū Bakr," came the reply.
>
> "Who then?" asked Ibn al-Ḥanafiyyah.
>
> "ʿUmar," replied ʿAlī رضي الله عنه.
>
> Muḥammad ibn al-Ḥanafiyyah says, 'I feared he would say ʿUthmān next if I asked him, so I said, "Then you."'
>
> ʿAlī رضي الله عنه replied, "I am but an ordinary man from the Muslims."[2]

---

1 Refer to al-Shaykhān, Abū Bakr al-Ṣiddīq, al-Balādhurī, p. 21.

2 *Ṣaḥīḥ al-Bukhārī*, Kitāb Faḍā'il Aṣḥāb al-Nabī صلى الله عليه وسلم, Ḥadīth no. 3671.

As for Tījānī's statement:

> **It is not possible for the faith of a man, who spent forty years of his life believing in polytheism and worshipping idols, to be greater than the faith of the entire nation of Muhammad, which has many God-fearing and pious people and martyrs and Imams, who spent all their lives fighting for the sake of Allah.**

We will respond to this from multiple perspectives:

a. The burden of proof lies with Tījānī. He has made an outlandish claim that Abū Bakr رَضِيَ اللَّهُ عَنْهُ used to worship idols for forty years. On the basis of this ridiculous claim Tījānī is prepared to reject the Prophet's صَلَّى اللَّهُ عَلَيْهِ وَسَلَّمَ words.

b. There has been no proof that Abū Bakr worshipped idols. He was a friend of the Prophet صَلَّى اللَّهُ عَلَيْهِ وَسَلَّمَ in the period of Jāhiliyyah. The Prophet صَلَّى اللَّهُ عَلَيْهِ وَسَلَّمَ was known not to have worshipped idols. It is not farfetched that Abū Bakr رَضِيَ اللَّهُ عَنْهُ was a *Ḥanīf* as well. There are some narrations whose integrity we do not rely on completely which read:

   > Abū Bakr once said in the company of the Prophet's صَلَّى اللَّهُ عَلَيْهِ وَسَلَّمَ Companions, "I never prostrated to an idol. That is because when I was close to puberty Abū Quḥāfah grabbed hold of my hand and took me to a closet in which was idols. He then said to me, 'These are your idols,' and left me alone in it and left. I drew close to the idol and said, 'I am hungry, feed me!' but he did not respond. Then I said, 'I am naked, clothe me!' but he did not respond. Then I threw a rock on top of it and it fell on its face."[1]

   Our defence of Abū Bakr is not in light of the above narration. We have merely cited it to show that there is some evidence contrary to what Tījānī has claimed. He bears the burden of furnishing evidence to back up his claim.

c. If we accept that Abū Bakr was engaged in idol worship during the Jāhiliyyah period, this is of no consequence after his Islam since Allah pardons all sins of the past:

قُل لِّلَّذِينَ كَفَرُوٓا۟ إِن يَنتَهُوا۟ يُغْفَرْ لَهُم مَّا قَدْ سَلَفَ

---

1 Refer to *al-Tārīkh al-Islamī* by Maḥmūd al-Shākir, vol. 3 p. 31; and *Mukhtaṣar al-Maḥāsin al-Mujtamiʿah* by ʿAbd al-Raḥmān al-Ṣafūrī, p. 38.

> Say to those who have disbelieved (that) if they cease, what has previously occurred will be forgiven for them.[1]

In a lengthy ḥadīth the Prophet ﷺ informed ʿAmr ibn al-ʿĀṣ رضي الله عنه:

أما علمت أن الإسلام يهدم ما كان قبله

Do you not know that Islam eradicates what came before it?[2]

Embracing Islam removes whatever sins the person committed and expiates it.

d. This reality is acknowledged by the Rāfiḍah as well. Al-Kulaynī narrates from Imām al-Bāqir in *al-Kāfī*, under the chapter, "the Muslim is not taken to task for what he did in his days of ignorance":

> Some people came to the Messenger of Allah ﷺ after they accepted Islam and said, "O Messenger of Allah, will a man amongst us be taken account of for what he did during his days of ignorance after accepting Islam?"
>
> The Messenger of Allah ﷺ said to them, "The person whose Islam is good, and the conviction in his īmān is correct, Allah will not take him to account for what he did during his days of ignorance. (On the other hand) whosoever's Islam is weak, and the conviction in his īmān is not correct, Allah will take into account all that he did from the first to the last (of his actions)."[3]

If anything it also shows the shallowness of Tījānī's claim where he says:

> **I have no enmity towards Abu Bakr or Umar or 'Uthman or Ali or even Wahshi, the killer of our master al-Ḥamzah, as long as he became a Muslim, and the Messenger of Allah ﷺ forgave him.**[4]

Why should Abū Bakr رضي الله عنه be taken to task for what he had allegedly done during the period of Jāhiliyyah? If he is to be taken to task then Tījānī's sentiments are self-contradictory.

e. Ibn Taymiyyah says:

---

1 Sūrah al-Anfāl: 38.

2 *Ṣaḥīḥ Muslim* with its commentary, Kitāb al-Īmān, Bāb ʿhal yuʿkhadh bi aʿmāl al-Jāhiliyyah.

3 *Uṣūl al-Kāfī*, vol. 2 p. 333.

4 *Then I was guided*, p. 82.

> Not every person born in Islam is better than the person who entered into Islam by himself such as Abū Bakr and ʿUmar. Indeed, it has been established that the greatest of all generations is the first generation and most of them accepted Islam on their own after unbelief. They are better than the second generation who were born into Islam.[1]

There remains his assertion that it is impossible for Abū Bakr's Īmān '*to be greater than the faith of the entire nation of Muḥammad, which has many God-fearing and pious people and martyrs and Imāms, who spent all their lives fighting for the sake of Allah*'.

The truth is that after Muḥammad ﷺ Abū Bakr is their leader. One has to appreciate the extent to which the Prophet ﷺ would become annoyed if anyone upset Abū Bakr رضي الله عنه.

Al-Bukhārī narrates from Abū al-Dardā':

> كنت جالسا عند النبي صلى الله عليه وسلم إذ أقبل أبو بكر آخذا بطرف ثوبه حتى أبدى عن ركبته، فقال النبي صلى الله عليه وسلم أما صاحبكم فقد غامر فسلم وقال إني كان بيني وبين ابن الخطاب شيء فأسرعت إليه ثم ندمت فسألته أن يغفر لي فأبى علي فأقبلت إليك فقال يغفر الله لك يابا بكر ثلاثا ثم إن عمر ندم فأتى منزل أبي بكر فسأل أثم أبو بكر فقالوا لا فأتى إلى النبي صلى الله عليه وسلم فسلم فجعل وجه النبي صلى الله عليه وسلم يتمعر حتى أشفق أبو بكر فجثا على ركبتيه فقال يا رسول الله والله أنا كنت أظلم مرتين فقال النبي صلى الله عليه وسلم إن الله بعثني إليكم فقلتم كذبت وقال أبو بكر صدق وواساني بنفسه وماله، فهل أنتم تاركو لي صاحبي مرتين فما أوذي بعدها

> I was sitting with the Prophet ﷺ when Abū Bakr headed towards us holding onto the edge of his cloak to the extent that he exposed his knees.
>
> The Prophet said, "As for your friend he is upset."
>
> Abū Bakr greeted and said, "O Messenger of Allah! Something happened between me and Ibn al-Khaṭṭāb (ʿUmar). I hastened (after the incident) towards him and regretted (my action) and asked him to forgive me but he refused. Therefore I came to you."

1 *Minhāj al-Sunnah*, vol. 8 p. 284.

The Prophet ﷺ said, "May Allah forgive you, O Abū Bakr, " repeating it thrice.

Then ʿUmar regretted his action and went to the house of Abū Bakr and asked, "Is Abū Bakr home," and they replied that he was not.

He then went to the Prophet ﷺ and when the Prophet ﷺ saw him, his face turned red to the point that Abū Bakr regretted (taking the matter to the Prophet ﷺ).

Abū Bakr sat up and said, "O Messenger of Allah! I was the one in the wrong," repeating it twice.

The Prophet ﷺ then said, "Allah sent me to you and you all said, 'You are lying,' and Abū Bakr said, 'You speak the truth,' he provided me with both physical and financial assistance. Will you not leave my Companion for my sake?" repeating it twice.

He (Abū Bakr) was never inconvenienced again after that.[1]

Abū ʿUthmān reports that ʿAmr ibn al-ʿĀṣ رضي الله عنه narrated when the Prophet ﷺ sent him with the army of Dhāt al-Salāsil:

أن النبي صلى الله عليه وسلم بعثه على جيش ذات السلاسل فأتيته فقلت أى الناس أحب إليك قال عائشة فقلت من الرجال فقال أبوها قلت ثم من قال ثم عمر بن الخطاب فعد رجالا

I went to him and said, "Who is most beloved person to you?"

The Prophet ﷺ replied, "ʿĀ'ishah."

I asked, "And from the men?"

He replied, "Her father."

I enquired, "Who thereafter?"

He said, "ʿUmar ibn al-Khaṭṭāb," and then mentioned a number of other men.[2]

---

1 *Ṣaḥīḥ al-Bukhārī*, Kitāb Al-Faḍā'il al-Ṣaḥābah, Ḥadīth no. 4361.

2 *Ṣaḥīḥ al-Bukhārī*, Kitāb Faḍā'il al-Ṣaḥābah, Ḥadīth no. 4362.

Abū Bakr was also considered the greatest of the Companions in terms of righteous actions. Muslim narrates with his chain to Abū Hurayrah who said:

> من أصبح منكم اليوم صائما قال أبو بكر أنا. قال فمن تبع منكم اليوم جنازة قال أبو بكر أنا قال فمن أطعم منكم اليوم مسكينا قال أبو بكر أنا قال فمن عاد منكم اليوم مريضا قال أبو بكر أنا. فقال رسول الله صلى الله عليه وسلم ما اجتمعن في امرئ إلا دخل الجنة

> One day the Messenger of Allah ﷺ asked, "Who amongst you is fasting?"
>
> Abū Bakr replied, "I am."
>
> The Prophet ﷺ then asked, "Who followed a Janāzah today?"
>
> Abū Bakr replied, "I did."
>
> The Prophet ﷺ said, "Who amongst you fed a needy person today?"
>
> Abū Bakr said, "I did."
>
> The Prophet ﷺ said, "Who amongst you visited the sick today?"
>
> Abū Bakr said, "I did."
>
> The Prophet ﷺ then said, "These (acts) are not combined in one person except that he enters Jannah."[1]

Notwithstanding all of the difficulty, hardship, and suffering that he endured from the earliest days of Islam. All of that without displaying any signs of cowardice, embarrassment, or failure. He gracefully defended the Messenger of Allah ﷺ, fighting the Mushrikīn at times with his hand, at times with his tongue, and at times with his wealth.[2]

ʿAlī رضي الله عنه said:

> قال لي رسول الله يوم بدر و لأبي بكر مع أحدكما جبريل و مع الأخر ميكائيل و إسرافيل ملك عظيم يشهد القتال أو يكون في القتال

1 *Muslim* with it commentary, Bāb Faḍā'il al-Ṣaḥābah, Ḥadīth no. 1028.

2 *Minhāj al-Sunnah*, vol. 8 p. 79.

> The Messenger of Allah ﷺ said to me and Abū Bakr on the Day of Badr, "Jibrīl was with one of you and Mīkā'īl was with the other. And Isrāfīl is a huge angel; he witnessed or partook in the battle."[1]

It is overwhelmingly clear that Abū Bakr رضي الله عنه was the leader of the righteous and Tījānī's snide comments are the result of nothing but prejudice.

I conclude this discussion with a narration recorded by the Twelver Shīʿī scholar, Abū al-Ḥasan al-Irbilī, in his book, *Kashf al-Ghummah*, from ʿUrwah ibn ʿAbd Allāh:

> I asked Abū Jaʿfar Muḥammad ibn ʿAlī (al-Bāqir) about adorning the swords and he said, "There is no problem with it. Indeed, Abū Bakr al-Ṣiddīq adorned his sword."
>
> I asked him, "Do you too say al-Ṣiddīq?"
>
> He jumped up and faced the Qiblah and said, "Yes, (he is) al-Ṣiddīq! Yes, (he is) al-Ṣiddīq! Yes, (he is) al-Ṣiddīq! The person who does not call (or regard) him as al-Ṣiddīq, Allah will not attest to a word he said in the world or in the hereafter."[2]

4. Tījānī's enlightenment and his attitude towards Abū Bakr

In these passages Tījānī opens up to the readers his religious persuasions and confesses the reasons for his conversion to the Twelver Shīʿī faith. He says:

> **The reasons behind my enlightenment are many, but I shall only mention a few of them here:**
>
> **The text regarding the succession to the Caliphate**
>
> **I have committed myself, before embarking on this study, to never depending on any reference unless it is considered authentic by the two parties, and to discarding those references that are solely referred to by only one of the parties.**
>
> **Thus, I shall investigate the idea regarding the preference between Abu Bakr and Ali ibn Abī Ṭālib, and that the succession of the caliphate was by**

1 *Musnad Abū Yaʿlā*, vol. 1 p. 340, *Musnad ʿAlī ibn Abī Ṭālib*, the editor commented and said: "Its sanad is authentic."

2 *Kashf al-Ghummah* by Irbilī, vol. 2 p. 360.

written text [Dictate] for Ali, as the Shiites claim, and not by election and Shura [consultation] as the Sunnis claim.

Any researcher in this subject, if he considers nothing but the truth, will find that the text in support of Ali is very clear, like the following saying by the Messenger of Allah ﷺ: Whoever considers me his master, then Ali is his master. He said it at the end of the Farewell Pilgrimage, when it was confirmed that Ali would succeed, and many people congratulated him on that, including Abu Bakr and Umar who were among the well-wishers, and who were quoted as having said to the Imam, "Well done, Ibn Abī Ṭālib, overnight you have become a master of all the believers."

This text has been agreed on by both Shiites and Sunnis, and in fact I have only referred in this study to some Sunni references and not to all of them, for they are so many.

If the reader wants more information, he may read "al- Ghadir" by al-Amini (thirteen Volumes) in which the writer classifies the sayings of the Prophet according to the Sunnis.[1]

Responding to Tījānī's enlightenment and his attitude towards Abū Bakr

We would have noticed Tījānī's endless reminders of his objectivity and impartiality; almost as if he anticipated that the reader would approach his book with a healthy dose of scepticism. All we have done is examine his objectivity and impartiality in the way he approached every claim that he made. Sadly, despite his repeated claims, we have found him wanting on many accounts when it came to objectivity throughout his book; and these we have pointed out along the way. We are confident that the discerning reader will see beyond Tījānī's sales pitch and evaluate the facts for what they are, based on accepted academic criteria.

Tījānī asserts that ʿAlī رضي الله عنه was unambiguously nominated by the Prophet ﷺ as his successor. This assertion is based on the doctrine that the Prophet's ﷺ successor was expressly appointed through divine text (Naṣṣ). In supporting his assertion Tījānī has alluded to the incident at Ghadīr Khum, when the Prophet ﷺ stopped to rest with those of his Companions who were returning to Madīnah with him after Ḥajj.

1 *Then I was guided*, p. 135.

Nomination of Khalīfah

Tījānī's generalized assertion that the Sunnīs only consider the khilāfah established through elections or shūrā is not entirely accurate. There is a minority view which holds that the candidacy of Abū Bakr رضي الله عنه for khilāfah was established through implicit texts. The preponderant view holds that the khilāfah of Abū Bakr was established on the basis of agreement between the people of *al-Ḥill wa l-ʿAqd* (executive authority). The textual evidence which is the basis of the minority is understood to be suggestions from the Prophet صلى الله عليه وسلم for his preferred candidate for Khilāfah.

These are some of the aḥādīth which are understood as implicit directives by some or Prophetic suggestions by the majority:

ʿĀ'ishah رضي الله عنها narrates:

> The Messenger صلى الله عليه وسلم said, "Indeed, I was on the verge of calling Abū Bakr and his son, and entrust leadership to him for fear that people might speak or aspire to things. But Allah and the Believers refuse to have anyone but Abū Bakr.[1]

In *Ṣaḥīḥ Muslim*, ʿUrwah narrates from ʿĀ'ishah رضي الله عنها:

> The Messenger said to me, "Call Abū Bakr and your brother for me so that I may write a letter. Indeed I fear that some aspiring person might say I am more deserving, but Allah and the Believers refuse to have anyone but Abū Bakr."[2]

Al-Bukhārī and Muslim narrate from Jubayr ibn Muṭʿim رضي الله عنه:

> A woman came to the Messenger and he instructed her to return to him later.
>
> She said, "What should I do if I return and I do not find you?" It was as if she was implying death.
>
> He replied, "If you do not find me then go to Abū Bakr."[3]

---

1 *Ṣaḥīḥ al-Bukhārī*, The Book of Laws, vol. 6, Ḥadīth no. 6791.

2 *Ṣaḥīḥ Muslim* with the commentary, vol. 15, Ḥadīth no. 2387.

3 *Ṣaḥīḥ al-Bukhārī*, The Chapter on the Merits of the Ṣaḥābah, Ḥadīth no. 3459; *Ṣaḥīḥ Muslim* with its commentary, The Chapter on the Merits of the Ṣaḥābah, vol. 15, Ḥadīth no. 386.

Al-Bukhārī and Muslim narrate also from Abū Hurayrah رَضِيَ اللَّهُ عَنْهُ that he heard the Messenger صَلَّى اللَّهُ عَلَيْهِ وَسَلَّمَ say:

> While I was sleeping I saw myself standing over a well with a bucket on it. I drew from it as much as Allah decreed. Then the son of Abū Quḥāfah (Abū Bakr) took it and drew a bucket or two. His drawing was somewhat weak but Allah overlooked it. Then it turned into a big bucket and ('Umar) Ibn al-Khaṭṭāb took it. I never saw a giant, draw water like he did, until people were fully satiated.[1]

The Messenger of Allah صَلَّى اللَّهُ عَلَيْهِ وَسَلَّمَ also instructed Abū Bakr to lead the people in ṣalāh and this continued till his demise. Al-Bukhārī narrates from Abū Mūsā رَضِيَ اللَّهُ عَنْهُ:

> The Messenger was ill and when his illness intensified, He said, "Order Abū Bakr to lead the people in ṣalāh!"
>
> 'Ā'ishah then said, "Indeed, he is a soft-hearted man. When he stands in your place he will be unable to lead the people in ṣalāh."
>
> She then repeated herself and he said, "Order Abū Bakr to lead the ṣalāh! Indeed you are like of the women of Yūsuf."

Anas ibn Mālik relates:

> Abū Bakr used to lead them in ṣalāh during the illness in which the Messenger صَلَّى اللَّهُ عَلَيْهِ وَسَلَّمَ passed away. On Monday while they were standing in their rows, the Messenger صَلَّى اللَّهُ عَلَيْهِ وَسَلَّمَ opened the curtain of the room and stood there gazing at us. As if his face was a page of the Qur'ān. He smiled and we were tempted to break our prayer out of happiness at the sight of the Messenger صَلَّى اللَّهُ عَلَيْهِ وَسَلَّمَ. Abū Bakr stepped backwards to reach the row behind him thinking that the Messenger صَلَّى اللَّهُ عَلَيْهِ وَسَلَّمَ had come out to the prayer. The Messenger صَلَّى اللَّهُ عَلَيْهِ وَسَلَّمَ, however, motioned to him to complete the prayer. He then lowered the screen and passed away later that day.[2]

If we were to assume that the office of Khilāfah requires textual nomination, as Tījānī claims, the minority view of the Ahl al-Sunnah provides for this situation as well. The issue now is where does one find the textual directive for the candidacy of the nominee? If we were to extend this assumption a bit further we would come

1 Op. Cit. Ḥadīth no. 4364.

2 *Ṣaḥīḥ al-Bukhārī*, Ḥadīth no. 648.

to realize that there were others who felt that other Companions of the Prophet ﷺ, or members of his family, were deserving of the office.

The Rāwandiyyah claim the Imāmah of ʿAbbās ibn ʿAbd al-Muṭṭalib. They argue that there is significant textual evidence to support their claim; very similar to the way in which the Rāfiḍah claim that there is textual evidence nominating ʿAlī. Qāḍī Abū Yaʿlā says:

> The Rāwandiyyah differ (amongst themselves), a group amongst them hold that the Prophet specified ʿAbbās by name and announced that explicitly, and state that the Ummah rejected this clear textual evidence and consequently turned apostate and opposed the Prophet's ﷺ instruction out of stubbornness. There are some amongst them who say that the textual evidence declares the right of ʿAbbās and his sons after him (to the khilāfah) until the Day of Judgement.[1]

Thus we find that the doctrine of the appointment of a specific candidate problematic. How do we reconcile the fact that numerous groupings claim the exclusive right to Khilāfah for different individuals? While it is plausible to infer that the evidence supporting those claims is spurious, the evidence in favour of Abū Bakr رضي الله عنه is not only tenable based on the fact that he led the prayers until the Prophet's ﷺ demise without objection, but it is highly credible in terms of the narrations. As for the textual evidence provided by Tījānī 'whoever considers me his Mawlā[2], then ʿAlī is also his Mawlā,'; this statement of the Prophet is not only ambivalent, but subject to context.

The Ḥadīth of Ghadīr

Tījānī says:

> **Any researcher in this subject, if he considers nothing but the truth, will find that the text in support of Ali is very clear, like the following saying by the Messenger of Allah ﷺ: Whoever considers me his master, then Ali is his master. He said it at the end of the Farewell Pilgrimage, when it was confirmed that Ali would succeed, and many people congratulated him on that, including Abu Bakr and Umar who were among the well-wishers, and**

1 *Minhāj al-Sunnah*, vol. 1 p. 500.

2 The meaning of this word will be explained shortly.

who were quoted as having said to the Imam, "Well done, Ibn Abī Ṭālib, overnight you have become a master of all the believers."[1]

Response to the Ḥadīth of Ghadīr

We, the Ahl al-Sunnah, acknowledge the reliability of the ḥadīth, "Whoever considers me his Mawlā, then ʿAlī is also his Mawlā." We do not merely reject aḥādīth or dismiss them for childish reasons as some 'objective researchers' do. The discussions surrounding this ḥadīth are focused on the context of the narration and its true meaning.

There are three core issues at hand:

- How was it understood by ʿAlī رضي الله عنه and the rest of the Ṣaḥābah رضي الله عنهم?
- What is the meaning of Mawlā?
- In what context did the Prophet صلى الله عليه وسلم say this?

Let us begin with the context.

Context of the Ḥadīth

There is consensus that the Prophet صلى الله عليه وسلم made this statement at a place called Ghadīr Khum, which is midway between Makkah and Madīnah. It served as a rest stop for travellers providing water and shade. On his return to Madīnah, after the Farewell Ḥajj, the Prophet صلى الله عليه وسلم stopped here to rest and pray. This is accepted as fact by both the Shīʿah and Ahl al-Sunnah.

This also means that the Prophet صلى الله عليه وسلم was only accompanied by the Ṣaḥābah who resided in Madīnah since those from the other parts of the Arabian Peninsula had taken off on their own paths, some to Ṭā'if, others to Yemen, others to Najd etc. The Prophet صلى الله عليه وسلم could have made any announcement during the period of Ḥajj which was attended by over one-hundred thousand pilgrims, but he chose to make a particular statement at Ghadīr Khumm where he was only accompanied by the Companions who resided in Madīnah.

This indicates to us that whatever the Prophet صلى الله عليه وسلم had to say was something that pertained to the people of Madīnah, and was not of absolute concern to

1 *Then I was guided*, p. 135.

the entire Muslim community. Why else did he wait until he was alone with the residents of Madīnah to announce what he had to say? We learn from this that this was a domestic issue and not one that affected the entire Muslim Ummah.

Why did the Prophet صَلَّى ٱللَّٰهُ عَلَيْهِ وَسَلَّمَ say this?

Prior to Ḥajj the Prophet صَلَّى ٱللَّٰهُ عَلَيْهِ وَسَلَّمَ sent ʿAlī رَضِيَ ٱللَّٰهُ عَنْهُ to Yemen to distribute the spoils after Khālid ibn al-Walīd's military campaign in Yemen. There were some people who were displeased with ʿAlī رَضِيَ ٱللَّٰهُ عَنْهُ and complained to the Prophet صَلَّى ٱللَّٰهُ عَلَيْهِ وَسَلَّمَ about him. These people felt that ʿAlī رَضِيَ ٱللَّٰهُ عَنْهُ was not entirely fair in his distribution and had treated them harshly. The Prophet صَلَّى ٱللَّٰهُ عَلَيْهِ وَسَلَّمَ realised that there had been a misunderstanding and that there was some bitterness towards ʿAlī رَضِيَ ٱللَّٰهُ عَنْهُ from those who had complained about him. Having realised this, and finding a suitable opportunity to address the matter, the Prophet صَلَّى ٱللَّٰهُ عَلَيْهِ وَسَلَّمَ addressed the entire gathering and said, "Whoever considers me his Mawlā, then ʿAlī is also his Mawlā."

The Meaning of Mawlā

The reader would have realised that we have not translated the word 'Mawlā'. The reason for this is that this word lends itself to multiple meanings and applying any one meaning without any contextual consideration would be misleading.

Let us look at how the word 'Mawlā' is understood lexically, as well as its usage in the Qur'ān and other aḥādīth. Once we have a comprehensive understanding of the term, it will then be appropriate to translate it.

Al-Rāzī says in *Mukhtār al-Ṣiḥāḥ*:

> Mawlā means *muʿtiq* (the one who sets free a slave), and *muʿtaq* (the freed slave), and *Ibn al-ʿAmm* (cousin), and *nāṣir* (helper), and *jār* (neighbour), and *Ḥalīf* (ally)... *Muwālāt* (friendship) is the opposite of *muʿādāt* (enmity)... *Wilāyah* (guardianship) with a *kasrah* means *sulṭān* (power/authority) and *wilāyah* or *walāyah* with a *kasrah* or a *fatḥah* means *nuṣrah* (assistance).[1]

Al-Fayrūzābādī says:

> *Walī* means *qurb* (closeness). *Walī* (guardian) is the noun derived from it and it means *muḥibb* (the one who loves), *ṣadīq* (friend), *naṣīr* (helper). (It is used

1 *Mukhtār al-Ṣiḥāḥ*, p. 306-307.

> in the following ways) *waliya al-shay* means he took responsibility for the thing. *ʿalayh al-wilāyah* or *walāyah* (It is his responsibility). With the *kasrah* it means *khiṭṭāh* (a plan), *imārah* (leadership), *sulṭān* (authority). (The word Mawlā) means *mālik* (owner), and *ʿabd* (slave), and *muʿtiq*, and *muʿtaq*, and *ṣāḥib* (companion), and *ibn* (son), and *ʿamm* (uncle), and *nazīl* (guest), *sharīk* (partner), and *ibn al-ukht* (sister's son), and *walī*, and *Lord* (owner), and *nāṣir* (helper), and *munʿim* (generous), and *munʿamʿalayh* (favoured), *muḥibb*, and *tābiʿī* (follower), and *ṣihr* (in-law).[1]

We learn that the word Mawlā contains a spectrum of meaning which include 'helper', among others. To project its meaning to *sulṭān* (authority) liberally is to ignore the ambiguity which is inherent in the term. There has to be additional evidence to identify a particular meaning beyond the term itself. Furthermore, it requires stretching the term Mawlā for it to mean *wālī* (governor).

Ibn Taymiyyah said:

> There is nothing in the statement which clearly indicates that it's (the word Mawlā) intended meaning is the khilāfah. That is because the word Mawlā is similar to the word walī. Allah says:
>
> إِنَّمَا وَلِيُّكُمُ اللّٰهُ وَرَسُوْلُهٗ وَالَّذِيْنَ اٰمَنُوْا
>
> *Your [Walī] ally is none but Allah, and also His Messenger and those who have believed.*[2]
>
> وَإِنْ تَظَاهَرَا عَلَيْهِ فَإِنَّ اللّٰهَ هُوَ مَوْلَاهُ وَجِبْرِيْلُ وَصَالِحُ الْمُؤْمِنِيْنَ وَالْمَلَآئِكَةُ بَعْدَ ذٰلِكَ ظَهِيْرٌ
>
> *But if you support one another against him – then indeed Allah is his [Mawlā] protector, as well as Jibrīl and all righteous believers, and the angels, moreover, are [his] assistants.*[3]

1 *Al-Qāmūs al-Muḥīṭ*, p. 1732.
2 Sūrah al-Mā'idah: 55.
3 Sūrah al-Taḥrīm: 4.

Allah explains that the Messenger is the *walī* (friend) of the believers and that they are his friends as well. In the same manner Allah is the friend of the believers and they are His friends, and likewise the believers are friends of one another, since friendship is the opposite of enmity and it is established from two sides.

If one of the two friends is greater than the other in status then his friendship is a form of goodwill and the friendship of the other is a form of obedience and worship. This is similar to the way Allah loves the believers and they love Him. Friendship is therefore the opposite of enmity, warring, and deception. The disbelievers do not love Allah and (instead) oppose Him and His Messenger and take Him as an enemy.

Allah says:

لَا تَتَّخِذُوْا عَدُوِّيْ وَعَدُوَّكُمْ أَوْلِيَآءَ

Do not take My enemies and your enemies as allies.[1]

In similar manner Allah says:

فَإِنْ لَّمْ تَفْعَلُوْا فَأْذَنُوْا بِحَرْبٍ مِّنَ اللّٰهِ وَرَسُوْلِهٖ

If you do not, then be informed of a war (against you) from Allah and His Messenger.[2]

Allah is the friend of the believers and their Mawlā, removing them from the darkness to the light. If that is the case then the meaning of Allah being the friend of the believers and their Mawlā, and the Messenger being their friend and their Mawlā, and ʿAlī (also) being their Mawlā, refers to friendship, good relationship and support.

The believers have pledged to Allah and His Messenger such allegiance that excludes the possibility of enmity. This ruling, however, applies to all believers. ʿAlī is included among the believers, whose description is that they take other believers as their friends and allies and they take him as their friend and ally.

1 Sūrah al-Mumtaḥinah: 1.

2 Sūrah al-Baqarah: 279.

This ḥadīth therefore establishes ʿAlī's allegiance inwardly and affirms that he is deserving of friendship inwardly and outwardly. This dispels whatever has been said against him by his enemies from the Khawārij and the Nawāṣib.

There is nothing in the ḥadīth to prove that the believers have no other Mawlā besides ʿAlī. How can that be inferred when the Prophet صلى الله عليه وسلم had many Mawlās, namely, the pious believers—which includes ʿAlī رضي الله عنه by way of priority—who took him as their friend? The Prophet صلى الله عليه وسلم said that the tribes of Aslam, Ghifār, Muzaynah, Juhaynah, Quraysh, and the Anṣār, had no Mawlā besides Allah and his Messenger[1]. Allah made them the Mawlās of the Messenger صلى الله عليه وسلم just as He made the pious believers His Mawlās, and Allah and His Messenger صلى الله عليه وسلم their Mawlā.

In summary, there is a slight difference between Walī and Mawlā, and a significant difference between these terms and *Wālī* (governor). The meaning of *Wilāyah* (the opposite of enmity) is at one end of the spectrum, and the term wilāyah referring to leadership is at the other. The wilāyah spoken of in the ḥadīth refers to the former and not the latter. The Prophet صلى الله عليه وسلم did not say, "Whoever I am his *wālī* (governor) ʿAlī is his wālī." The word used (in the ḥadīth) is "Whoever's Mawlā I am, ʿAlī is his Mawlā."

The word Mawlā cannot refer to *wālī* (governor) since friendship is established mutually. Indeed, the believers are the friends of Allah and He is their *Mawlā* (guardian).

As for the Prophet صلى الله عليه وسلم being more worthy of them (the believers) than themselves, this is only established for the Prophet صلى الله عليه وسلم as it is a unique feature of his nubuwwah. If we assume that he instated a khalīfah to be the leader after him that would not mean he is more worthy of every believer than himself in the same manner that the Prophet's صلى الله عليه وسلم wives will not be his wives. If this meaning was intended then he would have said, "Whoever I am more worthy of him than himself, ʿAlī is more worthy of him than himself," but no one has said this and no one has transmitted this, and its meaning is definitely false. The Prophet's صلى الله عليه وسلم being more worthy of every believer than himself is an established matter in his life and death.

The khilāfah of ʿAlī, on the assumption of its existence, only came into being after the Prophet's صلى الله عليه وسلم death. It did not exist during the Prophet's صلى الله عليه وسلم

1 Refer to *al-Bukhārī*, Kitāb al-Manāqib, Bāb dhikr Aslam, wa Ghifār, wa Muzaynah, wa Juhaynah, wa Ashjaʿ, Ḥadīth no. 3321.

> life. Therefore, it is not possible for ʿAlī رضي الله عنه to have been the khalīfah during the era of the Prophet صلى الله عليه وسلم and he could not therefore be more worthy of every believer than himself, rather, he could not have been the Mawlā of any believer if what is intended is the khilāfah. This is amongst the factors which prove that khilāfah was not intended. The fact that he is a friend of every believer is established during the era of the Prophet صلى الله عليه وسلم, whose implementation was not postponed until the Prophet's demise as opposed to the khilāfah which could only come into effect after the demise of the Prophet صلى الله عليه وسلم. Therefore, it is known that this (what is mentioned in the ḥadīth) is not that which the Rāfiḍah intend.
>
> ʿAlī being the Mawlā of every believer is true during the life of the Messenger صلى الله عليه وسلم, his death, and even after the death of ʿAlī. Even today ʿAlī remains the "Mawlā" of every believer even though he is not the governor over the people. In a similar manner all the believers are friends of one another living and deceased.[1]

We have learnt that the term 'Mawlā' has many meanings. Allah has described the believers as Mawlās for the Prophet صلى الله عليه وسلم. The term Mawlā is not used exclusively for the meaning of leadership in the Qur'ān and ḥadīth. The meaning of Mawlā is different from Wālī. If the term Mawlā meant Khalīfah, ʿAlī رضي الله عنه was not a Mawlā during the Prophet's life; however if it meant friend and ally it applies to him during the Prophet's صلى الله عليه وسلم life and remains applicable until the Day of Judgement.

How was it understood?

Tījānī projects the ḥadīth as an explicit nomination of ʿAlī رضي الله عنه for the office of Khilāfah by the Prophet صلى الله عليه وسلم. We have thus far shown that the context of the ḥadīth as well as the meaning of the term Mawlā suggests otherwise. An often overlooked element is whether ʿAlī رضي الله عنه, or any of the other Companions, considered this as appointment by Prophetic directive.

Al-Bukhārī narrates with his chain to al-Zuhrī

عن الزهري قال أخبرني عبد الله بن كعب بن مالك الأنصاري وكان كعب بن مالك أحد الثلاثة الذين تيب عليهم أن عبد الله بن عباس أخبره أن علي

1 *Minhāj al-Sunnah*, vol. 7 p. 322-325.

بن أبي طالب رضي الله عنه خرج من عند رسول الله صلى الله عليه وسلم في وجعه الذي توفي فيه فقال الناس يا أبا حسن كيف أصبح رسول الله صلى الله عليه وسلم فقال أصبح بحمد الله بارئا فأخذ بيده عباس بن عبد المطلب فقال له أنت والله بعد ثلاث عبد العصا وإني والله لأرى رسول الله صلى الله عليه وسلم سوف يتوفى من وجعه هذا إني لأعرف وجوه بني عبد المطلب عند الموت اذهب بنا إلى رسول الله صلى الله عليه وسلم فلنسأله فيمن هذا الأمر إن كان فينا علمنا ذلك وإن كان في غيرنا علمناه فأوصى بنا فقال علي إنا والله لئن سألناها رسول الله صلى الله عليه وسلم فمنعناها لا يعطيناها الناس بعده وإني والله لا أسألها رسول الله صلى الله عليه وسلم

Al-Zuhrī related from ʿAbd Allāh ibn Kaʿb ibn Mālik, and Kaʿb ibn Mālik was one of the three whom Allah pardoned,[1] that ʿAbd Allāh ibn ʿAbbās[2] informed him that ʿAlī ibn Abī Ṭālib emerged from the [home of the] Messenger of Allah ﷺ during his final illness and the people said, "O Abū al-Ḥasan; How is the Messenger of Allah ﷺ this morning?" He said, "All praise be to Allah, he is well this morning."

ʿAbbās ibn ʿAbd al-Muṭṭalib took him by the hand and said to him, "I swear by Allah, in three days' time you will be a subject. By Allah, I think that the Messenger of Allah ﷺ will die of this illness. I recognize the look of death in the faces of the Banū ʿAbd al-Muṭṭalib when they are dying. Let us go to the Messenger of Allah ﷺ and ask him who will take charge over this matter (Khilāfah). If it is for us, then we will know that, and if it is for someone other than us, we will know and he can advise him to look after us."

ʿAlī replied, "By Allah, if we ask him for it and he refuses us, then the people would never give it to us afterwards. By Allah, I will not ask it from the Messenger of Allah."

If ʿAlī رضي الله عنه was nominated by the Prophet ﷺ explicitly at Ghadīr Khum, why would ʿAbbās even bother to ask the Prophet about Khilāfah since it ought to be known that ʿAlī رضي الله عنه was given the directive for succession? Furthermore, why did

1 This information regarding Kaʿb is from al-Zuhrī. This is another example of al-Zuhrī's explanation while narrating a ḥadīth. See p. 234 of this book.

2 ʿAbd Allāh ibn ʿAbbās is also the narrator of the Ḥadīth regarding the Thursday Calamity.

ʿAlī not correct ʿAbbās and acknowledge that he was appointed? Why did ʿAlī fear the Prophet صَلَّى ٱللَّهُ عَلَيْهِ وَسَلَّمَ not granting him the Khilāfah if he was already appointed? The reaction of ʿAlī clearly indicates that he never considered himself appointed by any explicit directive.

Tījānī lambasted ʿUmar رَضِيَ ٱللَّهُ عَنْهُ for his audacity in the presence of the Prophet صَلَّى ٱللَّهُ عَلَيْهِ وَسَلَّمَ on the Thursday prior to his demise. We have demonstrated earlier in this book that ʿUmar رَضِيَ ٱللَّهُ عَنْهُ is innocent of all the false allegations cast against him by Tījānī and others[1]. There is, however, another significant element to bear in mind. If the Prophet صَلَّى ٱللَّهُ عَلَيْهِ وَسَلَّمَ nominated ʿAlī رَضِيَ ٱللَّهُ عَنْهُ at Ghadīr, why accuse ʿUmar of intervening in a matter already decided on. On the other hand, if whatever the Prophet صَلَّى ٱللَّهُ عَلَيْهِ وَسَلَّمَ was going to write was so significant, and the guidance of mankind depended on it, does that not call into question the unmistakable directive for succession at Ghadīr Khum? The implication of either argument cannot be reconciled with the other.

The argument against the Ṣaḥābah on the Thursday calamity is a self-inflicting injury to the argument of nomination based on the ḥadīth of Ghadīr. Any argument in favour of ʿAlī رَضِيَ ٱللَّهُ عَنْهُ based on the ḥadīth of Ghadīr Khumm exonerates the Ṣaḥābah on the issue of the Thursday calamity. The two are mutually exclusive, based on Shīʿī reasoning. It takes a special kind of logic to reconcile these two conflicting arguments. Tījānī's arguments bring to light unexplored dimensions of truth and objectivity!

On the other hand, the explanation and interpretation given by the Ahl al-Sunnah not only appears to be based on more persuasive evidence, but is free of ambiguity, accounts for all factors and possible objections, is in harmony with sound reasoning and aligns with the mutually accepted historical facts.

The alleged congratulatory procession

Tījānī claims that a procession was laid out for ʿAlī رَضِيَ ٱللَّهُ عَنْهُ and at the forefront of those who congratulated him at this 'magnificent' event were Abū Bakr and ʿUmar رَضِيَ ٱللَّهُ عَنْهُمَا. He references this dubious narration to a number of sources.

If we refer to *Musnad Aḥmad* we will find him mentioning the ḥadīth and in it:

1 Refer to p. 69 of this book.

فلقيه عمر بعد ذلك فقال هنيئا يا بن أبي طالب أصبحت وأمسيت مولى كل مؤمن ومؤمنة

Then ʿUmar met him after that and said, "Congratulations to you, O son of Abū Ṭālib! You have become the Mawlā of every believer, male and female."[1]

The narrator does not mention Abū Bakr رضي الله عنه at all.

A similar narration is reported in the book *Tadhkirat al-Khawāṣ*; however, there is no mention whatsoever of a procession nor of ʿUmar رضي الله عنه congratulating him; let alone Abū Bakr رضي الله عنه.

Al-Suyūṭī in his *al-Ḥāwī li al-Fatāwā*[2] records the narration which mentions ʿUmar رضي الله عنه congratulating ʿAlī رضي الله عنه, but here too there is no mention of Abū Bakr رضي الله عنه.

This narration appears a number of times in *Kanz al-ʿUmmāl* under the virtues of ʿAlī ibn Abī Ṭālib رضي الله عنه but you will not find any mention of Abū Bakr رضي الله عنه, let alone mention of a procession to congratulate him.[3]

Ibn Kathīr records it in *al-Bidāyah wa al-Nihāyah* with multiple and varying narrations and in it there is no mention of a procession of congratulations nor any mention of Abū Bakr al-Ṣiddīq رضي الله عنه.[4]

Tījānī's deceptive habits would have become apparent to the reader by now and here too he cannot resist distorting the narration to suit his preconceived version of events. The only reason he included the name of Abū Bakr رضي الله عنه was to fool the unwary reader—who is unable to research these multiple sources—into thinking that Abū Bakr رضي الله عنه usurped the khilāfah from ʿAlī رضي الله عنه despite acknowledging and even "congratulating" him upon his appointment. However the truth has been separated from falsehood and Tījānī's lies have once again been exposed.

As for the narration which contains the additional comment of ʿUmar رضي الله عنه, "Congratulations to you O ʿAlī! You have become the Mawlā of every believing male

1 *Musnad Aḥmad, Musnad al-Barā ibn Mālik*, vol. 6, Ḥadīth no. 18506.

2 Refer to *al-Ḥāwī li al-Fatāwā* by al-Suyūṭī, Bāb (mā warada fī al-tahni'ah bi al-ʿīd wa al-ʿamāl al-ṣāliḥah), vol. 1 p. 79, Dār al-Kutub al-ʿIlmiyyah.

3 *Kanz al-ʿUmmāl fī Sunan al-Aqwāl*, Faḍā'il ʿAlī, vol. 13, Ḥadīth no. 36340, 36341, 36342, 36343; and in vol. 11, Ḥadīth no. 32904, 32905, 32906, 32916.

4 *Al-Bidāyah wa al-Nihāyah*, vol. 7 p. 359-363.

and female," this portion of the ḥadīth is not authentic since it only appears in the narration of ʿAlī ibn Zayd ibn Judʿān who has been graded weak by the scholars.[1]

Tījānī sets out to deconstruct the doctrine of Shūrā notwithstanding his paltry arguments in favour of *Naṣṣ*. He says:

> **As for the alleged popular election of Abu Bakr on "The Day of al-Saqifah" and his subsequent acclamation in the mosque; it seems that it was just an allegation without foundation. How could it be by popular agreement when so many people were absent during the acclamation? People like: Ali, al-Abbas, most of the house of Bani Hashim, Usama ibn Zayd, al-Zubayr, Salman al-Farisi, Abu Dharr al-Ghifari, al-Miqdad ibn al-Aswad, Ammar ibn Yasir, Hudhayfa ibn al-Yaman, Khuzayma ibn Thabit, Abu Burayd al-Aslami, al-Bura ibn Azib, Abu Ka'b, Sahl ibn Hanif, Saad ibn Ubada, Qays ibn Saad, Abu Ayyub al-Ansari, Jabir ibn Saad, Khalid ibn Saad, and many others.**
>
> **So where was, that alleged popular agreement? The absence of Ali alone from the acclamation is sufficient to criticize that meeting because he was the only candidate for the caliphate, nominated by the Messenger of Allah ﷺ, on the assumption that there was no direct text regarding such a nomination.[2]**

Our comment:

The keystone concept that we alluded to at the beginning of this discussion is the concept of explicit nomination (Naṣṣ) by the Prophet ﷺ. This concept is foundationally flawed since no evidence exists to support it. The ḥadīth of Ghadīr Khumm is untenable because it is ambiguous and the only plausible interpretation of it enhances the Sunnī position on this issue as we have demonstrated earlier. ʿAlī رضي الله عنه did not even understand the ḥadīth of Ghadīr Khumm to be *Naṣṣ*.

Tījānī's objection to the nomination of a Khalīfah by Shūrā rests on the absence of the said Ṣaḥābah. To prove their absence he has referred us to the following sources, *al-Ṭabarī*, *Tārīkh ibn al-Athīr*, *Tārīkh al-Khulafā'*, *Tārīkh al-Khamīs*, *al-Istīʿāb*, without indicating to the volume or page numbers of any of the aforementioned sources.

---

1 Refer to *Taqrīb al-Tahdhīb*, vol. 1 p. 693, Ḥadīth no. 4750; And *Tahdhīb al-Kamāl fī Asmā' al-Rijāl*, vol. 21 p. 434, Ḥadīth no. 4070; al-Jūzajānī says about him in his book *al-Shajarah fī Aḥwāl al-Rijāl*, p. 194, "ʿAlī ibn Zayd: Wāhī al-Ḥadīth, ḍaʿīf, relates uncorroborated reports, his ḥadīth is not proof worthy." Refer also to *al-Silsilah al-Ṣaḥīḥah*, vol. 4 p. 344.

2 *Then I was guided*, p. 136.

Integrity of Tījānī's Quotes

It doesn't come as a surprise when the facts mentioned by Tījānī are inaccurate and the references quoted provide a different perspective. After consulting the references provided by Tījānī we have come to realise that his strategy in this section is deceit.

Under the heading, *Ḥadīth al-Saqīfah*, al-Ṭabarī presents a number of narrations, some of them authentic and some of them weak. He mentions also the ḥadīth of Ibn ʿAbbās when people suggested they would nominate such-and-such a person as a leader after ʿUmar's رضي الله عنه demise. ʿUmar gathered everyone in the Masjid and during the talk he mentioned the story of the Saqīfah. It reads:

وإنه قد كان من خبرنا حين توفى الله نبيه صلى الله عليه و سلم أن الأنصار خالفونا واجتمعوا بأسرهم في سقيفة بني ساعدة وخالف عنا علي والزبير ومن معهما تخلفوا عنا في بيت فاطمة واجتمع المهاجرون إلى أبي بكر فقلت لأبي بكر يا أبا بكر انطلق بنا إلى إخواننا هؤلاء من الأنصار فانطلقنا نريدهم فلما دنونا منهم لقينا منهم رجلان صالحان فذكرا ما تمالأ عليه القوم فقالا أين تريدون يا معشر المهاجرين ؟ فقلنا نريد إخواننا هؤلاء من الأنصار فقالا لا عليكم أن لا تقربوهم اقضوا أمركم فقلت والله لنأتينهم فانطلقنا حتى أتيناهم في سقيفة بني ساعدة فإذا رجل مزمل بين ظهرانيهم فقلت من هذا ؟ فقالوا هذا سعد بن عبادة فقلت ما له ؟ قالوا يوعك فلما جلسنا قليلا تشهد خطيبهم فأثنى على الله بما هو أهله ثم قال أما بعد فنحن أنصار الله وكتيبة الإسلام وأنتم معشر المهاجرين رهط وقد دفت دافة من قومكم فإذا هم يريدون أن يختزلونا من أصلنا وأن يحضنونا من الأمر . فلما سكت أردت أن أتكلم وكنت قد زورت مقالة أعجبتني أردت أن أقدمها بين يدي أبي بكر وكنت أداري منه بعض الحد فلما أردت أن أتكلم قال أبو بكر على رسلك فكرهت أن أغضبه فتكلم أبو بكر فكان هو أحلم مني وأوقر والله ما ترك من كلمة أعجبتني في تزويري إلا قال في بديهته مثلها أو أفضل منها حتى سكت فقال ما ذكرتم فيكم من خير فأنتم له أهل ولن يعرف هذا الأمر إلا لهذا الحي من قريش هم أوسط العرب نسبا ودارا وقد رضيت لكم أحد هذين الرجلين فبايعوا أيهما شئتم فأخذ بيدي وبيد أبي عبيدة بن الجراح

وهو جالس بيننا فلم أكره مما قال غيرها كان والله أن أقدم فتضرب عنقي لا يقربني ذلك من إثم أحب إلي من أن أتأمر على قوم فيهم أبو بكر اللهم إلا أن تسول لي نفسي عند الموت شيئا لا أجده الآن . فقال قائل من الأنصار أنا جذيلها المحكك وعذيقها المرجب منا أمير ومنكم أمير يا معشر قريش . فكثر اللغط وارتفعت الأصوات حتى فرقت من الاختلاف فقلت ابسط يدك يا أبا بكر فبسط يده فبايعته وبايعه المهاجرون ثم بايعته الأنصار

What happened when Allah took his Messenger is that the Anṣār had assembled under the canopy of Banū Sā'idah, whilst 'Alī and Zubayr and those with them were absent from us in the house of Fāṭimah. The Muhājirīn gathered around Abū Bakr and I said, "Let us go to our brothers from the Anṣār."

So we set of heading towards them. On the way two pious men who witnessed Badr met us and said, "Where are you heading, O Muhājirīn?"

We said, "We intend meeting our brothers from the Anṣār."

They said, "Return and discuss your matter amongst yourselves (Muhājirīn)."

We replied, "By Allah! We will go and see them."

(He said) We went to them and they were gathered at the meeting place of Banū Sā'idah and amongst them there was a man covered with his shawl.

I said, "Who is this?" and they replied, "Sa'd ibn 'Ubādah."

I asked, "What is the matter with him?" They replied, "He is sick."

Then a man amongst them stood up praised Allah and said, "Indeed we are the Anṣār and the legion of Islam and you are the Quraysh, the kinsmen of our Prophet, and a group of you has come to us ..."

'Umar says, "When I realised they intended to leave us without a say and exclude us from the matter... I had prepared an impressive speech in my mind which I intended to present before Abū Bakr in such a manner that it would pacify his anger somewhat (if I spoke out of turn). When I intended to speak he bade me to keep silent and I did not want to disobey him.

Then he stood up and praised Allah, and he was more composed and tolerant than me. He did not omit a single thing I had formulated in my mind that I intended to say if I had to speak except that he expressed it more eloquently.

He said, "O Anṣār! You have not mentioned a single virtue about yourselves except that you are worthy of it. (That being said) the Arabs do not recognise leadership except in this tribe of the Quraysh. They are the greatest of Arabs in terms of residence and lineage. I am pleased with either of these two men. Pledge your allegiance to either of the two you prefer", and he grabbed hold of my hand and the hand of Abū 'Ubaydah.

'Umar said, "By Allah, I approved of everything he said besides this statement. For me to be brought forward and have my neck chopped off was easier for me than to be selected as the leader of a community which included Abū Bakr.

When Abū Bakr completed his speech a man amongst them stood up and said, "I am the one with the solution and most deserving of consultation; a leader from amongst you and a leader from amongst us, O Quraysh!"

Then the voices started to rise and the noise started to increase. I said to Abū Bakr, "Extend your hand so that I can give you the pledge!" and he extended his hand and I gave him my pledge, and the Muhājirīn gave him their pledge, and the Anṣār gave him their pledge..."[1]

Then Ṭabarī narrates by way of Walīd ibn Jumay' al-Zuhrī, who said, 'Amr ibn Ḥurayth said to Sa'īd ibn Zayd:

"Did you witness the death of the Messenger?"

He said, "Yes."

He asked, "When was Abū Bakr given the pledge?"

He said, "The day the Messenger ﷺ passed away, they disliked remaining even a single day not as a congregation."

He asked, "Did anyone oppose them?"

He said, "No, except for an apostate or someone on the verge of apostasy, Allah saved the Anṣār (from that fate) and united them under him (Abū Bakr)."

He asked, "Did anyone from amongst the Muhājirīn refrain?" He said, "No, the Muhājirīn gave their pledge in succession without forsaking him."[2]

1 *Ṣaḥīḥ al-Bukhārī*, vol. 6, Kitāb al-Muḥāribīn, Ḥadīth no. 6442; Refer also to *Ṭabarī*, vol. 2 p. 234-235.

2 *Ṭabarī*, vol. 2, p. 236, events of 11 A.H.

Then al-Ṭabarī brings the narration of Ḥabīb ibn Abī Thābit[1], wherein he says:

> ʿAlī was in his home when someone came to him and said, "Abū Bakr has sat down for the pledge." He left the house in a shirt (a top) without an *izār* (lower garment) and without a *ridā* (overthrow) out of haste, to avoid lagging behind, and to give his pledge. Then he sat down and sent for his cloak, and went to him, honoured him and remained in his company.[2]

Then al-Ṭabarī forwards the ḥadīth[3] narrated by al-Bukhārī regarding Fāṭimah رضي الله عنها seeking her inheritance and this narration includes the pledge given by

1 Appearing in the isnād of this narration and the one before it is a narrator named Sayf ibn ʿUmar who is considered weak in Ḥadīth, and there is a divided opinion regarding his historical narrations. We have not quoted these narrations to prove the Baʿyah as this is established through abundant other narrations. The point being made is that Tījānī has made outlandish claims and provided references to sources which offer no support to those claims.

2 Ibid.

3 Ṭabarī adds: "A man asked, 'did he not give his pledge after six months?" He said, "No. He did not give his pledge and not anyone from Banū Hāshim." Ibn Ḥajar says, "Al-Bayhaqī has graded this narration weak on the premise that Zuhrī did not provide the full sanad of the narration and that the narration with the complete sanad from Abū Saʿīd is more authentic. Some scholars reconciled the two narrations suggesting that he gave his pledge after six months, a second time, to emphasize the first and to remove (any possible ill feelings that might have crept up) on account of what occurred as a result of the inheritance issue. Therefore, the statement of Zuhrī that ʿAlī did not give his pledge during those days is interpreted to mean his being close to him and being present with him and the like. This is because a person's distancing himself from his peer might lead some, who do not know the inner-workings of the situation, to believe that (ʿAlī's رضي الله عنه distancing himself from Abū Bakr) was on account of his displeasure with Abū Bakr's khilāfah. And the one who narrates the story unrestrictedly narrates it unrestrictedly. It is for this reason that ʿAlī openly gave his pledge to Abū Bakr after the demise of Fāṭimah, to remove this misconception." (*Fatḥ al-Bārī*, vol. 7 p. 566).
It is also possible to harmonise between the two aḥādīth by stating that ʿAlī رضي الله عنه gave his pledge twice, once at the beginning of the khilāfah and once again six months later in front of all the people and there is a narration with all of its transmitters reliable which offers that meaning.
ʿAbd Allāh ibn Aḥmad Ibn Ḥambal in Kitāb al-Sunnah mentions: "From Abū Naḍrah, who said, 'When the people gathered to give their pledge to Abū Bakr, he said, 'How is it that I do not see ʿAlī?' Then some men of the Anṣār left and brought him and Abū Bakr said to him, 'I said to myself, the cousin of the Messenger صلى الله عليه وسلم and his son-in-law?" ʿAlī said, 'There is no ill-feelings, O Khalīfah of the Messenger . Extend your hand!' Abū Bakr extended his hand and ʿAlī gave his pledge. Then Abū Bakr said, 'How is it that I do not see Zubayr?' Then some men of the Anṣār left and brought him. Abū Bakr said, 'O Zubayr, I said to myself the cousin of the Messenger صلى الله عليه وسلم and his disciple,' Zubayr said, 'There are no ill-feelings, O Khalīfah of the Messenger, extend your hand!' He extended his hand and he gave him his pledge." (Kitāb al-Sunnah, vol. 2, Ḥadīth no. 1292, the examiner of the book says: "Its sanad is reliable."

ʿAlī رضي الله عنه[1]. And finally he forwards the narration of Anas ibn Mālik regarding the general pledge to Abū Bakr after the pledge at Saqīfah. Al-Ṭabarī mentions nothing besides these narrations.

As for the book *Tārīkh Ibn al-Athīr*[2] there is no mention of those Tījānī claims were absent from giving the pledge to Abū Bakr. Under the chapter, "The ḥadīth of Saqīfah and the khilāfah of Abū Bakr', he narrates the ḥadīth of the Saqīfah and the narration relating ʿAlī giving his pledge to Abū Bakr at the beginning of the khilāfah when he heard about the pledge. Ibn Athīr says:

> The correct view is that Amīr al-Mu'minīn (ʿAlī ibn Abī Ṭālib) gave his pledge after six months.

Then he mentions the ḥadīth of Ibn ʿAbbās during the khilāfah of ʿUmar and his ascending the mimbar and mentioning the pledge which was previously mentioned. Then he mentions the narration of Abū ʿUmrah al-Anṣārī concerning the assembly in the Saqīfah which resulted in all the people giving their pledge to Abū Bakr. He also affirms that ʿAlī' and others from Banū Hāshim pledged allegiance to Abū Bakr after the passing of Fāṭimah رضي الله عنها. We have already discussed the interrupted chain in this narration, and that it contradicts the authentic narration on the subject. This is what Ibn al-Athīr mentioned in his *Tārīkh*, and he does not mention anything to give credibility to Tījānī claim.

As for the book *Tārīkh al-Khulafā'* which is ascribed to Ibn Qutaybah it is acceptable for us not to refer to it on account of the doubt, at the very least, in its authorship. This is the first reason. Secondly because of the reliable books we transmitted from, and thirdly he did not specify the page number to refer to. Any further discussion on this text by Ibn Qutaybah will only be a tedious repetition of what was mentioned earlier in the book.[3]

As for *Tārīkh al-Khamīs*, sadly, I could not find this book. I won't be surprised if this is a book of the Rāfiḍah.

Lastly, the book *al-Istīʿāb fī Maʿrifat al-Aṣḥāb* by Ibn ʿAbd al-Barr, is one where the author collects the greatest number of narrations proving the khilāfah of Abū Bakr;

---

1 Refer to p. 225 of this book - Ḥadīth of ʿĀ'ishah.

2 *Tārīkh Ibn al-Athīr*, 189-195, events of 11 A.H.

3 Refer to Ibn Qutaybah discussion on p. 214 of this book.

more than any other book. He relates the narration of Nazzāl ibn Sabrah (and what follows thereafter), from ʿAlī ﷛:

خير هذه الأمة بعد نبيها أبو بكر ثم عمر .(وروى محمد بن الحنفية وعبد خير وأبو جحيفة، عن علي مثله)

The best of this Ummah after its Prophet is Abū Bakr, then ʿUmar.

Ibn ʿAbd al-Barr says: "Muḥammad ibn Ḥanafiyyah and ʿAbd Khayr and Abū Juḥayfah narrate something similar from ʿAlī."

وكان علي رضي الله عنه يقول:سبق رسول الله صلى الله عليه وسلم وثنى أبو بكر وثلث عمر ثم حفتنا فتنة يعفو الله فيها عمن يشاء

ʿAlī ﷛ used to say, "The Messenger ﷺ preceded, Abū Bakr was second, ʿUmar was third, and then sedition (fitnah) enveloped us and Allah pardons whomsoever he wills."

وقال عبد خير: سمعت عليا يقول: رحم الله أبا بكر كان أول من جمع بين اللوحين

May Allah be merciful to Abū Bakr, he was the first to gather (the Qur'ān) between the two covers.

وروينا عن عبد الله بن جعفر بن أبي طالب من وجوه أنه قال: ولينا أبو بكر فخير خليفة أرحمه بنا وأحناه علينا وقال مسروق: حب أبي بكر وعمر ومعرفة فضلهما من السنة

And we narrated from ʿAbd Allāh ibn Jaʿfar ibn Abī Ṭālib from many chains that he said, "Abū Bakr reigned over us and he was a good khalīfah. Allah made him merciful and compassionate towards us."

Masrūq says, "Loving Abū Bakr and ʿUmar and acknowledging their merit is part of the Sunnah."

He also records the ḥadīth in which the Prophet ﷺ requested Abū Bakr ﷛ to lead the congregational prayer. He mentions the ḥadīth of Ḥudhayfah who narrates that the Messenger said:

اقتدوا بالذين من بعدي: أبي بكر وعمر، واهتدوا بهدي عمار، وتمسكوا بعهد ابن أم عبد

> Follow the two who come after me, Abū Bakr and ʿUmar, and be guided with the guidance of ʿAmmār, and hold onto the covenant of Ibn Umm ʿAbd (i.e. Ibn Masʿūd).

Then Ibn ʿAbd al-Barr comments:

> He was given the pledge the day the Prophet ﷺ passed on at Saqīfah of Banī Sā'idah. Then he was given the general pledge the Tuesday after that day. Saʿd ibn ʿUbādah, and a group of the Khazraj, and a group of the Quraysh, were absent from that pledge. Then they, at a later stage, gave their pledge with the exception of Saʿd. There is an opinion which states that no one amongst the Quraysh was absent from the pledge of that day. There is another opinion which suggests that from amongst the Quraysh ʿAlī, Zubayr, Ṭalḥah, Khālid ibn Saʿīd ibn al-ʿĀṣ, were absent (for the general pledge) but gave their pledge afterwards. There is also the opinion that ʿAlī only gave his pledge after the death of Fāṭimah and then remained obedient to him and praising him and honouring him.

He also quotes ʿAbd Allāh ibn Masʿūd:

> The Anṣār withdrew (from their position) the day of the Saqīfah on account of what ʿUmar said, "I remind you of Allah! Do you know that the Messenger commanded Abū Bakr to lead the ṣalāh for the people?"
>
> They said, "Yes!"
>
> He said, "So who amongst you is pleased with removing him from a position the Prophet placed him in?"
>
> They said, "None of us is pleased with that, we seek Allah's forgiveness."

Ḥasan al-Baṣrī narrates from Qays ibn ʿUbādah, who said:

> 'Alī ibn Abī Ṭālib said to me, "The Messenger ﷺ was sick for some days and nights when the call for the ṣalāh was proclaimed. He said, 'Instruct Abū Bakr to lead the ṣalāh.' When the Prophet ﷺ passed on I pondered about things and realised that the ṣalāh is the distinguishing mark of Islam and the

foundation of the dīn. We were, therefore, pleased for our worldly affairs with the one the Messenger ﷺ was pleased with for us in our religious affairs, and we gave our pledge to Abū Bakr."[1]

This is what Ibn ʿAbd al-Barr has mentioned in his book. Nothing mentioned by Ibn ʿAbd al-Barr, or in the previous books, confirms what Tījānī alleges. They all confirm the pledge of the Muslims to him at the Saqīfah of Banū Sāʿidah and the general pledge from all the people.

Does Tījānī think nothing of his readers that he would send them on a wild goose chase? Is it possible that he assumed that the once sceptic reader—who has read this far into his book—will be innocent enough to accept his quotes without verification?

Requirements for Valid Bayʿah

If we assume—momentarily and for the sake of argument— that the said Ṣaḥābah did not give their pledge to Abū Bakr رضي الله عنه it still does not compromise the pledge as it does not require the agreement of all the people. Rather, the agreement of the people of authority suffices. This is what the scholars have agreed on. Imām al-Nawawī says:

> As for the pledge, the scholars agree that the pledge of each and every person is not a requirement for it to be valid; nor is the pledge of each and every person of authority required. The only condition is that there should be agreement among those from whom it is possible to reach a consensus; amongst the scholars, leaders, and prominent persons.[2]

Al-Māzarī says:

> ʿAlī's justification for lagging behind in giving his pledge— notwithstanding the other excuses given by him—is that the pledge to the imām suffices if it originates from the people of authority. It is not necessary that all are included and it is not necessary for each person to be present and to place his hand into his hand. Rather, observing a disposition of obedience to him, following him, not opposing him, and not breaking away from him; is sufficient. This was the

1 Refer to the previous narrations in the book *al-Istīʿāb fī Maʿrifat al-Aṣḥāb* by Ibn ʿAbd al-Barr, vol. 3 p. 970-977, the edition examined by Muḥammad al-Bajāwī.

2 *Ṣaḥīḥ Muslim* with its commentary, vol. 12 p. 112-113.

> situation of ʿAlī. The only issue is that he delayed in coming to Abū Bakr and we mentioned the reason for that.[1]

Al-Sharīf al-Raḍī quotes ʿAlī on this matter in *Nahj al-Balāghah:*

> By my life! If leadership was not established until the general people were present it would not be possible. Rather, its people decide regardless of those who are absent from it. The one present does not have the right to retract and the one absent cannot choose.[2]

We realize that the absence of an individual or a small group does not affect the validity of the pledge. So Tījānī's conclusion, even though he doesn't accept Shūrā, is fundamentally challenged.

To summarize; we have shown that Tījānī has no evidence to prove that Khilāfah is established by direct nomination. In addition to this, the evidence that he uses to argue his point is inconclusive and irreconcilable with other evidence produced by him. The Sunnī interpretation of the same evidence does not require juggling between conflicting evidence, and is in harmony with fact and reason.

Tījānī's objection to Abū Bakr's Bayʿah evolves:

> **The acclamation of Abu Bakr was without consultation; in fact it took the people by surprise, especially when the men in charge of the Muslim affairs were busy preparing for the funeral of the Messenger of Allah صَلَّى ٱللَّٰهُ عَلَيْهِ وَسَلَّمَ. The citizens of al-Medinah were shocked by the death of their Prophet, and then they forced the acclamation on the people and even threatened to burn the house of Fatima if those who were absent from the acclamation refused to leave it. So how could we say that the acclamation was implemented through consultation and popular agreement?[3]**

Our comment:

If the pledge of Abū Bakr occurred without consultation and while the people were in a state of bewilderment then how does Tījānī reconcile this statement of his with his previous statement when he alleged that there was no consensus since a small group of the Ṣaḥābah delayed in giving their pledge? Subḥān Allah, Tījānī

1 *Fatḥ al-Bārī*, vol. 7 p. 565, Kitāb al-Maghāzī.

2 *Nahj al-Balāghah*, vol. 2 p. 368.

3 *Then I was guided.*

has devolved from misdirection and smokescreens to juggling tricks; all under the cloak of objectivity and impartiality.

He says that the pledge occurred without consultation with the Muslims. How can that be and we have confirmed from Tījānī's sources that it occurred with the consultation of the Muslims and Abū Bakr was given the pledge in the Saqīfah and in the general pledge of the Muslims in the Masjid?

> **He says, "The fate-stricken people of Madīnah were taken aback by the death of their Prophet and the people were coerced into offering the pledge,"**

Subḥān Allāh! Who coerced the Muslims of Madīnah into giving their pledge? Was it Abū Bakr رضي الله عنه? Was it ʿUmar رضي الله عنه? How did they force them? Did the angels assist them? Were the Muslims so small in number that Abū Bakr could coerce them?

If the Muslims did not pledge allegiance to him, then why did ʿAlī ibn Abī Ṭālib, the person nominated as the khalīfah through 'clear explicit textual evidence', and the rest of the people of authority, and the rest of the people of Madīnah, do nothing to stop Abū Bakr and the small band with him? How was Abū Bakr able to gain control of the khilāfah in spite of the opposition of the Ummah?

The reader will have to excuse us for a moment since the level of absurdity in Tījānī's line of reasoning has rendered us speechless.

Shīʿī Scholars Refute Tījānī's Allegation

We are going to overlook Tījānī's indiscretion momentarily and focus on the writings of some of the scholars which are trusted by the Twelver Shīʿah. We find even these scholars confirming this reality of Abū Bakr's pledge. Ḥasan ibn Mūsā al-Nawbakhtī, writes his book *Firaq al-Shīʿah*:

> The majority of the people sided with Abū Bakr. They remained with him and with ʿUmar supporting them and pleased with them.[1]

Ibrāhīm al-Thaqafī, one of the senior Shīʿī scholars, records an excerpt of alleged correspondence wherein ʿAlī ibn Abī Ṭālib رضي الله عنه wrote to one of his companions:

1 al-Nawbakhtī: *Firaq al-Shīʿah*, p. 4, Dār al-Aḍwā.

> Nothing alarmed me besides the swarming of the people around Abū Bakr and their hastening towards him to offer their pledge to him.[1]

The editor of the book explains:

> (The word) *inthiyāl* (translated as swarming) means their hasty approach from every direction (similar to the manner that dust scatters) towards Abū Bakr. Majlisī says, "*Ijfāl* means to hasten."[2]

As for Ibn Muṭahhar, he too was unable to deny this reality and tried to soften the blow. He says:

> Most people gave their pledge desiring material gain.[3]

Senior Shīʿī scholars could not hide from the reality of the pledge to Abū Bakr رضي الله عنه. Therefore, they sort to make light of it by insinuating that this was done only for material gain. Even if he buries his head in the sand, Tījānī cannot save himself the embarrassment of this gaffe.

We have dealt with the allegation of burning the house of Fāṭimah رضي الله عنها previously. It was proven that this was a fabrication and cannot be established. Reliable narrations indicate that there were healthy relations between the household of ʿAlī رضي الله عنه and the household of Abū Bakr رضي الله عنه after the Prophet's صلى الله عليه وسلم demise. Repeating the evidence here will prove tedious and redundant. Instead we refer the reader to the relevant section in this book.[4]

Tījānī's claim that ʿUmar Objected to Abū Bakr's Appointment

Tījānī goes on to say:

> **Umar ibn al-Khattāb himself testified that that acclamation was a mistake - may Allah protect the Muslims from its evil -, and that whoever repeated it should be killed, or he might have said that if someone called for a similar action there would be no acclamation for him or for those who acclaimed him."[5]**

---

1 al-Thaqafī: *Al-Ghārāt*, 305-306, Bāb: Risālat ʿAlī ilā Aṣḥābih.

2 Ibid.

3 Refer to *al-Minhāj*, vol. 2 p. 16.

4 Refer to p. 248 of this book - Tījānī's emotional outburst.

5 *Then I was guided*, p. 136.

Responding to Tījānī's claim that ʿUmar Objected to Abū Bakr's Appointment

This is not how the narration from ʿUmar رضي الله عنه goes. It does not appear this way in *al-Bukhārī* and any of the other books. It is an excerpt of a lengthier ḥadīth related by Ibn ʿAbbās رضي الله عنه which states that ʿUmar رضي الله عنه stood up one day addressing the people in order to correct a false notion circulated by some people. Included in what he said is the following:

> It has reached me that someone amongst you has said, "By Allah! Certainly, if ʿUmar dies I will offer my pledge to so and so." No one should delude himself and say that the pledge given to Abū Bakr occurred unexpectedly and was then concluded (therefore it will occur in this manner in the future). Indeed, it occurred in that manner but Allah protected (the Ummah) from its harm. There is none amongst you beyond reproach like Abū Bakr. So if any person gives the pledge of allegiance to somebody (to become a Khalīfah) without consulting the other Muslims, then the one he has selected should not be granted allegiance, lest both of them should be killed.[1]

The word ʿUmar رضي الله عنه used "*faltah*" means unexpectedly and without preparation. The pledge of Abū Bakr رضي الله عنه occurred in that manner, without preparation for it. However, Allah protected the Ummah from potential harm or its *fitnah* (sedition). ʿUmar's رضي الله عنه statement, "There is none amongst you beyond reproach like Abū Bakr," means there is none amongst you who has reached the status and virtue of Abū Bakr رضي الله عنه. The proofs indicating his legitimacy as the khalīfah are clear and the peoples' gathering around him is something beyond your capacity.

Al-Khaṭṭābī says:

> He meant, the most superior amongst them is unable to match Abū Bakr in rank and virtue. Therefore, no one amongst you should hope to achieve what Abū Bakr achieved in terms of receiving the pledge from a small group then from the Muslims in general as they gathered around him, not disputing his legitimacy. With Abū Bakr they did not require any verification and they did not require any additional consultation. No one is like him in that regard.[2]

Of course, the reason for this statement of ʿUmar رضي الله عنه is that he was aware someone had said, "When ʿUmar dies I will offer my pledge to so and so," in other words, that

---

1 *Ṣaḥīḥ al-Bukhārī*, Kitāb al-Muḥāribī, Ḥadīth no. 6442.

2 *Fatḥ al-Bārī*, vol. 12 p. 155.

person intended to replicate the situation and process by which the pledge was granted to Abū Bakr رضي الله عنه. ʿUmar رضي الله عنه considered it difficult, if not unlikely for the people to agree on the leadership of a specific individual as the Ṣaḥābah agreed upon the appointment of Abū Bakr رضي الله عنه. Therefore, whoever intended to receive the pledge in such a manner places his life in danger. That is why ʿUmar رضي الله عنه said, "in delusion and have themselves killed," in other words, whoever does that deludes himself and his companion, and places their life in danger.[1]

Tījānī reproduced this statement of ʿUmar رضي الله عنه and stripped it of its context. This was a desperate attempt to condemn the Khilāfah. Once we understand the reason behind ʿUmar's رضي الله عنه statement Tījānī's argument appears rather fatuous. ʿUmar's رضي الله عنه statement makes known the virtue and precedence of Abū Bakr رضي الله عنه and the plausibility in the manner he was nominated. It further indicates the unlikely future occurrence of such a pledge.

Tījānī's Claim That ʿAlī objected to Abū Bakr's Appointment

Tījānī does not realise what a terrible portrait he paints of our Master ʿAlī ibn Abī Ṭālib رضي الله عنه when he produces this questionable quote:

> **By Allah, Ibn Abī Quhafa has got it! And he knows that my position [regarding the caliphate] is like that of the pole in relation to the millstone! The torrent flows from me, and the bird will never reach me![2]**

Responding to Tījānī's Claim That ʿAlī objected to Abū Bakr's Appointment

Our respect for ʿAlī رضي الله عنه demands that we apply a prudent approach of verifying something before attributing it to him. This statement is not reliably proven from him, and appears peculiar to his disposition. ʿAlī رضي الله عنه was not power hungry and displayed the greatest amount of respect for Abū Bakr رضي الله عنه. This statement is anomalous with what has been reliably transmitted from ʿAlī رضي الله عنه and on these grounds disregarded.

ʿAlī's pledge to Abū Bakr رضي الله عنهما, whether immediately or after six months, is undeniably proven. How then can it be said that ʿAlī رضي الله عنه said what is attributed to him in what is called *al-Khuṭbah al-Shaqshaqiyyah*? If we say that he indeed gave

1 Ibid.

2 *Then I was guided*, 136.

his pledge and that the speech is a fabrication then this solves all problems. If it is asserted that ʿAlī رضي الله عنه gave the pledge and then practiced Taqiyyah, this becomes problematic. It does not befit ʿAlī رضي الله عنه to have the clear textual evidence with him and to withdraw from it because of any person and to display conformity with the pledge of Abū Bakr رضي الله عنه as this is the core of nifāq and cowardice. Allah knows that ʿAlī رضي الله عنه was neither a hypocrite nor a coward.

If we refer to the letters of ʿAlī رضي الله عنه we find it contradicting what Tījānī transmitted.[1] In one of his letters to Muʿāwiyah رضي الله عنه, ʿAlī رضي الله عنه writes:

> The people who gave me the pledge are the people who gave Abū Bakr the pledge, and ʿUmar, and ʿUthmān, upon the same conditions they gave their pledge to them. It is not befitting for the one present to choose (the position) and for the one absent to reject as the consultation is the right of the Muhājirīn and Anṣār. Therefore, when they concur upon a man and call him the Imām that is consent from them. If someone defects from their choice on account of some criticism or bidʿah they returned from where he left. If he refused they fought him on account of his following other than the way of the believers. Allah will give him what he deserves.[2]

Is it possible for the same person to have said, "Indeed, the son of Abū Quḥāfah appropriated it," and then write a letter emphasizing the legitimacy of his custodianship with these words, "The people who gave me the pledge are the people who gave Abū Bakr the pledge, and ʿUmar, and ʿUthmān"? Likewise the statement, "He knows that my position in relation to it (the khilāfah) is the position of the pivot," could it be possible to have been said by same person who said, "It is not befitting for the one present to choose and for the one absent to reject... the consultation is the right of the Muhājirīn and Anṣār. Therefore, when they concur upon a man and call him the Imām that is consent from them. If someone defects from their choice on account of some criticism or bidʿah they returned from where he left. If he refused they fought him on account of his following other than the way of the believers"?

I call upon people blessed with intelligence and reason to reflect; can there be a contradiction more ridiculous than this? Is that not a clear proof that the book *Nahj al-Balāghah* is not entirely transmitted from ʿAlī رضي الله عنه? The truth is that most

1 Such as his words, "Leave me and search for some besides me." *Nahj al-Balāghah*, vol. 1 p. 216.
2 *Nahj al-Balāghah*, 530.

of it is merely ascribed to him. ʿAlī رضي الله عنه used to advise against contradiction. How then can these blatant contradictions apply to him?

If we take the letter from ʿAlī to Muʿāwiyah, we discover that even the Shīʿī texts prove that Abū Bakr's pledge was not coerced upon any one, rather, it was through the pledge of the Muhājirīn and the Anṣār. When one considers this it becomes clear what a big blow this is to Tījānī's argument. How can it be said that ʿAlī's nomination was a result of Naṣṣ? Both Sunnī and Shīʿī sources indicate that Khilāfah was accomplished by Shūrā and no Naṣṣ exists. In the words of Tījānī, if one rids himself of bias and surrenders himself entirely to the truth, one will find that Khilāfah was established through Shūrā, and that the pledge was given to Abū Bakr رضي الله عنه.

Tījānī's next objection is that Saʿd ibn ʿUbādah launched an attack on Abū Bakr رضي الله عنه and attempted to prevent him from the khilāfah and had it not been that he was ill he would have opposed him and fought him to the end of this affair.

Our response:

Even if we assume this narration to be authentic it would be a criticism against Saʿd رضي الله عنه and not Abū Bakr رضي الله عنه. However, this fantasy in the narration is too alarming for it to have been the behaviour of a companion the likes of Saʿd ibn ʿUbādah رضي الله عنه.

We have repeatedly established that mere transmitting of information from the book *Tārīkh al-Khulafā'* ascribed to Ibn Qutaybah does not make it accurate. This is a report of that kind.

Instead of referring to texts from the Ahl al-Sunnah, once again I will respond with the quote from the Shīʿī book *Nahj al-Balāghah* when ʿAlī رضي الله عنه said that the Muhājirīn and the Anṣār gave their pledge to Abū Bakr, and that consultation was their right, and that anyone defected from their matter because of some criticism or bidʿah they returned him from whence he came.

On the assumption that what Tījānī claimed about Saʿd is actually true, then what made him deserving of praise? What proof is there for Saʿd to justify his attack on Abū Bakr and ʿUmar رضي الله عنهما when the Muhājirīn and the Anṣār had given him (Abū Bakr) their pledge?

Does this alleged action of Saʿd رَضِيَ ٱللَّهُ عَنْهُ undermine the consultation of the Muhājirīn and Anṣār? If his rebellion against them was on account of a criticism, or intending to fight them, would his action be justified or would it be necessary to deter him and even fight him on account of his following other than the way of the believers?

If Tījānī denies this then it is necessary to reject the important books relied upon by the Shīʿah, since denial in this instance is acknowledgement of the fact that these books are nothing but lies forged in the name of ʿAlī رَضِيَ ٱللَّهُ عَنْهُ and his family.

If Tījānī maintains the truthfulness of the statement then this results in one of two outcomes. Either one acknowledges that Saʿd's رَضِيَ ٱللَّهُ عَنْهُ statement and action were in opposition to the truth, and the consultation of the believers, and this would establish not only the validity of the Khilāfah, but the error in Saʿd's رَضِيَ ٱللَّهُ عَنْهُ judgement. The alternative conclusion—which is no doubt the actual case—is to acknowledge that what has been transmitted about Saʿd is a lie against him.

If we accept the latter conclusion it certainly proves that the book *Tārīkh al-Khulafā'* and what has been transmitted in it is false and has no basis, whether in its chain or text. The corollary of this conclusion further compels you to acknowledge the forgery in the narrations attributed to Fāṭimah رَضِيَ ٱللَّهُ عَنْهَا regarding her inheritance, and Abū Bakr and ʿUmar's رَضِيَ ٱللَّهُ عَنْهُمَا treatment of her.

All that is left to say to Tījānī on this discussion is: Which of the two statements do you objectively choose, O objective one?

5. Tījānī's proofs for the superiority of ʿAlī over Abū Bakr

Tījānī has a sectioned titled, "Alī is more worthy of being followed.' In this section he presents the reasons, both textual and rational, why he believes that ʿAlī رَضِيَ ٱللَّهُ عَنْهُ was superior to Abū Bakr رَضِيَ ٱللَّهُ عَنْهُ, and more deserving of the Khilāfah. He writes:

> **One of the reasons which led to my enlightenment and ultimately made me leave the tradition [Sunna] of my forefathers was the comparison between the positions of Ali ibn Abī Ṭālib and that of Abū Bakr, based on logical deductions and historical references.**
>
> **As I stated in earlier parts of this book, I only included in my research the references which have been agreed on by both, the Shiites and the Sunnis.**
>
> **I searched in the books of both parties and found that only Ali received total support, and both Shiites and Sunnis agreed on his leadership in accordance**

with the texts they approved of. However there is neither support nor agreement on the leadership of Abū Bakr except by a small group of Muslims, and we have mentioned what Umar said about his succession to the caliphate.[1]

Responding to Tījānī's proofs for the superiority of ʿAlī over Abū Bakr

The reasons given above could be expected from an individual who is trapped between the threshold of fantasy and reality. How else can the undertaking of objectivity be reconciled with such gross obfuscation of historical facts?

Let us pause for a moment. What would be a logical analysis of the situation after the Prophet's صَلَّى ٱللَّهُ عَلَيْهِ وَسَلَّمَ demise? How do we approach this delicate subject in a manner that is aligned with sound reasoning, yet detached from emotional bias? While we acknowledge the merit in a proposal to make sense of a murky situation based on mutually agreed upon facts, our objection against Tījānī is uncompromising since his execution of the said proposal ignores the very facts which he pledged to consider.

In the passages that follow we are going to demonstrate that the 'reasons for enlightenment' are not just a farce, but an insult to the intelligence of the astute reader. In order to proceed we will have to accept the following underlying assumptions:

1. ʿAlī رَضِيَ ٱللَّهُ عَنْهُ behaves in a rational manner and his behaviour is consistent
2. ʿAlī's رَضِيَ ٱللَّهُ عَنْهُ behaviour is an accurate indicator of how he interpreted situations

Bearing the underlying assumptions in mind, we can state with confidence that there is no disagreement on the fact that ʿAlī رَضِيَ ٱللَّهُ عَنْهُ fought Muʿāwiyah رَضِيَ ٱللَّهُ عَنْهُ with a formidable army at Ṣiffīn. Both the Ahl al-Sunnah and Shīʿah agree that ʿAlī رَضِيَ ٱللَّهُ عَنْهُ was the legitimate Khalīfah. Similarly there is no disagreement that Muʿāwiyah رَضِيَ ٱللَّهُ عَنْهُ resisted pledging allegiance to ʿAlī رَضِيَ ٱللَّهُ عَنْهُ, which is a point in favour of ʿAlī رَضِيَ ٱللَّهُ عَنْهُ in this unfortunate battle.

When the pledge was given to Abū Bakr رَضِيَ ٱللَّهُ عَنْهُ, there was no resistance from ʿAlī رَضِيَ ٱللَّهُ عَنْهُ. If ʿAlī رَضِيَ ٱللَّهُ عَنْهُ displayed no sign of resistance when Abū Bakr رَضِيَ ٱللَّهُ عَنْهُ was nominated as Khalīfah, and fought Muʿāwiyah رَضِيَ ٱللَّهُ عَنْهُ when Muʿāwiyah رَضِيَ ٱللَّهُ عَنْهُ resisted

1 *Then I was guided*, p. 140.

pledging allegiance; we are left with only two possible outcomes. Either ʿAlī رضي الله عنه acknowledged the legitimacy of Abū Bakr's رضي الله عنه khilāfah, hence no resistance, or—Allah forbid—ʿAlī's رضي الله عنه behaviour was erratic. It is the responsibility of the Rāfiḍah, like Tījānī, to explain the inconsistency in his behaviour since the understanding of the Ahl al-Sunnah is not only plausible, but portrays ʿAlī رضي الله عنه in the most positive light.

In a desperate attempt to show face, someone like Tījānī might say that ʿAlī رضي الله عنه was coerced and he had no alternative and had no army. The truth is that the army of Usāmah رضي الله عنه was camped at al-Jurf outside of Madīnah, which meant that Abū Bakr رضي الله عنه had no army as well. If there was support for ʿAlī رضي الله عنه from within Madīnah after the assassination of ʿUthmān, surely there would have been support for him after the Prophet's صلى الله عليه وسلم demise.

After the assassination of ʿUmar رضي الله عنه he nominated ʿAlī رضي الله عنه to be part of the six-member Shūrā from whom the new khalīfah ought to be elected. Why would ʿAlī رضي الله عنه agree to be a candidate, if he were nominated by authoritative text as Tījānī asserts? All he had to do was to announce his khilāfah. Why agree to a process of election if he was already the khalīfah? ʿUthmān رضي الله عنه had no army since he had not yet been elected. If ʿAlī رضي الله عنه was the only candidate to receive total support, why is it that the khilāfah went to ʿUthmān رضي الله عنه without resistance from ʿAlī رضي الله عنه?

If our expression appears a bit harsh it is only because the dignity of Sayyidunā ʿAlī رضي الله عنه is sacrificed at the altar of foolish arguments of people like Tījānī who do not realise the consequences of their rants. One wonders if Tījānī has no shame; to insinuate that ʿAlī رضي الله عنه displayed such erratic behaviour!

Another fact to consider is how was ijmāʿ on the leadership of ʿAlī رضي الله عنه attained when history testifies that an ijmāʿ was established on the leadership of Abū Bakr رضي الله عنه? It is given that no ijmāʿ existed regarding ʿAlī's رضي الله عنه leadership after the Prophet's صلى الله عليه وسلم demise from Sunnī sources; but it might come as an unpleasant surprise that no such ijmāʿ exists even in Twelver Shīʿah[1] sources.

Our argument is further reinforced by Tījānī's contradiction:

1 We have shown in earlier passages that Shīʿī scholars have reported that the pledge was given to Abū Bakr. Refer to p. 304 of this book.

However there is neither support nor agreement on the leadership of Abū Bakr except by a small group of Muslims.

Our comment:

If only a small group pledged their allegiance to Abū Bakr رضي الله عنه, as Tījānī alleges, why did ʿAlī رضي الله عنه not contest this? He went to war against Muʿāwiyah رضي الله عنه and he was a legitimate khalīfah by consensus. Why not here?

We ought to reiterate that the pledge of allegiance was initially given by those present at Saqīfah Banī Sāʿidah. Subsequently, the general Bayʿah took place where the entire community of Madīnah, including ʿAlī and Zubayr رضي الله عنهما, pledged their allegiance to Abū Bakr رضي الله عنه.

Then he says:

Furthermore there are many virtues and good deeds attributed to Ali ibn Abī Ṭālib by the Shiites and cited as authentic references in the Sunni books.[1]

Our comment:

The Ahl al-Sunnah do not deny the virtues of ʿAlī رضي الله عنه. They have compiled exclusive chapters about the virtues of ʿAlī رضي الله عنه in their ḥadīth collections. Similarly, many of the other Companions of the Prophet صلى الله عليه وسلم have virtues and merits. The difference between the Ahl al-Sunnah and the likes of Tījānī is that the Ahl al-Sunnah have scrutinised these narrations, whether they extol the virtues of ʿAlī رضي الله عنه or the rest of the Companions; in addition to understanding these narrations in their proper context.

Tījānī is finding it increasingly difficult to exercise restraint; his predilection for exaggeration manifests itself in his statement:

The sayings are full of the virtues of Ali, more than any other Companion ever received, and even Ahmed ibn Hanbal said: No one among the Companions of the Messenger of Allah صلى الله عليه وسلم had more virtues than Ali ibn Abi Talib.

Qadi Ismail, al-Nasa'i and Abu Ali al-Naisaburi said: "No Companion had as many virtues attributed to him as Ali."[2]

1 *Then I was guided*, p. 140-141.

2 *Then I was guided*, p. 141.

Our response:

What was intended by these scholars is that the narrators who transmit the virtues of ʿAlī رضي الله عنه are greater in number. They are not referring to the number of ḥadīth in terms of the Prophetic text; rather it is in reference to the vast number of chains of transmission by which these reports have been recorded. For example, the narration, "Whoever considers me his Mawlā, ʿAlī is his Mawlā." This ḥadīth has many chains even though it is one and the same narration.

We realise the reason for the abundant chains of narration for the aḥādīth which mention the virtues of ʿAlī رضي الله عنه is that he was subject to criticism by the Nawāṣib. This resulted in many ḥadīth scholars quoting these narrations and popularising them so that the rank and position of ʿAlī رضي الله عنه be properly recognised. It is for this reason that Ibn Ḥajar says:

> Aḥmad, Ismāʿīl al-Qāḍī, Nasāʾī, and Abū ʿAlī al-Naysābūrī, say, "There are not as many good narrations pertaining to any of the Ṣaḥābah as what has been transmitted about ʿAlī. Perhaps the reason was his late death. It was in his era that the Ummah split and he faced opposition. Therefore, the narration of his virtues spread as many of the Ṣaḥābah narrated it in order to respond to those who opposed him."[1]

Notwithstanding the abundant narrations which mention ʿAlī's رضي الله عنه merits, not all of them are reliable and true. Al-Dhahabī says in *Talkhīṣ al-Mawḍūʿāt*:

> The virtues of no Companion have been narrated as much as was been narrated about ʿAlī رضي الله عنه. Those narrations are of three categories:
>
> a. *Ṣaḥīḥ* (authentic) and *Ḥasan* (acceptable)
>
> b. A number of *ḍaʿīf* (weak) aḥādīth, and they are plenty,
>
> c. A number of *mawḍūʿāt* (fabricated), and they are many with perhaps some of them bearing misguidance and *zandaqah* (an effort to corrupt the dīn from the inside).[2]

---

1 *Fatḥ al-Bārī*, vol. 7 p. 89.

2 See the footnote of the book *al-Ṣawāʿiq al-Muḥriqah*, p. 186.

Therefore, not everything narrated about the virtues of ʿAlī رضي الله عنه is necessarily authentic. Rather, the liars fabricated a substantial number of narrations extolling his virtues. The Imāmiyyah Shīʿah confirm this. Ibn Abī al-Ḥadīd, the Shīʿī, says:

> The root of fabrications in ḥadīth in the genre of virtues stemmed from the Shīʿah. Indeed, they fabricated a number of aḥādīth relating to their Companion (ʿAlī) initially. Their enmity towards their adversaries motivated them to do that.[1]

Al-Kashshī confirms this in his book *Rijāl al-Kashshī*:

> From Ibn Muskān—from someone who narrated to him from our Companions—from Abū ʿAbd Allāh al-Ṣādiq whom I heard saying, "May Allah curse Mughīrah ibn Saʿīd. Indeed, he used to forge (aḥādīth) from my father and Allah made him taste the heat of the steel."[2]

He further states:

> From Yūnus, who said, "I visited ʿIrāq and found a group of the students of Abū Jaʿfar there. I found the students of Abū ʿAbd Allāh in abundance. I listened (to aḥādīth) from them and took their books (from them) and later presented it to Abū al-Ḥasan al-Riḍā. He denied a large number of the aḥādīth; that they could possibly be attributed to Abū ʿAbd Allāh, and said, "Indeed, Abū al-Khaṭṭāb forged a number of aḥādīth upon Abū ʿAbd Allāh. May Allah curse Abū al-Khaṭṭāb! Likewise the students of Abū al-Khaṭṭāb smuggle these aḥādīth into the books of the students of Abū ʿAbd Allāh until today."[3]

These are admissions from Shīʿī narrators found in reliable Shīʿī books. We do not have to refer to the Ahl al-Sunnah to confirm that a substantial number of narrations mentioning the virtues of ʿAlī رضي الله عنه are lies which have been forged by those who claim to be his Shīʿah!

Tījānī's subtle reference to Imām Aḥmad ibn Ḥambal might imply that he considered ʿAlī رضي الله عنه greater in status than Abū Bakr and ʿUmar رضي الله عنهما. The truth is that Imām Aḥmad held the view that the best of this Ummah after its Prophet صلى الله عليه وسلم was Abū Bakr then ʿUmar رضي الله عنهما.

1 Ibn Abī al-Ḥadīd: *Sharḥ Nahj al-Balāghah*, vol. 3 p. 17, Dār al-Fikr.

2 *Rijāl al-Kashshī*, p. 195.

3 Ibid.

ʿAbd Allāh ibn Aḥmad ibn Ḥambal says:

> I heard my father (Aḥmad ibn Ḥambal) saying, "As for superiority, I say, Abū Bakr, then ʿUmar, then ʿUthmān, then ʿAlī."[1]

He also says:

> I asked my father about superiority between Abū Bakr, ʿUmar, ʿUthmān, and ʿAlī and he replied, "Abū Bakr, ʿUmar, ʿUthmān, then ʿAlī, the fourth of the khulafā'." I said to my father, "Some people say he was not a khalīfah," and he replied, "This is an evil statement!"[2]

In the *Masā'il* of Ibn Hānī, he says:

> I heard Abū ʿAbd Allāh ibn Ḥambal saying about superiority (amongst the Ṣaḥābah), "Abū Bakr, then ʿUmar, then ʿUthmān and if someone should say ʿAlī I will not rebuke him," (then his son asked him about the khilāfah)."
>
> He says further, "I asked my father about the Imāms and he said, 'Abū Bakr, then ʿUmar, then ʿUthmān, then ʿAlī in terms of the khilāfah.'"[3]

This is the view of Aḥmad ibn Ḥambal regarding rank and khilāfah.

Tījānī goes on to say:

> **As for Abū Bakr, I searched in the books of the two parties, and found that the virtues attributed to him by the Sunnis were much less than that attributed to Ali...[4]**

Until he says:

> **Despite the fact that Abū Bakr was the first caliph, and had all the power and authority, despite the bribes and gifts that the Umayyad's gave to everyone who praised Abū Bakr, Umar and 'Uthman, and despite all the alleged virtues and good deeds that they invented for Abū Bakr, which filled many books ... despite all that, they did not amount to a fraction of the true virtues of Imam Ali.[5]**

1 Imām ʿAbd Allāh ibn Aḥmad ibn Ḥambal: *Al-Sunnah*, vol. 2 p. 573, Ḥadīth no. 1347.

2 Ibid.

3 *Masā'il Ibn Hānī*, vol. 2 p. 169, see the questions and the letters narrated from Imām Aḥmad ibn Ḥambal, compiled by ʿAbd al-Allāh al-Aḥmadī, vol. 1 p. 385.

4 *Then I was guided*, p. 141.

5 *Then I was guided*, p. 142-143.

Our comment:

It is amazing how Tījānī's objectivity could lead him to copious narrations of the merits of ʿAlī رضي الله عنه, yet blinded him from the aḥādīth which mention the merits of Abū Bakr رضي الله عنه. This is the same objectivity which led him to reject the aḥādīth mentioning the virtues of Abū Bakr because they are 'Umayyad-sponsored forgeries'. This eye of scrutiny was so focused on finding fault with narrations favouring Abū Bakr رضي الله عنه that it overlooked what is written in *Rijāl al-Kashshī*:

> From Ibn Muskān—from someone who narrated to him from our companions—from Abū ʿAbd Allāh al-Ṣādiq whom I heard saying, "May Allah curse Mughīrah ibn Saʿīd. Indeed, he used to forge (aḥādīth) from my father on account of which Allah made him taste the heat of the steal."[1]

This is a Jaʿfar al-Ṣādiq, the sixth of the twelve 'infallible' Imāms, cursing an individual who professes to be a Shīʿī yet forges narrations in the name of his Imāms. Is this the objective research that Tījānī was referring to? May Allah protect us all from such objectivity.

Furthermore, the onus is on Tījānī to provide evidence that supports his claim that the Umayyads gave gifts and bribes to narrators for forging aḥādīth about Abū Bakr, ʿUmar, and ʿUthmān رضي الله عنهم. Furthermore, what purpose would that serve since Abū Bakr رضي الله عنه was from the branch of Banū Taym and ʿUmar was from Banū ʿAdī? Their lineage meets up much later.

Little does Tījānī realise that some of the same narrators who narrate the virtues of ʿAlī رضي الله عنه are those who narrate the virtues of Abū Bakr and ʿUmar رضي الله عنهما! Are their narrations only sound if they narrate the virtues of ʿAlī رضي الله عنه? By Allah this is a unique brand of objectivity. The implication is even more damning if Tījānī insinuates that the forgers of ḥadīth were the Companions of the Prophet صلى الله عليه وسلم. May Allah have mercy on Imām Mālik for such a profound statement:

> These people criticise the Companions of the Messenger صلى الله عليه وسلم. They criticise his Companions and (nothing prevents) someone from saying, "(He was) an evil man and he had evil companions. If he was a good man he would have had good companions."[2]

1 *Rijāl al-Kashshī*, p. 195.

2 Ibn Taymiyyah: *Al-Fatāwā al-ʿIrāqiyyah*, p. 157.

Tījānī has not concluded his analysis. He seeks to elaborate further on his findings:

> **Furthermore, if we analyze the alleged sayings that were in favour of Abū Bakr, we find them incompatible with the historical facts, and no sensible man or creed could accept them.**[1]

Our comment:

One wonders if Abū Bakr رضي الله عنه is worthy of any virtue according to Tījānī? What seems evident here is that Tījānī's research is based on retrospective analysis from a point of absolute blind faith. Tījānī has failed to prove that ʿAlī رضي الله عنه was the prime candidate for khilāfah after the Prophet's صلى الله عليه وسلم demise, not by direct nomination—as he alleges—nor by the process of Shūrā. Tījānī's blind faith, however, is that ʿAlī رضي الله عنه was divinely appointed for the post. Regardless of what evidence is presented, he is going to dismiss it on any grounds as we have demonstrated earlier. Considering his blind faith in ʿAlī's رضي الله عنه leadership, every ḥadīth in favour of Abū Bakr رضي الله عنه must now be dismissed as a forgery and in conflict with reality. For him the virtues of ʿAlī رضي الله عنه and the virtues of Abū Bakr رضي الله عنه are mutually exclusive, absolutely incompatible. His logic is that any acknowledgement of virtues for Abū Bakr puts ʿAlī's candidacy in jeopardy; and since his faith is that ʿAlī is the divinely appointed leader any ḥadīth which mentions his virtue is validated regardless if it was narrated by a known forger.

The Ahl al-Sunnah, on the other hand, acknowledge virtues for both ʿAlī رضي الله عنه and Abū Bakr رضي الله عنه. The virtues and merits of one, does not detract from the other. Their merits and virtues are not based on the perception of the Ahl al-Sunnah in terms of their superiority in rank. Instead their merits are established from the narrations which are subject to scrutiny. The criteria of analysing narrations are not on the basis of any predisposition toward any of the Ṣaḥābah. The narrations are examined on the basis of their chain of transmission to establish whether they are reliable or not.

If we were to base these narrations on historical fact we find that Abū Bakr رضي الله عنه was the one who contributed to the cause of Islam financially in its early days. He was nearly beaten to death when he stood up in defence of the Prophet صلى الله عليه وسلم in the early days in Makkah.

---

1 *Then I was guided*, p. 143.

> ʿUrwah ibn al-Zubayr relates that he asked ʿAbd Allāh ibn ʿAmr ibn al-ʿĀṣ, "Tell me of the worst thing which the mushrikūn did to the Prophet?"
>
> He said, "While the Prophet صلى الله عليه وسلم was praying in the Ḥijr of the Kaʿbah; ʿUqbah ibn Abī Muʿayṭ came and put his garment around the Prophet's neck and throttled him violently. Abū Bakr came and caught him by his shoulder and pushed him away from the Prophet صلى الله عليه وسلم and said, "Do you want to kill a man just because he says, 'My Lord is Allah?'"[1]

Who was the Prophet's صلى الله عليه وسلم Companion during the *hijrah* (emigration)? ʿĀ'ishah رضي الله عنها narrates:

> Some Muslims emigrated to Abyssinia and Abū Bakr also prepared himself for the emigration, but the Prophet صلى الله عليه وسلم said (to him), "Wait, for I hope that Allah will allow me also to emigrate."
>
> Abū Bakr said, "May my father and mother be sacrificed for you. Do you expect to emigrate (soon)?"
>
> The Prophet said, "Yes." So Abū Bakr waited to accompany the Prophet صلى الله عليه وسلم and fed two she-camels he had on the leaves of an acacia tree regularly for four months. One day while we were sitting in our house at midday, someone said to Abū Bakr, "Here is the Messenger of Allah صلى الله عليه وسلم, coming with his head and a part of his face covered with a cloth at an hour he never used to come to us."
>
> Abū Bakr said, "May my father and mother be sacrificed for you, (O Prophet)! An urgent matter must have brought you here at this hour."
>
> The Prophet صلى الله عليه وسلم came and asked permission to enter, and he was allowed. The Prophet صلى الله عليه وسلم entered and said to Abū Bakr, "Let those who are with you excuse themselves."
>
> Abū Bakr replied, "There is no stranger; they are your family. Let my father be sacrificed for you, O Messenger of Allah!"
>
> The Prophet صلى الله عليه وسلم said, "I have been allowed to leave (Makkah)."
>
> Abū Bakr said, "Shall I accompany you, O Messenger of Allah, May my father be sacrificed for you?"

---

1 *Ṣaḥīḥ al-Bukhārī*, Kitāb Manāqib al-Anṣār, Ḥadīth no. 3856.

> The Prophet صَلَّى ٱللَّهُ عَلَيْهِ وَسَلَّمَ said, "Yes,"
>
> Abū Bakr said, "O Messenger of Allah! May my father be sacrificed for you. Take one of these two she camels of mine."
>
> The Prophet صَلَّى ٱللَّهُ عَلَيْهِ وَسَلَّمَ said, "I will take it only after paying its price."
>
> So we prepared their baggage and put their journey food in a leather bag; and Asmā' bint Abī Bakr cut a piece of her girdle and tied the mouth of the leather bag with it. That is why she was called Dhāt al-Niṭāqayn. Then the Prophet صَلَّى ٱللَّهُ عَلَيْهِ وَسَلَّمَ and Abū Bakr went to a cave in a mountain called Thawr and remained there for three nights. 'Abd Allāh ibn Abī Bakr, who was a young intelligent man, used to stay with them at night and leave before dawn so that in the morning, he would be with the Quraysh in Makkah as if he had spent the night among them. If he heard of any plot contrived by the Quraysh against the Prophet صَلَّى ٱللَّهُ عَلَيْهِ وَسَلَّمَ and Abū Bakr, he would understand it and (return to) inform them of it when it became dark. 'Āmir ibn Fuhayrah, the freed slave of Abū Bakr used to graze a flock of sheep for them and he used to take those sheep to them a while after the 'Ishā prayer. They would sleep till 'Āmir awakened them when it was still dark. He used to do that in each of those three nights..."[1]

Then he says:

> **Earlier on we explained the saying attributed to the Prophet صَلَّى ٱللَّهُ عَلَيْهِ وَسَلَّمَ: "If the faith of Abū Bakr and the faith of my nation are put on the balance, the faith of Abū Bakr will be heavier".**
>
> **If the Messenger of Allah صَلَّى ٱللَّهُ عَلَيْهِ وَسَلَّمَ was aware of this high degree of faith in Abū Bakr, he would not have appointed Usāmah to command the army; nor would he have refused to bear witness for him as he did for the martyrs of Uhud, and then said to him that he did not know what he was going to do after him, so that Abū Bakr cried.**[2]

Our comment:

Many of these criticisms have been dealt with in detail earlier in the book. Nonetheless, we will commit to brief comments here. I am taking the liberty of expressing Tījānī's argument as coherent as is possible:

1 *Ṣaḥīḥ al-Bukhārī*, Kitāb al-Libās, Ḥadīth 5807.

2 *Then I was guided*, 143.

How could Abū Bakr have īmān greater than the entire Ummah when someone as junior as Usāmah was appointed the leader of an army instead of him!

In the narration quoted above Tījānī has not only ignored the study of the chain of transmission for considerations that stand opposed to sound reason; but subtly implies that Usāmah رضي الله عنه was inadequate as a leader. This is the consequence of unprincipled reckless research. Tījānī has not realised that this insinuation of his undermines the objection which he raised against ʿUmar رضي الله عنه in the beginning of the book; even though he falsified the information there to implicate ʿUmar رضي الله عنه.

Furthermore, in his haste to reject this narration he has overlooked so many others. He has simply ignored the fact that the Prophet صلى الله عليه وسلم appointed Abū Bakr as the leader of prayer during his sickness. Similarly he has ignored the statement of ʿAlī رضي الله عنه when asked by his son Muḥammad ibn al-Ḥanafiyyah:

قلت لأبي أى الناس خير بعد رسول الله صلى الله عليه وسلم قال أبو بكر قلت ثم من قال ثم عمر وخشيت أن يقول عثمان قلت ثم أنت قال ما أنا إلا رجل من المسلمين

"Who is the best of all people after the Messenger of Allah صلى الله عليه وسلم?"

"Abū Bakr," was his reply.

"Who then?" asked Ibn al-Ḥanafiyyah.

"ʿUmar," replied ʿAlī.

Muḥammad ibn al-Ḥanafiyyah says, "I feared he would say ʿUthmān next if I asked him, so I said, "Then you.""

ʿAlī رضي الله عنه replied, "I am but an ordinary man from the Muslims."[1]

Earlier in the book we objected to the manner in which a phrase from the lengthier ḥadīth was translated

عن مالك عن أبي النضر مولى عمر بن عبيد الله أنه بلغه أن رسول الله صلى الله عليه وسلم قال لشهداء أحد هؤلاء أشهد عليهم فقال أبو بكر الصديق

1 *Ṣaḥīḥ al-Bukhārī*, Kitāb Faḍā'il Aṣḥāb al-Nabī صلى الله عليه وسلم, Ḥadīth no. 3671.

ألسنا يا رسول الله بإخوانهم أسلمنا كما أسلموا وجاهدنا كما جاهدوا فقال رسول الله صلى الله عليه وسلم بلى ولكن لا أدري ما تحدثون بعدي فبكى أبو بكر ثم بكى ثم قال أئنا لكائنون بعدك

Abū al-Naḍr, the freed-slave of ʿUmar ibn ʿUbaydillah said that it has reached him that the Messenger of Allah ﷺ said over the martyrs of Uhud, "I testify for them." Abū Bakr al-Ṣiddīq said, "O Messenger of Allah! Are we not their brothers? We entered Islam as they entered Islam and we strove as they strove." The Messenger of Allah ﷺ said, "Yes, but I do not know what you (all) will do after me." Abū Bakr wept profusely and said, "Are we really going to out-live you!"

The statement of Abū Bakr رضي الله عنه quoted earlier from the translation of *Then I was guided* read, "*We are going to alter many things after your departure.*"

At that instance it would have been unfair on us to raise this objection against Tījānī since the error was clearly with the translator in the manner in which the ḥadīth had been translated. However, here we find that the charge of distortion and interpolation against Tījānī is warranted. As a matter of fact, the translation has masked Tījānī's deception on this occasion.

The original wording quoted by the Prophet ﷺ responding to Abū Bakr رضي الله عنه using the pronoun which is plural i.e. "I do not know what you all will do after me." In the original version of his book Tījānī has substituted the plural pronoun for the singular; thus restricting the general mode of address by the Prophet ﷺ to Abū Bakr رضي الله عنه specifically. Ultimately, it is up to the discerning reader to decide how genuine the claim of impartiality and fair assessment of fact is.

Then he says:

In addition to that, the Prophet would not have sent Ali ibn Abi Talib to take "Surat Bara'a" from him and prevented him from transmitting it.[1]

Our comment:

Again, the facts have been distorted. It is unanimously accepted that the Prophet ﷺ instated Abū Bakr رضي الله عنه as the leader of the Ḥajj in the ninth year after the

1 Ibid.

hijrah. ʿAlī رضي الله عنه was subsequently sent to announce this during the Ḥajj as it was revealed after Abū Bakr's رضي الله عنه departure. After reviewing all the narrations which describe this, we cannot find a single narration which prohibits Abū Bakr رضي الله عنه from transmitting it.

Al-Ṭabarī, Isḥāq ibn Rāhūyah in his *Musnad*, Nasā'ī, Dārimī, Ibn Khuzaymah, and Ibn Ḥibbān all narrate by way of Ibn Jurayj, who says, "ʿAbd Allāh ibn ʿUthmān ibn Khaytham narrated to us—from Abū Zubayr—from Jābir who said:

> The Prophet صلى الله عليه وسلم, after his return from the ʿUmrah which commenced at Jiʿirrānah, sent Abū Bakr to lead the Ḥajj. We proceeded until we were close to al-ʿArj when the adhān for Fajr was called out and the sound of the Messenger's camel was heard and sitting on it was ʿAlī. Abū Bakr said to him, "Have you been sent as a leader or a messenger?" He said, "Rather, the Messenger صلى الله عليه وسلم sent me with (Sūrah) al-Barā'ah to recite to the people." We arrived in Makkah and one day before the Day of Tarwiyah, Abū Bakr came and addressed the people with regards to their rituals. Upon the completion of his address ʿAlī stood up and recited (Sūrah) al-Barā'ah to the people until he completed it. The Day of al-Naḥr passed by in the same manner and the Day of al-Nafr passed by in the same manner.[1]

During this Ḥajj, Abū Bakr رضي الله عنه proclaimed that no mushrik may perform Ḥajj after that year, and no person may perform ṭawāf in an unclothed state. He commanded his other Companions to do the same. This is supported by what al-Bukhārī narrates from Abū Hurayrah, who said:

> بعثني أبو بكر في تلك الحجة في مؤذنين يوم النحر نؤذن بمنى أن لا يحج بعد العام مشرك ولا يطوف بالبيت عريان قال حميد بن عبد الرحمن ثم أردف رسول الله صلى الله عليه وسلم عليا فأمره أن يؤذن ببراءة قال أبو هريرة فأذن معنا علي في أهل منى يوم النحر لا يحج بعد العام مشرك ولا يطوف بالبيت عريان.

> Abū Bakr sent me during that Ḥajj amongst the announcers on the Day of Naḥr at Minā that no mushrik may perform the Ḥajj after that year and no person may perform ṭawāf naked. Ḥumayd ibn ʿAbd al-Raḥmān says, "Then

1 *Fatḥ al-Bārī*, vol. 8 p. 171.

the Messenger ﷺ seated ʿAlī (on his camel) and instructed him to announce (recite Sūrah) al-Barā'ah (to the people)."

Abū Hurayrah says, "Then ʿAlī announced with us amongst the people in Minā the Day of al-Naḥr (Sūrah) al-Barā'ah and that no mushrik may perform the Ḥajj after that year and that no person may perform ṭawāf naked."[1]

The reason for sending ʿAlī was that since the Prophet ﷺ was a leader, it was Arab custom that only he, or someone from his household could convey this instruction.

Al-Ṭabarānī narrates from Abū Rāfiʿ, part of a lengthier report:

No one may convey it except you or a man from you![2]

The Prophet ﷺ sent ʿAlī رضي الله عنه for this reason and not to prevent Abū Bakr رضي الله عنه as stated by Tījānī. The Prophet ﷺ was the one who appointed him to lead the Ḥajj and ʿAlī رضي الله عنه was amongst Abū Bakr's رضي الله عنه Companions.

As for Tījānī's statement:

Nor would the Prophet have said in Khayber while presenting the flag: "Tomorrow I will give my flag to a man who loves Allah and His Messenger, ever going forward and never retreating, Allah had tested his heart with the faith" then he gave it to Ali and no one else.[3]

Our comments:

Firstly, he ascribes this narration to *Ṣaḥīḥ Muslim*.

Despite expending every effort we did not find this ḥadīth with this wording in *Ṣaḥīḥ Muslim*. The ḥadīth in *Ṣaḥīḥ Muslim* is the ḥadīth of Abū Hurayrah رضي الله عنه that the Messenger ﷺ said on the Day of Khaybar:

لأعطين هذه الراية رجلا يحب الله ورسوله ، يفتح الله على يديه ، قال عمر بن الخطاب : ما أحببت الإمارة إلا يومئذ ، قال : فتساورت لها ، رجاء أن أدعى لها ، قال : فدعا رسول الله صلى الله عليه وسلم ، علي بن أبي طالب

1 *Ṣaḥīḥ al-Bukhārī*, Kitāb al-Tafsīr, vol. 4, Ḥadīth no. 4378.

2 *Fatḥ al-Bārī*, vol. 8 p. 169.

3 *Then I was guided*, 143.

فأعطاه إياها ، وقال : إمش ولا تلتفت حتى يفتح الله عليك ، قال : فسار علي شيئا ، ثم وقف ولم يلتفت فصرخ : يا رسول الله : على ماذا أقاتل الناس ، قال : قاتلهم حتى يشهدوا أن لا إله إلا الله ، وأن محمدا رسول الله ، فإذا فعلوا ذلك ، فقد منعوا منك دماءهم وأموالهم إلا بحقها ، وحسابهم على الله

"I will most certainly give this flag to a man whom Allah and His Messenger love, Allah will grant victory at his hands."

'Umar said, "I did not wish for leadership except on that day."

'Umar then said, "Then I moved towards it hoping I would be called for it. The Messenger ﷺ called 'Alī and gave it to him and said, 'Walk and do not turn around until Allah gives victory by you.'"

'Alī travelled for a little while and then stopped and he did not turn around. Then he shouted, "O Messenger, on what basis should I fight the people?"

The Prophet ﷺ replied, "Fight them until they testify that there is no deity besides Allah and that Muḥammad is the Messenger of Allah! When they do that they prevent you from their blood and their wealth, except by its rights, and their reckoning is by Allah."[1]

No doubt this ḥadīth records the merits of 'Alī ibn Abī Ṭālib رضي الله عنه. However, there is no disparagement in it towards Abū Bakr رضي الله عنه whatsoever. The flag was not with Abū Bakr رضي الله عنه and then given to 'Alī رضي الله عنه. Also it is not logical to single out Abū Bakr for criticism here as it would apply to all the Companions as well, including those whom Tījānī loves.

If we study the statement of the Prophet, "I will give this flag to a man whom Allah and his Messenger love. Allah will give victory at his hands," no intelligent person will claim that this is exclusive to 'Alī رضي الله عنه. It is established that the Prophet ﷺ testified on behalf of 'Abd Allāh ibn Ḥammār when he came to receive the prescribed punishment for consuming alcohol more than once and a man amongst the people said, "O Allah curse him! How often he has perpetrated what he did." The Prophet said:

1 *Muslim* with its commentary, Kitāb Faḍā'il al-Ṣaḥābah, Ḥadīth no. 2405.

لا تلعنوه فوالله ما علمت أنه يحب الله ورسوله

Do not curse him, for indeed, I know him to love Allah and His Messenger.[1]

Will any intelligent person say that it is exclusive to ʿAbd Allāh ibn Ḥammār and excludes ʿAlī? Also it is well-known that the Ṣaḥābah were great in number and therefore it is not acceptable for all matters and praises and merits and precedence to restrict itself to a single Ṣaḥābī. Rather, every Ṣaḥābī is from the close friends of Allah having a certain status by the Prophet ﷺ and there is no doubt that the one whom Allah and His Messenger ﷺ affirm his Companionship; Allah and His Messenger love him. Therefore, proving ʿAlī's superiority over Abū Bakr with this ḥadīth is without merit.

Let us not forget that it is the same Abū Hurayrah رضي الله عنه—whom Tījānī is prepared to accuse of forging aḥādīth—who narrates this ḥadīth. Has the objectivity gone on lunch?

As for his statement:

> **If Allah knew that Abū Bakr had such a high degree of faith, and that his faith exceeded the faith of all Muslims, Allah - praise be upon Him - would not have had to threaten him that He would spoil his work when he raised his voice above the Prophet's voice.[2]**

Our response:

This verse was revealed to educate the Muslims in general and the Ṣaḥābah specifically with regards to their interaction with the Prophet ﷺ. The general address of this verse indicates how it should be understood, unless some evidence emerges to specify it.

Scholars have pointed out that there is more than one *sabab al-nuzūl* (reason for revelation) for this verse? One of these is that Abū Bakr and ʿUmar رضي الله عنهما argued with each other in the presence of the Prophet ﷺ so this verse was revealed which starts with the words, "O those who believe.." Thus we learn that the verse was revealed to discipline the Ṣaḥābah and educate them and inform them of the appropriate behaviour in the Prophet's ﷺ presence.

---

1 *Ṣaḥīḥ al-Bukhārī*, Kitāb al-Ḥudūd, Bāb: Mā Yuhrah min Laʿn Shārib al-Khamr, Ḥadīth no. 6397.

2 *Then I was guided*, p. 143.

Having acknowledged this, if we apply it to Abū Bakr رضي الله عنه then it is a divine acknowledgement to his belief as Allah addressed him as "O you who believe..."

Imām Muslim records a narration that indicates it was revealed regarding Thābit ibn Qays رضي الله عنه. Anas رضي الله عنه narrates:

لما نزلت هذه الآية يَا أَيُّهَا الَّذِينَ آمَنُوا لاَ تَرْفَعُوا أَصْوَاتَكُمْ فَوْقَ صَوْتِ النَّبِيِّ إلى آخر الآية ، جلس ثابت في بيته ، قال : أنا من أهل النار . واحتبس عن النبي - صلى الله عليه وسلم - فقال النبي - صلى الله عليه وسلم - لسعد بن معاذ : " يا أبا عمرو ، ما شأن ثابت ؟ أشتكى ؟ " فقال سعد : إنه لجاري ، وما علمت له بشكوى . قال : فأتاه سعد فذكر له قول رسول الله - صلى الله عليه وسلم - فقال ثابت : أنزلت هذه الآية ، ولقد علمتم أني من أرفعكم صوتا على رسول الله - صلى الله عليه وسلم - فأنا من أهل النار . فذكر ذلك سعد للنبي - صلى الله عليه وسلم - فقال رسول الله - صلى الله عليه وسلم - : " بل هو من أهل الجنة "

When this verse, "*O those who believe, do not raise your voices above the voice of the Prophet* صلى الله عليه وسلم..." was revealed, Thābit ibn Qays remained in his house and said (to himself), "I am from the dwellers of the fire," and he avoided the Prophet صلى الله عليه وسلم. Then the Prophet صلى الله عليه وسلم asked Saʿd ibn Muʿādh (about his whereabouts) and said, "O Abū ʿAmr, what is the matter with Thābit? Is he sick?" Saʿd replied, "He is my neighbour and I am not aware that he is sick." Then Saʿd went to him and mentioned to him the statement of the Prophet صلى الله عليه وسلم and Thābit replied, "This verse was revealed and you all know that I am the loudest amongst you when addressing the Prophet and I am therefore from the inmates of the Fire." Saʿd then mentioned that to the Prophet صلى الله عليه وسلم who said, "Rather, he is of the residents of Jannah!"[1]

If this explanation applies to Thābit ibn Qays; then what about Abū Bakr? He is one of those whom the Prophet gave the glad tidings of Jannah on a number of occasions, Ḥākim narrates in his book, *al-Mustadrak*, with a complete chain leading to the Prophet صلى الله عليه وسلم:

لما نزلت على النبي صلى الله عليه و سلم إِنَّ الَّذِيْنَ يَغُضُّوْنَ أَصْوَاتَهُمْ عِنْدَ رَسُوْلِ اللّٰهِ أُولٰئِكَ الَّذِيْنَ امْتَحَنَ اللّٰهُ قُلُوْبَهُمْ لِلتَّقْوٰى قال أبو بكر رضي الله

1 *Ṣaḥīḥ Muslim* with its commentary, Kitāb al-Īmān, vol. 2, Ḥadīth no. 119.

عنه فآليت على نفسي أن لا أكلم رسول الله صلى الله عليه و سلم إلا كأخي السرار

> When the verse, "*Indeed, those who lower their voices before the Messenger—they are the ones whose hearts Allah has tested for righteousness,*" was revealed, Abū Bakr narrated, "I said to the Messenger, 'I swear by Allah, I will not speak to the Messenger of Allah except as my secretive brother.'"[1]

In summary, Abū Bakr al-Ṣiddīq was not infallible. Rather he was correct at most times and erred at others, though he was informed about his error. The Qur'ān disciplined him and the Prophet ﷺ groomed him in character. If anything, this is a compliment to him. Furthermore, it is a divine certification of his īmān as he was addressed as one who believes.

Tījānī seeks to detract from Abū Bakr by implying that he had no right to suggest candidates less worthy if he was the most deserving of the khilāfah. This is what he seeks to convey in his statement:

> **And on the Day of Saqīfah he tossed down the matter to one of the two men, ʿUmar or Abū ʿUbaydah.[2]**

Our comment:

This issue has been dealt with adequately by Ḥāfiẓ Ibn Ḥajar in his book *Fatḥ al-Bārī*. He says:

> This statement of Abū Bakr has been regarded as dubious (by some) taking into consideration that he knew he was the most rightful for the khilāfah on account of his appointment to lead the ṣalāh among other signs. The answer to that is that he was too shy to nominate himself and say, for example, "I am happy to be your leader." This, in addition to the fact that he knew neither of them would accept that responsibility. ʿUmar clearly said this (in his account of) the story and (it may be inferred that) Abū ʿUbaydah (was not interested) to a greater extent as he was lower in rank than ʿUmar in terms of merit. This is unanimously agreed upon by the Muslim Ummah. It therefore sufficed Abū Bakr to leave open for himself the option (of assuming leadership) as no one denied him that (right). In that is an indication that he was the most rightful (for the position). It is therefore clear that there was nothing in his speech

1 *Fatḥ al-Bārī*, vol. 8 p. 456.

2 *Then I was guided*, p. 143.

which may be inferred from that he was discounting himself from assuming the leadership.[1]

Ibn Ḥajar says at another place:

Some Shīʿah hold tightly to Abū Bakr's statement when he said, "I am happy for you with one of these two men," and argue that he did not believe it necessary for him to be the leader and that he did not see himself fit for the position. The answer to this (misconception) is from many angles:

a. He said that out of humility,

b. He believed it permissible for the person lower of rank to lead in the presence of the person higher in rank, therefore, if it was his right to assume the leadership then it was his right to relinquish it,

c. He knew that neither of the two of them would be pleased with taking the lead ahead of him and he hinted to the fact that if he did not enter into that (the position of khalīfah) then the matter was between the two of them alone. Therefore, at the time of his death he instated ʿUmar as the leader after him because Abū ʿUbaydah was away in jihād in al-Shām, conquering it.

(The fact that ʿUmar رضي الله عنه was not interested in the position) is known from his statement, "for me to brought forth and my neck chopped..." supports the aforementioned claim.[2]

Another basis by which we can assess Tījānī's objectivity is to consider the extent to which he attempted to discredit Abū Bakr رضي الله عنه. He went out of his way to find trivial issues to build his case. If it hasn't already become clear, this ought to be glaring evidence that Tījānī approached his research with the objective of disparaging Abū Bakr رضي الله عنه. After he collected whatever possible data he could gather he retrospectively adapted his narrative to that of an unbiased researcher who had not yet formed an opinion and was going to go where the evidence leads him. The following passage is yet another example of how trivial he can be:

Let us consider the saying: If I was taking a close companion, I would have chosen Abū Bakr. This saying is like the previous one. Where was Abū Bakr

1 *Fatḥ al-Bārī*, vol. 7 p. 38-39, Kitāb Faḍā'il al-Ṣaḥābah.

2 Ibid. Kitāb al-Ḥudūd.

> **on the day of the small Brotherhood" in Mecca before the Hijra, and on the day of the great Brotherhood" in Medinah after the Hijra; when in both of them the Messenger of Allah ﷺ chose Ali as his brother then said to him, You are my brother in this life and in the Hereafter" and did not turn to Abū Bakr, thus depriving him of the brotherhood in the Hereafter and from the close companionship. I do not wish to go on about this subject, and it is sufficient to bring the above mentioned examples which I have found in the Sunni books. As for the Shiites, they do not recognize these sayings at all, and they have their own clear proof that they were invented sometime after the death of Abū Bakr.[1]**

Our comment:

The ḥadīth of the Prophet ﷺ, "If I were to take a Khalīl, I would have taken Abū Bakr; but he is my brother and my Companion (in Islam)," has been narrated with strong chains of narration and appear abundantly in the *Ṣaḥīḥ* collections. In addition to this, it has been reported from numerous companions; Abū Hurayrah, ʿAbd Allāh ibn Masʿūd, ʿAbd Allāh ibn ʿAbbās, Abū Saʿīd al-Khudrī, ʿAbd Allāh ibn al-Zubayr among others.

Even if we assumed the argument that Abū Bakr was not mentioned when the Prophet ﷺ said to ʿAlī, "You are my friend in this life and the next," is that sufficient reason to reject the ḥadīth above, despite its multiple authentic chains?

The ḥadīth about the minor and major *Mu'ākhāt* (bonds of brotherhood), "You are my brother in the world and the Hereafter," which Tījānī rests his argument on is considered baseless. Tirmidhī, Ibn ʿAdī, and Ḥākim all narrate it from a narrator called Ḥakīm ibn Jubayr—from Jamīʿ ibn ʿUmayr.

Ḥakīm ibn Jubayr is a weak narrator, whilst Jamīʿ ibn ʿUmayr is a known fabricator about whom Ibn Ḥibbān said:

> "He is a Rāfiḍī who fabricates aḥādīth."

Ibn Numayr said about him, "He was of the most deceitful people."[2]

Ibn Taymiyyah says about the aḥādīth of the mu'ākhāt, "It appears that all of them were fabricated."[3]

---

1 *Then I was guided*, 144.

2 al-Dhahabī: *Mīzān al-Iʿtidāl*, vol. 1 p. 421, no. 1552.

3 *Minhāj al-Sunnah*, vol. 7 p. 361; Refer also to *al-Silsilah al-Mawḍūʿah* by al-Albānī vol. 1 p. 355-366.

Let us put aside what both aḥādīth say for the moment. Both aḥādīth are alleged statements made by the Prophet ﷺ. These statements have been passed down in the form of reports. How do we know whether any of the reports is correct? We have to examine the source of these reports, and how reliable they are. If we are still uncertain about whether a report could have been a result of an inadvertent error, we could attempt to find some other supporting evidence that corroborates what is carried by the said report. This process is not unfamiliar with investigators or even professional journalists who wish to verify the integrity of information they receive. I am not inferring that the correctness of the process is established because it is used by investigators or journalists with integrity. Instead they use the process because it is so efficient.

Getting back to the narrations that we are investigating, the ḥadīth about Abū Bakr رضي الله عنه has been narrated with numerous chains. All the narrators in these chains are reliable transmitters of the Sunnah. Each narration is narrated from a different companion with different chains of narrators, which further corroborates the individual chains.

The ḥadīth about ʿAlī رضي الله عنه is restricted to a common chain. One of the narrators in the chain is considered weak and has not memorized his ḥadīth all that well. Another narrator is known to lie and forge aḥādīth.

Tījānī says the first ḥadīth must be a forgery because it contradicts what is mentioned in the second. Again, I ask; is this objective investigation; or is this simply a case of prejudiced reasoning?

Then he says:

> **As for the Shiites, they do not recognize these sayings at all, and they have their own clear proof that they were invented sometime after the death of Abū Bakr.[1]**

All the evidence points to the fact that aḥādīth were invented about ʿAlī رضي الله عنه. Notwithstanding that, we the Ahl al-Sunnah acknowledge that authentic aḥādīth do exist mentioning the merits of ʿAlī رضي الله عنه. We await practical demonstration to prove that the aḥādīth we have provided about Abū Bakr رضي الله عنه were forged after his death.

1 *Then I was guided*, p. 144.

Tījānī goes on to say:

> **History has recorded many facts telling us that Ali was the most knowledgeable man among all the Companions and they used to consult him on every important matter, and we do not know of any event in which he declined to give his advice.**
>
> **Abū Bakr said, "May Allah never put me in a predicament that Abu al-Ḥasan cannot solve."[1]**

Our comment:

The Ahl al-Sunnah wal-Jamāʿah consider ʿAlī رضي الله عنه from the *Fuqahā* (jurists) among the Ṣaḥābah, although knowledge alone is not the criteria for candidacy of khilāfah. Abū Bakr رضي الله عنه consulted ʿAlī رضي الله عنه just as he consulted numerous other Ṣaḥābah رضي الله عنهم. Abū Bakr رضي الله عنه didn't consult him because he was incapable of making a decision independently; rather he valued diversity of views and had high regard for ʿAlī's contribution.

If Abū Bakr had usurped the khilāfah from ʿAlī, why would he consult him on issues affecting the Ummah? Even stranger, why would ʿAlī—if he accepted himself the divinely appointed successor to the Prophet صلى الله عليه وسلم—give counsel to Abū Bakr رضي الله عنه since that is an implicit approval?

Returning to the issue of who is considered the most knowledgeable of the Ṣaḥābah after the Prophet صلى الله عليه وسلم, the Ahl al-Sunnah agree that it was Abū Bakr then ʿUmar رضي الله عنهما. More than one scholar has quoted *ijmāʿ* (consensus) on this matter. As a matter of fact it is established that ʿAlī رضي الله عنه acquired knowledge from Abū Bakr رضي الله عنه.

This narration appears in the *Sunan* from Asmā' bint al-Ḥakīm al-Fazārī who said:

> سمعت عليا رضى الله عنه يقول كنت رجلا إذا سمعت من رسول الله صلى
> الله عليه وسلم حديثا نفعنى الله منه بما شاء أن ينفعنى وإذا حدثنى أحد من
> أصحابه استحلفته فإذا حلف لى صدقته قال وحدثنى أبو بكر وصدق أبو
> بكررضى الله عنه أنه قال سمعت رسول الله صلى الله عليه وسلم يقول ما
> من عبد يذنب ذنبا فيحسن الطهور ثم يقوم فيصلى ركعتين ثم يستغفر الله

1 *Then I was guided*, p. 146.

إلا غفر الله له ثم قرأ هذه الآية والذين إذا فعلوا فاحشة أو ظلموا أنفسهم ذكروا الله إلى آخر الآية

I heard 'Alī saying, "I was a person when I heard (something) from the Messenger ﷺ, with which Allah benefitted me in a manner that He willed me to benefit and when one of his Ṣaḥābah related a ḥadīth to me I would request him to take an oath and when he took an oath for me I believed him. Abū Bakr رضي الله عنه related a ḥadīth to me, and Abū Bakr رضي الله عنه spoke the truth, he said, 'I heard the Messenger saying that there is no slave who commits a sin then diligently performs wuḍū, then stands and prays two raka'āt (of ṣalāh), then asks Allah for His forgiveness except that Allah forgives him, then he recited this verse, 'And those who, when they commit an immorality or wrong themselves (by transgression), remember Allah and seek forgiveness for their sins.'"[1]

This is in addition to 'Alī رضي الله عنه siding with Abū Bakr in the matter of attacking those who refused to give the zakāh.

Muslim, in his *Ṣaḥīḥ*, and Aḥmad in his *Musnad*, narrate part of a lengthier ḥadīth in which the Messenger ﷺ said:

فإن يطيعوا أبا بكر وعمر يرشدوا

If they obey Abū Bakr and 'Umar they will be rightly guided.[2]

Ibn Taymiyyah says:

It has been established from Ibn 'Abbās رضي الله عنه that he used to issue legal rulings through the Book of Allah سبحانه وتعالى, if he was unable (to issue a ruling from the Book of Allah) then the Sunnah of the Prophet ﷺ, and if was unable to do that he would align his ruling with the views of Abū Bakr and 'Umar. He never did the same in relation to 'Uthmān and 'Alī. Ibn 'Abbās رضي الله عنه was the *ḥabr* (learned man) of this Ummah and the most knowledgeable of the Ṣaḥābah رضي الله عنهم during his time and he used to issue legal rulings in accordance with the views of Abū Bakr and 'Umar رضي الله عنهما giving them preference over the views of others. It has been established that the Prophet ﷺ said, "O

1 *Sunan Abū Dāwūd*, Bāb Tafrī' Abwāb al-Witr, Ḥadīth no. 1521; See also *Ṣaḥīḥ Abū Dāwūd*, Ḥadīth no. 1346.

2 *Ṣaḥīḥ Muslim* with its commentary, Kitāb al-Masājid wa Mawāḍi' al-Ṣalāh, Ḥadīth no. 681.

> Allah, grant him (Ibn ʿAbbās رضي الله عنه) understanding in the dīn and teach him the interpretation (of the Qur'ān)."[1]

This indicates the deep understanding of the dīn Abū Bakr possessed. It is not known that he contradicted the texts in any matter where he exercised his discerning judgement. There are few cases where ʿUmar and ʿAlī issued rulings that do not align with the revealed texts, perhaps on account of them not being aware of those aḥādīth.

This is part of a lengthier ḥadīth found in *Ṣaḥīḥ al-Bukhārī* and *Ṣaḥīḥ Muslim* from Abū Saʿīd al-Khudrī, who said;

وكان أبو بكر أعلمنا (أي) بالنبي

> Abū Bakr was the most knowledgeable of us (in other words, about the Prophet صلى الله عليه وسلم).[2]

Ibn Ḥazm made a valuable contribution on this topic in his invaluable work *al-Fiṣal fī al-Milal wa al-Ahwā' wa al-Niḥal*, which I feel compelled to relate in full on account of its importance:

> Abū Muḥammad says, "They (the Rāfiḍah) argue that ʿAlī was the most knowledgeable amongst them (the Ṣaḥābah). The person who says this is a liar. The knowledge of a Ṣaḥābī is only known in one of two ways, there is no third way. Firstly: Abundance of his narrations and his *fatāwā* (legal rulings). Secondly: The frequency of the Prophet's صلى الله عليه وسلم use of his services. Therefore, it is impossible and false that the Prophet صلى الله عليه وسلم used the services of a person with no knowledge. These are the greatest testimonies of knowledge and its vastness."
>
> Then we researched the matter and we found that the Prophet صلى الله عليه وسلم appointed Abū Bakr to manage the ṣalāh for the entire duration of his illness when all the senior Ṣaḥābah were present; such as ʿAlī, ʿUmar, Ibn Masʿūd, Ubay, and others besides them but he preferred him (Abū Bakr) over them. This is different to his appointing a successor when he went on a campaign as such a successor is only left in charge of the females and those unable to join the campaign. It is necessary, therefore, to know that Abū Bakr was the

---

1 *Minhāj al-Sunnah*, vol. 7 p. 503.

2 *Ṣaḥīḥ al-Bukhārī*, Kitāb al-Ṣalāh, Bāb: al-Khawkah wa al-Mamarr fī al-Masjid, Ḥadīth no. 454; Refer also to *Minhāj al-Sunnah*, vol. 7 p. 507.

most knowledgeable with regards to the ṣalāh and its rulings and it is the foundation of the dīn.

We found the Prophet صلى الله عليه وسلم also using him (Abū Bakr) in matters of zakāh and this must mean that he had knowledge of zakāh, (knowledge) similar to others besides him from amongst the scholars of the Ṣaḥābah, not less but perhaps more, or perhaps not more as the Prophet صلى الله عليه وسلم employed others besides him (to fulfil that duty) as well. That being said the Prophet صلى الله عليه وسلم only employed a person knowledgeable of the duty he was entrusted with. The proof of our claim concerning the completeness of Abū Bakr's knowledge with regards to zakāh is that the aḥādīth relating to zakāh, the most authentic of them and the one practiced upon and not opposed is the ḥadīth of Abū Bakr running through the transmitter, ʿUmar. As for when the ḥadīth runs through the transmitter, ʿAlī, then there is some confusion in it and in those narrations is information which the scholars have neglected altogether such as the ruling that for every twenty five camels, five sheep are given in zakāh.

We also found the Prophet صلى الله عليه وسلم using Abū Bakr's services with regards to leading the ḥajj. Therefore, it is correct to say, by way of necessity, that Abū Bakr was the most knowledgeable of all the Ṣaḥābah with regards to the rites of ḥajj. And the aforementioned duties are the pillars of Islam.

Then we found the Prophet صلى الله عليه وسلم instating him as the leader of military campaigns. Therefore, it is correct to say that he had knowledge of the laws of jihād similar to the other leaders whom the Prophet صلى الله عليه وسلم instated as leaders of jihād, as the Prophet صلى الله عليه وسلم would not utilise the services of a person for a particular duty unless he was knowledgeable of it. Therefore, Abū Bakr had knowledge of jihād in the same way that ʿAlī had (knowledge of jihād) and all other leaders of military campaigns, not more and not less.

Therefore, it is correct to say that Abū Bakr was ahead of Alī and other than him in terms of knowledge of the ṣalāh, zakāh, and ḥajj; and he was similar to him in relation to the knowledge of jihād. This is the core of knowledge.

Then we found the Prophet صلى الله عليه وسلم keeping Abū Bakr in his company, and in his private conversations, and his travels, and in his residence and, consequently, Abū Bakr witnessed his issuing of laws more than what ʿAlī witnessed. Therefore, it is correct, by way of necessity, that Abū Bakr was more knowledgeable about it.

> Is there any knowledge remaining except that Abū Bakr is the leader who cannot be caught or a participant therein who cannot be beaten? Therefore, their claim is futile, and all praise is for Allah سُبْحَانَهُ وَتَعَالَىٰ.

Then he says:

> Indeed, we should not be suspected of intending to lower any Ṣaḥābī from his status and we should not be suspected of intending to raise anyone above his status. If we divert away from ʿAlī, may Allah سُبْحَانَهُ وَتَعَالَىٰ protect us from that, we tread the path of the Khawārij and indeed Allah has purified us from such fanaticism, and if we become extreme in our partisanship towards him we tread the path of the Shīʿah, and indeed Allah has protected us from this falsehood and fanaticism. Therefore, others besides us have either become disillusioned with him or fanatical about him and they are the ones who should be suspected either in his favour or against him.
>
> After all this it is impossible for the person subscribing to Islam to resist the evidence of the Ṣaḥābī's abundance of knowledge on account of the Messenger صَلَّى ٱللَّٰهُ عَلَيْهِ وَسَلَّمَ utilising those whom he utilised from amongst the Ṣaḥābah for what he utilised them for from the matters of the dīn.
>
> If the Rāfiḍah say that the Messenger صَلَّى ٱللَّٰهُ عَلَيْهِ وَسَلَّمَ made ʿAlī responsible for the *Akhmās* (the spoils of war) and for the governance of Yemen, we say to them: Yes, however, Abū Bakr's witnessing the Messenger's صَلَّى ٱللَّٰهُ عَلَيْهِ وَسَلَّمَ rulings is superior in knowledge and more established than what was by ʿAlī in Yemen. Indeed, the Prophet صَلَّى ٱللَّٰهُ عَلَيْهِ وَسَلَّمَ instated Abū Bakr رَضِيَ ٱللَّٰهُ عَنْهُ as leader of military campaigns in which there was Akhmās. Therefore, Abū Bakr's knowledge was equal to ʿAlī's knowledge without doubt as the Prophet صَلَّى ٱللَّٰهُ عَلَيْهِ وَسَلَّمَ did not select someone for a duty except that he was knowledgeable about what he appointed him to do. It is correct that Abū Bakr and ʿUmar issued fatāwā during the Messenger's صَلَّى ٱللَّٰهُ عَلَيْهِ وَسَلَّمَ lifetime, with the Messenger's صَلَّى ٱللَّٰهُ عَلَيْهِ وَسَلَّمَ knowledge, and it is impossible that the Prophet صَلَّى ٱللَّٰهُ عَلَيْهِ وَسَلَّمَ would allow them to do that except if they were more knowledgeable than those besides them. Indeed, he appointed Muʿādh ibn Jabal and Abū Mūsā al-Ashʿarī along with ʿAlī over the governance of Yemen. Therefore, ʿAlī had many partners in this trait including Abū Bakr and ʿUmar. Then we find Abū Bakr being unique in the majority of the fields previously mentioned.
>
> This Rāfiḍī says that ʿAlī was the best reciter of the Qur'ān amongst the Ṣaḥābah. This is slander from a number of angles. Firstly, it is a criticism

against the Prophet ﷺ as he said, "The best reader amongst you should lead the ṣalāh. If they are equal in their recitation then the most learned. If they are equal in their knowledge as well then the one earliest in hijrah," then we find the Prophet ﷺ giving preference to Abū Bakr with regards to leading the ṣalāh for the duration of his illness even though ʿAlī was present and the Prophet ﷺ saw him morning and evening. Despite that, he did not see anyone more fit for it than Abū Bakr. Therefore, it is correct to say that he was the best reader amongst them, the most learned amongst them, and the earliest amongst them in hijrah.

Sometimes the person who has not memorised the entire Qur'ān from memory is a better reciter than the person who memorised the entire Qur'ān, as he is better in his pronunciation of the words and better in terms of the pace at which he recites. This is on the premise that Abū Bakr, ʿUmar, and ʿAlī, none of them completed the memorisation of the entire Qur'ān. However, it is necessary to believe that Abū Bakr was a better reciter than ʿAlī because of his preferring Abū Bakr despite the presence of ʿAlī. The Prophet ﷺ would not have preferred for the *imāmah* (leading of the ṣalāh) the person with lesser knowledge in terms of reciting over the person with greater knowledge in terms of recitation and he would not have given preference to the person with lesser knowledge of fiqh over the person with greater knowledge of fiqh. The Rāfiḍah's efforts from this angle, therefore, are also null and void, and all praise is for Allah سُبْحَانَهُ وَتَعَالَىٰ.[1]

From this we come to realize the superiority of Abū Bakr in knowledge and his deep understanding of the religion.

Tījānī's petty arguments continue:

Abū Bakr was once asked about the meaning of the word "Abb" [herbage] in the words of Allah, the Most High:

وَفَاكِهَةً وَأَبًّا مَّتَاعًا لَّكُمْ وَلِأَنْعَامِكُمْ

And gardens of dense shrubbery. And fruit and grass

Abū Bakr replied, "Which sky would give me shade, and which land would carry me if I say something I do not know about the Book of Allah."[2]

1 Ibn Ḥaz:m *Al-Fiṣal fī al-Milal wa al-Niḥal*, vol. 4 p. 212-215.

2 *Then I was guided*, p. 147.

Our comment:

I am going to refer to the *Tafsīr al-Qur'ān al-ʿAẓīm* by Ibn Kathīr to clarify this matter. This particular narration is transmitted from Ibrāhīm al-Taymī from Abū Bakr; and the chain of transmission between Ibrāhīm and Abū Bakr is interrupted.

It should not be understood from this ḥadīth that Abū Bakr did not know the meaning of the word *Abb* as its meaning is very clear in that it refers to the produce of the earth as Allah says:

فَأَنۢبَتۡنَا فِيهَا حَبّٗا وَعِنَبٗا وَقَضۡبٗا وَزَيۡتُونٗا وَنَخۡلٗا وَحَدَآئِقَ غُلۡبٗا وَفَٰكِهَةٗ وَأَبّٗا
مَّتَٰعٗا لَّكُمۡ وَلِأَنۡعَٰمِكُمۡ

> *And caused to grow within it grain; and grapes and herbage. And olive and palm trees. And gardens of dense shrubbery. And fruit and grass —enjoyment (i.e. provision) for you and your grazing livestock.*

However, he could not specify the type of produce. In other words, he was unable to describe its form, its type, etc. This is what he meant by that statement.

It is similar to what Anas رضي الله عنه narrates about ʿUmar رضي الله عنه that he recited on the mimbar:

وَفَٰكِهَةٗ وَأَبّٗا

> And he said, "*This fruit we know; but what is al-Abb?*" Then he said to himself, "This is burdening oneself, O ʿUmar!"[1]

Therefore, some exegetes offer the meaning 'produce from the earth' as the general meaning for the word al-Abb, without specifying whether fruit, vegetable, herb etc., is implied.

> From Mujāhid, Saʿīd ibn Jubayr, and Abū Mālik (they say), "Al-Abb is *al-Kala* (grass)."

---

1 Bayhaqī in *Shuʿab al-Īmān*, Bāb fī Taʿẓīm al-Qur'ān, p. 424 with a reliable sanad; and Ḥākim in *al-Mustadrak*, vol. 2 p. 514, he says: "This is authentic according to the standards of Shaykhayn but they did not narrate it." Al-Dhahabī agreed with him.

> Mujāhid, Ḥasan, Qatādah, and Ibn Zayd say, "Abb is for domesticated animals what fruit is for human beings."
>
> From ʿAṭā, "Everything that grows on the face of the earth is Abb."
>
> Ḍaḥḥāk says, "Everything which the earth produces besides fruit is Abb."[1]

The meaning, as is clear, (of the word Abb) is "what grows on the earth" but the Ṣaḥābah did not specify it in terms of its type. This does not prove the absence of knowledge. If the Prophet صلى الله عليه وسلم had to clarify it by specifying its type then the Ṣaḥābah would have known about it. It is therefore, interpreted to mean everything which grows on the earth.

6. Tījānī criticises Abū Bakr for applying the Law of Allah

Tījānī says:

> **The second incident that involved Abu Bakr during the early days of his caliphate, which the Sunni historians recorded, was his disagreement with the nearest of all people to him, Umar ibn al-Khattāb. The incident revolves around Abu Bakr's decision to fight those who refused to pay Zakat [alms] and kill them, but Umar protested and advised him not to fight them because he had heard the Messenger of Allah صلى الله عليه وسلم saying: I have been ordered to fight the people until they say, "There is no other god but Allah and Muhammad is the Messenger of Allah." And he who says it can keep his wealth to himself and I have no right to his [blood], and he is accountable to Allah.**
>
> **This is a text cited by Muslim in his Ṣaḥīḥ: "The Messenger of Allah صلى الله عليه وسلم gave the flag to Ali on the Day of Khaybar, and Ali said, "O Messenger of Allah صلى الله عليه وسلم, what am I fighting them for?" The Messenger of Allah صلى الله عليه وسلم replied, "Fight them until they testify that there is no other god but Allah and that Muhammad is the Messenger of Allah صلى الله عليه وسلم, and if they do that then they will prevent you from killing them and taking their wealth, except by justice, and they will be accountable to Allah."**
>
> **But Abu Bakr was not satisfied with this tradition and said, "By Allah, I will fight those who differentiate between the prayers and Zakat because Zakat is justly charged on wealth." And also said: "By Allah if they refuse me a rope which they used to give to the Messenger of Allah صلى الله عليه وسلم I will fight them for it." After that Umar ibn al-Khattab was satisfied and said, "As soon as I saw Abu Bakr determined I felt very pleased."**

---

1 *Tafsīr Ibn Kathīr*, vol. 4 p. 504.

I do not know how Allah could please somebody who is preventing the tradition of the Prophet ﷺ.[1]

Our comment:

Tījānī objects to Abū Bakr's رضي الله عنه decision to fight those who refused to give their zakāh. The basis of Tījānī's criticism rests on the ḥadīth in which the Prophet ﷺ instructs ʿAlī رضي الله عنه to fight the Jewish tribes in the forts of Khaybar until they testify to the Oneness of Allah and the Prophethood of Muḥammad ﷺ; if they oblige in this then their lives and wealth become sacred and may not be taken except by valid cause. The question that needs to be asked is what did the Prophet ﷺ mean by this?

Context of the ḥadīth cited by Tījānī

If we consider that this was a military engagement wherein the dominant party may claim the spoils, then the Prophet ﷺ is simply defining the status of those who accept Islam among them. Those who accept Islam will be allowed to hold on to their possessions; whereas the possessions and wealth of those who do not accept Islam will form part of the spoils and will be distributed among the Muslims according to the discretion of the Muslim leader.

Tījānī appears to have suddenly grown a conscience—despite his wanton rejection of aḥādīth throughout his book—and objects to Abū Bakr's decision because it goes against the ḥadīth of the Prophet ﷺ.

I do not know how Allah opens the hearts of a people by their opposing the sunnah of their Prophet...

Fighting those who refuse to give zakāh

The decision to fight those who refused to give zakāh applies to a completely different set of circumstances. This is a situation where people who have already accepted the obligations of Islam refuse to uphold some of its most fundamental tenets.

We come to realise the soundness of Abū Bakr's decision due to it aligning with the what is mentioned in the Qur'ān as well as the established Sunnah; this in addition to the subsequent Ijmāʿ.

---

1 *Then I was guided*, p. 153-154.

Allah says in Sūrah al-Tawbah:

فَإِذَا انْسَلَخَ الْأَشْهُرُ الْحُرُمُ فَاقْتُلُوا الْمُشْرِكِيْنَ حَيْثُ وَجَدْتُّمُوْهُمْ وَخُذُوْهُمْ
وَاحْصُرُوْهُمْ وَاقْعُدُوْا لَهُمْ كُلَّ مَرْصَدٍ ۚ فَإِنْ تَابُوْا وَأَقَامُوْا الصَّلٰوةَ وَاٰتَوُا
الزَّكٰوةَ فَخَلُّوْا سَبِيْلَهُمْ ۚ إِنَّ اللّٰهَ غَفُوْرٌ رَحِيْمٌ

And when the sacred months have passed, then kill the polytheists wherever you find them and capture them and besiege them and sit in wait for them at every place of ambush. But if they should repent, establish ṣalāh, and give zakāh, let them (go) on their way. Indeed, Allah is All Forgiving and All Merciful.[1]

فَإِنْ تَابُوْا وَأَقَامُوا الصَّلٰوةَ وَاٰتَوُا الزَّكٰوةَ فَإِخْوَانُكُمْ فِي الدِّيْنِ ۗ وَنُفَصِّلُ
الْاٰيٰتِ لِقَوْمٍ يَّعْلَمُوْنَ

But if they repent, establish ṣalāh, and give zakāh, then they are your brothers in religion; and We detail the verses for a people who know.[2]

Sunnī Explanation

In these two verses the prerequisites for atonement are explained. The basic tenets which define the conditions of entering into Islam are the establishment of the ṣalāh and payment of zakāh. ʿAbd Allāh ibn Masʿūd رضي الله عنه says:

> You have been commanded with the establishment of the ṣalāh and the payment of the zakāh and not to distinguish between the two. The person who does not pay the zakāh has no ṣalāh.

Similarly, ʿAbd Allāh ibn ʿAbbās رضي الله عنهما explains:

> "But if they repent, establish ṣalāh, and give zakāh," this verse forbids the blood of the People of the Qiblah (the Muslims).[3]

This clearly indicates that their failure to uphold the prayer and payment of zakāh is grounds to fight them, until they re-establish it completely. This is exactly how Abū Bakr رضي الله عنه chose to deal with those who refused to pay zakāh.

1 Sūrah al-Tawbah: 5.

2 Sūrah al-Tawbah: 11.

3 *Tafsīr al-Ṭabarī*, vol. 6 p. 328.

In his explanation of this verse Ibn Kathīr says:

> For that reason, Abū Bakr al-Ṣiddīq relied on this and other honourable verses as proof for fighting those who refrained from paying the zakāh. These verses allowed fighting people unless and until they embrace Islam and implement its rulings and obligations. He also alerted those he argued against about the hierarchy of actions; that the noblest after the shahādatayn is the ṣalāh which is the right of Allah, and after it the payment of the zakāh, which is a benefit for the poor and the needy, and it is the noblest of deeds connected to the creation. It is for that reason Allah often combines between the ṣalāh and the zakāh.[1]

ʿAbd al-Raḥmān ibn Zayd says:

> Ṣalāh and zakāh were made compulsory together. They were not separated from one another. (Then he recited):
>
> فَإِنْ تَابُوْا وَأَقَامُوا الصَّلٰوةَ وَاٰتَوُا الزَّكٰوةَ فَإِخْوَانُكُمْ فِي الدِّيْنِ
>
> *But if they repent, establish ṣalāh, and give zakāh, then they are your brothers in religion.*[2]
>
> Allah refuses to accept the ṣalāh except with zakāh. (Then he said) May Allah shower His Mercy upon Abū Bakr; there was no one more knowledgeable than him.[3]

In the *Ṣaḥīḥayn* there is a ḥadīth from Ibn ʿUmar رضي الله عنهما:

> أمرت أن أقاتل الناس حتى يشهدوا أن لا إله إلا الله وأن محمدا رسول الله ويقيموا الصلاة ويؤتوا الزكاة فإذا فعلوا ذلك عصموا مني دماءهم وأموالهم إلا بحق الإسلام وحسابهم على الله
>
> I was instructed to fight the people until they bear witness that there is no God but Allah and that Muḥammad is the Messenger of Allah, and they establish the ṣalāh and pay the zakāh. When they do that they have protected their blood and their wealth except with the right of Islam and their judgement is with Allah.[4]

---

1 *Tafsīr Ibn Kathīr*, vol. 2 p. 349.

2 Sūrah al-Tawbah: 11.

3 *Tafsīr al-Ṭabarī*, vol. 6 p. 349.

4 *Ṣaḥīḥ al-Bukhārī*, Kitāb al-Īmān, Bāb: fa in Tābū wa Aqāmū al-Ṣalāh wa Ātū al-Zakāh fa Khallū Sabīlahum vol. 1, Ḥadīth no. 25; *Ṣaḥīḥ Muslim* with its commentary, Kitāb al-Īmān, Ḥadīth no. 22.

This authentic ḥadīth clearly proves that sanctity of blood and wealth is a consequence of true īmān. It further demonstrates that true īmān is only realised with the establishment of ṣalāh and payment of zakāh. Therefore, when people refuse to pay the zakāh they deserve to be fought, thus it will be taken from those whose obligation is to give and it will be given to those entitled to it. This is what Abū Bakr رضي الله عنه decided to do; and this is what Tījānī condemns him for.

Shīʿī Explanation

It appears that Tījānī is unaware of the view of the Twelver Shīʿah in this matter. It is evident from what is recorded in their books that zakāh is exactly like ṣalāh. Either that, or Tījānī has merely condemned Abū Bakr رضي الله عنه without grounds. The underlying relationship between ṣalāh and zakāh as understood from the Shīʿī books support the position taken by Abū Bakr رضي الله عنه.

Muḥammad al-Ḥurr al-ʿĀmilī, one of the senior scholars in the Shīʿī tradition, says in his book, *Wasā'il al-Shīʿah*:

> From Abū Jaʿfar (al-Bāqir) and Abū ʿAbd Allāh (al-Ṣādiq), they said, "Allah made zakāh compulsory along with ṣalāh."[1]

Al-Kulaynī produced another narration from Abū Jaʿfar:

> Indeed, Allah combines the (ruling of) zakāh with ṣalāh. He says, "Establish the ṣalāh and give the zakāh."[2] Therefore, whoever establishes the ṣalāh but has not given the zakāh has not established the ṣalāh.[3]

Muḥammad ibn ʿAlī ibn Bābuwayh al-Qummī, referred to as al-Ṣadūq; whose book, *Man Lā Yaḥḍuru al-Faqīh*, is considered one of the four books upon which Imāmiyyah law and belief is based, writes:

> From Abū ʿAbd Allāh (al-Ṣādiq), "Whoever refuses to give an inch of zakāh is not a Mu'min and he is not a Muslim. That is what is meant by Allah's words:
>
> حَتَّىٰٓ إِذَا جَآءَ أَحَدَهُمُ الْمَوْتُ قَالَ رَبِّ ارْجِعُونِ لَعَلِّيٓ أَعْمَلُ صَالِحًا فِيمَا تَرَكْتُ

1 *Wasā'il al-Shīʿah ilā Taḥṣīl Masā'il al-Sharīʿah* by ʿĀmilī, vol. 6 p. 5-11, Kitāb al-Zakāh, Abwāb mā Tajib fīhi al-Zakāh wa mā Tustaḥabb fīhi; Refer also to *Man Lā Yaḥḍuruhū al-Faqīh*, vol. 2 p. 11.

2 Sūrah al-Baqarah: 43.

3 al-Kulaynī: *Furūʿ al-Kāfī*, Bāb Manʿ al-Zakāh, vol. 3 p. 503, Ḥadīth no. 23.

> *Until, when death comes to one of them, he says, My Lord, send me back; that I might do righteousness in that which I left behind.*[1]

In another narration it appears, "No ṣalāh of his is accepted."[2]

Abū Jaʿfar (al-Bāqir) said:

> One day while the Prophet was in the Masjid he said, "You stand, and you stand, and you stand," until he hauled out five people. He then said, "Leave our Masjid and do not perform ṣalāh in it while you do not give the zakāh!"[3]

From Abū Baṣīr—from Abū ʿAbd Allāh (al-Ṣādiq):

> Whoever refuses to give a *qirāṭ* (a dry measurement) of zakāh then let him die either as a Jew or a Christian.[4]

But Abū ʿAbd Allāh does not stop there. Rather, he explicitly permits such a person's execution. It is narrated by way of Abān ibn Taghlib from al-Ṣādiq that he said:

> There are two bloods in Islam which are permissible by Allah and no one will judge concerning them (the two bloods) until Allah sends our al-Qā'im from the Ahl al-Bayt. When Allah sends our al-Qā'im from the Ahl al-Bayt he will judge them in accordance with the law of Allah. He will stone the *zānī muḥṣan* (the married person who committed zinā) and he will smite the neck of those who refuse to pay the zakāh.[5]

Tījānī's Conundrum

Tījānī is left in an awkward position. The Shīʿah say that *al-Qā'im* (their Mahdī) will smite the necks of those who refuse to pay zakāh. Abū Bakr decided that those who desisted discharging their zakāh were to be fought against, not necessarily killed, until they decided to pay. Despite his claims of examining the matter from both perspectives, Tījānī's condemnation is unsubstantiated either way. No matter how hard Tījānī tries to mask his hatred towards the Ṣaḥābah, the stench of his bias is unmistakeable.

---

1 Sūrah al-Mu'min: 99.

2 Ibn Bābuwayh al-Qummī: *Man Lā Yaḥḍuru al-Faqīh*, vol. 2 p. 12-13, Bāb Mā Jā' fī Māniʿi al-Zakāh.

3 Ibid. vol. 2 p. 13.

4 *Furūʿ al-Kāfī*, vol. 3 p. 502.

5 *Man Lā Yaḥḍuruh al-Faqīh*, vol. 2 p. 12; *Furūʿ al-Kāfī*, vol. 3 p. 500.

ʿUmar's Questioning

ʿUmar's رضي الله عنه initial objection against Abū Bakr رضي الله عنه is on account of him not realising the graveness of the situation immediately; as well as the basis for Abū Bakr's رضي الله عنه decision. Therefore, he said, "How can you fight the people whilst the Messenger صلى الله عليه وسلم said, 'I have been instructed to fight the people until they say there is none worthy of worship except Allah and Muḥammad is the Messenger of Allah. Whoever says there is none worthy of worship except Allah and Muḥammad is the Messenger of Allah, he has protected from me his wealth, blood, and life; except by valid cause and his judgement is with Allah'?"

ʿUmar's رضي الله عنه initial assessment of the situation was based on the general expression of the ḥadīth without considering the words, "except by valid cause". Abū Bakr made him realise that to fight those who differentiate between ṣalāh and zakāh is because zakāh is the right of the wealth; a valid cause. He equated the zakāh with the ṣalāh.

Abū Bakr's understanding is further supported by the ḥadīth narrated by Ibn ʿUmar رضي الله عنهما:

> I was instructed to fight the people until they bear witness that there is no God but Allah and that Muḥammad is the Messenger of Allah, and they establish the ṣalāh and pay the zakāh. When they do that they have protected their blood and their wealth except with the right of Islam and their judgement is with Allah.[1]

Notice the words with which it ends, "except by the right of Islam". The right of Islam, which guarantees the protection of blood and wealth, is a consequence of establishing of ṣalāh and discharging zakāh. Once ʿUmar رضي الله عنه realised the premise of Abū Bakr's رضي الله عنه decision he retracted his view and supported Abū Bakr رضي الله عنه when he said, "By Allah, as soon as I realised that Allah has expanded the chest of Abū Bakr to fight them, I knew that it was the truth."[2]

The ḥadīth of ʿAlī رضي الله عنه on the Day of Khaybar is understood in a similar manner. The practise of the Ṣaḥābah further endorses the preponderance of Abū Bakr's رضي الله عنه decision.

---

1 *Ṣaḥīḥ al-Bukhārī*, Kitāb al-Īmān, Bāb: fa in Tābū wa Aqāmū al-Ṣalāh wa Ātū al-Zakāh fa Khallū Sabīlahum vol. 1, Ḥadīth no. 25; *Ṣaḥīḥ Muslim* with its commentary, Kitāb al-Īmān, Ḥadīth no. 22.

2 *Ṣaḥīḥ al-Bukhārī*, Kitāb al-Iʿtiṣām bi al-Kitāb wa al-Sunnah, Ḥadīth no. 6854.

ʿUmar رضي الله عنه displayed his humility by retracting his objections when he realised the error in his judgement. Some 'objective researchers' have no idea how absurd their arguments are. Blinded by their said 'impartiality', these researchers misconstrue verses from the Qur'ān to support their outrageous presumptions:

> **This interpretation was used to justify their fight against Muslims although Allah had prohibited making war against them, and Allah said in His Glorious Book:**
>
> يَاأَيُّهَا الَّذِينَ آمَنُوا إِذَا ضَرَبْتُمْ فِي سَبِيلِ اللَّهِ فَتَبَيَّنُوا وَلَا تَقُولُوا لِمَنْ أَلْقَى إِلَيْكُمُ السَّلَامَ لَسْتَ مُؤْمِنًا تَبْتَغُونَ عَرَضَ الْحَيَاةِ الدُّنْيَا فَعِنْدَ اللَّهِ مَغَانِمُ كَثِيرَةٌ كَذَلِكَ كُنْتُمْ مِنْ قَبْلُ فَمَنَّ اللَّهُ عَلَيْكُمْ فَتَبَيَّنُوا إِنَّ اللَّهَ كَانَ بِمَا تَعْمَلُونَ خَبِيرًا
>
> ***O you who have believed, when you go forth (to fight) in the cause of Allah, investigate; and do not say to one who gives you (a greeting of) peace, "you are not a believer," aspiring for the goods of worldly life; for with Allah are many acquisitions. You (yourselves) were like that before; then Allah conferred His favour (i.e. guidance) upon you, so investigate. Indeed Allah is ever, with what you do, acquainted***[1]

Our comment:

Tījānī's complete disregard for the sabab al-nuzūl is a clear indication of where his argument will be going. He does not disappoint in that he rarely strays from the trick of connecting isolated incidents and pulling an objection out of his hat.

The circumstances surrounding the revelation of this verse, which will elaborate on its original context, has been narrated by ʿAbd Allāh ibn ʿAbbās رضي الله عنهما in *Ṣaḥīḥ al-Bukhārī*:

> ʿAbd Allāh ibn ʿAbbās says, "There was a man (standing) in his property. The Muslims met him and he greeted them but they killed him and took his property. Thereupon Allah revealed, 'aspiring for the goods of worldly life,' referring to that property."[2]

1 Sūrah al-Nisā': 94.

2 *Ṣaḥīḥ al-Bukhārī*, Kitāb al-Tafāsīr, Sūrah al-Nisā', Ḥadīth no. 4315.

As is evident this verse refers to a case where a person had been killed unjustly due to them being confused about the nature of his greeting, assuming it to be a mere ploy to save himself and not sincere. It is a generous stretch of the text to insinuate that it applies to Abū Bakr's رضي الله عنه decision to fight those who refused to give zakāh. Bear in mind that fighting is not a death sentence. Abū Bakr رضي الله عنه permitted fighting them, not because they were unbelievers but on account of them forsaking one of the duties of Islam. Those who refuse to pay the zakāh are rebels and it is necessary to take zakāh from them by force.

Abū Bakr رضي الله عنه did not instruct the Ṣaḥābah to kill them on grounds of heresy as was the case with Musaylamah al-Kadhdhāb and al-Aswad al-ʿAnsī. The latter were those whom Abū Bakr considered unbelievers and subsequently took military action against them which resulted in their families becoming slaves as part of the spoils. ʿAlī رضي الله عنه acknowledged the legitimacy of these wars when he took a slave girl captured from the Banū Ḥanīfah tribe. She bore him a son, Muḥammad, who is sometimes referred to as Muḥammad ibn al-Ḥanafiyyah.

There is no evidence to suggest that Abū Bakr رضي الله عنه fought those who refused to pay the zakāh for worldly gain. Rather, he fought them to preserve the integrity of this dīn.

With surgical precision, Tījānī carefully carves out a new argument. There are no surprises that this argument is born out of a predisposed attitude of scepticism towards Abū Bakr رضي الله عنه. Tījānī says:

> **Those who refused to give Abu Bakr their Zakat did not deny its necessity, but they only delayed it to investigate the matter. The Shiites say that these people were surprised by the succession of Abu Bakr, and some of them had been present with the Messenger of Allah صلى الله عليه وسلم at the Farewell Pilgrimage and had heard the text in which he mentioned Ali ibn Abī Ṭālib. Therefore they decided to wait for a while until they obtained a clarification as to what had happened, but Abu Bakr wanted to silence them lest they spoke the truth. Because I do not reason with nor protest against what the Shiites say, I will leave this issue to somebody who is interested in it.[1]**

Our comment:

1 *Then I was guided*, 154.

Why is that Tījānī, who had time to research petty issues, even from books that are falsely ascribed to authors, fails to produce even a shred of evidence to support his ridiculous claim that those who refused to pay the zakāh delayed in doing so in order to verify the matter but were surprised by the khilāfah of Abū Bakr رضي الله عنه? The vast extent of Tījānī's imagination allows for his book to be published as a work of fiction!

He goes on to say:

> **However, I should not forget to note here that the Messenger of Allah صلى الله عليه وسلم had an encounter with Tha'alabah who asked him repeatedly to pray for him to be rich and he promised Allah to give alms. The Messenger of Allah صلى الله عليه وسلم prayed for him and Tha'alabah became so rich that his sheep and camels filled al-Medinah, and he started to neglect his duties and stopped attending the Friday Prayers. When the Messenger of Allah صلى الله عليه وسلم sent some officials to collect the Zakat, he refused to give them anything saying that it was a Jiziah [head tax on free non-Muslims under Muslim rule] or similar to it, but the Messenger of Allah صلى الله عليه وسلم did not fight him nor did he order his killing, and Allah revealed the following verse about him:**
>
> وَمِنْهُم مَّنْ عَاهَدَ اللَّهَ لَئِنْ آتَانَا مِن فَضْلِهِ لَنَصَّدَّقَنَّ وَلَنَكُونَنَّ مِنَ الصَّالِحِينَ فَلَمَّا آتَاهُم مِّن فَضْلِهِ بَخِلُوا بِهِ وَتَوَلَّوا وَّهُم مُّعْرِضُونَ
>
> ***And among them are those who made a covenant with Allah, (saying), if He should give us from His bounty, we will surely spend in charity, and we will surely be among the righteous. But when He gave them from His bounty, they were stingy with it and turned away while they refused.***[1]
>
> **After the revelation of the above Quranic verse. Tha'alabah came to the Messenger of Allah صلى الله عليه وسلم crying and asked him to accept his Zakat, but the Messenger of Allah refused to accept it, according to the story.**
>
> **If Abu Bakr and Umar were following the tradition of the Messenger صلى الله عليه وسلم why did they allow the killing of all these innocent Muslims just because they refused to pay the Zakat?**
>
> **As for those apologists who were trying to correct Abu Bakr's mistake when he interpreted the Zakat as a just tax on wealth, there is no excuse for them**

1 Sūrah al-Tawbah: 75-76.

> **nor for Abu Bakr after considering the story of Tha'alabah who withheld the Zakat and thought of it as "Jiziah". Who knows, perhaps Abu Bakr persuaded his friend Umar to kill those who refused to pay the Zakat because otherwise their call would have spread throughout the Islamic world to revive al-Ghadir's text in which Ali was confirmed as successor [to the Messenger of Allah ﷺ]. Thus Umar ibn al-Khattab wanted to fight them, and it was he who threatened to kill and burn those who remained in Fatimah's house in order to extract the acclamation from them for his friend.[1]**

Our comment:

The truncated version of this narration provided by Tījānī conveniently omits the following passages:

> Tha'labah came to Abū Bakr after his appointment and said, "You know my position by the Messenger and my position amongst the Anṣār, so accept my zakāh."
>
> Abū Bakr said to him, "The Prophet did not accept it from you. Should I accept it from you?"
>
> Abū Bakr passed on and he did not accept it.
>
> When 'Umar became the khalīfah Tha'labah came to him and said, "O Amīr al-Mu'minīn, accept my zakāh!"
>
> 'Umar said, "The Prophet ﷺ did not accept it and Abū Bakr did not accept it. Do you expect that I would accept it?"
>
> He passed away and he did not accept it.
>
> Then 'Uthmān became the khalīfah and he came to him, and asked him to accept his zakāh.
>
> 'Uthmān said, "The Prophet ﷺ did not accept it, Abū Bakr did not accept it and 'Umar did not accept it. Should I accept it?"
>
> Tha'labah later died during the khilāfah of 'Uthmān.[2]

There is no prize for guessing why Tījānī concealed this part of the narration. Instead we will save him the trouble since this narration is weak, both in terms of

1 *Then I was guided*, p. 154-155.

2 Ṭabarānī: *Al-Mu'jam al-Kabīr*, vol. 8 p. 218, Ḥadīth no. 7873.

its chain of transmission and irregularities in the texts. Therefore, it is inadmissible as proof.

Let us begin by pointing out the flaws in the chain of transmission.

Central to the chain of this narration are two significant narrators: ʿAlī ibn Yazīd al-Alhānī and ʿAmr ibn ʿUbayd Abū ʿUthmān al-Baṣrī. Both of them are discredited as narrators by the experts in this science. These are the comments made by ḥadīth experts regarding ʿAlī ibn Yazīd:

> Ibn Ḥajar says, "He is weak."[1]
>
> Al-Bukhārī says, "He is *munkar al-ḥadīth* (censured for transmitting uncorroborated narrations)."
>
> Al-Nasā'ī says, "He is not reliable."
>
> Abū Zurʿah says, "He is not a strong transmitter."
>
> Al-Dāraquṭnī says, "He is *matrūk* (suspected of ḥadīth forgery)."[2]
>
> Yaḥyā ibn Maʿīn says, "'ʿAlī ibn Yazīd—from Qāsim—from Abū ʿUmāmah, they (the narrators from this chain) are all weak."
>
> Yaʿqūbī says, "He is weak in ḥadīth. He transmits many anomalies."
>
> Ḥākim says, "He is lenient in ḥadīth."[3]

As for ʿAmr ibn ʿUbayd:

> Ibn Maʿīn says about him, "His ḥadīth is not to be recorded."
>
> Nasā'ī says, "*Matrūk al-ḥadīth* (suspected of ḥadīth forgery)."
>
> Ayyūb and Yūnus say, "He lies."[4]
>
> Aḥmad ibn Ḥambal, "He is not someone from whom ḥadīth ought to be narrated."
>
> Yaḥyā ibn Maʿīn, "He is no good." This statement has very damaging implications by Ibn Maʿīn.

---

1 Ibn Ḥajar: *Taqrīb al-Tahdhīb*, vol. 1, biography no. 4883.

2 Dhahabī: *Mīzān al-Iʿtidāl*, vol. 3 p. 161, biography no. 5966.

3 Mizzī: *Tahdhīb al-Kamāl fī Asmāʾ al-Rijāl*, vol. 21, biography no. 4154.

4 *Mīzān al-Iʿtidāl*, vol. 3 p. 273, biography no. 6404.

ʿAmr ibn ʿAlī al-Fallās, "Matrūk al-ḥadīth and a person of innovation."

Ḥātim says, "Matrūk al-ḥadīth."[1]

This is the status of the chain and there is not much that can be further added to this besides the fact that the scholars have graded this narration extremely weak. To name a few of these scholars who have graded it as such:

1. Ibn Ḥazm
2. al-Bayhaqī
3. Ibn al-Athīr
4. al-Qurṭubī
5. al-Dhahabī
6. al-Haythamī
7. Ibn Ḥajar
8. al-Suyūṭī

The list carries on...

The text is problematic for the following reasons:

The story stands in stark contrast to the Qur'ān since it is a core principle in the Sharīʿah that Allah accepts the repentance of one who repents.

Allah says:

إِنَّمَا التَّوْبَةُ عَلَى اللّٰهِ لِلَّذِيْنَ يَعْمَلُوْنَ السُّوْٓءَ بِجَهَالَةٍ ثُمَّ يَتُوْبُوْنَ مِنْ قَرِيْبٍ فَأُولٰٓئِكَ يَتُوْبُ اللّٰهُ عَلَيْهِمْ ۗ وَكَانَ اللّٰهُ عَلِيْمًا حَكِيْمًا ﴿١٧﴾ وَلَيْسَتِ التَّوْبَةُ لِلَّذِيْنَ يَعْمَلُوْنَ السَّيِّئَاتِ ۚ حَتّٰى إِذَا حَضَرَ أَحَدَهُمُ الْمَوْتُ قَالَ إِنِّي تُبْتُ الْاٰنَ وَلَا الَّذِيْنَ يَمُوْتُوْنَ وَهُمْ كُفَّارٌ ۚ أُولٰٓئِكَ أَعْتَدْنَا لَهُمْ عَذَابًا أَلِيْمًا ﴿١٨﴾

1 *Tahdhīb al-Kamāl*, vol. 22 p. 123, biography no. 4406.

The repentance accepted by Allah is only for those who do wrong in ignorance (or carelessness) and then repent soon after. It is those to whom Allah will turn in forgiveness, and Allah is ever Knowing and Wise. But repentance is not (accepted) of those who (continue to) do evil deeds up until, when death comes to one of them, he says, "Indeed, I have repented now," or of those who die while they are disbelievers. For them We have prepared a painful punishment.[1]

The established Sunnah also indicates that there is repentance for all sins. The Prophet ﷺ said:

إن الله يقبل توبة العبد مالم يغرغر

Indeed, Allah accepts the repentance of the slave as longs as the soul does not reach the throat.[2]

The ḥadīth is an explanation of the verse

وَلَيْسَتِ التَّوْبَةُ لِلَّذِينَ يَعْمَلُونَ السَّيِّئَاتِ حَتَّىٰ إِذَا حَضَرَ أَحَدَهُمُ الْمَوْتُ قَالَ إِنِّي تُبْتُ الْآنَ

But repentance is not (accepted) of those who (continue to) do evil deeds up until, when death comes to one of them he says, "Indeed, I have repented now,"

The verse only excludes repentance in that condition and allows for repentance until the moment the person experiences the throes of death.

The story shows Thaʿlabah to be remorseful. So in addition to the severe weakness in the chain, the story of Thaʿlabah contradicts an established principle of the dīn. It also contradicts what the following verse indicates:

وَهُوَ الَّذِي يَقْبَلُ التَّوْبَةَ عَنْ عِبَادِهِ وَيَعْفُو عَنِ السَّيِّئَاتِ

And it is He who accepts repentance from His servants and pardons misdeeds.[3]

If it is claimed that Thaʿlabah was a munāfiq; Allah has opened the door of repentance wide open for them also.

---

1 Sūrah al-Nisā': 17-18.

2 *Tirmidhī*, Kitāb al-Daʿawāt, Ḥadīth no. 3537; Refer also to *Ṣaḥīḥ al-Tirmidhī*, Ḥadīth no. 2804.

3 Sūrah al-Shūrah: 25.

إِنَّ الْمُنَافِقِينَ فِي الدَّرْكِ الْأَسْفَلِ مِنَ النَّارِ وَلَن تَجِدَ لَهُمْ نَصِيرًا ﴿١٤٥﴾
إِلَّا الَّذِينَ تَابُوا وَأَصْلَحُوا وَاعْتَصَمُوا بِاللَّهِ وَأَخْلَصُوا دِينَهُمْ لِلَّهِ فَأُولَٰئِكَ
مَعَ الْمُؤْمِنِينَ ۖ وَسَوْفَ يُؤْتِ اللَّهُ الْمُؤْمِنِينَ أَجْرًا عَظِيمًا ﴿١٤٦﴾ مَّا يَفْعَلُ
اللَّهُ بِعَذَابِكُمْ إِن شَكَرْتُمْ وَآمَنتُمْ ۚ وَكَانَ اللَّهُ شَاكِرًا عَلِيمًا ﴿١٤٧﴾

Indeed, the hypocrites will be in the lowest depths of the Fire and never will you find for them a helper. Except for those who repent, correct themselves, hold fast to Allah, and are sincere in their religion for Allah, for those will be with the believers. And Allah is going to give the believers a great reward. What would Allah do with (i.e. gain from) your punishment if you are grateful and believe? And ever is Allah Appreciative and Knowing.[1]

Allah also says about the munāfiqīn:

فَإِن يَتُوبُوا يَكُ خَيْرًا لَّهُمْ

So if they repent, it is better for them.[2]

The story of Thaʿlabah leaves the sinner in a state of despair and despondency in the mercy of Allah; and that is disliked by Allah and His Messenger ﷺ.

The Messenger ﷺ told people that if they came to Allah with sins equivalent to the earth; and then repented to Him, He would forgive them. He informed people that if they did not repent, Allah would replace them with people who committed sin and repented and He would forgive them.

The Prophet ﷺ said:

قال اللّه يا ابن أدم إنّك ما دعوتني ورجوتني غفرت لك على ما كان فيك و لا أبالي يا ابن أدم لو بلغت ذنوبك عنان السّماء ثمّ استغفرتني غفرت لك و لا أبالي يا ابن أدم إنّك لو أتيتني بقراب الأرض خطايا ثمّ لقيتني لا تشرك بي شيئا لأتيتك بقرابها مغفرة

1 Sūrah al-Nisāʾ: 145-147.

2 Sūrah al-Tawbah: 74.

> Allah says, "O son of Ādam, as long as you call unto to Me and hope in Me I will forgive you no matter what sins you committed and it does not bother Me. O son of Ādam, if your sins reached the clouds in the sky then you seek My forgiveness I will forgive you and it does not bother Me. O son of Ādam if you should come to Me with an earth-load of sins having not associated partners with Me I will come to you with its amount in forgiveness."[1]
>
> والّذى نفسى بيده لو لم تذنبوا لذهب اللّه بكم ولجاء بقوم يذنبون فيستغفرون اللّه فيغفر لهم
>
> By the one whom my life is in his hand, if you did not commit sin, Allah would remove you and bring forth a nation who would sin and seek forgiveness from Allah and he would forgive them.[2]

These are among other factors that add to falseness of this story:

> The year in which Thaʿlabah passed away is not known exactly. There are many opinions with regards to the year of his death. Those who narrate this story place his death during the khilāfah of ʿUthmān. That view, however, is rejected as it, as well as the story, comes from the same weak chain. The second view is mentioned by Ibn ʿAbd al-Barr and Ibn Ḥajar placing his martyrdom at Uḥud or Khaybar respectively. Therefore, he was martyred during the life of the Prophet ﷺ which further contradicts the details of the story which claims that he died during the khilāfah of ʿUthmān رضي الله عنه.

Tījānī has nowhere to take this discussion. Abū Bakr's رضي الله عنه position has been proven from the Qur'ān, Sunnah, Ijmāʿ, and even Shīʿī law. Tījānī has shown us that the façade of impartiality can only last for so long.

7. Tījānī's condemnation of Abū Bakr for how he dealt with Khālid ibn al-Walīd

Tījānī says:

> **The third incident which took place during the early days of Abu Bakr's caliphate in which he found himself in disagreement with Umar, and for which certain Qur'anic and Prophetic texts were interpreted, was that of**

1 *Sunan Tirmidhī*, Kitāb al-Daʿwāt, Ḥadīth no. 3540; Refer also to *Ṣaḥīḥ al-Tirmidhī*, Ḥadīth no. 2805.

2 *Ṣaḥīḥ Muslim* with its commentary, Kitāb al-Tawbah, Bāb Suqūṭ al-Dhunūb bi al-Istighfār, Ḥadīth no. 2749.

Khalid ibn al-Walid who killed Malik ibn Nuwayrah and took his wife and married her on the same day. Umar said to Khalid, O enemy of Allah, you killed a Muslim man, then you took his wife ... by Allah, I will stone you."

But Abu Bakr defended Khalid, and said, "O Umar, forgive him, he made a mistake, but do not rebuke him!"

This is another scandal that history has recorded for a prominent Companion, and when we talk about him, we talk with respect and reverence; we even gave him the title "The ever drawn sword of Allah." What can I say about a Companion who did all that? Who killed Malik ibn Nuwayrah, the honourable Companion, leader of Bani Tamin and Bani Yarbu, famous for his courage and generosity, and furthermore the historians tell us that Khalid killed Malik and his followers after they put down their arms and stood together to pray. They were tied by ropes and with them was Leyla bint al-Minhal, wife of Malik, who was considered to be one of the most beautiful Arab ladies of her time, and Khalid was captured by her beauty. Malik said, "O Khalid, send us to Abu Bakr and he will be our judge. "And Abdullah ibn Umar together with Abu Qutadah al-Ansari intervened and urged Khalid to send them to Abu Bakr, but he refused and said, "Allah will never forgive me if I do not kill him."

Malik then turned to his wife Leyla and said, "This is the one who will kill me." After that Khalid ordered his execution and took his wife Leyla and married her that very night.[1]

Refuting Tījānī's condemnation of Abū Bakr for how he dealt with Khālid ibn al-Walīd

The hallmark feature of Tījānī's objectivity is that it ignores some narrations while he focuses on others. It is not surprising that the narrations presenting the Ṣaḥābah in a negative light are the only ones put on display; regardless of their credibility. While the sound narrations, which bring to the fore the reality of these murky situations, are conveniently ignored; although it is remotely possible that Tījānī was ignorant of them. Any other explanation would reveal his research to be nothing more than a calculated attack on the Ṣaḥābah رضي الله عنهم under the guise of academic enquiry.

These two narrations, which Tījānī has shielded his readers from, have been documented by the historians in relation to the incident of Mālik ibn Nuwayrah:

1 *Then I was guided*, p. 155.

The First Narration

When Khālid arrived in Biṭāḥ he sent out regiments instructing them with inviting to Islam and that they were to round up those who did not respond, and to kill anyone who further resists. Abū Bakr used to advise them to call out the adhān when they reached a locality [to establish if those people were Muslim], and if the people of the locality called out the adhān they were left to be. If they did not call out the adhān, then they were to be killed and their property seized. If they responded positively towards the call of Islam then they were to be questioned about zakāh. "If they confirm it (as part of the integrals of Islam) then accept it from them but if they refuse (to pay the zakāh) then fight them!" Thereupon Mālik ibn Nuwayrah, his own group, along with a band of riders from the Banū Thaʿlabah ibn Yarbūʿ arrived.

The Muslim regiment was divided about them (Mālik ibn Nuwayrah and his companions). Abū Qatādah was one of those who witnessed them calling out the adhān, and establishing the ṣalāh. As a result of their dispute the instruction was given that they be detained. Owing to the fact that it was a cold night Khālid instructed the announcer to call out, "Warm your detainees!" This expression, however, according to the language of the Kinānah (tribe) meant, figuratively, to kill them.

The people, therefore, assumed that Khālid wanted them executed; whereas he only meant for them to provide some warmth for them. The people killed them, and Ḍirār ibn al-Azwar killed Mālik ibn Nuwayrah. Khālid heard the commotion but only came out after the deed was done; he then said, "When Allah decrees a matter it occurs!"[1]

As for the second narration:

Khālid summoned Mālik ibn Nuwayrah and rebuked him on account of his following Sajāḥ (a false prophetess) and his refusing to pay the zakāh. He said to him, "Do you not know that zakāh is the partner of ṣalāh?" Mālik said, "That is certainly what your companion claims!" Khālid said, "Is he our companion and not yours? O Ḍirār, smite his neck!" and his head was severed.[2]

---

1 *Tārīkh al-Ṭabarī*, vol. 2 p. 273, 11th year after the hijrah; *Tārīkh Ibn al-Athīr*, vol. 2 p. 217, 11th year after hijrah; *al-Bidāyah wa l-Nihāyah*, vol. 6 p. 326; *Tārīkh ibn Khaldūn*, vol. 2 p. 500-501.

2 *Ṭabarī*, vol. 2 p. 273-274; *Tārīkh Ibn al-Athīr*, vol. 2 p. 216-217; *al-Bidāyah wa al-Nihāyah*, vol. 6 p. 326-327.

If we consider either of these narrations it becomes evident that Mālik ibn Nuwayrah and his party were either killed because the Muslim army misunderstood Khālid ibn al-Walīd, or that Mālik ibn Nuwayrah responded in a manner that caused Khālid ibn al-Walīd to doubt his Islam. The romantic element that Tījānī introduces in his version of this incident has no mention in any of these two narrations.

As a matter of fact, Tījānī's version with the romantic motive has been dismissed by the historians on account of its irregularity and anomalous nature. Tījānī references it to the following sources, *Tārīkh Abī al-Fidā*, *Tārīkh al-Yaʿqūbī*, *Tārīkh Ibn Saḥanah* and *Wafayāt al-Aʿyān*.

Interestingly, when we consulted these texts to investigate whether Tījānī has provided an honest presentation of the facts, we realised that our original suspicions were confirmed. Tījānī's snide remarks and accusations amount to nothing more than a premeditated attack on the Ṣaḥābah.

In *Wafayāt al-Aʿyān*, Ibn Khallikān provides a very different account of what happened. It does not corroborate the details of Tījānī's version. This is what Ibn Khallikān writes:

> When Khālid ibn Walīd departed to fight them during the khilāfah of Abū Bakr al-Ṣiddīq he captured Mālik ibn Nuwayrah who was the head of his people, Banū Yarbūʿ, and he had taken their zakāh and disposed of it. Khālid spoke to him about it and Mālik replied, "I uphold ṣalāh not zakāh!" Khālid said to him, "Are you not aware that the ṣalāh and the zakāh are inseparable, the one is not accepted without the other?" Mālik said, "Your companion (referring to the Messenger ﷺ) used to say that!" Khālid said, "Do you not consider him your companion? By Allah! I was on the verge of smiting your neck!" Then they spoke for a long time until Khālid said, "I am going to kill you!" Mālik said, "Did your companion instruct you to do that?" Khālid said, "This after that? By Allah! I will most definitely kill you!" ʿAbd Allāh ibn ʿUmar and Abū Qatādah al-Anṣārī were present and spoke to Khālid concerning him (Mālik ibn Nuwayrah) but he disliked their view. Mālik said, "O Khālid! Send us to Abū Bakr and let him be the one to judge us as you have sent to him others besides us whose crime was greater than our crime!" Khālid said, "My Allah will not forgive me if I do not kill you!" Ḍirār ibn al-Azwar al-Asadī came to the front to smite his neck and Mālik turned to his wife, Umm Mutammim, and said to Khālid, "This is the one who has killed me," as she was very beautiful. Khālid

> said to him, "Rather, Allah has killed you on account of your deserting Islam!" Mālik said, "I am upon Islam!" Khālid said to Ḍirār, "Smite his neck," and he removed his neck.[1]

This is Tījānī's account of Khālid's marriage to Laylā, Mālik's wife, "He took (married) Laylā, his (Mālik's) wife, and consummated the marriage the same night."

This is referenced to *Wafayāt al-Aʿyān* but when referring directly to the book it tells of something different:

> Khālid took his wife. It has been said that he purchased her from the booty and married her, and it has been said that she observed the ʿiddah for three menstrual cycles then Khālid proposed marriage to himself and she accepted.[2]

Tījānī has manipulated the details to provide a sensational story. It is not an accurate reproduction of what is mentioned in the original text that he refers to, albeit a late reference.

Ibn Khallikān completes the story and says at the end of it:

> This is how the previously mentioned Wathīmah and Wāqidī transmit this event in their respective books and the responsibility [of authenticity] is with them.[3]

In other words, he did not transmit it relying on the truthfulness of the report. Rather, he transmitted it as it comes in their books. Therefore, any criticism of the narration is their responsibility; or that of the researcher to verify the reliability from the earlier sources.

As for *Tārīkh al-Yaʿqūbī*, he narrates the incident in an undignified manner. He says:

> He wrote to Khālid to turn his attention to Mālik ibn Nuwayrah al-Yarbūʿī. He, therefore, marched towards them and it has been said that he incinerated them. Mālik ibn Nuwayrah stepped forward to debate him and his wife followed behind him. When Khālid saw her he was amazed with her beauty

1 Ibn Khalkhān: *Wafayāt al-Aʿyān wa Ambā Abnā al-Zamān*, vol. 6 p. 14, Dār Ṣādir: Beirut.

2 Ibid.

3 Ibid.

> and said, "By Allah! I will not attain what is in your house until I kill you and he looked at Mālik." Then he removed his neck and married his wife.[1]

This version of events might align with what Tījānī has written. However, it is necessary for us to be aware of who exactly al-Ya'qūbī actually is and how credible is his presentation of history.

Muḥammad ibn Ṣāmil al-Sulamī writes about the methodology of some of the early books on Islamic history. This is what he writes about al-Ya'qūbī:

> He presents the history of the Islamic empire from the Shī'ah Imāmiyyah perspective and he only acknowledges 'Alī's khilāfah and his sons in accordance with the line of A'immah by the Shī'ah. He calls 'Alī the *Waṣī* (the instated one). When documenting the khilāfah of Abū Bakr, 'Umar, and 'Uthmān he does not add the title of the khilāfah in front of their names. He simply says, "Such a person took control of the matter." Also, he does not spare any of them from criticism, even the senior Ṣaḥābah. He mentions many disparaging reports about 'Ā'ishah, and the same applies to Khālid ibn Walīd, 'Amr ibn 'Āṣ, and Mu'āwiyah ibn Abī Sufyān. He presents the incident of Saqīfah in a scandalous manner. He claims that there was a conspiracy against 'Alī ibn Ṭālib to remove him from the khilāfah as 'Alī was the Waṣī in his opinion. His extremism caused him to reach the point where he mentioned that Allah's words:
>
> اَلْيَوْمَ أَكْمَلْتُ لَكُمْ دِيْنَكُمْ وَأَتْمَمْتُ عَلَيْكُمْ نِعْمَتِيْ وَرَضِيْتُ لَكُمُ الْإِسْلَامَ دِيْنًا
>
> *This day I have perfected for you your religion and completed My favour upon you and have approved for you Islam as religion.*[2]
>
> He claims it was revealed concerning Amīr al-Mu'minīn, 'Alī ibn Abī Ṭālib on the Day of al-Nafr. His methodology in presenting the critical junctures in history is the methodology of his people from the Shī'ah and Rāfiḍah, which is: fabricating the entire report, or adding to the report, or presenting it outside of its context in order to distort its meaning.[3]

---

1 *Tārīkh al-Ya'qūbī*, vol. 2 p. 131.

2 Sūrah al-Mā'idah: 3.

3 Muḥammad ibn Ṣāmil al-Sulamī: *Manjaj Kitābah al-Tārīkh al-Islamī*, p. 430-431.

Thus, we realise that this account of what happened with Mālik ibn Nuwayrah is not only subjective and prejudiced, but suffers from a lack of credibility due to the predisposed hostile attitude towards the Ṣaḥābah by the author, al-Ya'qūbī. It is significant to note that this anomalous detail is only recorded by those with Shī'ī association, in addition to the defective chains of transmission.

We realise that, according to one version of reports, Khālid ibn Walīd instructed for Mālik ibn Nuwayrah to be killed considering him to have apostatised due to his rejecting the duty of zakāh. It is evident that the embellished fabricated versions of this report distort historical fact in the attempt to discredit Khālid wherein he is purported to have killed Mālik because of his wife. The other version refers to the misunderstanding of Khālid's instructions.

The next issue is Tījānī's claim that 'Umar رضي الله عنه said to Khālid رضي الله عنه, "O enemy of Allah! You killed a Muslim then you pounced on his wife! I will pelt you with stones!" He ascribed this narration to *Tārīkh al-Ṭabarī*, *Abū al-Fidā*[1], *al-Ya'qūbī* and *al-Iṣābah*. Not surprising; after consulting *Tārīkh al-Ya'qūbī* and *al-Iṣābah* we can safely confirm that they do not mention anything of this nature.

The narration found in *Tārīkh al-Ṭabarī* is problematic due to the severe weakness in the chain of transmission. Appearing in this chain is Muḥammad ibn Ḥumayd ibn Ḥayyān al-Rāzī, an untrustworthy narrator.

- Ya'qūb ibn Shaybah al-Sadūsī says about him, "He transmits many anomalies."
- Al-Bukhārī says, "His ḥadīth are problematic." Al-Bukhārī often uses this expression for one who has serious flaws in his narration.
- Al-Nasā'ī says, "He is not reliable."
- Al-Jūzajānī says, "He subscribes to a despicable school. He is not reliable."[2]
- Al-Dhahabī says, "A group of them have accepted him, but (after investigation) his position is among those whose narrations are abandoned."[3]

1 Sadly, I have not found *Tārīkh Abū al-Fidā* or *Ibn Saḥānah*. That being said, what we mentioned should satisfy the searcher of the truth.

2 *Al-Tahdhīb*, vol. 25 p. 102, biography no. 5167.

3 *al-Kāshif*, vol. 2 p. 166.

Furthermore, Muḥammad ibn Isḥāq, a narrator in this chain, is known for *Tadlīs* [omitting his actual source and ascribing the narration to someone further up the chain, whom he came into contact with, in a manner that is ambiguous]. In this narration he has not transmitted it in a way that establishes his original source.

This narration is therefore severely flawed in terms of its chain. This is in addition to the anomalous details found in the text. This has been pointed out by some researchers who examined this report:

> Abū Bakr summoned Khālid. When he arrived in Madīnah he entered the Masjid bearing the expression of a victorious general. Then ʿUmar went to him, took his arrows, and broke them into pieces, and made that threating statement to him about breaking the back, "You killed a Muslim then you pounced on his wife! I will pelt you with stones," all this while the hero of Islam, Khālid ibn Walīd did not respond to him considering that Abū Bakr shared these sentiments.
>
> I say (the author): If ʿUmar knew Abū Bakr's view on the issue, as mentioned in the narration, before Khālid's arrival as they had debated the issue and ʿUmar was critical of Khālid. However, Abū Bakr restrained him, and said to him, "Raise your tongue from (criticising) Khālid," and praised Khālid and vouched for him in the manner that the Prophet ﷺ vouched for him when he said, "Indeed Khālid is a sword Allah has unleashed upon the unbelievers, I will not shame him." How then could ʿUmar ibn Khaṭṭāb have interacted with Khālid in this manner which was in opposition of the view of the khalīfah? Someone might say, "Indeed ʿUmar ibn al-Khaṭṭāb was that stern person of the dīn who stood by his opinion and did not stand down from it on account of anyone else's opinion?" We then say: Where did that sternness disappear to after Khālid met Abū Bakr and conveyed to him the reality of the situation, as Abū Bakr and the Ṣaḥābah predicted? And where was that sternness when Khālid came to ʿUmar and threatened him with this belittling statement, "Come here, O son of Umm Shamlah"? ʿUmar knew that Abū Bakr was pleased with Khālid and therefore he did not speak to him and entered his house. ʿUmar knew this before his meeting Khālid and taking his arrows and shattering them into pieces. Did the transmitters forget or were they incompetent? Or did ʿUmar change his view and realise that Khālid was innocent of what he was accused of?[1]

---

1 Ṣādiq Ibrāhīm ʿArjūn: *Khālid ibn Walīd*, p. 166-167.

We are now assured that the report found in al-Ṭabarī is not only severely flawed in terms of its chain, but the report itself suffers from internal inconsistency. For some, it appears to be the pinnacle of objectivity that history be constructed on such shaky narrations.

As for Tījānī's statement:

> **This is another scandal that history has recorded for a prominent Companion, and when we talk about him, we talk with respect and reverence; we even gave him the title "The ever drawn sword of Allah". What can I say about a Companion who did all that? Amazing!**

The initial impression from Tījānī's statement above will lead one to think he is speaking about the chief of the munāfiqīn. Tījānī clearly expresses his disdain for anyone speaking about this Companion of the Prophet ﷺ in a respectful and honourable manner. But who cares whether Tījānī is pleased or offended, when it is the Leader of all the Prophets, Muḥammad ﷺ, who bestowed Khālid ibn al-Walīd with the epithet Sayf Allāh!

This is the narration as it appears in *Ṣaḥīḥ al-Bukhārī*:

> نعى زيدا وجعفرا وابن رواحة للناس قبل أن يأتيهم خبرهم فقال أخذ الراية زيد فأصيب ثم أخذ جعفر فأصيب ثم أخذ ابن رواحة فأصيب وعيناه تذرفان حتى أخذ الراية سيف من سيوف الله حتى فتح الله عليهم
>
> The Prophet announced the death of Zayd, and Jaʿfar, and Ibn Rawāḥah before the news of their martyrdom had reached the Companions (in Madīnah) and said, "Zayd took the flag and was killed, then Jaʿfar took the flag and was killed, then Ibn Rawāḥah took the flag and was killed," he said this while his eyes were flowing with tears, "Until a Sword from the swords of Allah took it and Allah granted them victory."[1]

Al-Tirmidhī narrates it by way of Abū Hurayrah:

> قال نزلنا مع رسول الله صلى الله عليه وسلم منزلا فجعل الناس يمرون فيقول رسول الله صلى الله عليه وسلم من هذا يا أبا هريرة فأقول فلان فيقول نعم عبد الله هذا ويقول من هذا فأقول فلان فيقول بئس عبد الله هذا

1 *Ṣaḥīḥ al-Bukhārī*, Kitāb Faḍā'il al-Ṣaḥābah, vol. 3, Ḥadīth no. 3547.

حتى مر خالد بن الوليد فقال من هذا فقلت هذا خالد بن الوليد فقال نعم عبد الله خالد بن الوليد سيف من سيوف الله

> We stopped over with the Messenger ﷺ at a place and the people started walking by. The Messenger ﷺ asked, "Who is this, O Abū Hurayrah?"
>
> I said, "It is so and so," and he said, "This is a good slave of Allah!"
>
> Then he asked, "Who is this?"
>
> I said, "It is so and so," and he said, "This is a bad slave of Allah."
>
> Then Khālid ibn Walīd passed by and he said, "Who is this?" I said, "This is Khālid ibn Walīd." and he said, "Khālid ibn Walīd is a good slave of Allah and a sword from the swords of Allah."[1]

Is Tījānī going to reject these authentic narrations on the basis of them not aligning with the spurious details he provided us with, from the books they are not even found in, with chains of transmission that are weaker than cotton wool? What a resourceful research! What innovative research methods!

Tījānī suddenly developed an affinity for the Companions as he theorises that Mālik ibn Nuwayrah was a noble Ṣaḥābī, despite their being no evidence to support this idea. It appears that anyone who was at variance with any of the popularly recognised Ṣaḥābah must have been from the category of good Ṣaḥābah, based on Tījānī's definition.

The historians confirm that Mālik ibn Nuwayrah apostatised after the Prophet's ﷺ demise and that he did not pay the zakāh but distributed in amongst his people. When he was brought to Khālid and argued with him about the issue of zakāh he made the statement, "Your companion used to claim that?" Thus implying that he did not acknowledge the obligation of zakāh. Secondly, he referred to the Prophet ﷺ with the words, "your companion," which was the phrase used by the Mushrikīn when referring to the Prophet Muḥammad ﷺ.

This version of events is mentioned by all the historians including Iṣfahānī in al-Aghānī and Ibn Khallikān. The only exception is al-Yaʿqūbī who is known for his lies. How then can it be said that Mālik ibn Nuwayrah was a noble Ṣaḥābī?

---

1 *Sunan al-Tirmidhī*, Ḥadīth no. 4117, Bāb Manāqib Khālid ibn Walīd; See also *Ṣaḥīḥ al-Tirmidhī*, Ḥadīth no. 3021.

The historians have produced further proof that supports the idea that Mālik ibn Nuwayrah died an apostate. They say:

> ʿUmar ibn al-Khaṭṭāb met Mutammim ibn Nuwayrah, Mālik's brother, and asked him to recite some verses of poetry in which he could mourn his brother's death. Mutammim then recited his poem which includes the following couplets:
>
> > We were close for a period of time to the point where it was said, "They will never part,"
> >
> > However, when we parted it was as if Mālik and I, despite the length of Companionship, did not spend a single night together.
>
> When ʿUmar heard that, he said, "By Allah! This is an eulogy. I wish I was skilled at poetry so I could express my mourning over the loss of my brother Zayd, as you have mourned your brother."
>
> Mutammim said, "If my brother died as your brother died (i.e. a martyr) I would not have mourned him."
>
> ʿUmar was pleased with Mutammim's remark and said, "No one consoled me about my brother as Mutammim consoled me."[1]

Mutammim's statement is even clearer in another narration:

> He said, "O Amīr al-Mu'minīn! Indeed your brother died as a believer while my brother died as an apostate." ʿUmar رضي الله عنه said, "No one consoled me in a better manner than the way Mutammim consoled me."[2]

Even the brother of Mālik mourns the fact that his brother died on apostasy!

There remains the matter of Khālid marrying Mālik's wife. Tījānī claims that he bedded her the same night. This is contrary to fact and is a serious allegation.

Ibn Kathīr mentions that Khālid رضي الله عنه observed praiseworthy traits in her and therefore, when she became lawful for him to marry, he married her.[3]

---

1 Muḥammad al-Sayyid al-Wakīl: *Jawlah Tārīkhiyyah fī ʿAṣr al-Khulafā' al-Rāshidīn*, p. 42; See also *Futūḥ al-Buldān* by Aḥmad al-Balādhurī, p. 108; and *Tārīkh Ibn al-Athīr*, vol. 2 p. 218.

2 *Kitāb al-Amālī* by ʿAbd Allāh al-Yazīdī, p. 25-26, *ʿĀlam al-Kutub* (Printing house).

3 Ibn Kathīr: *Al-Bidāyah wa al-Nihāyah*, vol. 6 p. 326.

Al-Ṭabarī mentions Khālid's marriage, "Khālid married Umm Tamīm, the wife (widow) of Mālik. He waited for her period of waiting to expire before wedding her."[1]

In *al-Kāmil* it comes, "Khālid married Umm Tamīm, the wife (widow) of Mālik."[2] He did not say, as Tījānī claims, that he bedded her the same night, rather, it says that he married her after she became lawful to marry (i.e. after the completion of her *'iddah*). If that was not the case Ibn al-Athīr would have mentioned that.

Ibn Khallikān whom Tījānī cites, says, "Khālid married his (Mālik's) wife (widow). It has been said that he purchased her from the booty and married her. It has (also) been said that she observed the 'iddah, then he proposed to her for himself and she responded (positively)."

So much for objectivity and fair representation!

Tījānī arrogantly continues his tirade:

> **What can I say about those Companions who trespassed on what Allah deemed to be forbidden; they killed Muslims because of personal whims and permitted themselves to have women that Allah had forbidden us to have. In Islam, a widow cannot be wed by another man before a definite period of time had elapsed, and this period of time has been specified by Allah in His Glorious Book. But Khalid followed his whims and debased himself.**[3]

Which continues until he says:

> **For what would this period of time [Iddah] mean to him after he had already killed her husband and his followers despite the fact that they were Muslims. Abdullah ibn Umar and Abu Qutadah have testified to this, and the latter became so angry about Khalid's behaviour that he returned to al-Medinah and swore that he would never serve in an army led by Khalid ibn al-Walid. [He references this to *Tārīkh al-Ṭabarī, Tārīkh al-Ya'qūbī, Tārīkh Abū al-Fidā*].**[4]

Our comment:

1 *Tārīkh al-Ṭabarī*, vol. 2 p. 273, the year 11 after the Hijrah.

2 Ibn al-Athīr: *Al-Kāmil*, vol. 2 p. 217, the year 11 after the Hijrah.

3 *Then I was guided*, p. 156.

4 Ibid. p. 156.

The initial complaint against one Ṣaḥābī has been amplified. Suddenly it becomes "those Companions", insinuating that there were many. Our previous comments have already pointed out the feeble evidence upon which Tījānī's argument rests. Furthermore, we have demonstrated the fictitious nature of the narration that says Khālid wed the widow of Mālik ibn Nuwayrah the next day. I merely want to remind the esteemed reader of Tījānī's deception; that a spurious narration is elevated to fact and conjecture is taken as reality. Tījānī has crossed the red line too many times to be taken seriously.

This narration referenced to *al-Ṭabarī* is the very narration whose severe weakness was pointed out in the previous pages.

The narration that mentions Abū Qatādah getting angry with Khālid cannot be found in *al-Iṣābah* even though Tījānī references it there. It appears that Tījānī falsifies the references, assuming that no one would verify them, in order to create the impression that he has researched the subject thoroughly. He does not realise that research methodology is equally important, and it is on that basis that we are able to reveal his deceit.

Tījānī cites a conglomeration of ideas from Ḥusayn al-Haykal's book *al-Ṣiddīq Abū Bakr*, which suffers from the lack of discretion between reliable and spurious narrations. He says:

> **May we ask Mr. Haykel and his like from our scholars, who would compromise in order to preserve the honour of the Companions: Why did Abu Bakr not bring Khalid to justice? And if Umar was an ideal example of firm justice, as Haykel puts it, why did he only remove him from the command of the army, and not bring him to justice so that he would not be a bad example for all Muslims of how to respect the Book of Allah, as he said. And did they respect the Book of Allah and discharge the laws of Allah? Nay! It was politics! It does wonders; it changes the truth and throws the Qur'anic texts over the wall.**[1]

Our comment:

Repeating the arguments that exonerate Khālid from the charge of murdering Mālik ibn Nuwayrah runs the risk of boring out the reader. We will, however, address some of the other issues raised.

---

1 *Then I was guided*, p. 157.

Tījānī advocates for the execution of Khālid ibn al-Walīd رَضِيَ ٱللَّهُ عَنْهُ. Assuming that Khālid was unjustified in what he had done, the most that can be said about this incident is that Khālid made a mistake in killing Mālik based on his interpretation of the situation. This, however, does not warrant his execution. In fact, a similar incident involving Usāmah ibn Zayd رَضِيَ ٱللَّهُ عَنْهُ occurred during the lifetime of the Prophet صَلَّى ٱللَّهُ عَلَيْهِ وَسَلَّمَ.

During a battle he killed a man who said, "*Lā ilāha illā Allāh.*"

When the Prophet صَلَّى ٱللَّهُ عَلَيْهِ وَسَلَّمَ came to know of this he said to him, "O Usāmah, did you kill him after he said *Lā ilāha illā Allāh*? O Usāmah, did you kill him after he said *Lā ilāha illā Allāh*? O Usāmah, did you kill him after he said *Lā ilāha illā Allāh*?"

In this ḥadīth the Prophet صَلَّى ٱللَّهُ عَلَيْهِ وَسَلَّمَ rebuked Usāmah for killing the man. That being said, he did not impose the Ḥadd upon him; nor blood money nor expiation.

Consider the explanation of this verse which al-Ṭabarī and others narrate from Ibn ʿAbbās and Qatādah:

وَلَا تَقُولُوا لِمَنْ أَلْقَىٰ إِلَيْكُمُ السَّلَامَ لَسْتَ مُؤْمِنًا

And do not say to one who gives you [a greeting of] peace, "You are not a believer"[1]

They say it was revealed concerning Mirdās, a man from the Ghaṭafān tribe. The Prophet صَلَّى ٱللَّهُ عَلَيْهِ وَسَلَّمَ sent an army to his people. Their leader was Ghālib al-Laythī. Mirdās's companions fled but he did not. He said, "I am a Muslim." When the cavalry arrived in the morning he greeted them but they killed him and took his possessions. Then Allah revealed this verse, and instructed the Prophet صَلَّى ٱللَّهُ عَلَيْهِ وَسَلَّمَ to return his wealth to his family and to pay them blood money. The Prophet صَلَّى ٱللَّهُ عَلَيْهِ وَسَلَّمَ forbade the Muslims from that in the future.

Likewise, there is an incident where Khālid ibn Walīd killed Banū Judhaymah on account of his interpretation of the situation and the Prophet صَلَّى ٱللَّهُ عَلَيْهِ وَسَلَّمَ raised his hands and said, "O Allah! I absolve myself from what Khālid did!" Despite that the Prophet صَلَّى ٱللَّهُ عَلَيْهِ وَسَلَّمَ did not execute him for the incorrect interpretation of the situation.

1 Sūrah al-Nisā: 94.

If the Prophet ﷺ refrained from executing him for killing more than one Muslim from Banū Judhaymah because he interpreted the situation incorrectly; then surely Abū Bakr رضي الله عنه cannot be censured for not executing him because of his killing Mālik ibn Nuwayrah, since the circumstances were in Khālid's favour to a greater extent.[1]

It is ironic that Tījānī presents the narration of Khālid with Banū Judhaymah as a complaint against Abū Bakr.

Even though he knows that the Prophet ﷺ did not execute him. Why did he not cite that in favour of Abū Bakr for not killing him? However, the one who follows his base desires it blinds him from following the truth.[2]

Now, let us pose the question to Tījānī: Why did the Prophet ﷺ not impose the Ḥadd upon Khālid? As a matter of fact, he did not even remove him from the leadership of the army. Instead, the Prophet ﷺ kept him in that position until he passed away? Is Tījānī going to point a finger at the Messenger ﷺ? Any finger to be pointed at Abū Bakr رضي الله عنه leads back to the Prophet ﷺ directly.

He goes on to say:

> **Some of our scholars tell us in their books that the Messenger of Allah ﷺ once became very angry when Usamah tried to mediate on behalf of an honourable woman accused of stealing, and the Messenger ﷺ said, "Woe unto you! Do you mediate about one of the laws of Allah? By Allah if it was Fatimah the daughter of Muhammad, I would cut her hand. He destroyed those before you because they would let the thief go if he was an honourable person, but would bring him to justice if he was a weak one." How could they be silent about the killing of the innocent Muslims, and the marriage of their widows on the same night despite the tragic loss of their husbands? I wish they had remained silent! But they try to justify Khalid's misdeed by inventing various virtues for him, they even called him "The ever drawn sword of Allah" I remember being surprised by a friend of mine, who used to like joking and changing the meaning of the words, when I mentioned the virtues of Khalid ibn al-Walid during my days of ignorance and called him "The ever drawn sword of Allah". He replied, "He is the crippled sword of the devil!"**

1 *Minhāj al-Sunnah*, vol. 5 p. 518.

2 Ibid.

I was surprised then, but after my research, Allah has opened my eyes and helped me to know the true value of those who seized the caliphate, changed the laws of Allah and violated the boundaries of Allah.[1]

Our response:

Bukhārī narrates the ḥadīth with the following wording:

عن عائشة رضى الله عنها أن قريشا أهمتهم المرأة المخزومية التي سرقت فقالوا من يكلم رسول الله صلى الله عليه وسلم ومن يجترئ عليه إلا أسامة حب رسول الله صلى الله عليه وسلم فكلم رسول الله صلى الله عليه وسلم فقال أتشفع في حد من حدود الله ثم قام فخطب قال يا أيها الناس إنما ضل من قبلكم أنهم كانوا إذا سرق الشريف تركوه وإذا سرق الضعيف فيهم أقاموا عليه الحد وايم الله لو أن فاطمة بنت محمد سرقت لقطع محمد يدها

'Ā'ishah narrates the (incident) of the Makhzūmī lady who stole and the Quraysh said, "Who will speak to the Messenger? There is none brave enough besides Usāmah, the beloved of the Messenger ﷺ."

He (Usāmah) went to speak to the Messenger ﷺ (and interceded on her behalf) and he replied, "Are you interceding concerning one of the prescribed punishments of Allah?"

Then he stood up and addressed (the people). He said, "O people! Those before you only went astray because when the noble (amongst them) stole they left him and when the weak (amongst them) they imposed upon him the prescribed punishment. By Allah! If Fāṭimah, the daughter of Muḥammad stole, Muḥammad would cut her hand!"[2]

This ḥadīth is one of the clearest arguments against Tījānī as it clearly discloses the fact that Usāmah intended to intercede on behalf of a woman whom it was clearly established that she stole. The Ḥudūd, as is well known, are warded off on account of ambiguities. Therefore, had there been ambiguity (in this particular case) Usāmah would not have been urged to intercede on behalf of the Makhzūmī lady. This is clear from the Prophet's ﷺ words, "Are you interceding in one of the prescribed punishments of Allah?"

1 *Then I was guided*, p. 157.

2 *Ṣaḥīḥ al-Bukhārī*, vol. 6, Kitāb al-Ḥudūd, Ḥadīth no. 6406.

This is in contrast to Khālid's case since he believed Mālik to have turned apostate after his argument with him and therefore killed him. The least that can be said is that he interpreted the situation and erred. What then if Mālik's apostasy has been established through clear proofs? If we consider the different circumstances, Tījānī's objection is obsolete.

Again it is ironic that Tījānī accuses the Ahl al-Sunnah of inventing lies and virtues for the warrior, Khālid ibn Walīd رضي الله عنه. He finds fault with the epithet "The Unsheathed Sword of Allah" even though it has been established that the Prophet ﷺ is the one who bestowed this on him. Why not; when it was he who led the Muslims from victory to victory? Why not; after the great service he rendered to Islam, fighting in the path of Allah such that nine swords were crushed in his hands on the day of Mu'tah and only a Yemenī sword stood firm with him?[1]

It has also been confirmed that he said, "Fighting in the path of Allah often prevents me from reading much of the Qur'ān."[2] When his end drew near, he uttered such profound words which deserve to be etched in gold. He said:

> A night in which my newly wedded bride is presented to me or (a night) in which I am given the news of a son born for me is not more beloved to me than a cold night in which I am in a military detachment with the Mujāhidīn waiting to attack the enemy in the morning. You have to go in Jihād![3]

Ibn ʿAbd al-Barr mentions in *al-Istīʿāb*:

> When death approached Khālid ibn Walīd he said, "I witnessed nearly one hundred military campaigns. There is not a single part of my body except that there is a strike (of a sword on it), or a stabbing (from a dagger on it), or a shot (from an arrow on it). Despite that, here I am on my bed dying like a stead. May the eyes of the cowards never sleep!"[4]

Even the scholars of the Rāfiḍah acknowledge the heroism and bravery of this honourable leader. Their great scholar, ʿAbbās al-Qummī, says in his book *al-Kunā wa l-Alqāb*:

---

1 *Ṣaḥīḥ al-Bukhārī*, Kitāb al-Maghāzī, Bāb Ghazwah Mu'tah min Arḍ al-Shām, vol. Ḥadīth no. 4017-4018.

2 *Siyar Aʿlām al-Nubalā'*, vol. 1 p. 375-376; Abū Yaʿlā also narrates it in the *Musnad*, vol. 13 under the aḥādīth of Khālid ibn Walīd, Ḥadīth no. 7188, the examiner of the book says, 'its chain is reliable'.

3 Ibn Ḥajar: *Al-Iṣābah*, vol. 2 p. 253.

4 Ibn ʿAbd al-Barr: *Al-Istīʿāb*, vol. 2 p. 430.

> He is the hero who witnessed many great battles and who used to say, according to what has been narrated about him, "I witnessed this battle and that battle. There is not a single part of my body except that there is a strike (of a sword on it), or a stabbing (from a dagger on it), or a shot (from an arrow on it). Despite that, here I am on my bed dying like a donkey dies and the eyes of cowards do not sleep."[1]

Look at Tījānī when he said to one of his friends during his 'days of ignorance' about Khālid ibn Walīd, that he was "The Unsheathed Sword of Allah", as the Prophet ﷺ referred him. His resentful friend responded that Khālid ibn Walīd was the "crippled sword of the devil." Thereafter Tījānī retracts that statement 'after research' in which 'Allah opened his eyes.' We seek Allah's protection from such 'guidance'.

Thereafter he says:

> **Historians have recorded that after this terrible misdeed, Abu Bakr sent Khalid on a mission to al-Yamamah, from which he came out victorious and subsequently married a girl from there in the same way as he had Leyla, before the blood of those innocent Muslims and the blood of the followers of Musaylama had dried. Later, Abu Bakr rebuked him about what he had done and used stronger words than those he used during the affair of Leyla.**
>
> **Undoubtedly, this girl's husband was killed by Khalid who took her for himself, in the same way as he had Leyla, the widow of Malik. It must have been so; otherwise Abu Bakr would not have rebuked him using stronger words than the previous event. The historians mention the text of the letter which Abu Bakr sent to Khalid ibn al-Walid in which he said, "O Ibn Umm Khalid. Upon my life you are doing nothing but marrying women, and in the yard of your house there is the blood of one thousand two hundred Muslims yet to dry!" When Khalid read the letter, he commented, "This must be the work of al-A'sar" meaning Umar ibn al-Khattab.[2]**

Our comment:

This narration is weak. Appearing in its chain is Muḥammad Ibn Ḥumayd ibn Ḥayyān al-Rāzī who is weak.[3] This tradition is severely flawed and cannot be relied upon.

---

1 ʿAbbās al-Qummī: *Al-Kunā wa al-Alqāb*, p. 38-39.

2 *Then I was guided*, p. 158.

3 Refer to p. 356 of this book.

Assuming its reliability still does not put Khālid in an awkward position. All that it amounts to is that he approached Majāʿah ibn Mirārah seeking to marry his daughter and he (Majāʿah) married him to his daughter. Is there anything in this proposal of marriage that disparages Khālid? His marriage to more than one wife is also not a reason for rebuke or a prohibition in Islam?

If we consider Abū Bakr's objection, then Khālid had done well to defend himself and justify his action with his statement:

> By my life! I did not marry any woman until consent was granted to me and the (people of the) household were pleased with me. I have married into the family of a man whom if I had to travel from Madīnah to propose I would not have bothered (myself about it). Indeed, I elicited my proposal to him from beneath my own feet. If you disapprove that for me on account of dīn or worldly matters then I disagree with you.
>
> As for the politeness of my condolences for the fallen Muslims, by Allah, if grief could keep the living alive or return the dead to the living then grief would have kept the living alive and returned the dead to the living for indeed I dived into situations to the point where I had lost hope in life and was certain of death.
>
> As for Majāʿah deceiving me, according to the opinion of some, I do not fault my opinion today but I do not have knowledge of the unseen. Indeed, Allah has decreed goodness for the Muslims. He has bequeathed to them the land and gifted the outcome to the pious.[1]

It appears that Tījānī cannot rid himself from his most distinguished quality; lying! He camouflages the truth with his statement, "*no doubt this other girl also had a husband who Khālid killed then pounced on her as he did with Laylā.*" I cannot believe that Tījānī who mentions this incident and references it to its sources in the footnotes of his book is unaware that this narration mentions that Khālid went to the father of this woman, namely Majāʿah, for her hand in marriage and he consented to Khālid's marriage with his daughter.[2]

What this narration does highlight though is Tījānī's resentment for Khālid ibn al-Walīd رضي الله عنه. Tījānī finds fault with him in unreliable narrations, even when there is no fault to be found.

1 Ṣādiq al-ʿArjūn: *Khālid ibn Walīd*, p. 201.

2 *Al-Ṭabarī*, vol. 2 p. 284, the year 11 after Hijrah.

Chapter Seven

Tījānī's Criticisms of the Second Khalīfah, ʿUmar ibn al-Khaṭṭāb

After his earlier diatribe on Ḥudaybiyyah, the Thursday calamity and the dispatching of Usāmah's battalion Tījānī, again, sets his target on the second Khalīfah, ʿUmar ibn al-Khaṭṭāb رَضِيَ اللَّهُ عَنْهُ. Fortunately, our detailed refutations of his arguments, and our exposé of his lies, misdirection and falsification of history suffices us from readdressing those issues[1].

Before addressing his criticisms I feel bound to elaborate, albeit briefly, on the personality and status of this Companion of the Prophet صَلَّى اللَّهُ عَلَيْهِ وَسَلَّمَ. I will present ʿUmar رَضِيَ اللَّهُ عَنْهُ as the Prophet صَلَّى اللَّهُ عَلَيْهِ وَسَلَّمَ described him. The Prophet صَلَّى اللَّهُ عَلَيْهِ وَسَلَّمَ said:

لقد كان فيمن كان قبلكم من بني إسرائيل رجال يكلمون من غير أن يكونوا أنبياء فإن يكن من أمتي منهم أحد فعمر

> There were men from those who preceded you, from the Banī Isrā'īl, who were inspired with guidance though they were not prophets. If ever there is such a person from my Ummah it is ʿUmar.[2]

The Prophet صَلَّى اللَّهُ عَلَيْهِ وَسَلَّمَ also attested to his knowledge when he said:

بينا أنا نائم رأيت الناس عرضوا على وعليهم قمص فمنها ما يبلغ الثدى ومنها ما يبلغ دون ذلك وعرض على عمر وعليه قميص اجتره قالوا فما أولته يا رسول الله قال الدين

> "I saw in a dream that some people were presented to me clad in shirts. Some of these reached the chest and others reached below that. ʿUmar رَضِيَ اللَّهُ عَنْهُ was presented to me wearing a shirt which he was dragging."
>
> They said, "How do you interpret it, O Messenger of Allah?"
>
> He replied, "The dīn!"[3]

---

1 Refer to p. 31 Ḥudaybiyyah discussion; p. 69 Thursday calamity discussion; and p. 91 Battalion of Usāmah discussion.

2 *Ṣaḥīḥ al-Bukhārī*, Kitāb Faḍā'il al-Ṣaḥābah, Ḥadīth no. 3486.

3 *Ṣaḥīḥ al-Bukhārī*, Kitāb Faḍā'il al-Ṣaḥābah, Ḥadīth no. 3487.

Abū Dharr رضي الله عنه is one of those Companions whom even the Shīʿah hold in high esteem. He said:

مر فتى على عمر فقال عمر نعم الفتى. فتبعه أبو ذر فقال يا فتى استغفر لي فقال يا أبا ذر أستغفر لك وأنت صاحب رسول الله صلى الله عليه وآله وسلم؟ قال استغفر لي. قال لا أو تخبرني. فقال إنك مررت على عمر فقال نعم الفتى.وإني سمعت رسول الله صلى الله عليه وآله وسلم يقول إن الله جعل الحق على لسان عمر وقلبه.

Once a young man passed by ʿUmar, and ʿUmar praised him saying, "What an excellent young man!"

So Abū Dharr رضي الله عنه followed him and said to him, "O young man, seek Allah's forgiveness for me."

The young man responded, "O Abū Dharr, how is it that you ask me to seek Allah's forgiveness for you whereas you are a Companion of the Prophet صلى الله عليه وسلم?"

Abū Dharr replied, "Seek Allah's forgiveness for me."

But the young man was persistent so Abū Dharr informed him, "When you passed by ʿUmar, I heard him commend you saying, 'What an excellent young man!', and I have heard the Prophet صلى الله عليه وسلم saying, 'Allah has placed the truth on ʿUmar's tongue and heart.'"[1]

Finally, we present a ḥadīth which demonstrates the lofty status of ʿUmar رضي الله عنه when the Prophet صلى الله عليه وسلم prayed for his Islam

عن عبد الله بن عمر رضي الله عنهما أن رسول الله صلى الله عليه وسلم قال اللهم أعز الإسلام بأحب هذين الرجلين إليك بأبي جهل بن هشام أو بعمر بن الخطاب قال وكان أحبهما إليه عمر

ʿAbd Allāh ibn ʿUmar رضي الله عنهما narrates that the Messenger of Allah صلى الله عليه وسلم said, "O Allah! Bring honour to Islam through the dearest of these two men to you: Abū Jahl ibn Hishām, or ʿUmar ibn al-Khaṭṭāb."

He said, "And the dearest of them to Him was ʿUmar."[2]

---

1 *Musnad Aḥmad*, Ḥadīth no. 5145.

2 *Sunan al-Tirmidhī*, Kitāb al-Manāqib, Ḥadīth no. 4045.

1. Tījānī's claim that ʿUmar Contradicted the Sunnah

Tījānī says:

> **The one who looks closely at narrations similar to this will find that they (the Ṣaḥābah) placed themselves above him (the Prophet ﷺ) and (will conclude that they) believed that he erred and they were correct. Indeed, this compelled some historians to regard the actions of Ṣaḥābah as correct even if it contradicted the action of the Prophet ﷺ or it projected that the level of some of the Ṣaḥābah's knowledge and piety was greater than the Prophet's ﷺ such as when they concluded that the Prophet ﷺ erred in the issue of the prisoners of Badr and ʿUmar got it right. They narrate concerning that false narrations in which the Prophet ﷺ said, "Had Allah afflicted us that day none would have been spared save ʿUmar."[1]**

Refuting Tījānī's claim that ʿUmar Contradicted the Sunnah

ʿUmar رضي الله عنه was sensitive to the greater objectives of the Sharīʿah. Often times his intuition on certain matters were in accordance to later revelation. There are a number of narrations wherein ʿUmar رضي الله عنه expresses his appreciation to Allah for this blessing as he recalls a few incidents when his suggestions on particular matters concurred with what Allah had later revealed in the Qurʾān. The following ḥadīth has been narrated by al-Bukhārī by way of Anas ibn Mālik رضي الله عنه, who quotes ʿUmar رضي الله عنه:

> وافقت ربي في ثلاث فقلت يا رسول الله لو اتخذنا من مقام إبراهيم مصلى فنزلت وَاتَّخِذُوْا مِنْ مَّقَامِ إِبْرَاهِيْمَ مُصَلًّى وآية الحجاب قلت يا رسول الله لو أمرت نساءك أن يحتجبن فإنه يكلمهن البر وفاجر فنزلت آية الحجاب واجتمع نساء النبي صلى الله عليه وسلم في الغيرة عليه فقلت لهن عسى ربه إن طلقكن أن يبدله أزواجا خيرا منكن فنزلت هذه الآية

> I concurred with my Lord on three issues.
>
> I said, "O Messenger of Allah perhaps we should take the Maqām Ibrāhīm as a place of ṣalāh." Later it was revealed, 'And take, [O believers], from the standing place of Ibrāhīm a place of prayer.'"

---

1 *Then I was guided*, p. 92.

> Similarly in case of the ḥijāb, I said, "O Messenger of Allah perhaps you ought to consider instructing your wives to conceal themselves as those who are good and bad both speak to them," whereupon, the verse of ḥijāb was revealed.
>
> On yet another occasion the wives of the Prophet ﷺ behaved inappropriately with him and I chastised them saying, "It is possible that if he divorces you, his Lord will replace you by granting him wives better than you!" Soon thereafter this verse was revealed.[1]

Al-Bukhārī narrates this in a different chapter with a slight variation in the wording:

قال عمر وافقت الله في ثلاث أو وافقني ربي في ثلاث قلت يا رسول الله لو اتخذت مقام إبراهيم مصلى وقلت يا رسول الله يدخل عليك البر والفاجر فلو أمرت أمهات المؤمنين بالحجاب فأنزل الله آية الحجاب قال وبلغني معاتبة النبي صلى الله عليه وسلم بعض نسائه فدخلت عليهن قلت إن انتهيتن أو ليبدلن الله رسوله صلى الله عليه وسلم خيرا منكن حتى أتيت إحدى نسائه قالت يا عمر أما في رسول الله صلى الله عليه وسلم ما يعظ نساءه حتى تعظهن أنت فأنزل الله عسى ربه إن طلقكن أن يبدله أزواجا خيرا منكن مسلمات الآية

> I concurred with Allah—or with my Lord—on three issues. I said, "O Messenger! Perhaps you should take the Maqām Ibrāhīm as a place of ṣalāh."
>
> On another occasion I said, "The good and the bad visit you, perhaps you should instruct the Mothers of the Believers to conceal (themselves)," and Allah revealed the verse of ḥijāb.
>
> (On another occasion) it reached me that the Prophet ﷺ reproached some of his wives so I went to them and said, "You better stop (with what you doing) or Allah will substitute for his Messenger better than you." I went to one of his wives and she said, "O 'Umar! Can the Prophet not rebuke his (own) wives that you come to exhort them?" Allah revealed, "Perhaps his Lord, if he divorced you [all], would substitute for him wives better than you..."[2]

Muslim also narrates those matters which 'Umar رضي الله عنه offered a suggestion that was in accordance with subsequent revelation:

---

1 *Ṣaḥīḥ al-Bukhārī*, Kitāb Abwāb al-Qiblah, Ḥadīth no. 393.

2 *Ṣaḥīḥ al-Bukhārī*, Kitāb al-Tafsīr, Sūrah al-Baqarah, Ḥadīth no. 4213.

قال عمر وافقت ربى في ثلاث في مقام إبراهيم وفي الحجاب وفي أسارى بدر

ʿUmar said, "I concurred with my Lord on three issues, the Maqām Ibrāhīm, the ḥijāb, and the captives of Badr."[1]

He also narrates from ʿUmar رضي الله عنه in a lengthy ḥadīth:

فلما أسروا الأسارى قال رسول الله صلى الله عليه وسلم لأبي بكر وعمر ما ترون في هؤلاء الأسارى فقال أبو بكر يا نبي الله هم بنو العم والعشيرة أرى أن تأخذ منهم فدية فتكون لنا قوة على الكفار فعسى الله أن يهديهم للإسلام فقال رسول الله صلى الله عليه وسلم ما ترى يا ابن الخطاب قلت لا والله يا رسول الله ما أرى الذي رأى أبو بكر ولكني أرى أن تمكنا فنضرب أعناقهم فتمكن عليا من عقيل فيضرب عنقه وتمكني من فلان نسيبا لعمر فأضرب عنقه فإن هؤلاء أئمة الكفر وصناديدها فهوي رسول الله صلى الله عليه وسلم ما قال أبو بكر ولم يهو ما قلت فلما كان من الغد جئت فإذا رسول الله صلى الله عليه وسلم وأبو بكر قاعدين يبكيان قلت يا رسول الله أخبرني من أي شيء تبكي أنت وصاحبك فإن وجدت بكاء بكيت وإن لم أجد بكاء تباكيت لبكائكما فقال رسول الله صلى الله عليه وسلم أبكي للذي عرض علي أصحابك من أخذهم الفداء لقد عرض علي عذابهم أدنى من هذه الشجرة شجرة قريبة من نبي الله صلى الله عليه وسلم وأنزل الله عز وجل ما كان لنبي أن يكون له أسرى حتى يثخن في الأرض إلى قوله فكلوا مما غنمتم حلالا طيبا فأحل الله الغنيمة لهم

When they took the captives, the Messenger ﷺ said to Abū Bakr and ʿUmar, "What is your opinion concerning these captives of war?"

Abū Bakr said, "O Prophet of Allah! They are relatives and family. My opinion is that you should release them after getting from them a ransom. This will be a source of strength to us against the disbelievers. It is quite possible that later Allah may guide them to Islam."

1 *Ṣaḥīḥ Muslim* with its commentary, Kitāb Faḍā'il al-Ṣaḥābah, Bāb min Faḍā'il Abī Bakr, Ḥadīth no. 2399.

The Prophet ﷺ said, "What is your opinion, O son of al-Khaṭṭāb?"

I said, "By Allah! No! O Messenger! I do not share the opinion of Abū Bakr. I am of the opinion that you should permit us to take off their heads. You should hand over ʿAqīl so that ʿAlī will remove his head, and allow me to take of the head of so and so ('Umar's relative), as these are the leaders of disbelief."

The Prophet ﷺ inclined towards Abū Bakr's opinion and he did not incline towards my opinion.

The next day I found the Messenger of Allah ﷺ and Abū Bakr sitting on the floor crying. I said, "O Messenger of Allah! Tell me what are you and your Companion crying about. If I find the tears I will weep, or I will at least pretend to cry in sympathy with you."

The Messenger ﷺ said, "I weep for what has happened to your Companions for taking ransom (from the prisoners). I was shown the punishment which would have afflicted them. It was brought to me as close as this tree. He pointed to a tree close to him. Allah revealed these verses:

مَا كَانَ لِنَبِيٍّ أَنْ يَكُوْنَ لَهٗ أَسْرٰى حَتّٰى يُثْخِنَ فِي الْأَرْضِ ۚ تُرِيْدُوْنَ عَرَضَ الدُّنْيَا ۖ وَاللّٰهُ يُرِيدُ الْاٰخِرَةَ ۗ وَاللّٰهُ عَزِيْزٌ حَكِيْمٌ لَوْلَا كِتٰبٌ مِنَ اللّٰهِ سَبَقَ لَمَسَّكُمْ فِيمَآ أَخَذْتُمْ عَذَابٌ عَظِيمٌ فَكُلُوْا مِمَّا غَنِمْتُمْ حَلٰلًا طَيِّبًا ۖ وَاتَّقُوا اللّٰهَ ۚ إِنَّ اللّٰهَ غَفُوْرٌ رَّحِيْمٌ

It is not for a Prophet to have captives (of war) until he has thoroughly defeated (Allah's enemies) in the land. You (i.e. some Muslims) desire the commodities of this world, but Allah desires (for you) the hereafter. And Allah is Exalted in Might and Wise. If not for a decree from Allah that preceded, you would have been touched for what you took by a great punishment. So consume what you have taken of war booty (as being) lawful and good, and fear Allah. Indeed, Allah is Forgiving and Merciful.[1]

And Allah permitted the spoils of war.[2]

---

1 Sūrah al-Anfāl: 67-69.

2 *Ṣaḥīḥ Muslim* with its commentary, Kitāb al-Jihād wa al-Siyar, Bāb al-Imdād bi al-Malāʾikah fī Ghazwah Badr wa Ibāḥāh al-Ghanāʾim, Ḥadīth no. 1763.

It is clear for all to see that these narrations appear in the authentic collections. There is no room for misplaced objections against the authenticity as these chains have withstood the rigorous test of ḥadīth critics. All content related criticism has no weight since there is nothing to suggest that these narrations have been compromised in any way.

By no means do these narrations suggest that some of the Ṣaḥābah were more knowledgeable or pious than the Prophet صَلَّى ٱللَّهُ عَلَيْهِ وَسَلَّمَ. On the contrary, the Prophet صَلَّى ٱللَّهُ عَلَيْهِ وَسَلَّمَ would at times consult his Companions on how to deal with a situation in the absence of revelation.

This was demonstrated on numerous occasions including the incident of Ifk; when the Messenger of Allah صَلَّى ٱللَّهُ عَلَيْهِ وَسَلَّمَ called ʿAlī ibn Abī Ṭālib and Usāmah ibn Zayd رَضِيَ ٱللَّهُ عَنْهُمَا and consulted with them about divorcing his wife. Usāmah ibn Zayd رَضِيَ ٱللَّهُ عَنْهُ told the Prophet صَلَّى ٱللَّهُ عَلَيْهِ وَسَلَّمَ about what he knew of his wife's innocence and his fondness for her saying, "O Messenger of Allah, she is your wife, and we do not know anything but good of her." On the other hand ʿAlī said, "O Messenger of Allah, Allah has not imposed restrictions on you, and there are plenty of other women besides her. If you ask her servant girl, she will be honest with you."[1]

No one claims that ʿAlī رَضِيَ ٱللَّهُ عَنْهُ was more knowledgeable or pious than the Prophet صَلَّى ٱللَّهُ عَلَيْهِ وَسَلَّمَ. The Prophet صَلَّى ٱللَّهُ عَلَيْهِ وَسَلَّمَ took ʿAlī's رَضِيَ ٱللَّهُ عَنْهُ advice and went to Barīrah; asking about ʿĀ'ishah رَضِيَ ٱللَّهُ عَنْهَا. Later on the verses were revealed in which she was exonerated.

We have alluded earlier that it was the Prophet's صَلَّى ٱللَّهُ عَلَيْهِ وَسَلَّمَ practice to seek the counsel of his Companions in matters which he had not yet received revelation; such was the case when he consulted them on the captives of Badr.

Similarly, in the absence of revelation, the Prophet صَلَّى ٱللَّهُ عَلَيْهِ وَسَلَّمَ used his discretion in matters which he considered would be of benefit for the Muslims. Most times Allah ratified this discretion but there were a few incidents wherein Allah pointed out that the most correct approach was different to what the Prophet صَلَّى ٱللَّهُ عَلَيْهِ وَسَلَّمَ first considered. One such occasion is when he prayed the Ṣalāt al-Janāzah for the head of the munāfiqīn, ʿAbd Allāh ibn Ubay. ʿUmar رَضِيَ ٱللَّهُ عَنْهُ said to him:

---

1 *Ṣaḥīḥ al-Bukhārī*, Kitāb al-Maghāzī, Ḥadīth no. 4141.

"O Messenger! Are you praying over him and Allah forbade you from praying over him?"

The Prophet ﷺ replied, "My Lord gave me the choice. He says, 'Ask forgiveness for them, (O Muḥammad), or do not ask forgiveness for them. If you should ask forgiveness for them seventy times—never will Allah forgive them,' I will pray for him more than seventy times."

'Umar said, "He is a munāfiq," but the Prophet ﷺ prayed over him. Then Allah revealed, "And do not pray (the funeral prayer, O Muḥammad), over any of them who has died—ever—or stand at his grave."[1]

This matter is confirmed in the Qur'ān which is obvious for all to see.

It is also established that the Prophet ﷺ reconsidered what he would have done had he not brought along his sacrificial animal during the Ḥajjat al-Wadā'. He said, "If I could change things I would not have brought these sacrificial animals; and had it not been for these sacrificial animals I would have released myself from Iḥrām and made this an 'Umrah [independent of the intention of Ḥajj]."[2]

Similarly when he pledged not to drink honey at the home of Zaynab bint Jaḥsh after indirect complaints from his wives, 'Ā'ishah and Ḥafṣah, Allah revealed:

يَأَيُّهَا النَّبِيُّ لِمَ تُحَرِّمُ مَا أَحَلَّ اللَّهُ لَكَ تَبْتَغِي مَرْضَاتَ أَزْوَاجِكَ وَاللَّهُ غَفُورٌ رَحِيمٌ

O Prophet, why do you prohibit (yourself from) what Allah has made lawful for you, seeking the approval of your wives? And Allah is Forgiving and Merciful.[3]

Since the Prophet ﷺ held the position of legislative authority, the only means by which his Ijtihād-based decisions could be redressed was through revelation. The handful of verses which amend decisions taken by the Prophet ﷺ were inevitable since these decisions yielded legislative authority and could only be redressed through divine intervention.

1 *Ṣaḥīḥ al-Bukhārī*, Kitāb al-Tafsīr, Sūrah al-Tawbah, Ḥadīth no. 4393.

2 *Ṣaḥīḥ al-Bukhārī*, Kitāb al-Ḥajj, Ḥadīth no. 1568, from Jābir ibn 'Abd Allāh.

3 Sūrah al-Taḥrīm: 1.

On the other hand, ʿUmar ibn al-Khaṭṭāb has no legislative authority. It was hence necessary for revelation to ratify his suggestions because of the lack of jurisdiction otherwise.

Revelation concurring with the suggestion of a Ṣaḥābī on an issue does not detract from the Prophet's ﷺ position; neither does it mean that some Ṣaḥābah were more knowledgeable than the Prophet ﷺ. One would only expect such reasoning from a foolish person.

An example of this appears in the glorious Qur'ān:

وَدَاوُدَ وَسُلَيْمَانَ إِذْ يَحْكُمَانِ فِي الْحَرْثِ إِذْ نَفَشَتْ فِيهِ غَنَمُ الْقَوْمِ وَكُنَّا لِحُكْمِهِمْ شَاهِدِينَ فَفَهَّمْنَاهَا سُلَيْمَانَ ۚ وَكُلًّا آتَيْنَا حُكْمًا وَعِلْمًا ۚ وَسَخَّرْنَا مَعَ دَاوُدَ الْجِبَالَ يُسَبِّحْنَ وَالطَّيْرَ ۚ وَكُنَّا فَاعِلِينَ

And [mention] Dāwūd and Sulaymān, when they judged concerning the field—when the sheep of a people overran it [at night], and We were witness to their judgment. And We gave understanding of the case to Sulaymān, and to each [of them] We gave judgment and knowledge. And We subjected the mountains to exalt [Us], along with Dāwūd and [also] the birds. And We were doing [that]. [1]

Thus we have established that the narrations that have been presented at the beginning of our response enjoy both strength of chain and soundness of purport. Only the eye of prejudice would see them differently.

Shīʿī scholars accept these narrations

In fact these narrations have been cited as proof by Rāfiḍī scholars when they debate one another? Dr ʿAlā' al-Dīn al-Qazwīnī cites the ḥadīth of Anas رضي الله عنه (mentioned above) as an argument against doctor Mūsā al-Mūsawī in his book *al-Shīʿah wa al-Taṣḥīḥ*. He says:

> For that reason it has been reported from Anas ibn Mālik (this is the narration of ʿUmar in which he says, "I concurred with my Lord on three issues"), he said that ʿUmar said, "I was informed of what some of his wives had said. Therefore, I went to them and I started questioning them, rebuking them and

1 Sūrah al-Ambiyā: 78 - 79.

among the things I said was, 'You all better stop (with what you doing) or Allah will substitute for him better than you,' until I came to Zaynab. She said, 'O 'Umar! Is the Messenger unable to exhort his own wives that you exhort us?' Then Allah revealed (the verse), 'Perhaps his Lord, if he divorced you (all), would substitute for him wives better than you...'"[1]

Then he mentions a number of narrations and says, "This is a collection of narrations from al-Ṣaḥīḥ (al-Bukhārī)."[2]

It is indeed an odd phenomena when the Rāfiḍah rely on some aḥādīth against the Ahl al-Sunnah they accept its authenticity. However, at other junctures they dismiss it as weak if it expresses some form of praise in it for a Ṣaḥābī.

Perhaps this explains Tījānī's methodology in ḥadīth. Any narration which he believes disparages a Ṣaḥābī becomes reliable, whilst any ḥadīth which professes praise for a Ṣaḥābī is rendered a false unacceptable ḥadīth, on grounds best known to him.

Tījānī forges aḥādīth

Tījānī is visibly annoyed with 'Umar رَضِيَ اللَّهُ عَنْهُ but he is cautious to unleash his blame on the Ahl al-Sunnah to create the impression that they invented the concept of Companions being more knowledgeable and pious than the Messenger of Allah صَلَّى اللَّهُ عَلَيْهِ وَسَلَّمَ. The truth is that if anything was invented it was the narration that he ascribes to the Prophet صَلَّى اللَّهُ عَلَيْهِ وَسَلَّمَ which reads:

"Had Allah afflicted us that day none would have been spared save 'Umar."

Naturally this is an original Tījānī forgery. Why would Allah afflict the Prophet صَلَّى اللَّهُ عَلَيْهِ وَسَلَّمَ and his Ṣaḥābah رَضِيَ اللَّهُ عَنْهُ with an affliction in the first place? This is an old strategy wherein he would ascribe ridiculous narrations to the Prophet صَلَّى اللَّهُ عَلَيْهِ وَسَلَّمَ assuming that the Ahl al-Sunnah would defend a predetermined position. Little does he realise that we do not have preconceived positions and then seek out evidence in support of it. The hallmark feature of the Ahl al-Sunnah is to follow the evidence in arriving at any conclusion.

---

1 Doctor 'Alā' al-Dīn al-Qazwīnī: Ma'a al-Duktūr Mūsā al-Mūsawī fī Kitābihī al-Shī'ah wa al-Taṣḥīḥ, p. 151.
2 Ibid. 152.

Tījānī goes on to say:

> In other words, they were saying, "If it was not for Umar, the Prophet ﷺ would have perished." God protect us from such a corrupt and shameful belief, and he who adheres to this kind of belief is surely far from Islam, and ought to review his thinking or rid himself of the devil. Allah says:
>
> أَفَرَأَيْتَ مَنِ اتَّخَذَ إِلَهَهُ هَوَاهُ وَأَضَلَّهُ اللّٰهُ عَلَىٰ عِلْمٍ وَخَتَمَ عَلَىٰ سَمْعِهِ وَقَلْبِهِ وَجَعَلَ عَلَىٰ بَصَرِهِ غِشَاوَةً فَمَنْ يَهْدِيْهِ مِنْ بَعْدِ اللّٰهِ أَفَلَا تَذَكَّرُوْنَ
>
> Have you seen he who has taken as his god his (own) desire, and Allah has sent him astray due to knowledge and has set a seal upon his hearing and his heart and put over his vision a veil? So who will guide him after Allah? Then will you not be reminded?[1,2]

Our response:

We have pointed out the forgery in Tījānī's citation. Therefore, we are not bound by the conclusion that follows. It is nothing but Tījānī's cunning construct. However, we do wish to hone in on Tījānī's judgment on persons holding that particular belief; that which raises 'some' individuals above the level of the Prophets and considers 'their' knowledge and piety superior to that of the Prophets.

Al-Kulaynī, in his book *al-Uṣūl min al-Kāfī*, reports that ʿAlī ibn Abī Ṭālib often used to say:

> I am God's partitioner between Jannah and Jahannam. I am the greatest criterion. I am the owner of the staff and the branding iron. All the angels, and the Rūḥ, and the Messengers have attested to me in the same way they attested to Muḥammad. Indeed, I have been empowered with the same power with which he was empowered, and that is empowerment of the Supreme Lord. I have been given characteristics which none before me share. I have been taught the appointed times of death, the tribulations to come, the lineages and the Final Judgement. What has preceded me has not passed me

---

1 Sūrah al-Jāthiyah: 23.
2 *Then I was guided*, 93.

> and what was absent from me did not escape me. I give glad tidings with the permission of Allah and execute on his behalf. All of that is from Allah who enabled me through His knowledge.[1]

The Rāfiḍah do not stop here, rather they consider the sons of ʿAlī greater than the Prophets. A famous Shīʿah scholar, Muḥammad Farrūkh al-Ṣaffār in his book *Faḍā'il Ahl al-Bayt*—quotes the following from ʿAbd Allāh ibn al-Walīd:

> Abū ʿAbd Allāh (al-Ṣādiq) said to me, "What do the Shīʿah say about ʿĪsā and Mūsā, and Amīr al-Mu'minīn?"
>
> I said, "They say that ʿĪsā and Mūsā are greater than Amīr al-Mu'minīn."
>
> He then said, "Do they claim that Amīr al-Mu'minīn knew what the Prophet knew?"
>
> I said, "Yes! But they do not prefer anyone above the Ulū al-ʿAzm from the Messengers."
>
> Abū ʿAbd Allāh said, "Argue against them using the Book of Allah!"
>
> I said, "Which place in it should I argue against them with?"
>
> He said, "Allah said to Mūsā:
>
> وَكَتَبْنَا لَهُ فِي الْأَلْوَاحِ مِنْ كُلِّ شَيْءٍ
>
> *And We wrote for him on the tablets from all things.*[2]
>
> He did not say: "We wrote for him all things."
>
> Allah said to ʿĪsā:
>
> وَلِأُبَيِّنَ لَكُمْ بَعْضَ الَّذِي تَخْتَلِفُونَ فِيهِ
>
> *And to make clear to you some of that over which you dispute.*[3]
>
> Whilst he said to Muḥammad ﷺ:

1 *Uṣūl al-Kāfī*, vol. 1 p. 152, Kitāb al-Ḥujjah, Bāb ʿan al-A'immah Hum Arkān al-Arḍ.

2 Sūrah al-Aʿrāf: 145.

3 Sūrah al-Zukhruf: 63.

وَجِئْنَا بِكَ شَهِيْدًا عَلَى هٰؤُلَاءِ وَنَزَّلْنَا عَلَيْكَ الْكِتَابَ تِبْيَانًا لِكُلِّ شَيْءٍ

And We will bring you, (O Muḥammad), as a witness over all of them And We have sent down to you the Book as clarification for all things.[1,2]

This fabrication implies that since Amīr al-Mu'minīn was equal to the Prophet Muḥammad ﷺ in knowledge, and these verses are meant to prove the superiority of his knowledge over that of Prophets Mūsā and ʿĪsā, the knowledge of Amīr al-Mu'minīn is superior to theirs!

Thereafter comes the next narration from Abū ʿAbd Allāh, Jaʿfar ibn Muḥammad ibn ʿAlī ibn Ḥusayn ibn ʿAlī ibn Abī Ṭālib, who allegedly said:

> Allah created the Ulū al-ʿAzm from the Messengers and honoured them with knowledge. And Allah caused us to inherit their knowledge and their honour. And he preferred us over them through their knowledge and the knowledge of the Messenger which they knew not. He taught us their knowledge and the knowledge of the Messenger.[3]

Tījānī claims to have examined the books of both sides before making his decision; I am sure he knows how to get out of his own trap.

2. Tījānī's claim that ʿUmar was Unjust

He says:

> **For example, we hear so much about Umar's justice which the "story-tellers" attributed to him. It was even said about him "You ruled with justice, therefore you can sleep." It has also been said that Umar was buried in a standing position so that justice would not die with him... and you could go on and on talking about Umar's justice. However, the correct history tells us that when Umar ordered that grants should be distributed among the people during the twentieth year of al-Hijrah, he did not follow the tradition of the Messenger of Allah ﷺ, nor did he confine himself to its rules. The Prophet ﷺ distributed the grants on an equal basis among all Muslims and did not differentiate between one person and another, and Abu Bakr did**

---

1 Sūrah al-Naḥl: 89.

2 Muḥammad al-Ṣaffār: *Faḍā'il Ahl al-Bayt* also known as *Baṣā'ir al-Darajāt*, p. 223-224, Bāb ʿan al-A'immah Afḍal min Mūsā wa al-Khiḍr.

3 Ibid. p. 224.

> **the same throughout his caliphate. But Umar introduced a new method. He preferred the early converts to Islam to those who came later. He preferred al-Muhajireen (immigrants from Mecca to Medinah) from Quraysh to other Muhajireen. He preferred all the Muhajireen to al-Ansar (followers of Prophet Muhammad ﷺ in Medinah who granted him refuge after the Hijra). He preferred the Arabs to the non-Arabs. He preferred the freeman to the slave. He preferred (the tribe of) Mudar to (the tribe of) Rabia for he gave three hundred to the former and two hundred to the latter. He also preferred al-Aws to al-Khazraj.**
>
> **Where is the justice in all this differentiation, O people who have minds?** [1]

Refuting Tījānī's claim that ʿUmar was Unjust

The idea of justice is subjective. Some advocate for justice as equality. Others promote the concept of need-based justice. While there are even others who call for merit-based justice. Since the concept of justice is so subjective, it is unfair to liberally dish out demerits based on a subjective perception of what justice actually is.

Secondly, the allegations against ʿUmar رضي الله عنه have to be seen against a particular backdrop. If there is a precedent which justifies his policy, the charge of injustice is nothing more than the reflection of bias and prejudice in the eyes of the accuser. If ʿUmar رضي الله عنه is found adopting a Prophetic precedent then it is not ʿUmar whom Tījānī has issue with; instead it is the Prophet ﷺ.

Tījānī accuses ʿUmar رضي الله عنه of injustice based on his grant distribution schedule [*ʿAṭā*]. ʿUmar رضي الله عنه had a tiered system by which he calculated people's monthly grant [*ʿAṭā*] from the state. This is a policy which has a precedent in the Sunnah.

Al-Bukhārī narrates in his *Ṣaḥīḥ* from Nāfiʿ—from Ibn ʿUmar, who said:

> قسم رسول الله صلى الله عليه وسلم يوم خيبر للفرس سهمين وللراجل سهما قال فسره نافع فقال إذا كان مع الرجل فرس فله ثلاثة أسهم فإن لم يكن له فرس فله سهم.
>
> The Prophet ﷺ distributed the spoils of war on the Day of Khaybar, for the horse two shares and for the infantry one share. Nāfiʿ interpreted it and

---

1 *Then I was guided*, p. 94-95.

said, "If the man had a horse with him he received three shares and if he did not have a horse with him he received one share."[1]

Ibn Taymiyyah says:

> Those who allow for disparate distribution say the general rule is parity (between all). The fact that the Prophet ﷺ used to favour at times proves permissibility of favouring. This view is the better view. In other words, the general rule is parity between all and that favouring is permissible on account of a favourable benefit. 'Umar did not show favour on account of preferential treatment or bias. Rather, he distributed the 'Aṭā according to religious merits and therefore favoured the Sābiqūn Awwalūn from the Muhājirīn and the Anṣār then those who came after them from the Ṣaḥābah. Also, he used to reduce his own share and the shares of his close family to less than their peers. He reduced the shares of his son and daughter to shares less than those they were superior to. Only the one who favours on the basis of his personal desires is criticised. As for the one whose goal is the pleasure of Allah, and obedience to the Messenger, and honouring those whom Allah and his Messenger honour, and giving preference to those whom Allah and his Messenger gave preference to; such a person is praised and not rebuked. It is for that reason that he gave 'Alī and his sons more than he gave to their peers and such was the way he treated the rest of the Prophet's ﷺ family. Had he distributed it equally they would only have received a portion of that.[2]

'Umar رضي الله عنه distributed the grant on a merit based system, and he divided them into categories based on a hierarchy of merit. The first category was the participants of Badr from the Muhājirīn, then the participants at Badr from the Anṣār. The next category was the Muhājirīn who did not participate in Badr but participated in the rest of the battles, then those who witnessed Ḥudaybiyyah, and then the Conquest of Makkah, then those who participated in the campaigns of al-Qādisiyyah and Yarmūk. He fixed stipends for some, like Ḥasan and Ḥusayn, at the highest tier despite them not fitting the brief.

Contrary to what Tījānī says, there was no distinction between Arab over non-Arab in terms of the distribution. He stipulated the same amount for those who participated

1 *Ṣaḥīḥ al-Bukhārī*, Kitāb al-Maghāzī, Bāb Ghazwah al-Khaybar, Ḥadīth no. 3988.

2 *Minhāj al-Sunnah*, vol. 6 p. 103-104.

at Badr, whether Arab or freed slave. He wrote to the leaders of the armies, "Those who you set free from the non-Arabs who have accepted Islam join them to their former masters with the same rights and duties. If they prefer to be independent then treat them as your family with regards to the ʿAṭā and general goodwill."[1] As for the method of distribution mentioned by Tījānī which he transmitted from Shīʿī sources, they have no reliable chains of narration for them.

3. Tījānī accuses ʿUmar of ignorance

Tījānī says:

> **We also hear so much about Umar's knowledge, to the extent he was described as the most knowledgeable Companion, and it has been said about him that he agreed with his God on many ideas that were revealed in various Qur'anic verses, and that he disagreed with the Prophet صَلَّى ٱللَّهُ عَلَيْهِ وَسَلَّمَ about them. But the correct history tells us that Umar did not agree with the Qur'an, even after it had been revealed. When one of the Companions asked him one day during his caliphate, "O Commander of the Believers, I am unclean, but I cannot find water to wash." Umar answered, "Do not pray." Then Ammar ibn Yasir had to remind him about Tayammum [ritual cleaning with earth], but Umar was not convinced, and said to Ammar, "You are responsible only for the duties which have been assigned to you".**
>
> **Where is Umar's knowledge regarding the Tayammum verse which had been revealed in the Book of Allah, and where is Umar's knowledge of the Tradition of the Prophet صَلَّى ٱللَّهُ عَلَيْهِ وَسَلَّمَ who taught them how to do Tayammum as well as Wudu [ritual ablution]?[2]**

Refuting Tījānī's accusation of ignorance

Contrary to what Tījānī attributed to the Ahl al-Sunnah, the general view is that the most knowledgeable of the Ummah after its Prophet صَلَّى ٱللَّهُ عَلَيْهِ وَسَلَّمَ was Abū Bakr رَضِيَ ٱللَّهُ عَنْهُ. That aside, Tījānī's façade is beginning to fade as can be seen from his petty objections against ʿUmar رَضِيَ ٱللَّهُ عَنْهُ. Tījānī is eager to condemn ʿUmar on account of a single incident that escaped his memory.

Al-Bukhārī from Saʿīd ibn ʿAbd al-Raḥmān ibn Abzā—from his father, who said:

---

1 Dr. Muḥammad Rawwās Qalʿah: *Mawsūʿāh Fiqh ʿUmar ibn al-Khaṭṭāb*, p. 541.

2 *Then I was guided*, p. 95.

جاء رجل إلى عمر بن الخطاب فقال إني أجنبت فلم أُصب الماء، فقال عمار بن ياسر لعمر بن الخطاب أما تذكر أنّا كنّا في سفر أنا وأنت، فأما أنت لم تُصلِّ، وأما أنا فتمعّكت فصلّيت، فذكرت ذلك للنبي صلى الله عليه وسلم فقال النبي صلى الله عليه وسلم : إنما كان يكفيك هكذا، فضرب النبي صلى الله عليه وسلم بكفيه الأرض ونفخ فيهما، ثم مسح بهما وجهه وكفيه

A man came to ʿUmar ibn al-Khaṭṭāb and said, "I was in a state of major ritual impurity but I could not find any water."

ʿAmmār ibn Yāsir said to ʿUmar ibn al-Khaṭṭāb, "Do you not remember when we were on a journey? You did not make ṣalāh but I rubbed myself with soil and performed ṣalāh. I then mentioned that to the Messenger ﷺ and the Messenger ﷺ said, "This would have sufficed you," and the Messenger ﷺ struck his hands on the earth and blew in it. Then he wiped his face and his hands (arms) with it."[1]

It is well-known that ʿUmar initially considered it incorrect for the *Junub* (person in the state of major ritual impurity) to take tayammum as a substitute for the mandatory Ghusl holding onto the apparent meaning of the verses:

وَإِنْ كُنْتُمْ جُنُبًا فَاطَّهَّرُوْا

And if you are in a state of Janābah then purify yourselves.[2]

وَلَا جُنُبًا إِلَّا عَابِرِيْ سَبِيْلٍ حَتّٰى تَغْتَسِلُوْا

Or in a state of Janābah except those passing through (a place of prayer), until you have washed (your whole body).[3]

ʿUmar maintained that position until ʿAmmār reminded him about the incident which involved the two of them but he could not recall. It is for that reason that ʿUmar said to ʿAmmār, as mentioned in the narration of *Ṣaḥīḥ Muslim*, "Fear Allah, O ʿAmmār!"

---

1 *Ṣaḥīḥ al-Bukhārī*, Kitāb al-Tayammum, Ḥadīth no. 331.

2 Sūrah al-Mā'idah: 6.

3 Sūrah al-Nisā': 43.

Al-Nawawī elaborates on this in his commentary of *Ṣaḥīḥ Muslim*:

> The meaning of ʿUmar's statement, "Fear Allah, O ʿAmmār," in other words, (fear Allah) with regards to what you narrate and be sure of it. Perhaps you forgot (something) or you are confused as I was with you and I do not remember anything about that.[1]

When ʿAmmār told him, "If you wish I will stop narrating it,"ʿUmar said to him, "We hold you responsible for what you have taken responsibility for," (and he did not say, "we burden you with what you burdened yourself with"), in other words:

> My inability to recall the incident does not mean it is untrue. Therefore, I will not prevent you from narrating it.[2]

The most that can be said about this matter is that ʿUmar رضي الله عنه did not remember this incident as he was not infallible.

The shallowness in Tījānī's objection is evident from this statement of his:

> **Where is Umar's knowledge regarding the Tayammum verse which had been revealed in the Book of Allah, and where is Umar's knowledge of the Tradition of the Prophet صلى الله عليه وسلم who taught them how to do Tayammum as well as Wudu [ritual ablution]?**

ʿUmar رضي الله عنه was aware of this verse just as he knew the manner of performing tayammum. The issue was whether or not Tayammum was applicable to the Junub (one in a state of major impurity) or not. Allah says:

وَإِنْ كُنْتُمْ مَرْضَىٰ أَوْ عَلَىٰ سَفَرٍ أَوْ جَآءَ أَحَدٌ مِّنْكُم مِّنَ الْغَآئِطِ أَوْ لَامَسْتُمُ
النِّسَآءَ فَلَمْ تَجِدُوْا مَآءً فَتَيَمَّمُوْا صَعِيْدًا طَيِّبًا

> *And if you are ill or on a journey or one of you comes from the place of relieving himself or you have contacted women and find no water, then seek clean earth and wipe over your faces and your hands (with it).*[3]

ʿUmar رضي الله عنه held the view that the Junub is not included in this verse. The 'contact' mentioned in the verse was understood to mean touching with the hand and not

1 *Fatḥ al-Bārī*, vol. 1 p. 544-545.

2 Ibid. p. 545.

3 Sūrah al-Nisā': 43.

sexual intercourse. Therefore, he held Tayammum necessary for the male who touched a female in the absence of water.

ʿUmar رضي الله عنه is not infallible. His Ijtihād was off mark on one issue but was spot on for so many others. One wonders whether it was Tījānī's impartiality that caused him to cast aside all the successful Ijtihād based opinions of ʿUmar, and only focus on one issue where he erred.

4. Tījānī accuses ʿUmar of contravening revealed text

Then he says:

> **He violated the Book of Allah and the Tradition of the Prophet and passed rules and judgements during his caliphate which contradicted the texts of the Holy Qur'an and the noble Tradition of the Prophet صلى الله عليه وسلم.[1]**

He says at another place:

> **Umar used to improvise and interpret the clear texts of the Prophet's tradition, and even the Holy Qur'anic texts. Like he used to say: "Two pleasures were allowed during the life of the Messenger of Allah صلى الله عليه وسلم but now I disallow them and punish those who commit them."[2]**

Refuting Tījānī's accusation of ʿUmar contravening revealed text

The word *Mutʿah* is very versatile in its application. In a technical sense it may apply to a temporary marriage. It is also used to describe a format of Ḥajj where the pilgrim dons the iḥrām during the months of Ḥajj with the intention of ʿUmrah. After completion of ʿUmrah a new intention is undertaken, this time for Ḥajj.

Tījānī is implying that ʿUmar رضي الله عنه unilaterally abolished these practises though they continued to be practised during the Prophet's صلى الله عليه وسلم time.

Mutʿah of Ḥajj

It was ʿUmar's رضي الله عنه policy to dissuade people from the Tamattuʿ format of Ḥajj since he noticed that people would delay ʿUmrah and perform it only with Ḥajj. The convenience of Tamattuʿ meant that ʿUmrah was at times neglected outside of the months of Ḥajj. ʿUmar رضي الله عنه wanted that the House of Allah never be empty

1 *Then I was guided*, 96.

2 Ibid. p. 109-110.

of pilgrims. Therefore ʿUmar رضي الله عنه did not forbid it, in the literal sense. Rather, his policy was of discouragement and not legal prohibition. There is strong evidence to prove that ʿUmar رضي الله عنه held the Tamattuʿ format of Ḥajj permissible.

Ibn ʿAbbās رضي الله عنهما narrates:

> I heard ʿUmar saying, "By Allah! I do not forbid you from Mutʿah (i.e. Tamattuʿ Ḥajj) as it is in the Book of Allah; and the Messenger did it," (meaning ʿUmrah during the months of Ḥajj)[1]

It is also reported in a lengthier ḥadīth from Ṣubayy ibn Maʿbad that he said to ʿUmar رضي الله عنه:

> I entered into Iḥrām intending the Ḥajj and ʿUmrah', and ʿUmar رضي الله عنه said to him, "You have been guided to the Sunnah of your Messenger صلى الله عليه وسلم."[2]

The superiority of ʿUmrah outside of the months of Ḥajj is the opinion of many of the jurists.

Abū Dharr is one of the Ṣaḥābah whom the Shīʿah view favourably and one of those whom Tījānī would happily include under the first category of Ṣaḥābah based on his own typology. Abū Dharr رضي الله عنه is well-known for forbidding Mutʿat al-Ḥajj (Tamattuʿ Ḥajj) in general.

The narration in *Ṣaḥīḥ Muslim* from Ibrāhīm al-Taymī—from his father—quotes Abū Dharr saying:

كانت المتعة في الحج لأصحاب محمد صلى الله عليه وسلم خاصة

The Mutʿah in the Ḥajj was for Muḥammad's Companions exclusively.[3]

If ʿUmar رضي الله عنه is guilty of violating the Book of Allah, and the Prophet's صلى الله عليه وسلم Sunnah, then surely the same applies to Abū Dharr رضي الله عنه. After all, Tījānī is a man of fairness and he has recently condemned ʿUmar رضي الله عنه for being unfair.

---

1 *Sunan al-Nasāʾī* with Ḥafiẓ's commentary and Sindī's sidenotes, Kitāb al-Ḥajj, Bāb al-Qurʾān, Ḥadīth no. 2719.

2 *Sunan al-Nasāʾī* with the commentary, Kitāb al-Ḥajj, Bāb al-Tamattuʿ, Ḥadīth no. 2736; *Musnad Aḥmad*, vol. 1, *Musnad ʿUmar ibn al-Khaṭṭāb*; See also: *Ṣaḥīḥ al-Nasāʾī* by Albānī, vol. 2, Ḥadīth no. 2548.

3 *Ṣaḥīḥ Muslim* with its commentary, Kitāb al-Ḥajj, Bāb Jawāz al-Tamattuʿ, Ḥadīth no. 1224.

Mut'ah of women

Tījānī attempts to pin the prohibition on temporary marriages on 'Umar ؓ. This is a farfetched accusation with the sole intent of passing 'Umar ؓ off as someone who altered the religion after the Prophet's ﷺ passing. Temporary marriages had been permanently banned by the Prophet ﷺ and this has been recorded by 'Alī ؓ among others.

Muslim narrates in his *Ṣaḥīḥ* from Rabī ibn Saburah al-Juhanī that his father narrated to him that he was with the Messenger ﷺ when he said:

يا أيها الناس إني قد كنت أذنت لكم في الاستمتاع من النساء وإن الله قد حرم ذلك إلى يوم القيامة فمن كان عنده منهن شيء فليخل سبيله ولا تأخذوا مما آتيتموهن شيئا

> O people! Indeed, I permitted Mutʻah (temporary marriage) for you (in the past) and indeed Allah has forbidden it until the Day of Judgement. Therefore, whoever has by him from them (a wife under such a contract) anything let him cancel it and do not take anything from what you gave them.[1]

Al-Bukhārī and Muslim narrate by way of al-Zuhrī—from Ḥasan ibn Muḥammad ibn 'Alī and his brother 'Abd Allāh—from their father:

> 'Alī said to Ibn 'Abbās, "Indeed, the Messenger forbade Mutʻah and the meat of donkeys during the Khaybar expedition."[2]

Ibn 'Abbās ؓ used to permit the Mutʻah marriage as well as the meat of donkeys. 'Alī ؓ corrected him on those matters. He said to him, "The Messenger forbade Mutʻah; and forbade the meat of donkeys the Day of Khaybar." Ibn 'Abbās retracted his view after the ḥadīth of the prohibition of those two issues reached him.[3]

A Shī'ī scholar seeking reform acknowledged that the prohibition for Mutʻah was not something 'Umar ؓ had invented. Instead he enforced the prohibition pronounced by the Prophet ﷺ; and 'Alī ؓ shared his view on the issue. He writes:

---

1 *Ṣaḥīḥ Muslim* with its commentary, Kitāb al-Nikāḥ, Bāb Nikāḥ al-Mutʻah, Ḥadīth no. 1406.
2 *Ṣaḥīḥ al-Bukhārī*, Kitāb al-Nikāḥ, Ḥadīth no. 4825, Bāb Nahy Rasūl Allāh ﷺ 'an Nikāḥ al-Mutʻah Ākhiran; *Muslim* with the commentary, Kitāb al-Nikāḥ, Ḥadīth no. 1407.
3 *Minhāj al-Sunnah*, vol. 4 p. 190.

> The legal opinion which states that Mut'ah was prohibited by the Khalīfah 'Umar ibn al-Khaṭṭāb is disproved by the action of 'Alī who confirmed its prohibition during his khilāfah and did not advocate its permissibility. According to the Shī'ī tradition and according to the view of our jurists the action of the Imām is a proof especially if he was unrestricted and he was able to disclose the correct view and explain the commands of Allah and His prohibitions. Imām 'Alī, as we know, initially excused himself from the khilāfah and he made it a condition for accepting it the right to exercise his scholarly discretion in the administration of the state. Therefore, Imām 'Alī's tacit approval of the prohibition means that Mut'ah was, indeed, prohibited since the Messenger's era. If that was not the case he would have opposed that ruling and explained the decree of Allah concerning it. The action of the Imām is a proof for the Shī'ah and I do not know how our jurists can ignore it.[1]

From this we know:

> That the Ahl al-Sunnah follows 'Alī and those besides him from the Khulafā' Rāshidīn in what they narrate from the Messenger ﷺ. The Shī'ah, on the other hand, oppose 'Alī regarding that which he narrated from the Messenger ﷺ and instead follow the view of those who oppose him.[2]

'Umar رضي الله عنه made a public announcement of the prohibition of Mut'ah due to the fact that some people were unaware of its prohibition. This is what is narrated by 'Abd Allāh ibn 'Umar رضي الله عنهما:

> لما ولي عمر بن الخطاب خطب الناس فقال إن رسول الله صلى الله عليه وسلم أذن لنا في المتعة ثلاثا ثم حرمها والله لا أعلم أحدا تمتع وهو محصن إلا رجمته بالحجارة إلا أن يأتيني بأربعة يشهدون أن رسول الله أحلها بعد إذ حرمها
>
> When 'Umar رضي الله عنه became the khalīfah he addressed the people and said, "The Prophet permitted Mut'ah then he forbade it. By Allah! Any person who practices Mut'ah and he is *Muḥṣan* (a person that is or has been married) I will stone him, unless he brings to me four witnesses to testify that the Messenger permitted it after having prohibited it."[3]

---

1 al-Mūsawī: *Al-Shī'ah wa al-Taṣḥīḥ*, p. 109.

2 *Minhāj al-Sunnah*, vol. 4 p. 190-191.

3 *Sunan Ibn Mājah*, Kitāb al-Nikāḥ, Bāb al-Nahy 'an Nikāḥ al-Mut'ah, Ḥadīth no. 1963; See also *Ṣaḥīḥ Sunan Ibn Mājah*, Ḥadīth no. 1597.

It is for this reason that Saʿīd ibn Musayyab said:

> May Allah have mercy on ʿUmar. Had he not forbidden Mutʿah, zinā would have become widespread.[1]

The question that remains for Tījānī is whether it is ʿUmar or the Shīʿah who have violated the Sunnah of the Messenger of Allah ﷺ.

Tījānī goes on to say:

> **Umar said, "If it was not for Ali, Umar would have perished."**

Tījānī presents this statement as if it is an insult. ʿUmar رضي الله عنه had the highest regard for ʿAlī رضي الله عنه and even wed his daughter. Tījānī's perception of the community in Madīnah reflects a schism in society, with the 'good Ṣaḥābah' on one side, and the 'evil Ṣaḥābah' on the other. If there is anything to be learnt it is that this perception of that society is far from accurate. The consequence of his flawed perception of that society has influenced the way Tījānī, and others besides him, interpret the entire historical narrative that followed. His warped understanding forces him to reconstruct what must have happened, as nothing is what it seems. Every statement in praise of any Ṣaḥābī must be viewed with suspicion.

This statement that he has quoted ought to be understood in its proper context. ʿUmar رضي الله عنه had ordered that a woman be stoned for adultery. ʿAlī رضي الله عنه intervened saying that she was insane. ʿUmar رضي الله عنه rescinded his original judgement after ʿAlī رضي الله عنه brought to his attention the detail of this woman's sanity. It is in this context that he made this statement. ʿUmar's رضي الله عنه humility ought to be appreciated in this respect.

In a variant version of this incident ʿUmar رضي الله عنه ordered for the stoning of a pregnant woman whereupon ʿAlī رضي الله عنه intervened. The remaining details appear quite similar. Again the context of the incident provides a great deal of perspective.

We are informed of this incident by Ibn ʿAbd al-Barr in *al-Istīʿāb*, Muḥibb al-Ṭabarī in *al-Riyāḍ al-Naḍirah*, as well as the Shīʿah scholar Ibn al-Muṭahhar who mentions these two narrations within this context.

Aḥmad narrates in *al-Faḍā'il* from Ibn Ẓabyān al-Jambī that ʿUmar ibn Khaṭṭāb رضي الله عنه ruled that a particular woman found guilty of adultery be stoned.

---

1 *Muṣannaf ibn Abī Shaybah*, Kitāb al-Nikāḥ, fī Nikāḥ al-Mutʿah wa Ḥuramatihā, vol. 3 p. 390.

When she was being taken to have the punishment enacted they passed ʿAlī رضي الله عنه who asked, "What did she do?"

They said, "She committed adultery and therefore ʿUmar commanded that she be stoned (to death)."

ʿAlī took her aside and instructed them to return to ʿUmar.

When they returned ʿUmar asked, "What brings you back?"

They said, "He (ʿAlī) sent us.

ʿUmar said, "ʿAlī would not do so unless he knew something (that we are unaware of)."

He then summoned ʿAlī. The anger on ʿAlī's face was visible when he entered. ʿUmar asked him, "What caused you to send these men back?"

ʿAlī said, "Did you not hear the Messenger صلى الله عليه وسلم saying, 'The pen has been lifted from three: from the sleeping person until he awakens, from the minor until he becomes an adult and from the insane person until he becomes sane'?"

Umar said, "Indeed I have heard it," and ʿAlī then said, "Perhaps the mental illness overcame her while he was with her."

ʿUmar said, "I did not consider that," and ʿAlī said, "I (also) do not know that. "ʿUmar, therefore, did not stone her.[1]

Despite numerous efforts, and cross-referencing this narration from multiple sources[2] none of them mention ʿUmar's statement, "Had it not been for ʿAlī, ʿUmar would be ruined!"

---

1 Aḥmad: *Faḍā'il al-Ṣaḥābah*, Ḥadīth no. 1209, p. 707 vol. 2, the examiner (of the book) says: its sanad is reliable.

2 Refer to *al-Musnad* vol. 1, Ḥadīth no. 1327, the *Musnad* of ʿAlī, p. 325; and Ibn Khuzaymah in his *Ṣaḥīḥ*, Kitāb al-Manāsik, Ḥadīth no. 3048, p. 348, vol. 4; Bukhārī mentioned it in a positive manner with a suspended (*Muʿallaq*) sanad, Kitāb al-Muḥāribīn, Bāb Lā Yurjam al-Majnūn wa al-Majnūnah, p. 2499, vol. 6; and *Abū Dāwūd*, Bāb fi al-Majnūn Yasriq aw Yuṣīb Ḥadd, Ḥadīth no. 4399, 4400, 4401, 4402; and *Sunan al-Dāraquṭnī*, Kitāb al-Ḥudūd wa al-Diyāt, Ḥadīth no. 173, vol. 3; and *Musnad Abī Yaʿlā*, vol. 1, *Musnad ʿAlī ibn Abī Ṭālib*, Ḥadīth no. 587, p. 440; and *Mustadrak al-Ḥākim*, Kitāb al-Ṣalāh, p. 257, vol. 1 and p. 59, Kitāb al-Buyūʿ, vol. 2 and p. 389, Kitāb al-Ḥudūd, vol. 4, Refer also to *ʿIlal al-Dāraquṭnī*, vol. 3, p. 72 and 291.

Notwithstanding the fact that we could not trace the statement, it only confirms that ʿUmar رضي الله عنه gave the ruling because he was unaware of the insanity of this woman. We know that from his statement, "I do not know that." Therefore, there is no doubt, in this instance, that ʿUmar رضي الله عنه was excused as he was unaware about this woman's insanity and there is no sin upon him as a result.

There is the other narration, which speaks of stoning a pregnant woman; found in *Muṣannaf ibn Abī Shaybah*:

> That there was a woman whose husband was away and when he returned he found her pregnant and raised the matter to ʿUmar who gave the instruction for her to be stoned.
>
> Muʿādh رضي الله عنه said, "(Even) if you have a right over her you do not have a right over what is in her womb!"
>
> ʿUmar رضي الله عنه said, "Imprison her until she gives birth!" Later she gave birth to a boy with two incisors. When his father saw him he said, "(This is) my son!"
>
> That then reached ʿUmar رضي الله عنه who said, "Women are unable to give birth to (sons) similar to Muʿādh رضي الله عنه. Had it not been for Muʿādh, ʿUmar would be ruined!"[1]

Then Ibn Abī Shaybah says:

> Khālid ibn al-Aḥmar narrated to us from Ḥajjāj—from Qāsim—from his father—from ʿAlī, a narration similar to it.[2]

In its chain is Ḥajjāj ibn Arṭāh who is a weak transmitter and often commits *Tadlīs* (conceals narrators). Al-Dhahabī says:

> Ḥajjāj ibn Arṭāh: His ḥadīth is not proof-worthy.[3]

This narration is therefore weak and is not proof-worthy.

As for the narration mentioned by Muḥibb al-Ṭabarī:

---

1 *Al-Muṣannaf ibn Abī Shaybah*, vol. 6, Kitāb al-Ḥudūd, p. 557.

2 Ibid.

3 Refer to: *Tahdhīb al-Kamāl*, vol. 5 p 420, biography no. 1112; (also) *Mīzān al-Iʿtidāl*, vol. 1, biography no. 1726.

> That ʿUmar intended to stone the woman who gave birth after six months and ʿAlī said to him, "Allah says, 'And his gestation and weaning (period) is thirty months,'[1] and He says, 'and his weaning is in two years,'[2] the gestation period is six months and the weaning period is two years." ʿUmar then decided against stoning her and said, "Had it not been for ʿAlī, ʿUmar would be ruined." This narration is transmitted by ʿUqaylī. Ibn Sammān also transmits it from Abū Ḥazm ibn Abū al-Aswad.[3]

Correction:

The name given, 'Abū Ḥazm', appears to be a mistake. The correct wording is Abū Ḥarb ibn Abū al-Aswad. Appearing in the chain of this narration is ʿUthmān ibn Maṭr al-Shaybānī.

> Yaḥyā ibn Maʿīn says, "He is weak. His ḥadīth is not documented. He is not much of a transmitter."
>
> ʿAlī ibn al-Madīnī says, "ʿUthmān ibn Maṭr is extremely weak."
>
> Abū Zurʿah says, "Weak in ḥadīth."
>
> Abū Ḥātim says, "Weak in ḥadīth. He is unacceptable in ḥadīth."
>
> Ṣāliḥ al-Baghdādī says, "His ḥadīth is not to be documented."
>
> Abū Dāwūd says, "Weak."
>
> Nasāʾī says, "He is not reliable."[4]
>
> Al-Bukhārī says, "He is unacceptable in ḥadīth."
>
> Ibn Ḥibbān says, "ʿUthmān ibn Maṭr was from amongst those who transmitted fabrications."[5]

Assuming the reliability of the narration, it displays ʿUmar's humility and reverence for the truth. He was not infallible so errors are to be expected from him. This is an isolated case not known to him about which he was enlightened, there are other

1 Sūrah al-Aḥqāf: 15.
2 Sūrah Luqmān: 14.
3 *Al-Riyāḍ al-Naḍirah*, vol. 2 p. 161.
4 *Tahdhīb al-Kamāl*, vol. 19 p. 494, biography no. 3863.
5 *Mīzān al-Iʿtidāl*, vol. 3 p. 53.

times where he forgot then someone reminded him, what is there to fault him on?[1]

However, if he is going to be judged only in light of a single error and thousands of issues are overlooked, that speaks of the extent of bias and prejudice by some 'impartial' researchers.

Tījānī's accusation regarding the knowledge of ʿUmar

Then Tījānī says:

> **This is Umar saying, "All people are more knowledgeable than I am, even women." He was once asked about the meaning of a Qur'anic verse, and his reaction was to rebuke the man and beat him until he bled, then he said, "Do not ask about matters which may appear bad to you."[2,3]**

Refuting Tījānī's accusation regarding the knowledge of ʿUmar

This narration is not narrated with the wording provided by Tījānī. Tījānī has been extremely careless with quoting statements throughout his book. The esteemed reader would have noticed that we repeatedly point out the correct wording. The translation of the wording in the narration that Tījānī alludes to is, "Everyone is better in understanding than ʿUmar."

No doubt Tījānī concealed the context of this statement so that the reader would get the impression that ʿUmar رضي الله عنه said that indiscriminately. The narration is recorded in its entirety in the *Sunan* of Saʿīd ibn Manṣūr, by way of al-Shaʿbī, who said:

> ʿUmar ibn al-Khaṭṭāb addressed the people. He praised Allah and extoled His Grace and said, "Do not be excessive in the *Ṣadāq* (wedding gift) of the women. It has reached me that some of you have given more than the Messenger صلى الله عليه وسلم gave. If you do not stop this practice I will take the surplus and place it in the Bayt al-Māl."
>
> Then he descended the mimbar and a woman from the Quraysh objected and said, "Is the Book of Allah better to follow or your view?"

1 *Minhāj al-Sunnah*, vol. 6 p. 42.

2 Sūrah al-Mā'idah: 101.

3 *Then I was guided*, p. 95 and 147.

He said, "The Book of Allah! Why do you ask that?"

She said, "You prohibited the people a short while ago about being excessive in the wedding gifts of the women while Allah says in his book:

وَأٰتَيْتُمْ إِحْدَاهُنَّ قِنطَارًا فَلَا تَأْخُذُوا مِنْهُ شَيْئًا أَتَأْخُذُونَهُ بُهْتَانًا وَإِثْمًا مُّبِينًا

And you have given one of them a great amount (in gifts); do not take (back) from it anything. Would you take it in injustice and manifest sin?[1]

ʿUmar then said, "Everyone is better in understanding than ʿUmar," twice or thrice.

Then he returned to the *mimbar* (pulpit) and said to the people, "I prohibited you from being excessive in the wedding gift of women. Let every man do what he sees fit in his wealth."[2]

Notwithstanding Tījānī's indiscretion when it comes to quoting, this narration is problematic in terms of its chain. There are two defects in the chain. The first is the interruption in the chain. Al-Bayhaqī says at the end of this narration:

This is an interrupted chain as Shaʿbī did not meet ʿUmar. Abū Zurʿah says in his book *al-Marāsīl*, "I heard my father and Abū Zurʿah saying, "Shaʿbī from ʿUmar is Mursal (interrupted)."[3]

The second defect in it is a narrator named Mujālid who is Ibn Saʿīd.

Al-Bukhārī says about him, "Yaḥyā ibn al-Qaṭṭān and Ibn Mahdī never used to transmit from him, from Shaʿbī."[4]

Nasāʾī says, "He is a Kūfī and he is weak."[5]

Al-Jūzajānī says, "Mujālid ibn Saʿīd, his ḥadīth is graded weak."[6]

---

1 Sūrah al-Nisā': 20.

2 *Sunan Saʿīd ibn Manṣūr*, vol. 1, Bāb ma Jā'a fī al-Ṣadāq, Ḥadīth no. 595, 569 and 579.

3 *Al-Qawl al-Muʿtabar fī Taḥqīq Riwāyah*, 'Kull Aḥad Afqah min ʿUmar', p. 20.

4 al-Bukhārī: *Al-Ḍuʿafā' al-Ṣaghīr*, p. 116, biography no. 368.

5 al-Nasa'ī: *Al-Ḍuʿafā' wa al-Matrūkīn*, p. 236, biography no. 552.

6 al-Jūzajānī: *Al-Shajarah fī Aḥwāl al-Rijāl wa Ayāt al-Nabawiyyah*, p. 144.

Ibn ʿAdī says, "I asked Aḥmad ibn Ḥambal about Mujālid and he said, 'He is not much of a transmitter. He elevated an anomalous ḥadīth (to the Messenger) which none besides him have.' (Ibn ʿAdī also said) Most of what he transmits is not documented."

Ibn Maʿīn said, "His ḥadīth is not proof-worthy." He also said, "He is a weak flimsy transmitter."[1]

Ibn Ḥajar said about him, "He is not a strong transmitter. He changed at the end of his life."[2]

There remains the assertion that ʿUmar رضي الله عنه beat the person who asked him about a verse in the Qur'ān until he bled, and said to him, "Do not ask about things which, if they are shown to you, will distress you," Tījānī has cited *Sunan al-Dārimī*, *Tafsīr Ibn Kathīr*, and *al-Durr al-Manthūr* as references. After exhaustive searching in these references there appears to be absolutely no trace of this narration in Tījānī's cited sources. In fact there is no trace for it at all. The books are available for all to study. We would be extremely grateful if someone can point out where this narration could be found. I fear that once again Tījānī has taken a chance assuming that he would get away with falsifying material.

Tījānī's accusation on ʿUmar concerning the meaning of Kalālah

Tījānī's nit-picking is far from over:

> **Also he was asked about "al-Kalalah" but he did not know what it meant.**
>
> **In his "commentary", al-Tabari stated that Umar once said the following, "My knowledge of al-Kalalah is more valuable to me than owning a palace similar to those in Syria."**
>
> **In one of his books, Ibn Maja quoted Umar as saying "There are three things, if they were explained by the Messenger of Allah صلى الله عليه وسلم, I would have loved them more dearly than anything in the world: Al-Kalalah, usury and the caliphate."[3]**

1 al-Mizzī: *Tahdhīb al-Kamāl*, vol. 27 p. 222, biography no. 5780.

2 *Taqrīb al-Tahdhīb*, vol. 2 p. 159, See the book *al-Qawl al-Muʿtabar*.

3 *Then I was guided*, p. 147.

Refuting Tījānī's accusation on ʿUmar concerning the meaning of Kalālah

Tījānī displays a unique skill of projecting someone's sincerity and humility as ignorance. Unfortunately many times this skill is accompanied with misdirection, fabrication or interpolation.

In order to demonstrate this I present the narration appearing in *Ṣaḥīḥ Muslim*. Compare what Tījānī has written to what appears in *Ṣaḥīḥ Muslim*. Maʿdān ibn Abī Ṭalḥah related:

> ʿUmar ibn al-Khaṭṭāb addressed (the people) one Friday and mentioned the Messenger صَلَّى ٱللَّهُ عَلَيْهِ وَسَلَّمَ and Abū Bakr. Then he said, "Indeed, I do not leave behind anything more important to me than the *Kalālah*[1]. I never consulted the Messenger about something as much as I consulted him about Kalālah and he was not stern with me about anything as much as he was stern about it (Kalālah). To the extent that (one day) he poked me with his finger against my chest and said, 'O ʿUmar! Does the verse of summer at the end of Sūrah al-Nisā not suffice you?' (ʿUmar رَضِيَ ٱللَّهُ عَنْهُ said,) If I live (long enough) I will issue a ruling concerning it that the person who reads the Qur'ān as well as the person who does not read the Qur'ān will judge according to it."[2]

We learn from this ḥadīth that ʿUmar's uncertainty about Kalālah was not out of lack of knowledge. Instead, the Prophet صَلَّى ٱللَّهُ عَلَيْهِ وَسَلَّمَ desired that the Ṣaḥābah apply their minds to extract laws from the revealed texts. Therefore he withheld the explanation and alerted ʿUmar to the verse which explains the meaning of the (word) Kalālah. This can be inferred from his statement, "O ʿUmar! Does the verse of summer at the end of Sūrah al-Nisā not suffice you?" Here the Messenger صَلَّى ٱللَّهُ عَلَيْهِ وَسَلَّمَ was referring to the verse:

يَسْتَفْتُونَكَ قُلِ اللَّهُ يُفْتِيكُمْ فِي الْكَلَالَةِ

> *They request from you a (legal) ruling. Say, Allah gives you a ruling concerning the Kalālah...*[3]

---

1 Kalālah: One having neither descendants nor ascendants as heirs, in which case his siblings will inherit.

2 *Ṣaḥīḥ Muslim* with its commentary, Kitāb al-Farā'iḍ, Bāb Mīrāth al-Kalālah, Ḥadīth no. 1617.

3 Sūrah al-Nisā': 176.

Al-Nawawī says:

> Perhaps the Messenger acted harshly with him out of fear that his and others dependence upon what he explicitly stated may result in them abandoning deducing from the texts. Indeed, Allah says:
>
> وَلَوْ رَدُّوْهُ إِلَى الرَّسُوْلِ وَإِلَى أُولِى الْأَمْرِ مِنْهُمْ لَعَلِمَهُ الَّذِيْنَ يَسْتَنْبِطُوْنَهُ مِنْهُمْ
>
> *But if they had referred it back to the Messenger or to those of authority among them, and then the ones who (can) draw correct conclusions from it would have known about it.*[1]
>
> Applying oneself in order to deduce rulings from the texts is of the most emphasised and required duties, as the clear texts only cover a few of the newer issues. When deduction from the texts is neglected the ability to issue legal decrees in newer cases, or at least some of them, is hindered. And Allah knows best![2]

ʿUmar رضي الله عنه shared the same view as Abū Bakr رضي الله عنه that the word *Kalālah* refers to a person with no father and no son. This is also the view of ʿAlī ibn Abī Ṭālib رضي الله عنه and the majority of the jurists from the Companions, and those who came after them. This only highlights the depth of ʿUmar's knowledge and understanding. Why not; when the Prophet صلى الله عليه وسلم said:

إن الله وضع الحق على لسان عمر يقول به

Indeed, Allah has placed the truth upon the tongue of ʿUmar.[3]

Al-Ṭabarī mentions fifteen narrations from ʿUmar ibn al-Khaṭṭāb about Kalālah in his Tafsīr. Among these narrations is the ḥadīth previously mentioned from *Ṣaḥīḥ Muslim*. Tījānī's 'objectivity' is so vast that all he sees is ʿUmar's statement,

---

1 Sūrah al-Nisā': 83.

2 Op. cit. vol. 11, p. 82.

3 *Sunan Abū Dāwūd*, Kitāb al-Kharāj wa al-Imārah wa al-Fay', Bāb fī Tadwīn al-Aṭā, Ḥadīth no. 2962; and *Sunan al-Tirmidhī*, Kitāb al-Manāqib, Bāb Manāqib ʿUmar ibn al-Khaṭṭāb, Ḥadīth no. 3946; and *Ibn Mājah fī al-Muqaddimah*, Bāb Faḍā'il Aṣḥāb al-Nabī صلى الله عليه وسلم, Bāb Faḍl ʿUmar, Ḥadīth no. 108; Refer also to *Ṣaḥīḥ Abū Dāwūd*, by Albānī, Ḥadīth no. 2566.

"Knowing the (meaning of the word) Kalālah is more beloved to me than having collecting the value of tax from the castles of Rome," not the castles of al-Shām, as Tījānī says. Subḥān Allāh! He could not transmit this part accurately! What more can be said of his objectivity!

All that the narration amounts to is ʿUmar's desire to have learnt the meaning of the word Kalālah from the Messenger ﷺ. This displays his eagerness for knowing the truth in this issue. Is this something that warrants criticism?

Tījānī's accusation on ʿUmar concerning the distribution of zakāh

Tījānī's tirade is far from over:

> **One of the first Companions to open the door of Ijtihad [interpretation] was the second Caliph who used his discretion vis-a-vis the Qur'anic Texts after the death of the Messenger of Allah ﷺ to stop the shares of those whose hearts inclined (to truth), although Allah had made its payment compulsory out of the Zakat, and said, "We do not need you."[1]**

Refuting Tījānī's accusation on ʿUmar concerning the distribution of zakāh

Ijtihād is an undisputed institution which dates back to the time of the Prophet ﷺ. As a matter of fact, the ḥadīth which Tījānī brought against ʿUmar رضي الله عنه is an example of ʿAmmār رضي الله عنه exercising his Ijtihād. The Prophet ﷺ did not disapprove of his Ijtihād, instead he corrected it.

There are countless examples of Ijtihād which are well established from senior Ṣaḥābah such as Abū Bakr, ʿUmar, ʿUthmān, ʿAlī, and Ibn Masʿūd رضي الله عنهم. It is in this regard that the Prophet ﷺ said:

> إذا حكم الحاكم فاجتهد ثم أصاب فله أجران وإذا حكم فاجتهد ثم أخطأ فله أجر
>
> When a judge gives a correct ruling after applying his scholarly discretion (*Ijtihād*), he will have a double reward; and if he errs after applying his scholarly discretion, he will have a single reward.[2]

1 *Then I was guided*, p. 165.

2 *Ṣaḥīḥ al-Bukhārī*, Bāb al-Iʿtiṣām bi al-Kitāb wa al-Sunnah, Ḥadīth no. 6919, vol. 6; and *Muslim* with its commentary, Bāb al-Aqḍiyah, Ḥadīth no. 1716, from ʿAmr ibn al-ʿĀṣ.

Their scholarly discretion was not in opposition of the Qur'ānic texts. On the contrary, their scholarly discretion was in the understanding of the Qur'ānic and prophetic texts, or finding solution to situations which had not been addressed directly in the Qur'ān and Sunnah. We ought to bear in mind that unlike Tījānī, the Ṣaḥābah were well aware of the context of the texts. They witnessed it being revealed and understood, first-hand the purport behind the legislation, and the circumstances in which verses were revealed or in which the Prophet صلى الله عليه وسلم said a particular statement. The lengthy period in which they accompanied the Prophet صلى الله عليه وسلم blossomed into a profound understanding of the Sharīʿah.[1]

There are rare cases where the Ijtihād of some of the Ṣaḥābah was in conflict with the revealed text. If we examine those cases we find that they were unaware of the revealed text on that matter. That being said, when they were made aware of the textual evidence, they retracted their views and adopted positions in line with the textual evidence.

ʿUmar رضي الله عنه understood the Zakāh distribution schedule of the Messenger صلى الله عليه وسلم to be based on specific benefits. Thus he considered the Prophet صلى الله عليه وسلم to have only assigned a portion for the Mu'allafah Qulūbuhum when the Muslims were in a state of weakness, to unite the hearts and in order to safeguard the Muslims from potential harm. After the Ummah established itself in terms of strength and ability to defend itself he no longer considered that category as worthy recipients for zakāh. This is definitely ʿUmar's scholarly discretion on this matter. This was not contested by the rest of the Ṣaḥābah hence their silence can be taken as approval which can be accepted as a form of *ijmāʿ* (consensus). It cannot be said that this was Ijtihād in the face of Qur'ānic texts. Rather, it was Ijtihād in determining the purpose of the text.

Tījānī's accusation on ʿUmar preventing Abū Hurayrah from transmitting the ḥadīth of glad tidings

Tījānī goes on to say:

> **There is another incident involving the Messenger of Allah صلى الله عليه وسلم and Umar which shows clearly the latter's mentality and how he allowed himself to argue and oppose the Messenger صلى الله عليه وسلم. The incident was about spreading**

---

1 Doctor ʿAbd al-Karīm Zaydān: *Al-Wajīz fī Uṣūl al-Fiqh*, p. 261.

the good news of Heavens. The Messenger of Allah صلى الله عليه وسلم sent Abu Hurayrah with the instruction that whenever he met a man who is absolutely convinced that "There is no other god but Allah" he was to give him the good news that he would end up in Heaven. Abu Hurayrah duly went out to spread the good news until he met Umar who prevented him from continuing his mission and beat him as he lay on the ground. Abu Hurayrah went back crying to the Messenger of Allah صلى الله عليه وسلم and told him about his encounter with Umar, so the Messenger صلى الله عليه وسلم asked Umar, "What made you do that?" Umar replied by asking the question, "Did you send him to spread the good news of Heaven to whoever convincingly believes that there is no other god but Allah!" The Messenger of Allah صلى الله عليه وسلم said, "Yes." Umar then said, "Do not do that, because I fear that all the people will rely on there is no other god but Allah."[1]

Refuting Tījānī's accusation on ʿUmar preventing Abū Hurayrah from transmitting the ḥadīth of glad tidings

It would not be an overstatement if we said that nearly every authentic ḥadīth that has been mentioned in praise of ʿUmar رضي الله عنه, or the other Ṣaḥābah for that matter, has been conveniently dismissed by Tījānī. Not because of any weakness in the chain of transmission; rather it did not fit in with his preconceived idea of what may or may not apply to them. This time he quotes a narration with unshakable confidence, not because the transmitters in the chain are trustworthy, rather, because of the potential disparagement of ʿUmar رضي الله عنه in it.

Without realising it, Tījānī has presented one of the greatest proofs for ʿUmar's profound understanding of the dīn. It comes as no surprise since the truth is always on his tongue. The Prophet صلى الله عليه وسلم said about him:

إن الله وضع الحق على لسان عمر يقول به

Indeed, Allah has placed the truth upon the tongue of ʿUmar.[2]

Ibn ʿUmar رضي الله عنه also narrates that the Prophet صلى الله عليه وسلم said:

رأيت كأني أتيت بقدح من لبن فشربت منه فأعطيت فضلي عمر بن الخطاب
قالوا فما أولته يا رسول الله؟ قال العلم

1 *Then I was guided*, p. 165.
2 Refer to p. 399 of this book.

> I saw (in a dream) as if I was brought a container of milk. Then I drank from it and gave my surplus to ʿUmar ibn al-Khaṭṭāb. They said, "How do you interpret it, O Messenger?" He said, "Knowledge."[1]

The ḥadīth that Tījānī quotes, also known as the ḥadīth of Tabshīr, has been narrated by Imām Muslim by way of Abū Hurayrah in a lengthy report:

> فقال يا أبا هريرة وأعطاني نعليه قال اذهب بنعلي هاتين فمن لقيت من وراء هذا الحائط يشهد أن لا إله إلا الله مستيقنا بها قلبه فبشره بالجنة فكان أول من لقيت عمر فقال ما هاتان النعلان يا أبا هريرة فقلت هاتان نعلا رسول الله صلى الله عليه وسلم بعثني بهما من لقيت يشهد أن لا إله إلا الله مستيقنا بها قلبه بشرته بالجنة فضرب عمر بيده بين ثديي فخررت لاستي فقال ارجع يا أبا هريرة فرجعت إلى رسول الله صلى الله عليه وسلم فأجهشت بكاء وركبني عمر فإذا هو على أثري فقال لي رسول الله صلى الله عليه وسلم ما لك يا أبا هريرة قلت لقيت عمر فأخبرته بالذي بعثتني به فضرب بين ثديي ضربة خررت لاستي قال ارجع فقال له رسول الله يا عمر ما حملك على ما فعلت قال يا رسول الله بأبي أنت وأمي أبعثت أبا هريرة بنعليك من لقي يشهد أن لا إله إلا الله مستيقنا بها قلبه بشره بالجنة قال نعم قال فلا تفعل فإني أخشى أن يتكل الناس عليها فخلهم يعملون قال رسول الله صلى الله عليه وسلم فخلهم

> The Messenger ﷺ said, "O Abū Hurayrah (and he handed me his sandals), go with these two sandals of mine and whoever you meet behind this wall that testifies that there is no God but Allah with conviction in his heart give him the glad tidings of Jannah."
>
> (Abū Hurayrah says) then the first person I met was ʿUmar who said, "What are these two sandals, O Abū Hurayrah?"
>
> I said, "These are the two sandals of the Messenger. He sent me with them to whomever I meet that testifies that there is no God but Allah with conviction in his heart to give him the glad tidings of Jannah."
>
> Then ʿUmar struck me with his hand in the middle of my chest and I fell on my rear.

---

1 Refer to p. 76 of this book.

He said, "Return, O Abū Hurayrah!"

So I returned to the Messenger, on the verge of crying. 'Umar followed me and was right behind me. The Messenger said to me, "What is the matter Abū Hurayrah?"

I said, "I met 'Umar and informed him about what you sent me with. Then he struck me in the middle of my chest and I fell on my rear and he told me to return."

The Messenger then said to him, "O 'Umar! What caused you to do that?"

He said, "O Messenger of Allah! May my mother and father be sacrificed for you! Did you send Abū Hurayrah with your two sandals to give everyone he meets that testifies that there is no God but Allah the glad tidings of Jannah?"

The Messenger ﷺ said, "Yes!"

He said, "I suggest that you do not do that as I fear that the people will rely on it. Leave them to perform good deeds!"

The Messenger then said, "Leave them."[1]

In this ḥadīth 'Umar رَضِيَ ٱللَّهُ عَنْهُ feared that the people would be negligent in the performance of righteous deeds after hearing the ḥadīth. Therefore he presented his suggestion to the Prophet ﷺ, who considered it and accepted it. Qāḍī 'Iyāḍ has said:

> 'Umar's action, and his consulting the Messenger ﷺ, was not an objection against him, or a refutation of his instruction. The Prophet ﷺ only sent Abū Hurayrah to appease the hearts of the believers and give them glad tidings. 'Umar felt withholding this announcement was more beneficial and more suitable so that they do not depend upon it only. When he presented his suggestion to the Messenger ﷺ he considered 'Umar's view correct. And Allah knows best.[2]

The Prophet ﷺ maintained this policy as can be seen from the ḥadīth of Anas:

---

1 *Ṣaḥīḥ Muslim* with its commentary, Kitāb al-Īmān, Ḥadīth no. 31.

2 *Ṣaḥīḥ Muslim* with its commentary, p. 325-326.

أنس بن مالك أن النبي صلى الله عليه وسلم ومعاذ رديفه على الرحل قال يا معاذ بن جبل قال لبيك يا رسول الله وسعديك قال يا معاذ قال لبيك يا رسول الله وسعديك ثلاثا قال ما من أحد يشهد أن لا إله إلا الله وأن محمدا رسول الله صدقا من قلبه إلا حرمه الله على النار قال يا رسول الله أفلا أخبر به الناس فيستبشروا قال إذا يتكلوا وأخبر بها معاذ عند موته تأثما

Anas ibn Mālik relates that the Prophet of Allah ﷺ addressed Muʿādh ibn Jabal as he was riding behind him, "O Muʿādh!" to which he replied, "I am at your service, and at your pleasure, Messenger of Allah!"

The Prophet ﷺ again called out, "Muʿādh!" and he gave a similar reply, and this continued for a third time before the Prophet ﷺ said,: "If anyone testifies (sincerely from his heart) that there is no God but Allah, and that Muḥammad is His slave and His messenger, Allah will grant him immunity from the Fire."

Muʿādh then said, "O Messenger of Allah, shall I not inform people of it so that they may rejoice?"

The Prophet ﷺ replied, "If that is the case they will rely on this alone (and not exert themselves in righteous deeds)." Muʿādh only transmitted this at the time of his death, to avoid sinning.[1]

When ʿUmar رضي الله عنه struck Abū Hurayrah رضي الله عنه in the chest it was not to push him to the ground or to harm him, he merely meant to stop him from proceeding. This was his way of getting his point across effectively.[2]

Is there anything as clear that proves that the truth is on ʿUmar's رضي الله عنه tongue and heart?

Tījānī's allegations against the Ahl al-Sunnah concerning the infallibility of the Prophet ﷺ

True to his strategy of misdirection Tījānī proceeds:

> **Looking at the various stances that Umar took regarding the Messenger of Allah ﷺ and his Tradition we could deduce that he never believed in**

1 *Ṣaḥīḥ al-Bukhārī*, Kitāb al-ʿIlm, Ḥadīth no. 128; *Ṣaḥīḥ Muslim*, Kitāb al-Īmān, Ḥadīth no. 55.

2 *Ṣaḥīḥ Muslim* with its commentary, p. 325.

the infallibility of the Messenger ﷺ; and he thought of him as any other man subject to right or wrong. Thus came the opinion adopted by the Sunni scholars and al-Jamaah that the Messenger of Allah ﷺ was infallible as regards the transmitting the Holy Qur'an, but that apart from that he was like any other human being, sometimes wrong and sometimes right. They (the Ahl al-Sunnah) cite as a proof for that (dogma) ʿUmar's directing his opinion on a number of occasions and on a number of issues.[1]

Refuting Tījānī's allegations against the Ahl al-Sunnah concerning the infallibility of the Prophet ﷺ

Tījānī's insult has no academic basis. He has exploited the forum of academic enquiry to malign ʿUmar رضي الله عنه. Not only is this a breach of conduct, but it is a blatant display of Tījānī's bias towards the Companions of the Prophet ﷺ. Moreover, he accuses the Ahl al-Sunnah of 'covering-up' for ʿUmar by retrospectively modifying their doctrine.

If Tījānī is fair in his adjudication of ʿUmar, the same disposition towards the Prophet ﷺ was recorded from ʿAlī رضي الله عنه on other issues. By what right does ʿAlī رضي الله عنه deserve exoneration and ʿUmar رضي الله عنه condemnation? If Tījānī cannot bring himself to excuse ʿUmar رضي الله عنه, in a manner that ʿAlī رضي الله عنه would be excused for—assuming Tījānī's breach of rank—then his claim to impartiality is nothing but a farce.

Al-Bukhārī narrates in his *Ṣaḥīḥ* by way of al-Zuhrī, from ʿAlī ibn Ḥusayn, that Ḥusayn ibn ʿAlī informed him that ʿAlī ibn Abī Ṭālib informed him:

> أن رسول الله صلى الله عليه وسلم طرقه وفاطمة بنت النبي عليه السلام ليلة فقال ألا تصليان فقلت يا رسول الله أنفسنا بيد الله فإذا شاء أن يبعثنا بعثنا فانصرف حين قلنا ذلك ولم يرجع إلي شيئا ثم سمعته وهو مول يضرب فخذه وهو يقول وكان الإنسان أكثر شيء جدلا

> The Messenger ﷺ knocked on his and Fāṭimah's door one night and said, "Are (the two of) you not performing ṣalāh?"
>
> I said, "O Messenger of Allah! Our souls are in the hands of Allah, if He decrees to wake us He wakes us."

1 *Then I was guided*, p. 166. This passage was omitted in the English translation.

> The Messenger of Allah left when I said that and he did not rebuke me with anything. Then I heard him as he was turning around and slapping his hand on his thigh saying, "But man has ever been, more than anything, (prone to) dispute."[1]

Would Tījānī infer that ʿAlī رَضِيَ ٱللَّهُ عَنْهُ refused the Prophet's صَلَّى ٱللَّهُ عَلَيْهِ وَسَلَّمَ request and angered him. Did he only consider the Prophet صَلَّى ٱللَّهُ عَلَيْهِ وَسَلَّمَ infallible regarding the conveying of the Qur'ān; and in all other matters he might have been correct or might have erred? Was he the same as the rest of mankind in that respect? Is it that he attached no importance to this request? Whatever answer Tījānī presents for ʿAlī رَضِيَ ٱللَّهُ عَنْهُ applies equally to ʿUmar رَضِيَ ٱللَّهُ عَنْهُ, provided that Tījānī doesn't consider ʿAlī greater than the Prophet صَلَّى ٱللَّهُ عَلَيْهِ وَسَلَّمَ.

Tījānī's claim that the scholars of the Ahl al-Sunnah only believe the Messenger of Allah صَلَّى ٱللَّهُ عَلَيْهِ وَسَلَّمَ infallible with regards to conveying the Qur'ān can only be taken seriously if he provided a single quote from their books to support his claim. Tījānī's academic integrity is as consistent as his impartiality, absent!

Tījānī's accusation on ʿUmar concerning the Devil fleeing from him

His rant continues:

> **Some ignorant people claim that the Messenger of Allah صَلَّى ٱللَّهُ عَلَيْهِ وَسَلَّمَ accepted the temptations of the devil in his home. Once he was lying on his back surrounded by women playing their tambourines and the devil sat joyfully next to him until Umar came, then the devil ran away and the women hid their tambourines under their seats. The Prophet صَلَّى ٱللَّهُ عَلَيْهِ وَسَلَّمَ said to Umar, "As soon as the devil saw you, he left by a different way from the way you came in."**
>
> **It is not therefore surprising that Umar has his own views on the religion and allowed himself to argue with the Messenger of Allah صَلَّى ٱللَّهُ عَلَيْهِ وَسَلَّمَ about political issues as well as religious ones, as we explained before regarding the good news about Heaven.**[2]

Refuting Tījānī's accusation on ʿUmar concerning the Devil fleeing from him

The ḥadīth books of Ahl al-Sunnah have been published on a large scale and are easily available in bookstores throughout the world. Despite this Tījānī still

1 *Ṣaḥīḥ al-Bukhārī*, Abwāb al-Tahajjud, Ḥadīth no. 1075.

2 *Then I was guided*, p. 166.

manages to quote a narration that cannot be found in any of these books. There is not a single ḥadīth in any of the books of the Ahl al-Sunnah with his wording.

There is no doubt that Tījānī is alluding to some authentic aḥādīth of which he is aware. However, his exhaustive research and impartiality got the better of him that he managed to interpolate two isolated narrations by combining them into one. I will present two isolated narrations which I believe Tījānī combined into what he calls "a narration from the Ahl al-Sunnah".

The first ḥadīth is narrated by al-Bukhārī in his *Ṣaḥīḥ*:

> عن عائشة قالت دخل علي أبو بكر وعندي جاريتان من جواري الأنصار تغنيان بما تقاولت به الأنصار يوم بعاث قالت وليستا بمغنيتين فقال أبو بكر أبمزمور الشيطان في بيت رسول الله صلى الله عليه وسلم وذلك في يوم عيد فقال رسول الله صلى الله عليه وسلم يا أبا بكر إن لكل قوم عيدا وهذا عيدنا
>
> From ʿĀ'ishah, she said, "Abū Bakr entered while there were two young girls from the Anṣār with me singing what the Anṣār sang at the Battle of Buʿāth. (She said) They were not singers. Abū Bakr then said, "The flutes of Shayṭān in the house of the Messenger?"
>
> That was a day of ʿĪd and the Messenger ﷺ said, "O Abū Bakr! Every nation has an *ʿĪd* (day of celebration) and this is our ʿĪd."[1]

The second ḥadīth is narrated by al-Tirmidhī in his *Sunan* from Buraydah, he says:

> خرج رسول الله صلى الله عليه وسلم في بعض مغازيه فلما انصرف جاءت جارية سوداء فقالت يا رسول الله إني كنت نذرت إن ردك الله صالحا أن أضرب بين يديك بالدف وأتغنى قال لها إن كنت نذرت فاضربي وإلا فلا ، فجعلت تضرب فدخل أبو بكر وهي تضرب ثم دخل علي وهي تضرب ثم دخل عثمان وهي تضرب ثم دخل عمر فألقت الدف تحت استها ثم قعدت عليه فقال رسول الله صلى الله عليه وسلم إن الشيطان ليخاف منك يا عمر إني كنت جالسا وهي تضرب فدخل أبو بكر وهي تضرب ثم دخل علي

1 *Ṣaḥīḥ al-Bukhārī*, Kitāb al-ʿĪdayn, Bāb Sunnah al-ʿĪdayn li Ahl al-Islām, Ḥadīth no. 909.

وهي تضرب ثم دخل عثمان وهي تضرب فلما دخلت أنت يا عمر ألقت الدف

> The Messenger ﷺ (once) came out for an expedition. When he returned a dark-skinned girl came to him and said, "O Messenger of Allah! I took an oath that if Allah returned you safely I would beat the drum in front of you and sing."
>
> The Messenger ﷺ said to her, "If you took an oath then beat (it) but if you did not then do not (beat it for me)!"
>
> Then she started beating (the drum) and Abū Bakr entered while she was beating (the drum). Then ʿAlī entered while she was beating (the drum), then ʿUthmān entered while she was beating (the drum), then ʿUmar entered while she was beating (the drum) and she threw the drum under her backside, then she sat on it.
>
> The Messenger ﷺ said, "Indeed, Shayṭān fears you, O ʿUmar!" I was sitting and she was beating (the drum), then Abū Bakr entered while she was beating (the drum), then ʿAlī entered while she was beating (the drum), then ʿUthmān entered while she was beating (the drum), then you entered, O ʿUmar, and she threw (aside) the drum."[1]

There is nothing objectionable in both these narrations. They are two authentic aḥādīth. The two girls mentioned in the first ḥadīth are two girls who had not yet reached puberty and they would sing during the day of ʿĪd. Naturally it was unlike the familiar forbidden music, which drives a person to follow the beat and stirs up passion. This is inferred from ʿĀ'ishah's words, "They were not singers".

Abū Bakr's رضي الله عنه reproach and subsequent comparison of the drum to the flutes of Shayṭān is because they distract the heart from Allah's remembrance and occupy the mind with amusement instead of being in a state of spiritual consciousness. Thereupon the Messenger ﷺ said to him, "Leave them," and justified that the circumstances allowed for it when he said, "Every nation has a day of ʿĪd (celebration) and this is our ʿĪd."

---

1 *Sunan al-Tirmidhī*, Bāb Manāqib ʿUmar ibn al-Khaṭṭāb, Ḥadīth no. 3690; See also *Ṣaḥīḥ al-Tirmidhī*, Ḥadīth no. 2913.

The second ḥadīth is one in which the girl said to the Prophet ﷺ that she took an oath to beat the drum if he returned safely, to which he responded, "If you took an oath then beat (it)," All that this amounts to is that the Messenger ﷺ permitted her to beat the drum in order to fulfil her oath, otherwise not.

Thereafter Abū Bakr رضي الله عنه entered, then ʿAlī رضي الله عنه, and ʿUthmān رضي الله عنه, until finally ʿUmar رضي الله عنه entered and that is when the girl threw the drum aside and sat on it. The Messenger ﷺ then made his statement—which disturbed Tījānī, "Indeed, Shayṭān is afraid of you, O ʿUmar." Can there any praise greater for ʿUmar after the Prophet ﷺ praised him?

Compare what appears in the two sound narrations with what Tījānī has written.

Tījānī's accusation that ʿUmar altered the rulings of the Prophet ﷺ

Tījānī says further:

> **After that Umar came and made things even worse, he permitted things which were forbidden by Allah and His Messenger and forbade what Allah and His Messenger had permitted**

Then he indicates in the footnote with the words:

> **Such as endorsing the three-fold divorce and his prohibition of the Mutʿah (Tamattuʿ) of the ḥajj and the Mutʿah marriage.[1]**

Refuting Tījānī's accusation that ʿUmar altered the rulings of the Prophet ﷺ

The issues of Mutʿah of Ḥajj and Mutʿah of women have been dealt with previously.[2] The discussion to follow will focus on the issue of triple-divorce.

At the outset I present the narration of Ibn ʿAbbās:

كان الطلاق على عهد رسول الله صلى الله عليه وسلم وأبي بكر وسنتين من خلافة عمر طلاق الثلاث واحدة فقال عمر بن الخطاب إن الناس قد استعجلوا في أمر قد كانت لهم فيه أناة فلو أمضيناه عليهم.فأمضاه عليهم

1 *Then I was guided*, p. 167.

2 Refer to p. 387 onwards of this book.

> The divorce during the Messenger's صلى الله عليه وسلم era, and Abū Bakr's رضي الله عنه era, and the first two years of ʿUmar's رضي الله عنه khilāfah, was that the three divorces (all at once) was regarded as one. Then ʿUmar ibn al-Khaṭṭāb رضي الله عنه said, "Indeed people are being hasty about a matter in which there was clemency (at one point). Perhaps I should pass it (the three-fold divorce all at once to be three) over them," then he passed it over them.[1]

This ḥadīth explains if a husband issued his wife with a triple divorce in one instance it was at times considered a single divorce. This continued until the khilāfah of ʿUmar. During the first two years it was maintained, but when he saw the people's carelessness about divorce and their abuse of it, he resorted to a stricter ruling to deter them from such carelessness and abuse and therefore he ruled the three-fold divorce at one instance constituted three.

This was his understanding of the issue, which was met with agreement from the Ṣaḥābah, including ʿAlī رضي الله عنه. This was not a case of making permissible what Allah and his Messenger صلى الله عليه وسلم prohibited as he did not abrogate the ruling. All he did was put it into perspective, and he was more knowledgeable of the Messenger's صلى الله عليه وسلم intent regarding the laws of divorce.

It is accepted that ʿUmar رضي الله عنه was of the noblest and among the most knowledgeable of the Ṣaḥābah. His Ijtihād in this regard is valid and has been upheld by the Ummah subsequently. Even on the assumption that he erred, he is excused on the basis of him being qualified for Ijtihād.

Senior companions have acknowledged his virtue and knowledge. Shaʿbī narrates from ʿAlī رضي الله عنه who said:

> We (the Companions of Muḥammad صلى الله عليه وسلم) had no doubt that ʿUmar was the voice of wisdom.[2]

Ibn Masʿūd said:

> ʿUmar was the most knowledgeable among us about Book of Allah, and the one with the best understanding of Allah's dīn. He had the best recognition

1 *Ṣaḥīḥ Muslim* with al-Nawawī's commentary, Kitāb al-Ṭalāq, Ḥadīth no. 1472.

2 Aḥmad: *Faḍā'il al-Ṣaḥābah*, vol. 1, p. 249, Ḥadīth no. 310, The examiner says, "its sanad is reliable."

> of Allah among us. By Allah! He was clearer than the path of those striving; meaning that this matter is clear and that the people recognise it.[1]

He also said:

> If ʿUmar's knowledge was placed on the one pan of a scale and the entire world's knowledge on the other, his (ʿUmar's) knowledge would outweigh their knowledge. (He said) I think that nine tenths of knowledge left the day ʿUmar left (this world).[2]

Mujāhid said:

> When people differed in a matter then search for what ʿUmar did and take it.[3]

In the spirit of fairness and impartiality I quote the Shīʿah sources on what the Waṣī, ʿAlī ibn Abī Ṭālib said in regards to the era of ʿUmar's Khilāfah:

> For Allah was the good showing of *Fulān* (so and so, with reference to ʿUmar).[4] He straightened the crookedness and he remedied the foundations. He pushed back fitnah and established the Sunnah. He left (this world) with a clean garment and few shortcomings. He procured the good of it (this world) and he hastened ahead of its evil. He executed his obedience towards Allah and was duly conscious of him. He passed on and left them (the people) upon many paths, the misguided not finding his way and the guided not certain (about his affairs).[5]

He also said:

> A leader governed them who straightened things (out) and was steadfast to the point where the dīn was firmly grounded.[6]

---

1 al-Haythamī: *Majmaʿ al-Zawāʾid*, vol. 9 p. 72 and 76, he says, "Ṭabarānī narrates it with many asānīd, the transmitters of one them are the transmitters of the *Ṣaḥīḥ* (al-Bukhārī)."

2 al-Haythamī: *Majmaʿ al-Zawāʾid*, vol. 9 p. 72, al-Haythamī says, "Ṭabarānī narrates this with many asānīd and transmitters. This is the transmitters of the *Ṣaḥīḥ* (of Bukhārī) besides Asad ibn Mūsā who is also a reliable transmitter."

3 Aḥmad: *Faḍāʾil al-Ṣaḥābah*, vol. 1 p. 264, Ḥadīth no. 343, the examiner says, "its sanad is reliable."

4 In the footnote of the book *al-Nahj*, it is the second khalīfah, ʿUmar ibn al-Khaṭṭāb رضي الله عنه.

5 *Nahj al-Balāghah*, vol. 2 p. 509.

6 Ibid. vol. 4 p. 793.

In the book *al-Ghārāt* by Ibrāhīm al-Thaqafī he mentions that 'Alī ibn Abī Ṭālib رضي الله عنه described the reign of 'Umar رضي الله عنه with these words:

> 'Umar stepped into office. He lived a praise-worthy lifestyle and had a blessed disposition.[1]

When 'Umar رضي الله عنه consulted him about leaving for the expedition of Rome, he said:

> Indeed, if you travel to the enemy and you meet them personally and you are afflicted with disaster then the Muslims will not have a place to resort to besides the furthest of their lands. There is no point of reference after you which people may resort to. Therefore, send to them an experienced man and incite to go with him some men with ability and goodwill. If Allah grants you victory then that is what you wanted. If it is the other (i.e. defeat) you will be a support for the people and a refuge for the Muslims.[2]

Another of their leaders, Muḥammad Āl Kāshif al-Ghiṭā says in his book *Aṣl al-Shī'ah wa Uṣūlihā*, which Tījānī claims he enjoyed reading:

> When he ('Alī ibn Abī Ṭālib) saw that the two khalīfah's, the first and the second (Abū Bakr and 'Umar), exerted all their efforts into the spreading of the call of Tawḥīd, and preparing armies, and expanding the conquests, and they did not appropriate and they did not act tyrannically, he gave the pledge and made peace.[3]

It is for that reason that 'Alī رضي الله عنه married his daughter to 'Umar ibn al-Khaṭṭāb رضي الله عنه. Not only that, he named one of his sons 'Umar, as acknowledged by al-Irbilī, in order to demonstrate his love and respect for the Khalīfah, 'Umar ibn al-Khaṭṭāb رضي الله عنه.

After all this, does it really matter that an 'impartial' researcher finds fault with his knowledge?

5. Tījānī's Claim That 'Umar Testified Against Himself

Tījānī says:

---

1 al-Thaqafī: *Al-Ghārāt*, vol. 1 p. 307, Risālah 'Alī ilā Aṣḥābīh.

2 *Nahj al-Balāghah*, p. 296-297.

3 *Aṣl al-Shī'ah wa Uṣūlihā*, p. 124.

In a chapter entitled "The virtues of Umar ibn al-Khattāb", al-Bukhārī wrote in his book: "When Umar was stabbed he felt great pain and Ibn Abbas wanted to comfort him, so he said to him, "O Commander of the Believers, you accompanied the Messenger of Allah and you were a good companion to him, and when he left you, he was very pleased with you. Then you accompanied Abu Bakr, and you were a good companion to him, and when he left you, he was pleased with you. Then you accompanied their companions and you were a good companion to them, and if you left them, they would remember you well." He said, "As for the companionship of the Messenger of Allah and his satisfaction with me, that is a gift that Allah- the Most High - has granted to me. As for the companionship of Abu Bakr and his satisfaction with me, that is a gift that Allah - Glory be to Him - has granted to me. But the reason you see me in pain is for you and your companions. By Allah, if I had all the gold on earth I would use it to ransom myself from the torture of Allah - Glory and Majesty be to Him - before I saw Him.

He has also been quoted as saying the following, "I wish I was my family's sheep. They would have fattened me up to the maximum. When they were visited by friends, they would have killed me and roasted part of me, and made *qadid* (meat cut into strips and dried) from the other part of it, then they would have eaten me, and lastly, they would have relieved me with their bowel evacuation ... I wish I had been all that, rather than a human being."[1]

Refuting Tījānī's claim that 'Umar testified against himself

Impartial eyes fail to notice the immense fear of Allah in this statement of 'Umar رَضِيَ ٱللَّهُ عَنْهُ. This is the disposition of those who are true in their commitment to Allah's dīn; they do not get ahead of themselves. Furthermore, they recognise Allah's grace in all the favours that they enjoyed. Similarly the purity of faith and deep conviction in Allah resonate with these words of 'Umar رَضِيَ ٱللَّهُ عَنْهُ.

Shaddād ibn 'Aws narrates that the Messenger of Allah صَلَّى ٱللَّهُ عَلَيْهِ وَسَلَّمَ said:

قال الله عز وجل و عزتي لا أجمع لعبدي أمنين و لا خوفين إن هو أمنني في الدنيا أخفته يوم أجمع فيه عبادي و إن هو خافني في الدنيا أمنته يوم أجمع فيه عبادي

1 *Then I was guided*, 111.

> Allah says, "By My Might! I will not combine for My slave two conditions of peace and two conditions of fear. If he felt safe from Me in the world, I will cause him to fear Me the day I gather in it My slaves. If he feared Me in the world, I will cause him to feel safe on the day I gather in it My slaves."[1]

If Tījānī is willing to accept this ḥadīth, he ought to accept the fact that the Prophet صلى الله عليه وسلم left this world pleased with ʿUmar رضي الله عنه as well. In addition to accepting that ʿUmar رضي الله عنه is a 'true' Ṣaḥābī based on Tījānī's warped tripartite definition. ʿUmar's رضي الله عنه fear of Allah highlights the fact of him being extremely consciousness of Allah even at the throes of death.

It is known that his killer was not a Muslim. He was a Persian unbeliever, whose shrine is visited and venerated by the Shīʿah in Irān to this day. The fact that he was murdered by an unbeliever bears merit since he was not killed by a believer. Muslim narrates in his *Ṣaḥīḥ* from ʿAwf ibn Mālik, from the Messenger of Allah صلى الله عليه وسلم:

> خيار أئمتكم الذين تحبونهم ويحبونكم ويصلون عليكم وتصلون عليهم وشرار أئمتكم الذين تبغضونهم ويبغضونكم وتلعنونهم ويلعنونكم
>
> Your best leaders are those whom you love and they love you, you pray for them and they pray for you. Your worst leaders are those whom you despise and they despise you, those whom you curse and they curse you.[2]

ʿUmar رضي الله عنه was a just leader whom his people loved and with whom they were pleased.

Al-Bukhārī narrates in his *Ṣaḥīḥ* by way of ʿAmr ibn Maymūn:

> فاحتمل إلى بيته فانطلقنا معه وكأنّ الناس لم تصبهم مصيبة قبل يومئذ، فقائل يقول لا بأس وقائل يقول: أخاف عليه فأتي بنبيذ فشربه فخرج من جوفه ثم أتي بلبن فشربه فخرج من جرحه فعلموا أنّه ميّتٌ، فدخلنا عليه وجاء الناس يثنون عليه وجاء رجل شابٌّ فقال أبشر يا أمير المؤمنين ببشرى الله لك من صحبة رسول الله صلى الله عليه وسلم وقدمٍ في الإسلام ما قد علمت، ثم وليت فعدلت

1 See reference on p. 211 of this book.

2 *Ṣaḥīḥ Muslim*, Kitāb al-Imārah, Bāb Khiyār al-A'immaf wa Shirāruhum, Ḥadīth no. 1855.

> Then he was carried to his house and we moved with him. It was as if an affliction had never befallen the people before that day. A man would say, "He is okay," and another man would say, "I fear for him." Then he ('Umar) was brought some juice and he drank from it but it exited out from his midsection. Then he was brought some milk and he drank it but it exited from his wounds. Then they knew he was going to die. Then we visited him, and the people visited him, and they started praising him. Then a young man came and said, "Take glad tidings, O Amīr al-Mu'minīn, from the company of the Messenger ﷺ, and earliness to Islam of what you know, then you governed (the Muslims) and you were just."[1]

Ibn Abī Mulaykah narrates the manner in which 'Alī رضي الله عنه lamented the passing of 'Umar رضي الله عنه:

> وضع عمر على سريره فتكنفه الناس يدعون ويصلون قبل أن يرفع وأنا فيهم فلم يرعني إلا رجل آخذ منكبي فإذا علي بن أبي طالب فترحم على عمر وقال ما خلفت أحدا أحب إلي أن ألقى الله بمثل عمله منك وايم الله إن كنت لأظن أن يجعلك الله مع صاحبيك وحسبت أني كنت كثيرا أسمع النبي صلى الله عليه وسلم يقول ذهبت أنا وأبو بكر وعمر ودخلت أنا وأبو بكر وعمر وخرجت أنا وأبو بكر وعمر
>
> 'Umar was placed on his bed. Then the people surrounded him supplicating and praying before he was raised and I was amongst them. Then a man alarmed me holding onto my shoulder and I noticed it was 'Alī. He prayed for Allah's mercy upon 'Umar and said, "I have not left behind anyone who I wished more to meet Allah with his deeds than you! By Allah! I think Allah will place you with you your two Companions, I remember I often used to hear the Prophet ﷺ saying, "Myself, and Abū Bakr, and 'Umar went... Myself, and Abū Bakr, and 'Umar entered... Myself, and Abū Bakr, and 'Umar left..."[2]

Many of the other issues raised by Tījānī have already been dealt under the response to "Abū Bakr's testifying against himself," the esteemed reader may refer to that section.[3]

---

1 *Ṣaḥīḥ al-Bukhārī*, Kitāb Faḍā'il al-Ṣaḥābah, Bāb Qiṣṣah al-Bay'ah, Ḥadīth no. 3497.

2 *Ṣaḥīḥ al-Bukhārī*, Kitāb Faḍā'il al-Ṣaḥābah, Bāb Manāqib 'Umar, Ḥadīth no. 3482.

3 Refer to p. 202 of this book - Tījānī's Claims that Abū Bakr Condemned Himself.

6. Tījānī's position on ʿUmar in the discussion, "A conversation with a scholar"

Tījānī says:

> **After that I opened the "Sahih" of al-Bukhari and read: Once Umar ibn al-Khattab came to Hafsah and found with her Asma bint Umays. When he saw her, he asked, "Who is she?" Hafsah answered, "Asma bint Umays." Umar said, "Is she that Ethiopian?" Asma replied, "Yes." He said, "We emigrated [that is to say from Mecca to Medinah] before you, so we are more entitled to the Messenger of Allah صَلَّى ٱللَّٰهُ عَلَيْهِ وَسَلَّمَ than you." She became very angry, then she said, "No, by Allah, you were with the Messenger of Allah صَلَّى ٱللَّٰهُ عَلَيْهِ وَسَلَّمَ, who fed your hungry people and advised the ignorant among you; whereas we were in a foreign land, in Abyssinia, for the sake of Allah and His Messenger صَلَّى ٱللَّٰهُ عَلَيْهِ وَسَلَّمَ, and whenever I ate or drank anything, I remembered the Messenger of Allah صَلَّى ٱللَّٰهُ عَلَيْهِ وَسَلَّمَ and we were hurt, and we were frightened. By Allah I will mention this to the Prophet صَلَّى ٱللَّٰهُ عَلَيْهِ وَسَلَّمَ without lying, adding anything or deviating from the subject." When the Prophet صَلَّى ٱللَّٰهُ عَلَيْهِ وَسَلَّمَ came, she said, "O Prophet of Allah صَلَّى ٱللَّٰهُ عَلَيْهِ وَسَلَّمَ, Umar said such and such." He asked, "What did you say to him?" She answered, "Such and such." He said, "I am not more entitled to him than to you." He and his companions had one emigration, but you, people of the ship, had two emigrations." She said, "I found Abu Musa and the people of the ship coming to me in groups and asking me about the Ḥadīth, very much delighted with what the Prophet صَلَّى ٱللَّٰهُ عَلَيْهِ وَسَلَّمَ had said to them."**

Then Tījānī says:

> **I said, "If the Messenger of Allah صَلَّى ٱللَّٰهُ عَلَيْهِ وَسَلَّمَ was the first to doubt Abu Bakr, and did not bear witness against him, because the Messenger صَلَّى ٱللَّٰهُ عَلَيْهِ وَسَلَّمَ did not know what would happen after him; and if the Messenger of Allah صَلَّى ٱللَّٰهُ عَلَيْهِ وَسَلَّمَ did not approve of the preference of Umar over Asma bint Umays, but indeed preferred her to him; then it is within my right to doubt and not to have a preference for anybody until I know the truth. Evidently, these Ḥadīths contradict and nullify all the known Ḥadīths in favour of Abu Bakr and Umar, because they are more realistic than these which mention their alleged virtues."[1]**

---

1 *Then I was guided*, p. 128-129.

Refuting Tījānī's position on ʿUmar in the discussion, "A conversation with a scholar"

Tījānī displays his flair of interpolation. I am amazed that he attempts to discredit ʿUmar رضي الله عنه by this ḥadīth. It is only possible to discredit him by deliberately misinterpreting it. All that the ḥadīth indicates is that the Prophet صلى الله عليه وسلم acknowledged the virtue of the people of the ship, those who migrated to Ḥabashah first and then to Madīnah, over those who migrated once from Makkah to Madīnah. This virtue was not unqualified. It was a virtue in terms of Hijrah only.

Tījānī's assumption, *"If the Prophet did not confirm the superiority of ʿUmar over Asmā' bint ʿUmays, rather, he preferred her over him,"* is symptomatic of his vitriolic disposition towards ʿUmar رضي الله عنه. When the Prophet صلى الله عليه وسلم responded to Asmā' رضي الله عنها, he said, "He does not have more right to me than you. He and his Companions migrated once while you and the people of the ship migrated twice," the Prophet صلى الله عليه وسلم did not indicate Asmā's virtue over ʿUmar only. He meant that in respect of Hijrah, those who undertook both Hijrahs had an added merit in that respect. Not that they held a higher status in general. If that were the case, Asmā' bint ʿUmays would be considered superior to all the Ṣaḥābah who migrated from Makkah to Madīnah, including ʿAlī ibn Abī Ṭālib رضي الله عنه since his Hijrah was to Madīnah only. Therefore, the merit mentioned in this ḥadīth applies only in respect to Hijrah.

Lastly, his statement,

> **It is well-known that these two aḥādīth contradict all the aḥādīth concerning the virtues of Abū Bakr and ʿUmar.**

Our response:

Why does it have to contradict all the ḥadīth concerning their virtues only? The general purport—if we take Tījānī's reasoning—implies that it contradicts all the aḥādīth concerning the virtues of ʿAlī and Fāṭimah رضي الله عنهما as they had only undertaken the Hijrah once, from Makkah to Madīnah.

Not only has Tījānī discarded the method of academic enquiry in terms of evaluating the reliability of ḥadīth, but he has completely ignored the context of the ḥadīth. In addition to this he displays complete ignorance of the principle of interpretation which dictate that specific matters be understood against the backdrop of more rigorously established general matters.

7. Tījānī's objections to ʿUmar's khilāfah

Tījānī says:

> **The acclamation of Uthman was a historical comedy: Umar nominated six people for the caliphate and told them to choose one candidate, and said if four agreed and two disagreed, then the two should be killed, however, if the six were divided into two equal camps, then the camp which was supported by Abdul Rahman ibn Awf should be considered. But if after a certain time passed and no agreement had been reached, the whole six should be killed. The story is long and rather strange, but the important thing is that Abdul Rahman ibn Awf chose Ali on the condition that he should rule in accordance with the Book of Allah [the Qur'an] and the tradition of His Messenger and the tradition of the two Shaykhs: Abu Bakr and Umar. Ali refused these conditions but Uthman accepted them, so he became caliph. Ali came out from the conference of the acclamation and knew in advance the result, and talked about it in his famous speech known as al-Shaqshaqiyya.[1]**

Refuting Tījānī's objections to ʿUmar's khilāfah

The narrations produced by Tījānī could easily be collected in an anthology of fiction. The onus is upon Tījānī to produce a reference for this fantasy-tale. It stands in stark contrast to the authentic version of what actually happened. It is mindboggling how Tījānī dismisses reality and fact with ease, and dresses up known lies as though they represent reality. They deny what has been authentically reported, and affirm that which has absolutely no basis. It is to people like Tījānī that Allah's words apply:

وَقَالُوْا لَوْ كُنَّا نَسْمَعُ أَوْ نَعْقِلُ مَا كُنَّا فِيْ أَصْحَابِ السَّعِيْرِ

And they will say, "If only we had been listening or reasoning, we would not be among the companions of the Blaze."[2]

The established truth on this issue is what al-Bukhārī narrates in his *Ṣaḥīḥ* in a lengthy ḥadīth from ʿAmr ibn Maymūn. The following passage contains the relevant portion:

---

1 *Then I was guided*, p. 145.

2 Sūrah al-Mulk: 10.

فقالوا أوص يا أمير المؤمنين استخلف قال ما أجد أحدا أحق بهذا الأمر من هؤلاء النفر أو الرهط الذين توفي رسول الله صلى الله عليه وسلم وهو عنهم راض فسمى عليا وعثمان والزبير وطلحة وسعدا وعبد الرحمن وقال يشهدكم عبد الله بن عمر وليس له من الأمر شيء كهيئة التعزية له فإن أصابت الإمرة سعدا فهو ذاك وإلا فليستعن به أيكم ما أمر فإني لم أعزله عن عجز ولا خيانة وقال أوصي الخليفة من بعدي بالمهاجرين الأولين أن يعرف لهم حقهم ويحفظ لهم حرمتهم وأوصيه بالأنصار خيرا الذين تبوءوا الدار والإيمان من قبلهم أن يقبل من محسنهم وأن يعفى عن مسيئهم وأوصيه بأهل الأمصار خيرا فإنهم ردء الإسلام وجباة المال وغيظ العدو وأن لا يؤخذ منهم إلا فضلهم عن رضاهم وأوصيه بالأعراب خيرا فإنهم أصل العرب ومادة الإسلام أن يؤخذ من حواشي أموالهم ويرد على فقرائهم وأوصيه بذمة الله وذمة رسوله صلى الله عليه وسلم أن يوفى لهم بعهدهم وأن يقاتل من ورائهم ولا يكلفوا إلا طاقتهم

They said, "Recommend (someone) O Amīr al-Mu'minīn! Select someone as your successor!"

He said, "I do not find anyone more suitable for this matter than these six (individuals) with whom the Messenger was pleased before he departed from this world." Then he named ʿAlī, ʿUthmān, Zubayr, Ṭalḥah, Saʿd, and ʿAbd al-Raḥmān.

He said, "ʿAbd Allāh ibn ʿUmar will oversee (the election process) but he has no say in the matter (it was as if he did that in order to console him). If the matter falls to Saʿd then that is that. If not, then whoever is made the khalīfah should seek his assistance as I did not withdraw him from his position on account of any inability or disloyalty."

He (ʿUmar) continued, "I remind the khalīfah after me about the first Muhājirīn, he should acknowledge their right and preserve their honour. I exhort him to be good to the Anṣār; those who were settled in Madīnah and were settled in faith before them (before the Muhājirīn came to them) he should accept the good amongst them and pardon the wrong amongst them. I encourage him to be good to the people of the (various) cities as they are the coat of Islam, and the collectors of wealth, and the irritation of the enemy. He should not take from them except their surplus and with their consent. I encourage him with goodness towards the Bedouin Arabs as they are the root of the Arabs and the core of Islam. He should take from the borders of their wealth and distribute it amongst their poor. I exhort him about the covenant of Allah and the covenant of his Messenger (with reference to the Ahl al-Dhimmah) that he should fulfil their rights according to their covenant, and that he should fight behind them (if an enemy of theirs attacks them), and that they should not be burdened beyond their ability."[1]

As is evidently clear, ʿUmar placed the matter in the hands of these six individuals with whom the Prophet ﷺ was pleased when he passed away. We can see from this narration that no command was given for anyone to be killed.

Assuming – momentarily – that there was a command for them to be killed, then in all probability its purpose would have been to prevent civil strife and deviation. Thus I ask: Would the command to have them killed have prevented civil strife or inflamed it? Would the execution of six of the best people of the Ummah have gone by without question? Would the Muslims have accepted that? In addition, if ʿUmar رضي الله عنه gave the command for their execution, as Tījānī claims, he would have commanded someone amongst the people to take responsibility for this duty; would Tījānī kindly direct us to the individual tasked with that responsibility? All these questions indicate to the fictitious nature of Tījānī's narration.

Tījānī asserts that ʿUmar رضي الله عنه said, "Then choose the view of the three ʿAbd al-Raḥmān ibn ʿAwf is amongst them." This is also a fabrication against ʿUmar رضي الله عنه as he handed the matter over to these six individuals to deal with among themselves. He did not instruct them to take the view of the group ʿAbd al-Raḥmān was a part of. The truth is that they nominated ʿAbd al-Raḥmān ibn ʿAwf as an arbitrator.

In the same ḥadīth the following is expressed:

اجتمع هؤلاء الرهط فقال عبد الرحمن اجعلوا أمركم إلى ثلاثة منكم فقال
الزبير قد جعلت أمري إلى علي فقال طلحة قد جعلت أمري إلى عثمان
وقال سعد قد جعلت أمري إلى عبد الرحمن بن عوف فقال عبد الرحمن
أيكما تبرأ من هذا الأمر فنجعله إليه والله عليه والإسلام لينظرن أفضلهم

1 *Ṣaḥīḥ al-Bukhārī*, Kitāb Faḍā'il al-Ṣaḥābah, Ḥadīth no. 3497.

في نفسه فأسكت الشيخان فقال عبد الرحمن أفتجعلونه إلي والله علي أن لا آل عن أفضلكم قالا نعم فأخذ بيد أحدهما فقال لك قرابة من رسول الله صلى الله عليه وسلم والقدم في الإسلام ما قد علمت فالله عليك لئن أمرتك لتعدلن ولئن أمرت عثمان لتسمعن ولتطيعن ثم خلا بالآخر فقال له مثل ذلك فلما أخذ الميثاق قال ارفع يدك يا عثمان فبايعه فبايع له علي وولج أهل الدار فبايعوه

When his burial was complete this group gathered together. ʿAbd al-Raḥmān said, "Make the matter between three amongst you!"

Then Zubayr said, "I pass my right to ʿAlī," and Ṭalḥah said, "I pass my right to ʿUthmān," and Saʿd said, "I pass my right to ʿAbd al-Raḥmān."

ʿAbd al-Raḥmān then said, "Which one of the two of you is willing to absolve himself from this matter so that we may place in front of him (the option of relinquishing his candidacy) considering (the other candidate), and Allah and Islam are watchful over him, the best from amongst them (to manage the responsibility of the khilāfah). The two Shaykhs (ʿUthmān and ʿAlī رضي الله عنهما) remained silent.

Then ʿAbd al-Raḥmān said, "Do you place the responsibility (of selecting the khalīfah) in front of me and Allah is watchful over me I will not fall short of making every effort in selecting the best of you (for the position)?

They said, "Yes!" He then grabbed hold of the hand of one of them and said, "You are closely related to the Messenger, and you entered into Islam very early as you know, By Allah, it is a duty upon you that if I choose you (to be the khalīfah) you be just and if I choose ʿUthmān you listen and obey!"

Then he went privately to the other and said something similar. When he had procured the agreement (from both of them) he said, "Raise your hand ʿUthmān," and he gave him his pledge. Then ʿAlī gave his pledge and then the people of the house entered and gave their pledge.

What more can be said of Tījānī's blatant lies!

Chapter Eight

Tījānī's Criticisms of the Third Khalīfah, ʿUthmān ibn ʿAffān

ʿUthmān ibn ʿAffān رضي الله عنه accepted Islam in its earliest days. He endured the persecution of the Quraysh of Makkah with the Prophet صلى الله عليه وسلم. When the persecution became unbearable ʿUthmān رضي الله عنه, along with a group of Muslims from Makkah, undertook the first Hijrah to Abyssinia. He was accompanied on this journey by his wife, Ruqayyah رضي الله عنها, the daughter of the Messenger صلى الله عليه وسلم. Later on they undertook the second Hijrah to Madīnah. Within two years she had passed away, whereupon the Messenger صلى الله عليه وسلم married him to his other daughter, Umm Kulthūm رضي الله عنها. Thus he was given the title *Dhū al-Nūrayn* (the possessor of the two lights), with reference to the privilege of being married to two of the Prophet's صلى الله عليه وسلم daughters, Ruqayyah and Umm Kulthūm رضي الله عنهما. As such, he was ʿAlī's رضي الله عنه brother-in-law twice. ʿUthmān رضي الله عنه was an embodiment of generosity. It is he who prepared the 'Army of Distress' during the Expedition of Tabūk.

When ʿUthmān رضي الله عنه brought a thousand gold coins to the Prophet صلى الله عليه وسلم at the occasion of Tabūk, the Prophet صلى الله عليه وسلم gave him the glad tidings of nothing being able to harm his Hereafter in the future. ʿAbd al-Raḥmān ibn Samurah narrates:

> عن عبد الرحمن بن سمرة قال جاء عثمان إلى النبي صلى الله عليه وسلم بألف دينار حين جهز جيش العسرة فنثرها في حجره قال عبد الرحمن فرأيت النبي صلى الله عليه وسلم يقلبها في حجره ويقول ما ضر عثمان ما عمل بعد اليوم مرتين
>
> ʿUthmān went to the Prophet صلى الله عليه وسلم with one thousand dīnārs when the 'Army of Distress' was being prepared. So he poured them into his lap. I saw the Prophet صلى الله عليه وسلم turning them over in his lap, saying, "No harm can come to ʿUthmān (in terms of his Hereafter) after what he has done today," (repeating it) twice.[1]

The Prophet صلى الله عليه وسلم promised that ʿUthmān would enter Jannah as well as be afflicted by tribulation before his death. Abū Mūsā al-Ashʿarī رضي الله عنه reports:

---

1 *Musnad Aḥmad*, Ḥadīth no. 20630; *Jāmiʿ al-Tirmidhī*, Ḥadīth no. 3701.

عن أبي موسى الأشعري رضي الله عنه ، أنه توضأ في بيته، ثم خرج فقال لألزمن رسول الله صلى الله عليه وسلم ، ولأكونن معه يومي هذا، فجاء المسجد، فسأل عن النبي صلى الله عليه وسلم فقالوا وجه ههنا قال فخرجت على أثره أسأل عنه حتى دخل بئر أريس، فجلست عند الباب حتى قضى رسول الله صلى الله عليه وسلم حاجته وتوضأ، فقمت إليه فإذا هو قد جلس على بئر أريس وتوسط قفها وكشف عن ساقيه ودلاهما في البئر فسلمت عليه ثم انصرفت فجلست عند الباب فقلت لأكونن بواب رسول الله صلى الله عليه وسلم اليوم فجاء أبو بكر رضي الله عنه فدفع الباب فقلت من هذا؟ فقال أبو بكر فقلت على رسلك ثم ذهبت فقلت يا رسول الله هذا أبو بكر يستأذن فقال ائذن له وبشره بالجنة فأقلبت حتى قلت لأبي بكر ادخل ورسول الله يبشرك بالجنة فدخل أبو بكر حتى جلس عن يمين النبي صلى الله عليه وسلم معه في القف ودلى رجليه في البئر كما صنع رسول الله صلى الله عليه وسلم وكشف عن ساقيه ثم رجعت وجلست، وقد تركت أخي يتوضأ ويلحقني فقلت إن يرد الله بفلان يريد أخاه خيراً يأت به فإذا إنسان يحرك الباب فقلت من هذا؟ فقال عمر بن الخطاب فقلت على رسلك ، ثم جئت إلى رسول الله صلى الله عليه وسلم فسلمت عليه وقلت هذا عمر يستأذن؟ فقال ائذن له وبشره بالجنة فجئت عمر فقلت أذن ويبشرك رسول الله صلى الله عليه وسلم بالجنة فدخل فجلس مع رسول الله صلى الله عليه وسلم في القف عن يساره ودلى رجليه في البئر ثم رجعت فجلست فقلت إن يرد الله بفلان خيراً يعني أخاه يأت به فجاء إنسان فحرك الباب فقلت من هذا ؟ فقال عثمان بن عفان فقلت على رسلك وجئت النبي صلى الله عليه وسلم فأخبرته فقال ائذن له وبشره بالجنة مع بلوى تصيبه فجئت فقلت له ادخل ويبشرك رسول الله صلى الله عليه وسلم بالجنة مع بلوى تصيبك فدخل فوجد القف قد ملئ فجلس وجاههم من الشق الآخر.
قال سعيد بن المسيب فأولتها قبورهم

One day, I performed ablution in my house. When I left home I did so with the idea of staying close to the Messenger of Allah ﷺ and spending the entire day with him. I came to the Masjid and enquired about him. The Companions said that he ﷺ had gone off in a particular direction. I continued enquiring about him until I came to Bi'r Arīs (a well in a particular area of Al-Madīnah). I sat down at the door until the Prophet صَلَّى ٱللَّهُ عَلَيْهِ وَسَلَّمَ relieved himself and performed ablution. Then I went to him and saw him sitting at the edge of the well with his shins uncovered and his legs dangling in the well. I greeted him and returned to the door of the garden, thinking to myself, "Today I will be the gatekeeper of the Messenger of Allah." Abū Bakr رَضِيَ ٱللَّهُ عَنْهُ came and knocked at the door.

I said, "Who is it?"

He said, "Abū Bakr."

I said, "Wait a moment."

Then I went to the Messenger of Allah صَلَّى ٱللَّهُ عَلَيْهِ وَسَلَّمَ and said, "O Messenger of Allah! Abū Bakr is at the door seeking permission to enter."

He said, "Allow him in and give him the glad tidings of Jannah."

I returned and said to Abū Bakr رَضِيَ ٱللَّهُ عَنْهُ, "You may enter and the Messenger of Allah صَلَّى ٱللَّهُ عَلَيْهِ وَسَلَّمَ has given you the glad tidings of Jannah."

Abū Bakr رَضِيَ ٱللَّهُ عَنْهُ came in, sat down on the right of the Messenger of Allah صَلَّى ٱللَّهُ عَلَيْهِ وَسَلَّمَ at the edge of the well, dangling his legs in the well with his shins exposed, as the Messenger of Allah صَلَّى ٱللَّهُ عَلَيْهِ وَسَلَّمَ had done. I returned to the door and sat down. I had left my brother at home while he was performing ablution and anticipated that he would join me. I said to myself, "If Allah intends good for him (i.e. to be blessed to come at this time and receive the glad tidings of entering Jannah), He will bring him here."

Someone knocked at the door and I said, "Who is it?"

He said, "ʿUmar ibn al-Khaṭṭāb."

I said, "Wait a moment."

Then I proceeded towards the Messenger of Allah صَلَّى ٱللَّهُ عَلَيْهِ وَسَلَّمَ. I greeted him and said, "ʿUmar is at the door, seeking permission to enter."

He said, "Allow him in and give him the glad tidings of Jannah."

I went back to ʿUmar رَضِيَ ٱللَّهُ عَنْهُ and said to him, "The Messenger of Allah has given you permission to enter, as well as glad tidings of Jannah."

He entered and sat down with the Messenger of Allah ﷺ on his left, dangling his feet into the well. I returned to the door and sat down and said to myself, "If Allah intends well for my brother, He will bring him here."

Someone knocked at the door and I said, "Who is it?"

He said, "'Uthmān ibn 'Affān."

I said, "Wait a moment."

I went to the Messenger of Allah ﷺ and informed him about his arrival. He said, "Let him in and give him glad tidings of entering Jannah together with a tribulation which he will have to face."

I came back to him and said, "You may enter; and the Messenger of Allah ﷺ gives you the glad tidings of entering Jannah together with a tribulation which will afflict you."

He entered and saw that the one side of the well was fully occupied. So he sat on the opposite side.

Sa'īd ibn al-Musayyab—a narrator in the chain—commented: The order in which they sat down indicated the places of their burial.[1]

The esteemed reader will notice that the Prophet ﷺ predicted that an affliction will affect 'Uthmān رضي الله عنه. The Prophet ﷺ also confirmed that 'Uthmān رضي الله عنه will be upon guidance when that communal strife affects the Ummah.

عن أبي الأشعث الصنعاني أن خطباء قامت بالشام وفيهم رجال من أصحاب رسول الله صلى الله عليه وسلم فقام آخرهم رجل يقال له مرة بن كعب فقال لولا حديث سمعته من رسول الله صلى الله عليه وسلم ما قمت وذكر الفتن فقربها فمر رجل مقنع في ثوب فقال هذا يومئذ على الهدى فقمت إليه فإذا هو عثمان بن عفان قال فأقبلت عليه بوجهه فقلت هذا قال نعم

Abū al-Ash'ath al-Ṣan'ānī said that people were delivering sermons in al-Shām, and among them were Companions of the Prophet ﷺ. Finally the last of them, a man called Murrah ibn Ka'b, stood up and said, "Were it not

1 *Ṣaḥīḥ al-Bukhārī*, Kitāb Faḍā'il Aṣḥāb al-Nabī ﷺ, Ḥadīth no. 3674; *Ṣaḥīḥ Muslim*, Kitāb Faḍā'il al-Ṣaḥābah, Ḥadīth no. 2403.

for a ḥadīth which I heard from the Messenger of Allah ﷺ, I would not have stood (to address you). He ﷺ mentioned tribulations, and that they would be coming soon. Then a man, who was concealed by a garment, passed by and he ﷺ said, 'This one will be upon guidance that day.' So I went towards him, and it was ʿUthmān ibn ʿAffān. I turned, facing him, and I said, 'This one?' He said, 'Yes.'"

In his final days, the Prophet ﷺ summoned ʿUthmān and consoled him over the difficulty he was to face in the future. ʿĀ'ishah رضي الله عنها relates the touching moments during the Prophet's ﷺ final days. She says:

عن عائشة قالت قال رسول الله صلى الله عليه وسلم في مرضه وددت أن عندي بعض أصحابي قلنا يا رسول الله ألا ندعو لك أبا بكر فسكت قلنا ألا ندعو لك عمر فسكت قلنا ألا ندعو لك عثمان قال نعم فجاء عثمان فخلا به فجعل النبي صلى الله عليه وسلم يكلمه ووجه عثمان يتغير قال قيس فحدثني أبو سهلة مولى عثمان أن عثمان بن عفان قال يوم الدار إن رسول الله صلى الله عليه وسلم عهد إلى عهدا وأنا صائر إليه وقال علي في حديثه وأنا صابر عليه قال قيس فكانوا يرونه ذلك اليوم

When the Messenger of Allah was ill he said, "I wish to have some of my Companions with me."

We said, "O Messenger of Allah! Shall we call Abū Bakr for you?"

But he remained silent so we said, "Shall we call ʿUmar for you?"

But he remained silent so we said, "Shall we call ʿUthmān for you?"

He said, "Yes."

So ʿUthmān came and he spoke to him in private. The Prophet ﷺ spoke to him and ʿUthmān's expression changed.

A narrator in this chain, Qays ibn Abī Ḥāzim, said, "Abū Sahlah, the freed slave of ʿUthmān, narrated to me that on the day he was assassinated in his home, ʿUthmān ibn ʿAffān said, 'The Messenger of Allah ﷺ told me what would come to pass and now I am coming to that day [Ṣā'ir].'" In another narration

> of the Ḥadīth, it appears, 'I am going to bear it with patience [Ṣābir].'"[1] Qays said, "They understood it to refer to the day he was assassinated."[2]

Tījānī does very little to hide his contempt for the Ṣaḥābah and has no qualms in falsifying history and altering the truth. Tījānī carefully reconstructs the events surrounding the murder of ʿUthmān, making sure to nudge his readers into a position where they are left to choose between the Ṣaḥābah in general, or ʿUthmān رضي الله عنه specifically. Similarly, our approach is to expose Tījānī as either deliberately misrepresenting the realities of what he speaks of, or that he failed to take all the facts into consideration, which consequently brings into question his claim of examining both sides and only being motivated by the truth.

Tījānī has previously revealed his prejudice when he condemned ʿUthmān رضي الله عنه for having wealth and spending it in the Path of Allah. He has also targeted him for praying in full during Ḥajj despite it being a matter of Ijtihād. These have been dealt with earlier in this book and we refer the esteemed reader to the relevant sections for the details.[3] Our focus here is to respond to the criticisms Tījānī constructed against ʿUthmān رضي الله عنه specifically.

Tījānī claims that the Ṣaḥābah unanimously conspired to kill ʿUthmān

Tījānī says the following:

> **When you ask them why the caliph of the Muslim's Uthman was murdered, they would say: It was the Egyptians - and they were not believers - who came and killed him, thus ends the subject with two words.**
>
> **When I had the opportunity to carry out research into history, I found that the main figures behind the killing of Uthman were the Companions themselves, and that Aishah led them, calling for his death publicly and saying: "Kill Na'thal (the old fool), for he was not a believer."**
>
> **Also we know that Talhah, al-Zubayr, Muhammad ibn Abi Bakr and other famous Companions besieged him in his house and prevented him from having a drink of water, so that they could force him to resign. Furthermore,**

---

1 The script of these two words are the same, the difference is one dot. As such it can be read in two different ways, even though neither negates the meaning of the other. - Translator.

2 *Musnad Aḥmad*, Ḥadīth no. 25797; *Sunan ibn Mājah*, Kitāb al-Muqaddimah, Ḥadīth no. 113.

3 Refer to Chapter 4, p. 173 and Chapter 5, p. 188 of this book.

the historians inform us that they did not allow his corpse to be buried in a Muslim cemetery, and that he was finally buried in "Hashsh Kawkab" without washing the corpse and without a shroud.

O Allah, praise be to You, how could they tell us that he was unjustly killed, and that those who killed him were not Muslims. This is another case similar to that of Fatimah and Abu Bakr: Uthman was either unjustly treated, therefore we may pass judgement on those Companions who killed him or those who participated in his killing that they were criminal murderers because they unlawfully killed the caliph of the Muslims, and threw stones at his funeral, and humiliated him when he was alive and then when he was dead; or that the Companions killed him because he committed certain deeds which were not compatible with Islam, as the historical sources tell us.

There is no third option, unless we dismiss the historical facts and accept the distorted picture that the Egyptians, who were not believers, killed Uthman. In both cases there is a definite rejection of the common belief that all the Companions were right and just, without exception, for either Uthman was unjust or his killers were not just, but all of them were Companions, and hence our proposition becomes void. Therefore we are left with the proposition of the followers of Ahl al-Bayt, and that is that some of the Companions were right and some others were wrong.[1]

Refuting Tījānī's claims that the Ṣaḥābah unanimously conspired to kill ʿUthmān

Tījānī's argument can be summarised in the following terms: The Ṣaḥābah all conspired to have ʿUthmān killed, which polarizes the community of Madīnah. Either ʿUthmān is upon truth, which implies that the rest of the Ṣaḥābah were evil; or ʿUthmān was upon falsehood which implies that the rest of the Ṣaḥābah were upon truth. To avoid this conundrum the Ahl al-Sunnah conveniently shifted the blame on a third party. This, in a nutshell, is the crux of Tījānī's argument. The *fait accompli*, in Tījānī's mind, is that since one of the parties must have been on falsehood, the only plausible explanation is that the Shīʿī division of Ṣaḥābah is accurate and that some of them are righteous whilst others had ulterior motives.

Tījānī does not present any reason for his rejection of the idea that a third party was responsible for ʿUthmān's murder except what has been ascribed to ʿĀ'ishah,

1 *Then I was guided*, 116-117.

and unreferenced ascriptions to Ṭalḥah, Zubayr, and Muḥammad ibn Abī Bakr (whom he claims was a senior Companion). Before we respond to Tījānī's twisting of history it is imperative that we point out the internal inconsistency in his own argument. He has overlooked the fact that if all the Companions where complicit in the murder of ʿUthmān, there is no evidence to exclude ʿAlī رضي الله عنه, Ḥasan, and Ḥusayn رضي الله عنهما. Furthermore, if we consider the ḥadīth of Murrah ibn Kaʿb mentioned above, ʿUthmān رضي الله عنه is clearly on guidance so where does that leave ʿAlī, Ḥasan, and Ḥusayn? One might go further and ask the question, who stood to gain from his death?

We have already pointed out that our response does not rest on the corollary of Tījānī's conundrum. Instead our argument investigates the facts with historical rigour. To begin with we state that the Ṣaḥābah were not involved in the murder of ʿUthmān رضي الله عنه. Rather it is they who volunteered to defend him with their lives. It was ʿUthmān's رضي الله عنه tender heart that prevented him from accepting their offer of defence. He was well aware of the fate that awaited him and feared the outbreak of further *fitnah* (communal strife). As proof for our stance we present a series of narrations that deny the involvement of the Ṣaḥābah رضي الله عنهم. I remind the esteemed reader that Tījānī did not substantiate his claims with historical proof.

Narrations negating the involvement of the Ṣaḥābah

ʿAbd Allāh ibn ʿUmar رضي الله عنهما remarked about the fitnah saying, "This person was killed in it unjustly," referring to ʿUthmān.[1]

In the lengthy narration of Abū Mūsā al-Ashʿarī رضي الله عنه, we find this detail in the book of al-Bukhārī:

ثم جاء آخر يستأذن فسكت هنيهة ثم قال ائذن له وبشره بالجنة على بلوى ستصيبه فإذا عثمان بن عفان

> Then another arrived. He remained silent for a short while then said, "Let him in and give him the glad tidings of Jannah upon a misfortune that will afflict him." It turned out to be ʿUthmān ibn ʿAffān.[2]

If the Ṣaḥābah conspired to kill him why narrate these virtues to begin with? Furthermore, they are on record offering to defend ʿUthmān رضي الله عنه. Why offer to

1 *Sunan al-Tirmidhī*, Kitāb al-Manāqib, Ḥadīth no. 3708; See also *Ṣaḥīḥ al-Tirmidhī*, Ḥadīth no. 2924.
2 *Ṣaḥīḥ al-Bukhārī*, Kitāb Faḍā'il al-Ṣaḥābah, Bāb Manāqib ʿUthmān ibn ʿAffān, Ḥadīth no. 3492.

defend him if you're going to kill him anyway? If questions are to be asked about who was involved in ʿUthmān's murder, who is the primary suspect? If the Ṣaḥābah were complicit in ʿUthmān's murder, why is it that ʿAlī رضي الله عنه would offer the following supplication?

ʿAbd al-Raḥmān ibn Laylā says:

> I saw ʿAlī raising his hands and saying, "O Allah! I declare my innocence before You of shedding the blood of ʿUthmān!"[1]

Similarly ʿUmayr ibn Saʿd says:

> We were with ʿAlī on the bank of the Euphrates when a ship passed by with its sail hoisted. ʿAlī said, "Allah says:
>
> وَلَهُ الْجَوَارِ الْمُنْشَآتُ فِي الْبَحْرِ كَالْأَعْلَامِ
>
> *And to Him belong the ships (with sails) elevated in the sea like mountains.*[2]
>
> I swear by the One who caused it to sail in one of its oceans, I did not kill ʿUthmān and I did not aid in his killing.

Jābir رضي الله عنه says:

> ʿAlī sent message to ʿUthmān, "I have five hundred coats of armour with me. Allow me and I will defend you against these people. "
>
> ʿUthmān said, "You will be rewarded with good (for your intention) but I do not wish for blood to be spilt because of me."[3]

Even ʿAlī's sons and the sons of some of the other Ṣaḥābah were ready to fight in defence of ʿUthmān ibn ʿAffān. Muḥammad ibn Sīrīn says:

> Ḥasan and Ḥusayn, Ibn ʿUmar, Ibn Zubayr, and Marwān, all of them, rushed (to ʿUthmān's house) fully armed until they entered the house and ʿUthmān said, "I order you to return, and leave your weapons, and to stay at your homes!"[4]

---

1 *Faḍā'il al-Ṣaḥābah*, vol. 1 p. 452, the examiner says, "Its sanad is good."

2 Sūrah al-Raḥmān: 24.

3 *Tārīkh Dimashq*, p. 403; See also the examined version of *Mawāqif al-Ṣaḥābah* by Muḥammad Amḥazūn, vol. 1, p. 469.

4 al-Khayyāṭ: *Tārīkh al-Khulafā'*, p. 173, See also the examined version of *Mawāqif al-Ṣaḥābah* by Muḥammad Amḥazūn, vol. 1 p. 468.

Kinānah, the freed slave of Ṣafiyyah, said:

> I witnessed the killing of ʿUthmān. Then I left the house and in front of me were four youngsters from the Quraysh stained in blood being lifted. They were warding off the attackers from ʿUthmān. They were Ḥasan ibn ʿAlī, ʿAbd Allāh ibn Zubayr, Muḥammad ibn Ḥāṭib, and Marwān ibn al-Ḥakam.[1]

Also, it has been narrated from Salamah ibn ʿAbd al-Raḥmān that Abū Qatādah al-Anṣārī and another man from the Anṣār visited ʿUthmān while he was under house arrest and requested his permission to perform the Ḥajj. He permitted them and they asked, "Who should we side with if this people take power?" He said, "Stick with the *Jamāʿah* (majority)!" They asked, "What if these people hurt you and they form a part of the majority?" He said, "Stick with the majority no matter who they are!" He said, "Then we left. When we reached the door of the house we met Ḥasan ibn ʿAlī رَضِيَ ٱللَّهُ عَنْهُ, who was entering the house. So we turned around in order to see what he intended. When Ḥasan entered the room of ʿUthmān he said, "O Amīr al-Mu'minīn! We are at your disposal. Instruct me with whatever you wish!" ʿUthmān رَضِيَ ٱللَّهُ عَنْهُ said, "O young man. Return to your home until Allah's decree comes into effect! I have no need for spilling blood!"[2]

Ibn Abī Shaybah narrates in *al-Muṣannaf* from ʿAbd Allāh ibn Zubayr, he says:

> I said to ʿUthmān on the Day of the House, "Go and fight them for indeed with you are a people whom Allah has granted victory with less than them! By Allah, fighting them is permissible!"
>
> ʿUthmān said, "By Allah! I will never fight them!"[3]

In another narration, Ibn Zubayr is on record having said:

> "Allah has permitted you to fight them."
>
> ʿUthmān said, "By Allah! I will never fight them!"[4]

---

1 Akram Ḍiyā ʿUmrī: *ʿAṣr al-Khilāfah al-Rāshidah*, p. 390, he says, "Ibn ʿAbd al-Barr narrates it in *al-Istīʿāb* with a good sanad."

2 Aḥmad: *Al-Faḍā'il*, vol. 1, Ḥadīth: 753, p. 464-465, the examiner says, "Its sanad is reliable."

3 *Muṣannaf Ibn Abī Shaybah*, vol. 8, Kitāb al-Fitan, Mā Dhakara fī ʿUthmān, p. 681-682.

4 *Ṭabaqāt Ibn Saʿd*, vol. 3 p. 70; the author of *ʿAṣr al-Khilāfah* says, "Its sanad is reliable."

It has also been narrated that Ibn ʿUmar wore his coat of arms twice the day ʿUthmān was surrounded and he unsheathed his sword until ʿUthmān instructed him to leave out of fear that he would be killed.[1]

Al-Khayyāṭ narrates from Abū Hurayrah:

> I said to ʿUthmān, "It pleases me to fight alongside you today."
>
> He said, "I command you to leave!"[2]

Ibn Abī Shaybah narrates from Muḥammad ibn Sīrīn:

> Zayd ibn Thābit came to ʿUthmān and said, "These Anṣār at the door are saying, 'If you wish we will be the Anṣār of Allah twice!'"
>
> He said, "As for fighting, no!"[3]

Qays ibn Ḥāzim, a trustworthy narrator, says:

> I heard Saʿīd ibn Zayd saying, "If Uḥud were to collapse on account of what happened to ʿUthmān it would have a good reason for doing so."[4]

Khālid ibn Rabīʿ al-ʿAbasī said:

> We heard about Ḥudhayfah's suffering. Therefore, Abū Masʿūd al-Anṣārī travelled to him in a group I was a part of to Madā'in. Then he mentioned the killing of ʿUthmān and said, "O Allah! I was not present, and I did not kill, and I was not pleased!"[5]

Jundub ibn ʿAbd Allāh says that when he met Ḥudhayfah he asked him about Amīr al-Mu'minīn, ʿUthmān, and he said:

> "Indeed, they will kill him!"
>
> I said, "Where is he?"

---

1 Ibid.; the author of *ʿAṣr al-Khilāfah* says, "Its sanad is reliable", p. 386.

2 Khalīfah al-Khayyāṭ: *Tārīkh al-Khulafā'*, p. 174; See the examined version of *Mawāqif al-Ṣaḥābah*, vol. 1 p. 468, with a reliable sanad; Refer also to *ʿAṣr al-Khilāfah*, p. 386.

3 *Al-Muṣannaf*, vol. 8, Kitāb al-Fitan, p. 682; The author of *ʿAṣr al-Khilāfah* says its sanad is good, p. 391.

4 Ibid. vol. 8 p. 682.

5 Ibid. vol. 8 p. 683.

He said, "In Jannah!"

I said, "Where are his killers?"

He said, "They are in the Fire!"[1]

Ibn Kathīr narrates in *al-Bidāyah wa al-Nihāyah* from Abū Bakrah:

> For me to fall from the heavens onto the earth is more beloved to me than to have participated in the killing of ʿUthmān.[2]

Abū ʿUthmān al-Nahdī says:

> Abū Mūsā al-Ashʿarī said, "If the killing of ʿUthmān had been guidance the Ummah would have derived milk from it but it was deviation and therefore the Ummah derived blood from it."[3]

Kulthūm ibn ʿĀmir, a Tābiʿī and a reliable transmitter, says:

> Ibn Masʿūd said, "It would not please me to throw a spear at ʿUthmān, whether it hits or not, in exchange for Mount Uḥud in gold."[4]

Ibn Shabbah narrates with a sanad leading to Rayṭah, the freed slave of Usāmah ibn Zayd, she says:

> Usāmah sent me to ʿUthmān saying, "If you wish we will burrow (for you) a hole in the house which you may escape through so that you reach a safe place for you. Then those who obey you will fight those who disobey you!"[5]

Al-Bukhārī narrates from Ḥārithah ibn ʿUthmān who witnessed Badr; he said to ʿUthmān while he was under siege, "If you wish, we will defend you."[6]

Aḥmad narrates in Faḍā'il al-Ṣaḥābah from ʿAbd Allāh ibn Salām, he said:

> Do not kill ʿUthmān! If you do so you will never pray together (again)![7]

---

1 *Tārīkh Dimashq*, p. 388; See the examined version of *Mawāqif al-Ṣaḥābah*, vol. 2 p. 28.

2 *Ibn Kathīr*, vol. 7 p. 203.

3 *Tārīkh Dimashq*, p. 490, See also *Mawāqif al-Ṣaḥābah*, vol. 2 p. 32.

4 al-Haytamī: *Majmaʿ al-Zawā'id*, vol. 9 p. 93.

5 Ibn Shabbah: *Tārīkh al-Madīnah al-Munawwarah*, vol. 3 p. 1211; See also *Mawāqif al-Ṣaḥābah*, vol. 2 p. 34.

6 al-Bukhārī: *Tārīkh al-Ṣaghīr*, vol. 1 p. 76; See also *Mawāqif al-Ṣaḥābah*, vol. 2 p. 34.

7 Aḥmad: *Faḍā'il*, vol. 1 p. 474, the examiner says, "Its sanad is reliable."

Ibn ʿAsākir narrates in his *Tārīkh* that Samurah ibn Jundub رضي الله عنه said:

> Indeed, Islam was well fortified. Then they breached a hole into Islam with their killing of ʿUthmān. Indeed, they will never cover their hole until the Day of Judgement. Indeed, the khilāfah used to be amongst the people of Madīnah but they removed it and it will never again be amongst them.[1]

Nāfiʿ, the freed slave of Ibn ʿUmar, narrates that Ibn ʿUmar رضي الله عنهما said:

> I met Ibn ʿAbbās and he was ʿUthmān's deputy for the Ḥajj season during the year of the killing. I informed him about his killing and said, "By Allah! He was amongst those who commanded towards justice. I wished I was killed that day."[2]

We have presented over twenty narrations which demonstrate the Ṣaḥābah's stance towards ʿUthmān ibn ʿAffān رضي الله عنه. We know with certainty that they did not participate, nor were they pleased with the killing of the third Khalīfah, Amīr al-Mu'minīn, ʿUthmān ibn ʿAffān, Dhū al-Nūrayn رضي الله عنه. The truth is that they offered to defend him and were prepared to give up their lives for him, but he would not have any blood spilt on his account. May Allah be pleased with these exemplary individuals!

Furthermore, Tījānī left his readers with two possible outcomes and now we also leave the discerning reader with two possible conclusions regarding Tījānī's research. The difference is that ours has been the result of academic enquiry and the facts have been substantiated by actual narrations. Thus we are absolutely certain that Tījānī either lied about examining all the narrations in this regard; or he lied about what really transpired. We leave it to the discerning reader to decide which lie is more probable.

Shīʿī scholars deny the Ṣaḥābah's involvement

Without wanting to appear overbearing we present some Shīʿī narrations which will confirm which lie Tījānī is guilty of. These narrations attest to the Ṣaḥābah's defence of ʿUthmān ibn ʿAffān رضي الله عنه, specifically that of ʿAlī ibn Abī Ṭālib and His two sons, Ḥasan and Ḥusayn.

1 *Tārīkh Dimashq*, p. 212; See also *Mawāqif al-Ṣaḥābah*, vol. 2 p. 37.

2 *ʿAṣr al-Khilāfah al-Rāshidah*, p. 397, the examiner said, "Its sanad is reliable."

Al-Masʿūdī, the Shīʿī, says in his book, *Murūj al-Dhahab*:

> When it reached ʿAlī that they intended killing him he sent his two sons, Ḥasan and Ḥusayn, with his freed slaves to ʿUthmān's door armed with swords in order to assist him and (he) commanded them to defend ʿUthmān from them. Zubayr sent his son ʿAbd Allāh, and Ṭalḥah sent his son Muḥammad. Most of the children of the Ṣaḥābah were sent by their fathers, following those who we mentioned before, and they blocked the enemies from the house.[1]

Ibn Abī al-Ḥadīd says in the commentary of *Nahj al-Balāghah*:

> A group of people stood up in Kūfah encouraging the people to support ʿUthmān, and the people of Madīnah also assisted him including ʿUqbah ibn ʿĀmir, ʿAbd Allāh ibn Abī Awfā, and Ḥanẓalah al-Kātib, all of the aforementioned are from the Ṣaḥābah. From the Tābiʿīn were Masrūq, al-Aswad, Shurayḥ, and others besides them.
>
> In Baṣrah ʿImrān ibn Ḥuṣayn, Anas ibn Mālik, and others besides them, stood up (in support of ʿUthmān). From the Tābiʿīn were Kaʿb ibn Sūr, and Haram ibn Ḥayyān, and others besides them.
>
> In al-Shām and Egypt a group of Ṣaḥābah and Tābiʿīn (also) stood up (in support of ʿUthmān).
>
> ʿUthmān came out one Friday, and led the people in ṣalāh, and ascended the mimbar, and said, "O you people (with reference to the rebels)! By Allah! The people of Madīnah know that you are cursed upon the tongue of Muḥammad. So erase the mistake with what is correct." Then Muḥammad ibn Salamah al-Anṣārī stood up and said, "Yes, indeed, I know that," and Ḥakīm ibn Jabalah sat him down. Then Zayd ibn Thābit stood up and Qutayrah ibn Saʿd sat him down. Then the rebels rose up against them and stoned them with pebbles until they forced them out of the Masjid. They even pelted ʿUthmān to a point where he fell down from the mimbar unconscious. He was brought to his house and a group of Madīnah residents remained with him including Saʿd ibn Abī Waqqāṣ, Ḥasan ibn ʿAlī, Zayd ibn Thābit, and Abū Hurayrah. Then ʿUthmān sent the message to them, "I command you to leave!" Then they left.[2]

---

1 al-Masʿūdī: *Murūj al-Dhahab*, vol. 2 p. 344-345.

2 Ibn Abī al-Ḥadīd: *Sharḥ Nahj al-Balāghah*, vol. 1 p. 162, under the sub-heading 'Fī Khurūj Ahl Miṣr wa al-Kūfah wa l-Baṣrah ʿalā ʿUthmān.

Who killed ʿUthmān?

These narrations indicate that the rebels and killers of ʿUthmān comprised of two groups. A further study will reveal that both groups were led by ʿAbd Allāh ibn Saba', who attempted to mislead the people. He constantly moved around from Ḥijāz, to Baṣrah, to Kūfah, then al-Shām from where he was expelled. Then he went to Egypt where he initiated the doctrine of Rajʿah and claimed that the successor after the Messenger ﷺ was ʿAlī. Many people of Egypt were charmed by this idea and these represent the first group. After developing his doctrine he sent his propagandists to the various regions. He wrote to those who were influenced by him in the various cities and they responded to him; they all secretly conspired to carry out his instructions. They form the second category of followers. They comprised largely of Bedouins and trouble-makers among the Arabs, many of whom turned apostate during Abū Bakr's era.

It was for this reason that ʿAlī رضي الله عنه was not in a position to deal with ʿUthmān's murderers right away. This is evident in his communication to Ṭalḥah and Zubayr when they demanded the *Ḥudūd* (prescribed punishments) be carried out on the killers of ʿUthmān:

> O my brothers! I am not ignorant of what you know. How do I do that with a people who are in charge of us and we are not in charge of them? Indeed, your slaves have revolted with them and your Bedouin Arabs have stood firm with them?[1]

This is confirmed by the Twelver scholar, al-Nawbakhtī. He says:

> A group of people turned apostate and left Islam. The Banū Ḥanīfah tribe claimed prophethood for Musaylamah, who had claimed prophethood (for himself) during the Messenger's ﷺ life. Abū Bakr sent the armies to them with Khālid ibn Walīd ibn Mughīrah al-Makhzūmī at their helm. They fought them and killed Musaylamah. Those who were killed were killed and those who returned (to Islam) returned to Islam. Those who returned were called Ahl al-Riddah and they remained united with the rest of the Ummah until they criticised ʿUthmān for some things which he innovated and (consequently) they were either conspirators or murderers, except for the special ones of the Ahl al-Bayt and a few others besides them until he (ʿUthmān) was killed.[2]

---

1 *Tārīkh al-Ṭabarī*, vol. 2 p. 702, the year 35 A.H.

2 al-Nawbakhtī: *Firaq al-Shīʿah*, p. 4.

Those who claimed responsibility for the attack upon ʿUthmān came from Egypt, led by al-Ghāfiqī ibn Ḥarb al-ʿAkbī. These people were known as the *Miṣriyyīn* (Egyptians). However, Tījānī denies that because, as he claims, he read the entire history! However, the books of history in addition to other resources confirm that the killers of ʿUthmān were indeed the Egyptians. Refer to *Tārīkh al-Ṭabarī*[1], *Tārīkh Ibn al-Athīr*[2], *al-Tamhīd wa l-Bayān*[3], *Murūj al-Dhahab*[4], *al-Bidāyah wa al-Nihāyah*[5], *Ṭabaqāt Ibn Saʿd*[6], *Sharḥ Nahj al-Balāghah*[7], *al-Istīʿāb* by Ibn ʿAbd al-Barr[8], *al-Tārīkh al-Islāmī*[9], and *al-Futūḥ* by Ibn al-Aʿtham.[10]

I repeat my earlier question, which history has Tījānī been reading?

ʿĀ'ishah's role

Tījānī has no qualms in pointing a finger at Umm al-Mu'minīn ʿĀ'ishah رضي الله عنها, accusing her of masterminding the assassination of ʿUthmān رضي الله عنه. He says:

> **Aishah led them, calling for his death publicly and saying: "Kill Na'thal (the old fool), for he was not a believer."**

Our response:

a. This narration, which Tījānī relies on, is weak as it revolves around a narrator called Naṣr ibn Muzāḥim.

> ʿUqaylī said about him, "He adopted Tashayyuʿ. There are internal inconsistencies in his narrations in addition to abundance of errors."[11]

---

1 *Tārīkh al-Ṭabarī*, vol. 3 p. 36, the year 35 (A.H).

2 *Tārīkh Ibn al-Athīr*, under the year 35 (A.H), vol. 3 p. 46.

3 Muḥammad ibn Yaḥyā al-Mālaqānī: *Al-Tamhīd wa l-Bayān fī Maqtal al-Shahīd ʿUthmān*, p. 109-118, under, 'Dhikr Ḥiṣār ʿUthmān'.

4 al-Masʿūdī al-Shīʿī: *Murūj al-Dhahab*, vol. 2, Khilāfah ʿUthmān ibn ʿAffān, p. 343.

5 *Al-Bidāyah wa l-Nihāyah* under 'the thirty sixth year entered and it occurred the killing of ʿUthmān.'

6 *Al-Ṭabaqāt*, under 'Dhikr al-Miṣriyyīn wa Ḥaṣr ʿUthmān I' vol. 3 p. 64.

7 Ibn Abī al-Ḥadīd: *Sharḥ Nahj al-Balāghah* under 'Fī Khurūj Ahl Miṣr wa l-Kūfah wa l-Baṣrah ʿalāʿUthmān' to 'Man ʿUthmān min al-Mā' wa Kayfiyyah Qatlih' vol. 1 p. 162-167, Dār al-Fikr Beirut.

8 *Al-Istīʿāb* 'Dhikr ʿUthmān ibn ʿAffān', vol. 3 p. 1037-1053.

9 Maḥmūd Shākir: *Al-Tārīkh al-Islāmī*, vol. 3, 'al-Bāb al-Thālith, ʿUthmān ibn ʿAffān.'

10 *Al-Futūḥ*, vol. 1, p. 44, under 'Dhikr Wuṣūl al-Miṣriyyīn ilā al-Madīnah.'

11 ʿUqaylī: *Al-Ḍuʿafā'* vol. 4, p. 300, biography no. 1899.

> Al-Dhahabī said (about him), "He was a staunch Rāfiḍī. They abandoned him (his aḥādīth)."
>
> Abū Khaythamah said about him, "He was a liar!"
>
> Abū Ḥātim said about him, "Weak in ḥadīth, *Matrūk* (suspected of forgery)."
>
> Al-Dāraquṭnī said about him, "Weak!"[1]
>
> Al-Jūzajānī says, "Naṣr was wayward from the truth, deviated (from it)."
>
> Ṣāliḥ ibn Muḥammad said, "Naṣr ibn Muzāḥim narrated many anomalous reports from the weak narrators."
>
> Ḥāfiẓ Abū al-Fatḥ Muḥammad ibn Ḥasan said, "Naṣr ibn Muzāḥim was extreme in his belief."[2]

Therefore, this narration is not reliable and is not considered proof-worthy in addition to the fact that it contradicts the authentic narrations.

b. The authentic narrations confirm that ʿĀ'ishah رضي الله عنها lamented the death of ʿUthmān رضي الله عنه and cursed his killers. Masrūq relates a conversation with ʿĀ'ishah رضي الله عنها:

> "You left him like a garment clean from any impurities. Then you drew him closer before slaughtering him like a ram."
>
> Masrūq said, "This is of your doing! You wrote to the people commanding them to rebel against him."
>
> ʿĀ'ishah said, "I swear by Him in whom the believers believe and the disbelievers belie, I never wrote anything to them even up to this moment!"
>
> Aʿmash said, "They were of the view that the letter was forged in her name."[3]

Aḥmad narrates in his *Faḍā'il* from ʿĀ'ishah رضي الله عنها that she used to say concerning the killing of ʿUthmān:

> If only I was in oblivion and forgotten. As for what happened to ʿUthmān, by Allah, I did not wish for a single right of ʿUthmān to be violated except that a

1 al-Dhahabī: *Al-Mīzān*, vol. 4 p. 253, biography no. 9046.

2 al-Baghdādī: *Tārīkh Baghdād*, vol. 13 p. 283.

3 Ibn Kathīr: *Al-Bidāyah wa l-Nihāyah*, vol. 7 p. 204, he said, "This is a reliable sanad."

similar right of mine be violated to the extent that if I wished for his killing, I would be killed instead...[1]

Ibn Shabbah narrated from Ṭalq ibn Ḥushshān:

I said to ʿĀ'ishah, "How was Amīr al-Mu'minīn, ʿUthmān, killed?"

She said, "He was killed unjustly. May Allah curse his killers!"[2]

Aḥmad narrates in his *Faḍā'il* from Sālim ibn Abī al-Jaʿd:

We were with Ibn Ḥanīfah in the mountain pass when he heard a man discrediting (someone) with Ibn ʿAbbās in his presence. Then he said, "O Ibn ʿAbbās! Did you hear Amīr al-Mu'minīn this morning? He heard a clamour coming from the direction of Marbad so he sent someone and told him, 'Go and investigate what this noise is!' When the person retuned he said, 'It is ʿĀ'ishah cursing ʿUthmān's killers and the people around her are saying Āmīn (to her supplications).' Then ʿAlī said, 'I too curse the killers of ʿUthmān's on the land and on the mountains. O Allah; Curse the killers of ʿUthmān! O Allah; Curse the killers of ʿUthmān on the land and on the mountain!'"

Then Ibn Ḥanīfah faced him and faced us and said, "Do you not find in Ibn ʿAbbās and me credible witnesses?"

We said, "We do!"

He said, "This indeed occurred!"[3]

c. It is well-known by all the historians that ʿĀ'ishah رضي الله عنها sought vengeance for ʿUthmān رضي الله عنه. Knowing that, how does one reconcile between demanding vengeance and the alleged statement, "Kill Naʿthal as he has disbelieved," unless it is a clear forgery upon her?

Roles of Ṭalḥah, Zubayr and Muḥammad ibn Abī Bakr

Tījānī says:

Also we know that Talhah, al-Zubayr, Muhammad ibn Abi Bakr and other famous Companions besieged him in his house and prevented him from having a drink of water, so that they could force him to resign

---

1 Aḥmad: *Faḍā'il al-Ṣaḥābah*, vol. 1 p. 462, its examiner says, "Its sanad is reliable."

2 Bukhārī: *Al-Tārīkh al-Kabīr*, vol. 4 p. 357, with a good sanad; See also *ʿAṣr al-Khilāfah*, p. 397.

3 Ibn Abī Shaybah: *Al-Muṣannaf*, vol. 8, Kitāb al-Jamal, p. 712, with a good sanad.

Our response:

a. Tījānī claims that Muḥammad ibn Abū Bakr was from the most famous Ṣaḥābah, this is an 'established fact' which cannot be denied. He was a companion no doubt! However, this Companionship lasted less than four months since the Prophet ﷺ passed away when Muḥammad ibn Abū Bakr was an infant, not even four months old! How can he be from amongst the most famous Ṣaḥābah?

b. Tījānī hasn't produced any evidence to substantiate his claim that Ṭalḥah and Zubayr رضي الله عنهما prevented 'Uthmān رضي الله عنه from leaving his house and that they were among those who laid siege to him. We know this to be a lie; not because of Tījānī's lack of evidence, but because there is sufficient evidence indicating their support for him.

c. The authentic narrations confirm that Ṭalḥah and Zubayr were deeply pained at the loss of 'Uthmān. They were prepared to defend him with their lives. Abū Ḥabībah relates:

> Zubayr sent me to 'Uthmān while he was restricted (to his house). I came to him on a clear day while he was sitting on a chair and Ḥasan ibn 'Alī, Abū Hurayrah, 'Abd Allāh ibn 'Umar, and 'Abd Allāh ibn Zubayr, were (all) with him.
>
> I said, "Zubayr sent me to you. He sends his greetings to you and says, 'I remain obedient (to you). I have not substituted (my obedience with disobedience) and I have not gone back on my pledge. If you wish I will enter the house and be one of the men (to defend you), and if you wish I will remain (where I am) as Banū 'Amr ibn 'Awf promised me they would be at my door in the morning and they will do what I instruct them to do.'"
>
> When he heard the message he said, "Allah Akbar! All praise is for Allah who protected my brother. Send my greeting to him and then say, 'If you enter the house you will merely be another person. I prefer that you remain where you are. Perhaps Allah will protect me through you.'"
>
> When Abū Hurayrah heard the message he stood up and said, "Should I not inform you what my ears heard from the Messenger?"
>
> They said, "Indeed!"

> He said, "I testify that I heard the Messenger saying, 'After me there will be trials and tribulations.' We asked, 'Where will the refuge be from it, O Messenger of Allah?' He said, 'With al-Amīn (the truthful one) and his group,' pointing towards ʿUthmān ibn ʿAffān."
>
> The people then stood up and said, "(This) knowledge justifies our position, so permit us to fight!"
>
> Then ʿUthmān said, "I instruct the person who considers it his duty to obey me not to fight!"[1]

Al-Dāraquṭnī narrates in *Faḍā'il al-Ṣaḥābah*:

> ʿUthmān overlooked the Masjid and saw Ṭalḥah sitting in the eastern wing of the Masjid. He said, "O Ṭalḥah!" and he said, "Here I am!"
>
> He said, "I remind you of Allah. Do you know that the Messenger said, 'Who will purchase a portion of land to expand the Masjid?' Then I bought it from my wealth."
>
> Ṭalḥah said, "Yes!"
>
> Then he (ʿUthmān) said, "O Ṭalḥah!" and he said, "Here I am!"
>
> He (ʿUthmān) said, "I remind you of Allah. Do you know that I carried in the Army of Distress one hundred?"
>
> Ṭalḥah said, "Yes!"
>
> Then Ṭalḥah said, "I only know ʿUthmān to have been oppressed."[2]

d. There is no disagreement in the fact that Ṭalḥah and Zubayr رضي الله عنهما were among the first to demand vengeance and retribution for ʿUthmān رضي الله عنه from his killers. Why then would they rebel, lay siege to ʿUthmān's رضي الله عنه house, and aid in murdering him? What purpose would demanding justice and vengeance for ʿUthmān's رضي الله عنه murder serve if they were responsible for killing him in the first place?

---

1 Aḥmad: *Al-Faḍā'il*, vol. 1, p. 511-512, the examiner says, "A good sanad."

2 *Taḥqīq Mawāqif al-Ṣaḥābah fī al-Fitnah*, vol. 2, p. 24.

ʿUthmān's burial

Tījānī goes on to say:

> **Furthermore, the historians inform us that they did not allow his corpse to be buried in a Muslim cemetery, and that he was finally buried in "Hashsh Kawkab" without washing the corpse and without a shroud.**

And at another place he says:

> **It became clear to me what the historians meant when they said that he was buried in "Hash Kawkab". Which was Jewish land.**

Our response:

This is Tījānī's desperate attempt to portray the Ṣaḥābah as a group of scum and savages who kill one another and even prevent them from being buried in the Muslim graveyard, that too without being washed or shrouded. That is quite interesting when one considers that the murderer of ʿUmar رضي الله عنه has a shrine built for him in some parts of the 'Muslim' world.

His allegation that the Ṣaḥābah prevented his burial in the Muslim cemetery hence he was buried in Ḥash Kawkab, a Jewish piece of land, only reveals his ignorance. Ḥash Kawkab is not a Jewish-owned piece of land. The (word) Ḥash means 'garden' and ʿUthmān purchased it from a man from the Anṣār named Kawkab.[1] When ʿUthmān رضي الله عنه passed away he was buried in his own garden which was purchased with his own wealth. Is there anything objectionable in that?

Then he adds and says:

> **It became clear to me what the historians meant when they said that he was buried in "Hash Kawkab". Which was Jewish land, because the Muslims refused to bury him in the Baqi' of the Messenger of Allah. When Muawiya seized power, he bought that land from the Jews and included it in al-Baqi', so that it contains the grave of his cousin Uthman. He who visits al-Baqi' today will see this fact very clearly.[2]**

Our response:

---

1 al-Nawawī: *Tahdhīb al-Asmā' wa l-Lughāt*, vol. 1, p. 323; Also: *al-Maʿālim al-Athīrah fī al-Sunnah wa l-Sīrah* by Muḥammad Ḥasan Sharāb, p. 101.

2 *Then I was guided*, p. 139.

Even toddlers know that the Jews were expelled from Madīnah during the Prophet's ﷺ lifetime, and not a single Jew remained during the period of the Khulafā'! There was no Jewish land in Madīnah. It exists only in Tījānī's 'unbiased' mind.

Prophetic inheritance

He goes on to say:

> **It is worth mentioning here a story related to the subject of inheritance that has been cited by many historians:**
>
> **Ibn Abi al-Hadid al-Mutazili said in his commentary on *Nahj al-Balagha*: Aisha and Hafsa came to see Uthman, during his caliphate, and asked him to give them their shares of what they had inherited from the Messenger of Allah ﷺ. Uthman was stretched on the sofa, so he sat up and said to Aisha: You and that woman sitting next to you brought a man who cleansed himself with his urine and testified that the Messenger of Allah ﷺ said, "We, the prophets, do not leave an inheritance." If the Prophet ﷺ truly did not leave any inheritance, why do you ask for it now, and if he left an inheritance, why did you deprive Fatimah of her legal share? After that, she left him feeling very angry and said: Kill Na'thal, for he has become an unbeliever.**[1]

Our comment:

I opened the commentary of *Nahj al-Balāghah* (volume 6, page 220-223) as he indicated in Tījānī's footnote, but I could not find the narration he alludes to. However, I did find this narration:

> Mālik—from Zuhrī—from 'Urwah—from 'Ā'ishah that when the Prophet ﷺ passed away, his wives intended to send 'Uthmān ibn 'Affān to Abū Bakr to ask for their share of the inheritance. She said, "I said to them, 'Did the Prophet not say, 'we are not inherited from. What we leave is charity.'"[2]

Al-Bukhārī and Muslim have narrated something similar to this narration which clearly contradicts the story Tījānī mentions in his book.

---

1 *Then I was guided*, p. 140.

2 *Sharḥ Nahj al-Balāghah*, vol. 4, p. 82, under the heading, Fī al-Akhbār al-Wāridah fī Fadak wa mā Ṣuni'ā fīhā, as for the copy which he relied upon and references it to vol. 16, it is not the copy I depended upon. That being said, I referred to the copy he depended upon, to the volume and page number the author indicated to but I did not find it there also.

That being said, the reliable aḥādīth and the biographies of ʿUthmān and ʿĀ'ishah رضي الله عنهما repudiate this report and reject it. And all praise is for Allah!

Tījānī criticises ʿUthmān's Ijtihād

Then he says:

> **When Uthman came to power after Umar, he went a long way in al-Ijtihad, and did more than any on his predecessors had done, until his opinions started to affect political and religious life generally, thus leading to the revolution, and he paid with his life as a price for his Ijtihad.[1]**

Look at Tījānī contradicting himself. Earlier on he was berating the Ṣaḥābah for the murder of ʿUthmān and now he blames ʿUthmān for his Ijtihād! Clearly it is a lie meant to shift attention from the rebels and the underground movement headed by Ibn Saba'. Responsibility for the Fitnah lies with them, and not ʿUthmān رضي الله عنه. That is clear from the ḥadīth of Murrah ibn Kaʿb, after the Prophet صلى الله عليه وسلم mentioned the imminent Fitnah he said:

> وذكر الفتن فقربها فمر رجل مقنع في ثوب فقال هذا يومئذ على الهدى فقمت إليه فإذا هو عثمان بن عفان قال فأقبلت عليه بوجهه فقلت هذا قال نعم
>
> He صلى الله عليه وسلم mentioned tribulations, and that they would be coming soon. Then a man, who was concealed by a garment, passed by and he صلى الله عليه وسلم said, "This one will be upon guidance that day."
>
> So I went towards him, and it was ʿUthmān ibn ʿAffān. I turned, facing him, and I said: "This one?"
>
> He said: "Yes."

Furthermore, the Ṣaḥābah stood by ʿUthmān رضي الله عنه and were prepared to defend him against the rebels. How then could one simply dismiss his murder as a consequence of his Ijtihād?

There are so many aḥādīth which confirm that ʿUthmān رضي الله عنه was upon truth and that those who rebelled against him were the people of sedition and falsehood.

---

1 *Then I was guided*, p. 167.

Al-Ḥākim narrates in al-Mustadrak, and Aḥmad in *Al-Faḍā'il*, by way of Mūsā ibn ʿUqbah, who said:

> Abū Ḥabībah narrated to me that he visited ʿUthmān while ʿUthmān was under siege and that he heard Abū Hurayrah seeking permission from ʿUthmān to speak and ʿUthmān permitted him. So he stood up, and praised Allah, and said, "Indeed, I heard the Messenger saying, 'You will encounter Fitnah and difference of opinion after me.' A man then said to him, 'What should we do, O Messenger of Allah?' He said, 'Stick with al-Amīn (with reference to ʿUthmān) and his party!'"[1]

The ḥadīth of Abū Mūsā al-Ashʿarī found in *Ṣaḥīḥ Muslim* was quoted in its entirety earlier on. We now reproduce the relevant part of it:

> فجلس النبى صلى الله عليه وسلم فقال افتح وبشره بالجنة على بلوى تكون قال فذهبت فإذا هو عثمان بن عفان قال ففتحت وبشرته بالجنة قال وقلت الذى قال فقال اللهم صبرا أو الله المستعان

> Then the Prophet ﷺ sat and said, "Open and give him the glad tidings of Jannah upon a trial which will afflict him!"
>
> I went and it was ʿUthmān ibn ʿAffān. So I opened the door and gave him the glad tidings of Jannah and related to him what the Prophet ﷺ had said.
>
> ʿUthmān said, "O Allah! (grant me) patience!" or he said, "Allah is the one whom help is sought from."[2]

Similarly Ibn ʿUmar said:

> The Prophet mentioned the Fitnah and said, "This person will be killed therein unjustly," pointing to ʿUthmān ibn ʿAffān.

The ḥadīth has emphatically declared ʿUthmān رضي الله عنه upon truth. We have presented over twenty narrations which clarify that the Ṣaḥābah stood by his side, supported him, and were prepared to fight in his defence which he forbade them from. All that remains is the party which is responsible for the murder of ʿUthmān. Tījānī has condemned the Ṣaḥābah, so he does not fall in that camp. He has castigated

1 Aḥmad: *Faḍā'il al-Ṣaḥābah*, vol. 1, p. 451, the examiner says, "Its sanad is reliable."

2 This ḥadīth has been previously cited p. 426 of this book.

ʿUthmān رضي الله عنه for his Ijtihād, so he cannot possibly be on ʿUthmān's side. Where does that leave Tījānī?

In conclusion we state:

ʿUthmān ibn ʿAffān رضي الله عنه ranks the third after the Prophets in terms of merit. He is only preceded by Abū Bakr and ʿUmar رضي الله عنهما. He is among those whom the Prophet صلى الله عليه وسلم confirmed is in Jannah. His generosity and spending in the path of Allah became an example for others to follow after him. He has the honour of extending the Prophet's Masjid using his own wealth. He purchased the well of Rūmah and endowed it for the benefit of the Muslims just as he prepared the 'Army of Distress'.

ʿUthmān's رضي الله عنه generosity is a reality which cannot be denied, not by Tījānī nor his mentors. Abū al-Fatḥ al-Irbilī, a Shīʿī scholar, writes in his book *Kashf al-Ghummah* about ʿAlī's marriage to Fāṭimah:

> ʿAlī said, "The Messenger faced (us) and said, 'O Abū al-Ḥasan! Go now and sell your coat of arms and bring its price so that I can prepare for you and my daughter what befits you.'"
>
> ʿAlī said, "Then I went and I sold it for four hundred Dirhams to ʿUthmān ibn ʿAffān. When I took hold of the dirhams and he took hold of the coat of arms from me he said, 'O Abū al-Ḥasan! Am I not more entitled to the coat of arms than you and you more entitled to the dirhams than me?' I said, 'Indeed!' He said, 'Indeed, the coat of arms is a gift from me to you.' So I took the coat of arms and the dirhams and headed to the Prophet صلى الله عليه وسلم and I placed the coat of arms and the dirhams in front of him and informed him about what happened with regards to ʿUthmān and the Prophet supplicated for him."[1]

The sons and grandsons of ʿAlī رضي الله عنه—who are considered infallible Imāms by the Shīʿah—displayed immense love and respect for ʿUthmān رضي الله عنه. It has been narrated from ʿAlī Zayn al-ʿĀbidīn that he said:

> A group of people from ʿIrāq came to him and uttered some disparaging remarks about Abū Bakr, ʿUmar, and ʿUthmān. When they completed what they had to say, he said to them, "Are you from those described by the verse:

1 al-Irbilī: *Kashf al-Ghummah*, vol. 1, p. 368-369, under the heading, 'Fī Tazwījihī Fāṭimah.'

الْمُهَاجِرِيْنَ الَّذِيْنَ أُخْرِجُوْا مِنْ دِيَارِهِمْ وَأَمْوَالِهِمْ يَبْتَغُوْنَ فَضْلًا مِّنَ
اللّٰهِ وَرِضْوَانًا وَيَنْصُرُوْنَ اللّٰهَ وَرَسُوْلَهٗ أُولٰٓئِكَ هُمُ الصَّادِقُوْنَ

The Muhājirīn who were expelled from their homes and their properties, seeking bounty from Allah and (His) approval and supporting Allah and His Messenger. Those are the truthful ones.[1]

The group from ʿIrāq replied, "No!"

Zayn al-ʿĀbidīn then asked, "Are you then from those described by the verse:

وَالَّذِيْنَ تَبَوَّءُوا الدَّارَ وَالْإِيْمَانَ مِنْ قَبْلِهِمْ يُحِبُّوْنَ مَنْ هَاجَرَ إِلَيْهِمْ
وَلَا يَجِدُوْنَ فِيْ صُدُوْرِهِمْ حَاجَةً مِمَّا أُوْتُوْا وَيُؤْثِرُوْنَ عَلٰى أَنْفُسِهِمْ
وَلَوْ كَانَ بِهِمْ خَصَاصَةٌ

And (also for) those who were settled in the abode (i.e. Madīnah) and adopted the faith before them. They love those who emigrated to them and find not any want in their breasts of what they (i.e. the Muhājirīn) were given but give them preference over themselves, even though they are in privation.[2]

The group from ʿIrāq replied, "No!"

Zayn al-ʿĀbidīn then said, "As for you, you have absolved yourselves from being from these two groups, and I testify that you are not from those regarding whom Allah says:

وَالَّذِيْنَ جَاءُوْا مِنْ بَعْدِهِمْ يَقُوْلُوْنَ رَبَّنَا اغْفِرْ لَنَا وَلِإِخْوَانِنَا الَّذِيْنَ
سَبَقُوْنَا بِالْإِيْمَانِ وَلَا تَجْعَلْ فِيْ قُلُوْبِنَا غِلًّا لِلَّذِيْنَ اٰمَنُوْا

And those who came after them, saying, "Our Lord, forgive us and our brothers who preceded us in faith and put not in our hearts (any) resentment toward those who have believed."[3]

---

1 Sūrah al-Ḥashr: 8.

2 Sūrah al-Ḥashr: 9.

3 Sūrah al-Ḥashr: 10.

> Zayn al-ʿĀbidīn said, "Get away from me! Allah will do with you what He wills!" [1]

This is how an 'infallible Imām' views ʿUthmān رضي الله عنه. It stands in stark contrast to Tījānī's stance on ʿUthmān رضي الله عنه. It does not come as a surprise that Tījānī's projection of events only fits a twisted version of history, riddled with internal inconsistencies which clearly identify it as false.

1 al-Irbilī: *Kashf al-Ghummah*, vol. 2, p. 291, under the heading, Faḍā'il al-Imām Zayn al-ʿĀbidīn.

Chapter Nine

Tījānī's criticism of Sayyidah ʿĀ'ishah, the Prophet's ﷺ wife

One of the most trying times during the Prophet's ﷺ life was when his wife, ʿĀ'ishah رضي الله عنها, Mother of the Believers, was accused of acts from which we shudder to mention. During this period the Prophet ﷺ experienced great incertitude, anxious for Divine intervention. Eventually the gloomy clouds were replaced by verses brighter than the sun in clearing her name, rebuking those who participated in the gossip and testifying to the sincerity of her faith. Allah says:

إِنَّ الَّذِيْنَ يَرْمُوْنَ الْمُحْصَنَاتِ الْغَافِلَاتِ الْمُؤْمِنَاتِ لُعِنُوْا فِي الدُّنْيَا وَالْأٰخِرَةِ وَلَهُمْ عَذَابٌ عَظِيْمٌ

Indeed, those who [falsely] accuse chaste, believing women who are unaware [of such indecency], are cursed in this world and the Hereafter; and they will have a great punishment![1]

We would like to draw attention to the fact that Allah described her as a believing, chaste woman, unaware of the indecency she had been accused of. In this regard Allah has rebuked those who speak ill of her, warning them of being cursed, while attesting to her sincerity of faith and chastity.

Prior to these verses Allah reaffirms the high status of Sayyidah ʿĀ'ishah رضي الله عنها by reminding the believers that they faced a severe punishment for speaking ill of her, were it not for Allah's prevailing grace and mercy. He says:

وَلَوْلَا فَضْلُ اللّٰهِ عَلَيْكُمْ وَرَحْمَتُهٗ فِي الدُّنْيَا وَالْأٰخِرَةِ لَمَسَّكُمْ فِيْ مَا أَفَضْتُمْ فِيْهِ عَذَابٌ عَظِيْمٌ

Yet were it not for the Grace of Allah upon you, and His Mercy in this world and in the Hereafter a great torment would certainly have afflicted you for that [gossip] in which you have indulged![2]

1 Sūrah al-Nūr: 23.

2 Sūrah al-Nūr: 14.

Such is the rank of al-Ṣiddīqah in the Sight of Allah, that He threatened anyone who dared to speak ill of Sayyidah ʿĀ'ishah رضي الله عنها after this. Allah says:

يَعِظُكُمُ اللّٰهُ أَنْ تَعُوْدُوْا لِمِثْلِهِ أَبَدًا إِنْ كُنْتُمْ مُؤْمِنِيْنَ

Allah admonishes you never to repeat the likes of this if you are truly believers![1]

The status that she enjoyed in the eyes of the Prophet صلى الله عليه وسلم exceeds the limitations of our vocabulary. She had once lost a necklace on a journey with the Prophet صلى الله عليه وسلم. He halted the entire army in a place without water. As a result Allah revealed the verses that permit dry ablution, *Tayammum*.

حدثنا عبد الله بن يوسف قال أخبرنا مالك عن عبد الرحمن بن القاسم عن أبيه عن عائشة زوج النبي صلى الله عليه وسلم قالت خرجنا مع رسول الله صلى الله عليه وسلم في بعض أسفاره حتى إذا كنا بالبيداء أو بذات الجيش انقطع عقد لي فأقام رسول الله صلى الله عليه وسلم على التماسه وأقام الناس معه وليسوا على ماء فأتى الناس إلى أبي بكر الصديق فقالوا ألا ترى ما صنعت عائشة أقامت برسول الله صلى الله عليه وسلم والناس وليسوا على ماء وليس معهم ماء فجاء أبو بكر ورسول الله صلى الله عليه وسلم واضع رأسه على فخذي قد نام فقال حبست رسول الله صلى الله عليه وسلم والناس وليسوا على ماء وليس معهم ماء فقالت عائشة فعاتبني أبو بكر وقال ما شاء الله أن يقول وجعل يطعنني بيده في خاصرتي فلا يمنعني من التحرك إلا مكان رسول الله صلى الله عليه وسلم على فخذي فقام رسول الله صلى الله عليه وسلم حين أصبح على غير ماء فأنزل الله آية التيمم فتيمموا فقال أسيد بن الحضير ما هي بأول بركتكم يا آل أبي بكر قالت فبعثنا البعير الذي كنت عليه فأصبنا العقد تحته

ʿĀ'ishah رضي الله عنها says, "We went out on a journey with the Messenger of Allah صلى الله عليه وسلم, and when we came to a place called al-Baydā' or Dhāt al-Jaysh, a necklace of mine fell off. The Messenger of Allah صلى الله عليه وسلم stopped to look for it and the people stopped with him. There was no water nearby and the people were not carrying any with them, so they came to Abū Bakr al-Ṣiddīq and said,

1 Sūrah al-Nūr: 17.

'Don't you see what ʿĀ'ishah has done? She has made the Messenger of Allah صلى الله عليه وسلم and the people stop when there is no water nearby and they are not carrying any with them.'"

ʿĀ'ishah continued, "Abū Bakr came whilst the Messenger of Allah صلى الله عليه وسلم was sleeping with his head on my thigh. Abū Bakr said, 'You have made the Messenger of Allah صلى الله عليه وسلم and the people stop when there is no water nearby and they are not carrying any with them!'

Abū Bakr reprimanded me and said whatever Allah willed him to say, and began to poke me in the waist. The only thing that stopped me from moving was that the Messenger of Allah صلى الله عليه وسلم had his head on my thigh. The Messenger of Allah صلى الله عليه وسلم slept until morning without water. Allah then revealed the verses of Tayammum, so they did Tayammum."

Usayd ibn Ḥuḍayr said, "This is not the first of your blessings, O family of Abū Bakr."

ʿĀ'ishah added, "We roused the camel I had been on, and found the necklace under it."[1]

The Prophet's صلى الله عليه وسلم fondness for Sayyidah ʿĀ'ishah رضي الله عنها is a matter which is beyond dispute. ʿAmr ibn al-ʿĀṣ رضي الله عنه was commissioned by the Prophet صلى الله عليه وسلم to lead the expedition of Dhāt al-Salāsil. Due to the Prophet's صلى الله عليه وسلم interaction with him he assumed that there was no one more beloved to the Prophet صلى الله عليه وسلم than him. He says:

أن رسول الله صلى الله عليه وسلم بعثه على جيش ذات السلاسل قال فأتيته فقلت أى الناس أحب إليك قال عائشة قلت من الرجال قال أبوها قلت ثم من قال عمر فعد رجالا

The Prophet صلى الله عليه وسلم deputed me to lead the Army of Dhāt al-Salāsil. I came to him and said, "Who is the most beloved person to you?"

He said, "'ʿĀ'ishah."

I asked, "Among the men?"

---

1 *Ṣaḥīḥ al-Bukhārī*, Kitāb Faḍā'il Aṣḥāb al-Nabī, Ḥadīth no. 3672; *Ṣaḥīḥ Muslim*, Kitāb al-Ḥayḍ, Bāb al-Tayammum, Ḥadīth no. 714.

He said, "Her father."

I said, "Who then?"

He said, "Then ʿUmar ibn al-Khaṭṭāb."

He then named other men.

Similarly the position she occupied in the Prophet's ﷺ heart was so well-known that people would send gifts to the Prophet ﷺ on the days that he was at the home of Sayyidah ʿĀ'ishah رضي الله عنها, knowing how jubilant he would be when visiting her.

عن عائشة رضي الله عنها أن نساء رسول الله صلى الله عليه وسلم كن حزبين فحزب فيه عائشة وحفصة وصفية وسودة والحزب الآخر أم سلمة وسائر نساء رسول الله صلى الله عليه وسلم وكان المسلمون قد علموا حب رسول الله صلى الله عليه وسلم عائشة فإذا كانت عند أحدهم هدية يريد أن يهديها إلى رسول الله صلى الله عليه وسلم أخرها حتى إذا كان رسول الله صلى الله عليه وسلم في بيت عائشة بعث صاحب الهدية بها إلى رسول الله صلى الله عليه وسلم في بيت عائشة فكلم حزب أم سلمة فقلن لها كلمي رسول الله صلى الله عليه وسلم يكلم الناس فيقول من أراد أن يهدي إلى رسول الله صلى الله عليه وسلم هدية فليهده إليه حيث كان من بيوت نسائه فكلمته أم سلمة بما قلن فلم يقل لها شيئا فسألنها فقالت ما قال لي شيئا فقلن لها فكلميه قالت فكلمته حين دار إليها أيضا فلم يقل لها شيئا فسألنها فقالت ما قال لي شيئا فقلن لها كلميه حتى يكلمك فدار إليها فكلمته فقال لها لا تؤذيني في عائشة فإن الوحي لم يأتني وأنا في ثوب امرأة إلا عائشة قالت فقالت أتوب إلى الله من أذاك يا رسول الله ثم إنهن دعون فاطمة بنت رسول الله صلى الله عليه وسلم فأرسلت إلى رسول الله صلى الله عليه وسلم تقول إن نساءك ينشدنك الله العدل في بنت أبي بكر فكلمته فقال يا بنية ألا تحبين ما أحب قالت بلى فرجعت إليهن فأخبرتهن فقلن ارجعي إليه فأبت أن ترجع فأرسلن زينب بنت جحش فأتته فأغلظت وقالت إن نساءك ينشدنك الله العدل في بنت ابن أبي قحافة فرفعت صوتها حتى تناولت عائشة وهي قاعدة فسبتها حتى إن رسول الله صلى الله عليه وسلم

لينظر إلى عائشة هل تكلم قال فتكلمت عائشة ترد على زينب حتى أسكتتها قالت فنظر النبي صلى الله عليه وسلم إلى عائشة وقال إنها بنت أبي بكر

The wives of the Messenger ﷺ were in two parties. One party consisted of ʿĀ'ishah, Ḥafṣah, Ṣafiyyah, and Sawdah; and the other party consisted of Umm Salamah and the other wives of the Messenger ﷺ. The Muslims were well aware of the Messenger's ﷺ love for ʿĀ'ishah, so if any of them had a gift for the Messenger ﷺ, they would delay it until it was ʿĀ'ishah's turn. That is when they chose to send gifts, knowing that the Messenger ﷺ would be in her home.

The party of Umm Salamah discussed the matter together and decided that Umm Salamah should request the Messenger ﷺ to tell the people to send their gifts to him at the home of whichever wife he was at. Umm Salamah conveyed to him what they had said, but he did not reply. Later they asked Umm Salamah about what transpired and she said, "He did not say anything to me." They asked her to talk to him again. She talked to him again when she met him on her day, but he gave no reply. When they asked her, she replied that he had given no reply. They said to her, "Talk to him till he gives you a reply." When it was her turn, she talked to him again. He then said to her, "Do not inconvenience me regarding ʿĀ'ishah as Revelation has never come to me under the sheets of anyone besides ʿĀ'ishah's." On that Umm Salamah said, "I seek Allah's repentance for inconveniencing you."

So the party of Umm Salamah called Fāṭimah, the Prophet's daughter, and sent her to the Messenger ﷺ to tell him, "Your wives request to treat them and the daughter of Abū Bakr on equal terms." Fāṭimah conveyed the message to him. The Prophet ﷺ responded, "O my daughter! Do you not love whom I love?" She replied in the affirmative and returned and told them of the situation. They requested her to go to him again but she refused.

They then sent Zaynab bint Jaḥsh who went to him and used firm words saying, "Your wives request you to treat them and the daughter of Ibn Abī Quḥāfah on equal terms." On that she raised her voice and reprimanded ʿĀ'ishah to her face so much so that the Messenger of Allah ﷺ looked at ʿĀ'ishah to see whether she would respond. ʿĀ'ishah started replying to Zaynab until she silenced her. The Prophet ﷺ then looked at ʿĀ'ishah and said, "She is certainly the daughter of Abū Bakr."[1]

---

1 *Ṣaḥīḥ al-Bukhārī*, Kitāb al-Hibah, Ḥadīth no. 2581.

It is ʿĀ'ishah رضي الله عنها about whom the Prophet صلى الله عليه وسلم said:

فضل عائشة على النساء كفضل الثريد على سائر الطعام

> The superiority of ʿĀ'ishah over all (other) women is like the superiority of Tharīd[1] over all other foods.[2]

The Prophet صلى الله عليه وسلم also said:

> Death was made easy for me as I was shown that you (referring to ʿĀ'ishah) are my wife in Jannah.

Notwithstanding the status of ʿĀ'ishah رضي الله عنها before Allah, His Messenger, and the entire Ummah; Tījānī saw it fit to find fault with the Prophet's صلى الله عليه وسلم wife, indirectly faulting the Prophet's صلى الله عليه وسلم judgment.

In his attacks on the Ṣaḥābah in general Tījānī accused ʿĀ'ishah رضي الله عنها of corrupting the religion, with specific reference to ṣalāh. This accusation has been dealt with in a fair amount of detail earlier in the book. To avoid unnecessary repetition I refer the esteemed reader to the earlier response to that issue.[3]

1. Tījānī accuses ʿĀ'ishah of sedition and provoking rebellion

Tījānī says:

> **We may ask a few questions about the war of al-Jamal, which was instigated by Umm al-Mumineen Aishah, who played an important role in it. How could Umm al-Mumineen Aishah leave her house in which Allah had ordered her to stay, when the most High said:**
>
> وَقَرْنَ فِي بُيُوتِكُنَّ وَلَا تَبَرَّجْنَ تَبَرُّجَ الْجَاهِلِيَّةِ الْأُولَى
>
> ***And abide in your houses and do not display yourselves as (was) the display of the former times of ignorance.[4]***
>
> **We may also ask, how could Aishah allow herself to declare war on the caliph of the Muslims, Ali ibn Abi Talib, who was the master of all Muslims? As**

1 A meal in which bread is broken up into small pieces and meat and gravy are poured over it.

2 *Ṣaḥīḥ al-Bukhārī*, Kitāb Faḍā'il al-Ṣaḥābah, Bāb Faḍl ʿĀ'ishah, Ḥadīth no. 3559, from Anas ibn Mālik.

3 Refer to p. 188 of this book.

4 Sūrah al-Aḥzāb: 33.

usual, our scholars, with some simplicity, answer us that she did not like Imam Ali because he advised the Messenger of Allah ﷺ to divorce her in the incident of al-Ifk. Seemingly these people are trying to convince us that that incident - if it was true - namely Ali's advice to the Prophet to divorce Aishah, was sufficient for her to disobey the orders of her God and her husband, the Messenger of Allah ﷺ. She rode a camel that the Messenger of Allah ﷺ forbade her from riding and warned her about the barking of al-Hawab's dogs, she travelled long distances from al-Medinah to Mekka then to Basrah, she permitted the killing of innocent people and started a war against the commander of the believers and the Companions who voted for him, and she caused the deaths of thousands of Muslims, according to the historians. She did all that because she did not like Ali who advised the Prophet ﷺ to divorce her. Nevertheless the Prophet ﷺ did not divorce her so why all this hatred towards Imam Ali?[1]

Our response:

The veneer of academic rigour in Tījānī's arguments have long been peeled off, all that remain exposed now are the untidy cracks. The cyclic internal inconsistencies are reappearing with rapid succession. However, before addressing these, it would be prudent to summarise the criticism presented by Tījānī.

Summary of Tījānī's argument

Tījānī asserts that Umm al-Mu'minīn, ʿĀ'ishah رضي الله عنها, led a rebellion against ʿAlī رضي الله عنه which resulted in open war at Jamal. Furthermore he accuses her of disregarding the Qur'ānic verse which describes the appropriate behaviour for the Prophet's ﷺ wives. Then he ascribes—without reference—an explanation of these events to the scholars of Ahl al-Sunnah; citing the underlying cause as a family squabble whose roots lie in a suggestion made by ʿAlī رضي الله عنه to the Prophet ﷺ during the incident of Ifk. He goes on to imply that the scholars of the Ahl al-Sunnah do not simply justify her 'rebellion' but implicitly acknowledge that ʿAlī رضي الله عنه was at fault on some levels.

The discerning reader will easily realise that he is building a straw man argument. If she was prepared to 'break the law' by riding on a camel and call for a rebellion wherein 'thousands' lost their lives then this suggests a more sinister agenda and

1 *Then I was guided*, p. 117-118.

not a trivial matter, such as to merely settle a 'score' with ʿAlī رضي الله عنه for suggesting that the Prophet صلى الله عليه وسلم is free to marry whom he wishes.

Underlying principles

Not only is Tījānī's conclusion misleading, but his premise is anything but sound. To begin with, the framework within which he proposes that we think it is flawed because it suffers from a black-or-white dilemma. He proposes that we think only within a framework where either ʿAlī رضي الله عنه is upon truth, and his opposition are destined for Hell, or they are upon truth, which leaves ʿAlī رضي الله عنه compromised. Tījānī disregards any other possible alternative.

As a point of departure the Ahl Sunnah view all the Ṣaḥābah favourably. The highest tier of virtue and merit, after the Prophets, is accorded to the four Khulafā'; in order of their Khilāfah. Thereafter those who remain from the ten who were given glad tidings of Jannah by the Prophet صلى الله عليه وسلم. The next tier belongs to *Ahl al-Badr* (the participants at Badr). The Ahl al-Sunnah considers all of them destined for Jannah. Similarly, the *Ummahāt al-Mu'minīn* (Mothers of the Believers), ʿĀ'ishah and the Prophet's صلى الله عليه وسلم other wives, are all considered from those destined for Jannah.

The Ahl al-Sunnah also acknowledge that being destined for Jannah does not result in infallibility. Therefore, it is possible that some of the Ṣaḥābah committed sins, sometimes major sins. However they have all repented and will thus enter Jannah. We have found that most incidents where the Ṣaḥābah's behaviour appears to be less than optimum have no historical basis. For those where the historical accuracy has been proven their conduct was the result of discretion in the form of Ijtihād, whilst an alternate view was shown to be closer to the truth. None of these detract from the status given to them by Allah and His Messenger صلى الله عليه وسلم. Having acknowledged that, the esteemed reader will certainly agree that the framework for discourse within the Sunni paradigm is much more accommodating for a faithful representation of history.

The stage in history where Muslims began fighting each other, often referred to as the first great Fitnah, is certainly a period in history which Muslims are not proud of. We find that the historical portrayal of what transpired can be accounted for through the framework referred to above. A great deal of what has been attributed to the Ṣaḥābah during this period is forged; whereas that which has been correctly reported of them was the result of Ijtihād.

The purpose of ʿĀ’ishah’s departure was for reconciliation and not battle

The claim that ʿĀ’ishah رَضِيَ ٱللَّهُ عَنْهَا was the instigator behind the Battle of the Camel is simply untrue. We have historical evidence that proves that ʿĀ’ishah رَضِيَ ٱللَّهُ عَنْهَا did not leave Makkah for Baṣrah for the purpose of fighting. On the contrary, she left with the hope of bringing about reconciliation as well as seeking retribution for ʿUthmān’s رَضِيَ ٱللَّهُ عَنْهُ murder. Her Ijtihād led her to the conclusion that leaving for Baṣrah would be in the best interest of the Muslims.[1] She certainly did not leave to fight ʿAlī رَضِيَ ٱللَّهُ عَنْهُ as ʿAlī رَضِيَ ٱللَّهُ عَنْهُ arrived with his army later on. How could she have sought to fight him if he was not in Baṣrah to begin with? If she intended to fight ʿAlī رَضِيَ ٱللَّهُ عَنْهُ, she needn’t go as far as Baṣrah. She could have merely gone to fight him in Madīnah.

The aftermath of the Battle of the Camel made her realise that it would have been more suitable had she returned to Madīnah from Makkah as she had not planned for any of this to happen. This is the reason for her weeping. She has been accurately quoted as having said, “I wish I was a branch [on a tree] and I did not undertake this journey.”[2]

Even if we were to assume that ʿĀ’ishah رَضِيَ ٱللَّهُ عَنْهَا, along with Ṭalḥah and Zubayr رَضِيَ ٱللَّهُ عَنْهُمَا, left with the purpose of fighting this is simply reduced to a case of Ijtihād. It does not compromise their faith since Allah said:

وَإِنْ طَائِفَتَانِ مِنَ الْمُؤْمِنِيْنَ اقْتَتَلُوْا فَأَصْلِحُوْا بَيْنَهُمَا فَإِنْ بَغَتْ إِحْدَاهُمَا عَلَى الْأُخْرٰى فَقَاتِلُوا الَّتِيْ تَبْغِيْ حَتّٰى تَفِيْءَ إِلٰى أَمْرِ اللّٰهِ فَإِنْ فَاءَتْ فَأَصْلِحُوْا بَيْنَهُمَا بِالْعَدْلِ وَأَقْسِطُوْا إِنَّ اللّٰهَ يُحِبُّ الْمُقْسِطِيْنَ إِنَّمَا الْمُؤْمِنُوْنَ إِخْوَةٌ فَأَصْلِحُوْا بَيْنَ أَخَوَيْكُمْ

And if two factions among the believers should fight, then make settlement between the two. But if one of them oppresses the other, then fight against the one that oppresses

1 *Tārīkh al-Ṭabarī* vol. 4 p. 498.

2 *Muṣannaf Ibn Abī Shaybah*, vol. 8, Kitāb al-Jamal fī Masīr “Ā’ishah, p. 718.

> *until it returns to the ordinance of Allah. And if it returns, then make settlement between them in justice and act justly. Indeed, Allah loves those who act justly. The believers are but brothers, so make settlement between your brothers.*[1]

Allah refers to the two parties that fight each other as believers, despite their fighting. If two fighting parties of general Muslims are considered believers according to the Qur'ān, certainly it applies to a greater extent to the Companions of the Prophet صَلَّى ٱللَّٰهُ عَلَيْهِ وَسَلَّمَ.

Tījānī accuses ʿĀ'ishah of adopting the ways of Jāhiliyyah

Tījānī asserts that by ʿĀ'ishah رَضِيَ ٱللَّٰهُ عَنْهَا departing from her home she has disregarded the Qur'ānic injunction and adopted the way of Jāhiliyyah. This is evident in his statement

> **"How could Umm al-Mu'minīn ʿĀ'ishah leave her house which Allah commanded her to remain in with His words, 'And abide in your houses and do not display yourselves as [was] the display of the former times of ignorance.'**[2]

In response to that I say:

This verse was revealed prior to the verses on Ḥijāb. The meaning of the verse did not change during the Prophet's صَلَّى ٱللَّٰهُ عَلَيْهِ وَسَلَّمَ lifetime, nor did it change after his departure from this world. Having taken that into consideration the incident of Ifk occurred after the verses of Ḥijāb were revealed. We know this because ʿĀ'ishah رَضِيَ ٱللَّٰهُ عَنْهَا acknowledges this when she describes the moment Ṣafwān رَضِيَ ٱللَّٰهُ عَنْهُ realised she had been left as he had seen her prior to the revelation of the verses of Ḥijāb.[3] If the instruction to remain within their houses was that of absolute obligation how did the Prophet صَلَّى ٱللَّٰهُ عَلَيْهِ وَسَلَّمَ take her along with him? We learn that the verse is not as direct as Tījānī would like us to believe. The second part of the verse implies the underlying rationale for this reasoning and that is *Tabarruj* [adornment]. This verse prohibits the adornment of the days of Jāhiliyyah. ʿĀ'ishah رَضِيَ ٱللَّٰهُ عَنْهَا, however, was properly clad, travelled with her nephew—ʿAbd Allāh ibn al-Zubayr, and undertook the journey with a religious motive in mind. None of this is in contravention of the verse of Sūrah al-Aḥzāb.

---

1 Sūrah al-Ḥujurāt: 9-10.

2 Sūrah al-Aḥzāb: 33.

3 *Ṣaḥīḥ al-Bukhārī*, Kitāb al-Shahādāt, Ḥadīth no. 2661.

Ibn Taymiyyah says:

> The command to remain at home is not in conflict with the permissibility of leaving home for a legitimate reason recognised by the Sharīʿah like Ḥajj or ʿUmrah. She undertook these journeys with her husband after this verse was revealed. Likewise the Prophet ﷺ travelled with his other wives subsequent to its revelation. For example, he travelled with ʿĀ'ishah and his other wives for Ḥajjat al-Wadāʿ. Similarly, he sent her with her brother, ʿAbd al-Raḥmān, and he placed her behind him (on his conveyance) and allowed her to perform ʿUmrah from Tanʿīm. The Ḥajjat al-Wadāʿ occurred less than three months before the Prophet's ﷺ demise, and was definitely after the revelation of this verse. It is for that reason that the Prophet's wives performed Ḥajj after his demise just as they performed it with him. During ʿUmar's khilāfah, he entrusted ʿUthmān and ʿAbd al-Raḥmān with their caravan. Therefore, it was permitted for them to travel where some benefit was anticipated. Thus, ʿĀ'ishah believed that undertaking this journey was a decision with the best interests of the Muslims in mind and that is how she interpreted the situation.[1]

Tījānī asserts that ʿĀ'ishah held a grudge against ʿAlī

Tījānī's carefully constructed straw man argument is that the scholars of Ahl al-Sunnah account for what transpired between ʿĀ'ishah and ʿAlī ibn Abī Ṭālib as nothing more than a personal grudge. She held a grudge against him after he advised the Prophet ﷺ to divorce her when the incident of Ifk occurred.

Our response:

a. The evidence of Tījānī's deception in this regard is his failure to produce a single reference to substantiate his allegation. Tījānī resorted to a false cause whilst assuming the mandate representation of the Ahl al-Sunnah by saying 'Our scholars...' Tījānī's position on this issue is nowhere close to the view that represents the Ahl al-Sunnah fairly.

b. The other matter brought up in Tījānī's loaded accusation is the ḥadīth of Ifk. In these verses Allah absolves ʿĀ'ishah رضي الله عنها from any indecency. In a portion of a lengthier ḥadīth, the Prophet sought consultation with some of his Ṣaḥābah about ʿĀ'ishah رضي الله عنها, and ʿAlī's رضي الله عنه view is reproduced below:

1 *Minhāj al-Sunnah*, vol. 4, p. 317-318.

لم يضيق الله عليك والنساء سواها كثير وسل الجارية تصدقك

> Allah has not restricted you. There are many women besides her. Ask the servant she will tell you the truth![1]

ʿAlī's رضي الله عنه words were not explicit in that he advised the Prophet صلى الله عليه وسلم to divorce ʿĀ'ishah رضي الله عنها because of suspicion of immorality; we seek Allah's protection from such thoughts! Instead, he implied that the Prophet صلى الله عليه وسلم consider taking another wife, due to the anxiety he experienced as a result of the delay in revelation. ʿAlī رضي الله عنه assumed that the Prophet صلى الله عليه وسلم would be more at ease if he parted ways with ʿĀ'ishah رضي الله عنها, though he could return to her if she were exonerated. Therefore, he suggested that the Prophet صلى الله عليه وسلم enquire from ʿĀ'ishah's رضي الله عنها servant if there was anything in her behaviour that might indicate something different. Ibn Ḥajar says:

> This statement made by ʿAlī is the result of his preference for the well-being of the Prophet صلى الله عليه وسلم. He was motivated to say that on account of what he saw in the Prophet صلى الله عليه وسلم in terms of anxiety and dejection from what had been said (about ʿĀ'ishah). The Prophet صلى الله عليه وسلم was fiercely protective (over his wives) and ʿAlī thought that if he divorced her the anxiety he was experiencing would subside on account of it; until her innocence was ascertained and he could then take her back. The principle of 'perpetrating the lesser harm in order to avoid the greater harm' is inferred from it.[2]

Al-Nawawī says:

> ʿAlī's statement was correct as far as he was concerned. He took the Prophet's صلى الله عليه وسلم goodwill into consideration. This is because he noticed the Prophet's صلى الله عليه وسلم uneasiness and anxiety as a result of this situation. He therefore intended to bring relief to the Prophet's heart and that was more important than anything else.[3]

Abū Muḥammad ibn Abī Jamrah says:

> ʿAlī was not overly assertive in his suggesting divorce as he followed it up with his statement, "Ask the servant! She will tell you the truth." Rather, he

---

1 A portion of a ḥadīth narrated by al-Bukhārī, Kitāb al-Tafsīr, Sūrah al-Nūr, Ḥadīth no. 4473, vol. 4.

2 *Fatḥ al-Bārī*, vol. 8 p. 324, Kitāb al-Tafsīr.

3 *Muslim* with its commentary, Kitāb al-Tawbah, p. 162-163.

entrusted the matter to the Prophet ﷺ. It was as if he said, "If you want to give your heart some peace then divorce her! If you do not want that then search for the truth until you uncover her innocence," as it was confirmed that Barīrah only informed him about what she knew and all she knew was ʿĀ'ishah's general innocence.[1]

Was ʿĀ'ishah responsible for bloodshed?

Tījānī blames ʿĀ'ishah رضي الله عنها for the shedding of Muslims blood at *Jamal* [The Battle of the Camel]. In an earlier chapter he accused her of being the mastermind behind ʿUthmān's رضي الله عنه murder. What motive would she have for wanting ʿUthmān رضي الله عنه killed? She would have known that the most prominent candidate to succeed ʿUthmān would be ʿAlī رضي الله عنه. If she had such a terrible relationship with ʿAlī رضي الله عنه as Tījānī suggests why would she undergo all the trouble to hand the Khilāfah over to ʿAlī رضي الله عنه? Keep these questions in mind while reading through Tījānī's words once again.

He says:

> **As usual, our scholars, with some simplicity, answer us that she did not like Imam Ali because he advised the Messenger of Allah to divorce her in the incident of al-Ifk. Seemingly these people are trying to convince us that that incident - if it was true - namely Ali's advice to the Prophet to divorce Aisha, was sufficient for her to disobey the orders of her God and her husband, the Messenger of Allah ﷺ. She rode a camel that the Messenger of Allah forbade her from riding and warned her about the barking of al-Hawab's dogs, she travelled long distances from al-Medinah to Mekka then to Basrah, she permitted the killing of innocent people and started a war against the commander of the believers and the Companions who voted for him, and she caused the deaths of thousands of Muslims, according to the historians.**

In his footnote Tījānī cites the following historians as reference: al-Ṭabarī, Ibn al-Athīr, al-Madā'inī, and others besides them who documented the events of the year thirty-six A.H.[2]

Our response:

1 *Fatḥ al-Bārī*, vol. 8 p. 324, Kitāb al-Tafsīr.

2 *Then I was guided*, p. 117-118.

We have referred to *Tārīkh al-Ṭabarī* which documents the events of the year thirty-six A.H. As expected, the version of events described by Tījānī, do not match what has been narrated about the Battle of the Camel. Not only do al-Ṭabarī's narrations expose the fraudulent referencing of Tījānī, but it confirms that ʿĀʾishah, Ṭalḥah, and Zubayr ﷢ set out for Baṣrah seeking reconciliation. Al-Ṭabarī relates that ʿAlī ﷠ sent Qaʿqāʿ ibn ʿAmr to the people of Baṣrah to inquire about the reason for their coming. The narration goes as follows:

> Then Qaʿqāʿ left until he arrived in Baṣrah. He first went to ʿĀʾishah. He greeted her and said, "O mother (of the believers)! What has brought you to this city?"
>
> She said, "The intention of reconciling the people."
>
> He said, "Send for Ṭalḥah and Zubayr so that you may hear our conversation!"
>
> She then sent for Ṭalḥah and Zubayr and they arrived.
>
> He said, "I asked the Mother of the Believers what has brought her to these cities and she replied, 'in order to reconcile the people'. What do the two of you say? Do you follow her (in her goal) or do you oppose her?"
>
> They said, "We follow her."[1]

This narration confirms that ʿĀʾishah, Ṭalḥah and al-Zubayr are innocent of any charge of sedition. We learn that those responsible for the death of thousands of Muslims were the killers of ʿUthmān ﷠ and those who were aligned with their underground movement.

He says:

> When the people had settled down and became content ʿAlī came and Ṭalḥah and Zubayr came. They agreed and spoke about their differences and they could not find a better solution than reconciliation and stopping the fight when they saw the unity (of the Ummah) being put at risk and that it could not be brought together (easily again). They departed agreeing to function as a single unit ʿAlī went to his camp and Ṭalḥah and Zubayr went to their camp. That night ʿAlī sent ʿAbd Allāh ibn ʿAbbās as a spokesperson to Ṭalḥah and Zubayr, and they sent Muḥammad ibn Ṭalḥah to ʿAlī as a spokesperson to speak to his companions and they all agreed to unity.

---

1 *Tārīkh al-Ṭabarī*, vol. 3 p. 29, the year 36 A.H; Also Ibn al-Athīr, vol. 3 p. 122-123, the year 36 A.H.

> When they went to sleep— that was during Jumād al-Ākhirah—Ṭalḥah and Zubayr sent word to the prominent figures among their companions and ʿAlī did the same. They all went to sleep that night having resolved all misunderstanding. It was to be a peaceful night, the like of which they had not experienced for a long time. They were relieved that they could reconcile without military engagement. However, those who incited the rebellion against ʿUthmān experienced the worst night; they were on the verge of failure. They discussed the situation the entire night until they all agreed to cause havoc in secret in order that their sinister motives come to pass. They left at dusk without those around them realising and infiltrated secretly while it was still dark. The Muḍarī went to the Muḍarī, and the Rabaʿī went to the Rabaʿī, and the Yamānī went to the Yamānī, and placed weapons amongst them. Then each group revolted against those they suspected...[1]

Al-Ṭabarī also says:

> ʿĀ'ishah said, "O Kaʿb! Leave the camel, and move forward with the Book of Allah, and call them to the Book of Allah, and she handed a *Muṣḥaf* (copy of the Qur'ān) over to him." Then he faced the people who were being led by the *Saba'iyyah* (followers of ʿAbd Allāh ibn Saba'), who feared a peace treaty (between the two groups). Kaʿb faced them with the Muṣḥaf and ʿAlī was behind them restraining them but they insisted on advancing. When Kaʿb called them (to the Book of Allah) they opened fire upon him all at once and killed him. They also shot (their arrows) at ʿĀ'ishah and hit her carriage. She started yelling, "O my sons! Fear Allah! Fear Allah! Remember Allah and the Day of Reckoning!" But they insisted on advancing. The first thing she did when they refused (to listen to her) she said, "O People! Curse ʿUthmān's killers and their supporters!" She started supplicating (against the killers of ʿUthmān) and the people of Baṣrah wept loudly upon hearing her supplication. ʿAlī ibn Abī Ṭālib (also) heard the noise and asked, "What is this clamour?" They said, "It is ʿĀ'ishah supplicating and they (the people) are supplicating with her against ʿUthmān's killers." Then ʿAlī started supplicating and saying, "O Allah! Curse ʿUthmān's killers and their supporters!"[2]

This is also what Ibn al-Athīr documents in his *Tārīkh*. I did not, however, find *Kitāb al-Madā'in*. When one considers what is described here, we realise that Tījānī either

1 Ibid. vol. 3 p. 39, the year 36 A.H.

2 Op. cit. vol. 3 p. 43, the year 36 A.H.

lied about what happened at ʿUthmān's murder, or he lied about what happened at Jamal. Tījānī cannot plea for ignorance in both cases.

The authentic narrations confirm that ʿĀ'ishah, Zubayr, and Ṭalḥah, as well as ʿAlī رضي الله عنه did not intend to fight one another. It is for that reason that ʿĀ'ishah رضي الله عنها regretted that journey of hers and remarked, "I wish I was a branch [on a tree] and I did not take this journey."[1] She also said, "I prefer to have lost ten children like al-Ḥārith ibn Hishām than to have taken this journey with Ibn Zubayr."[2]

If she wanted war and not peace then why regret? If she wanted war and not peace why did she go to Baṣrah when ʿAlī رضي الله عنه was in Madīnah? If she wanted war why did she encourage pledging allegiance to ʿAlī رضي الله عنه? The incoherence in Tījānī's reasoning is evident and requires very little elaboration.

Tījānī lies about ʿĀ'ishah hating ʿAlī

He says:

> **History has recorded some aggressive stances against Ali that could not be explained and these are some of them. When she was on her way back from Mekka Aishah was informed that Uthman was killed, so she was delighted, but when she learnt that people had voted for Ali to succeed him she became very angry and said, "I wish the sky would collapse on the earth before Ibn Abi Talib succeeds to the caliphate." Then she said, "Take me back." Thus she started the civil war against Ali, whose name she never liked to mention, as many historians agree.**

Our comment:

Tījānī's lie is exposed on account of a sound narration wherein al-Aḥnaf ibn Qays met ʿĀ'ishah رضي الله عنها in Makkah after ʿUthmān's رضي الله عنه murder and asked whom he ought to align with. In no uncertain terms she instructed him to pledge his allegiance to ʿAlī.[3]

Tījānī's comment on ʿĀ'ishah رضي الله عنها rejoicing at the death of ʿUthmān رضي الله عنه reveals the extent to which Tījānī lies as none of the historians mention that. Rather, they confirm that ʿĀ'ishah came to Baṣrah seeking retribution for ʿUthmān رضي الله عنه from

---

1 Mentioned previously on p. 459 of this book.

2 *Muṣannaf Ibn Abī Shaybah*, vol. 8 *Kitāb al-Jamal*, p. 716.

3 *Tārīkh al-Ṭabarī* vol. 4 p. 497, ibn Ḥajar graded this chain as sound in *Fatḥ al-Bārī* vol. 13 p. 38.

his killers. This begs the question: If ʿĀ'ishah was elated about ʿUthmān's death then why did she set out in the first place? Did she set out to prevent ʿAlī ibn Abī Ṭālib from taking control of the khilāfah? If so, then why did she instruct al-Aḥnaf ibn Qays— who was in Madīnah when all the commotion happened and came all the way to Makkah to seek her counsel—to pledge allegiance to ʿAlī? Why did she go to Baṣrah and not al-Madīnah?

Tījānī says that she disliked ʿAlī's رضي الله عنه Khilāfah and attempted to prevent him from taking control. When he is asked about the reason for that he says it is because she disliked him on account of his advising the Prophet ﷺ to divorce her. This time he does not say 'Our scholars,' so it refers to his independent view, or that of his real scholars, the Rāfiḍah. The simple response to this incredibly trivial reasoning is that ʿĀ'ishah رضي الله عنها, if she disliked ʿAlī رضي الله عنه because he suggested that the Prophet ﷺ divorce her, how do you explain the thousands who joined her? Does Tījānī have a logical reason to explain why these people stood by ʿĀ'ishah رضي الله عنها? Is it because ʿAlī رضي الله عنه suggested they get divorced as well?

Tījānī claims that the historians documented that ʿĀ'ishah رضي الله عنها did not want to even hear the mention of ʿAlī رضي الله عنه. This begs the question: Who are these historians? If Tījānī named a single historical reference to substantiate the claim he could avoid being called a liar yet again.

However, the truth is, and this is well known, that ʿĀ'ishah رضي الله عنها herself mentioned ʿAlī رضي الله عنه in a company of people. Shurayḥ ibn Hānī says:

> I asked ʿĀ'ishah about the *Masḥ* (wiping) over the socks and she said, "Go to ʿAlī! He is more knowledgeable than me."
>
> He says that ʿAlī said, "The Prophet used to instruct us to wipe over the leather socks for a day and a night, (if resident) and three days for the traveller."[1]

Muslim narrates with his chain to Shurayḥ ibn Hānī, who said:

أتيت عائشة أسألها عن المسح على الخفين فقالت عليك بابن أبي طالب

> I went to ʿĀ'ishah asking her about the Masḥ over the socks and she said, "Go to ʿAlī ibn Abī Ṭālib."[2]

1 Aḥmad: *Faḍā'il al-Ṣaḥābah*, vol. 2 p. 702, Ḥadīth no. 1199.

2 *Ṣaḥīḥ Muslim* with its commentary, Kitāb al-Ṭahārah, Bāb al-Tawqīt fī al-Masḥ ʿalā al-Khuffayn, Ḥadīth no. 276.

The famous ḥadīth in *Ṣaḥīḥ Muslim*[1], where the Prophet ﷺ took ʿAlī, Fāṭimah, Ḥasan, and Ḥusayn رضي الله عنهم all under his woollen shawl and supplicated for their protection, is narrated by ʿĀ'ishah رضي الله عنها.

Tījānī asks why ʿĀ'ishah ignored ʿAlī's merits

He asks why she held a grudge against him whereas the Anṣār recognised the hypocrites by their hatred for ʿAlī رضي الله عنه. I reproduce his words:

> **Had Aishah heard the saying of the Messenger of Allah ﷺ: "Loving Ali is believing and hating him is hypocrisy?" To the extent that some of the Companions used to say, "We recognized the hypocrites by their hatred of Ali." Had Aishah not heard the saying of the Prophet ﷺ: Whoever accepts me as his master, then Ali is his master? Undoubtedly she heard all that, but she did not like it, and she did not like mentioning his name, and when she learnt of his death she knelt and thanked Allah.[2]**

Our comment:

This is marvellous. 'Why?' The esteemed reader might ask. Well, it's a self-confirmation on how these narrations ought to have been understood. It is a clear demonstration of Tījānī's self-contradictory reasoning. Why single ʿĀ'ishah رضي الله عنها out for criticism in the wake of Jamal; whereas she ought to be condemned from the time of Abū Bakr's Khilāfah for not accepting ʿAlī as the destined successor? Why condemn her based on the stance of the Anṣār if he does not approve of the Anṣār pledging allegiance to Abū Bakr at the beginning? Their understanding of these narrations is either correct, which would validate Tījānī's argument against ʿĀ'ishah رضي الله عنها if it can be proven true from ʿĀ'ishah; or their understanding is incorrect, which Tījānī attempted to prove in the earlier chapters of this book, and in which case he has no argument to present as it is illogical to build an argument on a false premise.

Self-contradictions aside, let us focus on whether ʿĀ'ishah hated ʿAlī رضي الله عنه. ʿAbd Allāh ibn Shaddād came to visit ʿĀ'ishah رضي الله عنها soon after ʿAlī's رضي الله عنه assassination. The following conversation ensued, and was witnessed by a group of people:

---

1 *Ṣaḥīḥ Muslim*, Kitāb Faḍā'il al-Ṣaḥābah, Ḥadīth no. 2424.

2 *Then I was guided*, p. 118.

> ʿĀ'ishah enquired, "What were the remarks of ʿAlī upon learning of their rebellion as claimed by the People of ʿIrāq?"
>
> He said, "I heard him saying, 'Allah and His Messenger have spoken the truth.'"
>
> ʿĀ'ishah asked him for a second time to reassure if he really heard him saying only that. "These were the only words I heard him uttering," he replied.
>
> Upon this she remarked, "May Allah be pleased with him and may he shower his mercy upon him. This was his expression. Whenever he observed something strange he used to say, 'Allah and His Messenger have spoken the truth,' and now the people of ʿIrāq have begun fabricating things and ascribing it to him and adding from their own side to what he said."[1]

We can now safely state that she held him in a position of endearment and esteem but she disagreed with him. Her disagreement was for no reason other than requesting immediate retribution for ʿUthmān's رضي الله عنه murderers. She did not go to Baṣrah to fight him. Rather, she went there to bring back a sense of stability. Also, she went there because she was encouraged by people to attempt reconciliation. Ibn ʿImād says in *Shadharāt al-Dhahab*:

> When ʿAlī reached Baṣrah he went to ʿĀ'ishah and said, "May Allah forgive you," and she replied, "May Allah forgive you too. I did not come except for reconciliation."[2]

Ibn al-ʿArabī explains this:

> As for her coming out to the Battle of the Camel, she did not come out for war but the people attached themselves to her and complained to her about what they were heading towards civil strife [Fitnah] as people were in a state of confusion and suspicion. They hoped for her blessing in bringing about reform by process of reconciliation and they hoped that people would feel a sense of shyness if she stood up with the people (against ʿUthmān's conspirators) and she thought the same. It was for that reason that she came out in adherence to the words of Allah:

1 *Musnad Aḥmad*, vol. 2 p. 86, ḥadīth 656.

2 *Shadharāt al-Dhahab*, vol. 1 p. 42, See examined version of *Mawāqif al-Ṣaḥābah*, vol. 2 p. 115.

لَا خَيْرَ فِي كَثِيرٍ مِنْ نَجْوَاهُمْ إِلَّا مَنْ أَمَرَ بِصَدَقَةٍ أَوْ مَعْرُوفٍ أَوْ إِصْلَاحٍ بَيْنَ النَّاسِ وَمَنْ يَفْعَلْ ذَٰلِكَ ابْتِغَاءَ مَرْضَاتِ اللَّهِ فَسَوْفَ نُؤْتِيهِ أَجْرًا عَظِيمًا

No good is there in much of their private conversation, except for those who enjoin charity or that which is right or conciliation between people. And whoever does that seeking means to the approval of Allah — then We are going to give him a great reward.[1]

وَإِنْ طَائِفَتَانِ مِنَ الْمُؤْمِنِينَ اقْتَتَلُوا فَأَصْلِحُوا بَيْنَهُمَا فَإِنْ بَغَتْ إِحْدَاهُمَا عَلَى الْأُخْرَىٰ فَقَاتِلُوا الَّتِي تَبْغِي حَتَّىٰ تَفِيءَ إِلَىٰ أَمْرِ اللَّهِ فَإِنْ فَاءَتْ فَأَصْلِحُوا بَيْنَهُمَا بِالْعَدْلِ وَأَقْسِطُوا إِنَّ اللَّهَ يُحِبُّ الْمُقْسِطِينَ

And if two factions among the believers should fight, then make settlement between the two. But if one of them oppresses the other, then fight against the one that oppresses until it returns to the ordinance of Allah. And if it returns, then make settlement between them in justice and act justly. Indeed, Allah loves those who act justly.[2]

Ibn Ḥibbān narrates:

> ʿĀ'ishah wrote to Abū Mūsā al-Ashʿarī while he was the governor of Kūfah by ʿAlī's appointment, "You are well aware of ʿUthmān's situation. Indeed, I have come for the benefit of the people. Therefore, instruct those from your side to remain in their homes and to be pleased with their good health until the news of what you seek comes to you in terms of rectitude in the affairs of Muslim."

This was the reason for ʿĀ'ishah's رضي الله عنها emergence. It was not because she hated ʿAlī رضي الله عنه. Claiming that she hated him is nothing more than a baseless lie.

As for his statement,

> **In fact, when she heard about his death she prostrated to Allah in gratitude to him.**

1 Sūrah al-Nisā': 114.

2 Sūrah al-Ḥujurāt: 9.

He cited *al-Ṭabarī*, *Ibn al-Athīr*, *al-Fitnah al-Kubrā*, and all the historians who documented the events of the year forty after the hijrah, as his source for this allegation.[1]

We have consulted *al-Ṭabarī*, and *Ibn al-Athīr* in the section of the events of the fortieth year after the Hijrah and could not find a trace of evidence for this claim. What a liar he is! This is further compounded when we take into consideration that she supplicated for him, invoking Allah's mercy for him, in the incident with ʿAbd Allāh ibn Shaddād which we quoted earlier.

يَعِظُكُمُ اللَّهُ أَنْ تَعُودُوا لِمِثْلِهِ أَبَدًا إِنْ كُنْتُمْ مُؤْمِنِينَ

Allah admonishes you never to repeat the likes of this [lying against ʿĀ'ishah] if you are truly believers![2]

Who was wrong?

Tījānī reveals the black-or-white dilemma:

> **The same question crops up again. Who was right and who was wrong? Either, Ali and his followers were wrong or Aishah and her followers and Talhah and al-Zubayr and their followers were wrong. There is no third possibility. But I have no doubt that the fair researcher would take Ali's side and dismiss Aishah and her followers who instigated the civil war that devastated the nation and left its tragic marks to the present day.**
>
> **For the sake of further clarification and for the sake of my own satisfaction I mention here what al-Bukhari had to say in his book about the civil war. When Talhah, al-Zubayr and Aishah travelled to Basrah, Ali sent Ammar ibn Yasir and al-Ḥasan ibn Ali to al-Kufah. On their arrival, they went to the mosque and addressed the congregation, and we heard Ammar saying, "Aishah had gone to Basrah... and by Allah she is the wife of your Prophet in this life and the life hereafter, but Allah, the Most High, is testing you to know whom you obey: Him or her."[3]**

Our comment:

1 *Then I was guided*, p. 118 (In the footnote).

2 Sūrah al-Nūr: 17.

3 *Then I was guided*, p. 119.

Contrary to what Tījānī is cornering us into believing, there is a third possibility, and that is that both sides used their scholarly discretion in order to arrive at the truth and that neither of the two sides was the oppressor. The Fitnah of ʿUthmān's رضي الله عنه murder polarized the Ummah into two sides. The one side—which included the likes of Ṭalḥah, Zubayr, and ʿĀ'ishah رضي الله عنهم—held the opinion that it was necessary to execute ʿUthmān's رضي الله عنه killers immediately. The other side also felt it necessary to seek retribution for ʿUthmān رضي الله عنه by bringing his killers to justice but insisted on adopting a cautious approach bearing in mind the extent of the conspiracy. This view is the view of ʿAlī and his companions رضي الله عنهم.

These killers were the cause of the Battle of the Camel and neither of the two groups had any part in igniting the flame of war, as explained previously.

Tījānī seeks comfort in the statement of ʿAmmār رضي الله عنه when he announced to the people that Allah is testing people with ʿĀ'ishah رضي الله عنها to see whether they would obey Him or her. This has been taken beyond the context in which it was said, which is no surprise. Tījānī has overlooked the fact that in the ḥadīth ʿAmmār رضي الله عنه testifies that ʿĀ'ishah رضي الله عنها is the Prophet's wife in the world and the Hereafter (in Jannah). Is there an honour greater than that?

The context of ʿAmmār's رضي الله عنه statement, being from the party of ʿAlī رضي الله عنه, was that he wanted to encourage the people to join ʿAlī رضي الله عنه. However, they displayed hesitancy because the opposite party included great Ṣaḥābah, specifically Umm al-Mu'minīn, ʿĀ'ishah رضي الله عنها. Therefore, ʿAmmār رضي الله عنه sought to explain to them that since ʿAlī رضي الله عنه was the Khalīfah they were duty-bound to follow him. This right is in accordance with what Allah prescribed in terms of obedience to one's leader. This was before they learnt that Umm al-Mu'minīn only demanded justice against ʿUthmān's رضي الله عنه killers.

There is no doubt that Umm al-Mu'minīn, and Ṭalḥah and Zubayr also, genuinely believed that demanding action against ʿUthmān's رضي الله عنه killers was a priority and took precedence over standing down on the command of the Khalīfah ʿAlī رضي الله عنه as he was restricted in his decisions since he was surrounded by the troublemakers. She explained this to ʿUthmān ibn Ḥanīf when he sent message to her asking her the reason for her journey and she said:

By Allah! It is not befitting someone like me to travel with a hidden agenda and to conceal information. Indeed, the ruffians from the cities have attacked the Holy Sanctuary of the Messenger, they have innovated and given shelter to the innovators, they have brought the curse of Allah and the curse of his Messenger by killing the Imām of the Muslims without care, and for no reason. They have desecrated it by legitimising his blood, they have plundered wealth which is sacred, and they have made (forbidden things) permissible in the Sacred City and in the Sacred Month. They have violated peoples' honour and lives. They have settled in the homes of a people who disliked their settling. They are uncivilised and harmful, they are not beneficial and are not conscious (of Allah), they are unable to desist and they are not trustworthy. Therefore, I have come out amongst the Muslims to inform them about what these people are doing and about the condition of those behind us and what we require to bring about reform of this situation.

Then she recited:

لَا خَيْرَ فِيْ كَثِيْرٍ مِّنْ نَجْوَاهُمْ إِلَّا مَنْ أَمَرَ بِصَدَقَةٍ أَوْ مَعْرُوْفٍ أَوْ إِصْلَاحٍ بَيْنَ النَّاسِ وَمَنْ يَّفْعَلْ ذٰلِكَ ابْتِغَآءَ مَرْضَاتِ اللّٰهِ فَسَوْفَ نُؤْتِيْهِ أَجْرًا عَظِيْمًا

No good is there in much of their private conversation, except for those who enjoin charity or that which is right or conciliation between people. And whoever does that seeking means to the approval of Allah—then We are going to give him a great reward.[1]

(She said:) We rise up for reform on account of the command of Allah and the Messenger ﷺ for the young and the old, and the male and the female, this is our matter. We call towards good, and we forbid the evil, and we encourage you to change it.[2]

Added to that is the fact that these disreputable people were the first to nominate ʿAlī رضي الله عنه for the khilāfah and that they were in ʿAlī's رضي الله عنه army. If we take all of the above facts into fair consideration, the rational outcome that explains both stances is that each of the two sides believed the truth to be with them, and that they

1 Sūrah al-Nisā': 114.

2 *Tārīkh al-Ṭabarī*, vol. 3 p. 14, the year 36 A.H.

interpreted the 'mistake' of the other side with the most noble of interpretations. We know that each of the two groups sought rectitude though it be by different approach, as we have explained. Furthermore we are certain that both groups did not intend to fight each other but it happened nonetheless. In matters such as these the Ummah usually holds back from conducting an analysis of the events as it is a very trying period in Muslim history. However, when Tījānī, and others like him, insist on opening old wounds the potential for infection is too great and that is what brings us to write about what happened between the Ṣaḥābah رَضِيَ اللَّهُ عَنْهُمْ.

Tījānī's slanderous comments

Tījānī's stockpile of criticisms extend beyond the incident of Jamal. His hatred for ʿĀ'ishah رَضِيَ اللَّهُ عَنْهَا has brought about context-blindness. We are not entirely convinced that Tījānī had examined all the evidence that he cites since the references that he provides rarely reflect what he quotes, forget substantiating his claim. He goes on to say:

> **Also al-Bukhari wrote in his book a chapter about what went on in the houses of the Prophet's wives: Once the Prophet صَلَّى اللَّهُ عَلَيْهِ وَسَلَّمَ was giving a speech, and he indicated the house where Aishah was living, then said, "There is the trouble ... there is the trouble ... there is the trouble ... from where the devil's horns come out..."[1]**

Our response:

The English edition of '*Thumma ihtadayt*' contains the abridged translation of Tījānī's actual allegation. In the Arabic text, Tījānī speaks about opening *Ṣaḥīḥ al-Bukhārī* under '*Kitāb al-Shurūṭ*' (The Chapter of Conditions). After reading "The Chapter of Conditions" from *Ṣaḥīḥ al-Bukhārī* in its entirety we can conclude that this ḥadīth does not appear in this chapter. Instead it appears in the chapter under the heading "The Chapter of Khumus."

The significance of bringing up this point—which some might argue is trivial—is to point out the fallacy in Tījānī's claim of having studied the evidences first hand and considered both sides. What appears to be the case here is Tījānī merely borrowed the objection from the books of those scholars who enamoured him in Najaf. It is not fair on Tījānī to speculate, but it would not be farfetched if one had claimed

1 *Then I was guided*, p. 119.

that Tījānī's work relies completely on those books; without verifying the Sunnī perspective from original sources or seeking clarification from the erudite Sunnī scholars. We reiterate that we do not make this claim.

Tījānī cites this ḥadīth as proof against ʿĀ'ishah رضي الله عنها. He alleges, in light of it, that she is the source of the *fitan* (strife). This claim is easily defused since the Prophet ﷺ did not point to the home of ʿĀ'ishah رضي الله عنها that it would be the source of trouble. The Prophet ﷺ was indicating that trouble would emanate from the East i.e. from that direction, not from the home of ʿĀ'ishah رضي الله عنها. Had that been the case the narrator of the ḥadīth would have phrased the narration using the word *ilā* (to) and the not the word *nahw* (in the direction). The version of this ḥadīth which is narrated in *Ṣaḥīḥ Muslim* by way of Ibn ʿUmar رضي الله عنهما reads as follows:

خرج رسول الله صلى الله عليه وسلم من بيت عائشة فقال رأس الكفر من ها هنا من حيث يطلع قرن الشيطان يعنى المشرق

> The Messenger came out from ʿĀ'ishah's house and said, "The main source of disbelief is from there, from where the horns of Shayṭān rise," in other words the East.[1]

A similar narration is transmitted from Ibn ʿUmar:

أنه سمع رسول الله صلى الله عليه وسلم وهو مستقبل المشرق يقول ألا إن الفتنة ها هنا ألا إن الفتنة ها هنا من حيث يطلع قرن الشيطان

> He heard the Messenger ﷺ - whilst he ﷺ was facing the direction of the East – saying, "Indeed, the source of fitnah is from there! Indeed, the fitnah is from there, where the horns of Shayṭān emerge."[2]

If Tījānī actually resorted to the original texts he would have realised that this narration, also from Ibn ʿUmar رضي الله عنهما, appearing in *Ṣaḥīḥ Muslim*, relates that the Messenger ﷺ stood at the door of Ḥafṣah's house, and in another narration at the door of ʿĀ'ishah's house, waving his hand to the direction of the East, saying:

الفتنة ها هنا من حيث يطلع قرن الشيطان قالها مرتين أو ثلاثا

---

1 *Ṣaḥīḥ Muslim* with its commentary, Ḥadīth no. 2905, Kitāb al-Fitan, Bāb al-Fitnah min al-Mashriq min ḥayth Yaṭlaʿ Qarnā al-Shayṭān, vol. 18.

2 *Muslim* with its commentary, Ḥadīth no. 2905; *al-Bukhārī*, Kitāb al-Fitan, Ḥadīth no. 6680.

> "The fitnah is from there, where the horns of Shayṭān emerge!" he said this twice or thrice.[1]

After considering all these narrations we are left with only two possible outcomes. Unlike Tījānī's analysis of the Battle of Jamal, there is no third alternative here. Tījānī either studied these narrations first-hand, in which case he blatantly twisted the meaning of the ḥadīth and deliberately lied about their purport; or he was fed these narrations by way of the books he was gifted by the Shīʿah clergy of Najaf and he accepted the contents of those books blindly, not bothering to refer to the Sunnī references. In either scenario his claim of impartiality is fraudulent, it is only a matter of whether it was deliberate misrepresentation on his part, or the result of inadequate research wherein he merely relied on the evidences of one side and ignored those of the other.

He goes on to say:

> **Al-Bukhari wrote many strange things in his book about Aishah and her bad manners towards the Prophet صَلَّى ٱللَّٰهُ عَلَيْهِ وَسَلَّمَ to the extent that her father had to beat her until she bled.[2]**

Our comment:

Tījānī has loosely attributed this allegation to al-Bukhārī. He expends absolutely no effort in identifying where this information is to be found. The onus is upon Tījānī to furnish the reference for this outrageous claim. We have learnt that even when he provides references those do not support his accusations. Are we going to accept an accusation now, without a reference?

He writes further, ascribing these incidents to al-Bukhārī:

> **He also wrote about her pretention towards the Prophet until Allah threatened her with divorce... and there are many other stories but we are limited by space [3]**

The Ahl al-Sunnah maintain that none besides the Prophets صَلَّى ٱللَّٰهُ عَلَيْهِ وَسَلَّمَ are infallible. As such the latent potential for sin exists. However, the doors of repentance and

---

1 Ibid. Refer to the rest of the aḥādīth mentioning the East.

2 *Then I was guided*, p. 120.

3 *Then I was guided*, p. 120.

forgiveness are open as well. It is a reflection of the darkness in a person's heart if they condemn another on account of a sin from which they have repented.

Only a person with a darkened heart would dare condemn 'Alī رضي الله عنه for proposing to marry Abū Jahl's daughter while he was married to Fāṭimah رضي الله عنها whereupon the Prophet ﷺ became angry and said:

إن بنى هشام بن المغيرة استأذنوني أن ينكحوا ابنتهم علي بن أبي طالب فلا آذن لهم ثم لا آذن لهم ثم لا آذن لهم إلا أن يحب ابن أبي طالب أن يطلق ابنتي

> Indeed, Banū Hāshim ibn al-Mughīrah has sought my permission to marry their daughter to 'Alī ibn Abī Ṭālib; I do not grant them permission. Indeed, I do not grant them permission! Indeed I do not grant them permission! Unless, 'Alī ibn Abī Ṭālib wishes to divorce my daughter.[1]

The Ahl al-Sunnah are consistent in that they do not condemn 'Alī رضي الله عنه. They acknowledge that 'Alī رضي الله عنه sought forgiveness for his behaviour towards the daughter of the Prophet ﷺ. Similarly, the wives of the Prophet ﷺ sought forgiveness from their behaviour towards the Prophet ﷺ.

Tījānī's statement that Allah threatened 'Ā'ishah رضي الله عنها with divorce and replacement, is not accurate. Al-Bukhārī narrates by way of 'Umar رضي الله عنه who said:

واجتمع نساء النبي صلى الله عليه وسلم في الغيرة عليه فقلت لهن عسى ربه إن طلقكن أن يبدله أزواجا خيرا منكن فنزلت هذه الآية

> The wives of the Prophet ﷺ behaved in a possessive manner towards him and I said to them, "It is possible that if he divorces you, his Lord will replace him with wives better than you," and this verse was revealed.[2]

If one considers this verse carefully it appears to be a choice from Allah given to his Prophet ﷺ to divorce his wives, rather than a threat. It also explains why the verse is traditionally called *Āyat al-Takhyīr* (the verse of choice). That is in addition to the fact that the verse does not single out 'Ā'ishah رضي الله عنها but includes the rest of his wives.

---

1 Cited previously on p. 224 of this book.

2 *Ṣaḥīḥ al-Bukhārī*, Kitāb al-Tafsīr (al-Taḥrīm), Ḥadīth no. 4632.

If one were to assume that this verse applies to ʿĀ'ishah رضي الله عنها specifically and Allah has indeed threatened ʿĀ'ishah رضي الله عنها with divorce, the simple response is to ask whether there is any condemnation of ʿAlī رضي الله عنه when the Prophet صلى الله عليه وسلم threatened him with getting Fāṭimah divorced? Therefore whatever criticism is attributed to ʿĀ'ishah رضي الله عنها applies to ʿAlī رضي الله عنه as well. Likewise the excuse presented by Tījānī for ʿAlī رضي الله عنه in this instance, apply to ʿĀ'ishah رضي الله عنها as well.

Why respect ʿĀ'ishah?

Tījānī is long past the stage where he conceals his hatred and animosity towards ʿĀ'ishah رضي الله عنها. He writes:

> **After all that I ask how did Aishah deserve all that respect from the Sunnis; is it because she was the Prophet's wife? But he had so many wives, and some of them were better than Aishah, as the Prophet صلى الله عليه وسلم himself declared.[1]**
>
> **Or perhaps because she was Abu Bakr's daughter! Or maybe because she played an important role in the denial of the Prophet's will for Ali, and when she was told that the Prophet recommended Ali, she said, "Who said that? I was with the Prophet supporting his head on my chest, then he asked me to bring the wash bowl, as I bent down he died, so I cannot see how he recommended Ali."[2]**

Our response:

The Ahl al-Sunnah recite the Qur'ān in which they believe. They regard it as Allah's divine speech. When Allah says:

الْخَبِيْثَاتُ لِلْخَبِيْثِيْنَ وَالْخَبِيْثُوْنَ لِلْخَبِيْثَاتِ وَالطَّيِّبَاتُ لِلطَّيِّبِيْنَ وَالطَّيِّبُوْنَ لِلطَّيِّبَاتِ أُولَـٰئِكَ مُبَرَّءُوْنَ مِمَّا يَقُوْلُوْنَ لَهُمْ مَغْفِرَةٌ وَّرِزْقٌ كَرِيْمٌ

Evil women are for evil men, and evil men are for evil women. And good women are for good men, and good men are for good women. Those (good people) are declared innocent of what they (i.e. slanderers) say. For them is forgiveness and a noble provision.[3]

---

1 He references that claim to *Tirmidhī*, *al-Istīʿāb* and *al-Iṣābah*.

2 *Then I was guided*, p. 120.

3 Sūrah al-Nūr: 26.

The Ahl al-Sunnah believe that Allah is telling them that she is pure, the wife of the pure Prophet صَلَّى ٱللَّهُ عَلَيْهِ وَسَلَّمَ. Taking that into consideration the Ahl al-Sunnah believe that ʿĀ'ishah رَضِيَ ٱللَّهُ عَنْهَا deserves all that honour, respect and more.

This verse was understood to apply to ʿĀ'ishah رَضِيَ ٱللَّهُ عَنْهَا, from the earliest period already.

Ibn Kathīr writes in his *Tafsīr*:

> Mujāhid, ʿAṭā', Saʿīd ibn Jubayr, Shaʿbī, Ḥasan al-Baṣrī, Ḥabīb ibn Abī Thābit, and Ḍaḥḥāk, say it was revealed about ʿĀ'ishah and the incident of the *Ifk* (slander). This is (also) the opinion of Ibn Jarīr al-Ṭabarī.[1]
>
> As for the words, "Those are innocent of what they say," in other words, they are distant from what the slanderers and people of enmity are saying.[2]

As mentioned earlier, the Ahl al-Sunnah believe in the Qur'ān that they recite, and these verses from Sūrah al-Nūr put Tījānī in an awkward position. How does one reconcile belief in these verses with the attempt to prove that ʿĀ'ishah رَضِيَ ٱللَّهُ عَنْهَا was 'evil'? If that is not bad enough, is this not a criticism of the Prophet صَلَّى ٱللَّهُ عَلَيْهِ وَسَلَّمَ? How can it not be when Allah سُبْحَانَهُ وَتَعَالَىٰ says, "Evil women are for evil men."?

We respect ʿĀ'ishah رَضِيَ ٱللَّهُ عَنْهَا because she is our mother in īmān, Allah says:

النَّبِيُّ أَوْلَى بِالْمُؤْمِنِينَ مِنْ أَنفُسِهِمْ وَأَزْوَاجُهُ أُمَّهَاتُهُمْ

The Prophet is more worthy of the believers than themselves and his wives are (in the position of) their mothers.[3]

Tījānī's statement,

> **...is it because she was the Prophet's wife? But he had so many wives, and some of them were better than Aishah, as the Prophet صَلَّى ٱللَّهُ عَلَيْهِ وَسَلَّمَ himself declared.**

He references this to *al-Tirmidhī*, *al-Istīʿāb* and *al-Iṣābah*.[4]

---

1 *Tafsīr Ibn Kathīr*, vol. 3 p. 288, Sūrah al-Nūr.

2 *Tafsīr Ibn Kathīr*, vol. 3 p. 289, Sūrah al-Nūr.

3 Sūrah al-Aḥzāb: 6.

4 *Then I was guided*, p. 119.

Our comment:

We referred to *al-Tirmidhī*, under "the chapter of *Faḍā'il* (merits)" this is what we found under "the chapter of the merits of ʿĀ'ishah":

> كان الناس يتحرون بهداياهم يوم عائشة قالت فاجتمع صواحباتي إلى أم سلمة فقلن يا أم سلمة إن الناس يتحرون بهداياهم يوم عائشة وإنا نريد الخير كما تريد عائشة فقولي لرسول الله صلى الله عليه وسلم يأمر الناس يهدون إليه أينما كان فذكرت ذلك أم سلمة فأعرض عنها ثم عاد إليها فأعادت الكلام فقالت يا رسول الله إن صواحباتي قد ذكرن أن الناس يتحرون بهداياهم يوم عائشة فأمر الناس يهدون أينما كنت فلما كانت الثالثة قالت ذلك قال يا أم سلمة لا تؤذيني في عائشة فإنه ما أنزل علي الوحي وأنا في لحاف امرأة منكن غيرها قال أبو عيسى هذا حديث حسن غريب وقد روى بعضهم هذا الحديث عن حماد بن زيد عن هشام بن عروة عن أبيه عن النبي صلى الله عليه وسلم

> People used to seek out ʿĀ'ishah's day with the Prophet صلى الله عليه وسلم when giving their gifts. ʿĀ'ishah says, "Therefore, my co-wives went to Umm Salamah and said, 'O Umm Salamah! Indeed the people are seeking out ʿĀ'ishah's day (with the Prophet صلى الله عليه وسلم) when giving their gifts and we want the good in the same manner that ʿĀ'ishah wants the good. Go and speak to the Messenger صلى الله عليه وسلم so that he may instruct the people to give their gifts wherever he might be.' Umm Salamah mentioned that (to the Prophet) and he avoided her. Then he returned and she repeated herself and said, 'Indeed, my co-wives have mentioned that the people are seeking out ʿĀ'ishah's day (with you) for their gifts. Instruct the people to present their gifts wherever you may be!' On the third day (that he came to her) she said that (again) and the Prophet صلى الله عليه وسلم said, 'O Umm Salamah! Do not harm me with regards to ʿĀ'ishah for indeed revelation was not sent to me while I was in any of your beds besides hers!'"[1]

ʿAmr ibn al-ʿĀṣ رضي الله عنه narrates:

1 *Sunan al-Tirmidhī*, vol. 5, Kitāb al-Manāqib, Bāb Faḍl ʿĀ'ishah, Ḥadīth no. 3879.

أن رسول الله صلى الله عليه وسلم استعمله على جيش ذات السلاسل قال فأتيته فقلت يا رسول الله أى الناس أحب إليك قال عائشة قلت من الرجال قال أبوها

The Messenger placed him in charge of the army of Dhāt al-Salāsil. He said, "I went to him and asked, 'O Messenger of Allah, who is the most beloved person to you?' and he said, "Ā'ishah.'

I asked, 'and from amongst the men?' he replied, 'her father.'"[1]

Anas رضي الله عنه narrated:

قيل يا رسول الله من أحب الناس إليك قال عائشة قيل من الرجال قال أبوها

It was asked, "O Messenger of Allah! Who is the most beloved person to you?" He said, "ʿĀ'ishah." It was asked, "And from amongst the men?" He said, "Her father."[2]

ʿAbd Allāh ibn Ziyād al-Asadī narrates:

عبد الله بن زياد الأسدي قال سمعت عمار بن ياسر يقول هي زوجته في الدنيا والآخرة يعني عائشة رضى الله عنها

I heard ʿAmmār ibn Yāsir saying, "She is his wife in the world and the Hereafter," referring to ʿĀ'ishah رضي الله عنها.[3]

Anas رضي الله عنه narrated:

أن رسول الله صلى الله عليه و سلم قال وفضل عائشة على النساء كفضل الثريد على سائر الطعام

The Messenger ﷺ said, "The superiority of ʿĀ'ishah over other women is like the superiority of Tharīd over all other foods."[4]

1 *Sunan al-Tirmidhī*, Ḥadīth: 3886; *Bukhārī*, Ḥadīth: 3462.

2 Ibid. Ḥadīth no. 3890.

3 Ibid. Ḥadīth no. 3889.

4 Ibid. Ḥadīth no. 3887.

ʿĀ'ishah رضي الله عنها said:

قال لي رسول الله صلى الله عليه وسلم إن جبريل يقرأ عليك السلام فقلت وعليه السلام ورحمة الله وبركاته .

The Messenger of Allah ﷺ said to me, "Indeed, Jibrīl sends greetings upon you," and I said, "And may the mercy of Allah and His blessings be upon him."[1]

Abū Mūsā al-Ashʿarī رضي الله عنه said:

ما أشكل علينا أصحاب رسول الله صلى الله عليه وسلم حديث قط فسألنا عائشة إلا وجدنا عندها منه علما

Never did we, the Companions of the Messenger ﷺ, find difficulty in understanding a ḥadīth and then we asked ʿĀ'ishah about it except that she had some knowledge about it.[2]

Mūsā ibn Ṭalḥah رضي الله عنه narrates:

I did not meet anyone more eloquent than ʿĀ'ishah.[3]

Then we referred to "the chapter concerning the merits of the Prophet's wives" and found this ḥadīth from Ṣafiyyah bint Ḥuyay, she said:

دخل على رسول الله صلى الله عليه وسلم وقد بلغني عن حفصة وعائشة كلام فذكرت ذلك له فقال ألا قلت فكيف تكونان خيرا مني وزوجي محمد وأبي هارون وعمي موسى وكان الذي بلغها أنهم قالوا نحن أكرم على رسول الله صلى الله عليه وسلم منها وقالوا نحن أزواج النبي صلى الله عليه وسلم وبنات عمه

The Messenger ﷺ visited me after some statements from ʿĀ'ishah and Ḥafṣah had reached me, and therefore I mentioned that to him. Then he stood up and said, "Why did you not say, 'How can you be better than me when my husband is Muḥammad, and my father is Hārūn, and my uncle is Mūsā?'"

1 Ibid. Ḥadīth no. 3882.
2 Ibid. Ḥadīth no. 3883.
3 Ibid. Ḥadīth no. 3884.

> It had reached her that they said, "We are dearer to the Messenger than her, and we are the wives of the Messenger and the daughters of his uncles."[1]

These are the aḥādīth which have been transmitted about the merits of ʿĀ'ishah and Ṣafiyyah and thus we say:

a. There is no doubt that after Khadījah رضي الله عنها, ʿĀ'ishah رضي الله عنها was the best of the Prophet's صلى الله عليه وسلم wives because of the abundance of narrations in this regard. Many of them recorded in books such as al-Bukhārī and Muslim.

b. In reference to the ḥadīth of Ṣafiyyah, there is nothing in it which proves that she is better than ʿĀ'ishah or Ḥafṣah. The Prophet's words were meant as a response to them, not intrinsic superiority over them. This ḥadīth ought to be understood in light of the abundant sound narrations in which the Prophet صلى الله عليه وسلم emphasised the superiority of ʿĀ'ishah رضي الله عنها over all other women.

c. The authenticity of Ṣafiyyah's ḥadīth is called into question. Al-Tirmidhī, after quoting the ḥadīth, states:

> This is a gharīb[2] ḥadīth. We only recognise it from the narration of Hāshim al-Kūfī and its chain is not all that good.[3]

In *al-Istīʿāb*, Ibn ʿAbd al-Barr mentions the same ḥadīth, above, under Ṣafiyyah's رضي الله عنها biography. He does not mention anything besides that;[4] whereas under ʿĀ'ishah's رضي الله عنها biography he mentions many merits, and confirms that she was the most knowledgeable of the Prophet's صلى الله عليه وسلم wives. He narrates from Zuhrī:

> If ʿĀ'ishah's knowledge was to be compared with the knowledge of the other wives of the Prophet and the knowledge of all (other) women, ʿĀ'ishah's knowledge would be greater.[5]

Then he quotes the ḥadīth of ʿAmr ibn ʿĀṣ رضي الله عنه confirming that she is the best of women, and the best of the Prophet's صلى الله عليه وسلم wives. He also narrates the two narrations from Anas رضي الله عنه which have previously been mentioned.[6]

---

1 Ibid. Ḥadīth no. 3892.

2 A ḥadīth which is reported only by a single narrator in any point of this chain.

3 Albānī: *Ḍaʿīf Sunan al-Tirmidhī*, Ḥadīth no. 816.

4 *Al-Istīʿāb*, vol. 4, the letter Ṣād, p. 1872.

5 *Al-Istīʿāb*, vol. 4, the letter ʿAyn, p. 1883.

6 Ibid.

Besides the ḥadīth of Ṣafiyyah رضي الله عنها which we have presented earlier, there is not a single narration which clearly proves Ṣafiyyah's رضي الله عنها superiority over ʿĀ'ishah رضي الله عنها in *al-Iṣābah*. This is notwithstanding the authenticity of the narrations quoted.[1]

Our question is where did Tījānī find what he claims?

Tījānī's insolence

As for his statement,

> **Or maybe because she played an important role in the denial of the Prophet's will for Ali, and when she was told that the Prophet recommended Ali, she said, "Who said that? I was with the Prophet supporting his head on my chest, then he asked me to bring the wash bowl, as I bent down he died, so I cannot see how he recommended Ali."**

Our response:

Tījānī is referring to a narration appearing in *Ṣaḥīḥ al-Bukhārī* wherein ʿĀ'ishah رضي الله عنها is responding to a claim that ʿAlī رضي الله عنه was appointed by the Prophet صلى الله عليه وسلم as his successor. The argument that she makes is that it was not known until his final illness that he had appointed a successor. During his final illness he was being nursed in the home of ʿĀ'ishah رضي الله عنها. Had anything been said regarding succession she would have known as she had been the last person to see him alive. On this point Tījānī accuses her of concealing the fact that the Prophet صلى الله عليه وسلم nominated ʿAlī رضي الله عنه as his successor.

> عن الأسود قال ذكر عند عائشة أن النبي صلى الله عليه وسلم أوصى إلى علي فقالت من قاله لقد رأيت النبي صلى الله عليه وسلم وإني لمسندته إلى صدري فدعا بالطست فانخنث فمات فما شعرت فكيف أوصى إلى علي
>
> Al-Aswad relates that it was mentioned in the presence of ʿĀ'ishah رضي الله عنها that the Prophet صلى الله عليه وسلم had appointed ʿAlī as successor by bequest. Thereupon she said, "Who said so? I saw the Prophet, while I was supporting him against my chest. He asked for a tray, and then fell on one side and expired, and I did not feel it. So how (do the people say) he appointed ʿAlī as his successor?"

---

1 Refer to *al-Iṣābah*, vol. 7 p. 739-742.

ʿĀ'ishah رضي الله عنها did not play the major role in denying the Prophet's ﷺ instatement of ʿAlī رضي الله عنه as the khalīfah as Tījānī claims. If the Prophet ﷺ indeed instated ʿAlī رضي الله عنه as the khalīfah, ʿĀ'ishah would not have been able to deny it in the face of the entire Ummah. However, what she said was in light of her knowledge and that was that the Prophet ﷺ was ill and passed away while with her, and she did not hear anything about that. Let alone her, even ʿAlī رضي الله عنه did not know about it.[1]

Al-Bukhārī narrates with his chain to al-Zuhrī

عن الزهري قال أخبرني عبد الله بن كعب بن مالك الأنصاري وكان كعب بن مالك أحد الثلاثة الذين تيب عليهم أن عبد الله بن عباس أخبره أن علي بن أبي طالب رضي الله عنه خرج من عند رسول الله صلى الله عليه وسلم في وجعه الذي توفي فيه فقال الناس يا أبا حسن كيف أصبح رسول الله صلى الله عليه وسلم فقال أصبح بحمد الله بارئا فأخذ بيده عباس بن عبد المطلب فقال له أنت والله بعد ثلاث عبد العصا وإني والله لأرى رسول الله صلى الله عليه وسلم سوف يتوفى من وجعه هذا إني لأعرف وجوه بني عبد المطلب عند الموت اذهب بنا إلى رسول الله صلى الله عليه وسلم فلنسأله فيمن هذا الأمر إن كان فينا علمنا ذلك وإن كان في غيرنا علمناه فأوصى بنا فقال علي إنا والله لئن سألناها رسول الله صلى الله عليه وسلم فمنعناها لا يعطيناها الناس بعده وإني والله لا أسألها رسول الله صلى الله عليه وسلم

Al-Zuhrī related from ʿAbd Allāh ibn Kaʿb ibn Mālik—and Kaʿb ibn Mālik was one of the three whom Allah pardoned—that ʿAbd Allāh ibn ʿAbbās informed him that ʿAlī ibn Abī Ṭālib emerged from the [home of the] Messenger of Allah ﷺ during his final illness and the people said, "O Abū al-Ḥasan; How is the Messenger of Allah ﷺ this morning?"

He said, "All praise be to Allah, he is well this morning."

ʿAbbās ibn ʿAbd al-Muṭṭalib took him by the hand and said to him, "I swear by Allah, in three days' time you will be a subject. By Allah, I think that the Messenger of Allah ﷺ will die of this illness. I recognise the look of death in the faces of the Banū ʿAbd al-Muṭṭalib when they are dying. Let us go to the

---

1 *Ṣaḥīḥ al-Bukhārī*, Kitāb al-Maghāzī, Ḥadīth no. 4459.

> Messenger of Allah صلى الله عليه وسلم and ask him who will take charge over this matter (Khilāfah). If it is for us, then we will know that, and if it is for someone other than us, we will know and he can advise him to look after us."
>
> ʿAlī replied, "By Allah, if we ask him for it and he refuses us, then the people would never give it to us afterwards. By Allah, I will not ask it from the Messenger of Allah."[1]

Furthermore, had the Prophet صلى الله عليه وسلم intended to instate someone as the khalīfah it would have been necessary to do so publicly and he would not have satisfied himself with mentioning to his wife alone. Tījānī claims that the evidences that prove that the Prophet صلى الله عليه وسلم instated ʿAlī رضي الله عنه as the khalīfah are abundant and well-known. He has mentioned some of them in his book. He also claims that they are clear in nominating ʿAlī رضي الله عنه as the leader after the Prophet صلى الله عليه وسلم. If that were the case Tījānī is facing a conundrum. Why accuse ʿĀ'ishah رضي الله عنها of playing the major role in denying the instatement of ʿAlī رضي الله عنه as the khalīfah? If ʿĀ'ishah رضي الله عنها played a major role by concealing such important information, what does that say about the 'clear' proofs that Tījānī has presented?

Tījānī is not done venting. He says:

> **Or is it because she fought a total war against him and his sons after him, and even intercepted the funeral procession of al-Ḥasan - Leader of the Heaven's youth - and prevented his burial beside his grandfather, the Messenger of Allah صلى الله عليه وسلم, and said "Do not allow anybody that I do not like to enter my house."**
>
> **She forgot, or maybe ignored the Messenger of Allah's صلى الله عليه وسلم sayings about him and his brother, "Allah loves those who love them, and Allah hates those who hate them," Or his saying, "I am at war with those who fight against you, and I am at peace with those who appease you." And there are many other sayings in their honour. No wonder, for they were so dear to him![2]**

And he states further at another place:

> **Fatimah al-Zahra, as I mentioned earlier, stated in her will that she should be buried secretly; therefore, she was not buried beside her father. But what about her son, al-Ḥasan, why was he not buried beside his grandfather?**

1 *Ṣaḥīḥ al-Bukhārī* , Kitāb al-Maghāzī, Ḥadīth no. 4182.

2 *Then I was guided*, p. 120.

Aisha (Umm al-Mumineen) prevented that. When al-Husayn brought his brother to bury him by his grandfather, the Messenger of Allah, Aisha rode a mule and went around saying, "Do not bury someone I do not love in my house." Then, the houses of Bani Umayya and Hashim stood opposite each other ready to fight, but al-Husayn told her that he would only take the coffin of his brother around the grave of their grandfather then he would bury him in al-Baqi'. That was because Imam al-Ḥasan requested from his brother, that no blood should be shed for his sake. Ibn Abbas said a few verses regarding this event:

> ***She rode a camel, she rode a mule, if she had lived longer, she would have ridden an elephant, you have the ninth of the eighth, and you took everything.***[1]

Our comment:

Tījānī's proven track record for falsifying evidence obviates the need to repeatedly demonstrate his forgery. By this point any unsubstantiated quotation is to be ignored. If he lies when he cites references, what can be expected of those allegations which are bereft of any reference? Despite this we have attempted to find some mention of the accusations that he casts. We could not find a trace of it in any of the books of the Ahl al-Sunnah. Instead, the opposite is to be found.

Ibn al-Athīr describes Ḥasan's رضي الله عنه passing:

> Ḥusayn sought permission from ʿĀ'ishah to bury his brother and she permitted him.[2]

Ibn ʿAbd al-Barr writes in *al-Istīʿāb*:

> When Ḥasan passed away, Ḥusayn went to ʿĀ'ishah and requested that and she said, "Yes! It is an honour!"[3]

In *al-Bidāyah* it says:

> Ḥusayn sent someone to ʿĀ'ishah seeking permission and she permitted him.[4]

---

1 Ibid. p. 139-140.

2 Ibn al-Athīr: *Al-Kāmil*, vol. 3, p. 315, the year 49 A.H.

3 *Al-Istīʿāb*, vol. 1 p. 392, the letter Ḥā, Ḥasan ibn ʿAlī.

4 Ibn al-Kathīr: *Al-Bidāyah wa l-Nihāyah*, vol. 8, p. 46, the year 49 A.H.

Compare this to what Tījānī has written!

Ḥasan's true enemies are those who claim to be his supporters. They are among the most wretched and corrupt people. This is attested to by the Twelver Shīʿah themselves. Abū Manṣūr al-Ṭabarsī, a Twelver scholar, quotes Ḥasan ibn ʿAlī:

> By Allah! I believe that Muʿāwiyah is better for me than these people who claim to be supporters. They desire my death, and they are wary of my faults, and they take my wealth. By Allah! For me to make a covenant with Muʿāwiyah by which I protect my blood and the blood of my family is better for me than for them to kill me and consequently my family and household are ruined.[1]

These are the true enemies of Ḥasan رضي الله عنه, not ʿĀ'ishah رضي الله عنها! This is recorded by the Shīʿah, not the Ahl al-Sunnah!

The lines of poetry attributed to Ibn ʿAbbās رضي الله عنه lack poetic flair and fluency. These factors alone call into question their reliability, notwithstanding what he said about her at the time of her death.

Aḥmad narrates in *Al-Faḍā'il*—from Dhakwān, ʿĀ'ishah's freed slave:

> He asked ʿĀ'ishah permission for Ibn ʿAbbās to enter at the time of her death while her nephew, ʿAbd Allāh ibn ʿAbd al-Raḥmān, was with her.
>
> He said, "Ibn ʿAbbās is here seeking permission to visit you and he is of the best of your sons."
>
> She said, "I have no need of Ibn ʿAbbās, or your recommendation of him!"
>
> Then ʿAbd Allāh ibn ʿAbd al-Raḥmān said to her, "He is a reciter of the Book of Allah and knowledgeable of the dīn of Allah. Permit him to visit you so that he may greet you and bid you farewell!"
>
> She said, "Permit him then."
>
> He says, "Then I permitted him and ʿAbd Allāh ibn ʿAbbās entered, greeted, sat, and then said, 'Glad tiding O Mother of the Believers! The only thing between you and all harm and tiredness leaving you, and meeting your beloved ones, Muḥammad and his Companions, is for your soul to separate from your body.' And Ibn ʿAbbās said, 'You were the most beloved wife of the Messenger صلى الله عليه وسلم

1 al-Ṭabarsī: *Al-Ihtijāj*, vol. 2, p. 290.

> and he only loved what was pure. Also, Allah revealed your innocence from above the seven heavens and therefore, there is not a Masjid on the earth except that it is read during the nights and days. And your necklace fell the night of Abwā and the Prophet remained at that station with the people in search of it and the people woke up the next morning without water and Allah revealed, 'Then seek clean earth and wipe over your faces and your hands (with it)'[1], and in that was a concession for all people on account of you. By Allah! You are blessed!' She said, 'Leave me, O Ibn ʿAbbās! By Allah, I wish I was in oblivion, forgotten.'"[2]

Also, in his debate with the Khawārij he argued against them saying:

> I (Ibn ʿAbbās) said, "As for you statement, 'He fought but he did not take booty and he did not take slaves,' would you take your mother, ʿĀ'ishah, as a slave and make her permissible as you make others permissible when she is your mother? If you say, 'We make her permissible like we make others besides her permissible,' then you have turned apostate! And if you say that, 'She is not our mother,' then you have turned apostate as Allah says, 'The Prophet is more worthy of the believers than themselves and his wives are (in the position of) their mothers.' Therefore, you are between two deviations. So find a way out!" I said, "Are you leaving this?" and they said, "Yes..."[3]

These authentic narrations refute Tījānī's dubious narration. Who knows, it might be in Tījānī's imagination where it can be found!

Tījānī accuses ʿĀ'ishah of lying

Tījānī accuses her of fabricating narrations to yield support for her father:

> **The virtues of Abu Bakr that have been mentioned in historical books were narrated either by his daughter Aisha, whose position vis-a-vis Ali is well documented, and she tried hard to support her father, even by fabricating sayings.[4]**

Our response:

---

1 Sūrah al-Nisā': 43.

2 Aḥmad: *Faḍā'il al-Ṣaḥābah*, vol. 2, Ḥadīth no. 1639, the examiner says, "Its sanad is reliable."

3 Nasā'ī: *Khaṣā'iṣ Amīr al-Mu'minīn*, Ḥadīth: 185, the examiner say, "Its sanad is reliable."

4 *Then I was guided*, p. 141.

Considering the sheer extent of his forgeries one wonders if Tījānī knows what a *Ṣaḥīḥ* (authentic) narration looks like. One of the consequences of a fabricator of ḥadīth is that all their narrations are rejected.

If ʿĀ'ishah narrates fabricated aḥādīth then how can we know that ʿAlī, Fāṭimah, and her two sons are also included under the ambit of the *Verse of Taṭhīr*?[1] How do we know that Fāṭimah رضي الله عنها actually demanded her share of her father's inheritance? All of these are what ʿĀ'ishah رضي الله عنها narrates.[2]

If she was guilty of forging ḥadīth how could she be accused of concealing the Prophet's صلى الله عليه وسلم instating ʿAlī رضي الله عنه if she was unreliable to begin with? Why does Tījānī cite all these aḥādīth narrated by ʿĀ'ishah, acknowledge them, then claim that she narrates fabricated aḥādīth? Also, how is it that Ibn Bābuwayh al-Qummī, a prominent Shīʿī scholar, accepts her aḥādīth in his book *al-Khiṣāl*? Such double-standards!

1 *Then I was guided*, p. 119.
2 Ibid. p. 114.

Chapter Ten

Tījānī's Criticisms of Ṭalḥah and Zubayr

These two noble Companions, Ṭalḥah and Zubayr رضي الله عنهما, are among those whom the Prophet صلى الله عليه وسلم attested to as being of the people of Jannah.[1] Tījānī deemed it necessary to criticise them because they demanded retribution for the murder of ʿUthmān رضي الله عنه. Tījānī's weapon of choice in his scathing attacks is that of misrepresentation.

Tījānī claims, in the study of "the ḥadīth about their competing for the world," that they were amongst those who competed with one another for worldly acquisitions and that they hoarded gold and silver, etc. This ludicrous claim has been addressed earlier in this book which and therefore obviates the need of repeating the responses. Instead we refer the reader to the relevant passages which refute Tījānī's claim.[2]

Tījānī accused Ṭalḥah and Zubayr رضي الله عنهما of participating in the siege and rebelling against ʿUthmān رضي الله عنه. The answers to these allegations are the same answers which were provided in our refutation of Tījānī's allegations against ʿĀ'ishah رضي الله عنها.[1] If there is anything to be added it would be what follows. Who stood to gain from ʿUthmān's murder? Who endorsed ʿUthmān's nomination for the position of Khilāfah? Who sought retribution for ʿUthmān's murder? If we consider the fact that neither Ṭalḥah nor Zubayr رضي الله عنهما stood to benefit from ʿUthmān's رضي الله عنه murder. Both of them were not desirous of leadership. In a lengthy narration appearing in *Ṣaḥīḥ al-Bukhārī* we are told that after ʿUmar رضي الله عنه was stabbed he nominated a panel of six candidates for the position of Khalīfah. This is the significant part of the narration:

فقالوا أوص يا أمير المؤمنين استخلف قال ما أجد أحق بهذا الأمر من هؤلاء النفر أو الرهط الذين توفي رسول الله صلى الله عليه وسلم وهو عنهم راض. فسمى عليا وعثمان والزبير وطلحة وسعدا وعبد الرحمن .... فلما قبض خرجنا به فانطلقنا نمشي فسلم عبد الله بن عمر قال يستأذن عمر بن

1 Refer to *Tirmidhī*, Kitāb al-Manāqib, Ḥadīth no. 3747.

2 Refer to p. 173 of this book.

1 Refer to p. 456 of this book.

الخطاب قالت أدخلوه فأدخل فوضع هنالك مع صاحبيه فلما فرغ من دفنه اجتمع هؤلاء الرهط فقال عبد الرحمن اجعلوا أمركم إلى ثلاثة منكم. فقال الزبير قد جعلت أمري إلى علي. فقال طلحة قد جعلت أمري إلى عثمان. وقال سعد قد جعلت أمري إلى عبد الرحمن بن عوف

The people said to ʿUmar, "O Amīr al-Mu'minīn! Appoint a successor."

ʿUmar said, "I do not consider anyone more suitable for the task than the following persons, or group, whom the Messenger ﷺ had been pleased with before he died."

Then ʿUmar mentioned ʿAlī, ʿUthmān, Zubayr, Ṭalḥah, Saʿd and ʿAbd al-Raḥmān (ibn ʿAwf)... The narration continues until it mentions:

When ʿUmar breathed his last, we carried him out and began walking. ʿAbd Allāh ibn ʿUmar greeted (ʿĀ'ishah) and said, "ʿUmar ibn al-Khaṭṭāb seeks permission."

ʿĀ'ishah said, "Bring him in."

He was brought in and buried beside his two companions. When he was buried, the group (recommended by ʿUmar) held a meeting. Then ʿAbd al-Raḥmān said, "Reduce the candidates for leadership to three of you." Zubayr said, "I give up my candidacy to ʿAlī."

Ṭalḥah said, "I give up my candidacy to ʿUthmān,"

Saʿd, "I give up my candidacy to ʿAbd al-Raḥmān ibn ʿAwf."[1]

We learn from this narration that Ṭalḥah رضي الله عنه had given his candidacy to ʿUthmān رضي الله عنه. Why would he conspire to have ʿUthmān رضي الله عنه murdered when it was possible to withhold his nomination from the onset? This narration also brings to light the fact that Zubayr رضي الله عنه considered ʿAlī رضي الله عنه the prime candidate. It cannot be later said that he was an enemy to ʿAlī رضي الله عنه. In addition to this we know for a fact that the Muhājirīn and Anṣār, which includes Ṭalḥah and Zubayr رضي الله عنهما, were determined to defend ʿUthmān رضي الله عنه with their lives but it was ʿUthmān رضي الله عنه who did not permit anyone to fight in his defence. Finally if we consider the fact that neither of them was desirous of the Khilāfah after ʿUthmān's رضي الله عنه murder, it rules out any motive for rebelling against him.

---

1 *Ṣaḥīḥ al-Bukhārī*, Kitāb Faḍā'il Aṣḥāb al-Nabī ﷺ, Ḥadīth no. 3700.

Al-Aḥnaf ibn Qays relates:

سمعت الأحنف يقول أتيت المدينة وأنا حاج فبينا نحن في منازلنا نضع رحالنا إذ أتى آت فقال قد اجتمع الناس في المسجد فاطلعت فإذا يعني الناس مجتمعون وإذا بين أظهرهم نفر قعود فإذا هو علي بن أبي طالب والزبير وطلحة وسعد بن أبي وقاص رحمة الله عليهم فلما قمت عليهم قيل هذا عثمان بن عفان قد جاء قال فجاء وعليه ملية صفراء فقلت لصاحبي كما أنت حتى أنظر ما جاء به فقال عثمان أهاهنا علي أهاهنا الزبير أهاهنا طلحة أهاهنا سعد قالوا نعم قال فأنشدكم بالله الذي لا إله إلا هو أتعلمون أن رسول الله صلى الله عليه وسلم قال من يبتاع مربد بني فلان غفر الله له فابتعته فأتيت رسول الله صلى الله عليه وسلم فقلت إني ابتعت مربد بني فلان قال فاجعله في مسجدنا وأجره لك قالوا نعم قال فأنشدكم بالله الذي لا إله إلا هو هل تعلمون أن رسول الله صلى الله عليه وسلم قال من يبتاع بئر رومة غفر الله له فأتيت رسول الله صلى الله عليه وسلم فقلت قد ابتعت بئر رومة قال فاجعلها سقاية للمسلمين وأجرها لك قالوا نعم قال فأنشدكم بالله الذي لا إله إلا هو هل تعلمون أن رسول الله صلى الله عليه وسلم قال من يجهز جيش العسرة غفر الله له فجهزتهم حتى ما يفقدون عقالا ولا خطاما قالوا نعم قال اللهم اشهد اللهم اشهد اللهم اشهد

We arrived in Madīnah on the way for Ḥajj. We were at our lodgings, unloading our luggage, when someone called out, "They have gathered in the Masjid!" We rushed to the Masjid, I looked and found the people gathered, and in the midst of them was a group; there I saw ʿAlī, Zubayr, Ṭalḥah and Saʿd ibn Abī Waqqāṣ رضي الله عنهم. When I got closer it was said that ʿUthmān entered, he was wearing a yellowish cloak. I said to my companion, "Stay where you are until I find out what is happening."

ʿUthmān said, "Is ʿAlī here? Is Zubayr here? Is Ṭalḥah here? Is Saʿd here?"

They said, "Yes."

He said, "I beseech you by Allah, beside Whom there is none worthy of worship, are you aware that the Messenger of Allah said, 'Whoever buys the Mirbad [land for drying dates] of so and so clan, Allah will forgive him,' and

I bought it; then I came to the Messenger of Allah and told him, and he said, 'Add it to our Masjid and the reward for it will be yours'?"

They said, "Yes."

He then said, "I beseech you by Allah, beside Whom there is none worthy of worship, are you aware that the Messenger of Allah said, 'Whoever buys the well of Rūmah, Allah will forgive him,' so I came to the Messenger of Allah and said, 'I have bought the well of Rūmah.' He said, 'Make it public water for the Muslims, and the reward for it will be yours.'?"

They said, "Yes."

He said, "I beseech you by Allah, beside whom there is none worthy of worship, are you aware that the Messenger of Allah said, 'Whoever equips the army of al-ʿUsrah (i.e. Tabūk), Allah will forgive him,' so I equipped them until they were not lacking even a rope or a bridle?"

They said, "Yes."

So ʿUthmān said, "O Allah, bear witness, O Allah, bear witness, O Allah, bear witness."[1]

The narration appears in al-Ṭabarī with a similar chain but with more details of what transpired afterwards since al-Aḥnaf described what occurred in the early stages of the rebellion when ʿUthmān رضي الله عنه was not yet under siege. The narration in al-Ṭabarī provides the following details:

Later I met Ṭalḥah and Zubayr and asked them, "Whom do you instruct me with and are pleased with after ʿUthmān as I don't see an outcome other than ʿUthmān being killed?"

They said, "ʿAlī."

I asked them, "Are you pleased with him as a leader, and recommend him after ʿUthmān?"

They replied, "Certainly."

So I set off for Makkah. While I was there the news of ʿUthmān's murder reached me. I met ʿĀ'ishah in Makkah and asked her whom she is pleased

1 *Sunan al-Nasā'ī*, Kitāb al-Aḥbās, Bāb Waqf al-Masājid, Ḥadīth no. 3606.

with to lead the Ummah and whom I ought to pledge allegiance to, and she responded, "'Alī."[1]

Why would they recommend 'Alī رضي الله عنه if they were desirous of leadership? They had absolutely nothing to gain from 'Uthmān's رضي الله عنه murder. There is no evidence to suggest they had any part in 'Uthmān's رضي الله عنه murder.

Tījānī claims that Ṭalḥah and Zubayr gave false testimony

Tījānī says:

> **Let us move on, for I do not want to discuss the life of Umm al-Mumineen Aishah, but I have tried to show how many of the Companions violated the principles of Islam and disobeyed the orders of the Messenger of Allah صلى الله عليه وسلم, and it suffices to mention the following incident which happened to Aishah during the civil war, and on which all historians tend to agree. It has been said that when Aishah passed by the waters of al-Hawab and heard the dogs barking, she remembered the warning of her husband, the Messenger of Allah صلى الله عليه وسلم, and how he prevented her from being the instigator of "al-Jamal" war. She cried, then she said, "Take me back. Take me back!" But Talhah and al-Zubayr brought fifty men and bribed them, then made them testify that these waters were not al-Hawab's waters. Later she continued her journey until she reached Basrah. Many historians believe that those fifty men gave the first falsified testimony in the history of Islam. (al-Ṭabarī, and Ibn al-Athīr, and Madā'inī, and other historians who wrote about the year 40 A.H).**
>
> **O Muslims! You who have enlightened minds... assist us in solving this problem. Were these truly the honourable Companions, of whom we were always led to believe in their righteousness, and that they were the best people after the Messenger of Allah صلى الله عليه وسلم! How could they give a falsified testimony when the Messenger of Allah صلى الله عليه وسلم considered it to be one of the great sins, whose punishment is Hell.[2]**

Refuting Tījānī's claims that Ṭalḥah and Zubayr gave false testimony

Tījānī's accusation against these two noble Companions is that when 'Ā'ishah رضي الله عنها arrived at the waters of Ḥaw'ab she remembered a ḥadīth where the Prophet

---

1 *Tārīkh al-Ṭabarī* vol. 4 p. 497, Ibn Ḥajar graded this chain as sound in *Fatḥ al-Bārī* vol.13 p. 38.

2 *Then I was guided*, p. 118-119.

صَلَّى ٱللَّٰهُ عَلَيْهِ وَسَلَّمَ predicts that one of his wives will pass by the waters of Haw'ab and dogs will be barking. When she realised that it was her, she intended to return. The allegation against Ṭalḥah and Zubayr رَضِيَ ٱللَّٰهُ عَنْهُمَا comes here: they falsely claimed that this was not the water of Ḥaw'ab and bribed fifty people to corroborate their false testimony.

To begin with we know that Tījānī's eyes did not fall on a single page of the books he cited as reference because the incident of Jamal occurred well before 40 A.H. How do historians record the event four years after it occurred? It comes as no surprise that when we opened the books of al-Ṭabarī and Ibn al-Athīr we did not find any trace of this ḥadīth except for this narration:

> From Zuhrī, he said, "It reached me that when Ṭalḥah and Zubayr reached ʿAlī's house at Dhī al-Qār they diverted to Baṣrah and took al-Munkadir. Then ʿĀ'ishah heard the barking of the dogs and said, 'What river is this?' They said, 'Ḥaw'ab.' She said, 'To Allah do we belong, and to Him we return! It is me! Indeed, I heard the Messenger saying while his wives were with him, 'Which one of you will be barked at by the dogs of Ḥaw'ab!' Therefore, she intended to return but ʿAbd Allāh ibn Zubayr came to her and, it is claimed, that he said, 'Whoever says this is Ḥaw'ab is lying and he insisted until she continued (with her journey).'"

The narration of al-Ṭabarī and Ibn al-Athīr, as is clear, does not mention Ṭalḥah and Zubayr رَضِيَ ٱللَّٰهُ عَنْهُمَا. Rather, it only mentions ʿAbd Allāh ibn Zubayr رَضِيَ ٱللَّٰهُ عَنْهُ. Also, the expression, "It is claimed that he said," points to the fact that it cannot be proven that he said so. Furthermore, the interrupted narrations of al-Zuhrī are generally looked at suspiciously, and this is an interrupted narration.

Tījānī's claim that Ṭalḥah and Zubayr رَضِيَ ٱللَّٰهُ عَنْهُمَا bribed the people is evidently false as it is not supported by any reliable narration. Furthermore, the narration that he references is in conflict with narrations which have been transmitted by sound narrators. Qays ibn Abī Ḥāzim, a reliable narrator, reports:

> When ʿĀ'ishah reached some of the homes of Banū ʿĀmir the dogs barked and ʿĀ'ishah said, "What is this river?"
>
> They said, "Ḥaw'ab."
>
> She said, "I think I should return."

> Zubayr said, "No! Not until you arrived and the people see you and Allah reconciles them."
>
> She said, "I think I should return. I heard the Messenger saying, 'What will the condition of one of you be when the dogs of Ḥaw'ab bark at her?'"[1]

At the same time let us not forget the high status accorded to Ṭalḥah and Zubayr رضي الله عنهما by the Prophet صلى الله عليه وسلم

The Prophet صلى الله عليه وسلم said:

> Whoever would like to see a martyr walking on the face of the earth, let him look at Ṭalḥah ibn 'Ubayd Allāh.[2]

It is reported that Jābir said:

> On the day of Uḥud, when the people fled, the Messenger of Allah صلى الله عليه وسلم was on his own in some part of the battlefield with twelve men, including Ṭalḥah, and the disbelievers caught up with him. The Prophet صلى الله عليه وسلم said, "Who will confront these people?"
>
> Ṭalḥah said, "I will."
>
> He told him, "Stay where you are."
>
> One of the Anṣār said, "I will." and he fought until he was killed.
>
> Then the Messenger صلى الله عليه وسلم turned and looked at the disbelievers saying, "Who will confront these people?"
>
> Ṭalḥah said, "I will."
>
> He told him, "Stay where you are."
>
> One of the Anṣār said, "I will." and fought until he was killed.
>
> It continued like that until only Ṭalḥah was left with the Messenger of Allah صلى الله عليه وسلم

---

1 Al-Ḥākim narrates it in *al-Mustadrak*, vol. 3, p. 129; Abū Ya'lā in his *Musnad*, Ḥadīth no. 4868, p. 282, the examiner says, "Its sanad is reliable;" *Mawārid al-Ẓam'ān*, Ḥadīth no. 1831, Bāb fī Waq'ah al-Jamal, vol. 6 p. 73; Ibn Kathīr says in *al-Bidāyah*, vol. 6 p. 217, "This is a sanad on the level of the *Ṣaḥīḥayn* but they did not narrate it."

2 *Jāmi' al-Tirmidhī*, Abwāb al-Manāqib, Ḥadīth no. 3739.

> He said, "Who will confront these people?"
>
> Ṭalḥah said, "I will."
>
> Ṭalḥah fought like the eleven before him, until his fingers were cut off, then he said, "That is enough for me."
>
> The Messenger of Allah صلى الله عليه وسلم said, "If you had said, 'In the name of Allah,' the angels would have taken you up while the people were looking on."
>
> Then Allah drove back the polytheists.[1]

Qays ibn Abī Ḥāzim said:

> I saw the paralyzed hand of Ṭalḥah; he had protected the Messenger صلى الله عليه وسلم on the Day of Uḥud.[2]

On the Day of Uḥud, the Prophet صلى الله عليه وسلم wore two coats of mail. He tried to get up on a boulder but was not able to, so Ṭalḥah رضي الله عنه squatted under him, lifting the Prophet صلى الله عليه وسلم upon it such that he could sit on the boulder. The Prophet صلى الله عليه وسلم said:

> Ṭalḥah has made paradise incumbent (upon himself by this action of his).[3]

When Abū Bakr رضي الله عنه remembered the Day of Uḥud, he would say:

> That day was all for Ṭalḥah.[4]

Zubayr رضي الله عنه was the Prophet's صلى الله عليه وسلم cousin, the son of Ṣafiyyah رضي الله عنها, the cousin of ʿAlī رضي الله عنه, the husband of Asmā' رضي الله عنها, the son-in-law of Abū Bakr رضي الله عنه, the father of ʿAbd Allāh and ʿUrwah رضي الله عنهما; the Ḥawārī of the Messenger of Allah صلى الله عليه وسلم.

The Messenger of Allah صلى الله عليه وسلم said on the day of the Trench, "Who will bring me news of Banū Qurayẓah?" Zubayr said, "I will." So he went on a horse and brought news of them. The Messenger صلى الله عليه وسلم said that a second time and Zubayr said again, "I will." This happened a third time, whereupon the Messenger صلى الله عليه وسلم said:

---

1 *Sunan al-Nasā'ī*, Kitāb al-Jihād, Ḥadīth no. 3149.

2 *Ṣaḥīḥ al-Bukhārī*, Kitāb al-Maghāzī, Ḥadīth no. 4063.

3 *Jāmiʿ al-Tirmidhī*, Kitāb al-Jihād, Ḥadīth no. 1692.

4 *Fatḥ al-Bārī* vol. 7 p. 36.

> Every Prophet has a disciple, and my disciple is Zubayr.[1]

On the day of the Trench, the Messenger of Allah ﷺ said to him:

> May my father and mother be sacrificed for you.[2]

Zubayr رضي الله عنه was among the first Muslims and endured the difficulties of Makkah. He undertook the Hijrah to Abyssinia and later to Madīnah. He participated in all the military campaigns of the Messenger ﷺ and was one of the heroes at Yarmūk. He was instrumental in the conquest of Egypt as well.

At Jamal after ʿAmr ibn Jurmūz murdered Zubayr رضي الله عنه, he cut off his head and brought it to ʿAlī رضي الله عنه, assuming he would be praised. He sought permission to enter, and ʿAlī رضي الله عنه refused saying, "Give the killer of (Zubayr) Ṣafiyyah's son the tidings of the Fire!"[3]

Then ʿAlī رضي الله عنه said:

> I heard the Messenger of Allah ﷺ saying, "Every Prophet had a disciple, and my disciple is Zubayr." [4]

After all this Tījānī has the audacity to condemn them to Hell; for no reason other than a wretched conclusion from false narrations!

1 *Ṣaḥīḥ al-Bukhārī*, Kitāb al-Jihād, Ḥadīth no. 2846.

2 *Ṣaḥīḥ al-Bukhārī*, Kitāb Faḍā'il Aṣḥāb al-Nabī ﷺ, Ḥadīth no. 3720.

3 *Al-Ṭabaqāt*, vol. 3 p 105.

4 *Faḍa'il al-Ṣahabah*, vol. 2 p. 920.

Chapter Eleven

Tījānī's criticisms of Muʿāwiyah ibn Abī Sufyān

There is no dispute that Muʿāwiyah ibn Abī Sufyān رضي الله عنه was a leading figure who opposed ʿAlī's رضي الله عنه stance on dealing with the murderers of ʿUthmān رضي الله عنه. Muʿāwiyah رضي الله عنه demanded that action be taken immediately and withheld giving the pledge of allegiance to ʿAlī رضي الله عنه as leverage. ʿAlī رضي الله عنه insisted that he give the *Bayʿah* (pledge) and the matter of ʿUthmān's رضي الله عنه murder will be dealt with as soon as things become stable again. Muʿāwiyah رضي الله عنه felt that he was more entitled to seek retribution for ʿUthmān's رضي الله عنه murder as he was closer related to ʿUthmān رضي الله عنه. Eventually this resulted in the Battle of Ṣiffīn. Therefore, it is to be expected that Tījānī would pay special attention to him and accuse him of injustice and misguidance. What does it matter that Tījānī accuses this scribe of *Waḥī* (revelation) of misguidance after the Prophet صلى الله عليه وسلم said this about him:

اَللّٰهُمَّ اجْعَلْهُ هَادِيًا مَهْدِيًّا وَاهْدِ بِهِ

O Allah, make him a guide, rightly-guided, and guide (others) through him.[1]

Tījānī says:

> **Umar ibn al-Khattab, who was well known for his strictness towards his governors whom used to dismiss them on mere suspicions, was quite gentle towards Muawiyah ibn Abi Sufyan and never disciplined him. Muawiyah was appointed by Abu Bakr and confirmed by Umar throughout his life, who never even rebuked him or blamed him, despite the fact that many people complained about Muawiyah and reported him for wearing silk and gold, which was prohibited to men by the Messenger of Allah صلى الله عليه وسلم. Umar used to answer these complaints by saying, "Let him be, he is the Kisra (king) of the Arabs." Muawiyah continued in the governorship for more than twenty years without being touched or criticized, and when Uthman succeeded to the caliphate of the Muslims, he added to his authority further districts and regions, which enabled him to a mass great wealth from the Islamic nation and to raise armies to rebel against the Imam (Leader) of the nation and subsequently take the full power by force and intimidation. Thus he became**

---

1 *Sunan al-Tirmidhī*, Kitāb al-Manāqib, Bāb Manāqib Muʿāwiyah, Ḥadīth no. 3842; See *Ṣaḥīḥ al-Tirmidhī*, Ḥadīth no. 3108.

> **the sole ruler of all Muslims, and later forced them to vote for his corrupt and alcohol drinking son Yazid, as his heir and successor.**
>
> **This is another lengthy story in relation to its detail in this book.[1]**

Our comment:

Tījānī's ignorance of history is shocking. He appears to blurt out facts, and relate episodes with complete disregard for accuracy. Now he claims that Abū Bakr رضي الله عنه instated Muʿāwiyah رضي الله عنه, and ʿUmar رضي الله عنه endorsed this and retained him for the duration of his life. Contrary to what Tījānī has written, it is well-known by anyone who studied history—including students in primary school—that Abū Bakr appointed Yazīd ibn Abī Sufyān, the brother of Muʿāwiyah, as a commander of a battalion during the conquest of Syria. When the city of Damascus was conquered during ʿUmar's Khilāfah he was appointed as the governor over Syria and remained the governor over it until his untimely passing in the plague of ʿAmwās. After Yazīd's passing ʿUmar رضي الله عنه instated his brother, Muʿāwiyah ibn Abī Sufyān رضي الله عنه, as the governor over the region.[2]

There remains the matter of ʿUmar رضي الله عنه being excessively lenient with Muʿāwiyah رضي الله عنه and never holding him accountable for his actions. There appears to be no evidence to support this at all. One wonders where Tījānī finds this when he failed to record the history of Muʿāwiyah's رضي الله عنه appointment correctly.

That being said, there is evidence which is contrary to Tījānī's claim. Ibn al-Kathīr narrates in his encyclopaedia, *al-Bidāyah wa al-Nihāyah*:

> Muʿāwiyah visited ʿUmar wearing a green robe and the Ṣaḥābah stared at him. When ʿUmar saw that, he advanced towards him with a whip in his hand and started hitting him with it and Muʿāwiyah said, "O Amīr al-Mu'minīn, fear Allah concerning me!"
>
> ʿUmar then returned to his place and the people said to him, "Why did you hit him, O Amīr al-Mu'minīn, when there is none like him?"
>
> He said, "By Allah! I regard him to be a good person and I have only heard good things about him. If I had heard anything to the contrary about him, what

---

1 *Then I was guided*, p. 94.

2 *Siyar Aʿlām al-Nubalā'*, vol. 1 p. 329.

> you would have seen would be very different from what you just observed. Nevertheless, I saw him, gesturing with his hands, and I wanted to remove that sense of prominence from him."[1]

As for his statement:

> **Despite the fact that many people complained about Muawiyah and reported him for wearing silk and gold, which was prohibited to men by the Messenger of Allah ﷺ. Umar used to answer these complaints by saying, "Let him be, he is the Kisra (king) of the Arabs."**

Our comment:

This allegation is unfounded on numerous accounts. Firstly his statement, "Despite the many who complained against Muʿāwiyah," is called into question. Muʿāwiyah رضي الله عنه was an excellent appointment, well skilled at diplomacy. Historically there is no evidence of there being any major complaints against him. Muʿāwiyah رضي الله عنه ruled the people of Syria for forty years, twenty years as a governor and twenty as a Khalīfah. His relationship with them was so strong that they stood with him when he sought justice for the blood of ʿUthmān رضي الله عنه. A leader about whom there are abundant complaints will never be able to yield that level of loyalty.

It is farfetched that ʿUmar رضي الله عنه said Muʿāwiyah رضي الله عنه was the Kisrā of the Arabs when he learnt that he wore gold and silk, because ʿUmar hit Muʿāwiyah for wearing a fancy green robe, which is permitted, why then would he remain silent when he wore gold and silk which is forbidden.

The narration from ʿUmar رضي الله عنه which is narrated by Ibn Abī Dunyā from Abū ʿAbd al-Raḥmān al-Madanī, who said, "ʿUmar used to say when he saw Muʿāwiyah, 'This is the Kisrā of the Arabs.'"[2] The chain of this report is not very strong. Even if we were to accept it, there is no mention of Muʿāwiyah wearing gold or silk.

Tījānī goes on to say:

> **Muawiyah continued in the governorship for more than twenty years without being touched or criticized, and when Uthman succeeded to the caliphate of the Muslims, he added to his authority further districts and regions, which**

1 *Al-Bidāyah wa al-Nihāyah*, vol. 8, p. 128.

2 Ibid.

> **enabled him to a mass great wealth from the Islamic nation and to raise armies to rebel against the Imam (Leader) of the nation and subsequently take the full power by force and intimidation. Thus he became the sole ruler of all Muslims, and later forced them to vote for his corrupt and alcohol drinking son Yazid, as his heir and successor."**

Our comment:

In one sentence Tījānī contradicts himself. He just told us despite numerous complaints which were raised against Muʿāwiyah رضي الله عنه, ʿUmar رضي الله عنه did nothing. He now tells us that Muʿāwiyah رضي الله عنه was never criticized. If Tījānī stated from the outset that he dislikes the Ṣaḥābah for whatever reasons he presented, it would have been easier for him to compose his thoughts since he would have begun from a position of honesty. However, Tījānī chose the strategy of convincing his readers through a narrative that is meant to reflect his journey. The truth is that there was no journey since Tījānī constantly contradicts himself, cites false references, and invents history as he goes along. This contradiction is evidence of that.

There is no blame upon ʿUmar or ʿUthmān رضي الله عنهما for appointing Muʿāwiyah رضي الله عنه over Syria. The Prophet صلى الله عليه وسلم appointed his father, Abū Sufyān, over Najrān which lasted until the Prophet's صلى الله عليه وسلم demise. In fact, many of the Prophet's صلى الله عليه وسلم governors were from Banū Umayyah.

He appointed ʿAttāb ibn Usayd ibn Abū al-ʿĀṣ ibn Umayyah over Makkah, and he placed Khālid ibn Saʿīd ibn al-ʿĀṣ ibn Umayyah in charge of the charities of Madhḥaj and Ṣanʿā of Yemen, and he remained in that position until the Prophet صلى الله عليه وسلم passed away. He appointed ʿAmr as the governor of Taymā and Khaybar and the villages of ʿUraynah, and he appointed Abān ibn Saʿīd ibn al-ʿĀṣ as the governor of Baḥrayn, its land and its ocean, when he removed ʿAlā ibn al-Ḥaḍramī (from that position), and he remained in that position until the Prophet صلى الله عليه وسلم passed away, and before that he appointed him as the leader of a number of military expeditions from amongst them was the expedition to Najd.[1]

When Muʿāwiyah رضي الله عنه became the governor of Syria his manner of governance and interaction with his citizens was exemplary and his citizens loved him and he loved them.

---

1 *Minhāj al-Sunnah*, vol. 4 p. 460.

> Qubayṣāh ibn Jābir says, "I never saw anyone more forbearing and more dignified and more tolerant and more lenient and more open handed than Muʿāwiyah."
>
> Some people report that a man said some nasty and stern words to Muʿāwiyah. It was said to him, "Why do you not deal with him?" He said, "I feel embarrassed by Allah that my forbearance does not extend beyond the wrongs of one of my citizens."
>
> In one narration it mentions that a man said to him, "What makes you so forbearing?" He replied, "I am embarrassed that someone's crime can be greater than my forbearance."[1]

It is for that reason that they responded to him when he demanded retaliation against the killing of ʿUthmān رضي الله عنه and they gave him their pledge and trusted him with their lives and their wealth for that cause.

There remains Tījānī's claim that Muʿāwiyah رضي الله عنه took control of the economy and mobilised the armies and the Bedouin Arabs to stand up in rebellion against the Imām of the Ummah, and that he seized control of the governorship by force, and ruled oppressively over the Muslim. This is one of the many forgeries against Muʿāwiyah رضي الله عنه. He was certainly not desirous of leadership nor did he object to the legitimacy of ʿAlī ibn Abī Ṭālib's رضي الله عنه Khilāfah. All that he insisted on was that the killers of ʿUthmān رضي الله عنه be handed over to him, after which he would submit to ʿAlī رضي الله عنه.

Al-Dhahabī relates in his *Siyar*, from Yaʿlā ibn ʿUbayd, from his father, who said:

> Abū Muslim al-Khawlānī, and a group of people with him, came to Muʿāwiyah and said to him, "Are you contesting ʿAlī's right to the khilāfah or are you similar to him?"
>
> Muʿāwiyah said, "No, by Allah I know that ʿAlī is better than me and that he is more entitled to the leadership than me. However, do you not know that ʿUthmān was killed unjustly? I am his cousin and I am simply seeking retributivist punishment for ʿUthmān. So go to him and say that he should hand over to me ʿUthmān's killers and I will submit to him."

---

1 *Al-Bidāyah wa al-Nihāyah*, vol. 8 p. 138.

> They then went to ʿAlī and spoke to him concerning that (Muʿāwiyah's comments) but he did not hand them over to him.[1]

Muʿāwiyah continuously emphasised this sentiment with these words, "I only fought ʿAlī because of ʿUthmān's situation."

This is confirmed by ʿAlī from Twelver Shīʿah sources. Al-Sharīf al-Raḍī, in his book *Nahj al-Balāghah*, relates one of ʿAlī's sermons as follows:

> Our matter started when we met the people of Syria. What is clear is that our Lord is the same, our Prophet is the same, and our call to Islam is the same. We do not expect more from them in respect of their belief in Allah and their belief in the Messenger, and they do not expect more from us in terms of our belief in Allah and belief in the Messenger. There is only one issue in which we differ and that is concerning the blood of ʿUthmān, and we are innocent of it.[2]

Here ʿAlī رضي الله عنه emphasises that the only contention between him and Muʿāwiyah رضي الله عنه was concerning ʿUthmān's رضي الله عنه murder, not about the khilāfah or ruling with tyranny over the Muslims as Tījānī claims.

Tījānī asserts that Muʿāwiyah رضي الله عنه forced the Muslims to give their pledge to his drunkard son, Yazīd. This is a bold attempt at cloaking falsehood with the garb of truth. The blatant lie is that Muʿāwiyah did not coerce the people into giving their pledge to his son Yazīd. Rather, he sought to take the pledge from the people in order for Yazīd to be the heir apparent for the khilāfah and that is what occurred. Were it a case of coercion there would have been no excuse for the likes of ʿAbd Allāh ibn ʿUmar, Ḥusayn ibn ʿAlī, and ʿAbd Allāh ibn Zubayr رضي الله عنهم who withheld their pledge and were left to be. It was only after Muʿāwiyah's رضي الله عنه demise that Yazīd's governors began demanding that they pledge their allegiance.

It is disputed whether Yazīd was a drunkard and open sinner. There is no harm in presenting the testimony of Muḥammad ibn ʿAlī ibn Abī Ṭālib he lived during the reign of Yazīd and would certainly have more insight about him. Ibn Kathīr says in *al-Bidāyah*:

---

1 *Siyar Aʿlām al-Nubalāʾ*, vol. 3 p 140, the examiner of the books says, "Its transmitters are reliable."
2 *Nahj al-Balāghah*, vol. 3 p. 648.

When the people of Madīnah returned from Yazīd, ʿAbd Allāh ibn Muṭīʿ and his companions went to Muḥammad ibn al-Ḥanafiyyah with the intention of removing Yazīd (from office) but he refused.

Ibn Muṭīʿ said, "Indeed, Yazīd consumes alcohol, neglects the ṣalāh, and transgresses the command of the Book (of Allah)."

He said to them, "I did not see (from my time with him) what you are mentioning as I visited him and stayed with him. In fact, I saw him regular with ṣalāh, searching for good, asking about fiqh and holding to the Sunnah."

They said, "Indeed, that was pretentious from his side."

He said, "What does he fear or hope for that would cause him to display such humility to me? Did he openly display to you what you mentioned about drinking alcohol? If he was open about it with you then you are his partners in that (crime). If he did not display that to you, then it is not permissible for you to testify about what you do not know."

They said, "We consider that to be the truth even if we did not see it."

He said, "Allah refused that from the people who provide testimony. He says:

إِلَّا مَنْ شَهِدَ بِالْحَقِّ وَهُمْ يَعْلَمُوْنَ

But only those who testify to the truth [can benefit], and they know.[1]

(Muḥammad ibn ʿAlī continues) I am not at all with you."

They said, "Perhaps you dislike that someone besides you takes control of the matter (the khilāfah) therefore we entrust you with our matter."

He said, "What you ask of me, whether as a follower or a leader, I do not consider it permissible to fight for."

They said, "You fought with your father!"

He said, "Bring me someone similar to my father and for something similar to what he fought for!"

They said, "Then instruct your sons Abū al-Qāsim and Qāsim to fight with us!"

He said, "Had I instructed them, then I would fight."

1 Sūrah al-Zukhruf: 86.

They said, "Then stand with us so that we may encourage the people to fight!"

He said, "Subḥān Allāh! Should I command the people to do something I will not do and I am not pleased with? Then I have not displayed good towards the people for the sake of Allah."

They said, "Then we will force you!"

He said, "Then I will instruct the people to fear Allah and not to be obedient to the creation at the expense of the Creator." Then he left for Makkah.[1]

1. Tījānī accuses Muʿāwiyah of initiating the cursing of ʿAlī.

Tījānī says:

I looked for the reasons which led those Companions to change the Sunnah [the tradition] of the Messenger of Allah صَلَّى ٱللَّهُ عَلَيْهِ وَسَلَّمَ, and found that the Umayyads (and most of them were Companions of the Prophet صَلَّى ٱللَّهُ عَلَيْهِ وَسَلَّمَ) and Muawiah ibn Abi Sufian (writer of the revelation, as he was called) in particular used to force people to swear at Ali ibn Abi Talib and curse him from the pulpits of the mosques, as most of the historians have mentioned in their books.

Muslim, in his *Sahih*, wrote in a chapter entitled, "The virtues of Ali ibn Abi Talib", the following: Muawiah ordered his governors everywhere to take the curse [of Ali ibn Abi Talib] as tradition, and that all the speakers must include it in their speeches.[2]

He says at another place:

How could they judge him as a man who had worked hard to promote Islam and to reward him, after he forced the people to curse Ali and Ahl al- Bayt, the Family of the chosen Prophet (Muḥammad صَلَّى ٱللَّهُ عَلَيْهِ وَسَلَّمَ)?[3]

At another place he says:

He was the one who forced people to curse Ali and Ahl al-Bayt, the offspring of the Prophet, in every mosque, so that it became a followed tradition for sixty years.[4]

---

1 *Al-Bidāyah wa al-Nihāyah*, vol. 8 p. 236.

2 *Then I was guided*, p. 105.

3 Ibid. p. 122.

4 Ibid. p. 169.

Refuting Tījānī's accusation that Muʿāwiyah initiated the cursing of ʿAlī.

Tījānī displays little shame when he lies about Muʿāwiyah رضي الله عنه. There is absolutely no evidence to suggest that Muʿāwiyah رضي الله عنه was responsible for the despicable practise of cursing ʿAlī رضي الله عنه.

One cannot rely on the books of history blindly, especially when there was little care in regard to distinguishing the reliable narrations from the unreliable. The matter becomes more questionable when the historians who narrate something of this nature happen to be Shīʿah. Al-Ṭabarī says in the introduction of his work on history:

> The reader should know that with respect to all I have mentioned, and made it a condition to set down in this book of ours, I rely upon traditions and reports which I have transmitted and which I attribute to their transmitters. I rely only very exceptionally upon what is learned through rational arguments and produced by internal thought processes. For no knowledge of the history of men of the past, and of recent men and events, is attainable by those who were not able to observe them and did not live in their time, except through information and transmission provided by informants and transmitters. This knowledge cannot be brought out by reason or produced by internal thought processes. Therefore, any report in this book of mine which may (be found to) contain some information, mentioned by us on the authority of certain men of the past, which the reader may disapprove of, and the listener may find detestable, because he can find nothing sound, and there is no sense in it then let him know that it is not our fault that such information comes to him. Rather, it comes from some of those who transmitted it to us and I simply transmitted that in the manner it was transmitted to me.[1]

Therefore, any argument forwarded by Tījānī which relies on any book of history ought to be scrutinised in terms of its reliability. It is imperative that he mentions the exact narration which says that Muʿāwiyah رضي الله عنه instructed the people to curse ʿAlī رضي الله عنه from the pulpits. It is not sufficient to merely attribute this view to al-Ṭabarī.

Tījānī rests his case on a narration which appears in *Ṣaḥīḥ Muslim* under the chapter of the merits of ʿAlī رضي الله عنه. The narration in *Ṣaḥīḥ Muslim* is sound but Tījānī's

1 *Tārīkh al-Ṭabarī*, the Muqaddimah (introduction) p. 13.

distorted version of it is not; and the translators made sure of further distortion when rendering it into English. The narration under discussion is what ʿĀmir ibn Saʿd ibn Abī Waqqāṣ narrates from his father, who said:

أمر معاوية بن أبي سفيان سعدا فقال ما منعك أن تسب أبا التراب فقال أما ما ذكرت ثلاثا قالهن له رسول الله صلى الله عليه وسلم فلن أسبه لأن تكون لي واحدة منهن أحب إلي من حمر النعم سمعت رسول الله صلى الله عليه وسلم يقول له خلفه في بعض مغازيه فقال له علي يا رسول الله خلفتني مع النساء والصبيان فقال له رسول الله صلى الله عليه وسلم أما ترضى أن تكون مني بمنزلة هارون من موسى إلا أنه لا نبوة بعدي وسمعته يقول يوم خيبر لأعطين الراية رجلا يحب الله ورسوله ويحبه الله ورسوله قال فتطاولنا لها فقال ادعوا لي عليا فأتي به أرمد فبصق في عينه ودفع الراية إليه ففتح الله عليه ولما نزلت هذه الآية فقل تعالوا ندع أبناءنا وأبناءكم دعا رسول الله صلى الله عليه وسلم عليا وفاطمة وحسنا وحسينا فقال اللهم هؤلاء أهلي

Muʿāwiyah called for Saʿd and said, "What prevents you from abusing Abū al-Turāb?"

Thereupon he said, "It is because of three things which I remember Allah's Messenger ﷺ having said about him that I would not abuse him, and even if I find one of those three things for me, it would be dearer to me than red camels. I heard Allah's Messenger ﷺ say about ʿAlī as he left him behind in one of his campaigns. ʿAlī said to him, 'O Messenger of Allah, you leave me behind along with women and children?' Thereupon Allah's Messenger ﷺ said to him, 'Are you not pleased with being unto me what Hārūn was unto Mūsā but with this exception that there is no prophet after me.' And I (also) heard him say on the Day of Khaybar, 'I would certainly give this standard to a person who loves Allah and his Messenger, and Allah and his Messenger love him too.' We had been anxiously waiting for it, when he (the Prophet) said, 'Call ʿAlī,' he was called and his eyes were inflamed. He applied saliva to his eyes and handed over the standard to him, and Allah gave him victory. (The third occasion is this) when the (following) verse was revealed:

فَقُلْ تَعَالَوْا نَدْعُ أَبْنَآءَنَا وَأَبْنَآءَكُمْ

Let us summon our children and your children.[1]

> Allah's Messenger called ʿAlī, Fāṭimah, Ḥasan, and Ḥusayn and said, 'O Allah, they are my family.'"

This ḥadīth does not state that Muʿāwiyah instructed Saʿd to curse ʿAlī. Rather, as is apparent, Muʿāwiyah wanted to know what prevents him from abusing ʿAlī. Thereupon, Saʿd provided the reason. When Muʿāwiyah heard Saʿd's response he did not become angry or punished him. In fact Muʿāwiyah's silence is confirmation that he approved of Saʿd's view. If Muʿāwiyah was a tyrant, coercing the people to curse ʿAlī رضي الله عنه, as Tījānī claims, then he would not have remained silent and he would have coerced Saʿd into cursing him. However, that did not occur and therefore it is known that he was not instructed to curse and that he was not pleased with that.

Al-Nawawī says:

> This statement of Muʿāwiyah does not clearly mean that he requested him to curse ʿAlī. Rather, he asked the reason that prevents him from cursing. It is as if he is saying: Have you withheld out of piety, fear, or any other reason; so if it is out of piety and reverence for him then you have adopted the correct policy and if for any other reason there is a different response.
>
> Or perhaps Saʿd was with a group who used to curse but refrained from cursing and was not in a position to rebuke them so he asked the question prompting him, and thus providing the opportunity to object to those who were cursing.
>
> Some have said that it has the potential for an alternative interpretation and that it means why did you not object to his Ijtihād and make apparent to the people the correctness of our opinion and Ijtihād?[2]

Al-Qurṭubī said in *al-Mufhim*:

> This is not clear in that Muʿāwiyah demanded that ʿAlī be cursed. Instead it was a question regarding what was holding him back from doing so, so that Saʿd could bring out ʿAlī's virtues or praise for him as was clear from his response. When Muʿāwiyah remained silent after hearing Saʿd's response, he acknowledged the truth of what it was.[3]

---

1 Sūrah Āl ʿImrān: 61.

2 Op. cit. p. 250-252.

3 *Al-Mufhim* vol. 6 p. 276.

2. Tījānī's claim that Muʿāwiyah was not one of the Prophet's ﷺ scribes

He says:

> **And how could they call him "The writer of the Revelations" since the revelation came upon the Messenger of Allah ﷺ for twenty-three years, and Muawiyah was a polytheist for the first eleven years of them, and later, when he was converted to Islam, did not live in Medina (for we could not find any historical reference to support that), whereas the Messenger of Allah ﷺ did not live in Mecca after al-Fath [the conquer of Mecca by the Muslims]? So how could Muawiya manage to write the Revelation?[1]**

Refuting Tījānī's claim that Muʿāwiyah was not one of the Prophet's ﷺ scribes

The issue of Muʿāwiyah being one of the Prophet's ﷺ scribes is an established fact. Imām Muslim narrates in his *Ṣaḥīḥ* from Ibn ʿAbbās رضي الله عنه that Abū Sufyān رضي الله عنه made three requests to the Prophet ﷺ, one of them being:

قال ومعاوية تجعله كاتبا بين يديك. قال نعم

> He said, "And Muʿāwiyah, make him a scribe of yours."
>
> The Prophet responded, "Yes"

Aḥmad, in his *Musnad*, and Muslim in his *Ṣaḥīḥ*, narrate from Ibn ʿAbbās, who said:

> I was a young boy running around with the other children when the Messenger of Allah ﷺ happened to approach us from behind, I assumed that he did not seek anyone but me so I ran and hid behind a door of a house and I did not realise until suddenly he embraced me. He patted me between my shoulders and said, "Go and call Muʿāwiyah for me," and he [Muʿāwiyah] was his scribe, so I ran and said, "Respond to the call of the Messenger of Allah as he seeks you."[2]

Both these narrations confirm that Muʿāwiyah رضي الله عنه was one of the Prophet's scribes.

Tījānī goes on to state:

---

1 Ibid. p. 169.

2 *Musnad Aḥmad*, vol. 1, *Musnad Ibn ʿAbbās*, Ḥadīth no. 2618; *Ṣaḥīḥ Muslim* with the commentary, Kitāb al-Birr wa al-Ṣilah, Ḥadīth no. 2603.

> **When he embraced Islam after the Conquest of Makkah we did not come across a single narration that says he stayed in Madīnah, while the Prophet ﷺ did not reside in Makkah after the Conquest.**

Our comment:

Tījānī's glaring errors about history in general and about the Prophet's ﷺ sīrah specifically, ought to raise suspicion in the mind of any objective reader. It is very clear that Muʿāwiyah رضي الله عنه took up residence in Madīnah.

Fāṭimah bint Qays رضي الله عنها says:

> When I became lawful [for marriage] I mentioned to him [the Prophet ﷺ] that both Muʿāwiyah ibn Abī Sufyān and Abū Jahm have both proposed for me [in marriage] so the Messenger of Allah ﷺ said, "As for Abū Jahm he does not put his staff down from his shoulder, and as for Muʿāwiyah he is destitute and he does not have much wealth; marry Usāmah ibn Zayd [instead]..."[1]

Fāṭimah bint Qays was one of the early emigrants to Madīnah. None of the Muhājirīn returned to Makkah as a resident during the Prophet's ﷺ lifetime. This proposal would only have been possible if Muʿāwiyah رضي الله عنه was a resident of Madīnah.

However, it appears Tījānī understood that the Prophet ﷺ instructed Ibn ʿAbbās to call Muʿāwiyah from Makkah! Tījānī is not to be faulted for his statement, "*I did not come across a single narration*," as he spoke the truth: He did not search for it in the first place! It is from Allah that we seek protection from such 'objectivity'.

3. Tījānī's claim that Muʿāwiyah had Ḥujr ibn ʿAdī executed because he refused to curse ʿAlī

Tījānī says:

> **When some of the Companions protested very strongly against such a rule, Muawiah ordered their killing and burning. Among the famous Companions who were killed at the order of Muawiah were Hijr ibn Adi al-Kindi and his followers, because they protested and refused to curse Ali, and some of them were buried alive.[2]**

---

1 *Ṣaḥīh Muslim*, Kitāb al-Ṭalāq, Ḥadīth no. 1480.

2 *Then I was guided*, p. 105.

At another place he says:

> **How could they judge him as a promoter of Islam when he killed Hijr Ibn Adi and his companions and buried them in Marj Adhra in the Syrian desert because they refused to curse Ali ibn Abi Talib?[1]**

Refuting Tījānī's claim that Muʿāwiyah had Ḥujr ibn ʿAdī executed because he refused to curse ʿAlī

There is a difference of opinion regarding the status of Ḥujr ibn ʿAdī, whether he is a *Ṣaḥābī* (Companion) or a *Tābiʿī* (Follower). Ibn Saʿd has mentioned him in the fourth category of Companions and has mentioned that he had once visited the Prophet ﷺ. Thereafter he mentioned him in the first category of Tābiʿīn of the people of Kūfah. Al-Bukhārī, Ibn Abī Ḥātim, Khalīfah ibn Khayyāṭ, and Ibn Ḥibbān all mention him among the Tābiʿīn. Abū Aḥmad al-ʿAskarī has said, "Majority of the scholars of Ḥadīth do not consider him to be from the Companions."[2]

Muʿāwiyah رضي الله عنه did not kill Ḥujr because he refused to curse ʿAlī رضي الله عنه. This is a blatant mistruth. The historians discuss the cause of Ḥujr's death that Ziyād, the Amīr of Kūfah, by Muʿāwiyah's appointment[3], gave a lengthy sermon and Ḥujr ibn ʿAdī yelled out, 'Ṣalāh!' However, Ziyād continued with the sermon and Ḥujr and his companions began pelting him with stones. Ziyād then wrote to Muʿāwiyah about the disturbance caused by Ḥujr and his companions, since Ḥujr had done this before to the person who governed Kūfah before Ziyād. Muʿāwiyah then commanded that Ḥujr be sent to him, and when he arrived he instructed that he be executed. The reason for Muʿāwiyah's firmness in the execution of Ḥujr was that Ḥujr's behaviour could be the catalyst for a second rebellion against the leader of the community, and this would result once again in polarizing the Muslim community. Muʿāwiyah رضي الله عنه regarded it as provoking sedition. This was of serious concern since Kūfah was the city where some of the rebels against ʿUthmān رضي الله عنه had emerged from. ʿUthmān's رضي الله عنه leniency in this matter led to his murder. This resulted in bloodshed and brought about great civil strife in the Ummah. Indeed, Muʿāwiyah رضي الله عنه sought to 'nip the fitnah in the bud' with the execution of Ḥujr.

---

1 Ibid. p. 121.

2 *Al-Ṭabaqāt* vol. 6 p. 217, *al-Bidāyah wal-Nihāyah* vol. 11 p. 228 and *al-Iṣābah* vol. 1 p. 313.

3 The ummah at this point in history had submitted to Muʿāwiyah's رضي الله عنه khilāfah and they were safe from civil strife.

4. Tījānī's claim that Ḥasan al-Baṣrī disparaged Muʿāwiyah

Tījānī says:

> **Abu al-Aala al-Mawdudi wrote in his book "*Caliphate and Kingdom*": Abu al-Ḥasan al-Basri said:**
>
> **Muawiah had four features, and if he had only one of them, it would have been considered a great sin:**
>
> 1. **Making decisions without consulting the Companions, who were the light of virtues.**
> 2. **Designating his son as his successor. His son was a drunkard, corrupt and wore silk.**
> 3. **He claimed Ziyad [as his son], and the Messenger of Allah ﷺ said, "There is offspring for the honourable woman, but there is nothing for the whore."**
> 4. **His killing of Hijr and his followers. Woe unto him from Hijr and the followers of Hijr.**[1]

Refuting Tījānī's claim that Ḥasan al-Baṣrī disparaged Muʿāwiyah

This narration revolves around Abū Mikhnaf.[2] Abū Mikhnaf is Lūṭ ibn Yaḥyā al-Azdī al-Kūfī a prominent forger and liar.

Al-Dhahabī and Ibn Ḥajar say about him:

> A ruined historian who should not be trusted.[3]

Ibn Ḥajar says:

> Abū Ḥātim, and others, abandoned him.
>
> Al-Dāraquṭnī says, "Weak!"
>
> Ibn Maʿīn says, "He is definitely not reliable." (On one occasion he said,) He is not worth much as a transmitter."
>
> Ibn ʿAdī says, "He is a Shīʿī innovator."[4]

---

1 *Then I was guided*, p. 105-106.

2 Refer to *al-Ṭabarī*, vol. 3 p. 232, the year 51 A.H.

3 al-Dhahabī: *Mīzān al-Iʿtidāl*, vol. 3 p. 419, biography no. 6992; Also *Lisān al-Mīzān* by Ibn Ḥajar, vol. 4 p. 492.

4 *Mīzān al-Iʿtidāl* by al-Dhahabī, vol. 3 p. 419-420.

Al-Uqaylī counts him amongst the weak narrators.[1] Therefore, this narration is baseless.

The study of its text further indicates an inherent flaw in this narration. The assertion that Muʿāwiyah رضي الله عنه assumed leadership without any consultation is false. We know this since Ḥasan ibn ʿAlī رضي الله عنهما abdicated in favour of Muʿāwiyah رضي الله عنه, and the entire Ummah pledged allegiance to him. If they pledged allegiance to him whilst he was unqualified it would be an indictment on them and not him. The person who ought to bear the greatest responsibility in this regard would be Ḥasan ibn ʿAlī رضي الله عنه.

The ḥadīth of reconciliation between Ḥasan ibn ʿAlī and Muʿāwiyah رضي الله عنهم has been narrated by way of Ḥasan al-Baṣrī. Why would he narrate a ḥadīth wherein the Prophet صلى الله عليه وسلم praised a reconciliation which resulted in the appointment of a condemned individual as Khalīfah?

Qatādah relates from Ḥasan al-Baṣrī that some people had testified that Muʿāwiyah رضي الله عنه and his companions are in the Fire. He said, "May Allah curse them! What gives them the idea that he is in the Fire?"[2]

The narration provided by Tījānī is thus evidently a lie that has been carefully placed in the mouth of Ḥasan al-Baṣrī. It is flawed not only because it is only narrated by way of Lūṭ ibn Yaḥyā, Abū Mikhnaf the famous forger, but it contradicts that which has been accurately ascribed to Ḥasan al-Baṣrī in terms of his stance on Muʿāwiyah رضي الله عنه. We also learn the extent of desperation in Ṣaḥābah-haters like Tījānī, they have to resort to lies and forgery to argue their case!

5. Tījānī's perspective of Muʿāwiyah during the Fitnah

Tījānī says:

> **When we ask some of our scholars about Muawiah's war against Ali, who had been acknowledged by al-Muhajireen and al-Ansar, a war which led to the division of Islam into Sunnis and Shiites and left it scarred to this very day, they simply answer by saying, "Ali and Muawiah were both good Companions, and both of them interpreted Islam in his own way. However, Ali was right, therefore he deserves two rewards, but Muawiah got it wrong,**

1 al-ʿUqaylī: *Al-Ḍuʿafāʾ*, vol. 4 p. 18-19, biography no. 1572.

2 *Al-Sharīʿah* vol. 5 p. 2468; *Tārīkh Dimashq* vol. 59 p. 206.

therefore, he deserves one reward. It is not within our right to judge for them or against them, Allah- the Most High - said:

تِلْكَ أُمَّةٌ قَدْ خَلَتْ لَهَا مَا كَسَبَتْ وَلَكُم مَّا كَسَبْتُمْ وَلَا تُسْأَلُونَ عَمَّا كَانُوا يَعْمَلُونَ

***That was a nation which has passed on. It will have [the consequence of] what it earned and you will have what you have earned. And you will not be asked about what they used to do.*[1]**

Regrettably, we provide such weak answers that neither a sensible mind nor a religion, nor indeed a law would accept. O Allah, I am innocent of idle talk and of deviant whims. I beg You to protect me from the devil's touch.

How could a sensible mind accept that Muawiah had worked hard to interpret Islam and give him one reward for his war against the leader of all Muslims, and for his killing of thousands of innocent believers, in addition to all the crimes that he committed? He was known among the historians for killing his opponents through feeding them poisoned honey, and he used to say, "Allah has soldiers made of honey."

How could these people judge him as a man who worked hard to promote Islam and give him a reward for that, when he was the leader of a wrong faction? There is a well-known Ḥadīth of the Prophet ﷺ, and most of the scholars agree its authenticity, "Woe unto Ammar ... he will be killed by the wrong faction." And he was killed by Muawiah and his followers.

How could they judge him as a promoter of Islam when he killed Hijr Ibn Adi and his companions and buried them in Marj Adhra in the Syrian desert because they refused to curse Ali ibn Abi Talib?

How could they judge him a just Companion when he killed al-Ḥasan, leader of the Heaven's youth, by poisoning him?

How could they judge him as being correct after he had forced the nation to acknowledge him as a caliph and to accept his corrupt son Yazid as his successor, and to change the Shurah [consultative] system to a hereditary one?

How could they judge him as a man who had worked hard to promote Islam and to reward him, after he forced the people to curse Ali and Ahl al- Bayt, the Family of the chosen Prophet ﷺ, and killed those Companions who

1 Sūrah al-Baqarah: 134.

> **refused to do so, and made the act of cursing Ali a tradition? There is no power but in Allah, the Most High, the Great.**
>
> **The question crops up over and over again. Which faction was right, and which faction was wrong? Either, Ali and his followers were wrong, or Muawiah and his followers were wrong, and the Messenger of Allah ﷺ explained everything.**
>
> **In both cases, the proposition of the righteousness of all the Companions does not hold ground and is incompatible with logic.[1]**

Refuting Tījānī's perspective of Muʿāwiyah during the Fitnah

Tījānī's amazement at the explanation of the scholars of the Ahl al-Sunnah is an inexpensive escape from his prejudice. Would he display the same level of amazement if it were the Messenger ﷺ who suggested that both parties were upon guidance?

Al-Bukhārī narrates in his *Ṣaḥīḥ* by way of Abū Hurayrah that the Prophet ﷺ said:

لا تقوم الساعة حتى يقتتل فئتان دعواهما واحدة

> The last hour will not come until two groups fight one another,[2] their call will be the same.[3]

Muslim narrates in his *Ṣaḥīḥ* from Abū Saʿīd al-Khudrī رضي الله عنه, he said, the Messenger ﷺ said:

تمرق مارقة عند فرقة من المسلمين يقتلها أولى الطائفتين بالحق

> A faction will renegade at a time when there is division among the Muslims; and the party, among two parties, which is closer to the truth, will fight them.[4]

The narration of Abū Hurayrah رضي الله عنه is an explanation of what occurred between ʿAlī and Muʿāwiyah رضي الله عنهما; and there is no doubt that ʿAlī رضي الله عنه was closer to the

1 *Then I was guided*, p. 121-122.

2 Ibn Ḥajar says, "Intended thereby are those with ʿAlī and Muʿāwiyah when they fought at Ṣiffīn."*Fatḥ al-Bārī*, vol. 6 p. 713.

3 *Ṣaḥīḥ al-Bukhārī*, Kitāb al-Manāqib, Bāb ʿAlāmāt al-Nubuwwah fī al-Islām, Ḥadīth no. 3413.

4 *Ṣaḥīḥ Muslim* with the commentary, Kitāb al-Zakāh, Bāb Dhikr al-Khawārij wa Ṣifātihim, Ḥadīth no. 151.

truth than anyone else, and it was also ʿAlī رضي الله عنه who fought against the Khawārij renegades. In these narrations one finds a clear indication of the Islam of Muʿāwiyah رضي الله عنه since the Messenger of Allah صلى الله عليه وسلم said that 'Their call is one' and that 'the party closest to the truth among two parties' would fight the defectors. We understand that both parties sought the truth though they disputed about it.

Al-Nawawī has said in his commentary of *Muslim*:

> One finds that it contains an unequivocal pronouncement that both parties were believers; and they do not, on account of their fighting, exit the religion neither are they described with fisq [flagrant sin]; and this is our stance [i.e. the Ahl al-Sunnah].[1]

We have previously pointed out that Muʿāwiyah رضي الله عنه only fought ʿAlī رضي الله عنه because he considered himself the avenger of ʿUthmān رضي الله عنه due to him being a *Walī al-Dam* (blood heir). His position was the result of understanding that ʿUthmān رضي الله عنه was killed unjustly and the narrations describe those who rebelled against him as munāfiqīn. The ḥadīth under discussion is what al-Tirmidhī and Ibn Mājah narrate from ʿĀ'ishah رضي الله عنها, who said:

> قال رسول الله صلى الله عليه وسلم يا عثمان إن ولاك الله هذا الأمر يوما فأرادك المنافقون أن تخلع قميصك الذي قمصك الله فلا تخلعه يقول ذلك ثلاث مرات
>
> The Messenger صلى الله عليه وسلم said, "O ʿUthmān! If Allah should place you in charge of this matter one day and the munāfiqīn want you to remove your shirt which Allah clothed you with then do not remove it!" He said this thrice.[2]

Similarly, Kaʿb ibn Murrah confirmed this in front of Muʿāwiyah's رضي الله عنه army when he said:

> لولا حديث سمعته من رسول الله صلى الله عليه وسلم ما قمت وذكر الفتن فقربها فمر رجل مقنع في ثوب فقال هذا يومئذ على الهدى فقمت إليه فإذا هو عثمان بن عفان قال فأقبلت عليه بوجهه فقلت هذا قال نعم

---

1 *Al-Minhāj Sharḥ Ṣaḥīḥ Muslim*, vol. 7 p. 168.

2 *Sunan Ibn Mājah*, al-Muqaddimah, Bāb Faḍā'il Aṣḥāb al-Nabī صلى الله عليه وسلم, Ḥadīth no. 112; Refer also to *Ṣaḥīḥ Ibn Mājah*, Ḥadīth no. 90.

> Had it not been for a ḥadīth I heard from the Messenger ﷺ I would not have stood up! The Prophet ﷺ mentioned the trials and made them seem close by, then a man passed by wrapped in a shawl and he said, "This man on that day will be upon the truth." I rushed to him and it was ʿUthmān ibn ʿAffān. I turned his face towards him (the Prophet ﷺ) and asked, "This person?" and he replied, "Yes!"[1]

ʿAbd Allāh ibn Shaqīq ibn Murrah also narrates that the Prophet ﷺ said:

> Trials will erupt on this earth like the horns of the bull. Then a man clad in a robe passed by and the Messenger ﷺ said, "This man and his companions will be upon the truth on that day." So I rushed to him and uncovered his mask and I turned his face to the Messenger ﷺ and said, "O Messenger of Allah! Is it this person?" He said, "This is the person!" (ʿAbd Allāh said :) "And it was ʿUthmān ibn ʿAffān."[2]

Muʿāwiyah رضي الله عنه and his companions considered themselves upon the truth and guidance because of these narrations. When they found the rebels were embedded in ʿAlī's رضي الله عنه army they assumed it was permitted to fight them in light of the narrations they were aware of. This was a time of Fitnah, and the third force exploited the confusion.

It comes as no surprise that Muʿāwiyah's رضي الله عنه supporters said, "We will only give our pledge to someone who is fair to us and does not oppress us and if we give our pledge to ʿAlī, his people will oppress us in the same manner that they oppressed ʿUthmān. ʿAlī is unable to provide justice for us and therefore it is not compulsory upon us to give our pledge to someone who is unable to provide justice for us."[3]

They felt that since ʿUthmān's killers were in ʿAlī's army, and they were the oppressors who intended to transgress against us in the same manner that they transgressed against ʿUthmān رضي الله عنه, they will fight them in defence, in addition to the fact that they did not start the fight. This accounts for Muʿāwiyah رضي الله عنه and his comrades.

---

1 Narrated by al-Tirmidhī from Abū al-Ashʿath al-Ṣanʿānī, *Kitāb Al-Faḍā'il*, Ḥadīth no. 3704; Refer also to *Ṣaḥīḥ al-Tirmidhī*, Ḥadīth no. 2922.

2 Aḥmad: *Faḍā'il al-Ṣaḥābah*, vol. 1 p. 449-450, Ḥadīth no. 720, the examiner says, "its sanad is reliable."

3 Refer to *Minhāj al-Sunnah*, vol. 4 p. 384.

There was another group among the Ṣaḥābah who stayed out of the internal unrest because of narrations from the Prophet صلى الله عليه وسلم which encourage refraining from fighting. It was not mandatory or even recommended. For that reason, ʿImrān ibn Ḥuṣayn رضي الله عنه used to prohibit the sale of weapons during times of civil strife. He used to say, "Weapons are not sold during times of civil strife." This is also the view of Saʿd ibn Abī Waqqāṣ, Muḥammad ibn Maslamah, Ibn ʿUmar, Usāmah ibn Zayd رضي الله عنهم, and the majority of those who remained from the early Muhājirīn and the Anṣār[1] who avoided the fitnah and did not participate in the fighting. Therefore, many of the leaders of the Ahl al-Sunnah say:

> It is not a condition to fight the rebellious group as Allah did not order (us) to start the fight with them. Rather, he commanded us that when two groups are fighting one another to reconcile between them. Then if one of them transgresses against the other the transgressing group is fought.[2]

Therefore, Tījānī's claim that Muʿāwiyah was the one who called towards fighting ʿAlī is a blatant lie.

Ibn al-ʿArabī comments on this issue:

> That which will bring coolness to your chest is that the Prophet صلى الله عليه وسلم mentioned the communal strife and gave indications and warned about the Khawārij when he said, "The closest of the two groups to the truth..." so he explained that each of these two groups has an attachment with the truth; however the group of ʿAlī رضي الله عنه was closer to it. Allah says:
>
> وَإِنْ طَآئِفَتَانِ مِنَ الْمُؤْمِنِيْنَ اقْتَتَلُوْا فَأَصْلِحُوْا بَيْنَهُمَا فَإِنْ بَغَتْ إِحْدَاهُمَا عَلَى الْأُخْرَى فَقَاتِلُوا الَّتِي تَبْغِي حَتَّى تَفِيْٓءَ إِلَى أَمْرِ اللّٰهِ فَإِنْ فَآءَتْ فَأَصْلِحُوْا بَيْنَهُمَا بِالْعَدْلِ وَأَقْسِطُوْا إِنَّ اللّٰهَ يُحِبُّ الْمُقْسِطِيْنَ (٩) إِنَّمَا الْمُؤْمِنُوْنَ إِخْوَةٌ فَأَصْلِحُوْا بَيْنَ أَخَوَيْكُمْ وَاتَّقُوا اللّٰهَ لَعَلَّكُمْ تُرْحَمُوْنَ

1 Ibid. vol. 4 p. 391-391.

2 Ibid. vol. 4 p. 391.

> *If two groups of the believers fight each other, seek reconciliation between them. And if one of them commits aggression against the other, fight the one that commits aggression until it comes back to Allah's command. So if it comes back, seek reconciliation between them with fairness, and maintain justice. Surely Allah loves those who maintain justice."* [al-Ḥujurāt: 9]

> He did not exclude the rebellious party from the faith because their insubordination was on account of juristic interpretation; neither did He strip them of the description of brotherhood since He says after that "*Indeed the believers are brothers; so reconcile between your two brothers...*" [al-Ḥujurāt: 9]. The Messenger of Allah صلى الله عليه وسلم said of ʿAmmār, "The rebellious party will kill him," and he said with regards to Ḥasan رضي الله عنه, "This son of mine is a Sayyid; and perhaps Allah will bring about reconciliation at his hands between two major groups from the Muslims." So Ḥasan's رضي الله عنه part in all of this was that he abdicated and brought about reconciliation.[1]

Allah refers to both parties as brothers despite their fighting and rebelling against one another. For that reason, the Ahl al-Sunnah supplicates for mercy upon both groups as Allah says:

وَالَّذِينَ جَاءُوا مِنْ بَعْدِهِمْ يَقُولُونَ رَبَّنَا اغْفِرْ لَنَا وَلِإِخْوَانِنَا الَّذِينَ سَبَقُونَا
بِالْإِيمَانِ وَلَا تَجْعَلْ فِي قُلُوبِنَا غِلًّا لِلَّذِينَ آمَنُوا رَبَّنَا إِنَّكَ رَءُوفٌ رَحِيمٌ

And those who came after them, saying, "Our Lord, forgive us and our brothers who preceded us in faith and put not in our hearts (any) resentment toward those who have believed. Our Lord, indeed You are Kind and Merciful."[2]

Even if one were to assume that Muʿāwiyah رضي الله عنه was not motivated by Ijtihād, the oceans of Allah's mercy are vast and the doors of forgiveness had not been closed on him. Furthermore, Muʿāwiyah's رضي الله عنه actions after the truce all indicate a sense of piety which are a means of expiation of sins. Ibn Kathīr writes in *al-Bidāyah* from Miswar ibn Makhramah رضي الله عنه that he came to Muʿāwiyah رضي الله عنه. He says:

> When I entered upon him—the narrator says I think he said I greeted—he asked me, "What has come of your accusing the leaders, O Miswar?"

---

1 *Al-ʿAwāṣim min al-Qawāṣim*, vol. 1 p. 171-174.

2 Sūrah al-Ḥashr: 10.

I said, "Let us leave that aside; or let us discuss what I have come here for."

He said, "You shall speak what is on your chest."

Miswar said, "I did not leave anything with which I could fault him except that I told him about it."

Then he said, "I do not absolve myself from sins. Do you have sins that you fear destruction for yourself if Allah does not forgive you?"

I said, "Yes."

He said, "What makes you more deserving of hope in Allah's forgiveness than me? I swear by Allah, that which I take responsibility for with regards to resolving peoples disputes, upholding the penalties, engaging in jihād in the path of Allah, and the great matters which you cannot count, is much more than you have taken up on yourself. And I am upon a religion in which Allah accepts the good deeds and pardons the errors. And I swear by Allah, that whenever presented with a choice between Allah and others besides him I have always chosen Allah over anyone besides Him!"

Miswar said, "I reflected upon what he said and realised that he had proven his point to me in this discussion."

And whenever Miswar thought of him he would pray for him.[1]

Here Muʿāwiyah is elaborating the point raised earlier. He declares unapologetically that he was motivated by Allah's command and it was his Ijtihād that led him to do what he did. Even if it were not Ijtihād, surely he would have compensated for the wrong by the abundance of righteous deeds that he performed subsequent to the communal strife.

The ḥadīth, "Woe unto ʿAmmār. The rebellious group will kill him," is of the clearest proofs that ʿAlī was in the right. When the death of ʿAmmār reached ʿAmr ibn al-ʿĀṣ and his son, fear overwhelmed them. In the ḥadīth narrated by Aḥmad in the *Musnad* from Abū Bakr ibn Muḥammad ibn ʿAmr ibn Ḥazm, from his father, he said:

لما قتل عمار بن ياسر دخل عمرو بن حزم على عمرو بن العاص فقال قتل عمار وقد قال رسول الله صلى الله عليه وسلم تقتله الفئة الباغية فقام عمرو

1 *Al-Bidāyah wa al-Nihāyah*, vol. 7 p. 235.

بن العاص فزعا يرجع حتى دخل على معاوية فقال له معاوية ما شانك قال قتل عمار فقال معاوية قد قتل عمار فماذا قال عمرو سمعت رسول الله صلى الله عليه وسلم يقول تقتله الفئة الباغية فقال له معاوية دحضت في بولك أو نحن قتلناه إنما قتله علي وأصحابه جاؤوا به حتى القوه بين رماحنا أو قال بين سيوفنا

When ʿAmmār was killed, ʿAmr ibn Ḥazm went to see ʿAmr ibn al-ʿĀṣ and said, "ʿAmmār has been killed and the Messenger ﷺ said, 'The rebellious group will kill him.'"

Then ʿAmr ibn al-ʿĀṣ stood up anxiously saying, "To Allah we belong and unto Him shall we return," until he went to see Muʿāwiyah.

Muʿāwiyah said to him, "What is the matter with you?"

He said, "ʿAmmār has been killed."

Muʿāwiyah said, "What is it if ʿAmmār was killed?"

ʿAmr said, "I heard the Messenger ﷺ saying, 'The rebellious group will kill ʿAmmār.'"

Then Muʿāwiyah said to him, "You have slipped! Did we kill him? Rather, ʿAlī and his companions killed him. They brought him here and threw him between our arrows or swords." [1]

Then the people came out saying, "Those who brought ʿAmmār killed him," and confidence was restored within the army. The reason Muʿāwiyah رضي الله عنه interpreted this ḥadīth in this manner is because he could not imagine ʿUthmān's رضي الله عنه killers being upon the truth in light of the narrations which confirm that he was killed unjustly. Since ʿUthmān's رضي الله عنه killers were the wrongdoers there was no doubt in his mind that the rebellious group was within ʿAlī's رضي الله عنه army. However, the reality was somewhat different. While the transgressors might have formed part of ʿAlī's رضي الله عنه army, he remained the Khalīfah. It is imperative to obey the Khalīfah. Thus, ʿAmmār's رضي الله عنه death was a distinguishing marker to identify which party was in the right.

1 *Musnad al-Shāmiyyīn* from *Musnad al-Imām Aḥmad*, vol. 2, Musnad ʿAmr ibn al-ʿĀṣ, Ḥadīth no. 957, p. 163, the examiner says, "its transmitters are reliable."

Tījānī claims to find the truth with the Twelver Shīʿah school. One of the doctrines of the Twelver school is the infallibility of the Twelve Imāms. It is also a matter of consensus that Ḥasan رضي الله عنه, after having accepting the pledge from his people after his father passed away, abdicated in favour of Muʿāwiyah رضي الله عنه. If we assume Tījānī's perspective, any claim to follow sound reason is in jeopardy since the 'infallible' Imām surrendered the Khilāfah to Muʿāwiyah رضي الله عنه, which means that Muʿāwiyah's Khilāfah was valid according to the 'infallible' Imām, or the Imām is not infallible to begin with. For the Ahl al-Sunnah there is no problem since Ḥasan رضي الله عنه is not considered infallible, though his decision to abdicate in favour of Muʿāwiyah is the realisation of his grandfather's prophecy. The Prophet صلى الله عليه وسلم said, "This son of mine is a leader. Perhaps Allah will reconcile two groups of Muslims through him." Which view aligns with logic and reason?

Lastly, there is evidence in the Twelver Shīʿah books which confirms that ʿAlī and Muʿāwiyah رضي الله عنهما were both upon the truth and rewarded for their efforts. Surprisingly al-Kulaynī relates in al-Rawḍah min al-Kāfī, from Muḥammad ibn Yaḥyā, who said:

> I heard Abū ʿAbd Allāh al-Ṣādiq saying, "The dispute of the Banū al-ʿAbbās is inevitable, and the calling is inevitable, and the appearance of the al-Qā'im is inevitable."
>
> I said, "What is the calling?"
>
> He replied, "An announcer calls out at the beginning of the day, 'Indeed, ʿAlī and his supporters are the successful ones!'"
>
> He also said, "An announcer calls out at the end of the day, 'Indeed, ʿUthmān and his supporters are the successful ones!'"[1]

There is further evidence from the books of the Shīʿah where ʿAlī رضي الله عنه confirms that Muʿāwiyah رضي الله عنه and his supporters were believers and the fighting that resulted was one of scholarly discretion, each group believing itself to be upon the truth in terms of how it would deal with the murderers of ʿUthmān رضي الله عنه.

Al-Sharīf al-Raḍī mentions in *Nahj al-Balāghah* from ʿAlī رضي الله عنه that he said:

> Our matter started when we met the people of Syria. What is clear is that our Lord is the same, our Prophet is the same, and our call to Islam is the

---

1 *Rawḍah al-Kāfī*, vol. 8, p. 177.

> same. We do not request more from their belief in Allah and their belief in the Messenger, and they do not request more from us in terms of our belief in Allah and belief in the Messenger. There is only one issue in which we differ and that is concerning the blood of ʿUthmān and we are innocent of it.[1]

6. Tījānī's claim that Muʿāwiyah poisoned Ḥasan

Tījānī says:

> **How could they judge him a just Companion when he killed al-Ḥasan, leader of the Heaven's youth, by poisoning him?[2]**

He says at another place:

> **How could they judge him like that when he was the one who poisoned al-Ḥasan ibn Ali, leader of Heaven's youth? Perhaps they say, "This was an aspect of his Ijtihad [interpretation], but he got it wrong!"[3]**

Refuting Tījānī's claim that Muʿāwiyah poisoned Ḥasan

This claim is false for the following reasons:

No reliable evidence exists for this claim. The burden of proof lies with the one making the claim. The narrations that discuss Ḥasan's poisoning are unreliable. If we consider the fact that Ḥasan رضي الله عنه had an entire army behind him and still abdicated in favour of Muʿāwiyah رضي الله عنه, what would Muʿāwiyah رضي الله عنه have to fear that he had Ḥasan رضي الله عنه poisoned?

The correct policy, especially at the time of Fitnah, is to avoid suspicion. The historical reports, as weak as they are, only provide suspects and no culprits. On what grounds does Tījānī convert that suspicion into a conviction against Muʿāwiyah?

The person accused of poisoning Ḥasan رضي الله عنه was his wife. Some have suspected her father, al-Ashʿath ibn Qays, of instructing her to do so, and others have said it was Yazīd. This confusion about the one who poisoned Ḥasan رضي الله عنه indicates that the culprit cannot be identified or else there would have been no speculation.

---

1 *Nahj al-Balāghah*, vol. 3 p. 648.

2 *Then I was guided*, p. 121.

3 *Then I was guided*, p. 169.

However, Tījānī's 'impartiality' led him to Muʿāwiyah رضي الله عنه directly.

Ibn al-ʿArabī said in *al-ʿAwāṣim min al-Qawāṣim* regarding the allegation that Muʿāwiyah رضي الله عنه poisoned al-Ḥasan رضي الله عنه:

> It is a matter of the unseen known only to Allah. How can you place the blame on Muʿāwiyah without any proof; especially after such a long time? We cannot rely on a spurious report that has been transmitted among people of innovation; especially during a time of Fitnah when each party ascribes to the next that which is inappropriate. So nothing will be accepted of [such reports] except that which is evidently clear, and it will not be accepted except from one with great moral integrity.[1]

He states further:

> If it is said he secretly conspired to have Ḥasan poisoned, we say that this claim is far-fetched for two reasons, one of them was the fact that Ḥasan handed over the Khilāfah willingly and there was no incentive for Muʿāwiyah to have Ḥasan killed. Secondly the narration mentioning it is unreliable and a number of scholars have identified flaws in the narration.[2]

7. Tījānī's claim that Muʿāwiyah altered the Khilāfah from shūrā to monarchy

Tījānī says:

> **How could they judge him as being correct after he had forced the nation to acknowledge him as a caliph and to accept his corrupt son Yazid as his successor, and to change the Shurah [consultative] system to a hereditary one?[3]**

He says at another place:

> **After Ali, Muawiya took over the caliphate and changed it to a hereditary system within Bani Umayya, and after them came Bani al-Abbas where the caliphs succeeded one after the other either by personal nomination [from the previous caliph] or by means of force and seizure of power. From the beginning of the Islamic era until Kamal Ataturk - who abolished the**

---

1 *Al-ʿAwāṣim min al-Qawāṣim* vol. 1 p. 214.

2 Ibid.

3 *Then I was guided*, p. 121.

> **Islamic caliphate - there has been no correct acclamation except that for the Commander of the Believers Ali ibn Abi Talib.[1]**

He says at another place:

> **How could they judge his Ijtihad, when he was the one who took the nation's acclamation for himself by force, then gave it to his son Yazid after him, and changed the Shura system to a hereditary one?[2]**

Refuting Tījānī's claim that Muʿāwiyah altered the Khilāfah from shūrā to monarchy

Muʿāwiyah رضي الله عنه did not take the khilāfah by force. Rather, it was handed over to him by Ḥasan ibn ʿAlī after the reconciliation. It was the fruition of the Prophet's صلى الله عليه وسلم prediction when he said, "This son of mine is a leader. Perhaps Allah will reconcile two groups of Muslims through him."

Al-Bukhārī narrates in his *Ṣaḥīḥ* that Ḥasan al-Baṣrī said:

> استقبل والله الحسن بن علي معاوية بكتائب أمثال الجبال فقال عمرو بن العاص إني لأرى كتائب لا تولي حتى تقتل أقرانها فقال له معاوية وكان والله خير الرجلين أي عمرو إن قتل هؤلاء هؤلاء وهؤلاء هؤلاء من لي بأمور الناس من لي بنسائهم من لي بضيعتهم فبعث إليه رجلين من قريش من بني عبد شمس عبد الرحمن بن سمرة وعبد الله بن عامر بن كريز فقال اذهبا إلى هذا الرجل فاعرضا عليه وقولا له واطلبا إليه فأتياه فدخلا عليه فتكلما وقالا له فطلبا إليه فقال لهما الحسن بن علي إنا بنو عبد المطلب قد أصبنا من هذا المال وإن هذه الأمة قد عاثت في دمائها قالا فإنه يعرض عليك كذا وكذا ويطلب إليك ويسألك قال فمن لي بهذا قالا نحن لك به فما سألهما شيئا إلا قالا نحن لك به فصالحه فقال الحسن ولقد سمعت أبا بكرة يقول رأيت رسول الله صلى الله عليه وسلم على المنبر والحسن بن علي إلى جنبه وهو يقبل على الناس مرة وعليه أخرى ويقول إن ابني هذا سيد ولعل الله أن يصلح به بين فئتين عظيمتين من المسلمين

1 *Then I was guided*, p. 145.

2 *Then I was guided*, p. 169.

> Ḥasan faced Muʿāwiyah with military squadrons like mountains. Then ʿAmr said, "By Allah! I see military squadrons that will not turn back until they kill their opponents."
>
> Then Muʿāwiyah who was the better of the two men said, "O ʿAmr! If these people are killed then who will assist me with governing the people, who will assist me with their women, who will assist me with their vulnerable?"
>
> Then he sent to him two men from the Quraysh, from Banū ʿAbd al-Shams (tribe); ʿAbd al-Raḥmān al-Sumarah and ʿAbd Allāh ibn ʿĀmir ibn Kurayz. He said (to them), "Go to this man and present (the option of a peace treaty to him), and plea with him, and request it from him!" They went to him and got his audience and pleaded with him and requested from him.
>
> Ḥasan ibn ʿAlī said, "We are the Banū ʿAbd al-Muṭṭalib, we have acquired some of this wealth and this Ummah has squandered a lot of it in its blood."
>
> They said, "He offers you 'this and that' and requests from you 'this and that'."
>
> He said, "Who will guarantee for me this (the fulfilment of this agreement)?"
>
> They said, "We guarantee you that."
>
> Then he did not ask them anything except that they said, "We guarantee you that."
>
> Then he entered into the peace treaty with him. Ḥasan (al-Baṣrī) says, "I heard Abū Bakrah saying, 'I saw the Messenger صلى الله عليه وسلم on the mimbar while Ḥasan ibn ʿAlī was by his side. He faced the people and then faced Ḥasan and said, 'Indeed this son of mine is a leader. Perhaps Allah will reconcile between two groups of Muslims because of him.'"[1]

Tījānī's assertion that Muʿāwiyah رضي الله عنه forced people into acknowledging his Khilāfah is unfounded. How did he force Ḥasan رضي الله عنه, whereas Ḥasan رضي الله عنه had an entire army with him?

It is surprising that Tījānī accuses Muʿāwiyah رضي الله عنه of changing the Khilāfah and replacing it with monarchy since he does not acknowledge the validity of all the Khulafā' before Muʿāwiyah, nor does he approve of the manner of their appointment.

---

1 *Ṣaḥīḥ al-Bukhārī*, Kitāb al-Ṣulḥ, vol. 2, Ḥadīth no. 2557.

Safīnah رَضِيَ ٱللَّهُ عَنْهُ narrates that the Messenger صَلَّى ٱللَّهُ عَلَيْهِ وَسَلَّمَ said:

> Khilāfah will remain in my Ummah for thirty years, then it will become a monarchy after that.[1]

Ibn ʿAbbās رَضِيَ ٱللَّهُ عَنْهُ narrates that the Messenger صَلَّى ٱللَّهُ عَلَيْهِ وَسَلَّمَ said:

> The beginning of this affair is Prophethood and mercy, then it will be a Khilāfah and mercy, then monarchy and mercy, then leadership and mercy, then they will be biting each other for it as donkeys do, so it is your duty to engage in Jihād, and the best of your Jihād is in *Ribāṭ* [guarding the borders], and the best of your Ribāṭ is at *ʿAsqalān* [Ashkelon].[2]

Al-Haythamī commented saying, "Al-Ṭabarānī narrates it and the narrators are reliable."[3]

Ibn Taymiyyah responded to a question regarding Yazīd ibn Muʿāwiyah in *Jāmiʿ al-Masāʾil* saying:

> A wave of fitnahs emerged after the demise of Muʿāwiyah and disunity and fragmentation which is a confirmation of what the Prophet صَلَّى ٱللَّهُ عَلَيْهِ وَسَلَّمَ foretold since he said, "There will be Prophethood and mercy, then Khilāfah and mercy, then monarchy and mercy, then tyrannical monarchy." So the period of Prophethood was a period of mercy, as was the period of al-Khulafāʾ al-Rāshidūn, and the period of Muʿāwiyah's رَضِيَ ٱللَّهُ عَنْهُ rule was also a mercy, and after him began the cruel monarchy.[4]

He also said in his *Fatāwā*:

> By necessity the combination of Khilāfah and monarchy is allowed in our Sharīʿah, and that does not negate his moral, upright status; even though absolute Khilāfah is the best.[5]

With regards to the pledge of his son, Yazīd, no doubt Muʿāwiyah sought consent of the people. He consulted the Companions, and the leaders of the people, and the

---

1 *Musnad Aḥmad* vol. 5 p. 220, *Jāmiʿ al-Tirmidhī* Ḥadīth no. 2226, *Sunan Abī Dāwūd* Ḥadīth no. 4646, al-Nasāʾī in *al-Kubrā* Ḥadīth no. 8155.

2 *Al-Muʿjam al-Kabīr lil-Ṭabarānī* vol. 11 p. 88.

3 *Majmaʿ al-Zawāʾid* vol. 5 p. 190.

4 *Jāmiʿ al-Masāʾil* vol. 5 p. 154.

5 *Majmūʿ al-Fatāwa* vol. 35 p. 27.

governors of the provinces, and the consent came from most parts agreeing to the pledge for Yazīd. Many of the Companions gave their pledge to the point where al-Ḥāfiẓ ʿAbd al-Ghanī al-Maqdisī said:

> His khilāfah was valid. Sixty of the Ṣaḥābah gave their pledge including ʿAbd Allāh ibn ʿUmar.[1]

Also, it has been established in *Ṣaḥīḥ al-Bukhārī* that Ibn ʿUmar رضي الله عنه gave his pledge to Yazīd and when some civil strife arouse in Madīnah he gathered its people and warned them about rebelling against Yazīd. Nāfiʿ quotes him as having said:

> لما خلع أهل المدينة يزيد بن معاوية جمع ابن عمر حشمه وولده فقال إني سمعت النبي صلى الله عليه وسلم يقول ينصب لكل غادر لواء يوم القيامة وإنا قد بايعنا هذا الرجل على بيع الله ورسوله وإني لا أعلم غدرا أعظم من أن يبايع رجل على بيع الله ورسوله ثم ينصب له القتال وإني لا أعلم أحدا منكم خلعه ولا بايع في هذا الأمر إلا كانت الفيصل بيني وبينه
>
> When the people of Madīnah retracted their allegiance from Yazīd ibn Muʿāwiyah, Ibn ʿUmar gathered his servants and his children and said, "I heard the Messenger صلى الله عليه وسلم saying, 'A flag will be raised for every traitor on the Day of Judgement,' and indeed we gave our pledge to his man in the name of Allah and his Messenger صلى الله عليه وسلم. Certainly, I do not know of a treachery greater than a man giving his pledge of allegiance (to a man) in the name of Allah and the name of his Messenger صلى الله عليه وسلم then he starts a fight against him. Anyone amongst you who withdraws him (as his leader) and whoever follows this matter (the rebellion) it is the separation between him and me.[2]

There was opposition from Ibn al-Zubayr and Ḥusayn رضي الله عنهما, among others. No doubt Muʿāwiyah رضي الله عنه sought the consent of the Ummah for the pledge of succession for Yazīd. If Muʿāwiyah رضي الله عنه intended to rule autocratically and take the pledge for Yazīd by force, as Tījānī claims, he would have satisfied him with one pledge and forced it upon the people but Muʿāwiyah رضي الله عنه did not do that. Rather, those who opposed him opposed him but Muʿāwiyah رضي الله عنه did not take steps to coerce them upon the pledge.

---

1 Ibn Khaldūn: *Qayd al-Sharīd min Akhbār Yazīd*, p. 70.

2 *Ṣaḥīḥ al-Bukhārī*, Kitāb al-Ṣulḥ, vol. 2 Ḥadīth no. 2557.

Perhaps the reason for Mu'āwiyah رضي الله عنه taking the pledge for (the succession of) Yazīd was in order to avoid any further dispute and for the Ummah to maintain its stability. Therefore, he thought that appointing Yazīd was for the benefit of the Ummah and to remove the possibility of another fitnah with people contesting authority.

Lastly, what is indeed astonishing about Tījānī's rant is that the Rāfiḍah Ithnā 'Ashariyyah oppose, in principle, the standard of the shūrā and claim that it is necessary that the Prophet صلى الله عليه وسلم instated the leadership with a clear text. Indeed, Tījānī himself opposes the khilāfah of Abū Bakr, 'Umar, and 'Uthmān رضي الله عنهم, despite their appointment through shūrā. Why then does he pretend to cry about the shūrā system which he himself opposes? If Yazīd were to have been elected through shūrā would Tījānī and his Rāfiḍah brothers have accepted it? Or is the matter deliquescent to them? The answer is that they will never accept it even if the shūrā included all the Muslims. Why then is there this favouritism and false piety from Tījānī about the principle of shūrā?

Chapter Twelve

Tījānī's Criticisms of Abū Hurayrah

Abū Hurayrah رَضِيَ ٱللَّهُ عَنْهُ is the Companion of the Messenger صَلَّى ٱللَّهُ عَلَيْهِ وَسَلَّمَ who was most distinguished in terms of his phenomenal memory and the abundance of ḥadīth which he transmits. Despite the fact that he enjoyed the company of the Prophet صَلَّى ٱللَّهُ عَلَيْهِ وَسَلَّمَ for only a few years, Abū Hurayrah رَضِيَ ٱللَّهُ عَنْهُ clung to the Prophet صَلَّى ٱللَّهُ عَلَيْهِ وَسَلَّمَ whether at home or on a journey so that nothing of the Prophet's صَلَّى ٱللَّهُ عَلَيْهِ وَسَلَّمَ Sunnah would escape him. There is a difference of opinion among the scholars about his name, although the most famous is ʿAbd al-Raḥmān ibn Ṣakhr. Despite Abū Hurayrah's unrivalled contribution to Islam in terms of knowledge from the Prophet صَلَّى ٱللَّهُ عَلَيْهِ وَسَلَّمَ, he was not spared the wrath of the 'impartial researcher' who accuses him of forging aḥādīth against the Prophet صَلَّى ٱللَّهُ عَلَيْهِ وَسَلَّمَ. Some of the objections and criticisms against him will be listed below followed by the responses to them.

1. Tījānī's claims that Abū Hurayrah fabricated aḥādīth from the Prophet صَلَّى ٱللَّهُ عَلَيْهِ وَسَلَّمَ

Tījānī says:

> **Perhaps they assigned the second half of the religion to Abu Hurayrah, who told them what they wanted to hear, so they bestowed on him various honours: they gave him the governorship of al-Medinah, they gave him al-Aqiq palace and gave him the title of "Rawiat al-Islam" - the transmitter of Islam. He made it easy for the Umayyads to create a completely new religion which took whatever pleased them and supported their interests and power from the Holy Qur'an and the tradition of the Prophet صَلَّى ٱللَّهُ عَلَيْهِ وَسَلَّمَ.[1]**

He says at another place:

> **The virtues of Abu Bakr were also mentioned by Amr ibn al-'As, Abu Hurayrah...[2]**

He says also:

> **Then I read "Abu Hurayra" by Sharaf al-Din and Shaykh "al-Mudira" by Shaykh Mahmud Abu Rayyah al-Misri, and learnt that the Companions who**

1 *Then I was guided*, p. 120.

2 *Then I was guided*, p. 142.

changed after the departure of the Messenger of Allah ﷺ were two types. The first changed the rules because of its power and authority. The second changed the rules by attributing false Ḥadīths to the Messenger of Allah ﷺ.[1]

Refuting Tījānī's claims that Abū Hurayrah fabricated aḥādīth from the Prophet ﷺ

The assertion that Abū Hurayrah narrated aḥādīth in support of Banū Umayyah by virtue of which they compensated him by constructing a castle for and conferred upon him the title of Rāwiyat al-Islām is a blatant lie for a number of reasons:

a. Abū Hurayrah avoided the Fitnah and adopted a neutral position during these trying times. As a matter of fact he narrated some aḥādīth from the Prophet ﷺ which encourages seclusion at a time of communal strife. The following narration is a clear example of such aḥādīth:

ستكون فتن القاعد فيها خير من القائم والقائم خير من الماشي والماشي فيها خير من الساعي من تشرف لها تستشرفه فمن وجد ملجأ أو معاذا فليعذ به

> There will be tribulation. The one sitting when it occurs will be better off than the one standing, and the one standing will be better than the one walking, and the one walking will be better than the one running. The person who involves himself in it, it will overwhelm him. Therefore, the person who finds a shelter or a refuge let him take refuge in it.[2]

b. Abū Hurayrah رضي الله عنه only witnessed the era of Muʿāwiyah رضي الله عنه from the Umayyad rulers. He passed away before Yazīd assumed leadership. It is no surprise that Tījānī overlooks this considering his track record with Islamic history in general and the history of that period in particular. Furthermore, by the time that Muʿāwiyah رضي الله عنه became the Khalīfah Abū Hurayrah رضي الله عنه was not destitute, neither was his appointment over Madīnah the first time that he was tasked with governing. ʿUmar رضي الله عنه appointed him as governor

1 *Then I was guided*, p. 130.

2 *Ṣaḥīḥ al-Bukhārī*, Kitāb al-Fitan, Bāb Takūn Fitnah, al-Qāʿid fīha Khayr min al-Qāʾim, Ḥadīth no. 6670-6671.

over Baḥrayn during his era and by that time he had owned a considerable amount of wealth. Muḥammad ibn Sīrīn relates:

> ʿUmar appointed Abū Hurayrah as governor of Baḥrayn. Later he returned with ten thousand. ʿUmar said to him, "Did you prefer yourself with this wealth, O enemy of Allah and His Book?"
>
> Abū Hurayrah said, "I am not the enemy of Allah and I am not the enemy of his Book. Rather, I am the enemy of the one who transgresses them. "
>
> ʿUmar said, "Where did you get this wealth from?"
>
> Abū Hurayrah said, "Horses begotten, the profits of my slaves and gifts that poured forth."
>
> They looked into it and found it to be as he said. After some time ʿUmar summoned him to in order to appoint him as governor (once again) but he (Abū Hurayrah) refused.
>
> ʿUmar said, "You do not want to work and someone better than you, Yūsuf, requested work."
>
> He said, "Yūsuf was a Prophet, the son of a Prophet, the son of a Prophet, and I am Abū Hurayrah, the son of Umaymah. Also, I fear three and two things."
>
> ʿUmar said, "Why did you not say five things?" He said, "I fear that I will say something without knowledge, and I fear that I will pass a judgement without knowledge, and I fear that my back will be beaten, and I fear that my wealth will be taken, and I fear my honour will be insulted."[1]

c. Abū Hurayrah's رضي الله عنه appointment as governor of Madīnah during the Umayyad period was due to the fact that he was one of the few remaining senior Companions in Madīnah at the time. In addition to this he was a prime candidate for leadership in Madīnah especially when we consider that he was forwarded to lead the ṣalāh during the days of ʿAlī and Muʿāwiyah رضي الله عنهما. Whoever took charge of the affairs of the Muslims, whether the Umayyads or anyone besides them, would certainly have considered him a prime candidate to serve as the governor of Madīnah.

1 al-Dhahabī: *Siyar Aʿlām al-Nubalāʾ*, vol. 2 p. 612, the examiner says, "Its transmitters are reliable."

d. Tījānī's cheap attempt to portray Abū Hurayrah رضي الله عنه as someone covetous for the material gain, worldly acquisition and fulfilment of his base desires, signifies the weakness of his position and the feebleness of his accusations. Compare what Tījānī said about Abū Hurayrah رضي الله عنه with what Abū Hurayrah relates from the Prophet صلى الله عليه وسلم:

ثلاثة لا ينظر الله إليهم يوم القيامة ولا يزكيهم ولهم عذاب أليم رجل كان له فضل ماء بالطريق فمنعه من ابن السبيل ورجل بايع إماما لا يبايعه إلا لدنيا فإن أعطاه منها رضي وإن لم يعطه منها سخط...

Three persons, Allah will not look at them on the Day of Judgement, and he will not purify them, and for them is a painful punishment... (One of them is) A man who gives his pledge to a leader but only for a worldly benefit, therefore, when he gives him he is happy but when he does not give him he is upset...[1]

Also, how could he have been covetous for worldly prominence when he narrated from the Prophet صلى الله عليه وسلم:

لأن يحتطب أحدكم حزمة على ظهره خير من أن يسأل أحدا فيعطيه أو يمنعه

No doubt, it is better for any one of you to chop wood and carry it in a bundle over his back than to ask someone who may or may not give him.[2]

If Abū Hurayrah رضي الله عنه were a forger there is no doubt that he would conceal these narrations. Similarly, if Abū Hurayrah رضي الله عنه were to be as Tījānī described him he would have remained silent when evil was done in his presence. Muslim reports in his *Ṣaḥīḥ* from Abū Zurʿah, who said:

دخلت مع أبي هريرة في دار مروان فرأى فيها تصاوير فقال سمعت رسول الله صلى الله عليه وسلم يقول قال الله عز وجل ومن أظلم ممن ذهب يخلق خلقا كخلقي فليخلقوا ذرة أو ليخلقوا حبة أو ليخلقوا شعيرة

I entered Marwān's house along with Abū Hurayrah. Then he saw paintings in it and said, "I heard the Messenger صلى الله عليه وسلم saying that Allah says, 'Who is

1 *Ṣaḥīḥ al-Bukhārī*, Kitāb al-Musāqāt, Bāb Manʿ Ibn al-Sabīl min al-Māʾ, Ḥadīth no. 2230, vol. 2.
2 *Ṣaḥīḥ al-Bukhārī*, Kitāb al-Buyūʿ, Bāb Kasb al-Rajul wa ʿAmaluhu bi Yadih, Ḥadīth no. 1964.

> worse than the person who attempts to create a creation like My creation? Let them create corn, or let them create a seed, or let them create barley!'"[1]

Ḥākim narrates in his *Mustadrak* from Abū Maryam, Abū Hurayrah's freed slave, who said:

> Abū Hurayrah passed by Marwān while he was building his house in the middle of Madīnah. So I sat by him while the workers were working. He said, "Build something solid, and hope far into the future, and die very soon."
>
> Marwān said, "Abū Hurayrah must be narrating ḥadīth to the workers. What are you saying to them, O Abū Hurayrah?"
>
> He replied, "I said, 'build something solid, and hope far into the future, and die very soon,' O Quraysh (he repeated it thrice). Remember your condition yesterday and what you have become today! You employ your slaves, the Persians and the Romans; eat firm bread and fat meat. You do not eat one another and you do not bite your front teeth like horses. Be small today and you will be big tomorrow! By Allah, no man amongst you will ascend a single level except that Allah will bring him down on the Day of Judgement."[2]

Compare this Abū Hurayrah رَضِيَ اللَّهُ عَنْهُ with the Abū Hurayrah described by Tījānī. I am sure the reader notices the 'impartiality' in Tījānī's eyes.

Tījānī further accuses Abū Hurayrah رَضِيَ اللَّهُ عَنْهُ of forging ḥadīth to appease people. Similarly he accuses Abū Hurayrah of narrating forged aḥādīth about the merits of the Ṣaḥābah, especially Abū Bakr رَضِيَ اللَّهُ عَنْهُ. Tījānī has honestly pointed out that his convictions were further reinforced after reading the book Abū Hurayrah by ʿAbd al-Ḥusayn Sharaf al-Dīn and Maḥmūd Abū Rayyah.

Let us examine Tījānī's accusation:

a. There is no difference of opinion among the Companions about the merit of Abū Hurayrah رَضِيَ اللَّهُ عَنْهُ. Furthermore they attest to his integrity as a person as well as the keenness of his memory. They regard him among the most knowledgeable Companions when it comes to the Prophet's صَلَّى اللَّهُ عَلَيْهِ وَسَلَّمَ Sunnah.

---

1 *Muslim* with the commentary, Kitāb al-Libās wa al-Zīnah, Ḥadīth no. 2111.

2 Narrated by Ḥākim in the *Mustadrak*, vol. 4 p. 463; Refer also to *Aqbās min Manāqib Abī Hurayrah* by ʿAbd al-Munʿim Ṣāliḥ al-ʿAlī, p. 119.

Ibn ʿUmar رضي الله عنه once said to Abū Hurayrah رضي الله عنه:

يا أبا هريرة أنت كنت ألزمنا لرسول الله صلى الله عليه وسلم وأحفظنا لحديثه

> O Abū Hurayrah, you spent the most time with the Prophet among us and you the most knowledgeable with regards to his ḥadīth.[1]

Ibn ʿUmar was once asked, "Do you negate anything that Abū Hurayrah narrates?" He replied:

> No! But he is bold and we are cautious.[2]

Ashʿath ibn Salīm, relates from his father, who said:

> I came to Madīnah and I found Abū Ayyūb narrating from Abū Hurayrah from the Prophet صلى الله عليه وسلم. I said, "(Do you narrate from Abū Hurayrah) yet you accompanied the Prophet صلى الله عليه وسلم."
>
> He said, "He heard and I narrate from him from the Messenger صلى الله عليه وسلم. I find this more pleasing than narrating (directly) from the Prophet صلى الله عليه وسلم."[3]

Muʿāwiyah ibn Abī ʿAyyāsh al-Anṣārī relates:

> I was sitting with Ibn Zubayr when Muḥammad ibn Iyās ibn Bukayr came and asked about a man who divorced his wife thrice, before consummation (of the marriage). Then he sent him to Abū Hurayrah and Ibn ʿAbbās and both of them were by ʿĀ'ishah. Then he went and asked them, and Ibn ʿAbbās said to Abū Hurayrah, "Answer him, O Abū Hurayrah, as it is a complex question."
>
> He said, "The first (utterance of divorce) terminates it, and the three (divorces) prohibit her (from remarrying him)."
>
> Ibn ʿAbbās said something similar.[4]

Consider Abū Hurayrah's academic stature before Ibn ʿAbbās—who was a close ally and confidant of ʿAlī رضي الله عنه—that he considered him better suited to answer this problematic question. Would Ibn ʿAbbās رضي الله عنه consider Abū Hurayrah رضي الله عنه unreliable?

---

1 *Sunan al-Tirmidhī*, vol. 3, Bāb Manāqib Abī Hurayrah, Ḥadīth no. 3836.

2 *Siyar Aʿlām al-Nubalā'*, vol. 2 p. 608.

3 *Siyar Aʿlām al-Nubalā'*, vol. 2 p. 606.

4 Ibid. p. 607, the editor said, "Its chain is reliable."

The reason for his prolific transmission from the Prophet ﷺ is that he accompanied the Prophet ﷺ under all circumstances; whether the Prophet ﷺ was at home or on travel. Furthermore, Abū Hurayrah رضي الله عنه had no work commitment, nor wife to occupy his time. He was eager to be in the Prophet's ﷺ company whenever the opportunity presented itself.

Mālik ibn Abī ʿĀmir said:

> A man came to Ṭalḥah ibn ʿUbayd Allāh and said, "O Abū Muḥammad, what do you think about this Yemenī (referring to Abū Hurayrah)? Is he more knowledgeable about the Prophet's ﷺ aḥādīth than you? We hear things from him that we do not hear from you; is he saying things that the Prophet ﷺ did not say?"
>
> Ṭalḥah responded, "As for him hearing what we did not hear, I do not doubt (his having heard it). Let me tell you about his situation. We had families, livestock, and work (to attend to). We used to visit the Prophet ﷺ mornings and evenings. As for Abū Hurayrah, he was poor and a guest at the Prophet's ﷺ door. His hand was with his hand. Therefore, I have no doubt that he heard what we did not hear. You will not find any person who has any good in him forging lies upon the Prophet ﷺ."[1]

b. In addition to accompanying the Prophet ﷺ which contributed to him becoming the most prolific narrator of ḥadīth among the Companions, he also stood out on account of his retentive memory, accuracy of transmission, and his attention to detail. This is the result of the Prophet's ﷺ mercy and grace. Al-Bukhārī narrates by way of al-Zuhrī, who said:

سعيد بن المسيب وأبو سلمة بن عبد الرحمن أن أبا هريرة رضي الله عنه قال إنكم تقولون إن أبا هريرة يكثر الحديث عن رسول الله صلى الله عليه وسلم وتقولون ما بال المهاجرين والأنصار لا يحدثون عن رسول الله صلى الله عليه وسلم بمثل حديث أبي هريرة وإن إخوتي من المهاجرين كان يشغلهم صفق بالأسواق وكنت ألزم رسول الله صلى الله عليه وسلم على ملء بطني فأشهد إذا غابوا وأحفظ إذا نسوا وكان يشغل إخوتي من الأنصار

1 *Siyar Aʿlām al-Nubalāʾ*, vol. 2 p. 605-606, the examiner says, "Its transmitters are reliable."

عمل أموالهم وكنت امرأ مسكينا من مساكين الصفة أعي حين ينسون وقد قال رسول الله صلى الله عليه وسلم في حديث يحدثه إنه لن يبسط أحد ثوبه حتى أقضي مقالتي هذه ثم يجمع إليه ثوبه إلا وعى ما أقول فبسطت نمرة علي حتى إذا قضى رسول الله صلى الله عليه وسلم مقالته جمعتها إلى صدري فما نسيت من مقالة رسول الله صلى الله عليه وسلم تلك من شيء

> Saʿīd ibn Musayyab and Abū Salamah ibn ʿAbd al-Raḥmān narrated to me that Abū Hurayrah said, "Some of you say that Abū Hurayrah is abundant in what he relates from the Messenger ﷺ. You also say what is the matter with the Muhājirīn and the Anṣār that they do not narrate from the Prophet ﷺ like Abū Hurayrah narrates. Indeed, my brothers from the Muhājirīn were occupied with their dealings in the market place while I stuck to the Prophet ﷺ. Therefore, I witnessed (things) when they were absent, and I would remember when they forgot. My brothers from the Anṣār were occupied with their farms; while I was a poor man from the poor Companions of al-Ṣuffah and I remembered when they forgot. Also, the Prophet ﷺ once said, 'None amongst you will spread open (a garment) until I complete this talk of mine and then press it against himself except that he will remember what I say.' So I spread open a striped garment I was wearing until the Prophet ﷺ completed his talk then I pressed it against my chest and I did not forget anything since that speech of the Prophet ﷺ."[1]

c. It would be prudent to refer to one of the 'infallible' Imāms of the Shīʿah and hear what he says about Abū Hurayrah رضي الله عنه, whether he is trustworthy. We present the views of the fourth Imām, Zayn al-ʿĀbidīn, ʿAlī ibn Ḥusayn رضي الله عنهما, on Abū Hurayrah رضي الله عنه. Abū al-Ḥasan al-Irbilī, a senior Shīʿī scholar, relates in his book *Kashf al-Ghummah* from Saʿīd ibn Marjānah that he said:

> One day I was with ʿAlī ibn Ḥusayn and I said, "I heard Abū Hurayrah saying that the Messenger ﷺ said, 'Whoever frees a believing slave, Allah frees with every limb of his body a limb of his from the fire of Jahannam to the extent that he frees with the hand the hand, and with the foot the foot, and with the private parts the private parts.'"
>
> ʿAlī ibn Ḥusayn said, "You heard this from Abū Hurayrah?"

1 *Ṣaḥīḥ al-Bukhārī*, Kitāb al-Buyūʿ, Ḥadīth no. 1942.

> I replied that I did, on which he said to a slave of his, the most energetic of his slaves, whom ʿAbd Allāh ibn Jaʿfar had offered him one thousand dīnārs for but he refused to sell. He said "You are free, for the sake of Allah!"[1]

The extent of Abū Hurayrah's رضي الله عنه trustworthiness and honesty in the eyes of Imām ʿAlī ibn Ḥusayn is that he did not delay in practising upon a ḥadīth that reached him from Abū Hurayrah رضي الله عنه. Tījānī does not trust someone whom the 'infallible' Imām trusts. Subḥān Allah!

It is not strange then to find that one of the senior Imāmiyyah scholars in the field of ḥadīth transmitters ratifies him and places him amongst the category of praiseworthy transmitters. Ibn Dāwūd al-Ḥillī says:

> ʿAbd Allāh, Abū Hurayrah, is well-known and from amongst the Companions of the Messenger صلى الله عليه وسلم.[2]

Similarly Ibn Bābuwayh al-Qummī cited him in his book *al-Khiṣāl* at more than one place[3] and the examiner of the book, ʿAlī Akbar Ghifārī, does not subject him to criticism despite his footnotes on many of the transmitters in the book.

This is in addition to the fact that the person transmitting many of the aḥādīth from Abū Hurayrah is his son-in-law, Saʿīd ibn Musayyab. He is one of the most famous of his students, and the person who narrated the ḥadīth about the Prophet صلى الله عليه وسلم instructing to spread a garment which resulted in the extraordinary capacity for memorisation of ḥadīth. Al-Kashshī, a senior Shīʿī scholar in the field of transmitter criticism, says about him, "Saʿīd ibn Musayyab, he was raised by Amīr al-Mu'minīn."[4]

It has been narrated that Abū Jaʿfar al-Bāqir said:

> I heard ʿAlī ibn Ḥusayn saying, "Saʿīd ibn Musayyab is the most knowledgeable of people with regards to what preceded him of traditions and the person with the most understanding of his generation."[5]

---

1 *Kashf al-Ghummah*, vol. 2 p. 290, Faḍā'il al-Imām Zayn al-ʿĀbidīn.

2 *Rijāl Ibn Dāwūd al-Ḥalbī*, p. 198.

3 al-Qummī: *Al-Khiṣāl*, p. 31, 38, 164, 174, 176, and at other places as well.

4 *Rijāl al-Kashshī*, biography no. 54, p. 107.

5 Ibid. p. 110.

Does it matter what Tījānī says after ʿAlī, Zayn al-ʿĀbidīn, attested to his faithful representation of the Prophetic tradition and his reliability as a transmitter of Prophetic knowledge? If Zayn al-ʿĀbidīn could trust him, what stops Tījānī?

Tījānīs callous treatment of this noble Companion is further demonstrated by his statement:

> **The virtues of Abu Bakr were also mentioned by Amr ibn al-'As, Abu Hurayrah, Urwa and Ikrima, and all of them hated Ali and fought him either with arms or by plotting against him and attributing virtues to his enemies..."[1]**

Our response:

a. It is correct that ʿAmr ibn al-ʿĀṣ رضي الله عنه fought ʿAlī رضي الله عنه but this was not on account of enmity towards him. Rather, it was because he believed he was fighting in defence of the truth. The reason for conflict between Muʿāwiyah and ʿAlī رضي الله عنهما has already been dealt with so it suffices from repeating those discussions here. All that can be added is that ʿAmr ibn al-ʿĀṣ رضي الله عنه fought on the side of Muʿāwiyah رضي الله عنه. This is hardly any reason to forge aḥādīth on the virtues of Abū Bakr رضي الله عنه.

   ʿAmr ibn al-ʿĀṣ is also known for narrating the virtues of those who stood against him on the battlefield. He is one of the transmitters of the ḥadīth, "Pity ʿAmmār, the rebellious group will kill him." He narrates also that the Prophet صلى الله عليه وسلم said, "The one who kills him and takes his belongings is in the fire," and when someone objected to him and argued that he, ʿAmr, was fighting him he responded, "He (the Prophet صلى الله عليه وسلم) said the person who kills him and takes his belongings."[2]

   Is this what Tījānī refers to when he accuses him of 'fabrication' and 'inventing of merits for ʿAlī's enemies'.

   ʿAmr's رضي الله عنه real 'crime' is that he asked the Prophet صلى الله عليه وسلم:

   أى الناس أحب إليك قال عائشة فقلت من الرجال فقال أبوها قلت ثم من قال ثم عمر بن الخطاب فعد رجالا

---

1 *Then I was guided*, p. 142.

2 *Musnad Aḥmad*, vol. 6, Ḥadīth: 17791.

"Who is the most beloved person to you?"

He said, "'Ā'ishah."

I said, "And from the men?"

He said, "Her father!"

I said, "Then who?"

He said, "'Umar ibn al-Khaṭṭāb." And he mentioned other men.[1]

b. Abū Hurayrah رَضِيَ اللَّهُ عَنْهُ withdrew himself from the conflict between ʿAlī and Muʿāwiyah رَضِيَ اللَّهُ عَنْهُمَا. Therefore, from this perspective he did not attack ʿAlī رَضِيَ اللَّهُ عَنْهُ. However, apparently, he attacked him by 'fabricating' and 'inventing' merits for his enemies. These manifest in the form of what Abū Hurayrah رَضِيَ اللَّهُ عَنْهُ narrates from the Prophet صَلَّى اللَّهُ عَلَيْهِ وَسَلَّمَ about the Day of Khaybar:

لأعطين هذه الراية رجلا يحب الله ورسوله يفتح الله على يديه.فدعا رسول الله صلى الله عليه وسلم على بن أبي طالب فأعطاه إياها

I will most certainly hand over this flag to a man who loves Allah and His Messenger and Allah will grant victory at his hands... Then the Messenger صَلَّى اللَّهُ عَلَيْهِ وَسَلَّمَ called ʿAlī ibn Abī Ṭālib and gave him the flag.[2]

Not only this, he also narrated from the Prophet صَلَّى اللَّهُ عَلَيْهِ وَسَلَّمَ that he said:

Whoever loves them loves me, and whoever hates them hates me (referring to Ḥasan and Ḥusayn).[3]

He narrated also that the Prophet صَلَّى اللَّهُ عَلَيْهِ وَسَلَّمَ said:

O Allah! I love them so you love them![4]

Our question for Tījānī is whether these are fabrications? Or are they only fabrications when there is merit for Abū Bakr or ʿUmar رَضِيَ اللَّهُ عَنْهُمَا?

1 Previously cited on p. 453-454 of this book.

2 Previously cited on p. 321 of this book.

3 Aḥmad: *Faḍā'il al-Ṣaḥābah*, Ḥadīth no. 1395, the examiner says, "Its sanad is reliable."

4 *Al-Faḍā'il*, Ḥadīth no. 1371, the examiner says, "Its sanad is reliable."

Chapter Thirteen

The Final Study: Miscellaneous Issues

1. Tījānī's Proofs for ʿAlī's immediate succession

The ḥadīth, "I am the city of knowledge and ʿAlī is the door."

As proof for his claim for the pre-eminence of ʿAlī for leadership after the Prophet's صَلَّى ٱللَّٰهُ عَلَيْهِ وَسَلَّمَ demise, Tījānī presents what he believes to be mutually acceptable evidence. He says:

> **The prophetic traditions which persuaded me to follow Imam Ali were those I have read in the Sihahs of the Sunnis and were approved by the Shiites, and they have many more. But as usual I only referred to the prophetic traditions that have been agreed on by both parties, From those aḥadīth is, "I am the city of knowledge and Ali is the door."[1]**

Analysis of the ḥadīth, "I am the city of knowledge and ʿAlī is the door."

This narration has an unreliable chain, and its purport is problematic as well.

Ibn al-Jawzī has listed this narration in his book *Al-Mawḍūʿāt* and after a thorough examination of all of its variant narrations concluded that it is false.[2]

Ibn Ṭāhir al-Maqdisī mentioned it in his book *Tadhkirat al-Mawḍūʿāt* and said:

> Appearing in its chain is Abū al-Ṣalt. His name is ʿAbd al-Salām. Also appearing in its chain is ʿUthmān ibn Khālid and Ismāʿīl ibn Muḥammad ibn Yūsuf, all of whom are liars.[3]

Al-Suyūṭī mentions it in his book *al-La'ālī al-Maṣnūʿah*[4], as well al-Shawkānī in his book *al-Fawā'id al-Majmūʿah.*[5] The editor of al-Shawkānī's *al-Fawā'id*, ʿAbd al-Raḥmān al-Muʿallimī, provides a detailed discussion on this narration wherein he demonstrates that it is flawed by all counts.

---

1 *Then I was guided*, p. 146.

2 Ibn al-Jawzī: *Al-Mawḍūʿāt*, vol. 1 p. 349-354.

3 *Tadhkirat Al-Mawḍūʿāt*, p. 33.

4 *Al-La'ālī al-Maṣnūʿah*, vol. 1 p. 332.

5 *Al-Fawā'id al-Majmūʿah*, p. 348.

Ibn Taymiyyah said about it:

> This is a weak ḥadīth. Rather, it is a fabricated ḥadīth according to ḥadīth experts. That being said, al-Tirmidhī and others narrate it despite it being false.[1]

The words with which al-Tirmidhī narrates it is, "I am the house of wisdom and ʿAlī is its door." He goes on to comment, "This is a *gharīb munkar* (anomalous contradictory) ḥadīth."[2]

Ibn Kathīr mentions it in *al-Bidāyah* and says:

> This ḥadīth is known to pass through Abū al-Ṣalt al-Harawī. From him it was appropriated by Aḥmad ibn Salamah and a group of unreliable transmitters, who then fraudulently ascribed it to themselves.

He states further:

> Aḥmad ibn Muḥammad ibn Qāsim ibn Miḥraz relates from Ibn Maʿīn that he said, "Ibn Ayman narrated to me that Abū Muʿāwiyah narrated this ḥadīth initially but then refrained from it. He says, 'Abū al-Ṣalt was a wealthy man who used to honour the scholars and they used to narrate these aḥādīth to him.'"
>
> Ibn ʿAsākir forwards this ḥadīth with a weak sanad reaching the Prophet ﷺ, from Jaʿfar al-Ṣādiq, from his father, from his grandfather, from Jābir ibn ʿAbd Allāh; He also narrates it from a different path through Jābir. Ibn ʿAdī says, "That is also fabricated."

Abū al-Fatḥ al-Awdī says, "There is no authentic ḥadīth like this."[3]

Dāraquṭnī says, "This ḥadīth has irreconcilable inconsistencies and is not reliable."[4]

The wording of this narration suggests that it is problematic as well. The Prophet ﷺ is an ocean of knowledge. It is inconceivable that the knowledge of the Prophet ﷺ is only accessible via one door.

---

1 Ibn Taymiyyah: *Al-Aḥādīth al-Mawḍūʿah*, p. 40, the examiner says, "All its narrations are weak."

2 *Sunan al-Tirmidhī*, Kitāb al-Manāqib, Ḥadīth no. 3723.

3 Ibn Kathīr: *Al-Bidāyah wa al-Nihāyah*, vol. 8 p. 372.

4 *Al-ʿIlal al-Wāridah fī al-Aḥādīth al-Nabawiyyah*, vol. 3, question no. 386, p. 247.

It is well-known that knowledge has been transmitted from the Prophet ﷺ by other than ʿAlī رضي الله عنه. Much of Tījānī's claims have been based on narrations which have been conveyed from someone other than ʿAlī رضي الله عنه. Knowledge was spread in the different regions and cities based on whichever of the Companions had settled there. Much of ʿAlī's رضي الله عنه knowledge was spread in Kūfah. Despite that, the people of Kūfah began learning the Qur'ān and the Sunnah even before ʿUthmān's رضي الله عنه era.

Muʿādh رضي الله عنه was sent by the Prophet ﷺ to teach the people of Yemen. ʿAlī رضي الله عنه was in Yemen for a period of time, but Muʿādh رضي الله عنه remained for a considerable time. Therefore, the people of Yemen narrate more from Muʿādh رضي الله عنه than what they narrate from ʿAlī رضي الله عنه. Shurayḥ al-Qāḍī, in addition to many other Tābiʿīn, learnt from Muʿādh ibn Jabal رضي الله عنه.

When ʿAlī رضي الله عنه arrived in Kūfah, Shurayḥ was already appointed the judge. He and ʿAbīdah al-Salmānī learnt from others before ʿAlī رضي الله عنه. Therefore, Islamic knowledge preceded ʿAlī's رضي الله عنه arrival in Kūfah.[1]

Overlooking the weakness of this narration, there is nothing in it that proves ʿAlī's رضي الله عنه pre-eminence for succession. At most it could be said that he is a leader in terms of knowledge.

The ḥadīth, "O ʿAlī! You hold in relation to me the same position as Haroon held in relation to Moses."

Tījānī goes on to cite the second ḥadīth which he presents as mutually accepted proof:

> **The Prophetic tradition: O Ali! You hold in relation to me the same position as Haroon held in relation to Moses, except that there shall be no prophet after me.**
>
> **This tradition, as should be apparent to every sensible person, shows the special quality of the Commander of the Believers, Ali, which made him the right person to be the supporter, the guardian and the deputy [or successor] of the Messenger of Allah ﷺ as Haroon عليه السلام was the supporter, guardian and deputy of Moses عليه السلام when he went to meet his God. There is also the position of Ali vis-a-vis the Prophet ﷺ which is absolutely equal to the**

1 *Minhāj al-Sunnah*, vol. 7 p. 515-517.

relation between Haroon عَلَيْهِ السَّلَام and Moses عَلَيْهِ السَّلَام, except for the prophethood, which was excluded in the same tradition.

Furthermore, we find in the tradition the fact that Imam Ali was the best Companion, who only came second after the Messenger of Allah عَلَيْهِ السَّلَام.[1]

Analysis of the ḥadīth, "O ʿAlī! You hold in relation to me the same position as Haroon held in relation to Moses."

It is ironic that Tījānī presents the next ḥadīth which is narrated by way of Saʿd ibn Abī Waqqāṣ. Ideally he ought to have quoted a ḥadīth from ʿAlī رَضِيَ اللَّهُ عَنْهُ since the city of knowledge is meant to be accessed by its door! This ḥadīth is authentic and narrated by al-Bukhārī and Muslim by way of Saʿd ibn Abī Waqqāṣ رَضِيَ اللَّهُ عَنْهُ, who said:

خلف رسول الله صلى الله عليه وسلم على بن أبي طالب فى غزوة تبوك فقال يا رسول الله تخلفني في النساء والصبيان فقال أما ترضى أن تكون مني بمنزلة هارون من موسى غير أنه لا نبى بعدي

> The Prophet صَلَّى اللَّهُ عَلَيْهِ وَسَلَّمَ left ʿAlī ibn Abī Ṭālib behind for the Battle of Tabūk. He said, "O Messenger of Allah! Are you leaving me behind with the women and the children?"
>
> The Prophet صَلَّى اللَّهُ عَلَيْهِ وَسَلَّمَ said, "Does it not please you that you are to me, in the position Hārūn was to Mūsā (when he left to speak to his Lord) except that there is no Prophet after me?"[2]

This ḥadīth definitely demonstrates the merit of ʿAlī رَضِيَ اللَّهُ عَنْهُ and he is most deserving of merit and praise. The issue is not, however, whether or not ʿAlī رَضِيَ اللَّهُ عَنْهُ was praised. The issue is whether the Prophet صَلَّى اللَّهُ عَلَيْهِ وَسَلَّمَ intended to nominate ʿAlī رَضِيَ اللَّهُ عَنْهُ as his successor by this statement of his.

Before our investigation on the meaning of the ḥadīth it is necessary that we are aware of the background to it. The Battle of Tabūk was one wherein the Prophet صَلَّى اللَّهُ عَلَيْهِ وَسَلَّمَ did not permit anyone to remain behind. Thus, when he left ʿAlī رَضِيَ اللَّهُ عَنْهُ behind the munāfiqīn spread the rumour that the Prophet صَلَّى اللَّهُ عَلَيْهِ وَسَلَّمَ left him behind

1 *Then I was guided*, p. 148.

2 *Ṣaḥīḥ Muslim* with the commentary, Kitāb Al-Faḍā'il, Ḥadīth no. 2404; *Bukhārī*, Kitāb Al-Faḍā'il, Ḥadīth no. 3503.

because he was displeased with him. Al-Nasā'ī narrates in his book *Khaṣā'iṣ* ʿAlī from Saʿd ibn Abī Waqqāṣ رضي الله عنه, who said:

> When the Prophet صلى الله عليه وسلم left for the Battle of Tabūk he left ʿAlī, may Allah brighten his face, behind in Madīnah. They (the munāfiqīn) said concerning him, "He is tired of him and he dislikes his company." Therefore, ʿAlī followed the Prophet صلى الله عليه وسلم until he caught up with him in the road and said, "O Messenger of Allah! Are you leaving me behind with the women and the children and now they are saying, 'He is tired of him and dislikes his company'?"
>
> The Prophet صلى الله عليه وسلم replied, "O ʿAlī! I have left you behind to take care of my family that you are to me, in the position Hārūn was to Mūsā (when he left to speak to his Lord) except that there is no Prophet after me?"[1]

This version of the narration illustrates the reason that ʿAlī رضي الله عنه went to the Prophet صلى الله عليه وسلم and said to him what he said. Thereafter, the Prophet صلى الله عليه وسلم attempted to console ʿAlī رضي الله عنه and explained to him that remaining behind is not necessarily a shortcoming since Mūsā left Hārūn behind to assume responsibility for his people. How could it then be considered a shortcoming if it was at the instruction of the Prophet صلى الله عليه وسلم himself? We find that ʿAlī رضي الله عنه was satisfied with that explanation and said, "I am pleased, I am pleased," as it appears in the narration of Ibn al-Musayyab narrated by Aḥmad.[2] Therefore, the Prophet's صلى الله عليه وسلم statement was simply to console ʿAlī رضي الله عنه; not to appoint him as successor for the following reasons:

1. ʿAlī رضي الله عنه did not understand it to refer to Khilāfah or succession

   Al-Bukhārī narrates with his chain to al-Zuhrī

   عن الزهري قال أخبرني عبد الله بن كعب بن مالك الأنصاري وكان كعب بن مالك أحد الثلاثة الذين تيب عليهم أن عبد الله بن عباس أخبره أن علي بن أبي طالب رضي الله عنه خرج من عند رسول الله صلى الله عليه وسلم في وجعه الذي توفي فيه فقال الناس يا أبا حسن كيف أصبح رسول الله صلى الله عليه وسلم فقال أصبح بحمد الله بارئا فأخذ بيده عباس بن عبد

1 Nasā'ī: *Khaṣā'iṣ Amīr al-Mu'minīn*, Ḥadīth no. 43, the examiner says, "Its sanad is reliable."

2 Refer to *Fatḥ al-Bārī*, vol. 7 p. 92.

المطلب فقال له أنت والله بعد ثلاث عبد العصا وإني والله لأرى رسول الله صلى الله عليه وسلم سوف يتوفى من وجعه هذا إني لأعرف وجوه بني عبد المطلب عند الموت اذهب بنا إلى رسول الله صلى الله عليه وسلم فلنسأله فيمن هذا الأمر إن كان فينا علمنا ذلك وإن كان في غيرنا علمناه فأوصى بنا فقال علي إنا والله لئن سألناها رسول الله صلى الله عليه وسلم فمنعناها لا يعطيناها الناس بعده وإني والله لا أسألها رسول الله صلى الله عليه وسلم

> Al-Zuhrī related from ʿAbd Allāh ibn Kaʿb ibn Mālik—and Kaʿb ibn Mālik was one of the three whom Allah pardoned—that ʿAbd Allāh ibn ʿAbbās informed him that ʿAlī ibn Abī Ṭālib emerged from the [home of the] Messenger of Allah ﷺ during his final illness and the people said, "O Abū al-Ḥasan; How is the Messenger of Allah ﷺ this morning?"
>
> He said, "All praise be to Allah, he is well this morning."
>
> ʿAbbās ibn ʿAbd al-Muṭṭalib took him by the hand and said to him, "I swear by Allah, in three days' time you will be a subject. By Allah, I think that the Messenger of Allah ﷺ will die of this illness. I recognise the look of death in the faces of the Banū ʿAbd al-Muṭṭalib when they are dying. Let us go to the Messenger of Allah ﷺ and ask him who will take charge over this matter (Khilāfah). If it is for us, then we will know that, and if it is for someone other than us, we will know and he can advise him to look after us."
>
> ʿAlī replied, "By Allah, if we ask him for it and he refuses us, then the people would never give it to us afterwards. By Allah, I will not ask it from the Messenger of Allah." [1]

Why would ʿAlī رضي الله عنه fear the Prophet's refusal if he had already appointed ʿAlī رضي الله عنه as his successor prior to Tabūk?

2. It has been established in the *sīrah* (prophetic biography) that whenever he went on a journey or a military expedition the Prophet ﷺ would leave someone behind to take care of matters in Madīnah. However, he never said to anyone whom he left behind that he was to the Prophet ﷺ similar to Hārūn with Mūsā. The reason for that is every person whom the Prophet ﷺ left behind never considered this blameworthy and therefore the

1 *Ṣaḥīḥ al-Bukhārī*, Kitāb al-Maghāzī, Ḥadīth no. 4182.

Prophet ﷺ never needed to console him. This can easily be compared to an incident where a person once verbally abused a companion of the Prophet ﷺ who was found guilty of consuming alcohol. The Prophet ﷺ rebuked the person who uttered the insult saying, "Do not curse him because you do not know that he loves Allah and his Messenger!"[1] This statement of the Prophet ﷺ—and any rational person would agree—was not in negation of the faith of the person who cursed. Nor was it in affirmation of the faith of the person who drank because he drank. Instead, the Prophet's ﷺ statement was meant to prevent the curser from his cursing. In a similar manner, the reason the Prophet ﷺ said that to ʿAlī رضي الله عنه was to console him and not for him to feel crestfallen for being left behind.

3. It cannot be said that this was specific transfer of succession to ʿAlī رضي الله عنه merely on account of the Prophet ﷺ leaving him in charge of affairs in Madīnah in his absence since ʿAlī رضي الله عنه was tasked with taking care of the Prophet's immediate family; and the Prophet ﷺ appointed someone else, in charge of Madīnah during his absence. Therefore, leaving someone behind to take care of Madīnah does not automatically make the person left in charge a khalīfah.

4. Even if it were the case that the Prophet ﷺ left ʿAlī in charge of Madīnah there is no conference of succession because the Prophet ﷺ left someone besides ʿAlī رضي الله عنه in charge of Madīnah during the Farewell Ḥajj. Therefore, if leaving someone in charge means succession, then someone other than ʿAlī رضي الله عنه has a greater claim to it than him.

5. If we were to further concede that Tījānī is correct and that indeed ʿAlī رضي الله عنه was uniquely appointed; then this appointment would have been temporal and would have expired with either the appointment of Abū Bakr to lead the prayer, or with the Prophet's ﷺ passing. It would not have extended beyond his death because Hārūn عليه السلام was only Mūsā's عليه السلام deputy during his life and not after his death since there is consensus among the scholars that Hārūn عليه السلام passed away before Mūsā عليه السلام.[2] After all did Tījānī not say, "The position of Imām ʿAlī vis-a-vis to the Prophet ﷺ is absolutely equal

1 This ḥadīth was previously cited on p. 322 of this book.

2 *Fatḥ al-Bārī*, vol. 7 p. 93; *Sharḥ Muslim*, vol. 15 p. 249.

to the relation between Haroon and Moses, except for the prophethood" and here is the complete picture of Hārūn's succession of Mūsā. ʿAlī's succession only becomes the exact replica of Hārūn's عَلَيْهِ السَّلَام succession of Mūsā عَلَيْهِ السَّلَام when the succession remains within the Prophet's صَلَّى ٱللَّٰهُ عَلَيْهِ وَسَلَّمَ life.

In light of the aforementioned, it becomes clear to the unbiased reader that this ḥadīth does not prove ʿAlī's succession during the Messenger's صَلَّى ٱللَّٰهُ عَلَيْهِ وَسَلَّمَ life, let alone after his death.

The ḥadīth, "Whomsoever I am his Mawlā, then this is ʿAlī, he too is his Mawlā."

The third ḥadīth presented as proof by Tījānī is the following:

> **Whomsoever I am his Mawla, then this is Ali, he too is his Mawla. O Allah, befriend whoever he befriends and take as an enemy whoever he takes as an enemy, and assist whoever assists him and desert whoever deserts him, and cause the truth to follow him wherever he goes.**

Tījānī adds to this as follows:

> **This tradition alone is sufficient to reply to the allegations concerning the seniority of Abu Bakr, Umar and Uthman to Ali, who was appointed by the Messenger of Allah صَلَّى ٱللَّٰهُ عَلَيْهِ وَسَلَّمَ as the guardian after him of all the faithful. It is of no consequence for whoever tried to interpret the saying as the friend or the support in order to divert it from its original meaning so that the integrity of the Companions may be kept intact. The Messenger of Allah صَلَّى ٱللَّٰهُ عَلَيْهِ وَسَلَّمَ stood up in the terrible heat addressing the people, saying, "Do you witness that I have a prior right to and superior authority over all the faithful?" They replied, "Yes, O Messenger of Allah صَلَّى ٱللَّٰهُ عَلَيْهِ وَسَلَّمَ."Thereupon he said, "Ali is the master of all those whom I am a master . . . etc." This is a clear text indicating that the Messenger of Allah صَلَّى ٱللَّٰهُ عَلَيْهِ وَسَلَّمَ had appointed Ali as his successor to lead the nation [of Islam], and the fair and sensible person could not but accept this interpretation and refuse that of the others, thus preserving the integrity of the Messenger of Allah صَلَّى ٱللَّٰهُ عَلَيْهِ وَسَلَّمَ before preserving the integrity of the Companions. Those who give an alternative interpretation to the saying are in fact ridiculing the wisdom of the Messenger of Allah صَلَّى ٱللَّٰهُ عَلَيْهِ وَسَلَّمَ, who gathered the multitude of people, in that unbearable heat, to tell them that Ali was the friend and supporter of the faithful. And what do those, who misinterpret the text in order to preserve the integrity of their masters, say about the procession of congratulation that the Messenger of Allah صَلَّى ٱللَّٰهُ عَلَيْهِ وَسَلَّمَ**

organised for Ali? It started with the wives of the Messenger ﷺ, the mothers of the faithful, and then Abu Bakr and Umar came and said to him, "Well done Ibn Abī Talib, Overnight you became the guardian [master] of all the faithful."

In fact all the historical evidence gives clear indications that those who misinterpret the above tradition are liars. Woe to those who wrote what they wrote, and woe to them for what they are writing![1]

Allah says:

وَإِنَّ فَرِيْقًا مِّنْهُمْ لَيَكْتُمُوْنَ الْحَقَّ وَهُمْ يَعْلَمُوْنَ

But indeed, a party of them conceal the truth while they know [it].[2]

Analysis of the ḥadīth, "Whomsoever I am his Mawlā, then this is ʿAlī, he too is his Mawlā."

The common wording of the ḥadīth is authentic and in no uncertain terms establishes the virtue and lofty status of ʿAlī رضي الله عنه. Certainly he is our *Mawlā* and the *Mawlā* of all the believers.

This narration cannot be used to prove ʿAlī's رضي الله عنه pre-eminence for Khilāfah because the term Mawlā would be inconsistent with Khalīfah in this instance. We have demonstrated this in great detail in the study of Abū Bakr. We refer the reader to the relevant discussion to avoid unnecessary repetition![3]

The additional wording of the ḥadīth which Tījānī presents, "*and assist whoever assists him and desert whoever deserts him*," is an uncorroborated addition by the narrator, Sharīk ibn ʿAbd Allāh al-Qāḍī, who is weak of memory.[4] As such it will be treated as an irregular addition which means that these additional words are not considered to be the Prophet's ﷺ words.

Tījānī does not fail to deliver when it comes to invented narrations. He has quoted a version of this ḥadīth which has absolutely no basis, "*and cause the truth to follow*

1 *Then I was guided*, p. 148.

2 Sūrah al-Baqarah: 146.

3 Refer to p. 282 of this book.

4 *Al-Silsilah al-Ṣaḥīḥah*, vol. 4 p. 338; al-Jūzajānī says in *al-Shajarah wa Aḥwāl al-Rijāl*, p. 150, "Sharīk ibn ʿAbd Allāh: Weak of memory, confused in ḥadīth."

him wherever he goes." Despite exhaustive attempts we did not find this addition in all the various narrations of this ḥadīth.

As for his statement,

> **It is of no consequence for whoever tried to interpret the saying as the friend or the support in order to divert it from its original meaning so that the integrity of the Companions may be kept intact.**

It is ironic that Tījānī attributes an original meaning to this narration. He implicitly acknowledges that the term *Mawlā* has the latent capacity to present a spectrum of meanings. If Tījānī's ignorance of context is anything to go by, the reader will not find it strange that he struggles to understand the ḥadīth

He alleges that the Prophet صَلَّى ٱللَّٰهُ عَلَيْهِ وَسَلَّمَ stood up to give a sermon in the unbearable extreme heat in order to instate ʿAlī رَضِيَ ٱللَّٰهُ عَنْهُ as the khalīfah. It is preposterous to imply that standing in the heat to deliver a speech was the underlying sign of ʿAlī's رَضِيَ ٱللَّٰهُ عَنْهُ appointment. It would be more sensible if the Prophet صَلَّى ٱللَّٰهُ عَلَيْهِ وَسَلَّمَ gave a specific instruction for everyone to gather at Ghadīr Khumm before announcing ʿAlī's رَضِيَ ٱللَّٰهُ عَنْهُ appointment. However, reality paints quite a different picture. No announcement was made for the people to gather at Ghadīr Khumm. Instead the Prophet صَلَّى ٱللَّٰهُ عَلَيْهِ وَسَلَّمَ waited until his return from the Farewell Ḥajj, and when he stopped for water and rest at Ghadīr Khumm he addressed those who were present with him. This tells us that the reason for addressing the Companions at this point was never to announce ʿAlī's رَضِيَ ٱللَّٰهُ عَنْهُ khilāfah because if that were the case he would have mentioned it during the Farewell Ḥajj, wherein he delivered numerous sermons about the most important matters for the entire Ummah to know. However, because this was not something to be conveyed to the people he did not mention it. After delivering those sermons he said, "Have I conveyed? O Allah, be my witness!"

This reinforces the view that says that the word Mawlā was not used with the intention of Khilāfah. Why wait until after Ḥajj, after the majority of Muslims have returned to their respective destinations, and appoint the Khalīfah with language—that even Tījānī accepts—is ambivalent?

What further demonstrates the Prophet's صَلَّى ٱللَّٰهُ عَلَيْهِ وَسَلَّمَ intention behind the term Mawlā is a narration recorded by Imām Aḥmad in *Al-Faḍā'il* from Ibn Buraydah from his father, who said:

> The Messenger صلى الله عليه وسلم dispatched us and appointed ʿAlī (as the leader) over us. When we returned he asked us, "How did you find your companion's (i.e. ʿAlī's) company?" Either I was going to complain about him or someone else was going to complain about him. I raised my head, being a man from Makkah, and the Prophet's صلى الله عليه وسلم face was red. He said, "Whoever I am his Mawlā, ʿAlī is his Mawlā!"[1]

Ibn ʿAbbās رضي الله عنه also narrated from Buraydah, who said:

> I went out with ʿAlī to Yemen and noticed some harshness about him. I went to the Prophet صلى الله عليه وسلم and complained about ʿAlī and criticised him. Then the Prophet's صلى الله عليه وسلم face started to change (and he said), "Buraydah! Do I not have more right over the believers than they have over themselves?" I said, "Yes, O Messenger of Allah!" He said, "Whoever I am his Mawlā, ʿAlī is his Mawlā."[2]

If we take these narrations into consideration we realise that the Prophet's صلى الله عليه وسلم intention by the term Mawlā was support and assistance since his statement was a form of rebuke for their criticism of ʿAlī رضي الله عنه.

As for his statement:

> **And what do those, who misinterpret the text in order to preserve the integrity of their masters, say about the procession of congratulation that the Messenger of Allah صلى الله عليه وسلم organised for Ali? It started with the wives of the Messenger صلى الله عليه وسلم, the mothers of the faithful, and then Abu Bakr and Umar came and said to him, "Well done Ibn Abi Talib, Overnight you became the guardian [master] of all the faithful.**

Our comment:

Firstly we would like to point out how Tījānī selectively presents these narrations! When he mentioned this ḥadīth in the study, "Reasons for Enlightenment," he did not mention the Prophet's صلى الله عليه وسلم wives among those who congratulated ʿAlī رضي الله عنه. Here he is trying to eliminate the possibility of interpretation of this ḥadīth so he includes them. He makes it appear as though there was a formal procession.

1 *Khaṣāʾiṣ Amīr al-Muʾminīn*, Ḥadīth no. 77; Aḥmad in *Al-Faḍāʾil*, Ḥadīth no. 947; the examiners of the two books say, 'reliable'.

2 Aḥmad: *Al-Faḍāʾil*, Ḥadīth no. 989; Nasāʾī in *al-Khaṣāʾiṣ*, Ḥadīth no. 79, the examiners say, "It is reliable."

The detail about some Companions congratulating ʿAlī رضي الله عنه is reported by ʿAlī ibn Zayd who is a weak transmitter.[1] That is not as significant as the fact that there is no mention of Abū Bakr in the version of the ḥadīth[2] which has been narrated by ʿAlī ibn Zayd ibn Judʿān.

After deliberately lying and interpolating the weak narration of ʿAlī ibn Zayd ibn Judʿān, Tījānī is not ashamed to say:

> **In fact all the historical evidence gives clear indications that those who misinterpret the above tradition are liars. Woe to those who wrote what they wrote, and woe to them for what they are writing. Allah - the Most High - said. "...a party of them most surely conceal the truth while they know it"[3]**

Besides the fact that the grandson of ʿAlī رضي الله عنه, Ḥasan ibn Ḥasan al-Muthannā, interpreted it to mean support and fondness[4], all that remains is for us to say, "Āmīn," to Tījānī's supplication against the liars!

The ḥadīth, "ʿAlī is from me and I am from ʿAlī"

Then Tījānī mentions the fourth ḥadīth and says:

> **The Prophetic tradition: Ali is from me and I am from Ali and no one can discharge my duty except myself or Ali.**
>
> **This honourable tradition [92] is another clear indication that Imam Ali was only one whom the Messenger صلى الله عليه وسلم authorized to discharge his duties. The Messenger صلى الله عليه وسلم said it on the day of the great pilgrimage when he sent Ali with Surat Bara'a instead of Abu Bakr, who came crying and asked, "O Messenger of Allah صلى الله عليه وسلم! Reveal something for me." The Messenger صلى الله عليه وسلم answered, "My Lord ordered me that nobody can discharge my duty except myself or Ali."**
>
> **There is another supporting tradition that the Messenger of Allah صلى الله عليه وسلم, said on another occasion in honour of Ali, "O Ali! You will show them the right path when there will be dissension among them after me ..."[5]**

---

1 Return to p. 289-290 for more clarity.

2 Return to p. 289 of this book in order to ascertain the scope of Tījānī's distortion of the texts.

3 *Then I was guided*, p. 148.

4 *Al-Iʿtiqād wa al-Hidāyah*, p. 232.

5 *Then I was guided*,p. 149.

Analysis of the ḥadīth, "ʿAlī is from me and I am from ʿAlī"

This ḥadīth is authentic and established. However, Tījānī misinterprets it.

The phrase "from me," in the Prophet's ﷺ statement, "ʿAlī is from me and I am from ʿAlī," is not exclusive to ʿAlī رضي الله عنه since the Prophet ﷺ used this phrase with other Companions as well. Al-Bukhārī and Muslim narrate from Abū Mūsā al-Ashʿarī رضي الله عنه who said that the Prophet ﷺ said:

إن الأشعريين إذا أرملوا في الغزو أو قل طعام عيالهم بالمدينة جمعوا ما كان عندهم في ثوب واحد ثم اقتسموه بينهم في إناء واحد بالسوية فهم مني وأنا منهم

> When the provisions of the Ashʿariyyīn run low during time of war, or food for their families is scarce when at home, they gather what they have with them in one container and then divide it between themselves equally. They are from me and I am from them.[1]

He said something similar to Julaybīb رضي الله عنه:

كان في مغزى له فأفاء الله عليه فقال لأصحابه هل تفقدون من أحد قالوا نعم فلانا وفلانا وفلانا ثم قال هل تفقدون من أحد قالوا نعم فلانا وفلانا وفلانا ثم قال هل تفقدون من أحد قالوا لا قال لكنى أفقد جليبيبا فاطلبوه فطلب فى القتلى فوجدوه إلى جنب سبعة قد قتلهم ثم قتلوه فأتى النبى صلى الله عليه وسلم فوقف عليه فقال قتل سبعة ثم قتلوه هذا منى وأنا منه هذا منى وأنا منه

> The Prophet ﷺ was on an expedition and Allah granted him victory. Then he said to his Ṣaḥābah, "Are you missing anyone?"
>
> They said, "Yes, this person and this person and this person."
>
> Then he said, "Are you missing anyone?"
>
> They said, "Yes, this person and this person and this person."
>
> Then he said, "Are you missing anyone?"

1 *Ṣaḥīḥ al-Bukhārī*, Kitāb al-Shirākah, Ḥadīth no. 2353; *Ṣaḥīḥ Muslim*, Faḍā'il al-Ṣaḥābah, Ḥadīth no. 2499.

> They said, "No."
>
> He said, "But I am missing Julaybīb. So search for him!"
>
> Then they searched amongst the fallen and found him next to seven men who he killed and they killed him.
>
> Then the Prophet ﷺ came and stood over him and said, "He killed seven and then they killed him. This person is from me and I am from him. This person is from me and I am from him."[1]

Therefore, this statement of his was not unique for ʿAlī رضي الله عنه since it was said to others as well. It would hence be invalid to infer that this narration proves his pre-eminence.

The basis for the Prophet's ﷺ statement, "No one can act on my behalf besides me or ʿAlī," is that it was the habit of the Arabs when they discussed something amongst themselves relating to abrogating, or consenting, or reconciliation, or abandoning, that the only persons who execute that was the chief or his closest relative. They would not accept anyone besides them.[2]

The Prophet ﷺ sent ʿAlī رضي الله عنه to join up with Abū Bakr and inform him about the revelation of Sūrah al-Barā'ah. Notwithstanding this he was sent as a follower under the command of Abū Bakr رضي الله عنه, as Abū Bakr رضي الله عنه was the leader of the Ḥajj at that point. So the Prophet's ﷺ dispatching ʿAlī رضي الله عنه under the command of Abū Bakr رضي الله عنه does not prove ʿAlī's رضي الله عنه rightfulness to the khilāfah. Rather, it is the other way around. It proves that Abū Bakr رضي الله عنه was the most rightful person to the khilāfah as he was the leader of the Ḥajj.

The narration which Tījānī produced, "You, O ʿAlī, will clarify to my Ummah what they dispute about after me..." is a fabricated ḥadīth. We know this on account of the narrator Ḍirār ibn al-Ṣurad.

> Al-Bukhārī and others say about him, "He is *matrūk* (suspected of ḥadīth forgery)."
>
> Yaḥyā ibn Maʿīn, "There were two distinguished fabricators in Kūfah, Ḍirār ibn al-Ṣurad and Abū Naʿīm al-Nakhaʿī."

---

1 *Ṣaḥīḥ Muslim* with the commentary, Kitāb Faḍā'il al-Ṣaḥābah, Bāb Faḍā'il Julaybīb, Ḥadīth no. 2472.

2 al-Mubārakfūrī: *Tuḥfah al-Aḥwadhī* (commentary of Tirmidhī), vol. 10 p. 152.

Al-Nasā'ī says, "He was not reliable."

Abū Ḥātim says, "Reasonable but not proof-worthy."

Al-Dāraquṭnī says, "A weak transmitter."[1]

This ḥadīth is also narrated via another chain from 'Alī ibn 'Ābis, which has been narrated by Ibn al-Jawzī in his book *Al-Mawḍū'āt.*

He says, "This ḥadīth is not reliable."

Yaḥyā ibn Ma'īn says, "Alī ibn 'Ābis is not a good transmitter."[2]

Al-Jūzajānī, al-Nasā'ī and al-Azdī say, "He is a weak transmitter."

Ibn Ḥibbān says, "His mistakes are dreadful to the point that deserves to be abandoned (as a transmitter)."[3]

Ibn Ḥajar says, "He is a weak transmitter."[4]

The ḥadīth, "This is my brother, my trustee and my deputy [caliph] after me."

Tījānī has failed to produce a single 'mutually agreeable' narration that supports his claim until this point. He cites the final ḥadīth and says:

> **The Prophetic tradition of the House on the day of Warning:**
>
> **The Prophet of Allah صَلَّى ٱللَّٰهُ عَلَيْهِ وَسَلَّمَ said, indicating Ali. "This is my brother, my trustee and my deputy [caliph] after me, so listen to him and obey him."**
>
> **This is yet another correct tradition cited by many historians at the beginning of the prophetic mission, and considered as one of the Prophet's miracles. However, political intrigues distorted the facts.[5]**

Analysis of the ḥadīth, "This is my brother, my trustee and my deputy [caliph] after me."

This ḥadīth is false both in terms of its chain and its text.

1 al-Dhahabī: *Mīzān al-I'tidāl*, vol. 2 p. 327-328, biography no. 3951.

2 Ibn al-Jawzī: *Al-Mawḍū'āt*, vol. 1 p. 376-377.

3 *Al-Mīzān*, vol. 3 p. 134-135, Ḥadīth no. 5872.

4 *Taqrīb al-Tahdhīb*, vol. 1 p. 697.

5 *Then I was guided*, p. 150.

Appearing in the chain of this narration is a pair of unreliable narrators, namely; ʿAbd al-Ghaffār ibn al-Qāsim and ʿAbd Allāh ibn ʿAbd al-Quddūs.

As for ʿAbd al-Ghaffār ibn al-Qāsim, he is *matrūk* (suspected of forgery) as a transmitter and is not proof-worthy. Al-Dhahabī says about him:

> He is Abū Maryam al-Anṣārī, he is a Rāfiḍī. He is not reliable.
>
> ʿAlī ibn al-Madīnī said about him: "He fabricates aḥādīth."
>
> It is also said about him that he is amongst the leaders of the Shīʿah.
>
> ʿAbbās ibn Yaḥyā narrates, "He is no good (as a transmitter)."
>
> Al-Bukhārī says, "He is not a strong transmitter according to them."
>
> Aḥmad ibn Ḥambal says, "Abū ʿUbaydah when he used to relate ḥadīth to us from Abū Maryam the people would become noisy and say, "We do not want him (his aḥādīth)."
>
> Aḥmad said, "Abū Maryam used to narrate imperfections of ʿUthmān."[1]

Ibn Ḥibbān says:

> He was amongst those who narrated the imperfections concerning ʿUthmān. He drank alcohol until he became drunk. In addition to that he used to distort information. It is not permissible to cite him as proof. Aḥmad ibn Ḥambal and Yaḥyā ibn Maʿīn suspected him of forgery.[2]

Ibn Kathīr says about him:

> He is matrūk, a liar, a Shīʿī, ʿAlī ibn al-Madīnī and others accuse him of fabricating aḥādīth and the a'immah (of transmitter criticism) grade him weak.[3]

As for ʿAbd Allāh ibn Quddūs, al-Dhahabī says about him:

> He was a Kūfī, Rāfiḍī. He settled in Ray. He narrates from al-Aʿmash and others.
>
> Ibn ʿAdī says about him, "Most of what he narrates relates to the merits of the Ahl al-Bayt."

---

1 al-Dhahabī: *Mīzān al-Iʿtidāl*, vol. 2 p. 640.

2 Ibn Ḥibbān: *Kitāb al-Majrūḥīn*, p. 143.

3 *Tafsīr Ibn Kathīr*, vol. 3 p. 363.

> Yaḥyā says, "He is no good (as a transmitter). He is a Rāfiḍī, malicious."
>
> Al-Nasā'ī and others say, "He is not reliable."
>
> Al-Dāraquṭnī says, "He is a weak transmitter."
>
> Abū Maʿmar says, "'Abd Allāh ibn al-Quddūs, he was a Rāfiḍī."[1]
>
> Aḥmad ibn ʿAlī al-Abār says, "I asked Zanīj, Rāzī's teacher, about ʿAbd Allāh ibn al-Quddūs and he said, 'I have abandoned him (as a transmitter). I did not write anything from him and he was not pleased with it.'"[2]

The purport of the narration is also problematic for the following reasons:

The narration mentioned by Tījānī is not the complete version. Rather, the narration in its complete form reads:

> When this verse, "And warn, (O Muḥammad), your closest kindred," was revealed upon Muḥammad, he called me and said, "O ʿAlī! Allah has instructed me 'to warn your close relatives,' but I find that difficult. I know that when I open this discussion with them I will see from them what I dislike. Therefore prepare a meal for them with a leg of lamb and milk. Then gather the sons of ʿAbd al-Muṭṭalib for me so that I may speak to them and convey to them what I have been instructed with."
>
> Then I did what he instructed me to do and I invited them to come and see him. They were approximately forty on that day and amongst them were his paternal uncles Abū Ṭālib, Ḥamzah, ʿAbbās, and Abū Lahab. When they were all there he summoned me to bring the food I had prepared for them. Then I brought it and when I placed it down the Prophet ﷺ took a chunk of meat and cut into it with his teeth and then spread it out at the corners of the plate. Then he said, "Take, with the name of Allah!" The people ate until they were satisfied. I could only see their hands. Then he said, "Bring the drinks," and I brought them the milk and they drank until they all were quenched.
>
> When the Prophet ﷺ intended to address them Abū Lahab preceded him in speaking and said, "Indeed, your companion has bewitched you," and the people left and the Prophet ﷺ did not speak to them.

---

1 *Mīzān al-Iʿtidāl*, vol. 2 p. 458.

2 al-ʿUqaylī: *Al-Ḍuʿafāʾ*, vol. 2 p. 279.

Then the Prophet ﷺ said, "Tomorrow, O ʿAlī! Indeed, this person preceded me to what you heard from him of speech and the people left before I could speak to them. Prepare the food again as you did before. Then gather them by me." Then I did that and gathered them and the Prophet ﷺ summoned me to bring the food. I presented the food and they ate to their fill, as the previous day. Then he said, "Quench them." and I brought the milk until all of them were quenched. Then the Messenger ﷺ spoke and said, "O Banī ʿAbd al-Muṭṭalib! By Allah! I do not know of a youth amongst the Arabs who has brought to his people what I am bringing you. I bring to you the best of this world and the next. Indeed, Allah has instructed me to call you to him. Who will assist me with this and he will be my brother, and my executor, and my khalīfah amongst you?"

(ʿAlī says) All of them desisted and I said, and I was the youngest amongst them, and the one with the smallest eyes, and the sternest amongst them, and the most zealous amongst them, "Me, O Messenger of Allah! I will be your assistant upon it!"

The Prophet ﷺ took me by the shoulder and said, "This is my brother, and my executor, and my khalīfah amongst you! Therefore, listen to him, and obey him!" The people stood up laughing and saying to Abū Ṭālib, "Indeed, he instructs you to listen to your son and to obey him!"

(In another narration it comes with the wording) No one responded to him. Then ʿAlī stood up and said, "Me, O Messenger of Allah!"

He said, "Sit down."

Then he repeated his request a second time but the people remained silent.

Then ʿAlī stood up again and said, "Me, O Messenger of Allah!"

He said (for a second time), "Sit down."

Then he repeated himself for a third time and (once again) no one responded. Then ʿAlī stood up (for a third time) and said, "Me, O Messenger of Allah!"

The Messenger ﷺ said, "Sit down! You are my brother, and ..."[1]

---

1 Muḥammad Marʿī al-Anṭākī: *Li Mādhā Ikhtarta Madh-hab al-Shīʿah*, p. 137-143; *Al-Murājaʿāt Murājaʿah*, p. 20 and 123.

The reason for Tījānī's concealing this part of the ḥadīth is no surprise; it brings to light the evidence of his lies and fabrications. We know this text to be forged because:

- In the ḥadīth it tells us that the sons of ʿAbd al-Muṭṭalib, "Were approximately forty on that day." However, history tells us that they were not even twenty men in number, let alone forty!

> Scholars agree that only four of the sons of ʿAbd al-Muṭṭalib had sons to perpetuate the family name. They were ʿAbbās, Abū Ṭālib, Ḥārith, and Abū Lahab. As for the uncles and the cousins, Abū Ṭālib had four sons: Ṭālib, ʿAqīl, Jaʿfar, and ʿAlī. As for ʿAbbās all of his sons were minors as none of them were adults when in Makkah. But for argument's sake, let us assume they were all adult men then they were ʿAbd Allāh, ʿUbayd Allāh, and Faḍl. As for Qutham, he was born afterwards. The eldest amongst them was Faḍl and it was with that name he was called by in his agnomen. As for Ḥārith ibn ʿAbd al-Muṭṭalib and Abū Lahab, their sons were fewer. Ḥārith had two sons: Abū Sufyān and Rabīʿah, both of them accepted Islam later. They were amongst those who accepted Islam upon the Conquest of Makkah. Similarly, the sons of Abū Lahab, they too accepted Islam upon the Conquest of Makkah. He had three sons, two of whom accepted Islam, ʿUtbah and Mughīth.[1]

- This narration contradicts another narration which the ḥadīth scholars agree is authentic and established. Al-Bukhārī and Muslim narrate in their Ṣaḥīḥs from Ibn ʿAbbās رضي الله عنه who said:

> لما نزلت وأنذر عشيرتك الأقربين صعد النبي صلى الله عليه وسلم على الصفا فجعل ينادي يا بني فهر يا بني عدي لبطون قريش حتى اجتمعوا فجعل الرجل إذا لم يستطع أن يخرج أرسل رسولا لينظر ما هو فجاء أبو لهب وقريش فقال أرأيتكم لو أخبرتكم أن خيلا بالوادي تريد أن تغير عليكم أكنتم مصدقي قالوا نعم ما جربنا عليك إلا صدقا قال فإني نذير لكم بين يدى عذاب شديد فقال أبو لهب تبا لك سائر اليوم ألهذا جمعتنا فنزلت تبت يدا أبي لهب وتب ما أغنى عنه ماله وما كسب

> When the verse, "And warn, (O Muḥammad), your closest kindred," was revealed, the Prophet صلى الله عليه وسلم ascended al-Ṣafā and started exclaiming, "O

1 *Minhāj al-Sunnah*, vol. 7 p. 304-305 with some alterations.

sons of Fihr! O sons of ʿAdī!" to all the clans of the Quraysh until all of them were gathered together. Those unable to attend sent a messenger to find out what the commotion was about. Then Abū Lahab and the Quraysh came.

The Prophet ﷺ said, "If I should tell you that there is an army in the valley ready to attack you will you believe me?"

They said, "Yes, we have only experienced truthfulness from you."

He said, "Then certainly I am a warner unto you before a severe punishment."

Abū Lahab said, "May you be ruined for the rest of the day! Did you gather us here for this?"

Then the following verse was revealed:

تَبَّتْ يَدَا أَبِي لَهَبٍ وَّتَبَّ مَا أَغْنَىٰ عَنْهُ مَالُهُ وَمَا كَسَبَ سَيَصْلَىٰ نَارًا ذَاتَ لَهَبٍ وَّامْرَأَتُهُ حَمَّالَةَ الْحَطَبِ فِي جِيدِهَا حَبْلٌ مِّن مَّسَدٍ

May the hands of Abū Lahab be ruined and ruined is he. His wealth will not avail him or that which he gained. He will (enter to) burn in a Fire of (blazing) flame. And his wife (as well)—the carrier of firewood, around her neck is a rope of twisted fibre.[1]

This narration claims that the Prophet ﷺ said to ʿAlī, after his people desisted from assisting him, "This is my brother, my executor, and my khalīfah amongst you! Therefore, listen to him, and obey him!" The people stood up laughing and saying to Abū Ṭālib, "Indeed, he instructs you to listen to your son and to obey him!"

Here I ask astonished: How could the Prophet ﷺ say to a people who had refused to assist him, rather, they waged war against him, "This is my brother, and my executor, and my khalīfah amongst you! Therefore, listen to him, and obey him"?

By Allah! They did not obey the divinely sent Prophet ﷺ, would they follow a small boy? If we assume that Tījānī argues (that the wording), "This is my brother, my executor, and my khalīfah (after me)" is correct and the words, "amongst you",

1 *Ṣaḥīḥ al-Bukhārī*, Kitāb al-Tafsīr, Bāb Wa Andhir ʿAshīrataka al-ʿAqrabīn, Ḥadīth no. 4492.

as in the above narration, is not authentic, then we ask were they obedient to the Prophet ﷺ at that point in time that they would obey his khalīfah after him? It is as if the address was for all Muslims and not for the leaders of the Quraysh.

After all of the above proofs can anyone still accept the authenticity of this ḥadīth?

2. Tījānī's proofs for the obligation of following the Ahl al-Bayt

Tījānī argues that it is necessary to follow the Ahl al-Bayt in all matters. He attempts to substantiate his claim by citing a number of aḥādīth.

a. Ḥadīth al-Thaqalayn

The first of his proofs is often referred to as ḥadīth al-Thaqalayn:

> **The Prophetic tradition of the two weighty things:**
>
> **The messenger of Allah ﷺ said,**
>
> **O People, I leave amongst you two things which if you follow, you will never go astray. They are the Book of Allah and my Ahl al-Bayt [family].**
>
> **He also said: The messenger of my God is about to come to me and I shall answer. I am leaving with you the two weighty things: The first is the Book of Allah, in which you find guidance and enlightenment, and the people of my household. I remind you, by Allah, of the people of my household... I remind you by Allah of the people of my household."**
>
> **If we examine with some care this honourable tradition, which has been cited by the Sihahs of the Sunnis and al-Jamaah, we will find that the Shiites alone followed the two weighty things: "The Book of Allah and honourable members of the Prophet's ﷺ Household". On the other hand, the Sunnis and al-Jamaah followed the saying of Umar "The Book of Allah is sufficient for us", but I wish they had followed the Book of Allah without interpreting it in their own ways. If Umar himself did not understand the meaning of al-Kalalah and did not know the Qur'anic verse regarding the Tayammum and other rules, so how about those who came later and followed him without the ability to interpret the Qur'anic texts?**
>
> **Naturally they will answer me with their own quoted saying, and that is: "I have left with you the Book of Allah and my tradition [Sunnah]!"**

This tradition, if it were correct - and it is correct in its general meaning - would correspond to the tradition of the two weighty things, because when the Prophet صَلَّى ٱللَّٰهُ عَلَيْهِ وَسَلَّمَ talked about his Household (Ahl al- Bayt) he meant that they should be consulted for two reasons. Firstly, to teach the tradition [Sunnah], or to transmit to people the correct tradition because they are cleared from telling any lies, and because Allah سُبْحَانَهُ وَتَعَالَىٰ made them infallible in the purification verse. Secondly, to explain and interpret the meanings and aims of the tradition, because the Book of Allah is not enough for guidance. There are many parties who claim to follow the Qur'an but in actual fact they have gone astray, and the Messenger of Allah صَلَّى ٱللَّٰهُ عَلَيْهِ وَسَلَّمَ said, "How many are the readers of the Qur'an whom the Qur'an curses! The Book of Allah is silent and could be interpreted in various ways, and it contains what is vague and what is similar, and to understand it we have to refer to those who are well endowed with knowledge as regards the Qur'an, and to Ahl al-Bayt, as regards to the Prophet's صَلَّى ٱللَّٰهُ عَلَيْهِ وَسَلَّمَ traditions.

The Shiites referred everything to the infallible Imams of Ahl al-Bayt [the Prophet's صَلَّى ٱللَّٰهُ عَلَيْهِ وَسَلَّمَ Household], and they did not interpret anything unless it had a supporting text.

We refer in every case to the Companions, whether it concerns Qur'anic commentary or the confirmation of the Sunnah and its explanation, and we know about the Companions and their interpretations and their personal opinions vis-a-vis the clear texts, and there are hundreds of them, so we cannot rely upon them after what they have done.

If we ask our religious leaders, "Which Sunnah do you follow?" They answer categorically, "The Sunnah of the Messenger of Allah صَلَّى ٱللَّٰهُ عَلَيْهِ وَسَلَّمَ!"

But the historical facts are incompatible with that, for they claim that the Messenger of Allah said, "Take my Sunnah and the Sunnah of the Rightly Guided Caliphs after me. Hold firmly to it." But the Sunnah they follow is often the Sunnah of the Rightly Guided Caliphs, and even the Messenger's صَلَّى ٱللَّٰهُ عَلَيْهِ وَسَلَّمَ Sunnah which they claim to follow is in fact transmitted by those people.

However, we read in our Sihahs that the Messenger of Allah صَلَّى ٱللَّٰهُ عَلَيْهِ وَسَلَّمَ prevented them from writing his Sunnah so that it was not confused with the Qur'an. Abu Bakr and Umar did the same thing during their caliphate, we therefore have no proof for the saying, "I left you my Sunnah!"[1]

---

1 *Then I was guided*, p. 151-152.

Analysis of Ḥadīth al-Thaqalayn

To begin with it would be prudent to reproduce the ḥadīth as it appears in *Ṣaḥīḥ Muslim* and let that be our frame of reference:

عن يزيد بن حيان قال انطلقت أنا وحصين بن سبرة وعمر بن مسلم إلى زيد بن أرقم فلما جلسنا إليه قال له حصين لقد لقيت يا زيد خيرا كثيرا رأيت رسول الله صلى الله عليه وسلم وسمعت حديثه وغزوت معه وصليت خلفه لقد لقيت يا زيد خيرا كثيرا حدثنا يا زيد ما سمعت من رسول الله صلى الله عليه وسلم قال يا ابن أخي والله لقد كبرت سني وقدم عهدي ونسيت بعض الذي كنت أعي من رسول الله صلى الله عليه وسلم فما حدثتكم فاقبلوا وما لا فلا تكلفونيه ثم قال قام رسول الله صلى الله عليه وسلم يوما فينا خطيبا بماء يدعى خما بين مكة والمدينة فحمد الله وأثنى عليه ووعظ وذكر ثم قال أما بعد ألا أيها الناس فإنما أنا بشر يوشك أن يأتي رسول ربي فأجيب وأنا تارك فيكم ثقلين أولهما كتاب الله فيه الهدى والنور فخذوا بكتاب الله واستمسكوا به فحث على كتاب الله ورغب فيه ثم قال وأهل بيتي أذكركم الله في أهل بيتي أذكركم الله في أهل بيتي أذكركم الله في أهل بيتي فقال له حصين ومن أهل بيته يا زيد أليس نساؤه من أهل بيته قال نساؤه من أهل بيته ولكن أهل بيته من حرم الصدقة بعده قال ومن هم قال هم آل علي وآل عقيل وآل جعفر وآل عباس قال كل هؤلاء حرم الصدقة قال نعم

Yazīd ibn Ḥayyān narrates, "Ḥusayn ibn Sabrah, ʿAmr ibn Muslim and I all went to visit Zayd ibn Arqam. As we sat at his side Ḥusayn (ibn Sabrah) said to him, 'O Zayd! You witnessed much good. You saw the Messenger of Allah ﷺ you heard his speech, participated in military campaigns with him and prayed behind him in Ṣalāh. O Zayd! You witnessed such good; relate to us some of what you had heard from the Prophet ﷺ.'

He responded, 'O my nephew! By Allah, I have become very old and a long time has passed (since the Prophet's passing) and I have forgotten some of what I used to remember from the Prophet ﷺ. Accept from me what I relate and do not impose upon me (to narrate) what I no longer remember.'

He went on to say, 'One day the Messenger ﷺ stood up to deliver a sermon at a watering stop known as Khumm, which is situated between Makkah and

Madīnah. He praised and glorified Allah, admonished and reminded us and said, "Listen O people, I am merely a human being. A Messenger from my Lord will soon approach me and I will respond to his call. I am leaving behind two weighty things; the First is the Book of Allah which contains guidance and illumination. So accept the Book of Allah and hold firmly to it."

He emphasized practising on the Book of Allah and holding firmly onto it. Then he said, "(And the second is) My family (Ahl Baytī). I remind you of Allah with regards to fulfilling the rights of my family. I remind you of Allah with regards to fulfilling the rights of my family.'"

Ḥusayn said to Zayd, 'O Zayd! Who is his family? Are his wives not part of his family?'

Zayd responded, 'His wives are part of his family, but his family (in terms of blood relation) are those whom charity is unlawful for.'

Ḥusayn asked, 'Who are they?'

Zayd replied, 'They are the family of ʿAlī, family of ʿAqīl, family of Jaʿfar, and the family of Ibn ʿAbbās.'

Ḥusayn then asked, 'Is it not permitted to give charity to all of them?'

Zayd replied, 'Yes.'"[1]

If we examine the various elements mentioned in the ḥadīth we realise the following:

1. The Prophet ﷺ was about to depart from this world.
2. The Prophet ﷺ left behind two weighty things.
3. He advised how to deal with each of these weighty things differently.
4. One of them is the Book of Allah; which he exhorted towards in terms of holding on to and abiding by its injunctions.
5. The second was his family, the Ahl al-Bayt for whom the Prophet ﷺ invoked our fear in Allah in terms of respecting them, honouring them, and safeguarding them.

---

1 *Ṣaḥīḥ Muslim*, Kitāb al-Fāḍā'il al-Ṣaḥābah, Ḥadīth no. 5920.

Now that ḥadīth cited by Tījānī is placed in its proper context we realise that this was said at Ghadīr Khumm. The next task is to identify the meaning of the term Ahl al-Bayt and to whom this term applies. The reader will notice that Tījānī appears to present this narration as proof for the absolute obedience to Ahl al-Bayt vis-à-vis the Sunnah. The term Ahl al-Bayt used in the ḥadīth has been applied to various meanings according to its context. In a sense it could refer to one's followers, specifically those who are knowledgeable among them. It also refers to a man's entire family, and this mode of expression is consistent with the Qur'ān's usage of the term Ahl al-Bayt. By the admission of Zayd ibn al-Arqam رضي الله عنه, the narrator of this ḥadīth, the wives of the Prophet صلى الله عليه وسلم are included in the definition of the term Ahl al-Bayt.

The question now arises as to the meaning of this ḥadīth? Tījānī and those who think like him are inclined to think that this refers to ʿAlī رضي الله عنه specifically, whereas this stands in stark contrast with reality since the Prophet صلى الله عليه وسلم would not have used such an encompassing phrase if he only intended a particular individual. It is quite evident that this ḥadīth be understood in a framework other than that which Tījānī argues from.

One of the ways of understanding this narration is that it refers to the people of knowledge and piety among the Ahl al-Bayt who hold onto the Book of Allah and the Sunnah of the Prophet. This is what is referred to in the version of the ḥadīth, "O People! I leave amongst you what if you hold onto it you will never go astray, the Book of Allah and my offspring, the people of my household (Ahl al-Bayt)." This version of the ḥadīth has been called into question in terms of its reliability since the narrators are not all sound.

There is another way of looking at it, and this seems to be a more accurate representation of the ḥadīth of Zayd ibn Arqam رضي الله عنه, especially if the wording is considered. According to this understanding the ḥadīth calls for love for the Ahl al-Bayt, respecting them, honouring them, and safeguarding them.

The Ahl al-Bayt, in terms of the Sunnī understanding, refers to the Prophet's صلى الله عليه وسلم entire family, whereas according to the Twelver Shīʿah it applies only to twelve individuals among them. Interestingly, Fāṭimah رضي الله عنها is excluded from the twelve. The view of Ahl al-Sunnah is further supported by the clarification of Zayd ibn Arqam رضي الله عنه, who was a follower of ʿAlī رضي الله عنه, when he pointed out that the

Prophet's ﷺ wives were part of the Ahl al-Bayt, as well as the members of the four famous lines mentioned in the ḥadīth.

Tījānī's contention is that it applies exclusively to ʿAlī رضي الله عنه and his sons رضي الله عنهما. The problem with this reasoning is that there is nothing to substantiate the exclusive application to one part of the family since comprehensive form of expression Ahl al-Bayt encompasses the other branches as pointed out by the narrator, Zayd ibn Arqam رضي الله عنه.

In addition to this, we know that not all his relatives were on Islam. The Prophet ﷺ instructed us to hold onto the Ahl al-Bayt, was the command then to hold onto to every person who subscribes to the Ahl al-Bayt even if they oppose the Qur'ān and the Sunnah? No doubt this view is incorrect. Therefore, he instructed us to follow those from the Ahl al-Bayt who hold onto the Book of Allah and the Sunnah. In this regard we also understand the ḥadīth, "You must follow my Sunnah and the Sunnah of the Rightly Guided Khulafā' after me. Hold on to it with your molar teeth!"[1]

As well as the ḥadīth:

إني لا أدري ما بقائي فيكم فاقتدوا باللذين من بعدي وأشار إلى أبي بكر وعمر

> "Indeed, I do not know how long I will remain amongst you. Therefore, follow the two after me," and he pointed to Abū Bakr and ʿUmar.[2]

Collectively these aḥādīth encourage holding onto the Sunnah and cannot be understood to apply exclusively to ʿAlī رضي الله عنه.

Al-Qārī comments on the meaning of the words, "holding onto," as they appear in the weaker narrations bearing the words, "my ʿitrah," and the narrations about the Khulafā' respectively:

> Intended by them are the people of knowledge, those who study his biography, those who know his methodology and know its ruling and its wisdom.
>
> Ibn Mālik says, "The meaning of holding onto the ʿitrah is to love them and follow their guidance and their lifestyles." Jamāl al-Dīn adds, "When it does not contradict the dīn."[3]

1 *Sunan al-Tirmidhī*, Kitāb al-ʿIlm, Ḥadīth no. 2676; Refer also to *Ṣaḥīḥ al-Tirmidhī*, Ḥadīth no. 2157.

2 *Sunan al-Tirmidhī*, Kitāb al-Manāqib, Ḥadīth no. 3663; Refer also to *Ṣaḥīḥ al-Tirmidhī*, Ḥadīth no. 2896.

3 *Mirqāt al-Mafātīḥ Sharḥ Mishkāt al-Maṣābīḥ*, vol. 10 p. 531.

Some scholars say:

> The ʿitrah of a man is his household and his close kin. The word ʿitrah has many usages. The Prophet ﷺ explained it with his words, "My Ahl al-Bayt," so that it could be known that he intended with it his progeny, his close relatives, and his wives.[1]

It is similar to Allah's instruction to the Prophet's ﷺ wives in the verse:

وَاذْكُرْنَ مَا يُتْلَى فِي بُيُوتِكُنَّ مِنْ آيَاتِ اللَّهِ وَالْحِكْمَةِ

And remember what is recited in your houses of the verses of Allah and wisdom.[2]

The word, 'wisdom', carries the meaning of 'Sunnah'.

So the meaning of the Prophet's ﷺ words, "You must follow my Sunnah and the Sunnah of the Rightly Guided Khulafā'," according to al-Qārī:

> It is because they only practice my Sunnah. His ascribing (the Sunnah) to them was either because of their knowledge of it, or because their extracting rules and principles from it and their choosing it.[3]

Ibn Rajab says:

> This is his prediction about what was going to occur in his Ummah after him in terms of disputes in the fundamentals and branches of the dīn, and in terms of statements and actions and beliefs. This supports what was narrated from him about the splitting of his Ummah into seventy odd branches and that all of them were in the fire besides one, that group being the group that followed him and his Ṣaḥābah.
>
> Similarly, in this ḥadīth there is the instruction to hold onto his Sunnah and the Sunnah of the Rightly Guided Khulafā' after him at the time of the splitting of this Ummah.
>
> The Sunnah is the chosen path and that includes holding onto what the Prophet ﷺ and the Rightly Guided Khulafā' were upon in terms of beliefs, and actions, and statements. This is the complete Sunnah and it was for this reason that the predecessors used the term to include all of that.[4]

1 Op. cit. vol. 10 p. 530; *Tuḥfah al-Aḥwadhī*, vol. 1 p. 196.

2 Sūrah al-Aḥzāb: 34.

3 *Tuḥfah al-Aḥwadhī*, vol. 7 p. 367.

4 Ibn Rajab: *Jāmiʿ al-ʿUlūm wa al-Ḥukm*, p. 120.

From the aforementioned we conclude that the command to hold onto the Sunnah of these people refers to holding onto what they have with them in terms of knowledge and this knowledge was not restricted to ʿAlī رضي الله عنه or his sons after him. How could that be when the ḥadīth proving this has been narrated by others besides ʿAlī رضي الله عنه and his sons?

In Tījānī's framework of understanding, Ḥadīth al-Thaqalayn is in conflict with the ḥadīth of holding to the Book and Sunnah. Since the version of the ḥadīth of holding on to the Book and Sunnah appears with an interrupted chain he infers that the concept of the Book and Sunnah is a Sunnī construct and the Book and Ahl al-Bayt is the Shīʿī understanding. He does not realise that he has subconsciously associated the Sunnah with the Khulafā'. Secondly he ignores the obligation of following the Sunnah of the Prophet صلى الله عليه وسلم. He does not realise that his reasoning inherently denies the need to follow to Sunnah. This is the result of his inability to understand ḥadīth al-Thaqalayn in its proper context.

The Qur'ān encourages returning to the Sunnah:

لَقَدْ مَنَّ اللّٰهُ عَلَى الْمُؤْمِنِيْنَ إِذْ بَعَثَ فِيْهِمْ رَسُوْلًا مِّنْ أَنْفُسِهِمْ يَتْلُوْ عَلَيْهِمْ آيَاتِهِ وَيُزَكِّيْهِمْ وَيُعَلِّمُهُمُ الْكِتَابَ وَالْحِكْمَةَ وَإِنْ كَانُوْا مِنْ قَبْلُ لَفِيْ ضَلَالٍ مُّبِيْنٍ

Certainly did Allah confer (great) favour upon the believers when He sent among them a Messenger from themselves, reciting to them His verses and purifying them and teaching them the Book (i.e., the Qur'ān) and wisdom, although they had been before in manifest error.[1]

Al-Shāfiʿī said:

> Allah mentions the Book and that is the Qur'ān, and he mentions the wisdom and I heard from someone I am pleased with from the people of knowledge of the Qur'ān, he said, "The wisdom refers to the Prophet's Sunnah."[2]

Similar instructions are to be understood from the verse:

---

1 Sūrah Āl ʿImrān: 164.

2 Jalāl al-Dīn al-Suyūṭī: *Miftāḥ al-Jannah fī al-Iʿtiṣām bi al-Sunnah*, p. 18.

وَمَا آتَاكُمُ الرَّسُوْلُ فَخُذُوْهُ وَمَا نَهَاكُمْ عَنْهُ فَانْتَهُوْا وَاتَّقُوا اللّٰهَ إِنَّ اللّٰهَ شَدِيْدُ الْعِقَابِ

> And whatever the Messenger has given you—take; and what he has forbidden you—refrain from. And fear Allah; indeed, Allah is severe in penalty.[1]

Muḥammad Jawwād al-Maghniyyah, a senior contemporary Imāmī scholar, says in the Tafsīr of this verse:

> Allah says: Practice the Qur'ān! If you do not find in it a clear text for what you intend then return to the prophetic Sunnah![2]

When we study these verses alongside the previous aḥādīth, which encourage holding onto the Sunnah of the 'itrah and the Khulafā' because of their knowledge of the Sunnah, we know with certainty that there is harmony in understanding the instruction to follow the Sunnah, the Rightly-guided Khulafā' and the 'itrah.

Al-Kulaynī narrates in his book *Uṣūl al-Kāfī* from Ayyūb ibn al-Ḥurr, who said:

> I heard Abū 'Abd Allāh (al-Ṣādiq) saying, "Everything returns to the Qur'ān and the Sunnah. Every ḥadīth that does not agree with the Book of Allah is vanity.[3]

Abū 'Abd Allāh (al-Ṣādiq), he said:

> The Prophet ﷺ addressed us at Minā and said, "O People! Whatever comes to you from me in agreement with the Book of Allah then I said it. And what comes to you (from me) opposing the Book of Allah I did not say it."[4]

From Ibn Abī 'Umayr, from some of his companions, who said, I heard Abū 'Abd Allāh (al-Ṣādiq) saying:

> Whoever opposes the Book of Allah and the Sunnah of Muḥammad ﷺ has become an unbeliever.[5]

---

1 Sūrah al-Ḥashr: 7.

2 *Al-Tafsīr al-Mubīn*, p. 731.

3 al-Kulaynī: *Uṣūl min al-Kāfī*, vol. 1, Kitāb Faḍl al-'Ilm, Bāb al-Akhdh bi al-Sunnah wa Shawāhid al-Kitāb, p. 55.

4 Ibid. p. 56.

5 Ibid.

From Abān ibn Taghlib, from Abū Jaʿfar (al-Bāqir):

> He was asked about something and he answered. Then the man said, "The jurists do not say this!"
>
> He said, "Woe unto you! Do you recognise the jurist only? Indeed, the jurist, the true jurist, is the ascetic in this world, and desirous of the hereafter, and the one who holds onto the prophetic Sunnah!"[1]

Their senior scholar in the field of transmitter biographical information, in his book *Rijāl al-Kashshī*, forwards from Abū ʿAbd Allāh (al-Ṣādiq) saying:

> Fear Allah and do not accept upon us what opposes the word of Allah and the Sunnah of the Prophet ﷺ because when we speak we say, "Allah says, and the Messenger ﷺ says."[2]

Yūnus said when the books of the companions of Abū ʿAbd Allāh (al-Ṣādiq) were presented to Abū al-Ḥasan (al-Riḍā) he denied many of the aḥādīth saying that they could not have been from the aḥādīth of Abū ʿAbd Allāh, he said:

> Indeed Abū al-Khaṭṭāb has forged (aḥādīth) upon Abū ʿAbd Allāh. May Allah curse Abū al-Khaṭṭāb and the companions of Abū al-Khaṭṭāb who inserted these aḥādīth (into the ḥadīth collections) and those who up until today insert in the books of the companions of Abū ʿAbd Allāh! Therefore, do not accept from us anything in conflict with the Qur'ān.[3] For indeed, when we speak we speak in conformity with the Qur'ān and in conformity with the Sunnah. Either from Allah or from his Messenger do we speak! We do not say,

1 Ibid.

2 *Rijāl al-Kashshī*, p. 195, al-Mughīrah ibn Saʿd.

3 Therefore, everything the Rāfiḍah ascribe to Abū ʿAbd Allāh or his father in terms of the claim of the existence of the Muṣḥaf of Fāṭimah, which is not in agreement with our copy of the Qur'ān, or the apostasy of all the Ṣaḥābah besides three or seven, or the claim that the Imāms have been divinely appointed by Allah and his Messenger ﷺ, and everything that has been narrated upon his tongue in terms of statements which equates to unbelief, and extremism in relation to the Imāms, is a lie and false. The best proof for that is that Abū ʿAbd Allāh said that Mughīrah use to forge statements of unbelief and sacrilege against his father and used to ascribe them to his companions. Then he instructed them to spread it amongst the Shīʿah. Therefore, everything that was in the books of the companions of my father in terms of extremism that is what Mughīrah ibn Saʿd inserted in their books. *Rijāl al-Kashshī*, p. 196.

"Such and such a person said,"[1] and then our speech becomes contradictory.[2]

Can anyone doubt, after the aforementioned, that the members of the Ahl al-Sunnah are the true followers of the Prophet صَلَّى ٱللَّٰهُ عَلَيْهِ وَسَلَّمَ by following the Qur'ān and the Sunnah?

Tījānī says:

> **The meaning of ʿitrah in the Prophet's statement in the previously cited ḥadīth of al-Thaqalayn is to return to my household so that they may teach you, firstly, my Sunnah, or so that they may transmit to you the authentic aḥādīth because they were above lying on account of the verse of Taṭhīr.**

Our response:

The purpose of infallible according to Tījānī is to avoid the possibility of error, whether deliberate or accidental in the transmission of the ḥadīth of the Prophet صَلَّى ٱللَّٰهُ عَلَيْهِ وَسَلَّمَ. The problem with this reasoning is that it required fallible narrators to prove the infallibility of the infallibles. Not only is that a paradox but an exercise in futility.

Tījānī claims that those intended by the words Ahl al-Bayt are the Imāms of the Twelvers from the sons of ʿAlī ibn Abī Ṭālib, after Ḥasan, from the line of Ḥusayn to Jaʿfar al-Ṣādiq. According to them Imāmah continues with Mūsā ibn Jaʿfar al-Kāẓim, in contrast to the Ismāʿīliyyah who consider to continuity of Imāmah to be with his son, Ismāʿīl ibn Jaʿfar.

Then another sect emerged, the Kaysāniyyah, who consider Imāmah to have continued with Muḥammad ibn al-Ḥanafiyyah. Then a group followed them and claimed that the Ahl al-Bayt is ʿAbbās and his sons. This group is known as al-Rāwandiyyah.[3]

---

1 What is strange is that Imāmiyyah do return the matters of the religion to the statements of men. Their legal school in terms of the branches (of the religion) relies upon the Jaʿfar's (al-Ṣādiq) legal school. How can that be if he commands with following the Book (the Qur'ān) and the Sunnah and discarding the views of men? Can the Ahl al-Sunnah then be rebuked after that for following the Book (Qur'ān) and the Sunnah?

2 *Rijāl al-Kashshī*, p. 195-196.

3 Refer to *Firaq al-Shīʿah* by al-Nawbakhtī, p. 23, 33, 68; *al-Farq bayn al-Firaq* by al-Baghdādī, p. 60; *ʿAqā'id al-Thalāth wa al-Sabʿīn Firqah* by Abū Muḥammad al-Yamanī, vol. 2.

There are also other sects who subscribe to the Ahl al-Bayt and each of these sects claims the right for itself, and that it is following the path of the Ahl al-Bayt, and it declares the other groups as unbelievers or innovators. Also, each one of them claims to take the authentic Sunnah from those who they believe the Imāmah passed through them. How does the idea of adhering to an infallible overcome this diverse interpretation and multiple claims of leadership? How do we determine which of these interpretations of Ahl al-Bayt to follow?

b. The Ḥadīth, "My Ahl al-Bayt are like the Ark of Noah."

Then Tījānī cites the second ḥadīth and says:

> **The Prophetic tradition of the Ship:**
>
> **The Messenger of Allah صَلَّى ٱللَّهُ عَلَيْهِ وَسَلَّمَ said, Behold! My Ahl al-Bayt are like the Ark of Noah, whoever embarked in it was saved, and whoever turned away from it was drowned.**

In another ḥadīth:

> **My Ahl al-Bayt are like the Gate of Repentance of the children of Israel; whoever entered therein was forgiven.[1]**

Analysing the Ḥadīth, "My Ahl al-Bayt are like the Ark of Noah."

This ḥadīth revolves around a series of weak and abandoned narrators. In the chain is Ḥasan ibn Abī Jaʿfar and he is *matrūk* (suspected of forgery), and ʿAlī ibn Zayd who is a weak transmitter.

In al-Ṭabarānī's chain of this ḥadīth appears ʿAbd Allāh ibn Dāhir and he is matrūk.[2]The editor of the published version of *Faḍā'il al-Ṣaḥābah* of Aḥmad agrees because a narrator in the chain Mufaḍḍal ibn Ṣāliḥ al-Naḥḥās al-Asadī who the scholars of verification grade as weak. Al-Dhahabī says about him, "Mufaḍḍal is weak."[3]

Tījānī referenced the second ḥadīth to *Majmaʿ al-Zawā'id* by al-Haythamī but when we referred to the book we found:

---

1 *Then I was guided*, p. 160.

2 Refer to *Muʿjam al-Ṭabarānī al-Kabīr*, Ḥadīth no. 2632, 2637, 2638, 12388.

3 *Faḍā'il al-Ṣaḥābah*, vol. 2, Ḥadīth no. 1402.

From Abū Dharr, who said, the Messenger ﷺ said, "The likeness of my Ahl al-Bayt is the likeness of Noah's ark. Whoever boards it is saved and whoever lags behind drowns. And whoever fights at the end of days he is like the one who fights Dajjāl." This is narrated by al-Bazzār and Ṭabarānī in the three. In al-Bazzār's sanad is al-Ḥasan ibn Abī Jaʿfar al-Jaʿfarī and in Ṭabarānī's sanad is ʿAbd Allāh ibn Dāhir and both of them are matrūk.

From Ibn ʿAbbās, he said, the Messenger ﷺ said, "The likeness of my Ahl al-Bayt is the likeness of Noah's ark. Whoever boards it is saved and whoever lags behind drowns." This is narrated by al-Bazzār and Ṭabarānī and in it is al-Ḥasan ibn Abī Jaʿfar and he is matrūk.

From ʿAbd Allāh ibn Zubayr that the Prophet ﷺ said, "The similitude of my Ahl al-Bay is the similitude of Noah's ark. Whoever mounts it is saved and whoever lags behind drowns." This is narrated by al-Bazzār and in it is Ibn Lahīʿah and he is a weak transmitter.

From Abū Saʿīd al-Khudrī, he said, I heard the Messenger ﷺ saying, "The example of my Ahl al-Bay amongst you is the example of Noah's ark. Whoever mounts it is saved and whoever lags behind drowns. And the example of my Ahl al-Bay amongst you is the example of the door of Ḥiṭṭah amongst the Banī Isrā'īl. Whoever enters it is forgiven.' This is narrated by Ṭabarānī in the *al-Ṣaghīr* and in *al-Awsaṭ* and in it is a group (of transmitters) I do not know.[1]

If Tījānī actually referred to *Majmaʿ al-Zawā'id* it means that he knowingly cited spurious narrations. That speaks volumes for his objectivity in proving an undeniable tenet of his faith!

c. The Ḥadīth, "Whoever wishes to live and die like me..."

The third narration which he presents is the following:

The Prophetic tradition: "He who wishes to live like me."

The Messenger of Allah ﷺ said: "Whoever wishes to live and die like me, and to abide in the Garden of Eden after death should acknowledge Ali as his patron and follow Ahl al-Bayt after me, for they are my Ahl al-Bayt and they have been created out of the same knowledge and understanding as myself. Woe unto those followers of mine who will deny the Ahl al-Bayt their

1 Al-Haythamī: *Majmaʿ al-Zawā'id wa Mambaʿ al-Fawā'id*, vol. 9 p. 167.

distinctions and who will disregard their relationship and affinity with me. May Allah, never let them benefit from my intercession."[1]

Analysing the Ḥadīth, "Whoever wishes to live and die like me..."

This ḥadīth is fabricated. Its transmitters are all unknown with the exception of Ibn Abī Rawwād:

> Everyone besides Ibn Abī Rawwād is unknown. I do not find (any scholar) who mentions them. However, I am of the opinion that Aḥmad ibn Muḥammad ibn Yazīd ibn Sulaym is in actual fact Ibn Muslim al-Anṣārī al-Aṭrābalsī, also known as Ibn Abī al-Ḥanājir. Ibn Abī Ḥātim says, "We wrote him as a *ṣadūq* (average transmitter)." There is some biographical information about him in *Tārīkh Ibn ʿAsākir*. As for the rest of them I do not recognise them. Therefore, one of them fabricated this ḥadīth which is apparent in its falseness and make up. The merit of ʿAlī is beyond having to prove it with such fabrications which the Shīʿah cling onto and blacken their books with tens of them citing them in order to establish that which no one today denies and that is the merit of ʿAlī رضي الله عنه.[2]

Tījānī indicates in the footnotes to the sources of this ḥadīth include *al-Ḥilyah* of Abū Nuʿaym, and *Tārīkh Ibn ʿAsākir*, but he concealed their evaluation of these two narrations that they are weak. So much for fair representation and avoiding prejudice!

Abū Nuʿaym said about it, "(This is a) strange (ḥadīth),"[3] indicating to its weakness.

Ibn ʿAsākir narrated it in his *Tārīkh* and said about it, "This is a contradictory ḥadīth and it has more than one unknown transmitter."[4]

He confirms his ignorance when he says:

> **It is worth noting here that at the early stage of my research, I felt doubtful about the authenticity of this tradition and I thought it carried a great threat to those who are not in agreement with Ali and Ahl al-Bayt, especially when the tradition does not allow any scope for interpretation. I became rather**

1 *Then I was guided*, p. 161.

2 *Al-silsilah al-Aḥādīth al-Mawḍūʿāh*, vol. 2 p. 298.

3 Abū Nuʿaym: *Al-Ḥilyah*, vol. 1 p. 86.

4 *Tarīkh Dimashq*, vol. 12 p. 120.

> **worried when I read the book "Al- Isabah" in which Ibn Hajar al-Asqalani gives the following commentary on the tradition: "...I based the tradition on what Yahya ibn Ya'la al-Muharibi had said, and he is feeble." In fact Ibn Hajar removed some of the doubt that remained in my minds for I thought that Yahya ibn Ya'la al-Muharihi fabricated the tradition and could not be a reliable transmitter. But Allah—Praise be to Him the Most High —wanted to show me the whole truth. I read a book entitled Ideological discussions on the writings of Ibrahim al-Jabhan. This book clarified the situation and it became apparent to me that Yahya ibn Ya'la al-Muharibi was a reliable transmitter of Ḥadīth and the two Shaykhs, Muslim and al-Bukhari depended on what he transmitted. I myself followed his case and found that al-Bukhari cited a few traditions transmitted by him regarding the Battle of al-Hudaybiyah, and they were put in Volume 3, Page 31. Muslim also cited a few traditions in his *Sahih* Volume 5 in a chapter entitled "The Boundaries" Page 119. Even al-Dhahabi, with all his restrictions, considered him a reliable transmitter, together with the Imams of al-Jarh and al-Ta'deel (criteria applied to Ḥadīths to find out the reliable and unreliable transmitter), and of course the two Shaykhs [Muslim and al-Bukhari] used him as a reliable reference. So why all this intrigue, falsification and deception about a man who was considered to be a reliable transmitter by the authors of al-Sihah?**

Our response:

Tījānī repeatedly exposes his ignorance. The ḥadīth he cites, "Whoever wants to live my life," is not transmitted by way of the narrator Yaḥyā ibn Yaʿlā al-Muḥāribī. Rather, Tījānī confuses the ḥadīth we are discussing with another ḥadīth which reads:

> Whoever wishes to live my life and die my death and live the everlasting garden which Allah promised me, he planted its trees with his own hands; let him take ʿAlī ibn Abī Ṭālib as his guardian. Indeed, he will not remove you from guidance and he will not enter you into misguidance.

It appears that Tījānī merely followed his guru, ʿAbd al-Ḥusayn al-Mūsawī, in his book *al-Murājaʿāt* when he mentioned the same ḥadīth and also brought Ibn Ḥajar's statement about Yaʿlā al-Muḥāribī and said:

> I say: This is strange from someone the like of al-ʿAsqalānī as Yaḥyā ibn Yaʿlā al-Muḥāribī is reliable by consensus.[1]

---

1 Mūsawī: *Al-Murājaʿāt*, p. 27, in the footnote.

In Tījānī's haste to relate this statement of Mūsawī he overlooked the fact the he was referring to a different ḥadīth!

As for Ibn Ḥajar's statement, "In its chain is Yaḥyā ibn Yaʿlā al-Muḥāribī and his is a weak transmitter," it appears to be an oversight on the part of Ibn Ḥajar and instead of saying Yaḥyā ibn Yaʿlā al-Aslamī, who is one of the transmitters of this ḥadīth, said, "al-Muḥāribī." The proof for that is that Ibn Ḥajar himself grades al-Muḥāribī as reliable in his biography when he said, "Yaḥyā ibn Yaʿlā ibn al-Ḥārith al-Muḥāribī al-Kūfī is a reliable transmitter," and he said in the biography of al-Aslamī, "Yaḥyā ibn Yaʿlā al-Aslamī al-Kūfī is a Shīʿī and a weak transmitter."[1]

In the chain of the ḥadīth above is Yaḥyā ibn Yaʿlā al-Aslamī. Despite Tījānī's powers of observation and in-depth research he failed to distinguish between two aḥādīth. Therefore, he narrates one ḥadīth and studies the chain of another!

3. Tījānī's Confusion about the salutation[2] appearing after ʿAlī's name in *Ṣaḥīḥ al-Bukhārī*

Tījānī says:

> One day while I was talking to my friend I asked him to answer me frankly, and the following dialogue took place:
>
> I said: You place Ali, may Allah be pleased with him, and may He honour him, at the same level as the prophets, because whenever I hear his name mentioned you say "Peace be on him".
>
> My friend: That is right whenever we mention the name of the Commander of the Faithful [Imam Ali or one of the Imams of his off-spring we say "Peace be upon him", but this does not mean that they are prophets. However, they are the descendants of the Prophet, and Allah has ordered us to pray for them, therefore we are allowed to say "May Allah bless them and grant them peace" as well.
>
> I said: No brother, we do not say "May Allah bless him and grant him peace" except on the Prophet Muhammad ﷺ and on the Prophets who came before him, and there is nothing to do with Ali or his descendants, may Allah be pleased with them all, in this matter.

---

1 Ibn Ḥajar: *Taqrīb al-Tahdhīb*, vol. 2 p. 319.
2 Referring to the words: ʿalayh al-Ṣalāh wa al-Salām or ʿalayh al-Salām, usually said after the mention of a Prophet of Allah عَلَيْهِ السَّلَام.

(Then his Shīʿī friend cites some proofs against his statement and later says to Tījānī :) "What do you think of al Bukhari?"

I said, "He is a great Sunni Imam and his book is the most reliable book after the book of Allah [the Qur'an]."

Then, he stood up and pulled "Sahih al-Bukhari" from his library and searched for a particular page he wanted and gave it to read: "We have been informed by so and so that Ali [may Allah grant him peace] ..." I could not believe my eyes and was very surprised to the extent that I thought it was not "Sahih al-Bukhari", and looked at the page and the cover again, and when my friend sensed my doubtful looks, he took the book from me and opened another page, it read: "Ali ibn al-Husain—may Allah grant them peace..." After that I could only say to him, "Glory be to Allah." He was satisfied with my answer, so he left the room and I stayed behind thinking, reading those pages again and making sure of the book's edition, which I found had been published and distributed by al-Halabi & Sons Co. in Egypt.

(Then Tījānī said): O my God, why should I be so arrogant and stubborn, for he gave me a tangible reasoning, based on one of our most reliable books, and al-Bukhari was not Shi'i at all, in fact he was a Sunni Imam and scholar. [1]

Our comment:

Before expounding on the multiple views among the Ahl al-Sunnah on a secondary issue such as this, I would like to draw the esteemed reader's attention to the fact that Tījānī's own narrative is a testament to his ignorance. Tījānī speaks about being arrogant and stubborn in the beginning. It appears that it was not arrogance or stubbornness, rather a case of ignorance. He was discussing matters that he was unqualified to discuss. It is extremely hard to believe that he began his journey of enlightenment from a position of neutrality because his ignorance of a simple detail in *Ṣaḥīḥ al-Bukhārī*—which is evident to novice students who study the text, let alone experts who have poured over it in significant detail—indicates that he was unprepared for the tidal wave of Shīʿī propaganda that was about to hit him. His abandoning the school of the Ahl al-Sunnah was inevitable if he was to study the material for himself since he would be clearly unaware of the unfaithful representation of history, and the forgeries in the ḥadīth presented. Any acknowledgement of stubbornness and arrogance is accounted for during his

1 *Then I was guided*, p. 29-31.

enlightenment since he ignored seeking professional help and attempted to study these texts with the guide of Shīʿī propaganda.

The Ahl al-Sunnah differs about the ruling of independently invoking salutations upon others besides the Prophets عَلَيْهِمُ السَّلَامُ.

The view of Mālik, al-Shāfiʿī, and al-Majd ibn Taymiyyah from the Ḥambalīs is one of prohibition. Their argument is that Ibn ʿAbbās رَضِيَ اللَّهُ عَنْهُ said:

> To say al-Ṣalāh upon anyone other than the Prophet صَلَّى اللَّهُ عَلَيْهِ وَسَلَّمَ is not correct. Instead, Istighfār is (seeking forgiveness) for the Muslims, male and female (is what one is meant to say).

Aḥmad ibn Ḥambal, and most of his adherents, the likes of al-Qāḍī, Ibn ʿAqīl, and al-Shaykh ʿAbd al-Qādir, consider it permissible. They cite what has been narrated from ʿAlī رَضِيَ اللَّهُ عَنْهُ that he said to ʿUmar رَضِيَ اللَّهُ عَنْهُ, "*Ṣallāt Allāh ʿalayka!*"[1] (May the mercy and salutations of Allah be on you)

Al-Nawawī, the authoritative jurist of the Shāfiʿī school, says:

> The correct opinion—which the majority is upon—is that it is Makrūh, *Karāhat al-Tanzīh* (discouraged), because it is the symbol of the people of bidʿah.[2]

Therefore, it is originally permissible. Also, they agree that it is permissible to say it for others besides the Prophets عَلَيْهِمُ السَّلَامُ in a secondary capacity, i.e. after having said it for the Prophets عَلَيْهِمُ السَّلَامُ. In other words, it may be said in the manner mentioned below, since it is prescribed in a sound aḥādīth that we are required to do so in the *Tashahhud*. Similarly, the early Muslims were recorded as having done so outside of the ṣalāh.[3]

اَللّٰهُمَّ صَلِّ عَلٰى مُحَمَّدٍ وَّ عَلٰى اٰلِ مُحَمَّدٍ وَّ أَصْحَابِهِ وَ أَزْوَاجِهِ وَ ذُرِّيّٰتِهِ وَ أَتْبَاعِهِ

> O Allah! Send al-Ṣalāh upon Muḥammad and family of Muḥammad, and his Ṣaḥābah, and his wives, and his progeny, and his followers.

1 Refer to *Majmūʿ al-Fatāwā*, vol. 22 p. 472-474.

2 Imām al-Nawawī: *Al-Adhkār*, p. 176.

3 Op. cit. p. 177; See also *Masā'il min Fiqh al-Kitāb wa al-Sunnah* by ʿUmar al-Ashqar, p. 62-63.

From this we understand the permissibility of conferring this mode of salutation for any person as long as it does not become a symbol, as the Rāfiḍah do with ʿAlī ibn Abī Ṭālib رَضِيَ اللَّهُ عَنْهُ. So if any scholar, or author, convers *Ṣalāt* and *Salām* upon ʿAlī, it does not necessarily mean that he is a Shīʿī. Furthermore it is not proven beyond doubt that al-Bukhārī singled out ʿAlī and his sons with the Ṣalāt and Salām. Tījānī's citing the publication of Bābī al-Ḥalabī is not much of an argument since *Ṣaḥīḥ al-Bukhārī* has been extant before al-Ḥalabī and his publishing house were established. It is highly possible that the addition of salutations upon ʿAlī رَضِيَ اللَّهُ عَنْهُ was done by later scribes as this does not interfere with the integrity of the text of *Ṣaḥīḥ al-Bukhārī.*

If one refers to different editions of the text as well as some of the manuscripts, the terms "*ʿAlayhi al-Salām*" are found in some and in others "*Raḍi Allā ʿanhū*" is used for ʿAlī رَضِيَ اللَّهُ عَنْهُ.

The issue at hand has been dealt with by the most prolific commentator of *al-Bukhārī*, al-Ḥāfiẓ ibn Ḥajar al-ʿAsqalānī. When the issue of conferring Ṣalāt and Salām to others besides the Prophets عَلَيْهِ السَّلَام came to his attention he mentioned the difference of opinion among Ahl al-Sunnah on this issue:

> This ḥadīth has been cited to prove the permissibility of saying the ṣalāh for other than the Prophet صَلَّى اللَّهُ عَلَيْهِ وَسَلَّمَ because of his words, "and upon his family". Those who prohibit respond by saying its permissibility is restricted to when it is said after it is said for the Ambiyā' (as explained previously), and that it is prohibited to say it individually (for other than the Ambiyā'). The proof for the prohibition is that it has become a symbol of the Prophet صَلَّى اللَّهُ عَلَيْهِ وَسَلَّمَ and therefore no one should share it with him. For that reason no one says, "Abū Bakr صَلَّى اللَّهُ عَلَيْهِ وَسَلَّمَ," even if its meaning is not problematic. However, one can say, "*Ṣallā Allāh ʿalā Muḥammad wa ʿalā Ṣadīqihī, aw Khalīfatihī.*" In a similar manner no one says, "*Muḥammad ʿAzza wa Jall,*" even if its meaning is not problematic, as this type of praise has become uniquely used for Allah and therefore no one should share in it.
>
> There is no proof for the person who permits sending ṣalāh individually (for other than the Ambiyā') in Allah's words, "and invoke (Allah's blessings) upon them," or in the Prophet's words, "O Allah! Send ṣalāh upon the family of Abū Awfā," or in the statement of Jābir's wife, "Send ṣalāh upon me and my husband," and Prophet صَلَّى اللَّهُ عَلَيْهِ وَسَلَّمَ said, "O Allah! Send ṣalāh on the both of them," because all of that was from the Prophet صَلَّى اللَّهُ عَلَيْهِ وَسَلَّمَ and the owner of a

> right may share it with whom he wishes. However, someone else may not share it without his permission and his permission has not been confirmed concerning that.
>
> The view of prohibition is stronger when one takes into consideration that saying the ṣalāh for other than the Prophet صلى الله عليه وسلم has become a symbol of the people of deviation who say the ṣalāh for those who they glorify from the Ahl al-Bayt and other than them.
>
> (The question then is) That prohibition: Is it *Ḥarām* or *Makrūh* or *Khilāf al-Awlā* (the worse of two permissible options)? Al-Nawawī relates those three views and validates the second.
>
> Ismāʿīl ibn Isḥāq narrates in his book Aḥkām al-Qur'ān with a good sanad from ʿUmar ibn ʿAbd al-ʿAzīz that he wrote, "As to what follows: There are people who seek the work of the world with the work of the hereafter, and there are people from the story-tellers who have innovated the ṣalāh for their leaders in the same manner that ṣalāh is for the Prophet صلى الله عليه وسلم. Therefore, when this letter of mine reaches you then command them to let their ṣalāh be only for the Ambiyā' and their supplications for the Muslims; and let them say everything besides that!" Then he narrated from Ibn ʿAbbās with a reliable sanad that he said, "Ṣalāh upon anyone other than the Prophet is not correct. Rather, Istighfār is for the Muslims, male and female."
>
> Abū Dharr mentions that the command of the ṣalāh for the Prophet صلى الله عليه وسلم occurred during the second year after the hijrah. There is a weaker opinion that says it occurred during the night of Isrā'.[1]

As you can see Ibn Ḥajar did not bring up al-Bukhārī saying *ʿalayhī al-Salām* for ʿAlī رضي الله عنه at all; which indicates that al-Bukhārī did not use the term of salutation and that it was of the addition of some of the later scribes.

4. Tījānī's claim that the four Schools of Fiqh are traced back to Jaʿfar al-Ṣādiq

Tījānī's academic prowess was tested when he encountered a group of young boys who studied in the Shīʿah institutes of learning, or Ḥawzahs. By virtue of the immaturity of the arguments and Tījānī's failure to respond one wonders on what

1 *Fatḥ al-Bārī*, vol. 8 p. 394-395.

basis he set out to undertake his independent research of the history of Islam in its formative period. The Tījānī who challenges narrations in *Ṣaḥīḥ al-Bukhārī* and sifts through books of history to question the reliability of Abū Hurayrah رَضِيَ ٱللَّهُ عَنْهُ was unable to disarm these young boys of their superficial objections. It is very hard to believe that the tenacious Tījānī was docile and mute in the face of such frail objections. He says:

> **One of the boys asked me, "Which Madhhab (religious school) is followed in Tunis'?" I said, "The Maliki madhhab." And noticed that some of them laughed, but I did not pay much attention. He asked me, "Do you not know the Jafari Madhhab?" I said, "What is this new name? No we only know the four Madhahibs, and apart from that is not within Islam."**
>
> **He smiled and said, "The Jafari Madhhab is the essence of Islam, do you not know that Imam Abu Hanifah studied under Imam Jafar al-Sadiq? And that Abu Hanifah said, "Without the two years al-Numan would have perished." I remained silent and did not answer, for I had heard a name that I had never heard before, but thanked Allah that he - i.e. their Imam Jafar al- Sadiq - was not a teacher of Imam Malik, and said that we are Malikis and not Hanafis. He said, "The four Madhahibs took from each other, Ahmed ibn Hanbal took from al-Shafii, and al-Shafii took from Malik, and Malik took from Abu Hanifah, and Abu Hanifah from Jafar al- Sadiq, therefore, all of them were students of Jafar ibn Muhammad, who was the first to open an Islamic University in the mosque of his grandfather, the Messenger of Allah صَلَّى ٱللَّهُ عَلَيْهِ وَسَلَّمَ and under him studied no less than four thousand jurisprudents and specialists in Ḥadīth (prophetic traditions).**[1]

Refuting Tījānī's claim that the four Schools of Fiqh are traced back to Jaʿfar al-Ṣādiq

The Ahl al-Sunnah venerate the Ahl al-Bayt, and Jaʿfar al-Ṣādiq is certainly one of those whom the Ahl al-Sunnah love and admire. The Ahl al-Sunnah consider him an outstanding scholar, and one worthy of taking knowledge from. The reality, however, is that this feeble attempt at portraying Jaʿfar al-Ṣādiq as a Mujtahid Imām from whom all the Sunnī schools trace their academic heritage is misleading on a number of accounts.

---

1 *Then I was guided*, p. 35-36.

Firstly, it assumes that the scholars of the Ahl al-Sunnah adopted an adversarial approach to this great-grandson of the Prophet صلى الله عليه وسلم, which is not true since the ḥadīth of Jaʿfar al-Ṣādiq is found in the ḥadīth collections of the Ahl al-Sunnah. The Ahl al-Sunnah consider Jaʿfar al-Ṣādiq, his father al-Bāqir, and their fathers up to ʿAlī رضي الله عنه scholars and Imāms of Ahl al-Sunnah. Similarly Imām Jaʿfar al-Ṣādiq narrated from the scholars of the Ahl al-Sunnah, the likes of ʿUrwah ibn al-Zubayr, ʿAṭā' ibn Abī Rabāḥ, Ibn Shihāb al-Zuhrī as well as his father Muḥammad ibn ʿAlī and his maternal grandfather, Qāsim ibn Muḥammad, the grandson of Abū Bakr and nephew of ʿĀ'ishah رضي الله عنها.

The second fallacy in the argument is that it assumes the practise of the Shīʿah throughout history to be in conformity with the Fiqh of Jaʿfar al-Ṣādīq. This is a known fallacy since the practise of the Twelver Shīʿah are the teachings of people like Zurārah ibn Aʿyan and Abū Baṣīr among others who were cursed at the hands of the Imāms for forging ḥadīth in their names.

The third misleading element in the argument is that it portrays the differences between the Ahl al-Sunnah and the Shīʿah as differences in practice, whereas the primary differences lie in core beliefs like Imāmah, Ghaybah, etc.

Abū Ḥanīfah's academic heritage traces its way, via the study circle of the Masjid in Kūfah, to Ḥammād ibn Abī Sulaymān who was Imām Abū Ḥanīfah's primary instructor and mentor in the discipline of Fiqh. Ḥammād received his instruction at the hands of Ibrāhīm ibn Yazīd al-Nakhaʿī, who succeeded al-Aswad and ʿAlqamah, the two outstanding students of ʿAbd Allāh ibn Masʿūd رضي الله عنه. Thus, Imām Abū Ḥanīfah was the heir to a long standing Fiqh tradition in Kūfah. In terms of receiving ḥadīth, Imām Abū Ḥanīfah had taken from the father of Jaʿfar, Muḥammad al-Bāqir. Whatever Imām Abū Ḥanīfah narrates by way of Imām Jaʿfar al-Ṣādiq is minimal on account of them being contemporaries, Imām Abū Ḥanīfah being a few years senior.

It would be a stretch of ones imagination to assert that Abū Ḥanīfah received instruction and formal training at the hands of Jaʿfar al-Ṣādiq. Furthermore it is not proven that Imām Mālik had studied under Imām Abū Ḥanīfah, nor has it been proven that Imām Abū Ḥanīfah studied under Imām Mālik. Academic debates ensured between these two scholars but their relationship was that of contemporaries rather than student-teacher.

The fabricated narrations appearing in the books of the Shīʿah give the impression that Abū Ḥanīfah was an adversary of the father of Jaʿfar, let alone being a student of Jaʿfar al-Ṣādiq. Al-Kulaynī narrates in *Uṣūl al-Kāfī*:

> From Sadīr, he said, "I heard Abū Jaʿfar (al-Bāqir) while we were out. He took my hand, then faced the Qiblah and said, 'O Sadīr! All the people have to do is to come to these stones and circle them. Then they come to us and announce to us their support for us and that is the meaning of the verse,
>
> وَإِنِّي لَغَفَّارٌ لِمَنْ تَابَ وَآمَنَ وَعَمِلَ صَالِحًا ثُمَّ اهْتَدَى
>
> *But indeed, I am the Perpetual Forgiver of whoever repents and believes and does righteousness and then continues in guidance.*[1]
>
> Then he pointed to his chest (and said), 'Our support!'
>
> Then he said, 'O Sadīr! I will show you those who prevent others from the dīn of Allah. Then he looked at Abū Ḥanīfah and Sufyān al-Thawrī at that time and they were in circles in the Masjid and said, 'These are the ones who prevent others from the dīn of Allah without any guidance from Allah, and no clear book. Indeed, these useless people, if they sat in their homes and the people started searching (for people to teach them) and they did not find anyone to teach them about Allah and his Messenger ﷺ until they came to us and we would have informed them about Allah and his Messenger ﷺ.'"[2]

The mention of more than four thousand scholars of fiqh and ḥadīth studying at the hands of Imām Jaʿfar al-Ṣādiq is something which has been circulated by the Shīʿah.

> Some people from the outskirts from the Shīʿah sought permission to visit Abū Jaʿfar and he permitted them. They entered and asked him in one sitting three thousand issues and he answered them. He was ten years old at the time.[3]

It is the good fortune of the Ahl al-Sunnah that they narrate some of the ḥadīth of Imām Jaʿfar al-Ṣādiq, else his entire academic legacy would have been exhausted by the lies of the Shīʿah who forged narrations in his name!

---

1 Sūrah Ṭāhā: 82.

2 *Al-Uṣūl min al-Kāfī*, vol. 1, Kitāb al-Ḥujjah, p. 323; we do not believe this could have come from Jaʿfar. Perhaps it is of the forgeries of al-Mughīrah ibn Saʿīd.

3 Ibid. vol. 1 Kitāb al-Ḥujjah, Bāb Mawlid Abū Jaʿfar p. 415.

5. The Rāfiḍah Deny the Existence of Shīʿī sects which consider ʿAlī Divine

Tījānī apologises to al-Khū'ī for the stance of Ahl al-Sunnah regarding the Shīʿah in general. He says:

> **I said, "We consider the Shia to be harder on Islam than the Christian and Jews, because they worship Allah and believe in the Message of Musa may Allah grant him peace, but we hear that the Shia worship Ali and consider him to be sacred, and there is a sect among them who worship Allah but put Ali at the same level as the Messenger of Allah صَلَّى ٱللَّهُ عَلَيْهِ وَسَلَّمَ." Also I told him the story about how the angel Gabriel betrayed his charge - as they say - so instead of giving the message to Ali he gave it to Muhammad صَلَّى ٱللَّهُ عَلَيْهِ وَسَلَّمَ.**
>
> **Al-Sayyid remained silent for a little while, with his head down, then he looked at me and said, "We believe that there is no other God but Allah, and that Muhammad صَلَّى ٱللَّهُ عَلَيْهِ وَسَلَّمَ is the Messenger of Allah صَلَّى ٱللَّهُ عَلَيْهِ وَسَلَّمَ, and that Ali was but a servant of Allah." 'He turned to his audience and said, indicating to me "Look at these innocent people how they have been brain-washed by the false rumours; and this is not surprising for I heard more than that from other people - (so we say) there is no power or strength save in Allah, the Highest and the Greatest."!"[1]**

Our comment:

There are sects among the Shīʿah that deify ʿAlī. This is a fact which will only be denied by an ignorant person or someone who deliberately seeks to mislead

The Saba'iyyah sect, the followers of the Jew, ʿAbd Allāh ibn Saba', believed in ʿAlī's رَضِيَ ٱللَّهُ عَنْهُ divinity. His followers came to ʿAlī رَضِيَ ٱللَّهُ عَنْهُ and said to him, "You are Him!" He said, "And who is He?" They said, "You are Allah!" ʿAlī رَضِيَ ٱللَّهُ عَنْهُ took the matter very seriously and instructed for a fire to be kindled and he burnt them at the stake.[2]

This is a fact which Rāfiḍah are unable to deny. Al-Kashshī, an authority in the field of Shīʿah narrator criticism, reports:

> Abū Jaʿfar (al-Bāqir) said, "ʿAbd Allāh ibn Saba' indeed claimed prophethood. He also claimed that Amīr al-Mu'minīn was Allah; and Allah is free from that.

---

1 *Then I was guided*, p. 49-50.

2 Ibn Ḥazm: *Al-Faṣl fī al-Milal wa al-Ahwā' wa al-Niḥal*, vol. 5, p. 46-47; Ibn Ṭāhir: *al-Farq bayn al-Firaq*, p. 213.

> This claim reached Amīr al-Mu'minīn who summoned him ('Abd Allāh ibn Saba') and asked him (about that) and he confirmed it. He said, 'Yes, you are Allah. Indeed it was revealed to me that you are Allah and I am a Prophet.' Amīr al-Mu'minīn said to him, 'Woe unto you! Shayṭān is mocking you! Refrain from this and repent!' He refused and 'Alī imprisoned him and instructed him to repent for three days but he did not repent. Thereafter he burnt him at the stake and remarked, 'Indeed Shayṭān tempted him and he was the one who would come to him and inspired him towards that."[1]

There is also a group that claims that Jibrīl عَلَيْهِ السَّلَام betrayed the Divine trust when Allah sent him to 'Alī رَضِيَ اللَّهُ عَنْهُ. He erred and went to the Prophet صَلَّى اللَّهُ عَلَيْهِ وَسَلَّمَ instead. This sect is known as the *Ghurābiyyah.*

The Twelver scholar, al-Nawbakhtī confirms the fact that there were numerous groups among the Shī'ah that ascribe divinity to 'Alī رَضِيَ اللَّهُ عَنْهُ and his household. He writes about these sects in his book *Firaq al-Shī'ah*:

> These sects are the *Kaysāniyyah*, the *'Abbāsiyyah*, the *Ḥārithiyyah*, and from them came the *Kharmadīniyyah*, and from them started the extremism in statements to the point where they claimed the Imāms to be deities, and that they are Prophets, and that they are angels, and they are the ones who speak about reincarnation of the souls.[2]

When he speaks about the *Manṣūriyyah* sect he says:

> Abū Manṣūr was from Kūfah from 'Abd al-Qays. He had a house but he grew up in the desert. He was unlettered unable to read. He claimed after the death of Abū Ja'far Muḥammad ibn 'Alī ibn Ḥusayn that he entrusted him with the matter and made him his executor after him. Then he climbed the ranks to the point where he said, "'Alī was a Prophet and a Messenger. Similarly, Ḥasan, and Ḥusayn, 'Alī ibn Ḥusayn, and Muḥammad ibn 'Alī, and I (too) am a Prophet and a Messenger. Nubuwwah will be in six of my progeny. After me they will be prophets the last of whom will be the Qā'im."[3]

Al-Nawbakhtī further states:

---

1 *Rijāl al-Kashshī*, p. 99, the biography of 'Abd Allāh ibn Saba'.

2 al-Nawbakhtī: *Firaq al-Shī'ah*, p. 36.

3 Ibid. p. 37.

> And a sect that said, "Ja'far ibn Muḥammad is Allah; and Allah is free from that."[1]
>
> (He also said about them) They say that Muḥammad was, the day he said this, a slave and a Messenger. Abū Ṭālib sent him and he was the light which was Allah in 'Abd al-Muṭṭalib, then it went into Abū Ṭālib, then it went into Muḥammad, then it went into 'Alī ibn Abī Ṭālib. Therefore, all of them are Gods.[2]

Then he mentions another sect:

> They say, "The Imām is knowledgeable of all things and he is Allah," and Allah is aloof from all that they say! This group is called the *Rāwandiyyah*.[3]

He also says:

> One sect stands out from amongst those sects claiming the Imāmah of 'Alī ibn Muḥammad during his life. They claim the Imāmah of a man called Muḥammad ibn Nuṣayr al-Namīrī. He used to claim he was a Prophet sent by Abū al-Ḥasan al-'Askarī (the eleventh Imām). He used to call towards reincarnation and extremism with regards to Abū al-Ḥasan as he used to claim his divinity. He also believed in the permissibility of marrying the *Maḥārim* (blood relatives) and he permitted men marrying men and anal intercourse with them. He claimed that it was a form of humility, and that it was one of the natural desires and from amongst the wholesome permissible matters, and that Allah never prohibited any of it.[4]

These are statements in the books of the Twelver Shī'ah which confirm that there are Shī'ī sects which deify 'Alī رضي الله عنه, whilst there are others which place him at the level of the Prophet صلى الله عليه وسلم. Others went further and deified his sons as well.

Al-Sayyid al-Khū'ī claims that 'Alī رضي الله عنه is a slave from the slaves of Allah. How honest was he in this claim? The sects that have been referred to are those where there is explicit deification of 'Alī رضي الله عنه, or unequivocal elevation to the status of Prophethood. What can be said of implicit elevation to such a status, or even higher?

1 Ibid. p. 44.
2 Ibid. p. 45.
3 Ibid. p. 52.
4 Ibid. p. 93.

The undisputed authority in the Shīʿah tradition, Muḥammad ibn Yaʿqūb al-Kulaynī, relates dozens of narrations in *Uṣūl al-Kāfī*, rather, he devotes complete chapters to explain the status of ʿAlī رضي الله عنه and his sons. He also equates the ḥadīth of the Messenger صلى الله عليه وسلم in terms of their authority to the ḥadīth of ʿAlī رضي الله عنه and his sons. He relates:

> Hishām ibn Sālim, Ḥammād ibn ʿUthmān, and others say, "We heard Abū ʿAbd Allāh (al-Ṣādiq) saying, 'My ḥadīth is like the ḥadīth of my father, and the ḥadīth of my father is like the ḥadīth of my grandfather, and the ḥadīth of my grandfather is like the ḥadīth of Ḥusayn, and the ḥadīth of Ḥusayn is like the ḥadīth of Ḥasan, and the ḥadīth of Ḥasan is like the ḥadīth of Amīr al-Mu'minīn, and the ḥadīth of Amīr al-Mu'minīn is like the ḥadīth of the Messenger صلى الله عليه وسلم, and the ḥadīth of the Messenger صلى الله عليه وسلم is the word of Allah.'"[1]

He dedicates an entire chapter to the following topic, "(The chapter proving) that the A'immah, the angels enter their homes and tread on their carpets and bring them information (of the unseen)".[2] Then he mentions some narrations supporting the heading. From Abū Ḥamzah al-Thumālī, who says:

> I visited ʿAlī ibn Ḥusayn (Zayn al-ʿĀbidīn) and I waited for a while, then I entered the room while he was picking something up from the ground and he entered his hand behind the veil and gave it to whoever was in the house. I said to him, "May I be ransomed for you! What was it that I saw you pick up?"
>
> He said, "The surplus of the angels fluff. We gather it when they leave us and make it into clothing for our children."
>
> I said, "May I be sacrificed for you! Do they visit you?"
>
> He said, "O Abū Ḥamzah! Indeed, they crowd us on our seats."[3]
>
> (And from Abū al-Ḥasan (al-Riḍā) He said, I heard him saying, "There is not a single angel that Allah sends down on a mission except that he starts with the Imām. He presents that (mission) to him. Indeed, the place where the angels

---

1 al-Kulaynī: *Al-Uṣūl min al-Kāfī*, vol. 1 p. 42, Kitāb Faḍl al-ʿIlm.

2 Ibid. vol. 1 p. 323, Kitāb al-Ḥujjah.

3 Ibid. vol. 1 p. 323.

descend (when they descend) from Allah is the place of the one in control of this matter."[1]

Abū Jaʿfar Muḥammad ibn Farrūkh al-Ṣaffār, goes even further in his book *Baṣā'ir al-Darajāt* under the chapter stating, "They (the Imāms) are addressed, and that they hear the voice. Creation superior in rank to Jibrīl and Mīkā'īl visit them."[2]

He reports from Abū Baṣīr:

> I heard Abū ʿAbd Allāh (al-Ṣādiq) saying, "Indeed, among us are those who see, and among us are those whom something is carved in his heart, and among us are those who hear similar to a chain falling into a basin."
>
> I said, "Those who see, what do they see?"
>
> He said, "A creation greater than Jibrīl and Mīkā'īl."[3]
>
> (From Abū ʿAbd Allāh (al-Ṣādiq) He said, "Indeed from amongst us is the one who is inspired in his heart, and from amongst us is the one who hears with his ears, and the best is the person who hears."[4]

Does the Prophet صَلَّى ٱللَّٰهُ عَلَيْهِ وَسَلَّمَ compare to these individuals based on the narration above?

These are some of the chapters which al-Kulaynī has dedicated for explaining the status of the Imāms.

He says:

> Chapter: The Imāms inherited the Prophet's knowledge and the knowledge of all the Ambiyā' and executors before them.[5]
>
> Chapter: The Imāms possess all the books that were revealed by Allah and that they understand them despite the difference in languages.[6]
>
> Chapter: What the Imāms possess from the signs of the Ambiyā'.[7]

1 Ibid. vol. 1 p. 323.

2 *Baṣā'ir al-Darajāt*, p. 325.

3 Ibid.

4 Ibid.

5 *Al-Uṣūl min al-Kāfī*, Kitāb al-Ḥujjah, vol. 1 p. 173.

6 Ibid. vol. 1 p. 177.

7 Ibid. vol. 1 p. 180.

> Chapter: The Imāms know all the branches of knowledge given to the angels, and the Ambiyā', and the Messengers.[1]

> Chapter: The Imāms, when they want to know something, they know it.[2]

> Chapter: The Imāms know when they are going to die and that they only die by their choosing.[3]

> Chapter: The Imāms possess knowledge of the past and the knowledge of the future and that nothing is hidden from them.[4]

> Chapter: Allah did not teach the Prophet ﷺ anything except that he instructed him to teach it to Amīr al-Mu'minīn and that he was his partner in knowledge.[5]

> Chapter: The A'immah if they were concealed they would have informed every person about what would benefit him and what would harm him.[6]

These are some of the chapter headings to be found in al-Ṣaffār's book *Baṣā'ir al-Darajāt:*

> Chapter: Concerning the A'immah that they are the proof of Allah, and the door of Allah, and the governors of Allah's command, and the face of Allah which he is arrived at, and the side of Allah, and the eyes of Allah, and the treasure of Allah's knowledge.[7]

> (It is narrated from Hishām ibn Abī ʿAmmār, he said:) I heard Amīr al-Mu'minīn saying, "I am the eye of Allah, and I am the hand of Allah, and I am the side of Allah, and I am the door of Allah."[8]

> Chapter: Concerning the knowledge of the A'immah concerning what is in the heavens and the earth, and Jannah and Jahannam, and what has occurred and what will occur until the Day of Judgement.[9]

---

1 Ibid. vol. 1 p. 199.
2 Ibid. vol. 1 p. 201.
3 Ibid. vol. 1 p. 202.
4 Ibid. vol. 1 p. 203.
5 Ibid. vol. 1 p. 205.
6 Ibid. vol. 1 p. 207.
7 al-Ṣaffār: *Baṣā'r al-Darajāt*, p. 75.
8 Ibid. p. 75.
9 Ibid. p. 131.

> Chapter: Concerning the A'immah that by them is the scroll containing the names of the people of Jannah and the names of the people of the Jahannam.[1]

Notwithstanding all of this al-Khū'ī says:

> "ʿAlī is but a slave from the slaves of Allah!" Who are those innocent people who have been condemned by false rumours?

Did all of this escape the industrious Tījānī?

6. Tījānī presents al-Khū'ī's defence of the Shīʿah on the issue of distortion

Tījānī's discussion continues with al-Sayyid al-Khū'ī:

> **Then he turned to me and said, "Have you read the Qur'an?" I answered, "I could recite half of it by heart before I was ten." He said, "Do you know that all the Islamic groups, regardless of their sects agree on the Holy Qur'an, for our Qur'an is the same as yours?" I said, "Yes I know that." He then said, "Have you not read the words of Allah, praise be to Him the Sublime:**
>
> وَمَا مُحَمَّدٌ إِلَّا رَسُوْلٌ قَدْ خَلَتْ مِنْ قَبْلِهِ الرُّسُلُ
>
> ***Muḥammad is not but a Messenger. (Other) Messengers have passed on before him.[2]***
>
> مُحَمَّدٌ رَسُوْلُ اللّٰهِ وَالَّذِيْنَ مَعَهٗ أَشِدَّآءُ عَلَى الْكُفَّارِ
>
> ***Muḥammad is the Messenger of Allah; and those with him are forceful against the disbelievers.[3]***
>
> مَا كَانَ مُحَمَّدٌ أَبَا أَحَدٍ مِّنْ رِّجَالِكُمْ وَلَكِنْ رَّسُوْلَ اللّٰهِ وَخَاتَمَ النَّبِيِّيْنَ
>
> ***Muḥammad is not the father of (any) one of your men, but (he is) the Messenger of Allah and seal (i.e., last) of the ambiyā'.[4]***

1 Ibid. p. 189.

2 Sūrah Āl ʿImrān: 144.

3 Sūrah al-Fatḥ: 29.

4 Sūrah al-Aḥzāb: 40.

I said, "Yes I know all these Qur'anic verses." He said, "Where is Ali then? If our Qur'an says that Muhammad صَلَّى ٱللَّٰهُ عَلَيْهِ وَسَلَّمَ is the Messenger of Allah, so where did this lie come from?"[1]

Our comment:

All statements which claim that the Qur'ān is not distorted is certainly welcome. Similarly the Muṣḥaf from which the Shī'ah recite is not different from that which is recited by the Ahl al-Sunnah. However, there is no denying the fact that Twelver Shī'ah authorities have espoused a belief of corruption in the Qur'ān which we continue to recite today. The claim that the Qur'ān was distorted by the Ṣaḥābah has been a doctrine found in many of the most authoritative and reliable Shī'ah books. Scholars in the early and later period have declared that the Qur'ān that was revealed to Muḥammad صَلَّى ٱللَّٰهُ عَلَيْهِ وَسَلَّمَ was with 'Alī رَضِيَ ٱللَّٰهُ عَنْهُ and his sons.

The early authority in Tafsīr, 'Alī ibn Ibrāhīm al-Qummī, writes in his *Tafsīr al-Qummī*:

> The Qur'ān has within it the *Nāsikh* (abrogating verse) and the *Mansūkh* (abrogated verse), and it has within it the *Muḥkam* (clear) verse and the *Mutashābih* (ambiguous) verse, and it has within it the *'Ām* (general) verse and the *Khāṣ* (specific) verse, and within it is the delayed and the advanced, and within it is the independent and the combined, and within it is the letter in place of another letter, **and it contains other than what Allah revealed.**[2]

Then he forwards some examples of what he considers as 'other than what Allah revealed'.

He cites the verse:

كُنْتُمْ خَيْرَ أُمَّةٍ أُخْرِجَتْ لِلنَّاسِ تَأْمُرُوْنَ بِالْمَعْرُوْفِ وَتَنْهَوْنَ عَنِ الْمُنْكَرِ وَتُؤْمِنُوْنَ بِاللّٰهِ

You are the best nation produced [as an example] for mankind. You enjoin what is right and forbid what is wrong and believe in Allah.[3]

1 *Then I was guided*, p. 37.

2 *Tafsīr al-Qummī*, vol. 1 p. 17, the introduction of the book.

3 Sūrah Āl 'Imrān: 11.

Abū ʿAbd Allāh (al-Ṣādiq) said (as they claim), "Did the reciter of this verse (You are the best nation) kill Amīr al-Mu'minīn, and Ḥasan and Ḥusayn?"

It was said to him, "How was it revealed, O son of the Messenger?"

He said, "It was revealed as...

كُنْتُمْ خَيْرَ أَئِمَّةٍ أُخْرِجَتْ لِلنَّاسِ

You are the best of A'immah produced (as an example) for mankind.

Do you not know praise for them at the end of the verse?

تَأْمُرُوْنَ بِالْمَعْرُوْفِ وَتَنْهَوْنَ عَنِ الْمُنْكَرِ وَتُؤْمِنُوْنَ بِاللّٰهِ

You enjoin what is right and forbid what is wrong and believe in Allah."

Similar to it is when a verse was recited to Abū ʿAbd Allāh (al-Ṣādiq):

وَالَّذِينَ يَقُوْلُوْنَ رَبَّنَا هَبْ لَنَا مِنْ أَزْوَاجِنَا وَذُرِّيَّاتِنَا قُرَّةَ أَعْيُنٍ وَّاجْعَلْنَا لِلْمُتَّقِيْنَ إِمَامًا

And those who say, "Our Lord! grant us from among our wives and offspring comfort to our eyes and make us a leader (i.e. example) for the righteous."[1]

It was said to him, "O son of the Messenger ﷺ, how did it descend?"

He said, "It descended as...

الَّذِينَ يَقُوْلُوْنَ رَبَّنَا هَبْ لَنَا مِنْ أَزْوَاجِنَا وَذُرِّيَّاتِنَا قُرَّةَ أَعْيُنٍ وَّاجْعَلْ لَنَا مِنَ الْمُتَّقِيْنَ إِمَامًا

And those who say, "Our Lord, grant us from among our wives and offspring comfort to our eyes and **make for us from the righteous a leader**."

Also:

لَهُ مُعَقِّبَاتٌ مِنْ بَيْنِ يَدَيْهِ وَمِنْ خَلْفِهِ يَحْفَظُوْنَهُ مِنْ أَمْرِ اللّٰهِ

1 Sūrah al-Furqān: 74.

For him (i.e. each one) are successive (angels) before and behind him who protect him by (literally: from) the decree of Allah.[1]

Abū ʿAbd Allāh (al-Ṣādiq) said, "How can something be protected from the decree of Allah? And how can the Muʿaqqib (literally: pursuer) be in front of him?"

It was said to him, "how was it revealed, O son of the Messenger?"

He said, "It descended as...

لَهُ مُعَقِّبَاتٌ مِّنْ خَلْفِهِ وَ رَقِيْبٌ مِّنْ بَيْنِ يَدَيْهِ يَحْفَظُوْنَهُ مِنْ أَمْرِ اللّٰهِ

He has pursues (angels) **from behind him and a guard from in front of him** who protect him from the decree of Allah."

And there are many examples like this![2]

Then he elaborates further, saying, "As for what distorted, it is like the words of Allah:

لٰكِنِ اللّٰهُ يَشْهَدُ بِمَا أَنْزَلَ إِلَيْكَ – فِي علي – أَنْزَلَهُ بِعِلْمِهِ وَالْمَلَآئِكَةُ يَشْهَدُوْنَ

*But Allah bears witness to that which He has revealed to you—**concerning ʿAlī**—He has sent it down with His knowledge.*[3]

And the verse:

يَاأَيُّهَا الرَّسُوْلُ بَلِّغْ مَا أُنْزِلَ إِلَيْكَ – فِي علي – وَإِنْ لَمْ تَفْعَلْ فَمَا بَلَّغْتَ رِسَالَتَهُ

O Messenger, announce that which has been revealed to you—concerning ʿAlī—and if you do not, then you have not conveyed His message.[4]

1 Sūrah al-Raʿd: 11.

2 *Tafsīr al-Qummī*, vol. 1 p. 22-23.

3 Sūrah al-Nisāʾ: 166.

4 Sūrah al-Māʾidah: 67.

And the verse:

إِنَّ الَّذِيْنَ كَفَرُوْا وَظَلَمُوْا -آل محمد حقهم - لَمْ يَكُنِ اللّٰهُ لِيَغْفِرَ

*Indeed, those who disbelieve and commit wrong (or injustice)—**against the family of Muḥammad**—never will Allah forgive them.*[1]

And the verse:

وَسَيَعْلَمُ الَّذِيْنَ ظَلَمُوْا - آل محمد حقهم - أَيَّ مُنْقَلَبٍ يَّنْقَلِبُوْنَ

*And those who have wronged—**the family of Muḥammad**—are going to know to what (kind of) return they will be returned.*[2]

And the verse:

وَلَوْ تَرَى - الذين ظلموا آل محمد - فِيْ غَمَرَاتِ الْمَوْتِ

*And if you could but see those—**who wrong the family of Muḥammad**—in the overwhelming pangs of death.*[3]

And there are many examples like this which we will mention in the appropriate place![4]

It is odd that al-Khū'ī ratifies al-Qummī as a transmitter of sacred knowledge and testifies to his high religious status. He says about him:

> And we declare all of ʿAlī ibn Ibrāhīm al-Qummī's teachers trustworthy, all of those from whom he narrates in his *Tafsīr* with a chain which leads to one of the infallibles.[5]

The irony is that Maqbūl Jadīd, a Shīʿī author, in his book *Tuḥfat al-ʿAwāmm*, describes an invocation called "the prayer (against) the two idols of the Quraysh,"

---

1 Sūrah al-Nisā': 168.

2 Sūrah al-Shuʿarā': 227.

3 Sūrah al-Anʿām: 93.

4 *Tafsīr al-Qummī*, vol. 1 p. 23.

5 Abū al-Qāsim al-Khū'ī: *Muʿjam Rijāl al-Ḥadīth*, vol. 1 p. 63.

which refers to Abū Bakr and ʿUmar.[1] These are the words which form part of that 'prayer':

> And curse the two idols of the Quraysh; who oppose your command; **and distort your book**; O Allah! **Curse them with every verse they distorted**![2]

His books alleges to only quote material which meets the criteria of acceptance by six of their scholars, amongst them al-Khū'ī.[3] If al-Khū'ī accepts this narration it means that he has indirectly acknowledged some distortion in the Qur'ān.

Muḥammad al-ʿAyyāshī, one of their reputable scholars in the field of Tafsīr, relates in his *Tafsīr*:

> From Abū ʿAbd Allāh (al-Ṣādiq), he said, "If the Qur'ān was recited the way it was revealed you would find us named therein!"[4]

Al-Fayḍ al-Kāshānī, he too is of their senior scholars, says in his *Tafsīr al-Ṣāfī*:

> I say: What is learnt from all of these reports and other than them from the Ahl al-Bayt is that the Qur'ān which is in front of us is not in the complete form as it was revealed to Muḥammad ﷺ. Rather, in it is what is opposite to what Allah revealed and in it is what has been changed and distorted. Indeed, many things have been erased from it such as ʿAlī's name at many places, and the words, "the family of Muḥammad," at more than one place, and the names of the munāfiqīn at its places, and other than the aforementioned. Also, it is not in the sequence desired by Allah and his Messenger ﷺ.[5]

Al-Kulaynī confirms the existence of a *Muṣḥaf* other than the copy we are familiar with. He narrates a lengthy narration from Abū ʿAbd Allāh (al-Ṣādiq), a portion of which is a s follows:

---

1 Their Imām Muḥammad Āghā Buzruk mentions in his book *al-Dharīʿah ilā Taṣānīf al-Shīʿah* that Abū Bakr and ʿUmar were the two intended with the words, "the two idols of the Quraysh." vol. 1 p. 9, published by al-Najaf. Al-Fayḍ al-Kāshānī in *Qurrat al-ʿUyūn*, p. 326, published by Dār al-Kitāb al-Libnānī.

2 Manẓūr Ḥusayn: *Tuḥfah al-ʿAwāmm Maqbūl Jadīd*, p. 422.

3 Refer to the cover of *Tuḥfat al-ʿAwāmm*.

4 *Tafsīr al-ʿAyāshī*, the introduction, p. 25.

5 *Tafsīr al-Ṣāfī*, vol. 1 p. 44.

> Then he said, "And indeed, with us is the Muṣḥaf of Fāṭimah. And what will make them realise what the Muṣḥaf of Fāṭimah is?"
>
> I asked, "What is the Muṣḥaf of Fāṭimah?"
>
> He said, "A Muṣḥaf similar to this Qur'ān of yours (but) three times (greater). By Allah! There is not a single letter of it in your Qur'ān!"[1]

This is further emphasised in what al-Kulaynī narrates elsewhere:

> Abū ʿAbd Allāh (al-Ṣādiq) said, "Indeed, the Qur'ān that Jibrīl brought to Muḥammad صلى الله عليه وسلم contains seventeen thousand verses."[2]

Where is this Muṣḥaf? Who will bring it? Al-Ṣaffār has the answer in his book *Baṣā'ir al-Darajāt* under the chapter, "The Imāms possess the entire Qur'ān revealed to Muḥammad صلى الله عليه وسلم." He narrates from Jābir (al-Juʿfī):

> From Abū Jaʿfar (al-Bāqir) that he said, "No person is able to say that he has compiled the entire Qur'ān, the apparent and the hidden, besides the successors."[3]
>
> (Jābir also said) I heard Abū Jaʿfar (al-Bāqir) saying, "No person is able to say that he has gathered the entire Qur'ān as Allah revealed it except a liar. No one besides ʿAlī ibn Abī Ṭālib and the Imāms who succeeded him have gathered it and memorised it as Allah revealed it."[4]

Al-Ṭabarsī provides greater clarity, without being ambiguous in any way, in his book *al-Iḥtijāj*. He presents a narration from Abū Dhar, who allegedly said:

> When the Messenger صلى الله عليه وسلم passed away, ʿAlī documented the Qur'ān, and brought it to the Muhājirīn and the Anṣār. He presented it to them in accordance with the bequest of the Rasūl صلى الله عليه وسلم. When Abū Bakr opened it, their ignominies appeared on the first page, then ʿUmar jumped and said, "O ʿAlī take it back, and we have no need of it." He then took it and departed. Thereafter he called for Zayd ibn Thābit who was a great Qārī of the Qur'ān, and ʿUmar said to him, "Indeed ʿAlī came to us with a copy of Qur'ān, in it is

---

1 *Al-Uṣūl min al-Kāfī*, vol. 1 p. 186, Kitāb al-Ḥujjah.

2 *Al-Uṣūl min al-Kāfī*, vol. 2 p. 463, Kitāb Faḍl al-Qur'ān, Bāb al-Nawādir.

3 *Baṣā'ir al-Darajāt*, p. 191.

4 Ibid.

> the ignominies of the Muhājirīn and the Anṣār, we want you to document the Qur'ān for us, together with omitting any ignominy and degradation of the Muhājirīn and the Anṣār," and Zayd agreed to that.
>
> Thereafter he said, "When I am done with the documentation of the Qur'ān in the manner that you asked me to do, and 'Alī exposes what he documented, would not your effort be in vain?"
>
> 'Umar enquired, "What would be the solution then?"
>
> Zayd replied, "You know better."
>
> 'Umar said, "The only solution is to kill him to become free of him."
>
> Then he plotted that Khālid ibn al-Walīd should kill him, but he failed to do so. So when 'Umar was appointed as Khalīfah, he asked 'Alī to hand the Qur'ān over to them, so that they could distort it amongst themselves. He said, "O Abū al-Ḥasan if you brought the Muṣḥaf to Abū Bakr, bring it to us as well so that we may agree upon it."
>
> 'Alī said, "Never! That is impossible, I only brought it to Abū Bakr as a proof against you, so that you do not say on the Day of Judgment, 'We were unmindful about this,' nor say, 'You did not show it to us.' Indeed the Qur'ān that is with me none can touch it except the pure and the successors from my sons."
>
> 'Umar said, "Is the time of its exposition known?"
>
> 'Alī said, "Yes, when my son, al-Qā'im, comes, he will expose it and take it to the people and the Sunnah will be established through it."[1]

Then he forwards a lengthy narration explaining that there are two Qur'āns and not one. This is a portion of it:

> Then, when 'Alī saw their betrayal and their lack of trustworthiness he remained at home and focused his attention upon compiling and collecting the Qur'ān and he did not leave until he collected all of it. Therefore, he wrote in the manner it was revealed including the Nāsikh and the Mansūkh.
>
> Then Abū Bakr summoned him, "Come out of your house and give your pledge!"

---

1 al-Ṭabarsī: *Al-Iḥtijāj*, vol. 1 p. 155-156.

ʿAlī sent message to him, "I am busy. Indeed, I took an oath that I would not get dressed except for the ṣalāh until I have compiled the Qur'ān and gathered it."

Then he gathered it in a garment and sealed it and went to the people and they were gathered with Abū Bakr in the Masjid of the Messenger ﷺ and he yelled out at the pitch of his voice, "O people! I have been busy since the time the Messenger ﷺ passed away, (first) with his ghusl, then with the Qur'ān until I gathered all of it in this garment. There is not a verse in it except that the Prophet ﷺ taught it to me and taught me its meaning!"

They said, "We have no need for it. We have something similar to it!"[1]

Therefore, there is a Qur'ān belonging to ʿAlī رضي الله عنه which is different to our Qur'ān. Al-Ṭabarsī is not the only one to openly state this. Rather, al-Kulaynī and al-Ṣaffār confirm it as well. The narration appears by way of Sālim ibn Salamah:

A man read to Abū ʿAbd Allāh (al-Ṣādiq) and I heard him reciting letters different to what the people recite. Abū ʿAbd Allāh said, "Quiet, quiet! Refrain from this recital! Recite the way the people recite until al-Qā'im appears. When he appears, then recite the Qur'ān in its correct manner!"

Then he took out the Muṣḥaf which ʿAlī عليه السلام wrote and said, "ʿAlī brought it to the people when he completed its collection and writing and said to them, 'This is the Book of Allah as Allah revealed it to Muḥammad and I have gathered it between these two covers!"

They said, "We have with us a comprehensive Muṣḥaf and in it is the Qur'ān. We have no need for it!"

He said, "You will not see it after today! My duty was only to inform you about it when I gathered it so that you could read it!"[2]

The question that now arises: Is al-Sayyid al-Khū'ī any different from Tījānī when it comes to misrepresentation?

Then al-Khū'ī says:

---

1 Ibid. vol. 1 p. 82.

2 *Al-Uṣūl min al-Kāfī*, vol. 2 p. 462-463, Kitāb Faḍā'il al-Qur'ān; Also, *Baṣā'ir al-Darajāt*, p. 191-192.

> **The Shia and the Sunnis only differ on issues regarding jurisprudence, in the same way that the different schools of jurisprudence in the Sunni school differ among each other; as Malik did not agree all the way with Abu Hanifah who himself did not agree all the way with al-Shafii ... and so on![1]**

Our comment:

If al-Khū'ī was telling the truth then Tījānī's book would be an exercise in futility. Does Mālik differ with Abū Ḥanīfah about the superiority of 'Alī رضي الله عنه over the rest of the Ṣaḥābah رضي الله عنهم? Does Aḥmad differ with al-Shāfi'ī about the legitimacy of Abū Bakr's khilāfah? Does Abū Ḥanīfah differ with al-Shāfi'ī about the categorisation of the Ṣaḥābah? Is al-Shāfi'ī's view that all the Ṣaḥābah رضي الله عنهم are trustworthy while Abū Ḥanīfah says that the munāfiqīn are a category of people among the Ṣaḥābah رضي الله عنهم? Do they differ with one another about whether one ought to hold on to the Sunnah, or whether one ought to discard the Sunnah and hold on to selected members from the Ahl al-Bayt and only accept what people like Zurārah and Jābir al-Ju'fī relate from them?

Tījānī's book is a more honest refutation of al-Sayyid al-Khū'ī's responses than an enlightening alternative perspective of both traditions.

7. Tījānī on the significance of the addition in the Adhān, "'Alī Walī Allāh"

Tījānī recalls his interaction with al-Sayyid Bāqir al-Ṣadr. He says:

> **I asked al-Sayyid al-Sadr about Imam Ali and why they testify for him in the Adhan [the call for prayers] that he is "Waliy Allah" [the friend of Allah]. He answered me in the following way:**
>
> **The Commander of the Believers, Ali, may Allah's blessings be upon him, was one of those servants of Allah whom He chose and honoured by giving them the responsibilities of the Message after His Prophet. These servants are the trustees of the Prophet صلى الله عليه وسلم, since each prophet has a trustee, and Ali ibn Abi Talib is the trustee of Muhammad صلى الله عليه وسلم.**
>
> **We favour him above all the Companions of the Prophet صلى الله عليه وسلم because Allah and the Prophet favoured him, and we have many proofs of that, some of them are deduced through logical reasoning, others are found in the Qur'an and al- Sunnah [the Tradition of the Prophet Muhammad صلى الله عليه وسلم],**

1 *Then I was guided*, p. 38.

> **and these proofs cannot be suspect, because they have been scrutinized, and proven right, by our own learned people (who wrote many books about the subject) and those of the Sunni Madhahibs. The Umayyad regime worked very hard to cover this truth and fought Imam Ali and his sons, whom they killed. They even ordered people, sometimes by force, to curse him, so his followers - May Allah bless them all started to testify for him as being the friend of Allah. No Muslim would curse the friend of Allah in defiance of the oppressive authorities, so that the glory was to Allah, and to His Messenger and to all the believers. It also became an historical land mark across the generations so that they know the just cause of Ali and the wrong doing of his enemies. Thus, our learned people continued to testify that Ali is the friend of Allah in their calls to prayer, as something which is commendable. There are many commendable things in the religious rites as well as in ordinary mundane dealings, and the Muslim will be rewarded for doing them, but not punished for leaving them aside..**[1]

Our comment:

The claim that testifying to ʿAlī رضي الله عنه during the adhān and iqāmah is a legally recommended (mustaḥabb) act requires evidence. The technical definition for a Mustaḥabb act is, "An action encouraged by the Sharīʿah whose omission does not warrant reproach,"[2] or, in other words, "Its recommendation is proven in the Sharīʿah without obligation."[3] This definition is in harmony with the understanding of the term Mustaḥabb within the Twelver Shīʿī framework as well. Jamāl al-Dīn al-Ḥillī defines a recommended action in his book, *Mabādi' al-Wuṣūl ilā ʿIlm al-Uṣūl*, wherein he defines the various legal rulings:

> If his action is preferable in the Sharīʿah then it is Mustaḥabb, and Mandūb, and Nafl, and Taṭawwuʿ, and Sunnah.[4]

We learn from the definitions of both legal frameworks that an act will only be considered Mustaḥabb if it is supported by evidence which recommends it from the Legislator. The absence of any such evidence means that it cannot be considered Mustaḥab.

---

1 *Then I was guided*, p. 42-43.

2 Imām al-Ḥaramayn: *Al-Burhān fī Uṣūl al-Fiqh*, vol. 1 p. 214.

3 Muḥammad al-Yānūnī: *Al-Ḥukm al-Taklīfī fī al-Sharīʿah al-Islāmiyyah*, p. 162.

4 Ḥillī: *Mabādi' al-Wuṣūl*, p. 83.

The next question is to request the proof from the Sharīʿah for the recommendation of including the testimony ʿAlī as Walī Allāh in the adhān and the iqāmah. In the absence of any proof this testimony ought to be considered an innovation [*Bidʿah*] in the Sharīʿah and impermissible to act upon.

The translator of Tījānī's original text has economised on detail. The original Arabic attributes a statement to al-Sayyid al-Ṣadr wherein he denies that the testimony of ʿAlī رضي الله عنه being Walī Allah is part of the original Adhān and Iqāmah. Instead he justifies the action based on the good sentiments of the Mu'adhdhin who gives expression to his love for ʿAlī though it is not part of the original Adhān. He goes on to say that if these two expressions are chanted as part of the adhān it would be invalidated. His statement, however, stands in stark contrast to the opinion of Āyat Allāh al-ʿUẓmā al-Sayyid Muḥammad al-Shīrāzī, who writes in his book *al-Masā'il al-Islāmiyyah*:

> The preponderant view is that the words, "I testify that ʿAlī is the walī of Allah," is part of the adhān and the iqāmah. Indeed, I have indicated towards that in the narrations in general.[1]

There appears to be some inconsistency within the tradition which had to be taken only from 'infallibles' because the potential for error was too great if knowledge was transmitted from fallible Companions رضي الله عنهم. On the one hand al-Sayyid al-Ṣadr claims that there is no evidence and this statement is the personal announcement of the Mu'adhdhin which would invalidate the Adhān and Iqāmah if uttered as words of the Adhān and Iqāmah. On the other hand is Āyat Allah al-Uẓmā al-Sayyid al-Shīrāzī who considers these words part of the Adhān, the utterance of which is Mustaḥab.

This leaves us in a conundrum since if it is to be considered Mustaḥabb there ought to be evidence, though we cannot find such evidence. If these words are said as part of the Adhān, despite the lack of evidence to proof their status as Mustaḥab, they are considered Bidʿah. Al-Ṣadr says they are not part of the Adhān and Iqāmah, whilst al-Shīrāzī says they are. Oh why is this so confusing?

Ibn Bābuwayh al-Qummī has commented on this issue in his book *Man Lā Yaḥḍuruhū al-Faqīh*. He begins by citing a narration:

---

1 al-Shīrāzī: *Al-Masā'il al-Islāmiyyah*, p. 281, Mas'alah no. 928.

> Abū Bakr al-Ḥaḍramī and Kulayb al-Asadī narrate from Abū ʿAbd Allāh (al-Ṣādiq) that he related to them the adhān and said:
>
> اَللّٰهُ أَكْبَرُ اَللّٰهُ أَكْبَرُ اَللّٰهُ أَكْبَرُ اَللّٰهُ أَكْبَرُ أَشْهَدُ أَنْ لَّا إِلٰهَ إِلَّا اللّٰه أَشْهَدُ أَنْ لَّا إِلٰهَ إِلَّا اللّٰه أَشْهَدُ أَنَّ مُحَمَّدً رَّسُوْلُ اللّٰه أَشْهَدُ أَنَّ مُحَمَّدً رَّسُوْلُ اللّٰه حَيَّ عَلَى الصَّلَاة حَيَّ عَلَى الصَّلَاة حَيَّ عَلَى الْفَلَاح حَيَّ عَلَى الْفَلَاح حَيَّ عَلٰى خَيْرِ الْعَمَلِ حَيَّ عَلٰى خَيْرِ الْعَمَلِ اَللّٰهُ أَكْبَرُ اَللّٰهُ أَكْبَرُ لَا إِلٰهَ إِلَّا اللّٰهُ.
>
> (He said) This is how the adhān is said. As Taqiyyah there is no problem in saying:
>
> اَلصَّلَاةُ خَيْرٌ مِّنَ النَّوْم
>
> After the words, (Ḥayya ʿalā Khayr al-ʿAmal) in the adhān for the Fajr Prayer.[1]

Then he comments:

> This is the correct adhān! Nothing should be added or subtracted from it! The Mufawwiḍah, may Allah curse them, have fabricated aḥādīth and added to these words to the adhān (Muḥammad and the family of Muḥammad are the best of creation, twice). In some of their narrations after the words (Ashhadu anna Muḥammadan Rasūl Allah) they add the words (Ashhadu Ann ʿAlī Walī Allāh, twice).
>
> Some of them narrate instead of that the words (Ashhadu Ann ʿAlī Amīr al-Mu'minīn Ḥaqqan, twice). There is no doubt in ʿAlī being the Walī of Allah, and there is no doubt that he is truly Amīr al-Mu'minīn, and there is no doubt that Muḥammad and his family are the best of the creation. However, that (narration) refers to the original adhān. I only mentioned that so that those suspected of Tafwīḍ, who deceive amongst us, may be identified.[2]

No amount of bias or prejudice can help Tījānī out of this rut.

---

1 Ponder about the meaning of Taqiyyah according to them!

2 Ibn Bābuwayh al-Qummī: *Man Lā Yaḥḍuruhū al-Faqīh*, vol. 1 p. 290, Bāb fī al-Adhān wa l-Iqāmah wa Thawāb al-Mu'adhdhinīn, Dār al-Aḍwā publishers, Beirut; Refer also to vol. 1 p. 188, Tehran Publishers.

8. The proof for self-flagellation during the commemoration of Ḥusayn's murder

Tījānī says:

> **I asked, with reference to our master al-Husayn, may Allah's blessings be upon him, "Why do the Shia cry and beat their cheeks and other parts of their bodies until blood is spilt, and this is prohibited in Islam, for the Prophet صَلَّى ٱللَّٰهُ عَلَيْهِ وَسَلَّمَ said: He who beats the cheeks, tears the pockets and follows the call of al-Jahiliyyah is not one of us."**
>
> **Al-Sayyid replied the saying is correct and there is no doubt about it, but it does not apply to the obsequies of Abu Abdullah, for he who calls for the avenging of al-Husayn and follows his path, his call is not of the Jahiliyyah. Besides, the Shias are only human beings, among them you find the learned and not so learned, and they have feelings and emotions. If they are overcome by their emotions during the anniversary of the martyrdom of Abu Abdullah, and remember what happened to him, his family and his companions from degradation to captivity and then finally murder, then they will be rewarded for their good intentions, because all these intentions are for the sake of Allah. Allah - praise be to Him, the Highest - who rewards people according to their intentions.**
>
> **Last week I read the official reports from the Egyptian government about the suicide incidents that followed the death of Jamal Abdul Nasser. There were eight such incidents in which people took their lives by jumping from buildings or throwing themselves under trains, besides them there were many injured people. These are but some examples in which emotions have overcome the most rational of people, who happen to be Muslims and who killed themselves because of the death of Jamal Abdul Nasser, who died of natural causes, therefore, it is not right for us to condemn the Sunnis and judge them to be wronged.**[1]

Our comment:

To claim that beating one's chest in lament of Ḥusayn رَضِيَ ٱللَّٰهُ عَنْهُ is not a call of Jāhiliyyah requires specific evidence to exclude it from the general prohibition. There is no evidence that excludes lamenting Ḥusayn رَضِيَ ٱللَّٰهُ عَنْهُ from the general prohibition.

1 *Then I was guided*, p. 44-45.

The Prophet ﷺ lost his beloved uncle, Ḥamzah, at the Battle of Uḥud. Despite this he did not behave in the way the Shīʿah behave. Ḥusayn رضي الله عنه was a martyr who was murdered over ten centuries ago. If it is argued that they want to mourn him? Why do they not do the same for his father, ʿAlī ibn Abī Ṭālib, as he too was killed unjustly and he is superior to Ḥusayn رضي الله عنه by consensus?

To assert that they are rewarded for their action because their intention was to please Allah begs the question on how do we know their intentions are for the sake of Allah? Even under the assumption that their intention is to please Allah, is that sufficient for the acceptance of an action condemned by the Prophet ﷺ as the mourning of Jāhiliyyah?

Strangely, the actions of the Shīʿah are justified by deflecting the lack of evidence and referring to the actions of some ignorant people who committed suicide and some other people who hurt and injured themselves upon hearing the news of the death of the tyrant Jamāl ʿAbd al-Nāṣir! Did Tījānī consider Jamal ʿAbd al-Nāṣir an equal to Sayyidunā al-Ḥusayn رضي الله عنه that he accepted such a ridiculous explanation? Where was his scepticism then? Did his 'objective thinking' only get activated when he wished to discredit the Ṣaḥābah?

The books of the Ahl al-Sunnah prohibit suicide on account of a walī. What then about a tyrant who allowed the spilling of innocent Muslim blood and violation of their honour? The legal framework for the Ahl al-Sunnah is rooted in the Qur'ān and the Sunnah, not on the basis of people's actions.

If anything, his response proves that the legal framework within the Shīʿī tradition is influenced greatly by the later actions carried out by people. There is no other way of explaining such evasive reasoning. This is further demonstrated in the ensuing discussion.

Tījānī says:

> **I asked, "Why do the Shia decorate the graves of their saints with gold and silver, despite the fact that it is prohibited in Islam?"**
>
> **Al-Sayyid al-Sadr replied, this is not done just by the Shia, and it is not prohibited. Look at the mosques of our brothers the Sunnis in Iraq or Egypt or Turkey or anywhere else in the Islamic world, they are all decorated with gold and silver. Furthermore, the mosque of the Messenger of Allah**

> **ﷺ in al-Madinah al-Munawarah and the Kaba, the House of Allah, in the blessed Mecca is covered every year by a cloth decorated by gold which costs millions. So such a thing is not exclusive to the Shia.**[1]

In his eagerness to please the masses it appears that al-Ṣadr is prepared to forgo the Prophetic prohibition in embellishment of Masājid as it is among the signs of Qiyāmah.

Anas relate that the Prophet ﷺ said:

لا تقوم الساعة حتى يتباهى الناس في المساجد

> The Day of Judgement will not occur until people boast about the Masjids.[2]

There is another narration which has reached us by way of Ibn ʿAbbās, who said that the Messenger ﷺ said:

ما أمرت بتشييد المساجد قال ابن عباس لتزخرفنها كما زخرفت اليهود والنصارى

> "I have not been commanded to decorate the Masjids."
>
> Ibn ʿAbbās said, "Indeed, you will embellish it like the Jews and the Christians embellished it."[3]

Why was Tījānī speechless? He either lacked knowledge or was still finding his impartiality!

9. Explanation of the ḥadīth of division in the Ummah.

Tījānī says:

> **I read the saying of the Prophet ﷺ: The sons of Israel were divided into seventy-one groups, and the Christians were divided into seventy-two groups, and my people will be divided into seventy-three groups, all of which, except one group will end up in Hell.**

---

1 Ibid.

2 *Sunan Abū Dāwūd*, Kitāb al-Ṣalāh, Bāb fī Banā al-Masājid, Ḥadīth no. 449; See also *Ṣaḥīḥ Abū Dāwūd* by Albānī, Ḥadīth no. 432.

3 *Sunan Abū Dāwūd*, Ḥadīth no. 448; See also *al-Ṣaḥīḥ*, Ḥadīth no. 431.

> **Here is not the place to talk about the various religions which claim to be the right one and that the rest are wrong, but I am surprised and astonished whenever I read this saying. My surprise and astonishment is not at the saying itself, but at those Muslims who read it and repeat it in their speeches and brush over it without analysing it or even attempting to find out which the group is going to be saved and which are going to be doomed.**
>
> **The interesting thing is that each group claims that it is the saved one. At the end of the saying came the following: "Who are they, O Messenger of Allah?" He answered, "Those who follow my path and the path of my Companions." Is there any group that does not adhere to the Book [Qur'an] and Sunnah (the prophetic tradition), and is there any Islamic group that claims otherwise? If Imams Malik or Abu Hanifah or al-Shafii or Ahmed ibn Hanbel were asked, wouldn't each and every one of them claim that he adheres to the teachings of the Qur'an and the Right Sunnah'?'**
>
> **These are the Sunni Madhahib, in addition to the various Shii-groups, which I had believed at one time to be deviant and corrupt. All of them claim to adhere to the Qur'an and the correct Sunnah which has been handed down through Ahl al-Bayt (the Prophets صلى الله عليه وسلم Family) who knew best about what they were saying. Is it possible that they are all right, as they claim? This is not possible, because the Prophets صلى الله عليه وسلم saying states the opposite, unless the saying is invented or fabricated. But that is not possible either, because the saying is accepted by both the Shia and Sunnis. Is it possible that the saying has no meaning? God forbid that His Messenger صلى الله عليه وسلم could utter a meaningless and aimless saying, as he only spoke words of wisdom. Therefore we are left with one possible conclusion: that there is one group which is on the right path and that the rest are wrong.[1]**

Our comment:

The differences between the four Imāms are not about the fundamentals of the religion. As a matter of fact, they are in agreement on those issues. Their differences are limited to secondary issues of practise which could be the result of a varied approach towards the text which resulted in alternative understandings of particular text which advocated practise.

The division being referred to in the ḥadīth applies to the fundamentals and not secondary issues of practise.

1 *Then I was guided*, p. 49-50.

The only group which holds fast to the Qur'ān and Sunnah is safe. The Prophet ﷺ indicated that salvation is to be found with his Companions when he said, "What I, and my Ṣaḥābah, are upon." Thus we come to realise that the group worthy of salvation is the Ahl al-Sunnah wa l-Jamāʿah. Tījānī's book is a criticism of the Ṣaḥābah from beginning to end. Where does this place him?

10. Tījānī distorts the ḥadīth of the Bedouin urinating in the Masjid

Tījānī says:

> **Allow me to tell you the story of the man who urinated in the mosque of the Messenger of Allah ﷺ and in his presence, and some of his Companions drew their swords to kill him, but he stopped them and said: Let him go and do not harm him, and pour some water on the place where he urinated. We are sent to make things easy and not difficult. We are sent to spread the good words and not to make people keep away from us.**
>
> **The Companions obeyed his orders, and the Messenger of Allah ﷺ asked that man to come and sit next to him and spoke to him nicely. He explained to him that the place was the House of Allah and should not be dirtied, and the man seemed to have understood the point, for he later was seen in the mosque wearing his best and cleanest clothes.[1] Allah speaks the truth when he says:**
>
> وَلَوْ كُنْتَ فَظًّا غَلِيظَ الْقَلْبِ لَانْفَضُّوْا مِنْ حَوْلِكَ
>
> ***And if you had been rude (in speech) and harsh in heart, they would have disbanded from you.[2]***

Our comment:

The ḥadīth he cites is not narrated with the above wording. The correct wording, as narrated in *Ṣaḥīḥ al-Bukhārī* from Abū Hurayrah, is as follows:

> قال قام أعرابي فبال في المسجد فتناوله الناس فقال لهم النبي صلى الله عليه وسلم دعوه وهريقوا على بوله سجلا من ماء أو ذنوبا من ماء فإنما بعثتم ميسرين ولم تبعثوا معسرين

1 *Then I was guided*, p. 56-57.

2 Sūrah Āl ʿImrān: 159.

> A Bedouin stood up and urinated in the Masjid. The people reproached him and the Prophet صلى الله عليه وسلم said, "Leave him and pour a bucket of water over his urine. You were sent as facilitators of ease, and not to make things difficult."[1]

Tījānī's imagination was activated as he needed to somewhat soften his blows against the Ṣaḥābah. To accomplish this task he resorted to distortion when he said, "When the Ṣaḥābah stood up towards him with swords unsheathed in order to kill him." All the variations of this ḥadīth show this to be a lie. Despite the numerous variation of wordings for this narration, "Some people stood up towards him," and "The people yelled out," and "The people rushed towards him," and "The people reproached him," and "The Companions of the Messenger صلى الله عليه وسلم said, 'Be quiet! Be quiet!'" none of these narrations impressed Tījānī. His task could only be accomplished by distorting the wording of the ḥadīth in a meagre attempt to display the Ṣaḥābah رضي الله عنهم as savages with no other concern but killing and dishonouring people.

Tījānī's imaginary version states that the Prophet صلى الله عليه وسلم spoke kindly to the Bedouin who later accepted Islam, and was only seen after that wearing his best clothes when attending the Masjid. Was the Bedouin an unbeliever that he needed to accept Islam? The narration appearing in *Abū Dāwūd*, from Abū Hurayrah confirms that he was a believer prior to this incident:

> أن أعرابيا دخل المسجد ورسول الله صلى الله عليه وسلم جالس فصلى قال ابن عبدة ركعتين ثم قال اللهم ارحمنى ومحمدا ولا ترحم معنا أحدا فقال النبى صلى الله عليه وسلم لقد تحجرت واسعا ثم لم يلبث أن بال فى ناحية المسجد فأسرع الناس إليه فنهاهم النبى صلى الله عليه وسلم وقال إنما بعثتم ميسرين ولم تبعثوا معسرين صبوا عليه سجلا من ماء أو قال ذنوبا من ماء

> A Bedouin entered the Masjid while the Messenger صلى الله عليه وسلم was seated. Then he performed ṣalāh (Ibn ʿAbdah says, two rakʿāhs) and said, "O Allah! Have mercy on me and Muḥammad and do not show mercy to anyone with us!"
>
> The Prophet صلى الله عليه وسلم said, "You have narrowed down something vast."
>
> Shortly thereafter he urinated in the corner of the Masjid and the people rushed towards him but the Prophet صلى الله عليه وسلم stopped them and said, "You

1 *Ṣaḥīḥ al-Bukhārī*, Kitāb al-Wuḍū, Ṣabb al-Mā' ʿalā al-Bawl fī al-Masjid, Ḥadīth no. 217.

> have been sent as facilitators of ease, you have not been sent to make things difficult. Pour a bucket of water over it!"[1]

This is the version narrated in *Musnad Aḥmad*:

> The Prophet ﷺ went to him and said, "This house has been built for the remembrance of Allah, and for ṣalāh, and we do not urinate in it."
>
> Then he called for a bucket of water and he poured (the water) over it. The Bedouin, after he understood (what the Prophet had taught him), said, "The Prophet approached, by my mother and my father, and he did not curse me or reprimand me or beat me."[2,3]

Did Tījānī even look at this ḥadīth in the books of ḥadīth or was he cautiously led to this false account of the ḥadīth?

11. Tījānī's criticism of ʿAbd Allāh ibn ʿUmar

Tījānī says:

> **Or by Abdullah ibn Umar, who was never close to Ali, and he was one of those who refused to pay homage to Ali despite the popular support he had received. Abdullah ibn Umar used to say that the best people after the Prophet were Abu Bakr then Uthman, and after that everybody was equal. Thus, he made Imam Ali like any other ordinary person, without preferences or virtues.**
>
> **What was Abdullah ibn Umar's attitude towards the facts that had been mentioned by the leading personalities of the nation that "No companion had as many virtues attributed to him as Ali." Had Abdullah ibn Umar not heard about even one of Ali's virtues? Yes, by Allah, he had heard and understood, but political intrigues tend to distort the facts![4]**

Our comment:

Tījānī denigrates ʿAbd Allāh ibn ʿUmar رضي الله عنهما for merely relating a narration which—in Tījānī's mind—amounts to defamation of ʿAlī رضي الله عنه. Such an attitude could be anticipated from such a prejudiced mind; a mind which would merely reject

1 *Sunan Abū Dāwūd*, vol. 1, Kitāb al-Ṭahārah, Bāb al-Arḍ Yuṣībuhā al-Bawl, Ḥadīth no. 380; Refer also to *Ṣaḥīḥ Abū Dāwūd*, Ḥadīth no. 366; Narrated also by al-Tirmidhī, Ḥadīth no. 147.

2 He did not say kill.

3 *Musnad Aḥmad*, vol. 3, Ḥadīth no. 10538, p. 572, *Musnad Abū Hurayrah*.

4 *Then I was guided*, p. 141, 142.

the narrations in favour of Abū Bakr and ʿUmar رضي الله عنهما for no logical or academic reason.

ʿAbd Allāh ibn ʿUmar رضي الله عنهما never intended to defame ʿAlī رضي الله عنه nor he did not consider him without merit. However, in the aforementioned ḥadīth he was referring to the rank of those Companions who were of the same generation. ʿAlī رضي الله عنه, in terms of his age, was of a generation younger than that. The narration is to be understood within the framework of best-suited for Khilāfah. Ibn Ḥajar states:

> This means superiority in terms of suitability for khilāfah. Therefore, Ibn ʿAsākir narrates from ʿAbd Allāh ibn Yasār—from Sālim—from ʿAbd Allāh ibn ʿUmar, who said, "Indeed, you all know that we used to say during the Prophet's صلى الله عليه وسلم time, Abū Bakr, and ʿUmar, and ʿUthmān—referring to the khilāfah."
>
> Similarly, ʿUbayd Allāh narrates from Nāfiʿ—from Ibn ʿUmar, "We used to say during the Prophet's time, 'Who is the best person to take charge of this matter?' And we used to say, 'Abū Bakr and ʿUmar.'[1]

ʿAbbās al-Qummī, in his book *al-Kunā wa l-Alqāb*, confirms the merit and fair-mindedness of Ibn ʿUmar. He writes:

> ʿAbd Allāh ibn ʿUmar is a famous Ṣaḥābī. Ibn ʿAbd al-Barr says about him in al-Istīʿāb, "He was of the people of piety, knowledge, and strict emulation of the Prophet صلى الله عليه وسلم. He was extremely cautious in issuing of rulings and in everything he undertook. The Prophet صلى الله عليه وسلم once said to his wife, Ḥafṣah, ʿUmar's daughter, 'Indeed, your brother is a pious man. If only he stood for a portion of the evening (for ṣalāh).' Ibn ʿUmar never missed Qiyām al-Layl (after that)."[2]

Even Ibn Bābuwayh al-Qummī cites Ibn ʿUmar's رضي الله عنه narrations in his book *al-Khiṣāl*[3] validating them, as well as the editor who annotated and published the book.

If Ibn ʿUmar رضي الله عنه considered ʿAlī رضي الله عنه without virtue how is it that he narrates from the Prophet صلى الله عليه وسلم that he said:

1 *Fatḥ al-Bārī*, vol. 7 p. 21

2 al-Qummī: *Al-Kunā wa l-Alqāb*, vol. 1 p. 363, Maktabah al-Ṣadr Publishers: Tehran.

3 *Al-Khiṣāl*, p. 29, 31, 67, 72, 163, 184, 191.

الْحسن والحسين سيدا شباب أهل الجنة وأبوهما خير منهما

> Ḥasan and Ḥusayn are the leaders of the youth of Jannah. And their father is better than them.[1]

This is in addition to what appears in *Ṣaḥīḥ al-Bukhārī* from Saʿd ibn ʿUbaydah, who said:

جاء رجل إلى ابن عمر فسأله عن عثمان فذكر عن محاسن عمله قال لعل ذاك يسوؤك قال نعم قال فأرغم الله بأنفك ثم سأله عن علي فذكر محاسن عمله قال هو ذاك بيته أوسط بيوت النبي صلى الله عليه وسلم ثم قال لعل ذاك يسوؤك قال أجل قال فأرغم الله بأنفك انطلق فاجهد على جهدك

> A man came to Ibn ʿUmar and asked him about ʿUthmān. Ibn ʿUmar spoke highly of him mentioning some of his good actions and said to the man, "Perhaps these facts annoy you?"
>
> He said, "Yes!"
>
> Ibn ʿUmar said, "May Allah make your nose grovel in sand!"
>
> Then the man asked about ʿAlī and Ibn ʿUmar spoke highly of him mentioning some of his good actions and said, "His house is the vastest of the Prophet's houses."
>
> Then he said (to the man), "Perhaps these facts annoy you (as well)?"
>
> He said, "Yes!"
>
> He said, "May Allah make your nose grovel in sand! Move from here! Try your best to harm me (let us see how far you come)!"[2]

This ḥadīth has also been narrated by way of ʿAṭā with a slightly varied wording:

> The man said, "I hate him!"
>
> Ibn ʿUmar said to him, "May Allah hate you!"[3]

---

1 *Sunan Ibn Mājah*, Bāb Faḍā'il Aṣḥāb al-Nabī ﷺ, Ḥadīth no. 118.

2 *Ṣaḥīḥ al-Bukhārī*, Kitāb Al-Faḍā'il, Bāb Faḍā'il ʿAlī, Ḥadīth no. 3501.

3 *Fatḥ al-Bārī*, vol. 7 p. 91; See also *Khaṣā'iṣ ʿAlī*, p. 104-105, the examiner says, "authentic."

Ibn ʿUmar's رضي الله عنه statement that ʿAlī's رضي الله عنه house is the vastest of the Prophet's صلى الله عليه وسلم houses means, "The best of his houses."[1]

Do these aḥādīth indicate in any way that Ibn ʿUmar رضي الله عنه carried a grudge against ʿAlī رضي الله عنه or considered him without merit? Tījānī's lack of familiarity with the literature coupled with his bias and prejudice blinds him from these narrations. All that he is aware of is what fraudsters like al-Sayyid al-Khū'ī and al-Sayyid al-Ṣadr have fed him in terms of narrations in this regard. Tījānī's ignorance was fuelled by his underlying prejudice. This resulted in '*Then I was guided*,' to which we respond: Rather, misguided!

12. Tījānī ridicules some of the Ṣaḥābah calling them *al-Munqalibīn* (those who turned back on their heels)

Tījānī says:

> **I have changed the Companions who turned back on their heels, like Muawiah, Amr ibn al-As, al-Mughira ibn Shu'ba, Abu Hurayra, Ikrima, Ka'b al-Ahbar and others, for the grateful Companions who never broke the promise they gave to the Prophet صلى الله عليه وسلم, like Ammar ibn Yasir, Salman al-Farisi, Abu Dharr al-Ghifari, al-Miqdad ibn al-Aswad. Khuzayma ibn Thabit - Dhu al-Shahadetain - and others, and praise be to Allah for this enlightenment.[2]**

Our comment:

It appears that the 'infallible' Imām, Ḥasan ibn ʿAlī رضي الله عنهما handed the khilāfah over to someone who turned back on their heels. Ḥusayn رضي الله عنه rose up against Yazīd, but he pledged allegiance to Muʿāwiyah رضي الله عنه. One 'infallible' handed the Khilāfah over to a person who turned back on his heels, another 'infallible' pledged allegiance to someone who turned back on his heels. Either the 'infallibles' were wrong or Tījānī is making up history as he goes.

All that ʿAmr ibn al-ʿĀṣ رضي الله عنه could be guilty of was that he supported Muʿāwiyah رضي الله عنه. Since it is known that Muʿāwiyah رضي الله عنه became the khalīfah by the nomination of both Ḥasan and Ḥusayn رضي الله عنهما, whatever applies to Muʿāwiyah رضي الله عنه applies to ʿAmr رضي الله عنه.

---

1 *Fatḥ al-Bārī*, vol. 7 p. 91.

2 *Then I was guided*, p. 133.

One wonders what was the reason for Tījānī accusing al-Mughīrah, ʿIkrimah, and Kaʿb' al-Aḥbār (who was not even a companion), of turning back on their heels? Tījānī did not mention anything against these three which would indicate why they deserved such callous treatment. Perhaps it could be a case of him having opened the door through which he accuses people of leaving the religion; so he used this opportunity to cast out as many of the Ṣaḥābah as he could

Abū Hurayrah's only sin was that he transmitted the merits of the Abū Bakr and ʿUmar رضي الله عنهما. This was sufficient for Tījānī to accuse him of going back on his heels.

There is not much more that can be said of Tījānī's self-claimed 'impartiality'. Instead of refuting him we urge the reader to consider whether Tījānī's views are the result of an academic enquiry; or whether he adopts a view and then searches for anything that could be used to support his preconceived ideas.

13. Tījānī associates the term Ahl al-Sunnah wa l-Jamāʿah with Muʿāwiyah

Tījānī says:

> **Who was the first to use the term Ahl al-Sunnah [Sunni Traditions] and al-Jamaah? I have searched through the history books and found that they agreed to call the year in which Muawiyah seized power "the year of al-Jamaah". It was called thus because the nation became divided into two factions after the death of Uthman: The Shia of Ali and the followers of Muawiyah. When Imam Ali was martyred and Muawiyah seized power after his pact with Imam Ḥasan which enabled him to become commander of the believers the years was then called "al-Jamaah". Therefore the name Ahl al-Sunnah [Sunnah Traditionists] and al-Jamaah indicates the Sunnah [tradition] of Muawiyah, and the agreement on his leadership, and does not mean the followers of the Sunnah [tradition] of the Messenger of Allah صلى الله عليه وسلم.[1]**

Our comment:

Lexically, the term Sunnah is defined as a pattern, path, life, history. The word Jamāʿah is defined in contrast with separation. This is the lexical basis for both the terms Sunnah and al-Jamāʿah.

Technically, the word Sunnah refers to what the Prophet صلى الله عليه وسلم and his Ṣaḥābah رضي الله عنهم were upon in terms of moderation in belief, speech, and action.[2]

1 *Then I was guided*, p. 170.

2 ʿUthmān ʿAlī: *Manhaj al-Istidlāl ʿalā Masāʾil al-Iʿtiqād ʿinda Ahl al-Sunnah wa l-Jamāʿah*, vol. 1 p. 28.

Ibn Ḥazm defines it as follows:

> The Ahl al-Sunnah are the *Ahl al-Ḥaq* (people of the truth) and everyone besides them are *Ahl al-Bidʿah* (people of innovation). Indeed, the Ahl al-Sunnah were the Ṣaḥābah رضي الله عنهم, and those who followed their path from the best amongst the Tābiʿīn , then the scholars of Ḥadīth, and those who followed them from amongst the jurists; generation after generation until present times. This includes those who followed them from the general masses from East to West.[1]

Ahl al-Sunnah is a term used to refer to those who follow the Prophet's صلى الله عليه وسلم Sunnah.

The technical meaning of *al-Jamāʿah* refers to the *Jamāʿah* (group) who follow the truth, in reference to the Ṣaḥābah رضي الله عنهم. We know from the Prophetic ḥadīth that it applies to them, "What I and my Ṣaḥābah are upon."[2] This is mentioned unambiguously in another narration wherein the Prophet صلى الله عليه وسلم said, "They are the Jamāʿah!"[3] It is for that reason that Abū Shāmah said:

> Whenever the command comes to stick to the Jamāʿah, then the intended meaning is stick to the truth and following it even if those who hold onto it are few and those who oppose it are many as the truth is what the first Jamāʿah were upon, i.e. the Prophet صلى الله عليه وسلم and his Ṣaḥābah رضي الله عنهم. The abundance of people of falsehood who came later are not to be looked at (to determine the way of the Jamāʿah).[4]

Ibn Masʿūd رضي الله عنه said, "The Jamāʿah is what is aligned with the truth even if you are alone!"[5] Therefore, the person who subscribes to the Qur'ān, Sunnah, and ijmāʿ is from the Ahl al-Sunnah wa l-Jamāʿah.[6]

This is the definition of the term Ahl al-Sunnah wa l-Jamāʿah.

---

1 Ibn Ḥazm: *Al-Faṣl fī al-Milal wa al-Ahwā wa al-Niḥal*, vol. 2 p. 271.

2 *Sunan al-Tirmidhī*, Kitāb al-Īmān, Bāb Mā Jā fī Iftirāq hādhīh al-Ummah, Ḥadīth no. 2641, vol. 5; Refer also to *Ṣaḥīḥ al-Tirmidhī*, Ḥadīth no. 2129.

3 *Sunan Ibn Mājah*, Kitāb al-Fitan, Bāb Iftirāq al-Umam, Ḥadīth no. 3992; See also *Ṣaḥīḥ Ibn Mājah*, Ḥadīth no. 3226, 3227.

4 Abū Shāmah: *Al-Bāʿith ʿalā Inkār al-Bidaʿ wa al-Ḥawādith*, p. 91; See also *Manhaj al-Istidlāl*, vol. 1 p. 39.

5 Ibid. p. 92.

6 *Majmūʿ al-Fatāwā*, vol. 3 p. 346.

14. Tījānī claims that the Prophet ﷺ mentioned the Twelve Imāms by name

Tījānī says:

> **How could you follow religious leaders that have been appointed by the Umayyads and the Abbasids for political reasons, and leave other religious leaders although the Messenger of Allah ﷺ pointed out their number and their names?**
>
> **How could you follow somebody who did not know the Prophet very well and leave the gate to the city of knowledge, whose relation to the Messenger ﷺ was the same as the position of Harun to Musa?**
>
> **(He refers in the footnotes to *al-Bukhārī* and *Yanābīʿ al-Mawaddah*)[1]**

Our comment:

Tījānī refers to what al-Bukhārī narrates from Jābir ibn Samurah regarding the Prophet ﷺ "specifying" their number, he said:

> يكون اثنا عشر أميرا فقال كلمة لم أسمعها فقال أبي إنه قال كلهم من قريش
>
> "There will be twelve leaders," then he said something I could not hear. My father said that he ﷺ said, "Each of them is from the Quraysh."[2]

It is amazing that Tījānī cites this ḥadīth to argue his case. By the twelve Khulafā' he refers to the sons of ʿAlī رضي الله عنه though and it is well-known that none of them became a khalīfah besides ʿAlī ibn Abī Ṭālib رضي الله عنه. Ḥasan ibn ʿAlī رضي الله عنه accepted the Khilāfah initially but later abdicated in favour of Muʿāwiyah رضي الله عنه. The rest of them passed away before any one of them could become a leader. How then can Tījānī use this ḥadīth as a proof?

The scholars of the Ahl al-Sunnah are unanimous that the first four Khulafā' are included in the twelve. The only difference among them is whether this applied to the Khulafā' after the demise of ʿAlī ibn Abī Ṭālib رضي الله عنه in succession or if it refers to the periods of strength throughout history.

---

1 *Then I was guided*, p. 170.

2 *Ṣaḥīḥ al-Bukhārī*, Kitāb al-Aḥkām, Bāb al-Istikhlāf, Ḥadīth no. 6796; *Muslim* with the commentary, Kitāb al-Imārah, Bāb al-Nās Tabʿ li Quraysh, Ḥadīth no. 1821.

It is necessary to demonstrate the flaws in Tījānī's argument

The narration uses a specific description to identify the tribe from which these Khulafā' will emerge, namely the Quraysh. The tribe of Quraysh comprises of multiple branches:

- Banū ʿAbd al-Dār
- Banū ʿAbd Manāf
- Banū Nawfal
- Banū Muṭṭalib
- Banū Hāshim: ʿAlī
- Banū ʿAbd Shams:- Banū Umayyah: ʿUthmān ibn ʿAffān, Muʿāwiyah
- Banū Makhzūm
- Banū Zuhrah
- Banū Taym: Abū Bakr al-Ṣiddīq
- Banū ʿAdī: ʿUmar ibn al-Khaṭṭāb
- Banū Asad
- Banū Sahm
- Banū Jumah

The Twelver Shīʿah consider the Imāms to be these individuals according the sequence in which they are mentioned:

1. ʿAlī ibn Abī Ṭālib,
2. His son, al-Ḥasan ibn ʿAlī,
3. His brother, al-Ḥusayn ibn ʿAlī,
4. His son, ʿAlī ibn al-Ḥusayn ibn ʿAlī [Zayn al-ʿĀbidīn],
5. His son, Muḥammad ibn ʿAlī ibn al-Ḥusayn [al-Bāqir],
6. His son, Jaʿfar ibn Muḥammad [al-Ṣādiq],

7. His son, Mūsā ibn Jaʿfar [al-Kāẓim],
8. His son, ʿAlī ibn Mūsā [al-Riḍā],
9. His son, Muḥammad ibn ʿAlī [al-Jawwād],
10. His son, ʿAlī ibn Muḥammad [al-Hādī],
11. His son, al-Ḥasan ibn ʿAlī [al-ʿAskarī],
12. Finally his son, Muḥammad ibn al-Ḥasan [al-Mahdī] whom it is disputed whether he was even born, and if so whether he survived his infancy.

The Prophet ﷺ said that all twelve will be from Quraysh. We can see that the four rightly-guided Khulafā' are all from Quraysh, so there is no contradiction to the ḥadīth. The problem lies with the Twelver Shīʿah since they bear the responsibility to explain why the Messenger ﷺ used such a broad, comprehensive description (Quraysh) if he only intended the individuals from the descendants of ʿAlī ibn Abī Ṭālib, and only specific individuals from that line. In fact, it would be very clumsy and irrational to use such a broad term if only a handful of individuals from a single line were intended.

However, it is impossible that he intended the Twelve Imāms whom the Rāfiḍah belief are the 'infallibles' as all of them died without claiming to be the Khalīfah; with the exception of Muḥammad ibn al-Ḥasan al-ʿAskarī who entered the cave when he was five years old and he will come out at a specific time, as the Rāfiḍah claim.

Limiting the number to twelve leaders does not conform to the ideology of the Rāfiḍah who claim that the first of the twelve Imāms is ʿAlī رضي الله عنه. The number fluctuates between twelve and thirteen leaders as we will come to see.

Al-Ṭabarsī confirms this in what he narrates in his book, *Iʿlām al-Warā bi ʿAlām al-Hudā*:

> From Abū Jaʿfar (al-Bāqir), from Jābir ibn ʿAbd Allāh al-Anṣārī, he said, "I visited Fāṭimah and she had a board in front of her with the names of all the twelve executors from her sons. I counted twelve with the last of them being the Qā'im, three of them were Muḥammad and four of them were ʿAlī."[1]

---

1 Abū Faḍl al-Ṭabarsī: *Iʿlām al-Warā*, p. 366, al-Faṣl al-Thānī fī Dhikr baʿḍ al-Ikhbār allatī Jā'at min Ṭarīq al-Shīʿah Imāmiyyah fī al-Naṣṣ ʿalā Imāmat al-IthnāʿAsharah min Āl Muḥammad.

If twelve of her sons were to be Imāms, where does that leave ʿAlī? The Thirteenth?

Al-Ṭabarsī narrates from Zurārah, who said:

> I heard Abū Jaʿfar (al-Bāqir) saying, "From the family of Muḥammad there will be twelve. Each one of them will be inspired. From the sons of the Messenger of Allah and the sons of ʿAlī ibn Abī Ṭālib . Therefore, the Messenger and ʿAlī are the parents."[1]

If twelve of ʿAlī's sons are to be Imāms there is no space left for him. This is the consequence of forging. The forger overlooks simple elements such as this which we have just pointed out.

The claim that the Prophet صَلَّى ٱللَّٰهُ عَلَيْهِ وَسَلَّمَ appointing the Imāms by name is a clear lie as it cannot be established with reliable evidence.

It is not sufficient to reference it to *Yanābīʿ al-Mawaddah*, since this is a book of the Rāfiḍah and Tījānī undertook to produce mutually acceptable evidence. In addition to this the various Shīʿah sects dispute the names of the Imāms. Some believe that Imāmah continued through Ḥusayn's رَضِيَ ٱللَّٰهُ عَنْهُ sons until Jaʿfar. Then they differ amongst themselves with one group considering it continued with Mūsā ibn Jaʿfar, they are the Imāmiyyah, another group said it went to Ismāʿīl ibn Jaʿfar, they are the Ismāʿīliyyah, and another group said it continued in Muḥammad ibn al-Ḥanafiyyah, and so on. The fact that the Shīʿah have different sects among themselves is evidence of the fact that the Prophet صَلَّى ٱللَّٰهُ عَلَيْهِ وَسَلَّمَ did not appoint them, let alone by name. Reality proves the inconsistency of Tījānī's argument.

15. Tījānī claims that the Ṣaḥābah killed ʿAlī

Tījānī says:

> **Whereas the Companions of Moses plotted against Aaron and tried to kill him, some of the Companions of Muhammad killed his Aaron and pursued his sons and followers everywhere. They removed their names from the Diwan (account books of the treasury) and prohibited anyone to be named after them.[2]**

---

1 Ibid. p. 369, *al-Nuṣūṣ al-Wāridah ʿalā al-Aʾimmah al-Ithnā Asharah.*

2 *Then I was guided*, p. 106.

Our comment:

Is there any book that mentions that the Ṣaḥābah رضي الله عنهم killed ʿAlī رضي الله عنه? Subḥān Allāh! Blinded by his ignorance Tījānī has reached the point where he contradicts undisputed reality and confirmed history.

What is well-known and accepted both by the Ahl al-Sunnah and the Shīʿah is that ʿAlī's killers were a group from the Khawārij and the dreadful deed was carried out by the accursed Ibn Muljam. Since when are the Khawārij included among the Ṣaḥābah? Unless Tījānī wishes to divide the Ṣaḥābah into four categories?

It is absolutely ridiculous to claim that they prevented anyone from adopting his name. How is it that there are so many scholars from the Ahl al-Sunnah who still kept the name ʿAlī in the early period? How was it possible that his grandchildren kept the name ʿAlī? Tījānī's ignorance of history has reached an all-time low!

16. Another distortion of ḥadīth by Tījānī

Tījānī says:

> **They claim that some of the early Companions were not reliable transmitters of the Prophet's صلى الله عليه وسلم tradition; therefore they removed what they did not like, especially if these traditions included some of the last instructions of the Messenger of Allah صلى الله عليه وسلم before his death.**
>
> **Al-Bukhari and Muslim both write about the fact that the Messenger of Allah صلى الله عليه وسلم advised three things on his death-bed:**
>
> - **Remove all the polytheists from the Arabian Peninsula**
> - **Reward the delegation in the same way as I have done and the narrator then said, "I forgot the third."**
>
> **It is possible that those Companions who were present at the death-bed and heard the three instructions forgot the third one, when we know that they used to learn by heart a whole epic after hearing it once? No. It is politics that forced them to forget it and not to mention it again. This is indeed another of those comedies organized by the Companions, because there is no doubt about the first instruction of the Messenger صلى الله عليه وسلم.[1]**

1 *Then I was guided*, p. 163.

Our comment:

Tījānī does not realise that this ḥadīth is a portion of the ḥadīth which he calls, "The Thursday Calamity." Tījānī has either taken this narration from the books of the Shīʿah, or he has deliberately manipulated the texts. How else can one reconcile a condemnation of the Ṣaḥābah from a 'forged' ḥadīth?

It also proves that the Messenger صَلَّى ٱللَّهُ عَلَيْهِ وَسَلَّمَ did not expel them from his room. How else would they be able to relate this information? More significant is the fact that the Prophet صَلَّى ٱللَّهُ عَلَيْهِ وَسَلَّمَ made these bequests to the Ṣaḥābah رَضِيَ ٱللَّهُ عَنْهُمْ after he decided against 'writing something which would cause them never to go astray after him.' This ḥadīth is one of the clearest proofs that the intention behind writing the book was not imperative but a personal choice. It exonerates ʿUmar رَضِيَ ٱللَّهُ عَنْهُ from any accusations of misconduct since the demeanour of the Prophet صَلَّى ٱللَّهُ عَلَيْهِ وَسَلَّمَ indicates that ʿUmar رَضِيَ ٱللَّهُ عَنْهُ had understood the situation correctly.

The person who said, "I forgot the third," is the Tābiʿī, Saʿīd ibn Jubayr. In one narration it appears as follows, "He remained silent about the third or he said, 'I forgot it.'" So, the narrator who forgot was Saʿīd ibn Jubayr, and he was not a Ṣaḥābī. Thus, Tījānī's statement, "Is it conceivable that the Ṣaḥābah present, who heard the Prophet's three bequests and the time of his death, forgot the third bequest," is actually egg on his face since the Ṣaḥābah رَضِيَ ٱللَّهُ عَنْهُمْ did not forget the ḥadīth. Instead, the narrator, Saʿīd ibn Jubayr, who narrated the ḥadīth from the Ṣaḥābah, was the one who forgot it. How could the Ṣaḥābah رَضِيَ ٱللَّهُ عَنْهُمْ be held responsible for one of the narrators forgetting a part of the ḥadīth?

17. Tījānī claims that the differences between the four Imāms is symptomatic of contradiction between Qur'ān and Ḥadīth

Tījānī says:

> **Because of the vast differences between the four religious Islamic schools, they cannot be from Allah or from His Messenger, for the Messenger did not contradict the Holy Qur'an.**[1]

Our comment:

1 *Then I was guided*, p. 127.

Our purpose here is not to defend the four Imāms or elaborate the reasons for their legal differences. However, I want to comment on his statement that the "differences of the Imāms prove that it is not from Allah and not from his Messenger." What would Tījānī say if we present to him the statement of *Shaykh al-Ṭā'ifah al-Ithnā ʿAshariyyah*, Abū Jaʿfar al-Ṭūsī, who confirms that the differences among the Shīʿah vastly exceeds the differences of the four schools of fiqh. He says in his book *ʿUddah al-Uṣūl:*

> I mentioned what has been transmitted from them, the Imāms, of different aḥādīth which relate to fiqh (the legal discipline) in my book called *al-Istibṣār*. In my book *Tahdhīb al-Aḥkām* (I have mentioned) more than five thousand aḥādīth and I mentioned, in relation to most of them, the differences of the school in terms of application, and that is so well-known that it cannot be hidden. In fact, if you ponder about their differences in law you will find it greater than the differences between Abū Ḥanīfah and al-Shāfiʿī and Mālik.[1]

---

1 al-Ṭabarsī: *ʿUddah al-Uṣūl*, vol. 1 p. 356-357, Sayyid al-Shuhadā Publishers, Distributed by the Āl al-Bayt foundation, al-Najaf.

Made in the USA
Monee, IL
08 January 2025

76169668R00350